English Theatre Music in the Eighteenth Century

FISKE, Roger. English theatre music in the eighteenth century. Oxford, 1973. 648p il. 40.00.   ISBN 0-19-316402-7

There are precious few occasions when a scholarly, complete, and voluminous historical book is also very entertaining. Fiske's book on London theater music from the death of Purcell (1695) to the death of Storace (1796) is one of these. The text covers all major genres of drama and their music; it is thus a good reference for both theater and music historians (as well as being one of the very few references for this period). Fiske also presents a marvelous verbal picture of 18th-century English theaters and audiences. He includes bits of information which one enjoys collecting, such as appendices of extant works and scores, numerous and illustrative musical examples, and detailed descriptions of several works which may well be considered the more important ones of the period, so that one comes away from the book feeling that a period of music-theater, heretofore quite neglected, has just been unearthed. Recommended for undergraduates, graduates, and scholars.

Title-page of *The Judgment of Paris* ('The Prize') by Eccles.

English Theatre Music
in the
Eighteenth Century

ROGER FISKE

London

OXFORD UNIVERSITY PRESS

NEW YORK   TORONTO

1973

Oxford University Press, Ely House, London W.1

GLASGOW NEW YORK TORONTO MELBOURNE WELLINGTON
CAPE TOWN SALISBURY IBADAN NAIROBI DAR ES SALEM LUSAKA ADDIS ABABA
BOMBAY CALCUTTA MADRAS KARACHI LAHORE DACCA
KUALA LUMPUR SINGAPORE HONG KONG TOKYO

ISBN 0 19 316402 7

Printed in Great Britain
by W & J Mackay Limited, Chatham

Preface

This book is about London theatre music from the death of Purcell in 1695 to the death of Storace in 1796. By chance this period roughly corresponds with the eighteenth century, and it makes a satisfactory unit of history because, at the one end, new composers came to the fore as soon as Purcell died, and, at the other end, Storace's more important rivals gave up theatre music within a year or two of 1800. Thus the period has a beginning and an end. It includes the damaging rise of Italian Opera early in the century, the popularizing of pantomime and ballad opera in the 1720s, and the proliferation of dialogue operas after the success of *Love in a Village* in 1762.

In the last forty years of the century the sheer quantity of operatic music performed at the playhouses is astonishing, yet it has been consistently played down or ignored by both music and theatre historians. The fact is that at this period many people went to the playhouses more for the music than the speaking. In winter most of them heard music nowhere else, and their desire for it was such that the chief theatrical successes of the time were as often as not operatic. This theatre music was known and loved by much the same minority that enjoyed the novels of Fielding and Sterne, the poetry of Pope and Gray, and the paintings of Hogarth and Gainsborough. All these writers and artists, and others as well, have inspired a steady succession of books in modern times, but not our composers, and the accepted reason for this is that our composers were not of comparable merit. Even if this were true, there should surely be a book about them. In my opinion it is not true, and indeed one would hardly expect a country that showed solid achievement in the other arts to show none in music.

Needless to say, we shall find no composers the equal of Bach, Handel, Haydn, or Mozart. We would not find any in Italy either, or in France apart perhaps from Rameau. But in recent years less exalted composers have been giving increasing pleasure, and at the Vivaldi-Paisiello level English composers can compete with confidence. They have, however, been more dogged by ill fortune than their continental rivals, in particular by early deaths and by the attitude of our own critics, both professional and amateur. Even in the days when Purcell had no equal in Europe, many Londoners managed to prefer foreign composers to their own, and our weakness for self-denigration was even more apparent in the century that followed. If Purcell's music could not silence such critics, it is not to be expected that the music of his successors should do so. As Addison put it in *Spectator* No. 18:

> We are transported with anything that is not *English*: So it be of a foreign Growth, let it be *Italian*, *French* or *High-Dutch*, it is the same thing. In short, our *English* Musick is quite rooted out . . .

Dr. Burney gave near-permanence to this rooting out in his *History of Music*, for he found nothing to praise in the English music of his own century. His influence was such that later historians accepted his views without troubling to flip through more than a page or two of what they were condemning. Though the Italian composers Burney so admired are almost all forgotten today, his views on English composers are all too persistent.

Theatre historians have been equally unsympathetic. I can think of none in recent times who thought playhouse music worth considering. A famous book on Drury Lane completely ignores operatic works, even though they comprised half the repertoire in the late eighteenth century. Books on English Pantomime make what they can of the verbal evidence, which is scanty, and take no account of the musical evidence, with is considerable. All editors of Sheridan that I know of print *The Duenna* and *Pizarro* incomplete because they have never looked at the vocal scores. Had they done so, they would have found several authentic lyrics that were regularly sung but never sent to the printer presumably because Sheridan had forgotten to keep a copy. Just as Burney conditioned our music historians to think ill of English music, so the great theatre historian Genest conditioned his followers to think the same. Music gave him no pleasure. Faced with the English adaptation of Piccini's *La buona figliuola*, which was widely popular abroad, he dismissed it with his usual cliché: 'This is a mere opera.'

The result of this indifference has been a sad lack of modern books about our theatre music. Eric Walter White's on English Opera in general stands virtually alone so far as this period is concerned. However there has recently been an increasing number of informed articles on the subject in our music periodicals, and this suggests a rise of interest that is encouraging.

With information so hard to come by, I have thought it necessary to describe, if only in brief, every dramatic work of the period of which the music survives in published score or in MS. In the last quarter of the century there are so many such items that I have inevitably been in danger of producing a work of reference rather than a book for reading. Both, perhaps, are needed, and I hope I have not been too unsuccessful in my attempt at a compromise. Two recent large-scale publications have been of the greatest help to me: *The British Union-Catalogue of Early Music*, which gives the location of everything published before 1800 that is to be found in our major libraries, and *The London Stage*, which comprises eleven large volumes listing every known performance with its cast at every theatre in London's West End from 1660 to 1800. The information comes mainly from newspaper advertisements.

I have had unfailing help from librarians in the British Museum, in the Parry Room at the Royal College of Music, in the Bodleian, and at the BBC. I am grateful for help to Edward Croft-Murray, Charles Cudworth, Charles Farncombe, Dr. John Hayes, Julian Herbage, Edgar Hunt, Dr. H. Diack Johnstone, R. A. Lynex, David Marsh, the late Dr. C. B. Oldman, Richard Platt, Dr. Alan Tyson, and Dr. Alexander Weinmann.

Contents

6 *Garrick's Influence, 1747–1760*

7 *Interlude*

8 *Arne's 'Artaxerxes' and 'Love in a Village', 1760–1770*

List of plates

Plates I, II, IV, VII, VIII, XI, XII(b), and XVI are reproduced by permission of the Victoria and Albert Museum; III, V(a), and VI by permission of the Bodleian Library; V(b), V(c), and XII(a) by permission of the National Portrait Gallery; X and XV(a) by permission of the British Museum; XII(c) and (d) by permission of Dulwich College; XIII(a) by permission of Exeter Museums; XIV by permission of Sir John Kellaway and the Paul Mellon Centre for Studies of British Art; XV(b) by permission of Greater London Council as Trustees of the Iveagh Bequest, Kenwood; and XV(c) by permission of Erik Smith, Esq.

Abbreviations

THEATRES		
	BF	Bartholomew Fair
	CG	Covent Garden
	DG	Dorset Garden
	DL	Drury Lane
	GF	Goodman's Fields
	KT	King's Theatre (in the Haymarket)
	LIF	Lincoln's Inn Fields
	LT	Little Theatre (in the Haymarket)
	MG	Marylebone Gardens
	QT	Queen's Theatre (= KT)
	RC	Royal Circus
	RG	Ranelagh Gardens
	RT	Royalty Theatre
	SW	Sadler's Wells

The term 'Haymarket Theatre' is not used in this book because it has caused so much confusion. Deutsch's 'Haymarket' is on the opposite side of the road to the one in *The London Stage*; in Paul Henry Lang's *Handel* the map shows the one 'Haymarket', the text the other. Even Baker used the term for two buildings, though he understood the difference.

1. Vanbrugh's large theatre, the home of Italian Opera, was on the west side of the road, on the site of the modern Her Majesty's. Early in the century it was often called 'The Theatre in the Haymarket', or just 'The Haymarket'. Later it was known as the King's Theatre.

2. The small theatre opposite was on the site of the modern Haymarket Theatre. It was known first as 'The New Theatre in the Haymarket', later as 'The Little Theatre in the Haymarket', and by the end of the century as the Haymarket.

LIBRARIES		
	BM or L	British Museum
	CUM	Cambridge University Music School
	CFM	Cambridge, Fitzwilliam Museum
	L	British Museum
	LAM	London, Royal Academy of Music
	LCM	London, Royal College of Music
	LGC	London, Gresham College Library in the Guildhall

LK   London, King's Music Library in the British Museum
M   Manchester Public Library
O   Oxford, the Bodleian Library

Except for 'BM', all the above are used in *The British Union-Catalogue of Early Music*

OTHER SOURCES

BUCEM	*The British Union-Catalogue of Early Music*
LS	*The London Stage*
M&L	*Music and Letters*
MT	*The Musical Times*
BMA	*Proceedings of the Royal Musical Association*
STR	*The Society for Theatre Research*
TN	*Theatre Notebook* (published by the STR)

I am sorry it is (in this Age) so much the Vanity of some of our English Gentry to admire that in a Foreigner, which they either slight, or take little notice of, in one of their own Nation.

John Playford
The Preface to the Third Book
of his Choice Ayres and Songs
(1681)

. . . fiddlers, pipers, and *id genus omne*; most unedifying and unbecoming company for a man of fashion.

Lord Chesterfield
Letter to his son, 6 June 1751

I

English Masque versus Italian Opera, 1695–1720

1 PROLEGOMENA

THROUGHOUT the eighteenth century, London normally had only two theatres presenting plays and operas in English. One was Drury Lane, built by Wren in 1672. In 1693 Christopher Rich, then the manager, enlarged the auditorium at the expense of the stage area, after which the house held an audience variously estimated at 663 and 'nearly a thousand'; by 1794, lavishly rebuilt, Drury Lane held over three thousand. But it was always a smaller theatre than these figures imply, for people sat more tightly packed than we or the present Lord Chamberlain would tolerate. In winter it was proximity more than anything else that kept an audience warm.

Until 1732 Drury Lane's rival changed site and name with some frequency. A small theatre in Lincoln's Inn Fields was active under Thomas Betterton from 1695 to 1705, in which year most of the company were absorbed in the new Queen's Theatre in the Haymarket, known after Anne's death as the King's Theatre. This was a much larger building designed by the dramatist and architect Sir John Vanbrugh, and though it was visually imposing, the 'extra-ordinary and superfluous Space' under the domed roof

> occasion'd such an Undulation, from the Voice of every Actor, that generally what they said sounded like the Gabbling of so many People, in the Isles in a Cathedral—The Tone of a Trumpet, or the Swell of an Eunuch's holding Note, 'tis true, might be sweeten'd by it; but the articulate Sounds of a speaking Voice were drown'd, by the hollow Reverberations of one Word upon another.[1]

In 1709 the resonance was reduced by lowering the ceiling and other means, but the theatre still favoured singing rather than speaking, and after a performance of *Macbeth* on 18 November 1710 it presented little but Italian operas and singers for the rest of the century. In 1714 a new theatre was opened

[1] Colley Cibber's *Apology* (2nd ed.), Ch. IX.

on the Lincoln's Inn Fields site under John Rich, whose company provided powerful opposition to Drury Lane both before and after its transfer to Covent Garden in 1732. For the rest of the century Drury Lane and Covent Garden enjoyed a virtual monopoly.

London's playhouses were limited to two as a result of patents granted by Charles II to Thomas Killigrew and William Davenant in 1663; patents that gave them the exclusive right to present plays in English. (The subject is complex, and only brief generalizations will be attempted here.) The two companies were in effect servants of the Crown, and subject to the Lord Chamberlain, who was not above intervening in their affairs. He even went so far as to sack Christopher Rich for disregarding one of his directives. The Licensing Act of 1737 strengthened his powers of preventing rival theatres being built and of insisting that all plays should be submitted in advance for censorship. Among the very few entertainments he ever banned was John Gay's ballad opera *Polly*. Companies were sometimes allowed to perform under licence, and it was under licence that Vanbrugh and Congreve opened the Queen's Theatre in 1705. When this house turned to Italian Opera it no longer needed legal permission because it no longer presented spoken dialogue in English. Thus it was never a 'patent' theatre or a Theatre Royal, as were Drury Lane and Covent Garden.

A poor relation to the two playhouses was the New Theatre in the Haymarket, later known as the Little Theatre. Built by John Potter, it opened in 1720 with a season of French comedies, and it relied in the main on foreign companies, exhibitions of dancing and acrobatics, and concerts, all of which could be presented without a patent. Occasionally, and more especially just before the Act of 1737, the theatre was prepared to break the law and offer haphazard seasons of plays in English, but the other playhouses often intrigued to have such activities stopped, and for long periods the house was closed. It did not become a permanent part of London's theatrical life until 1767 when, under Samuel Foote, it was granted a patent for those summer months when Drury Lane and Covent Garden were closed.

Each theatre employed singers whom they taught so far as was possible to act, and encouraged actors to sing. The orchestra was continuously busy, for even in 'straight' comedies and tragedies there were occasional songs with orchestral accompaniment. Intervals, if not graced with dances and short ballets, were filled with Corelli concertos and Handel overtures.

In the 1760s the proportion of operas to plays rose sharply, and from then on they were nearly all published in vocal score. Very few full scores, either published or MS, survive from this later period, but we have quite a number from the earlier years when operas were comparatively few. In this early period there were two grades of publication. Masques were sometimes issued in handsome full scores, and these included the overture and all the arias. Orchestral parts were not published because it was taken for granted that they would be specially copied in the provinces from the published scores. There was no demand at provincial concerts for the recitatives and choruses, so these were normally not given in the score. There was also a lower grade of publication mainly for home consumption. Songs were offered in single sheets engraved on only one side and costing only a few pence. There were only two staves, a vocal line and a bass line for the accompaniment. Sometimes this was all the composer had written, for simple continuo songs occurred in the grandest operas, but if there were an introduction and independent instrumental parts, the publisher cut them to save space and expense. In any case those who bought sheet music wanted little more than the tune and the words. When a song survives only in this form, it is sometimes impossible to tell whether the original accompaniment was simple or elaborate. Publishers sometimes bound several songs together and offered them as a vocal score. Even when every aria was included, as is the case with Clayton's operas, the score may give little or no idea of what the orchestra played. Many such scores leave out as many arias as they include.

Women learnt their songs at the spinet, men on the flute; sheet songs nearly always found space at the bottom for a flute arrangement. There were even solo flute arrangements of complete operas. The instrument was the one we know as the recorder, and when in the third quarter of the century the recorder was super-seded by the more difficult cross flute, flute arrangements became less common.

For much of the century male sing-songs were popular, notably in the coffee-houses; early on a vast anthology eventually known as *Pills to purge Melancholy* was much used when ladies were not present. This was compiled by the dramatist and wit, Thomas D'Urfey, and the first two volumes appeared in 1699 and 1700. There were several revisions, and other volumes were added one by one. Nearly all the songs were printed with their melody lines; there were no basses. All references in what follows are to the final six-volume edition of 1719–20, which contains well over a thousand songs. A modern reprint with the same pagination is available. More often than not D'Urfey does not bother to give the composer's name, but in fact at least ninety known composers have been identified as contributors. Nearly a hundred songs are by Henry Purcell. Samuel Akeroyd, John Barrett, John Blow, Jeremiah Clarke, John Eccles, Thomas Farmer, Robert King, Richard Leveridge, Daniel Purcell, and John Weldon all reach double figures. As well as bawdy items, the collection contains a large number of opera songs, as also some of folk origin, and its influence was enormous, especially on ballad operas, which borrowed tunes from it by the dozen.

I shall return to the ways of theatres and publishers in more detail in the middle of this book, by which period far more information is available.

2 THE ENGLISH MASQUE BEFORE PURCELL'S DEATH

To Purcell an opera was a spoken play with interpolated all-sung masques, the interest of the music transcending the interest of the dialogue. The word masque can be puzzling, and it may even be necessary to stress that it was invariably dramatic; that is, it was performed in costume in front of scenery. Before the Restoration masques were hardly ever public entertainments. They were performed privately by and for aristocrats, and though a few were given in country houses and castles, for instance Milton's *Comus* (1634), most that have in some degree survived were presented in Whitehall Palace. One of the first was Ben Jonson's *The Masque of Blackness* (1605), performed by the Queen, eleven of her ladies, and some professional instrumentalists. The last in this period was William Davenant's *Salmacida Spolia* (1640), in which, unusually, both Lords and Ladies performed led by Charles I and Henrietta Maria. Charles had been taking part in Court masques since 1619 when he was a boy of nineteen. In Italy and France royalty also prided themselves on their acting, and even in eighteenth-century England we shall find occasional examples of aristocrats putting on masques in their Stately Homes for the excellent reason that they wished to perform themselves. There were no court masques between 1640 and the Restoration because of the Civil War, and only isolated examples thereafter.

After 1660 and throughout the eighteenth century masques were nearly always all-sung, but early masques, for instance *Comus*, included a good deal of spoken dialogue. This was in heroic couplets or blank verse for the more estimable characters, but Jonson's masques sometimes included working-class characters who spoke prose. The dialogue in Court masques is so full of contemporary allusions that it is often hard or impossible to understand.

About two dozen of Jonson's librettos survive, and the earlier ones tell us a great deal about the visual side of the entertainment. This was the responsibility of Inigo Jones. After his quarrel with Jonson in 1630 Jones and his pupil John Webb worked with other poets, latterly with Davenant; a surprising number of their entrancing sets and dress designs survive at Chatsworth.[1]

Court masques were probably the first English entertainments given with scenery, as also the first in which women took part. The scenery was elaborate and included splendid palaces, 'streets in perspective', and landscape settings. About half way through a masque it was usual for a pair of 'shutters' to divide and astonish the audience with something quite different revealed behind; for instance 'a glorious Bower'. By 1609 there was conventionally a contrast between the debased and often deformed characters and the morally uplifting ones. The latter sometimes represented the classical gods, but more often they were personifications of various virtues; either way they symbolized the Royal House triumphing over its enemies. Thus in Jonson's *The Masque of Queens* (1609) the first scene was 'an ugly Hell: Which flaming beneath, smoked unto the top of the Roof'; all the characters were witches. But half way through the masque the scene suddenly changed to 'a magnificent Building, figuring the

[1] See Roy Strong's *Festival Designs by Inigo Jones* (Chatsworth Collection Catalogue).

House of Fame', and various legendary queens were conjured up by characters called Heroic Virtue and Fame. Such personifications pervade English opera for a century and a half, as also our paintings and sculptures. We shall also find many eighteenth-century masques extolling royalty under various guises, even though royalty no longer took part in them.

By 1615 the evil characters in Court Masques were conventionalized into two 'antimasques'. Usually the antimasquers capered about without speaking. Thus in Jonson's *The Vision of Delight* (1617) the dialogue is suddenly interrupted by a stage direction:

> Here the first Anti-Masque enter'd. A She-Monster deliver'd of Six Burratines, that dance with Six Pantaloons.

(Twelve was a conventional number for a dance group.) The dialogue is then resumed without reference to the antimasque. We shall find that in early pantomimes the 'comic' or mimed scenes are indicated in precisely the same uninformative way. There was also an increasing tendency in Court masques to group the songs together at the end, linking them with the new-fangled recitative that Charles's picture-buyer, Nicholas Lanier, had learned about in Italy. Here again there is a striking parallel with early pantomimes, which also ended with some twenty minutes of operatic music.

Not much music survives from our Court masques,[1] but there are many references to it in Jonson's stage directions. As early as in *The Masque of Blackness* there is a song, 'Daughters of the subtle Flood', with 'a double Eccho, from several parts of the Land', and this operatic effect was so successful that another double-echo song was written for its successor, *The Masque of Beauty*. 'Loud Musick' is specified in the latter, and at the start of *The Golden Age Restored* (1615) it is contrasted with soft. This masque called for 'two Drums, Trumpets and confusion of Martial Musick', *Pleasure Reconciled to Vertue* has Comus dancing to 'Musick of Cymbals, Flutes and Tabers', and *Neptune's Triumph* (1624) ends with 'five Lutes, three Cornets, and ten Voices'. In *The Irish Masque* (1613–14?), besides two harps, there was 'a Bagpipe and other rude musick'. Rude musick was a long-lived pleasure to the English. Bottom, in a wood near Athens, had called for the tongs and the bones, and in a sketch for *Britannia Triumphans* (Davenant, 1638) Inigo Jones showed that you held the tongs in your left hand and hit the forked end—not in this case with a bone but with a large metal key. Another of his lively drawings for the same masque shows a man scraping a gridiron with a metal shoehorn. We shall find these and other 'instruments' still being used for humorous purposes in the eighteenth century by Fielding and Henry Carey; even the great Dr. Burney asked for them in his mock St. Cecilia's Day Ode.

There is no need here for a detailed account of opera in the Restoration

[1] BM Add. 10444 is the most fruitful source.

period for information is easily available.[1] But a few generalizations will be needed to make clear what English eighteenth-century opera took and what it rejected. It took almost nothing from the very few Court masques the period can show. The tradition for these had been largely lost, and in any case they could not compete scenically with the playhouses. Blow wrote his all-sung *Venus and Adonis* about 1681 so that one of Charles II's mistresses and their small daughter could show off their voices at Court in front of the king, but Purcell, writing for the public theatres, found himself in control of an art-form that was developing along quite different lines. In his day the playhouse masque was never self-sufficient, being an interpolation in some spoken play, and it hardly ever had what we would accept as a plot. The dialogue in *The Fairy Queen* was taken from *A Midsummer Night's Dream*, but none of Shakespeare's characters were called upon to sing. The first interpolated masque was performed in Act II for the entertainment of Titania, the main singers representing Night, Mystery, Secrecy, and Sleep. The next comes in Act IV after the reconciliation of Oberon and Titania and the characters are personifications of the four seasons. The last is performed in Act V for the entertainment of Theseus and his Court. There are songs in the other acts as well, and so much music in the whole that the result can reasonably be called an opera. The distinction between an opera and a play is one of emphasis; it is nearly always easy to tell the difference between a piece whose main interest lies in the words and one whose main interest lies in the music. Purcell decorated many plays with songs; *The Fairy Queen* has the effect of an opera that Shakespeare decorated with dialogue

Though *Venus and Adonis* might be sung at court and *Dido and Aeneas* (1689)[2] in a Chelsea girls' school, Blow and Purcell never attempted an all-sung opera for the playhouses. Davenant's *The Siege of Rhodes* (1656) is often cited as an example, but in fact it had continuous music only because in Cromwellian times spoken dialogue was forbidden. As soon as the ban was lifted Davenant showed no further interest in all-sung opera, which was a great rarity at the playhouses for the rest of the century.

There was a sensible reason for the interpolated masque. Like the Florentines who started opera in 1600, the English were conscious of an incompatibility between stage action and singing, for singing must surely destroy the illusion of reality. Yet it was enjoyable and emotionally moving. The best way of making it dramatically viable was to confine it to a play within the play, the masque that the speaking characters arranged for their own entertainment. This transferred the onus of accepting what was dramatically false from the audience in the theatre to the one on the stage. Even so, it was important for the interpolations to be sung by characters with no pretensions to reality. Personifica-

---

[1] See, for instance, R. E. Moore's *Henry Purcell and the Restoration Theatre*.
[2] For this date see 'Dating Purcell's "Dido and Aeneas"' by John Buttrey, RMA Proceedings 1967–8.

tions such as Honour and Liberty were acceptable because they were no less real when singing than when speaking. Immediately after Purcell's death there was a sudden increase in masques with a plot. As in continental operas these plots were taken from mythology or Ancient History to reduce the silliness of people singing who in real life would speak. Back in the Golden Age, for all that anyone knew, gods and shepherds habitually sang when conversing, and it was not wholly unreasonable that they should do so in a theatre.

But throughout the eighteenth century most Englishmen continued to believe that in opera the plot should be carried forward by means of spoken dialogue. It was a belief that sprang from Restoration practice, and it was scarcely shaken by all-sung entertainments from Italy. Yet, if Roger North is to be believed, the belief was not at first very wide-spread. 'Some come for the play and hate the musick, others come onely for the musick, and the drama is pennance to them, and scarce any are well reconciled to both.'

3 ENGLISH OPERA AFTER PURCELL'S DEATH

During Purcell's lifetime other composers were allowed few opportunities in the playhouses. As Dryden put it ('On the Death of Mr. Purcell'):

> So ceas'd the rival Crew, when Purcell came,
> They sung no more, or only sung his Fame.

But once he was out of the way their chances suddenly increased, and for nearly ten years they made surprisingly full use of them. Much the most active were John Eccles (born about 1672), Daniel Purcell (Henry's brother, born about 1660) and a Moravian immigrant called Gottfried Finger.

Eccles was the grandson of Solomon Eccles, a notoriously turbulent Quaker, and the son of another Solomon who played the violin in the Royal Band from 1685. He was contributing songs to plays from an early age, and their popularity is shown by the large number that were published. In *Pills to purge Melancholy*, there are some forty of his songs, many of them operatic; this is less than half Henry Purcell's contribution but double that of any other composer. During Betterton's tenure of the theatre in Lincoln's Inn Fields (1695–1705) Eccles was the 'house' composer, on call for anything that was wanted. It thus happened that he wrote a great deal of his music for Mrs. Bracegirdle, the only example in the period of a good actress who could sing. He was immensely talented. Much that he wrote is of Purcellian calibre, and its neglect is hard to comprehend.

Daniel Purcell worked mainly for the rival theatre, Drury Lane. From 1689 until about 1695 he had been organist at Magdalen College Oxford, where his more extended works were performed. These included a setting of a St. Cecilia's Day Ode by Joseph Addison, who then held a Demyship at Magdalen. Burney described Daniel as 'a wicked punster and no less wicked composer', and since then writers have generally been content to dismiss his music without going to the trouble of looking at it. Certainly his invention can be rather feeble, but every now and again it takes wing so fascinatingly that one longs for someone to give him the attention he deserves.

Of Finger, who was a foreigner and who left the country in 1701, little need be said; which is as well for very little is known. He collaborated with both Eccles and Daniel Purcell; though rivals, they all seem to have been friendly. Other collaborators were Jeremiah Clarke and Richard Leveridge, who worked only in a junior capacity.

I shall discuss first the full-length operas of these composers and then certain interpolated masques of an unusual nature. The full-length operas are remarkable both for their number and for the fact that though none of them was published complete most of them survive in manuscript full score. They all resemble *The Fairy Queen* in plan, though they do not all have so much music.

Purcell (D): *Brutus of Alba* (Tate etc.) A few songs survive	DG late 1696
Purcell/Clarke(?): *Cinthia and Endimion* (D'Urfey) Only one song survives	DL Dec. 1696
Purcell/Clarke: *The World in the Moon* (Settle) About 10 songs survive	DG June 1697
Eccles: *Europe's Revells* (Motteux) FS—BM Add. 29378	Court 4.11.97
Eccles: *Rinaldo and Armida* (Dennis) FS—BM Add. 29378	LIF Nov. 1698
Purcell/Clarke: *The Island Princess* (Fletcher) FS—BM Add. 15318 (Leveridge also collaborated)	DL Nov. 1698
Purcell: *The Grove* (Oldmixon) FS—LCM MS 988	DL Feb. 1700
Purcell/Finger: *The Rival Queens* (Lee) FS—CFM 23.H.12	DL 1701 (?)
Finger: *The Virgin Prophetess* (Settle) FS—CFM 23.H.12 and LCM MS 862	DL May 1701

The first two of these operas have uninteresting and badly written librettos. *Brutus of Alba* is set in Ancient Britain, with scenes on the Thames and on the cliffs of Dover. In spite of this, an assortment of Greek gods and goddesses appear in the later acts; indeed in the last act they appear in a barely credible way. 'A very large Machine descends', says the stage direction; 'in this Machine sits Apollo, Cupid, Mars, Vulcan, Juno, Venus etc.' Probably they were cardboard figures; if human, the descent must have been hazardous in the extreme.

Cinthia and Endimion was presented at Court before it was given at Drury Lane. The libretto mentions 'A Symphony of Flutes and Hautboys' in the first act, and we shall find that pieces for woodwind alone become quite common in operas of this period. The masque in Act II is introduced without any attempt at plausibility. It is not known who wrote the music, but one song by Clarke survives and it is likely that he was collaborating with Daniel Purcell.

The World in the Moon deserves attention even though so little of the music can be found, for Settle devised an original and intelligent way of introducing the masques. He wrote a short comedy in prose on normal 'Restoration' lines about young Londoners in pursuit of girls. Frank Wildblood is an uninhibited chaser, but his friend Palmerin Worthy is more principled when courting the heroine, Jacintha. Her father, needless to say, wants her to marry an elderly alderman. A country yokel called Tom Dawkins comes to London with his mother to see Frank Wildblood, whose tenants they are. So far all is conventional; what happens is not.

In the opening dialogue there are references to some play which, at seven o'clock, is judged to be half over. Time enough, says Frank, who plans to go to the theatre after the play is over to see 'a general Practice of the Musick and Machines of some part of the new Opera', called *The New World on the Moon*. At the end of Act I the stage becomes itself, and we see part of this opera; the music is by Clarke, who also composed the Prologue. In Act II Palmerin plans to disguise himself as the alderman's servant, and Jacintha treats the old gentleman to a surprising barrage of invective which drives him out of the house screaming 'I shall be ravished'. Back at the opera rehearsal, we find that Wildblood has brought his tenant Tom with him, and they are welcomed by the famous comedian, Joe Haines, representing himself. For a joke they plan to dress Tom up in grand clothes, and he is thrilled at the thought of meeting the operatic 'Queen'. From now on we can leave the prose comedy to take its predictable course. In those parts of the next two acts that take place at the opera rehearsal, the ridiculous Tom slips in and out of the action, much inconvenienced by his mother who thinks his morals are being ruined. However when he is seen in a great stage bed waiting for his 'Queen' (presumably the Queen of the Moon) there is a clap of thunder and the whole bed falls out of sight. By the end of the fourth act reality declines, for the 'Nuptial Entertainment' seems not to be part of the opera rehearsal but something Jacintha conjures up to plague her alderman. Nevertheless this is a striking attempt at a credible opera. All the music from Act II onwards was by Daniel Purcell.

Europe's Revells on the Peace was a court production celebrating the Peace of Ryswick, and though it was acted it was hardly in the English opera tradition. *Rinaldo and Armida* was the only Purcell-type opera that Eccles wrote, and very good it is. John Dennis took his characters and plot from Tasso, but claimed to have made Rinaldo more principled and Armida less wanton. The entire action takes place on Armida's magic island a few hours before her death, and because she is a sorceress it was easy for Dennis to introduce the masques. The score omits the overture, as does the score of Purcell's *The Grove*, and the probable reason is that these overtures were published in parts and the manuscript had to be sent to the engraver. In fact no copies survive, but the Royal College of Music does have the published 'Overture and Ayres' of Finger's *The Virgin Prophetess*, music which is not to be found in this library's manuscript score of the rest of the opera. Other instrumental pieces in *Rinaldo and Armida* were no doubt published with the overture, and it is especially sad that we do not have a piece referred to in the libretto as 'The Serpent and Basses softly under the Stage'. Eccles had a flair for ghost music, a flair that is especially apparent in Act IV of this opera, and we shall find him using a serpent for similar reasons in his *Macbeth* music.

The Grove also ends sadly. The plot was claimed by Oldmixon to be of his own invention, and though it has a certain atmosphere inherent in the title it is dully written. A number of high-born Greeks find themselves in a delightful grove on the Gulf of Venice, and at the end of the opera one pair of lovers elects to stay there rather than rule in Thrace. Inevitably shepherds and shepherdesses feature in the masque interpolations. Act II has a 'symphony' for flutes, oboes, and bass (presumably bassoon) on their own, the intention apparently being to represent the birdsong of the Grove. As in all Daniel Purcell's operas there is a great deal of trumpeting. This one has two Trumpet Sonatas on the lines of the one attributed without certainty to his brother Henry; in each case there are three movements, the trumpet being silent in the central slow one. The first of these Sonatas is a little unusual in being in the key of C, but the D major one that starts Act III is more spirited, and quite as good, one might think, as Henry's. There are also some songs with trumpet obbligato and a fine chorus at the end in which trumpets and drums are added to the strings and oboes. At the very beginning of the score there is antiphonal writing for strings and oboes, and the bass line below the oboes is marked 'bassoon'.[1]

The same copyist who produced this beautifully-written score of *The Grove* was also responsible for a magnificent volume in the Fitzwilliam Library at Cambridge. As well as two works I shall come to later, this volume includes Purcell's *The Rival Queens* and Finger's *The Virgin Prophetess*, and it would seem that it was made for Drury Lane in or about 1702. *The Rival Queens*, a tragedy by Nathaniel Lee, had had some performances the year before with Purcell's additions, usually under the alternative title of *Alexander*. The queens of the title are the two wives of Alexander the Great, Roxana and Statira. At the end Roxana stabs her rival, and Alexander dies too. It is remarkable how many of these operas end tragically, in contrast to Italian operas later in the century when the curtain was expected to fall on a general reconciliation. There is a masque in Act IV of 'Indian Singers and Dancers'.

The Virgin Prophetess of Finger's opera was Cassandra. At the start of Act II she organizes a short masque to appease the gods, but it must have antagonized them for by Act III she is held prisoner by the Greeks. Ulysses advises

[1] See p. 22 for another very early bassoon part.

that she shall be put to death but King Menelaus insists on a magnanimous release, and at this point a short masque about Cupid makes an unprepared appearance. Back in Troy Cassandra conjures up a 'Garden with Fountains, Arbours, Golden Fruit etc' which is an excuse for a song or two. Much more original and effective must have been the last act, in which the dialogue switches from verse to prose because the speakers are members of a mob of Trojans who have tried to drink their cares away. 'All snug in a jovial tippling Crowd', they sing, but the opera ends with Troy on fire and Helen leaping into the flames. Finger's style is markedly different from Purcell's. Perhaps he learnt his craft in Paris, for he often writes for a five-part string band like Lully's, the middle parts looking as though they had been added by a hack. In spite of a masque in Act III for the entertainment of Paris and Helen, there is much less music in *The Virgin Prophetess* than there is in *The Grove* or *Rinaldo and Armida*.

The *Island Princess* differs from the other operas of its time in two respects which are in fact related. It was by far the most successful English opera before *The Beggar's Opera*, and though for the most part tragic in feeling it ended in reconciliation. This may in part have been why it was liked, for the mood, though deriving from such tragi-comedies as *The Winter's Tale*, must have seemed modern and in accord with that of Handel's operas. There were revivals almost every season for nearly thirty years. The libretto was based on a tragi-comedy of the same name by John Fletcher; the lyrics were added, and the blank-verse dialogue revised by Peter Motteux.[1] The scene is the Spice Islands in the East Indies, and the plot concerns a noble Portuguese, Armusia, who becomes betrothed to the Island King's sister, Quisara. Both are un-justly vilified, imprisoned, and condemned to be sacrificed, but the truth is un-covered in time and there is a happy ending. Most of the songs and dialogues (duets) were published separately, and Walsh assembled some of these sheet songs into a fragmentary vocal score. The British Museum has a manuscript full score of virtually the whole opera. This is said to be in Clarke's hand, but it looks to me as though two or even three writers had worked on it.[2] It includes all the spoken dialogue, and it is the sole source for the many instrumental pieces, the choruses, and a few of the songs.

The *Island Princess* is similar in scale and design to *The Fairy Queen*. No other operas of the time begin, as do these, with 'First Musicke' and 'Second

---

[1] Peter Motteux (1660–1718) was a Huguenot refugee, who worked mainly with Eccles. Dryden described him as 'So Great a Poet and so Good a Friend' (*Epistle to Peter Anthony Motteux*). By 1711 he was in the City selling 'China and Japan Wares, Tea, Fans, Muslins, Pictures, Arrack, and other *Indian* goods' (see his letter, *Spectator* 288). His unhappy end in a brothel when 'trying a very odd Experi-ment' is recorded in Baker but without details.

[2] Add. 15318. It omits Leveridge's tuneful Prologue, Clarke's Epilogue (for which see *Pills* v, pp. 348 and 339), and a charming song by D. Purcell sung in Act III by Quisara's page, 'Lovely Charmer'.

Musicke' (two binary-form dances in each) for the benefit of those who have come into the theatre early. Each act except the last ends with an 'Act Tune' for the interval. All the instrumental music seems to be by Clarke. The rest of the score consists in the main of three masques. Near the end of Act II, to celebrate the betrothal of Armusia and Quisara, there is an 'Entertainment of Musick and Dancing' presented by shepherds and composed by Daniel Purcell. His three-movement Trumpet Sonata would be worth salvaging. Act IV begins with Armusia 'lying on a Bank in a Grove of Orange Trees', and being entertained by a dialogue composed by Leveridge, who was also one of the singers, and it ends with a long 'Incantation' sung at night with many references to 'infernal powers'. As well as a trumpet song there is a striking 'Symphony of flat Trumpets' in which three trombones play one slow chord a bar, much as in Henry Purcell's music for Queen Mary's Funeral. All this Incantation is by Daniel Purcell except for an 'Enthusiastick Song' with soft and loud markings by Leveridge.

The longest section of uninterrupted music ends the last act. Clarke's Masque of the Four Seasons 'or Love in Every Age' is for the entertainment of the reunited hero and heroine, and it includes a dance and a love-making dialogue appropriate to each of the four seasons. The Spring dialogue is sung by 'A Girl of 13 or 14 and a Youth', and begins 'Must I a Girl for ever be?' A 'Sumer Dance by Blacks' is followed by an Autumn dialogue for a widow and a rake. Finally the masque comes full circle with a Winter dialogue in which a widow complains to an old man:

> Hold, good Mr. Fumble! By what do you mean
> To court my Grand Daughter? She's scarce yet fifteen.

A jubilant D major chorus with trumpets rounds off the entertainment. Clarke is here at his best, and the whole masque would make agreeable entertainment today.

In his *Essay of Dramatick Poesie* (1665) Dryden wrote that the plays published as by Beaumont and Fletcher

> are now the most pleasant and frequent entertainments of the stage; two of theirs being acted through the year for one of Shakespeare's or Johnson's: the reason is, because there is a certain gaiety in their comedies, and pathos in their more serious plays, which suits generally with all men's humours.

This was equally true in 1700 when Dryden died; except that in fact it was the plays Fletcher wrote alone that were liked rather than those he wrote in collaboration. They were mostly tragi-comedies ending in romantic reconciliation, and their gallimaufry of moods made them well-suited to musical additions. Shakespeare's superiority over Fletcher and Jonson, though suspected by Dryden, was not fully appreciated until well on in the eighteenth century.

The full-length operas described above were for the most part written for Dorset Gardens or Drury Lane. At Lincoln's Inn Fields Betterton preferred the single interpolated masque with a mythological plot, and the result must have been much closer to Italianate opera. There had been very occasional experiments in this direction earlier in the century. For instance in the 1670s Matthew Locke's *Orpheus and Euridice* had been included in performances of Settle's *The Empress of Morocco*. But Betterton was the first to interpolate such masques as a considered policy, and it is tragic that none of them survive in full score.

Eccles } Finger }	*The Loves of Mars and Venus* (Motteux) in *The Anatomist* (Ravenscroft)	LIF 14.11.96 (?)
Eccles	*Hercules* (Motteux) in *The Novelty* (Motteux)	LIF May (?) 1697
Eccles	*Ixion* (Taverner) in *The Italian Husband* (Ravenscroft)	LIF Dec. 1697 (?)
Eccles	*Acis and Galatea* (Motteux) in *The Mad Lover* (Fletcher)	LIF 1700 (?)
Eccles (?)	*Peleus and Thetis* (Granville) in *The Jew of Venice* (Shakespeare etc.)	LIF May (?) 1701

Published librettos of all these masques survive, but there seems to be no music for *Ixion*, *Hercules* or *Peleus and Thetis*. Hercules was treated as a comic character. George Granville, author of *Peleus and Thetis*, later became Lord Lansdowne. His masque was performed in a version of *The Merchant of Venice* for the entertainment of Antonio and Shylock in Bassanio's house, and it was later set by Boyce.

Like Elkanah Settle in *The World in the Moon*, Edward Ravenscroft tried to introduce the musical interpolations in his farce *The Anatomist* as naturally as possible. In the very first line, Angelica the doctor's daughter remarks 'Is my Mother ready, is she coming to hear the Musick?' There is to be a rehearsal in the doctor's house of a masque in four scenes about Mars and Venus, and we see two of them in Act I (with dialogue in between) and the others ('We'll hear the rest after dinner' says Angelica's mother) at the ends of Acts II and III. Right at the start we learn that Angelica's lover is sitting in the orchestra heavily disguised, and later, purporting to be a surgeon, he prescribes pills to a woman because she has lost her dog, and sets about a supposed corpse with a butcher's knife with a view to a dissertation on anatomy. In fact he is no more than a servant in love above his station, and behaving in the absurd but delightful way audiences later came to expect of Harlequin. The farce remained popular throughout the eighteenth century, but the musical inserts seem to have lasted only about ten years. According to the libretto Finger set the first and last sections and Eccles the middle two. Bowman and Mrs. Bracegirdle sang the title roles, and dozen songs were published mostly with just a bass for accompaniment. Those by Eccles are noticably longer and more Italianate than those by Finger, and there is a good duet of his with trumpet obbligato. The music was much liked, but it fell from favour when Italian opera became the rage.

Acis and Galatea had a contrary fate. The masque, written for a revival of a tragi-comedy by Fletcher, survived and *The Mad Lover* did not. The date of the revival is unknown, but by 11 December 1702 the masque was being performed on its own. This is the first known occasion on which a full-length play was followed by a half-length afterpiece, and it would seem that the afterpiece tradition, fully established by about 1730, originally arose because there was no other way of presenting a short masque as a self-contained entity. This one has a clodhopping underplot in which Joan is briefly diverted from her betrothed, Roger, by the charms of Acis. There is a happy ending. Instead of being crushed under a rock thrown by Polyphemus, Acis survives to wed Galatea. He was played by Mrs. Bracegirdle as a breeches part, as is revealed in *Pills* (v, pp. 287–8, 299). These and two other songs were also published with a bass, and described as coming from *The Mad Lover*. The masque was especially popular in the 1720s, the date of the only libretto I have found.

We now have a context in which we can place the performances at Lincoln's Inn Fields of Henry Purcell's *Dido and Aeneas*. In 1700 Charles Gildon freely adapted *Measure for Measure*, inserting Purcell's opera act by act as had been done with *The Loves of Mars and Venus*; the interpolations were described as *The Loves of Dido and Aeneas*, and they were ostensibly performed for the entertainment of Angelo.[1] Later, because of the success of *Acis and Galatea* on its own, *Dido and Aeneas* was allowed a few continuous performances as a self-contained work, the first of them probably in 1704.

Drury Lane's more conservative policy is shown in Dryden's virtually plotless *Secular Masque* (1700), inserted into Fletcher's *The Pilgrim*. The music was by Daniel Purcell and Finger, and the first half by Purcell survives complete,[2] but of the second half by Finger we have nothing but one published song. Years later Dryden's marvellous masque was re-set by Boyce.[3]

In 1701 English composers had the opportunity of writing a more extended all-sung masque than usual, and the occasion proved a happy one for John Weldon. His Purcellian and very lovely setting of 'Take oh take those Lips away' was probably written for the *Measure for Measure* production mentioned above. He came from Chichester, and he had been a pupil of Henry Purcell, and organist of New College, Oxford. At the age of twenty-four

---

[1] See Eric Walter White in *Henry Purcell: Essays on his Music*, ed. Imogen Holst. His suggestion that Daniel Purcell set the missing scene is improbable; Daniel worked only for Drury Lane. It is more likely that Eccles set it.

[2] BM Add. 29378. It includes some enterprising writing for trumpets, and a fine setting of Chronos's 'Weary, weary'.

[3] See p. 210.

Weldon entered the famous competition for setting a masque libretto that Congreve wrote for the occasion, *The Judgment of Paris*. £200 was offered as prize money, and the entries were all performed at Dorset Garden, which by then was not in regular use and shortly to be pulled down. The version by Eccles was given on March 21, Finger's a week later, Daniel Purcell's on April 11, and Weldon's on May 6. Then on June 3 'All the Pieces of Musick contending for the Prize' were given in turn, and 'the victorys decided by the judgment of the subscribers'.[1] Paris's apple must have been intended as a symbol of the prize offered to the composers, and the idea may well have been sparked off by Motteux in his preface to *The Loves of Mars and Venus*. Finger and Eccles, it will be remembered, had collaborated, and Motteux remarked on the high quality of the music, 'the two great Composers having, as it were, nobly strove to outdo one another, and thus excelled even themselves'.

The only detailed description of 'The Prize' is in a letter Congreve wrote to his Dublin friend, Joseph Keally, just after the Eccles performance. This, says Congreve, was 'universally admired', and he goes on:

> I don't think any one place in the world can show such an assembly. The number of performers, besides the verse singers, was 85. The front of the stage was all built into a concave with deal boards; all of which was faced with tin, to increase and throw forward the sound . . . the boxes and pit were all thrown into one; so that all sat in common; and the whole was crammed with beauties and beaux, not one scrub being admitted. The place where formerly the music used to play, between the pit and the stage, was turned into White's chocolate-house; the whole family being transplanted thither with chocolate, cool'd drinks, ratafia, portico, etc., which every body that would call'd for, the whole expence of every thing being defray'd by the subscribers.

No doubt it was high prices that kept out the scrubs. The well-dressed audience partaking of elaborate refreshments at no extra cost suggests our country-house entertainments in which the wine is thrown in with the ticket. The orchestra and chorus must have been exceptionally large, and if, as seems implied, the former sat on the stage in front of the tin resonators there cannot have been much room for the acting.

Congreve certainly envisaged both acting and scenery. After Mercury has warned Paris what is to happen,

Juno, Pallas, *and* Venus, *are seen at a distance descending in several Machins.*

Each in fact descends in turn, to sing a song and claim the prize. Paris says he is dazzled by so much beauty, and he asks to view the goddesses separately:

[1] *Roger North on Music*, ed. John Wilson, p. 354.

> Apart let me view then each Heav'nly Fair,
> For Three at a time there's no Mortal can bear;
> And since a gay Robe an ill Shape may disguise,
> When each is undrest
> I'll judge of the best,
> For 'tis not a Face that must carry the Prize.

The flippant tone was intended; Congreve's libretto is surprisingly subtle, with much more softly worded lyrics for Venus than for the other two goddesses. Presumably some degree of disrobing now takes place, after which Juno sings 'Let Ambition fire thy mind', in which she offers Paris the bribe of political prestige. A chorus joins in both here and after Pallas Athene's songs offering military distinction; and yet again when Venus offers Helen. Paris finds Venus and her offer irresistible and he gives her the Golden Apple.

> *Several* Cupids *descend, the three* Graces *alight from the Chariot of* Venus, *they call the* Howrs, *who assemble; with all the Attendants on* Venus. *All join in a Circle round her, and sing the last grand* Chorus; *while* Juno *and* Pallas *ascend.*

Congreve managed his simple story without once asking for recitative, as indeed did Motteux in *The Loves of Mars and Venus*.

A postscript in the Congreve letter quoted above reveals that in the Eccles version Mrs. Hodgson sang Juno and Mrs. Bowman Pallas; the latter 'was not quite so well approv'd'. Venus was Mrs. Bracegirdle, with whom Congreve was in love; she 'perform'd to a miracle'. The music shows that Paris was a counter-tenor, whereas in Weldon's version he was a baritone. It may be that the same women singers were used for all four versions, that performances were well spaced so that they had time to learn the next one, and that in spite of this the difficulty of learning four settings of the same words was such that they insisted on having the music in their hands and giving a concert performance. During the next five years the Eccles, Purcell, and Weldon masques were each given two or three isolated performances in the London theatres, and these surely were acted in costume, with a full complement of machines and Cupids.

Burney and Baker both give the winner of the competition as Weldon, with Eccles and Purcell second and third and Finger last, and it is strange and perhaps significant that only the Eccles and Purcell scores were published. There may well have been a feeling among the knowledgable that Weldon did not deserve his success. Certainly Eccles was somewhat needled by the result, as he shows in the dedication of his score. After asking Lord 'Hallifax' for 'a continuance of your patronage', he goes on

> As to the following Composition, my Labour in it was more then [*sic*] requited, by your Lordship's Allowance of it at the Practice; if at the publick performance, besides the kind Approbation which it received

from the Greater part of the Audience, it had also had the fortune to have pleas'd them who came prepar'd to Dislike it, I might have been too vain of my Success, and maybe not have thought my selfe obliged (as I now think I am) by my future care to Endevour to Obtain their good Opinions Whome it is my Ambition to please and from whome I am sorry not to have already Deserv'd more Encouragement.

Clearly there had been some attempt to prejudice the result by means of a claque hostile to Eccles.

The Eccles and Purcell scores were published in full by Walsh and Hare, who used the same splendid title-page for both. This depicts the three more-or-less naked goddesses and describes each work not as a Masque but as a Pastoral. The quality of the music is high, especially in the Eccles which is a masterpiece. The scoring is unusually lavish, each composer being free to introduce as many instruments as he liked. Indeed Daniel Purcell emphasises the orchestra at the expense of the singers. As well as a four-movement overture with oboes, trumpets, and drums added to the string band, he has the inevitable three-movement 'Trumpet Sonata' modelled on his brother's for the entrance of the war-minded Pallas Athene, and a three-movement 'Symphony' for trumpet and strings before her final song. In smaller compass there is a one-movement 'Symphony' for Paris, in which Purcell uses the rare combination of flutes and oboes over lower strings, while Juno is characterized by a stormy string piece with every instrument hurrying in semiquavers. Venus is conventionally portrayed by the amorous sound of flutes over a chromatically descending ground bass which persists in her song, a lovely one.

The association of Venus (i.e. love) with flutes (i.e. recorders) was to be a convention for nearly fifty years. Before the Commonwealth, recorders had been required in the theatres for funerals, portents and miracles,[1] but the new attitude is apparent in one of Dryden's stage directions for Grabu's all-sung opera, *Albion and Albanius* (1685):

> A Machine rises out of the Sea; it opens and discovers Venus and Albanius sitting in a great Scallop-shell richly adorned . . . the Shell is drawn by Dolphins; it moves forward while a Symphony of flutes-doux etc. is playing . . .

'Flutes-doux' are recorders. About the same time these instruments were accompanying amorous words in Act I of Blow's *Venus and Adonis*, and four years later Dryden immortalized the association in his *Song for St. Cecilia's Day*:

> The soft complaining Flute
> In dying Notes discovers
> The Woes of hopeless Lovers.

[1] See J. S. Manifold's *The Music in English Drama from Shakespeare to Purcell.*

For the most part Daniel Purcell's level of inspiration in what came to be known as *The Prize* fell below the skill of his orchestration. Thus the last movement of the overture begins gallantly with seven bars for trumpets and drums on their own, but the theme is too banal to support the gesture. The preceding movement, for strings alone, seems to be influenced by the Adagio in the overture to his brother's *St. Cecilia's Day Ode* of 1692; nevertheless it is a remarkable experiment in discord:

Eccles never lets the orchestra hold up the action as Daniel Purcell does, and he keeps his flashier effects till near the end, his overture being scored for a single trumpet and strings. His themes are stronger and more individual than Daniel Purcell's, and he is far more adventurous in his modulations, in the overture passing easily through F sharp major in the course of an opening movement in D. The whole overture is inventive. We may profitably compare the two settings of the song Paris sings when he first sets eyes on the three goddesses. Both composers see this as a highly emotional moment, but their reactions are utterly different. Daniel Purcell gives his counter-tenor free rhapsodical melismata, on the lines of ''Tis Nature's Voice' in his brother's *St. Cecilia's Day Ode*, and the result is one of his most moving songs.

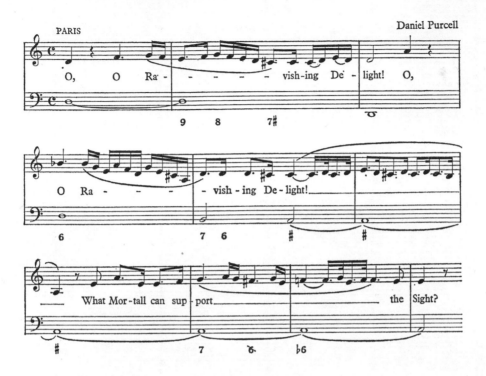

Eccles conveys a rather different sort of feeling with a beautifully shaped vocal line—the word-setting is exemplary—and a remarkable richness of harmony in the accompaniment, which is none the worse for a suggestion of 'Dido's Lament':

For Pallas Athene Eccles makes his great gesture, introducing no less than four trumpets in her last song.

This is the introduction; sudden explosions on the four trumpets and the drums punctuate the song itself, and the effect at the first performance must have been overwhelming. For the splendid chorus that follows Eccles devised a fugue subject within the trumpet's capabilities, and he keeps all four trumpets going with entries of their own:

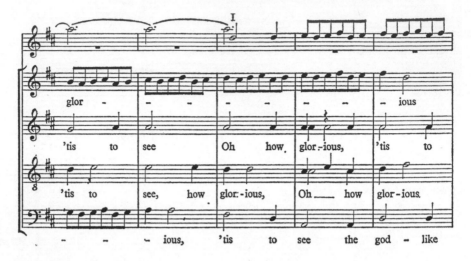

The *Judgment of Paris* by Eccles was given its only stage performance for more than two centuries by Anthony Bernard at Hampton Court in 1951, but the vogue for Baroque music had scarcely begun, and the production aroused little attention.

Weldon's *Prize* music, though inexplicably never published, survives in MS full score in the Folger Library, Washington. It starts with a 'Pastoral Symphony by Paris and other Shepherds on Ida's top while Mercury descends'. The action must have begun immediately with actors miming the opening 'Canon 4 in 1' for flutes and oboes with what looks like tabor accompaniment; the canon is not very clever, for it is based on C major arpeggios throughout. It is soon clear why Weldon won, for the score is full of simple catchy songs; also it is a little more modern in style than the Eccles. Juno's 'Let Ambition fire the Mind' was especially liked, the many repeats fixing it in everyone's mind, and sixty years later it renewed its appeal as the first song in *Love in a Village*. But there are also moments of deeper beauty, and even of passion, as when Paris sees the three goddesses descend.

That is similar in style to the Daniel Purcell setting already quoted, but it is more dramatic in feeling, and Weldon covers the ground more briskly. Pallas Athene arrives to a remarkable symphony that is antiphonal throughout; trumpet, first violins, and bass violins alternate with oboe, second violins, and curtill (bassoon). This is one of the first individual parts for a bassoon in English music;[1] there is another antiphonal symphony with a bassoon stave just before Venus makes her claim for the trophy. It is for Venus that Weldon reserves his loveliest music. Here for instance is the start of her song 'on a Ground', 'Stay, lovely Youth'; it is nearly all in three-bar phrases.

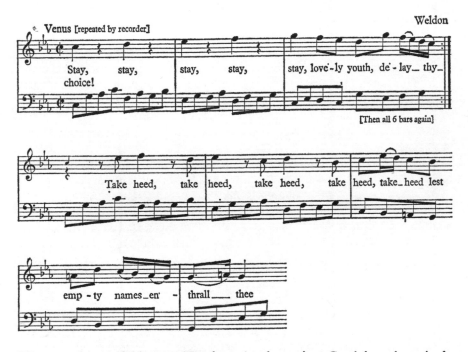

The second part of this song, 'Far from thee be anxious Care', has a hauntingly beautiful tune.

Finger was so angry at coming last that he left England for good and got a job in Berlin, where he continued to write operas. 'The best musician perhaps among the candidates the fourth', remarked Burney with his usual anti-British prejudice; he can never have seen Finger's music which does not survive. At least his conscience made him add 'perhaps'. He would also have praised, had he ever heard of it, a fifth setting of Congreve's words by the elderly German composer Johann Franck, who had been living in London on and off since 1690. This was given at York Buildings (2.2.02), being 'Compos'd for three Quires, and in quite a different way from the others, not used here before'. Perhaps

[1] There is also a curtill part in Weldon's overture; and see p. 10.

Franck's entry arrived after Closing Day; nothing of it survives. Much later in the century Congreve's libretto was re-set by both Giuseppe Sammartini and Thomas Arne.

It is astonishing how much theatre music our composers wrote at this period, and astonishing also that so much of it should survive; by contrast the twenty years from 1710 onwards are a desolate featureless waste. Composers were especially in demand for a type of incidental music, purely instrumental, that Henry Purcell had often written. It can be exemplified by his music for *Abdelazer*, and it consisted of an overture and some eight or ten short dances and 'Act Tunes'. In 1697 his 'Collection of Ayres compos'd for the Theatre' was published, and with such success that similar music by other composers was soon being published too. At least forty-five sets had appeared by 1708,[1] and at least eight more survive in manuscript. The boom years were 1701–2, in each of which six to eight sets were printed. The real number must have been much higher, for most of the sets I have seen survive precariously in only one library. In March 1706 Walsh and Hare advertised 'Mr. Eccles Musick in the Play call'd Ulysses' but no copy survives and no doubt there have been many other such losses. The number of new plays presented in London at this period was prodigious.

I have attempted a tentative list of this incidental music in an appendix.[2] Nearly all of it was written for plays no one today would think of reviving, but there are also examples of Congreve's *Love for Love* by Finger, for Farquhar's *The (Beaux') Stratagem* by the French emigré, Jean Claude Gillier, and for Vanbrugh's *The Relapse* by Daniel Purcell. Only six sets have operatic associations; I list them with the interpolated masque, if any, in brackets.

Eccles	*The Italian Husband* (Ravenscroft) (*Ixion* by Taverner)	LIF 1698; O (MS)
Barrett	*The Pilgrim* (Fletcher) (*Secular Masque* by Dryden)	DL 29.4.00; L (PP)
Eccles	*The Mad Lover* (Fletcher) (*Acis and Galatea* by Motteux)	LIF 1701 (?); LCM (PP)
Finger	*The Virgin Prophetess* (Settle)	DL May 1701; LCM (PP)
Corbett	*The British Enchanters* (Lansdowne)	QT 21.2.06; L (PP incomplete)
Smith	*Wonders in the Sun* (D'Urfey)	QT 5.4.06; L (PP)

All this music survives in four separate string parts; the grander type of overture with trumpets and drums was either not published in this form or these instruments were omitted from such music as was published. It is impossible to assess the merit of these pieces without making a score from the parts. Judged

[1] The last was Barrett's *The Fine Lady's Airs*, mistitled *The Lady's Fine Airs*.
[2] Appendix B, p. 591.

superficially by the tunes given to the first violin, much of it seems well up to Henry Purcell standards, and it would be a mistake to expect excellence only in composers one has heard of. The dances in *Wonders in the Sun* are of good quality, though written by a violinist called John Smith of whom nothing at all is known.

Fifteen different composers are named in the appendix listing this incidental music. Those most in demand were Finger (9 sets), John Lenton (7), Daniel Purcell (6), Barrett and Corbett (5), Croft and Paisible (4). The dances include a high proportion of gavottes, hornpipes and jigs; allemands and sarabandes occur but are rare. There are also a good many labour-saving pieces called 'Round O' and a number of Scotch Tunes none of which shows the allegedly typical 'snap'. Much the longest pieces are the occasional Chaconnes, presumably written for stage processions. This type of music nearly always brought out the best in English composers, and those by Croft in *The Funeral* and *The Lying Lover* look well worth playing.

It is strange that after his success in the 'Prize' John Weldon wrote no incidental music for the theatres. Like Croft he ran from the Italian invaders and took refuge in church music; in fact he seems to have run several years before anyone else did. However he was lured back to the stage on at least one important occasion, as we shall see in the next section.

4 SHAKESPEAREAN MASQUES

The masques that were interpolated in Shakespeare's *Macbeth* and *The Tempest* are so different in style and in the degree of their success from anything so far described that they merit a section to themselves.

Shakespeare himself had inserted a masque in *The Tempest*, and perhaps would not have objected to similar intrusions in his other comedies. I have already mentioned *The Fairy Queen*. Apart from one act, this was never given in the eighteenth century apparently because the score was mislaid, but the entrancing masque Purcell composed for *Timon of Athens* remained popular for some years, and was heard in other plays as well. As already stated, *Dido and Aeneas* was performed in *Measure for Measure*, and *Peleus and Thetis* in *The Jew of Venice*. In the epilogue to the latter Granville went so far as to question Shakespeare's drawing power without the assistance of music:

> How was the Scene forlorn, and how despis'd
> When Timon, without Musick moraliz'd?
> *Shakespeare's* sublime in vain entic'd the Throng
> Without the Charm of *Purcel's* Syren Song.

Unlike the interpolations so far mentioned, those in *Macbeth* and *The Tempest* were lastingly popular. They also had one other very curious characteristic in common.

In 1664 Pepys described *Macbeth* as 'one of the best plays for a stage, and a variety of dancing and music, that ever I saw', and it is obvious that he was writing of a very different *Macbeth* from the one we know. He had in fact seen William Davenant's adaptation, not published until ten years later. Davenant cut some of the minor characters, built up the parts of Macduff and Lady Macduff (who comes on much earlier than she does in the original), and added (or established) short masques performed by the witches in the three middle acts. The first of these occurs in a new scene during which the weird sisters predict what fate has in store for the Macduffs—and indeed for everyone else; there is much singing of the vast quantities of blood that will be spilt. Davenant probably found the masque words for Acts III and IV in the old acting copies of the play, for they are referred to in the First Folio version. Shakespeare's III 5, a suspect scene, introduces Hecate and ends with the stage direction:

Music and a Song within, 'Come away, come away' etc.

In the equally suspect Hecate scene at the start of IV i we find:

Music and a Song, 'Black Spirits' etc.

These words are the first lines of *scenas* for music in dialogue form in *The Witch* (1610) by Thomas Middleton. The original settings, one of which survives, were probably by Robert Johnson, and apparently they were so successful that they were lugged into early performances of *Macbeth* as well. (But the other Hecate scenes are not to be found in *The Witch*.) The Act III masque consists of macabre badinage between Hecate and her attendant crew, who enter from aloft in a 'Machin'. The one in Act IV is an incantation as the witches prepare a hellish brew in their cauldron; it alone has some relevance to Shakespeare's *Macbeth*.

Matthew Locke set the masques for Davenant, and at the end of the century they were set again by Eccles, presumably for unrecorded performances at Lincoln's Inn Fields. By 1702 Locke's music was probably thought too old-fashioned,[1] and on 21 November Drury Lane advertised a performance 'with Vocal and Instrumental Musick, all new Compos'd by Mr. Leveridge, and perform'd by him and others'. Astonishingly, this music survived Garrick's restoration of the play to something like its proper self and was used for all London productions right up to 1875. Yet it is hardly an exaggeration to say that today no one knows a note of it.

Richard Leveridge, a bass singer and a minor composer, spent close on sixty years on the London stage, singing one of the leads in Purcell's *The Indian Queen* in 1695 and what Hawkins described as any pantomime part 'in which a

[1] Of Locke's music only two tunes survive (see my article 'The "Macbeth" Music', M&L, April 1964). The British Museum and the Royal College of Music each own two early manuscripts of Eccles's *Macbeth*: BM Add. 12219 appears to be his autograph.

long beard was necessary' as late as the 1750s, by which time he was well over eighty. 'Being a man of rather coarse manner', says Hawkins,

> and able to drink a great deal, he was by some thought a good companion. The humour of his songs, and indeed of his conversation, consisted in exhortations to despise riches and the means of attaining them; to drown care by drinking; to enjoy the present hour, and to set reflection and death at defiance.

This attitude, Hawkins wrily adds, made him very popular. His best-known song was the one you would have expected him to write, 'The Roast Beef of Old England' (CG 15.4.35 as an interval song);[1] in old age this was the only type of music within his powers. But as a young man he aspired to higher things, even aping the Italian style. We have seen how he collaborated in 1699 with Daniel Purcell and Clarke in *The Island Princess*.

The *Macbeth* music of three years later looked backwards rather than forwards in its short solid choruses, but there is some interesting arioso-like solo writing to offset the conscious archaisms. The scoring is for strings alone, and the orchestral preludes to Acts II and IV, specially mentioned in the advertisements, are curiously static and banal, and much less dramatic than the corresponding preludes by Eccles. There seems to have been a traditional style for witch music. Chords repeated very quickly in semiquavers apparently had a spine-chilling effect, and Eccles and Leveridge resort to them freely. There is MS. evidence that one of Locke's tunes was so treated. Also there is a family likeness between the three settings of the Act II song;

[1] Leveridge took the idea and the first verse from Fielding's ballad opera, *Don Quixote in England* (LT 5.4.34).

(Locke's tune survives only instrumentally—in Playford's *Musicks Delight upon the Cithren* of 1666 as 'A Jigg called Macbeth', and in Greeting's *The Pleasant Companion* of 1680 for the 'flagelet', but it fits the above words too well for coincidence.) In general Eccles was more ambitious than Leveridge, using a serpent with eerie effect in his opening Symphony, and writing antiphonally for soloists and chorus up aloft and similar groups down on the stage. Perhaps it was the extreme difficulty of such writing that led to his version being superceded by Leveridge's more practical one.

Fitzwilliam 23.H.12, a manuscript already mentioned, positively names Leveridge as the composer of the *Macbeth* score that remained popular into the nineteenth century, and it must have been copied within a year or two of its composition. Almost as early is British Museum Egerton 2957, from which the composer's name seems to have been maliciously removed. This excision was a major cause of the music's extraordinary history later on. It was not published until 1770, when the title page described it as 'Composed by Matthew Locke . . . Revised and Corrected by Dr. Boyce'. Boyce printed an approximation to Egerton 2957, which at that time he owned, together with two unidentified dances at the end on two staves. In 1785 Harrison & Co. brought out a vocal score of the same music which they attributed to Purcell. By this time the score was receiving ecstatic praise from everyone. Burney, believing it to be by Locke, a composer he could admire without prejudice to any Italian, went so far as to write that 'its rude wild excellence cannot be surpassed'—words he would have been horrified at using of Leveridge. Controversy between the Locke and Purcell schools of thought was still raging in Victorian times, and the first edition of *Grove's Dictionary* gave it four columns. The growing realization that the music was probably by neither composer naturally made people think much less highly of it, and today it is forgotten. Yet such critics as Dr. Johnson, Coleridge, and Hazlitt can never have seen *Macbeth* without Leveridge's music. Shelley as a boy at Eton was remembered by a friend as 'singing with the buoyant cheerfulness in which he often indulged, as he might be running nimbly up and down stairs, the Witches' songs in *Macbeth*', while Samuel Palmer, according to his son, used to sing Locke's *Macbeth* music with fellow art students 'by night in hollow clefts and deserted chalk pits'.

The history of the music for *The Tempest* is strangely similar. Again Davenant produced an operatic adaptation in early Restoration times, and again the Restoration music was found old-fashioned in Queen Anne's reign and replaced. Davenant's text was revised by both Dryden and Shadwell in quick succession, and the play was saddled with a second pair of lovers—Hippolito, the boy who had never seen a girl, and Dorinda, Miranda's sister. Dryden contrived much sly fun from the sexual innocence of the two girls and Hippolito. The play also acquired in Act II a masque of devils who plague Alonzo and the other conspirators; 'Arise, ye subterranean Winds' was sung by one of them. Act III had several isolated songs, most of them for Ariel; two even had words by Shakespeare. But for some reason Ariel never sang 'Where the Bee sucks' in Restoration times. Shadwell wrote a marine masque for Act V; it replaced Shakespeare's in Act IV about Ceres and Juno, and it was staged by Prospero for the pleasure of his guests. The character sinclude Neptune, Amphitrite, and Aeolus.

For one or other of the Restoration versions of *The Tempest* Matthew Locke wrote the instrumental movements, Pelham Humfrey the masques, and John Banister most of the single songs; John Hart and the Italian Draghi also contributed. Nearly all this music survives. Late in the century Hart's rather touching song in Act IV (*Pills* iii, p. 178) was replaced by Purcell's 'Dear pretty Youth', which was also sung by Dorinda, and this was published in *Orpheus Britannicus*. The existence of this song led later musicians to attribute to Purcell all the music commonly used for the play in the middle of the eighteenth century. In Dublin it was performed as Purcell's as early as 1749,[1] and a curious publication of 1761, *The Words of such Pieces as are most usually performed by the Academy of Ancient Music* attributes to Purcell the masques in both *The Tempest* and *Macbeth*. The *Tempest* music was published as Purcell's about 1790, and it has been admired ever since as one of his finest achievements. As might be expected, it has nothing in common with the Locke–Humfrey–Banister music mentioned above.

Some years ago the Purcell attribution was questioned by Dennis Arundell and others who found the word-setting uncharacteristic, and recently it has been demolished by Dr. Margaret Laurie.[2] Her evidence hinges largely on a Drury Lane advertisement for 30 July 1716: 'All the Musick compos'd by Mr. Weldon, and perform'd Compleat, as at the Revival'. *The Tempest* had been continuously in the Drury Lane repertoire since 7 January 1712, clearly the date of the 'revival'. Among other arguments, Dr. Laurie suggests that Weldon would never have been asked to write this music if there had been a

---

[1] Sheldon, p. 333; the *Macbeth* music was played as Purcell's at the same time.
[2] *RMA Proceedings* 1963–4: 'Did Purcell set *The Tempest*?'

score available by the still very popular Purcell; that its Italianate style accords much better with 1712 than with 1695, the date of Purcell's death; that there is nothing from *The Tempest* in his *Ayres compos'd for the Theatre* (1697) or, with the one exception, in *Orpheus Britannicus*, and there would have been had he written the music; that the obsession with the key of C in each act is uncharacteristic of Purcell, as is the absence of trumpets and of a grand chorus at the end; that the scoring for strings alone (plus one oboe in 'Halcyon Days') is less ambitious, and the word setting less subtle than Purcell's. Weldon's *The Judgment of Paris* shows a similar inability to escape from the key of C. Dr. Laurie's case is arguably not proven, but to me it is completely convincing.

Early manuscripts of the *Tempest* music contain no overture. Perhaps Weldon borrowed one from some other work. He certainly borrowed the violin melody of a 'Dance of the Winds' from Lully's *Cadmus et Hermione*, which had been given in London in 1687, as also Purcell's 'Dear pretty youth', which no doubt was thought irreplaceable. He alone deserves credit for the splendid Italianate music in the final masque (a shortened version of the Shadwell one set by Humfrey back in 1674), as also for such beauties as the well-known chorus of 'Full fathom five', with its heaven-sent false relations. It may be salutary to look at these bars with Weldon's name in mind instead of Purcell's.

Eccles, Daniel Purcell, and Weldon must have watched the Italian take-over bid with something approaching horror. For the first four or five years of the century they could still get their music performed, and the future seemed reasonably secure. But when Eccles wrote a full-length all-sung English opera in 1706 (it was a setting of Congreve's *Semele*, later re-set by Handel), the result was never performed at all. Eccles washed his hands of the London theatres, and retired to Kingston upon Thames where he devoted his remaining twenty-five years to writing Court Odes and fishing. No doubt he found time for some grumbling too. His brother Henry, a good violinist, left the country to live in Paris, where he got some of his instrumental music published; he had found this impossible in London. Yet another brother took to drink. Clarke committed suicide in 1707. Weldon, apart from producing his score for *The Tempest*, wrote little but church music; he succeeded Blow as organist at the Chapel Royal in 1708. As for Daniel Purcell, he was just forgotten.

5 THE RISE AND TRIUMPH OF ITALIAN OPERA

I must now describe how

> The *Italian* Opera began first to steal into *England*; but in as rude a disguise and unlike itself, as possible; in a lame, hobling Translation, into our own Language, with false Quantities, or Metre out of Measure, to its original Notes, sung by our own unskilful Voices, with Graces mis-apply'd to almost every Sentiment, and with Action lifeless and unmeaning through every Character.
>
> Colley Cibber's *Apology* 2nd ed., p. 261

The disease itself is beyond the scope of this book, but its onset cannot be avoided. The first virulent germs were carried to this country by Thomas Clayton, one-time violinist in the Royal Band of William and Mary, who returned from a visit to Italy with librettos and arias on which he drew for his own two operas. Significantly these were the only works he ever published. On 16 January 1705 Drury Lane staged his *Arsinoe, Queen of Cyprus*. It was the first full-length all-sung English opera to survive, as also the first that was wholly in the Italian style. The libretto, by one Stanzani, had been written back in 1677, and it was translated by Motteux. Clayton explained in the Preface that

> The Design of this Entertainment being to introduce the Italian Manner of Musick on the English Stage, which has not before been attempted; I was oblig'd to have an Italian Opera translated: In which the Words, however mean in several Places, suited much better with that manner of Musick, than others more Poetical would do.

Having been thoroughly rude to Motteux, Clayton now proceeded to antagonize his singers.

> The Stile of this Musick is to express the Passions which is the Soul of Musick: And though the Voices are not equal to the Italian, yet I have engaged the Best that were to be found in England; and I have not been wanting, to the utmost of my Diligence, in the instructing of them.

Finally he touched on a point that was to be argued for the rest of the century:

> The Musick being Recitative, may not, at first, meet with that general Acceptation, as it is to be hop'd for from the Audiences being better acquainted with it.

As *Spectator* 258 makes clear, Clayton was associated in this venture with two foreign musicians. Nicola Haym, an Italian of German descent, was both cellist and composer. He later wrote opera librettos for Handel as well as a book on medals, and he collected material for a history of music that he did not live to write. Charles Dieupart was a French violinist who also played the harpsichord. Haym is known to have played in *Arsinoe*, and the conclusion is irresistible that he and Dieupart provided the continuo accompaniments, a task that might well have been beyond any English performers. Eric Walter White has suggested that they also composed some of the arias.

Clayton never claimed to have written all the music, and his name is not given on the pictorial title page of the published score. Hawkins thought the music consisted largely of Italian thefts, but Burney felt that 'nothing so mean in melody and incorrect in counterpoint' could possibly come from an Italian composer. Certainly the arias are for the most part poor. The score is a binding together of songs printed on one side of the page and issued separately, and it may be that we should take their headings literally. Of the thirty-seven songs, twenty-three are said to have been 'set by Mr. Tho. Clayton'; perhaps those without this ascription were filched from Italian sources that Clayton brought back from his travels. The score omits the recitatives. All the songs are given on two staves and appear to have only continuo accompaniment. Fifteen have no introduction, but introductions were often omitted by engravers to save space. There are no indications of violin parts except in the very short two-movement overture, which is on three staves for violins and bass. It ends with a minuet of unbeatable banality.

The libretto was utterly different from that of any previous English opera. It contained no speaking, no masques (apart from a very short Epithalamium at the end), no machines or scenic effects, and no probability in the action. The cardboard characters, the involved relationships, the silly misunderstandings, and the final reconciliation are such as we often find in Handel. The opera starts with Queen Arsinoe improbably asleep in a garden at night and being saved

Clayton's *Arsinoe*; Sir James Thornhill's designs for I i ('Arsinoe sleeping. By Moon light')
and I iii ('A Room of Stait, with Statues and Bustoes. Arsinoe on a Couch').

Pantomime sets: Drury Lane's *Harlequin Dr Faustus*, scene i (1723) see p. 68; Dibdin's *The Mirror* (1779), 'The Principal Scene' by Richards.

from an assassin by Ormondo, one of her generals. At the end of Act II he saves her again in the same garden, this time from a dagger wielded by his ex-girl-friend, Dorisbe. The situations arise because the first rescue has led to Ormondo and Arsinoe falling in love, to the fury of those they loved before. Iago's handkerchief trick is introduced to make Arsinoe suspect Ormondo's fidelity, and, distraught because of her apparent charge of heart, he obliges with a 'Simile Aria', probably the first that London audiences had heard:

> Thus sinking Mariners,
> In sight of Land are lost;
> Dash'd on the Rocks
> And cannot reach the Coast.

In the last act there is the inevitable prison scene, with Ormondo, the prisoner, talking in his sleep and thereby revealing both that he is innocent of the charges made against him, and also that in reality he is Pelops, son of the King of Athens. 'I stand amaz'd,' sings Arsinoe, and follows this cliché with another: 'Ha! who comes here? I'll hear her business and retire.' It is, of course, Dorisbe, heavily veiled and eager to save Ormondo if only he will love her. But he won't. Dorisbe stabs herself on a balcony, but the opera being Italianate and this being the end of it, she remarks 'The Wound's not dangerous, I believe', and when forgiven by Arsinoe and Ormondo she seems in excellent health.

It is tragic that playhouse audiences were taken in by this nonsense. *Arsinoe* was monstrously successful, the silliness of both words and music passing unnoticed. There were twenty-four performances the first season and a dozen more the next. Arsinoe was sung by Mrs. Tofts. Her beauty, popularity, and what Colley Cibber called 'the sweet silver tone of her voice' contributed much to this otherwise undeserved success. Mrs. Cross was Dorisbe, the counter-tenor Hughes sang Ormondo, and Leveridge was Arsinoe's former lover, Feraspe. James Thornhill, famous for his magnificent work at the Royal Naval Hospital, Greenwich, designed the scenery.

The Queen's Theatre in the Haymarket opened its doors with no great show of enthusiasm some twelve weeks later on 9 April 1705. The joint managers, Vanbrugh and Congreve, had considered four projects for their opening night, and significantly they were all operas. The theatre was finished too late for *Arsinoe* and too early for Eccles's *Semele*. Daniel Purcell's projected *Orlando Furioso* seems never to have been written. In the end they offered an unnamed opera sung by 'a new Sett of Singers arriv'd from Italy', and Loewenberg identified it as *The Loves of Ergasto* by Jakob Greber, claiming it as the first London opera sung entirely in Italian. The identification is supported by an anonymous letter to Sir Richard Newdigate:

On Monday next (April 23) the new theatre in the hay market . . . is to be opened at which a new Italian pastoral called the Loves of Ergasto set to music by the famous Italian Jacomo Greber will be acted.[1]

The anonymous libretto was published with the Italian and its English translation on facing pages, and this became the usual way of printing Italian librettos.

In spite of all this evidence, the occasion is shadowy with doubt. An opera sung in Italian would surely have aroused comment, especially at a brand-new and much discussed theatre. *The Loves of Ergasto* aroused no comment at all. In his *Apology* Cibber states that the Queen's Theatre opened with an opera called *The Triumph of Love*; presumably he was confused by the titles of two slightly later Italianate operas, *The Temple of Love* and *Love's Triumph*. But though we can believe that he forgot the name, we can hardly believe that he forgot the language; Cibber specifically states that it was 'a translated Opera, to Italian Musick'. Nor can we credit that an Italian company would have been willing to learn a new opera by a man who was not Italian. They would have brought with them an opera they had already performed in Italy. Greber was a German violinist long resident in London, and his insignificance as a composer is itself a stumbling-block.

In my view there is only one explanation that covers the facts. Vanbrugh and Congreve were desperate because their various projects had all fallen through. They felt that after *Arsinoe* only an Italianate opera would serve for the occasion, and they went for advice and help to Margherita de l'Epine, the Italian soprano who had been singing in London for some years; they may also have approached Margherita's sister, Maria Gallia. Margherita was familiarly known at this time as 'Greber's Peg', no doubt because she was his mistress. She had sung at a Lincoln's Inn Fields concert for which Greber composed the music as early as June 1703. If approached by Vanbrugh and Congreve, she might well have suggested a new opera by her lover, and offered to attract other Italian singers from abroad to take part in it. The latter may well not have arrived. It seems certain that the production was staged without due preparation, and with English singers as well as Italian. Margherita herself often sang in English in concerts, and later she did so in operas as well. The original intention no doubt was to perform the opera in Italian, but almost certainly it was sung in English.

One would also expect Mrs. Bracegirdle to have sung on this momentous occasion, for she was both the best singer and the most popular actress in the company. In fact she only spoke the Epilogue. This was written by Congreve, and one might hope that it would offer some clues as to the nature of the entertainment; as indeed it does, but in such veiled language that we are not much forrader:

This Day, without Presumption, we pretend

---

[1] Quoted in J. H. Wilson's article in TN, Spring 1961. Greber was not Italian and the date is a fortnight too late.

With Novelty entire you're entertain'd;
For not alone our House and Scenes are new,
Our Song and Dance, but ev'n our Actors too.
Our Play itself has something in't uncommon,
Two faithful Lovers, and *one* constant Woman.
In sweet *Italian* strains our Shepherds sing,
Of harmless Loves our painted Forests ring
In Notes, perhaps, less Foreign than the *thing*.
To Sound and Show at first we make pretence,
In time we may regale you with some Sense,
But that, at present, were too great Expence.

The fourth line of this extract suggests that some of the performers were new to London, and it might well mean that they all were. But if so, how are we to account for the last line, which would then imply that it was cheaper to present an opera with singers brought from abroad than a play acted by the resident English company? Are we to give any weight to the word 'pretend' in the first line? What does line 9 mean?

Passing from speculation to fact, we may note that Greber's opera was given in Vienna in 1706 as *Gli Amori d'Ergasto*, and according to Loewenberg the manuscript is in the Vienna National-Bibliothek. In London there were five performances, after which the Queen's Theatre turned to plays, as had always been the intention, with the elderly Betterton and Mrs. Bracegirdle in the chief roles.

As Congreve was London's leading dramatist, and Eccles its leading composer, it must have been expected that they would collaborate in an opera for the new theatre, especially as Congreve was one of its managers. Unfortunately he soon resigned, disappointed at its lack of success. That *Semele* was never produced was yet another item in the list of disasters suffered by English opera, for its intelligent attempt to fuse English and Italian elements might well have had followers. The autograph score in London's Royal College of Music lacks the overture, the start of the first scene, and the final pages; also the dances and the strange mimed scene at the end of Act II, though it includes the stage directions for these. Thus there are no extended instrumental pieces. What we have is scored entirely for strings; perhaps resources were strained in early days at the Queen's Theatre. But within narrow limits Eccles is fastidious. For the introductions to his arias he sometimes asks for '6 1st violins' and '6 2nd violins', cutting down to three of each when the voice comes in, or even to a single instrument. He never seems to have in mind more than two 'tenors' (violas). Act III, as Handel addicts will recall, starts in 'The Cave of Sleep, the God of Sleep (Somnus) lying on his bed'. It was not within Eccles's powers to equal Handel's marvellous prelude starting with cellos and bassoons, but his pizzicato introduction was highly original for its day:

All the instruments strike the strings with their fingers

Eccles

Juno and Iris bustle in to the same sort of music as Handel wrote at this point, and the aria for Somnus that follows, 'Leave me, loathsome Light', is marked 'Loads upon the Instruments'; that is, they are muted.

Some of the arias in *Semele* have a Purcellian turn of phrase, and some venture into Italianate figuration, three being in *Da Capo* form. But, many of them have a highly individual quality. Congreve, it may be remembered, had managed without recitative in *The Judgment of Paris*, but his preface to *Semele* shows him well aware of its character, and he saw that it might just as well be in free verse as in any regular metre.

> It was not thought requisite to have any Regard either to Rhyme, or Equality of Measure, in the Lines of that Part of the Dialogue which was design'd for the *Recitative Style* in Musick. For as that Style in Musick is not confin'd to the strict Observation of Time and Measure, which is requir'd in the Composition of Airs and Sonatas, so neither is it necessary that the same exactness in Numbers, Rhymes or Measure, should be observ'd in Words design'd to be set in that manner . . . *Recitative* is only a more tuneable Speaking; it is a kind of Prose in Musick; its Beauty consists in coming near Nature, and in improving the natural Accents of Words by more Pathetick or Emphatical Tone.

When Congreve dropped into regular metre, he was presumably inviting an aria, but if Eccles felt that an aria would hold up the action he resorted to a kind of arioso,[1] more tuneful than his recitative and somewhat in the declamatory style of Blow and Purcell. His recitative was not at all Italian in style, a fact that

---

[1] See Stoddard Lincoln's 'The First Setting of Congreve's "Semele"', M&L, April 1963; also TN, Autumn 1963, in which the same writer shows how often Eccles and Mrs. Bracegirdle were associated. He thinks *Semele* was not performed because of Mrs. Bracegirdle's retirement in 1707.

Addison for one should have welcomed. Italian music suited the Italian language well enough, but something different was required to fit the inflections and 'improve the natural Accents' of English words. Here is the first recitative in what survives of Eccles's score, together with Handel's setting of the same words:

The two settings have nothing in common, and it is hard to resist a preference for what Eccles wrote. In particular the words 'passion' and 'must' are managed with a much better sense of English emphasis, as also of dramatic feeling.

It is extraordinary that this remarkable score should never have been performed in London until 20 April 1972, when it was given by Opera da Camera. Naturally it does not reach the heights of Handel at his very best, but in its gentle way it holds the interest completely, seldom slipping into the well-mannered clichés that bedevil so much music of the period, and often being lit from within by what is best described as musicality. Many examples might be given. Here is one that does not have to compete with Handel, who happened to omit these words.

Fond__ de-sir - ing.

During the next few years the rivalry between Drury Lane and the Queen's Theatre ran so complex a course that a plan will be needed for reference. Only the main operatic events are noted; before *Idaspe*, Drury Lane staged four Italianate operas in English, or partly so, as against seven at the Queen's. Theatrical seasons ran from September until the following May or June.

	DRURY LANE	QUEEN'S
1704–5	Plays and Operas *Arsinoe*, first all-sung opera	Plays and Operas Opened 9.4.05 under Vanbrugh and Congreve with *Loves of Ergasto*
1705–6		
1706–7	*Thomyris*, first opera with an Italian castrato	Plays only
1707–8	Plays only. Rivalry suspended	Operas only (from 13.1.08), and only on Tuesdays and Saturdays
1708–9		*Pyrrhus and Demetrius*; first bilingual opera and first with Nicolini
1709–10	Plays and Operas (from 23.11.09), Rivalry resumed. Aaron Hill the leading manager	Plays and Operas from September. Better acoustics. Cibber the leading manager. *Idaspe* (23.3.10) first opera sung wholly in Italian
1710–11	Rivalry abandoned. From 18.11.10 the managers were Swiney, Wilkes, Cibber, Dogget	Italian Operas only, from 22.11.10. Handel's *Rinaldo* (24.2.11). Hill and Collier the managers

1711–12: Swiney and Collier exchanged as managers

We shall find the Queen's Theatre pursuing a labyrinthine path in its search for the opera of the future, until at last the huge success of Handel's *Rinaldo* clarified the way ahead.

Though plays provided the bulk of the repertoire at Drury Lane, the success of *Arsinoe* meant that opera could not be ignored, and the problem at both theatres was whether to attempt Purcellian opera with spoken dialogue, masques, dancing, and lavish scenic effects, or Italianate opera with no speaking and the emphasis on the solo aria and good singing. George Granville was not alone in thinking the English language unsuited to recitative, and accordingly his opera *The British Enchanters* (QT 21.2.06) had spoken dialogue in heroic couplets. Dr. Johnson admired the libretto, which is set in ancient Britain and appears to be influenced by Dryden's *King Arthur*; in fact it was taken from Lully's *Amadis de Gaule*.[1] A wicked enchantress, Urganda, does her utmost to destroy the hero and heroine, Amadis and Oriana, who are eventually saved by various benevolent 'enchanters'. Of curiosity value for us is a scene with someone called Florestan in a prison. Towards the end of Act V there is the usual masque-like entertainment which 'concludes with Variety of other Songs and Dances', a stage direction that enabled absolutely anything to be dragged in. The music is lost, apart from a song by Eccles (*Pills* v, p. 203) and the overture and instrumental 'ayres' by William Corbett.[2] This Purcell-type opera had a modest success.

Of more interest, though less successful, was *The Temple of Love* (QT 7.3.06), in which the managers switched to Italian opera. The words were a translation by Motteux, and the music was by Giuseppe Fedelli Saggione, known to present-day dictionaries as Fedelli. Downes tells us the opera consisted entirely of singing and dancing, the dancers being French, but except for Maria Gallia, who by now was Saggione's wife, the singers were all English and included Mrs. Bracegirdle. The arias, (though not the overture, dance movement and recitatives) were published in the usual way, with the same pictorial title-page as had been used for *The Judgment of Paris*. The music is a great improvement on that of *Arsinoe*. With so much dancing, there was room for only eighteen arias, less than half the number in Clayton's work. One of the two with recorder parts, 'Warbling the Birds enjoying' (the addition of more lines would not clarify the sense), is a coloratura song for Gallia, and a very early example of bird-song imitation. The recorder, 'perform'd by Mr. Paisible' (who was French), echoes the voice much as it was to do in so many eighteenth century 'bird' songs. Fourteen of the eighteen arias are in *Da Capo* form, a much higher proportion than in *Arsinoe* (seven out of thirty-seven).

By staging two utterly different kinds of opera within three weeks, the

[1] See *RMA Research Chronicle* No. 1 for 4.11.04, which suggests unrecorded performances of *Amadis de Gaule* at Lincoln's Inn Fields with music by Eccles.

[2] There is a good drawing of Corbett by William Hoare in the Menstrie Museum, Bath.

managers of the Queen's Theatre doubtless hoped to learn which kind Londoners preferred. Evidence was far from conclusive, but it seemed to point towards Purcellian opera, and for their next production the theatre tried the rather desperate expedient of a thoroughly low-brow example with plenty of trick-staging. *Wonders in the Sun, or The Kingdom of the Birds* (QT 5.4.06) lasted only six nights and lost money, yet its influence was considerable. It even anticipated *The Beggar's Opera* in some respects. D'Urfey's libretto boasts on the title page of a 'great Variety of *Songs* in all kinds set to Musick by several of the most Eminent Masters of the Age', and then adds rather lamely 'Several of the Songs will be omitted the Performance being too long'. Three songs and three dialogues were published as a rudimentary vocal score, and most of these together with five other items can be found in *Pills*. Some of the tunes were borrowed from earlier sources, and several of these are of the popular type we associate with ballad operas.

The all-sung Prologue includes a dialogue between a Satyr and the nymph Calliope, given in the 'vocal score', and this is followed by 'The Song of Orpheus charming the Birds, Beasts, Trees etc. to follow him . . . Set to the Tune call'd the Czar' (*Pills* i, p. 170). With delightful frankness the libretto adds that the words were written to fit 'a pretty but very difficult Tune of Mr. Eccles', and this may reflect troublesome rehearsals. The admission that the tune was pre-existing is significant. Orpheus, it turns out, wants to lure all the birds and the beasts to the Sun, which is where the rest of the opera takes place.

Act I, set in 'a bright luminous Country', starts in best Science Fiction style with Gonzales, a Spaniard, and his Sancho-like servant Diego, in 'a Machin hanging in the Air at a small distance with Ganzas harness'd to it'. The story is to be a sequel to the then well-known romance by Bishop Godwin, *The Man in the Moone* (1638),[1] in which Gonzales was drawn to the moon by a team of mythical birds for which the bishop devised the name 'ganzas'. The word caught people's fancy, and it turns up in Butler's *Hudibras* and elsewhere. D'Urfey's hero is lucky enough to have the service of Socrates as interpreter, and he explains that everything on the Sun is the opposite to what it is on earth. Riches accrue to the unworthy (but is this the opposite?), and punches and slaps are a sign of friendliness. Much gibberish is spoken, but never sung. There are a great many birds which, forming the opinion that Gonzales is an ostrich from Earth, feed him on nails and old iron. As in that later and not wholly dissimilar work *Gulliver's Travels*, one frequently suspects a double meaning, though in D'Urfey's farrago the first meaning is hard enough to unravel. In the end, Gonzales and Diego, much confused by all they have seen, return to their Machine and are pulled back to Earth by the ganzas.

As in Purcellian operas, the music came mostly at the ends of the acts, for the entertainment of Gonzales. These embryonic masques have virtually no plot,

---

[1] It includes one of the first musical ciphers; see article by H. Neville Davies, M&L, Oct. 1967.

though individual 'dialogues' are often dramatic, and such as would be all the more effective with stage action. The entertainment at the end of Act III is typical. Early on, 'Mrs. Willises Girle' indulged in some farmyard imitations in a song not forgotten even today:

Later verses introduced imitations of owls, sheep, turkeys, hens and ducks. Pigs were kept for a quite different song in another act, 'The Pigg's March' (*Pills* ii, p. 87), in which Dogget, representing the servant Diego, told of a soldier marching through Flanders with a pig 'cramm'd' in his knapsack. Each verse has the refrain

> *Weeck, Weeck, Weeck*, squeak'd the Pig,
> *Ogh, Ogh, Ogh*, grunts the Sow.

We are a long way from the high-flown sentiments of *Arsinoe*. After the song by 'Mrs. Willises Girle', Mr. Pack, representing Sport, and Mrs. Bradshaw, representing Maturity, sang a 'dialogue' in which Sport slowly worked his way round to thoughts of wedded bliss, until Maturity, tiring of the argument, wrapped the subject up with the words:

> We'll Wed and we'll Bed,
> There's no more to be said,
> And I'll ne'er go a-Milking more. (*Pills* i, p. 100)

The act ends with another 'dialogue' in which Rash Ignorance and Timorous Housewife (Sport and Maturity a few years later?) quarrel because he is off to the wars, leaving her to look after 'all the Brats' as well as the farm. The song was topical for the Marlborough Wars had just begun, and we can trace such duets in English opera right through the century. In the end the wife always gives way to better feelings, and thus there was an element of propaganda in the outcome. Another topical song in *Wonders in the Sun* came in Act II, 'What are these Ideots doing?' (*Pills* i, p. 80); in this Mr. Pack, now representing Moderation, warned the audience of the dangers of being kind to the French.

We have seen that personifications were common in the Jacobean masques of Ben Jonson, and they continued to be welcomed in European theatres for most of the eighteenth century. Had the abstract virtues seemed as uninteresting on the stage as they do today, the device would not have lasted so long. In England Britannia was an especially favourite abstraction. Even as late as the 1760s, Haydn wrote an 'Applausus' cantata in which the soloists represented such inspiring concepts as Fortitudo and Temperantia, and later still Sir Joshua Reynolds was depicting personified virtues in stained glass in New College Chapel, Oxford. Thousands of examples might be given, in paintings and sculptures as well as in operatic masques. Perhaps these abstractions were sometimes another form of propaganda, a method of raising morale for the better conducting of the inevitable war in progress or in prospect.

The words of the *Wonders in the Sun* duet in which the husband leaves for the wars were written to fit a French tune, 'the famous Cebell of Signior Baptist Lully' (*Pills* i, p. 139). This was the 'Invocation to Cybele' from Lully's opera *Atys* (1676); the word 'Cebell', sometimes used to mean a gavotte, was a corruption of Lully's title. As *Pills* reveals time after time, D'Urfey made a practice of writing words to fit tunes he had in his head, even instrumental ones by Purcell, and no doubt there were other examples in this opera besides the lyrics he wrote for tunes by Lully and Eccles. He anticipated John Gay and *The Beggar's Opera* in other ways as well; for instance in his liking for tunes of the kind known today as 'traditional'. The word is little more than an expression of ignorance, but it does perhaps give a picture of a four-square melody of popular type—possibly of folk origin but more probably a composition by one of D'Urfey's friends. Such a melody is the one sung at the end of Act I of

Wonders in the Sun by Mrs. Willis as 'the Dame of Honour or Hospitality.' It was known as 'The World turn'd upside down' (*Pills* i, p. 212), and began:

Anon.

Some twenty-five years later this tune seemed very much at home in such popular ballad operas as *The Devil to pay* and *The Jovial Crew*; also in Gay's *Polly*. The borrowing and lending of tunes, exemplified in *Wonders in the Sun*, is equally characteristic of operas at the end of the century.

The music-hall flavour of many songs in *Wonders in the Sun* will already be apparent. Other examples were a 'Song representing the going of a Pad' (*Pills* ii, p. 190), in which the onomatopoeic tune plods when the horse walks, trips when it trots, and bursts into $\frac{12}{8}$ when it gallops; and, at the very end of the opera, a song in which Mrs. Baldwin imitated a nightingale (*Pills* i, p. 83) and thus helped to establish the convention started a few weeks earlier in *The Temple of Love*.

Of the six songs in the 'vocal score' of *Wonders in the Sun*, five have no introduction and only a bass line by way of accompaniment. Those performed immediately after spoken dialogue must have had introductions for practical reasons, and we must postulate an engraver omitting them to save space and expense. He had plenty of precedent, for songs in *Pills* and other melody line publications were invariably given without introductions. The point may seem academic, but it becomes important in connection with *The Beggar's Opera* and other ballad operas, whose songs, as I hope to show, were performed with introductions but published without because for years that had been the normal way.

The comparative failure of *Wonders in the Sun* turned the Queen's Theatre against operas, and in the 1706–7 season they gave none at all. We must now turn to the rival theatre, Drury Lane, which, under Christopher Rich, was much more inclined to accept Italianate opera as a durable art form. *Camilla* (DL 30.3.06), an adaptation by Haym of an opera by M. A. Bononcini, was to prove popular for a quarter of a century. The songs were published in the usual way, and the translation was by Owen Swiney, a remarkable Irishman whom we shall meet again. *Rosamond* (DL 4.3.07), with a new libretto by Addison and ostensibly new music by Clayton, was not successful at all. It was the most notable and influential operatic failure of the century.

As a young man Joseph Addison had been Demy and Fellow of Magdalen College, Oxford, after which his eager interest in the arts and aptitude for languages were stimulated by a prolonged Grand Tour, financed in part by the Government with an eye to his political future. In September 1699 he sailed for France and was abroad for four years and a half. In Paris he saw operas by Lully, and in Venice and Florence operas by various forgotten Italians. By 1703 he was in Vienna, and later that year in Hamburg where he saw an opera by Keiser and perhaps met Handel. He came back to England in February 1704.

Addison might well have returned from foreign parts boasting like Burney many years later of the operas he had heard, and deriding all English attempts at emulation. He did no such thing. But with acute perception he realized that mere imitation was not enough. In France Lully had

> acted like a Man of Sense . . . knowing the Genius of the People, the Humour of their Language, and the prejudiced Ears he had to deal with, he did not pretend to extirpate the *French* Musick, and plant the *Italian* in its stead; but only to cultivate and civilize it with innumerable Graces and Modulations which he borrowed from the *Italian*.[1]

English opera should have an English story in English. Translations from the Italian could be no more than a second-best, and in any case such Italian librettos as he knew were either improbable, incomprehensible, or both. His own opera should have a simple story anyone could follow, and he fastened on the popular legend of Rosamond, mistress of King Henry II. The events, supposed to take place little more than five hundred years previously, were by many centuries the most modern that Londoners would encounter in any serious opera before Handel's *Riccardo Primo* (1727). Some of Addison's sentiments were neatly expressed in a Prologue to *Rosamond* by Thomas Tickell,[2] though not in time for the performances.

> The Opera first Italian Masters taught,
> Enrich'd with Songs but innocent of Thought.
> Britannia's learned Theatre disdains
> Melodious Trifles and enervate Strains:
> And blushes on her injur'd Stage to see
> Nonsense well tun'd, and sweet Stupidity.

[1] *Spectator* 29.
[2] Tickell was Addison's protégé, and later his Under-Secretary when Addison was Secretary of State. The Prologue was printed in the third edition of *Rosamond* (1713).

Addison's *Spectators* written some four or five years after the *Rosamond* débâcle, are full of interesting paragraphs about opera, many of them written with his delightful blend of benevolence and contempt. No. 29 is especially good on recitative:

> There is nothing that has more startled our *English* Audience, than the *Italian Recitativo* at its first Entrance upon the Stage. People were wonderfully surprized to hear Generals singing the Word of Command, and Ladies delivering Messages in Musick.

Yet Italian recitative was, he thought,

> much more just than that which prevailed in our *English* Opera before this Innovation: The Transition from an Air to Recitative Musick being more natural, than the passing from a Song to plain and ordinary Speaking, which was the common Method in *Purcell's* Operas. The only Fault I find in our present Practice is the making use of *Italian Recitativo* with *English* Words.

He then explains how each nation has its own type of speech melody, and that recitative, being 'only the Accents of their Language made more Musical and Tuneful', must be specially written to suit whatever language is being sung. A translation must lead to absurdities and incongruities, unless new music is written to fit that translation. He himself wrote for recitative in octosyllabic couplets.

It seems likely that Addison drew for his libretto on a poem in heroic couplets called 'The Death of Rosamond' by Thomas May, who had earned notoriety in the Civil War by suddenly switching from the Cavalier to the Roundhead cause. But Addison saved his heroine from her legendary fate because happy endings were becoming an operatic convention, and he further lightened the libretto with a pair of comic attendants. The plot pleased him the more for observing the unity of time, being confined to a single day, and, as so often in his *Spectators*, he managed to include some estimable moral precepts, mainly on the sanctity of marriage. What he wrote has considerable merit as literature, together with one very obvious defect. Reacting against the complexities of Italian librettos, Addison went too far; in *Rosamond* scarcely anything happens.

In Act I we learn that King Henry keeps a mistress, Rosamond, in a bower at Woodstock; she is looked after by a buffoon called Sir Trusty and his wife, Grideline. In Act II Henry's wife, Queen Eleanor, seems to poison Rosamond. In Act III, after a prophetic vision of angels, Henry admits the error of his ways to the Queen, who reveals that the poison has incapacitated Rosamond only temporarily.

Burney remarked with some truth that 'the loss of Rosamond in the second act is not compensated by a single interesting event in the third', but in fact the topicality of the vision scene had many admirers. The angels not only foretold the victories at Crecy and Agincourt, but also the one at Blenheim and the building of Blenheim Palace for its victor. At the time Vanbrugh's building was still in the planning stage, and Addison's description is not much like what visitors see today.

1st Angel	Behold the glorious Pile ascending!	*(Scene changes to*
	Columns swelling, Arches bending,	*the Plan of*
	Domes in awful Pomp arising,	Blenheim *Castle.)*
	Art in curious Strokes surprising,	
	Foes in figur'd Fights contending,	
	Behold the glorious Pile ascending!	
2nd Angel	He sees, he sees the great Reward	
	for Anna's mighty Chief prepar'd.	

The scene, deriving perhaps from the fourth act of *Macbeth*, influenced a number of later English masques, for instance Arne's *Alfred*, and was surprisingly admired by Dr. Johnson, who pointed out in his *Lives of the Poets* that 'the praise of Marlborough, for which the scene gives an opportunity, is, what perhaps every human excellence must be, the product of good luck, improved by genius'. He found the versification in *Rosamond* 'easy and gay', the drama 'airy and elegant', the whole 'one of the first of Addison's compositions'. Yet the opera had but three performances.

The truth is that since *Arsinoe* Londoners had been able to hear enough medium-quality Italian arias by M. A. Bononcini and others to form standards of judgement, and their ears told them that Clayton's music in *Rosamond* was cretinous. Hawkins described it as 'mere noise' and 'confused chaos'. The best thing in the published score is the picture on the title page of the Queen prowling near Rosamond's bower with a cup of poison in one hand and a dagger in the other. Unlike the title-page of *Arsinoe*, this one does credit Clayton with all the music. The overture is not saved by its unusual and close-packed contrasts between 'loud' and 'soft'. The forty-two songs are mostly very short, some absurdly so; eleven are in *Da Capo* form, and for some reason ten of these occur in the first act. There are more introductions than in *Arsinoe*, but again these consist of a bass line only, and again there is no sign of violins or any other melody instruments joining in. There seems little point in following Hawkins and presenting an example of Clayton at his worst. His best is almost more damning:

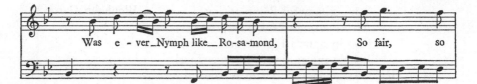

Music criticism is such that the shift into three time in bars 2–3 can, according to taste, be either hailed for its subtlety or condemned for its incompetence. Another setting of the same words will be found on page 138. Clayton could not complain of his cast. The counter-tenor Hughes sang King Henry, Mrs. Tofts the Queen, Gallia Rosamond, and, inevitably, Leveridge Sir Trusty.

A month later Drury Lane staged its fourth and last all-sung Italianate opera, *Thomyris, Queen of Scythia,* and this was far more successful than *Rosamond.* The music was selected in the main from Alessandro Scarlatti and Giovanni Bononcini, and Motteux concocted a story and lyrics of fit the tunes, mentioning in a preface the difficulty of doing this. Pepusch composed the recitatives, and Margherita de l'Epine (his future wife) sang Thomyris, with Mrs. Tofts as the Persian princess, Cleora. A startling innovation was that Orontes, the hero and Thomyris's son, was taken alternately by Hughes and the Italian castrato Valentino. According to Angus Heriot, the latter's full name was Valentino Urbani, he was about forty-seven, and he had never been in the front rank. Drury Lane, not having seen a castrato before in opera,[1] was hugely intrigued. Needless to say, Valentino sang in Italian, while everyone else stuck to English; in the libretto, his arias, and his alone, are printed in both languages. Much of the music, notably Bononcini's overture, looks rather good.

It will not be supposed that Italian singers and Italianate music were accepted with enthusiasm by everyone. Violent hostility was expressed by the critic John Dennis in his *Essay on the Operas after the Italian Manner, which are about to be*

---

[1] But see *RMA Research Chronicle I,* entry for 15 April 1699.

Stage set by Lediard for *Britannia* (1733) see p. 134.

The Little Theatre in 1736. Note stage chandeliers and boxes, and cramped orchestra facing the actors for the sake of ensemble.

establish'd on the English Stage: With some Reflections on the Damage which they may bring to the Publick (1706). He believed that operas 'which are entirely Musical' should be banned: otherwise they would drive plays and dramatic poetry from our theatres as they had already done in Italy. Jeremy Collier had done enough damage when he attacked the morality of the stage and thereby pushed men into the evils of gaming who might otherwise have profited from an evening in the theatre. In point of fact, operas were more pernicious than 'the most licentious play', for experience

> shows what influence the soft and effeminate Measures of the Italian Opera have upon the Minds and Manners of Men. The modern Italian men . . . are neither Vertuous, nor Wise, nor Valiant; and they who have reason to know their Women, never trust them out of their sight.

How different were the ancient Romans! Only opera can account for the difference. Dramatic poetry uplifts; soft, effeminate music degrades. 'Notions of Liberty . . . public Virtue and public Spirit, and a noble Contempt of Death' all come from poetry, never from music, which is 'incapable of informing the Understanding, or reforming the Will; and for that reason utterly unfit to be made a public Diversion'. One reason for this is that moral precepts demand forceful expression, and this in turn demands 'a great many Consonants . . . which cannot be pronounc'd without very frequently shutting the Mouth, which is diametrically oppos'd to the expressing of Musick'. Dennis ends by going overboard with what I believe to be the first condemnation in our literature of the musician as such; it is a view with which Lord Chesterfield would have agreed, as also many legions of Victorian fathers, and its prevalence may partly explain the alleged inferiority of our musicians to our novelists, poets and painters in the next two centuries:

> An *Englishman* is deservedly scorn'd by *Englishmen*, when he descends so far beneath himself, as to sing or to dance in publick; because by doing so, he practises Arts which Nature has bestow'd on effeminate Nations, but deny'd to him, as below the Dignity of his Country, and the Majesty of the *British* Genius.

Colonel Blimp could not have put it better, and it is no surprise to read Pope's lines on Dennis in his *Essay on Criticism* (line 585):

> But Appius reddens at each Word you speak,
> And stares, tremendous, with a threatening Eye,
> Like some fierce Tyrant in old Tapestry.

It was early suspected that Italianate opera might profitably be attacked with ridicule, but London's theatre-goers were not yet prepared to have their idols made fun of, and *Prunella* had only one performance (DL 12.2.08). Its author was Richard Estcourt, the original Sergeant Kite in Farquhar's *The Recruiting*

Officer and one of the managers of Drury Lane; he was also famous as a mimic. The humour of *Prunella* lay partly in the chaotic plot and hum-drum London characters (in this Estcourt anticipated Gay), and partly in having banal words sung to well-known tunes from *Arsinoe*, *Thomyris*, and *Camilla*. There was no need to publish the music for, recitatives apart, it was already available. Prunella is the daughter of Racina, 'a Grocer in the Piazza in *Conventino Hortensi*', and her opening recitative runs:

> This well-known Place, this spacious, spacious Square,
> Where Fruiterers do sell their Ware,
> Is where we Girls do use to meet,
> When our House was in *Russel-street*.

Unfortunately the casual line-lengths and tenses of this passage presage an excess of casualness in all the writing, and the libretto is less amusing than it promises to be. A few touches linger in the memory; for instance the solemn aria to words which paraphrase 'Girls and Boys come out to play', and the moment when Prunella's lover is being chased by Bailiffs, and she routs them with a single glance of her lovely eyes.[1]

Drury Lane could safely attack Italianate opera because in the previous month (January 1708) the no-rivalry arrangement had been initiated, whereby Drury Lane staged only plays and the Queen's only operas. We left the Queen's managers undecided as to what type of opera to support, and then ignoring opera altogether. When they returned to it, they found the problem solved for them, and they opened with *Thomyris*, the entire production transported from Drury Lane. During the two seasons and a half that the no-rivalry arrangement was honoured, the Queen's initiated four bilingual Italianate operas. *Love's Triumph* did not succeed, but in *Pyrrhus and Demetrius* (QT 14.12.08) they at last found a winner, largely because of the singing of Nicolini, the first great castrato Londoners had heard.[2] For some years he was the chief cause of Italian opera's popularity at the Queen's. The libretto was yet another translation by Swiney, and Haym chose the music mainly from Scarlatti; he himself composed the overture and several arias. There were twenty-three performances the first season and several more later. In this opera, as in its successor, *Clotilda* (QT 2.3.09), there were more Italian singers in the cast than English, and a number of London performers found themselves being quietly edged out of their jobs.

And then, as Addison put it in a famous sentence, 'the Audience grew tired of understanding half the Opera; and therefore to ease themselves intirely of

[1] Baker, deceived by errors in Chetwood, has Nicolini singing in *Prunella*; he had not then arrived in England. There is an obituary of Estcourt by Steele in *Spectator* 468.

[2] See TN No. 14 (1959–60) for an interesting article by Eric Walter White about Marco Ricci's painting of an opera rehearsal. Of Ricci's many versions six are reproduced; the earlier ones show Nicolini and Mrs. Tofts rehearsing *Pyrrhus and Demetrius*.

the Fatigue of Thinking, have so ordered it at present, that the whole Opera is performed in an unknown Tongue'. Burney thought *Almahide* (QT 10.1.10) was the first to be so performed, though he mentions Intermezzi sung between the acts by Dogget, Mrs. Lindsay, and Mrs. Cross. (He guessed that the anonymously-published music was by Bononcini.) But the libretto shows that these three singers played minor characters in the opera itself, and they must have sung in English because the song words were published 'in Italian and English as they are perform'd at the Queen's Theatre'. But *Idaspe* (QT 23.5.10), deceptively advertised as *Hydaspes*, was sung entirely in Italian by Italians. Francesco Mancini wrote the music, and the audience was equally captivated by the glorious singing and by the grotesque presence in the cast of a lion, immortalized in one of Addison's most delightful *Spectators* (No. 13). Both these operas were presented in a season mainly devoted to plays, but their huge success brought about the last shuffling between London's two theatres, and from 18 November 1710 the Queen's Theatre decided to give all its energies to Italian opera, and in the main continued to do so for the rest of the century. This change of policy was confirmed the following February by the production of Handel's *Rinaldo*, with music far superior to anything of the kind that Londoners had heard before. Handel did not cause the fever for Italian opera, but he ensured its continuance.

The fever had been brought on more by the beauty of the new singing than by the beauty of the new music. If Roger North is to be believed, English theatre singing had too often been out-of-tune. Also it was unexciting compared with Italian singing. 'Come into the theater or musick-meeting', he wrote about 1700, 'and you shall have a woman sing like a mouse in a cheese scarce to be heard, and for the most part her teeth shutt'. Nor was good ensemble cultivated. 'What a fulsome thing it is to see a performer upon a stage not know when to begin, but the *basso continuo* must stay or skip for them, which by the way they are not very good at; and then a flute must be at the lasses ear to give her the tone, and that often thro' the whole air, or else she would fall a semitone and sing on as assuredly as if she were in no fault. All this a knowledge of musick would prevent'.[1]

North was often a sour critic, but it cannot be doubted that castrati had far more 'knowledge of musick' than most English singers, and far more powers of thrilling an audience.

6 ENGLISH ATTEMPTS TO COMBAT THE ITALIANS

Dr. Johnson's famous description of Italian Opera as 'an exotick and irrational entertainment, which has been always combated, and always has prevailed' occurs in his Life of one of those who combated it most strenuously, John

---

[1] John Wilson's *Roger North on Music*, pp. 215–217.

Hughes (1677–1720). It is ironic that just when English Opera vanished into an abyss we were unusually well equipped with literary men who felt enthusiasm for it. Addison, Hughes, and Aaron Hill agreed in wanting an all-sung Italianate opera based on original English texts of literary merit, and it was their misfortune and ours that they could find no English composer of talent with whom to collaborate. Purcell need have lived only until he was forty-seven to cap *Arsinoe*; at forty-nine he could have set Addison's *Rosamond*, and at fifty-four Hughes's *Calypso and Telemachus* with the experience of hearing *Rinaldo* behind him.

After Handel's arrival, politics allowed Addison no more time for opera, but Hughes and Hill made several assaults on the Italian position. Aaron Hill (1685–1750) was a man of vast energy and resource. At the age of fifteen he set off on his own for Constantinople to visit the English ambassador, who was a relative. Subsequent travels in Palestine and Egypt led to a *History of the Ottoman Empire*, written when he was little more than a youth. Hill returned to London by land through the Balkans, and at twenty-four became one of the managers of Drury Lane; he switched to the Queen's just before Handel's arrival. He got rid of Clayton (who twice wrote to the *Spectator* to complain), knocked up a plan for the libretto of *Rinaldo* (which Rossi put into Italian for Handel to set), and explained in the preface that he had included elaborate 'Machines and Decorations' of the sort used in Purcellian opera because their absence had caused earlier Italian operas to be 'heard and seen to considerable disadvantage'. He aimed to please the eye as well as the ear. In *Spectator* 5 Addison made famous fun of the result, but Hill's theory was sensible, and indeed reflects Addison's own belief in a compromise between Italian and English taste. About 1713 Hill married an heiress and left the Queen's Theatre, disillusioned perhaps by the fact that his co-manager, Owen Swiney,[1] had just absconded with all the takings. He returned to theatre management in the early days of the Little Theatre, but gave most of his attention to some surprising commercial undertakings, raising £25,000 for making oil from beechnuts, dabbling in agricultural development in what was later known as the state of Georgia, and initiating both a plan to make potash and a huge forestry scheme in the Highlands of Scotland with a view to building ships there. In between times he found energy for putting the Lord's Prayer and the Sermon on the Mount into heroic couplets, and writing to actresses to tell them they were not putting their pauses in the right place. He even thought at one time of starting a Drama School. Pope made him one of the contestants in *The Dunciad*, and Hill retaliated with a portrait of Pope that had a good deal of truth in it:

[1] Swiney spent over twenty years in Italy, occasionally advising Handel about the capabilities of Italian singers. In 1735 he returned unconvincingly disguised as Owen Macswiney and was strangely rewarded with a job in H.M. Customs, from which he made a fortune he eventually left to Peg Woffington. His portrait by Van Loo shows a handsome persuasive man with a beard, a rare appendage in those days.

> Desiring and deserving, others' praise,
> Poorly accepts a fame he ne'er repays:
> Unborn to cherish, *sneakingly approves,*
> And wants the soul to *spread* the worth he loves.

He then sent Pope 'a gentle complaint' about *The Dunciad*; Pope replied that he had intended no reference to Hill, and then had to make a number of alterations in the second edition to susbtantiate this lie. Later he and Hill became surprisingly friendly.

John Hughes, a less forceful personality, was that rare creature, a poet with a deep knowledge of music. He had written an ode *In Praise of Music* in 1703, and in a letter[1] to Steele of 1711, he damned Clayton's serenata, *The Passion of Sappho*, with some detailed technical criticism of a calibre seldom attained in the eighteenth century even by professional musicians. His views on the musical problems of his day are skilfully expressed in the prefaces to Pepusch's Six Cantatas (1710), and Galliard's opera *Calypso and Telemachus* (1712), for both of which Hughes supplied the words. In the former, referring to Italian music in general, he remarks:

> If Reason may be admitted to have any Share in these Entertainments, nothing is more necessary than that the Words shou'd be understood, without which the End of *Vocal Musick* is lost.

Obvious? It did not seem so to admirers of Nicolini in 1710. Hughes then suggests that a composition which is agreeable with poor words will be even more enjoyable with good ones, and he calls on 'our best poets' to help. 'Since Poetry and Musick are so nearly ally'd, it is a Misfortune that those who excel in one, are often perfect Strangers to the other.' As for recitative (and in the Cantatas he had written some of his words specially for this type of music), people were biased against it from their belief 'that all Musick shou'd be Air'. In fact recitative is 'a kind of improv'd Elocution' (and as such 'wholly at the Mercy of the Performer'), its purpose being 'to relieve the Ear with a Variety, and to introduce the Airs with the greater Advantage'. In the preface to *Calypso and Telemachus* Hughes elaborated some of these points with special reference to opera. He thought it right that we should do justice to the Italian variety, from which we have much to learn, but

> There is likewise a Justice due to ourselves . . . I know not how it comes to be a late opinion among some, that English Words are not proper for Musick . . . The great Pleasure in hearing Vocal Musick, arises from the Association of the Ideas rais'd at the same time by the Expressions (i.e. the words) and the Sounds. When these Ideas are separated, half the Impression is wanting. . . It is impossible that Recitative should give Pleasure, which can raise no such Ideas.

[1] Quoted by J. Merrill Knapp, in an article about Galliard, M&L, Jan. 1961.

Many of us today are just as deaf to these simple truths as they were in Hughes's day, though how anyone in any century could deny the stark fact of his last sentence is beyond comprehension.

Though Weldon and Daniel Purcell were available, Hughes turned to Johann Ernst Galliard, a Hanoverian oboist who had come to England in 1706 when only nineteen. He lived in London for over forty years, becoming a naturalized Englishman with a good command of the English language. From the time of *Rinaldo* to that of *The Beggar's Opera*, some seventeen years, he and Pepusch, both of them Germans, were the only composers of the slightest distinction working in the London Playhouses. Burney blasted the pair of them in one sentence when he wrote of Galliard (whom he liked as a person) 'I never saw more correctness or less originality in any author I have examined, of the present century, Dr. Pepusch always excepted'. This unflattering opinion was largely the result of studying Galliard's *The Hymn of Adam and Eve*, a boring work, but some of his masques and his set of bassoon sonatas are still worth occasional hearing today. Galliard was quite talented enough to have started, with Hughes, a school of English opera in opposition to the Italian, but their *Calypso and Telemachus* was cruelly handicapped. Aaron Hill accepted it for the Queen's Theatre, against considerable opposition, and it was first performed on 17 May 1712, but the Lord Chamberlain, goaded by his Italian wife (herself in league with her compatriots at the theatre) was persuaded 'to take off the Subscription for it, and to open the House at its lowest Price, or not at all. This was design'd to sink it.' Even Dr. Johnson, no friend of opera, expressed stern disapproval of the ethics of the arrangement, the point being that the production was an expensive one and could not survive low prices. There were only five performances.

Hughes was a member of Button's, the largely Whig club over which Addison presided, and he probably discussed with Addison the subject of the libretto. This was based on *Les Aventures de Télémaque, Fils d'Ulysse*, a poem by Fénelon, Archbishop of Cambrai; its publication in 1699 had been something of a sensation. Boileau told Addison that year that it gave a modern reader a better idea of Homer than any translation could do, and he added, apparently by way of praise, that Fénelon made his characters preach whereas Homer showed moral purpose only through actions. Not much of the preaching survives in Hughes's libretto, but the writing is agreeable, and the plot easily intelligible without being inert.

Calypso, mourning the departure of Ulysses, is delighted when Telemachus comes to her island in search of his father. To hold him, she tells him Ulysses is dead. But when he falls in love, it is with her attendant, Eucharis, who is herself loved by the uncouth sea-god Proteus. Calypso and Proteus are thus allied by a common jealousy, and as a result of their scheming, Proteus finds the lovers in a wood, separates them with a mist, and for good measure turns himself into a tree. In the last act Minerva (Mentor) appears, saves Telemachus from being killed by Proteus in a cave, and takes him back to Ithaca. Marghe-rita de l'Epine and Mrs. Barbier played Calypso and Telemachus, Signora Manina was Eucharis, and Leveridge Proteus.

Walsh's excellent full score omits recitatives and final chorus. Arias and ensembles are mostly in *Da Capo* form (24 out of 32). Apart from the strings, the only instruments used are oboes and, in one aria, 'traversi'; this is probably the first demand for cross flutes in an English opera. Telemachus has a 'Hunt-ing Aire', 'Hark the hollow Groves resounding', in which the violin writing suggests hunting horns, but it could not in fact be played by natural horns, which probably did not reach theatre orchestras until after their revolutionary use in Handel's *Water Music* some five years later. In this aria Hughes gave Galliard every encouragement to work in conventional echo effects, but Galliard ignored the possibilities almost entirely. About half the vocal numbers are accompanied by a single independent violin line and bass; nine have only continuo accom-paniment; five have one or more oboes. Apart from the 'traversi', there is nothing striking about the scoring, and the same can be said of the music. Though it never sinks to the best of Clayton, it never rises above the worst of Handel, and the unvarying level of inspiration has a somewhat deadening effect; if Galliard had been more unequal there might have been more to admire. Nearly a century later Samuel Arnold told Dr. Kitchener (who scribbled the remark into his copy of the opera, now in the British Museum) that 'Mr. Handel had so high an opinion of *Calypso and Telemachus* as to have declared he would sooner have composed it that any one of his own operas'. Either Handel spoke carelessly or Arnold exaggerated; yet Handel must have expressed praise for Galliard's music in some measure, and *Calypso and Telemachus* does possess a certain solid worth.

It will have been noticed that the hero's role, Telemachus, was taken by Mrs. Barbier. The playhouses were much handicapped by having no voices to set against the castrati in the Italian operas. The exciting vocal quality of these singers is legendary, but their curiosity value was equally good box-office, Wycherley's *The Country Wife* shows how fascinated many women were by men they thought impotent, and Angus Heriot's *The Castrati in Opera* adds many unexpected details. No wonder the playhouses were shy of operas when their chief attraction was denied to them. In Purcell's day audiences had happily accepted counter-tenors as the heroes of operas because for years many perfectly normal men had chosen to sing falsetto; for instance, Sir Francis Drake, and perhaps Purcell himself. But the establishment of the castrati deprived perfectly normal men of their pleasure in singing counter-tenor, for they found themselves viewed with the same amused and patronizing contempt as the castrati but without the compensation of an equally heroic and profitable voice. In our own time the renaissance of the counter-tenor soloist is still bedevilled by the unease such singing occasions in some circles, an unease born of the triumphs of Nicolini. It would scarcely have been understood before 1700. For the playhouses there was the added difficulty that the counter-tenor voice had been cultivated at the expense of what we would regard as the true tenor. Thus when counter-tenors were put to shame, the hero's role in operas and masques was given to women because there was no one else to give it to. Also there was a convention, prolonged by the castrati but very strange to us, that heroes should sing with 'unbroken' voices.

After the Queen's Theatre turned exclusively to Italian opera, Drury Lane for some years gave all its energies to plays, and it was not until 1715 that any real attempt was made on behalf of English opera. Colley Cibber, the most active of the managers, fixed on Pepusch as his composer. Pepusch was a Prussian who reached England about 1700 when he was thirty-three, married when fifty-one the famous singer Margherita de L'Epine (who had just retired), sailed for Bermuda when fifty-seven to help 'erect a college' but returned after being shipwrecked, and acquired immortality when sixty-one by his somewhat casual arrangements for *The Beggar's Opera*. He disliked Handel's music, says Burney, but admired Corelli's, 'treating all other Musick in which there was fancy or invention with sovereign contempt'.

Pepusch's first work for the theatre was the masque *Venus and Adonis* (DL 12.3.15), in which his future wife sang Adonis and Mrs. Barbier Venus. Cibber himself wrote the libretto, and in his preface described the masque as 'an Attempt to give the Town a little good Musick in a Language they understand'. As well as repeating some of Hughes's views on Opera in English, he tried to answer those who complained that when opera *was* sung in English it was very bad English. Two of the five characters in *Calypso and Telemachus* had not been at home in their adopted language, and there was not likely to be much improvement in *Venus and Adonis*.

> It is hoped (wrote Cibber) that this undertaking, if encourag'd, may in time reconcile Musick to the *English* Tongue. And, to make the union more practicable, it is humbly mov'd, that it may be allow'd a less inconvenience, to hear the Performer express his meaning with an imperfect Accent, than in Words, that (to an *English* Audience) have no meaning at all: And at worst, it will be an easier matter to instruct two or three Performers in tolerable *English*, than to teach a whole Nation *Italian*.

The better solution of teaching more English performers to sing seems to have occurred to nobody.

Venus and Adonis was said to be 'Compos'd after the Italian Manner', and the overture and all the songs were published in full score. The former is well written, with plenty of individual work for oboes and bassoon. The third and last movement is an Allegro (really a minuet) and 'Trio'; this may be the first time in English music that the word was used to mean 'central section'. Three of the seventeen songs were avowedly borrowed from unspecified Italian sources, and one of these, 'Swain, thy foolish Sports give o'er', has some delightful syncopations. Those by Pepusch are full of charm and scored with unexpected variety. Oboes and bassoon are given plenty to do. One aria has an obbligato for a 'flageletto', and another near the end has what appears to be a recorder part full of pathetic suspensions:

The first act ends with a duet of real beauty, 'Farewell, Venus'.

The published score omits recitatives and the final chorus, but these can be found in the MS full score and parts at the Royal College of Music. The parts are for Oboe I and Oboe II (doubling flutes), Violino I (two copies), Violino II (three copies), 'Tenore', 'Basso' (two copies), and 'Double Bass'. In the aria quoted above the solo part is marked 'Flute Almain' (cross flute), and there are accompanying chords in minims for the strings. Just before Adonis sings in recitative 'Hark how the cheerful Horn Proclaims the wasting Morn', there are five bars of repeated As marked 'Hunting Horns in the Distance'; the notes are cued into the first oboe part, and the oboist presumably played them off-stage on the short horn used by huntsmen. As we have seen, there are no certain orchestral horn parts in English music until *The Water Music* of 1717 In the very first aria in *Venus and Adonis* the words cry out for horns, but their sounds are imitated by the oboes. There is some evidence that the masque was in part a skit on fox-hunting, which was becoming increasingly popular.

The following season Pepusch wrote three much less successful masques for Drury Lane. *Myrtillo* (DL 5.11.15) also had words by Cibber, but only six of the songs were published. *Apollo and Daphne* (DL 12.1.16) was not published even in part, but again the Royal College of Music possesses a complete MS score. Nothing at all survives of *The Death of Dido* (DL 17.4.16), the one literary attempt of the famous actor Barton Booth. All these masques were advertised as being 'Compos'd after the Italian Manner', but it is possible to sense in *Apollo and Daphne* anticipations of the lyrical minuet song which in Arne's hands sounds thoroughly English.

The above is the introduction. Apollo then sings the same tune to the words

> Fair blooming Creature,
> Each tender feature
> Speaks thee by Nature
> For Love design'd.

(Pepusch managed to spell the last word 'desing'd' on every occasion.) A single oboe doubles the voice, and for accompaniment the violins play the bass line an octave higher. The E flat in the first bar gives the music a touch of individuality; a year or two later Bach was to succeed with much the same trick in the Minuet of his first Brandenburg Concerto. The part of Apollo was sung by Margherita de l'Epine, who had also been the hero in *Myrtillo*; in the Booth masque Aeneas was sung by Mrs. Barbier.

Drury Lane also staged a distantly Shakespearean comic masque, *Pyramus and Thisbe*, written by Leveridge for his own benefit (11.4.16) but popular for several years. Except for a song or two, only the libretto survives, and this reveals that Leveridge anticipated Benjamin Britten in presenting the mechanicals' play as a skit on the Italian opera. Leveridge himself played the Prologue and Bottom. Apart from *Pyramus and Thisbe*, Drury Lane's attempt to re-establish the masque petered out in the summer of 1717.

The new theatre in Lincoln's Inn Fields had been opened in December 1714. Christopher Rich, who built it, did not live to see the opening night, and his twenty-three-year-old son, John Rich, took over, beginning a career of management that was to last nearly half a century. He was a good deal more sympathetic towards opera than Cibber, but for some years he could not collect enough singers to do much about it. However early in 1717 several of the best singers at Drury Lane transferred their services to Rich, either because they were dissatisfied with the work Cibber found for them or because Rich offered them more money. Having nothing new on the stocks, Rich began by reviving *Thomyris* in May and *Camilla* in July, and their success showed how hungry his public was for opera in a language they could follow. *Thomyris*, spruced up with some new arias by Pepusch, held the repertoire throughout the 1720s, and *Camilla* was especially popular in the 1726–7 season when London supported it through as many as twenty-six performances. That lifelong Handelian Mrs. Delany saw one of them, and liked it 'for old acquaintance sake, but there is not many of the songs better than ballads', a remark that reflects the progress of Italian opera since the first decade of the century. Those who valued 'old acquaintance sake' may have taken pleasure in seeing Leveridge still sustaining the roles he had created many years before, but there were no counter-tenors available for the heroes, let alone a castrato; Turnus and Orontes were sung by the ubiquitous Mrs. Barbier.

Rich saw that he must have a composer at his beck and call if he were to develop the operatic side of his repertoire, and late that summer he engaged Galliard; the arrangement was to prove profitable to both parties. A revival of *Calypso and Telemachus* was disappointing, but early in 1718 Galliard wrote music for two new masques with words by Lewis Theobald, *Pan and Syrinx* and *Decius and Paulina*, and the following year he even attempted a full-length all-sung opera, *Circe*, the words a revision of an old libretto by Charles Davenant. *Circe* had seven performances, and thus was no failure by standards of the time, but none of the music was ever printed, and Galliard's contribution to *Decius and Paulina* does not survive either. This, a semi-flippant insertion in *The Lady's Triumph*, an old play by Elkanah Settle, was sufficient for the whole to be described as 'A New Comic-Dramatic Opera'. A mildly coarse song that

Galliard wrote for the play itself, 'On a Bank of Flowers', was published, and found its way into several ballad operas. Being introduced into *The Duenna* by Sheridan, it was later mistaken by Thomson for a Scotch Song; he got Burns to write new words for it and Kozeluch to arrange it.

Pan and Syrinx (LIF 14.1.18) was much the most successful of Galliard's ventures at this time, and is of special interest because all the music survives in the composer's autograph. Oddly enough, none of it seems ever to have been printed. The score, which describes itself as an Opera, includes all the recitatives and most of the stage directions, as well as a quantity of additional music at the end written for a revival in 1726. Pan, not being the sort of god a woman could decently portray, was played by Leveridge, and the nymph Syrinx by Mrs. Barbier. By 1726 they must have been a somewhat elderly pair of lovers. One can only agree with Burney that much of the music is correct but dull. There are however some unusually imaginative touches towards the end when Syrinx is turned into a reed. She has an excellent *Allegro* duet with her uncouth pursuer, Syrinx singing 'Thy Passion is in vain', and Pan 'Thy Resistance is in vain'. Pan turns out to be wrong about this, for during the quick-running orchestral music at the end Syrinx 'wrests herself from Pan and fly's away', the music admirably expressing her haste and apprehension. Then comes a splendid aria for Pan, beginning with an imitation of the flowing stream that has seemed an important part of the story from the first. Galliard's unusual choice of the darkly-coloured viola for the solo is a subtle stroke; viola solos at this period are an extreme rarity.

In the next bar Pan starts singing of his surprise at Syrinx's behaviour, but before he has got very far, three recorders are unobtrusively worked into the texture, and he gradually becomes aware that they are the voice of his transformed nymph:

By the end of the aria the recorders are dominating the score, and the viola has petered out.

    Winton Dean has pointed out that some of these masques, more particularly the Hughes–Pepusch *Apollo and Daphne*,[1] had a good deal of influence on John

---

[1] He wrongly states (p. 158) that the music does not seem to survive.

Gay's libretto for *Acis and Galatea*, which was probably performed for the first time in the summer of 1718 at Cannons, Edgware. It is sad that this master-piece was not taken up by either playhouse until many years later, for it is as actable as any English masque, and its production might both have encouraged English opera and interested Handel in its problems. John Hughes and Aaron Hill were still on hand, and eager for a renaissance that only faltered for lack of a good composer. Alas, both Handel and the English masque were about to turn aside in very different directions, the latter deflected for pantomime purposes.

7 ITALIAN OPERA IN LONDON: HANDEL

My main subject is playhouse music, but it will be necessary from time to time to give a brief generalized summary of the progress of Italian Opera; its in-fluence on playhouse music was never very strong, but it was sometimes very real. Changes in policy do not correspond with those in the playhouses, and it will be a convenience in this section to stray in time beyond the limits of the previous sections to the break-up of the Royal Academy of Music in the summer of 1728.

During this period conventions similar to those of Italian operas in other countries were quickly established. Opera plots, which at the start of the cen-tury had usually included one or two comic characters, became in general more serious and more unreal. Librettos, often adapted from earlier operas by other composers, purported to be about heroic figures in ancient legend or in ancient history, but often bore no relation to what we today know of the subject. Atalanta runs no race in Handel's opera of that name, and a reading of Xenophon is no help towards an understanding of *Serse*. Events always occur, or are described, during the often-very-long recitatives. Nothing ever happens during the arias and ensembles, which express at length a mood arising out of the situa-tion left in mid-air at the end of the previous recitative. Plots had to be suffi-ciently complex to allow each of the main characters to sing arias in a wide variety of moods, and it was the expression of these moods rather than what happened that the audience enjoyed. The number of arias sung by each char-acter was controlled by a sort of etiquette all too well understood by the castrati. As the Venetian playwright and librettist Goldoni put it,

> The three principal personages of the drama ought to sing five airs each; two in the first act, two in the second, and one in the third. The second actress and the second soprano can have only three, and the inferior characters must be satisfied with a single air each, or two at the most. The author of the words must furnish the musician with the different shades which form the *chiaroscuro* of music, and take care that two pathetic airs do not succeed one another. He must distribute with the same precaution

the bravura airs, the airs of action, the inferior airs, and the minuets and rondeaus. He must, above all things, avoid giving impassioned airs, bravura airs, or rondeaus, to inferior characters.[1]

Hampered by such restrictions, it is not surprising that librettists seldom produced a dramatic situation that was both credible and lively.

With so few people able to understand Italian, the events would have had no impact on the audience but for the publication of librettos that included an English translation. They also gave the cast, and they could be bought as you went into the theatre. Today we would call them programmes. There was probably enough light in the auditorium for the translation to be read while the recitatives were being sung. Operas always ended with a reconciliation scene, during which the villains were forgiven and undertook to reform their ways. Londoners were used to such endings in the plays of John Fletcher, but in operas they were more absurd because they were unmotivated.

The arias, especially those sung by the great castrati, were the main attraction. There was always a 'chorus' of principals at the end, and perhaps one or two duets and ensembles, but arias predominated overwhelmingly over other musical forms. Handel towered over his contemporaries because his vocal lines and accompaniments constantly gave emotional depth to conventional lyrics and situations. Much more than his contemporaries, he thought dramatically, and even descriptively. Most of his arias were in *Da Capo* form, with the long opening section repeated after a middle section that was usually short and sometimes perfunctory. This repeat encouraged the singers to add difficult decorations and flourishes of their own devising, and audiences revelled in the skill with which they transformed the original vocal line into something rich and strange.

Like English operas of the time, Italian operas were invariably composed to suit a known cast of singers. Each season opera houses employed a then-famous composer and poet who assessed the capabilities of the company and wrote accordingly. But it was impossible to provide a complete repertoire in this way, and when an opera composed for some other company was chosen, it had to be revised, with some arias cut and others inserted, to suit the resident company. Often it was thought less trouble to compile a pastiche. Singers would suggest arias from their repertoire which showed off their voices to advantage, and the resident poet would link them and other suitable arias into some sort of dramatic sequence. Handel himself sometimes composed new arias for pastiche operas or supplied new recitatives. When his old operas were revived he nearly always replaced some of the arias because the original singers were no longer available and the new ones needed music of a different range or style.

Castrati usually had the range of a modern counter-tenor, and were at their

[1] Goldoni's *Memoirs*, Eng. ed. 1814, i, pp. 185–6, quoted in 'The Aria in Opera Seria, 1725–1780', by M. F. Robinson, *RMA Proceedings*, 1961–2.

best in the octave above Middle C. Later in the century the most notable castrati were sopranos, but Handel seldom had the use of such voices. The leading castrato normally took the part of the hero, but Handel was willing on occasions for the hero to be sung by a woman. Female contraltos were a rarity, and tenors were mostly limited to minor roles.

Opera seasons began in November or January, and might last until the following June or July. In Handel's day there were only two performances a week; with such taxing music singers could not be expected to appear more often. When Handel wanted new singers he usually went abroad himself to search them out, and when he had found good ones he tried to engage them for several seasons on end.

For the first few years after the production of *Rinaldo* in 1711 Handel spent more time abroad than in England. Londoners were regaled with pastiche operas and such oddities as Gasparini's *Ambleto*; the librettist, Apostolo Zeno, is said to have had no knowledge of Shakespeare's tragedy. Nicolini delighted audiences until he left England in 1714, in which year Anastasia Robinson began her career. At this early date there was much less opposition to English singers than obtained in the 1720s and early 1730s. Mrs. Barbier, also English-born, was also tolerated between the autumn of 1711 and 1714; she sang in Handel's *Il Pastor Fido* and *Teseo*. Mrs. Robinson had learnt her music from Croft and her Italian style from a minor composer called Sandoni.[1] She herself could speak fluent Italian. For ten years she sang the second woman in nearly all London's Italian operas, and it is curious that she never sang in English operas or masques. In 1722 she secretly married the Earl of Peterborough, and shortly afterwards she left the stage, having taken part in the first performances of no less than six Handel operas.

A good standard of performance needed more than the composer directing at the harpsichord; it needed also a good leader of the violins, and the first whose name has a small niche in today's memories was Veracini, who was in London in 1714. (More than twenty years later he returned as an opera composer.) Veracini was succeeded by Castrucci, a pupil of Corelli and the violinist that Hogarth portrayed as 'The Enraged Musician'.

In 1714 Queen Anne died, and the Queen's Theatre became the King's. The arrival of George I from Hanover soon led to the return of his employee, Handel. For some time Handel worked for the Duke of Chandos at Cannons, an immense mansion near Edgware. The Duke had made a rather shady fortune from his position as Paymaster-General during the Marlborough Wars, and he aspired to be a patron of the arts. However, he does not seem to have been much interested in opera, though Handel's *Acis and Galatea* was presumably staged at Cannons during Handel's time there. We have seen that Dr. Pepusch was also on his payroll, as also a number of minor singers and instrumentalists to be mentioned later.

[1] He later married Cuzzoni.

By 1719 Italian Opera was dying of inanition. To prevent the completion of this process, a group of wealthy aristocrats led by the Lord Chamberlain (the Duke of Newcastle) formed what was called the Royal Academy of Music. They asked for annual subscriptions, and the sixty-two original subscribers all guaranteed a minimum sum of £200; some of them guaranteed as much as £1000. Handel was deputed to go abroad and 'make Contracts with such Singer or Singers as you shall judge fit to perform on the English Stage', and in particular he was instructed to engage the famous castrato Senesino.[1] Two other composers were also engaged to help Handel provide a repertoire, Giovanni Bononcini and Attilio Ariosti, and all three worked for the Academy until its collapse. Handel captured Senesino by offering him the then enormous salary of £2,000 a year, but Senesino was unable to come for the first season, which opened with Handel's *Radamisto* (KT 27.4.20). The title role was sung by the company's leading soprano, Margherita Durastanti. It looks as though Handel thought more of vocal quality than appearance, for Durastanti was approaching middle age and was described by the librettist Rolli as 'an Elephant'. When *Radamisto* was revived in the following season, she yielded up the title role to Senesino (it was his first Handelian role) and switched to the heroine.

Senesino sang for the Academy for eight seasons in a row. The great soprano Francesca Cuzzoni joined him in January 1723, making her début in Handel's *Ottone*, and the company was further strengthened in May 1726 by the arrival of Faustina. Her rivalry with Cuzzoni made *Admeto* (KT 31.1.27) one of the most popular operas of the decade. By the following season squabbling inside the company was rife, and Senesino was widely thought to be getting too big for his boots. With the Royal Academy of Music struggling hopelessly against financial difficulties, its demise was predictable. It had presented more than thirty different operas during its reign, thirteen of them by Handel.[2] His enthusiasm seems to have grown with time, and latterly he often wrote two operas on end for the one season. During the final season of the Academy no less than three Handel operas were given their first performance, though *Riccardo Primo* had in fact been written somewhat earlier. It is also of interest that Handel's operas were increasingly revived as the decade progressed. There is no point in listing all their titles here. *Flavio* (KT 14.5.23) was unusual for its touches of humour, and *Giulio Cesare* (KT 20.2.24) was the most lavishly scored; Senesino took the title role, and Cuzzoni was Cleopatra.

Audiences at the King's Theatre seem to have been scarcely aware of Handel's superiority over Bononcini and Ariosto, whose operas were often almost as popular. This was perhaps because they tended to be simpler and easier to follow at a first hearing. But they were not revived so often as Handel's, presumably because it became apparent that they did not bear repetition so well. The three composers seem to have worked together in reasonable harmony.

[1] Deutsch, p. 90.
[2] He had written only four operas for London in the 1710s.

In the summer of 1728 Ariosto left the country, together with the three singers who had done so much to make Italian opera popular in recent years: Senesino, Cuzzoni, and Faustina. In the following season there was no Italian opera, and the lack of it was not unconnected with the nation's enthusiasm for *The Beggar's Opera*.

There was never in England a widespread enthusiasm for Italian Opera. As in more recent years, it affected only a coterie of society people and intellectuals; the middle and lower class theatregoer inevitably preferred the playhouses where he could understand the words. But opera in a foreign tongue has always had a strong snob appeal for those few who wish to be thought cleverer than they are. Even if they could make nothing of the music, there was the fascination of watching those only-just-mentionable creatures, the castrati, strutting about in their monstrous pride. It is doubtful if Italian opera would ever have got established without them. Castrati had the additional allure of being foreign, and dozens of quotations can be produced to show that in the eighteenth and indeed the nineteenth centuries it was widely believed that foreigners by their very nature were better at music than Britons.

Yet the appeal of Italian Opera to intellectuals was fully justified. Handel's music was of superb quality, a quality that could seldom be matched in the playhouses, and castrato singing had a thrill about it that could never be matched in the playhouses. In this one fantastic field Drury Lane and Covent Garden could not hope to compete on equal terms, and it was not until they struck out on their own (which was after 1762) that English opera became truly popular. It then became popular not only in London but also in the provinces, where Italian Opera had never penetrated.

2
Pantomime
1700–1728

1 THE RISE OF ENGLISH PANTOMIME
1700–1723

IN a study of English nineteenth-century opera no writer would treat panto-mime as an important offshoot, but in the eighteenth century pantomimes and operas were composed by the same composers and sung by the same singers. Pantomimes always contained a number of arias, and there were usually recita-tives, ensembles, and choruses as well. Between the vocal items there was a string of short instrumental pieces which accompanied the miming, and they were known as, and published as, 'The Comic Tunes', this being a generic name for music intended for mime whether it was comic or not. In the second half of the century Comic Tunes were increasingly descriptive, reflecting the action or situation they accompanied. Pantomime music was continuous; there was no speaking before about 1780, and usually there was none right up to 1800. Thus composers were driven into treating dramatic situations musically, whereas in most eighteenth-century operas dramatic situations were developed in the dialogue without any music at all. It could be argued that some com-posers, notably William Shield, were more operatic in their pantomimes than they were in their operas. Pantomimes were historically important because the long stretches of miming to orchestral accompaniment led directly to the *ballet d'action*.

Eighteenth-century pantomimes were very different from anything we our-selves can ever have seen in this country. They were invariably afterpieces lasting under an hour, and until Linley composed his *Robinson Crusoe* in 1781 and Shield his *Aladdin* in 1788, the stories were not those we associate with the form today. Early plots were mostly mythological, but any story both familiar and macabre was likely to be pressed into service. For preference there had to be a scene in Hades, and it is not surprising that the Orpheus and Proserpine legends were especially popular. Devils and monsters on earth were found almost as compelling, and the mediaeval tale of Dr. Faustus was a perennial attraction.

It may seem surprising that such titles as *Jupiter and Europa* and *Apollo and Daphne* also proved alluring, for to us they offer little or no promise of sensationalism, but theatre-goers of the 1720s were influenced by the suggestive pictures of classical love-making on view at Sadler's Wells 'Musick-House' and elsewhere, pictures of which these particular love affairs were often the subject.

A peculiarly English form of harlequinade was usually superimposed on what might be called the variable element in the entertainment. Harlequin and Columbine were hero and heroine, and by the second quarter of the century Harlequin was identified with the hero of the associated story. Thus in the Shield pantomime mentioned above, Harlequin and Aladdin were the same person, while the Plate no. II shows that as early as 1723 Dr. Faustus wore Harlequin's lozenge-patterned leotard under his scholar's gown. He bore little resemblance to Marlowe's hero, and none at all to any harlequin seen on the stage this century. The one in *Carnaval*, the ballet by Fokine, is a poetic, graceful, moonlit creature, whereas the eighteenth-century variety was robust, earthy, and not poetic at all. Addison described the Italian *arlecchino* as 'made up of Blunders and Absurdities. He is to mistake one Name for another, to forget his Errands, to stumble over Queans and to run against every post that comes his way'. So far he sounds like the servants in Shakespeare's early Italianate comedies, for instance the Dromios in *The Comedy of Errors*, but we must include in the picture some vigorous love-making and a tendency to make everyone else on the stage seem unimportant. The English Harlequin was sharperwitted than the Italian, though still something of a buffoon, and above all he was a magician. Indeed it was stage conjuring tricks, his sudden disappearances and transformations, his changing of bailiffs into ostriches and whole villages into deserts, that filled the theatres.

Two other *commedia dell'arte* characters were popular. Pantaloon, Columbine's fat old father, and his servant the Clown spent most of their time chasing Harlequin and Columbine through the streets of London or down into Hell (or both) with a view to preventing their union. By 1800 Grimaldi's genius for playing the Clown had raised that character to the position of chief comic, thereby starting Harlequin on his gradual decline into insignificance, but for most of the eighteenth century the Clown was a subordinate character. The other *commedia dell'arte* personages, for instance Brighella and Scaramouche, never really established themselves in England. It is sometimes forgotten that those who developed the English pantomime into the most profitable stage entertainment of the century knew little or nothing of the Italian variety at first hand.

Pantomime fever was fully developed by 1723, after a rather uncertain build-up of some six years. By French and Italian standards this was late in the day, but Londoners had been allowed glimpses of Harlequin and his antics long before this. Two influential plays of the seventeenth century were written as a direct result of seeing *commedia dell'arte* abroad. Sir Aston Cokain had this enviable experience in Venice in the 1630s, and drew on his memories of the occasion for *Trappolin suppos'd Prince*, a play published in 1658. It was probably not acted until 1684, when Nahum Tate rewrote it, to its disadvantage, as *A Duke and No Duke*. Trappolin, a comic servant, is changed by a magician into an exact likeness of the Duke of Florence, who happens to be away. This allows Trappolin to usurp his place and reverse his decisions. When the Duke returns, the two rage round the stage spreading confusion, but not meeting until it is time for the piece to end. *A Duke and No Duke* held its place in the playhouse repertoire for much of the eighteenth century.

More influential was a play called *The Emperor of the Moon* by the remarkable Mrs. Aphra Behn. In Paris in 1684 she had seen *Arlequin, Empereur dans la Lune*, of which the French scenes were published but not the Italian interludes which were improvised. Mrs. Behn claimed to have taken no more than 'a very barren and thin hint' from what she had seen. Harlequin is servant to Cinthio, the juvenile lead, while Scaramouche is servant to Dr. Baliardo, the heroine's father. The doctor is obsessed by the moon, and there is much horseplay deluding him into thinking he sees lunar creatures through an enormous telescope. (Haydn's *Il mondo della luna* surely derives from the same source.) At several points miming takes over from dialogue, as for instance when Harlequin and Scaramouche are groping round in a dark room unaware that the other is there, until at last Scaramouche squats down,

> his Mouth stretch'd wide, and his Eyes staring. Harlequin, groping, thrusts his Hand in his Mouth, he bites him, the other dares not cry out.

There are far more stage directions than usual in this play, though not nearly as many as in an English pantomime libretto. Other early plays with *commedia dell'arte* characters were *Scaramouche* (1677) by Ravenscroft and Motteux's *The Novelty* (1697).

More positive steps towards English pantomime were taken by the dancing-master, John Weaver, 'a little dapper cheerful Man' who wrote *A History of the Mimes and Pantomimes* in 1728. In this he claimed that

> The first Entertainment that appear'd on the English Stage where the Representation and the Story was carried on by Dancing, Action and Motion only, was perform'd with Grotesque Characters after the modern Italians such as Harlequin, Scaramouch etc.; and was call'd *The Tavern Bilkers*, compos'd by Weaver and first perform'd at Drury Lane in 1702.[1] The next was many years after.

In other words *The Tavern Bilkers* was not a success. Though nothing is known of it, we may presume a silent Harlequin miming to continuous music. That same year Drury Lane advertised a 'Night Scene by a Harlequin and a

[1] Most of Weaver's dates are wrong, but this one is correct.

Scaramouch, after the Italian manner, by Serene and another Person lately arriv'd in England'. It was performed in one of the intervals of Brome's comedy, *The Jovial Crew*, and there were many other occasions in the next few years when a Harlequin filled an interval with a short dance. Judging by the music of other much-advertised interval dances, for instance 'The Black Joke', they were probably only about a minute in length; all through the first half of the century the tiniest dances were held out as a carrot to entice Londoners into the playhouses. But in 1717 Weaver talked Drury Lane into some much more elaborate dances and mimes.

In his *Apology* Colley Cibber tried to maintain that Drury Lane entered the pantomime field only because Lincoln's Inn Fields had done so first and with much profit. In fact Drury Lane itself seems to have been the pioneer, and it is clear that this theatre turned to pantomime because the recent experiment with masques by Pepusch suggested that English opera could not succeed. Cibber himself made this point:

> Our *English* Musick has been so discountenanced, since the Taste of *Italian* Operas prevail'd, that it was to no purpose, to pretend to it. Dancing therefore was, now, the only Weight in the opposite Scale, and as the New Theatre sometimes found their Account in it, it could not be safe for us, wholly to neglect it. To give even Dancing therefore some Improvement, and to make it something more than Motion without Meaning, the fable of *Mars* and *Venus*, was form'd into a connected Presentation of Dances in Character, wherein the Passions were so happily expressed, and the whole Story so intelligibly told, by a mute Narration of Gesture only, that even thinking Spectators allow'd it both a pleasing and a rational Entertainment.

Weaver's *Loves of Mars and Venus* was advertised as 'A New Dramatick Entertainment of Dancing after the Manner of the Antient Pantomimes' and first performed at Drury Lane on 2 March 1717. Weaver himself danced the part of Vulcan.

In a non-speaking pantomime, there is some hope of two constituents surviving: a printed 'Description' of the action, including the song-words if any; and the music. 'Description' was a generic word for pantomime librettos, and about twenty survive from the period 1717–1750. No doubt many more were printed; the interest in such booklets was ephemeral, and they were far more likely to be thrown away than plays or opera words. They were usually very short and very cheap, their purpose being to lure the customer into the theatre by describing the wonderful tricks he would see there. Wags said that they saved you the trouble of going at all, but these synopses must have been efficacious for they continued to be printed to the end of the century and beyond.

We are fortunate in having an especially interesting Description for *The Loves of Mars and Venus*, and it is unusual but by no means unique in being padded out with material that is only marginally relevant.[1] Weaver's preface is full of grandiose claims that would most impress those who did not bother to think about them. He was imitating not the modern Italian *commedia dell'arte* but 'the Pantomimes of the Ancient Greeks and Romans', and making 'the first Trial of this Nature that has been made since the Reign of *Trajan*, as far as I have been able to trace it'. He goes on:

> these *Mimes* and *Pantomimes* were *Dances* that represented a Story or Fable in Motion and Measure: They were Imitators of all things, as the name of *Pantomime* imports, and perform'd all by Gesture and the Action of the Hands, Fingers, Legs, and Feet, without making use of the Tongue. The Face or Countenance had a large Share in this Performance, and they imitated the Manners, Passions, and Affections by the numerous Variety of Gesticulations . . . for Nature assign'd each Motion of the Mind its proper Gesticulation and Countenance . . .

Pages later, in the middle of the description proper, Weaver breaks off to list some of these conventional 'gesticulations'. I quote two of them; the first is the more stylized.

ADMIRATION

> *Admiration* is discover'd by the raising up of the right Hand, the Palm turn'd upwards, the Fingers clos'd; and in one Motion the Wrist turn'd round and Fingers spread; the Body reclining, and Eyes fix'd on the Object.

ANGER

> The left Hand struck suddenly with the Right; and sometimes against the Breast; denotes *Anger*.

Similarly '*Impatience* is seen by the smiting of the Thigh, or Breast with the Hand'. In classical ballets, for instance Tchaikovsky's *Swan Lake*, emotions are conventionally expressed in surprisingly similar ways; such gestures may well derive in both instances from the same French source.

The Loves of Mars and Venus had four scenes. In the first, after 'a Martial Overture', the four followers of Mars dance a Pyrrhic Dance to a March, and later Mars himself joins in and 'appears engaged sometimes with two at a time and sometimes with all four'. Weaver then digresses rather boresomely to explain what he means by a Pyrrhic Dance. Scene ii starts with a 'Symphony of flutes' and shows Venus at her toilet. She dances a 'Passacaile', in which she is joined by the Graces and Hours. Vulcan enters to 'a wild rough air', and he and Venus perform a dance together

[1] Weaver was influenced by the *livres de ballet* published in association with the *ballets de cour* in France; these too were programmes rather than librettos, and like so many pantomine Descriptions, included thumb-nail sketches of the principal characters.

> *in which Vulcan expresses* his Admiration; Jealousie; Anger; *and* Despite:
> *And Venus shews* Neglect; Coquetry; Contempt; *and* Disdain.

This is Weaver's cue for listing the gestures by means of which such emotions can be conveyed. Scene iii shows the Cyclops making a net in Vulcan's 'shop', and scene iv a garden. During 'A Prelude of Trumpets, Hautbois, Violins and Flutes alternate', Mars enters on one side with his followers, and Venus on the other with hers. Mars shows adoration and Venus 'wishing Looks'. Vulcan catches Mars in the net and executes 'an Insulting Performance', after which he exhibits his captives to Jupiter and Juno, who liberate them.

This reads much more like the synopsis of a ballet than of a pantomime, and there is no sign that the 'grotesque characters' of the harlequinade took any part in the entertainment. As we shall see, the pantomime did not go Weaver's way in the next ten years, and it is predictable that he should have been bewailing its decline in his book of 1728. Nevertheless Weaver had shown that mythological stories familiar in masques could be danced without any singing at all, and in the 1720s we shall meet two kinds of mythological pantomime, neither of them the same as Weaver's kind, yet both of them influenced by it. In the one the gods and goddesses sang exactly as they had done in the masques while the 'grotesque characters' were limited to unscripted interludes. In the other the 'grotesque characters' were identified with the gods and goddesses, who thus were played by dancers, while the singing was given to subordinate characters. It was the latter type of pantomime that prevailed in the end.

It is sad that no music survives from *The Loves of Mars and Venus*; we do not even know who composed it. We can be certain that no use was made of the music Eccles had written twenty years earlier for the masque of the same name, for this was entirely vocal, whereas Weaver's pantomime had no singing in it at all. But there was singing in the next pantomime, the much less successful *Shipwreck, or Perseus and Andromeda*. 'Thomas, I cannot', which must have been sung by a *commedia dell'arte* character, was published in *The Dancing Master* (1719) and from there made its way into *The Beggar's Opera* as 'I like a Ship in Storms was tost'. Weaver himself was Perseus,[1] and the cast included 'a Monster Crocodile'. In 1728 this pantomime was revived and revised, and we know far more about the later and much more successful version.

It was John Rich more than anyone who turned pantomime from the high-flown style of 'the Ancient Greeks and Romans' into a mass cult. As well as managing Lincoln's Inn Fields and its successor Covent Garden, he himself played Harlequin regularly from 1717 to 1741, and occasionally thereafter until 1748. He always billed himself as 'Lun', which, according to Tate Wilkinson,[2] 'had been the name of the famous man who represented Harlequin

---

[1] He must have been about forty-five; according to Lonsdale (p. 6) he was 'more than seventy years old' when, about 1743, he was teaching dancing in Shrewsbury to young Charles Burney.

[2] *Memoirs* iv, p. 153, and *The Wandering Patentee* i, p. 124.

at Paris'. Wilkinson also reveals that he was 'remarkably short in stature'; he was by far the greatest Harlequin of the century. In his early days Rich occasionally attempted tragedy and comedy, no doubt because his rival manager Cibber did so, but he soon realized he had no aptitude in these directions. The story that he never learnt to read is hard to credit, but if he read only with difficulty that alone might have deterred him from acting; Harlequins did not need to read. In private life he was a curiosity, with his quantities of cats and his inability to remember anybody's name. According to Wilkinson he even called Garrick 'Grifkin'. But he had some appreciation of music and was always a good friend to Handel, providing a home for his operas whenever the King's Theatre was being 'difficult'. When Handel's operas were published, Rich was usually among the subscribers, and he bought as many as three sets of the op. 6 concertos, no doubt with a view to their constant use as interval music. Handel, the first to die by two years, left his organ to Rich in his Will; it was used at Covent Garden for background music and accompaniments until it was destroyed in the great fire of 1808.

Rich seldom devised the pantomimes in which he took part, though he surely exercised overriding control. As might be expected, he found it easier in the end to work with a literary man than with another dancer. In May 1715 he had brought over from Dublin for his new company at Lincoln's Inn Fields John Thurmond and his wife, who both acted. Their son, another John, was a trained dancer, and he was soon making his mark as Scaramouche in various interval dances. Two years later he was Scaramouche to Rich's Harlequin in Lincoln's Inn Fields' first pantomimes, *The Cheats, or The Tavern Bilkers* (22.4.17), and *The Jealous Doctor* (29.4.17). The latter was much the most successful of Rich's early pantomimes, and though nothing is known of its story or music, newspaper advertisements show that the *commedia dell'arte* characters were identified with those of the 'outside' story, Harlequin being called Underplot, Scaramouche Plotwell, and Columbine Mrs. Townley. It was several years before Rich thought of combining pantomime with mythology, and by that time he had got rid of young Thurmond and taken up with Lewis Theobald. But he still had Thurmond with him in the 1717–18 season, when he pushed pantomime fairly hard. He gave forty-eight performances of six different examples, and twice capped a Drury Lane pantomime with another of the same name, in the one case slapping it together in a mere six days. He was to continue this bitchy policy in the 1720s, though by this time pantomimes were much more elaborate and took far longer to prepare. In 1718–19 and again the following winter, Rich brought over a French company from Paris which gave plays and pantomimes one or two nights a week at Lincoln's Inn Fields. In fact London was able to enjoy the French players four winters running, for Aaron Hill gave two similar seasons between 1720 and 1722 at the newly-opened Little Theatre in the Haymarket. This was *commedia dell'arte* at only one remove, and Rich must have learned much from what he saw. But he did not care to exhibit his own pantomimes alongside those of the French, and both London theatres conserved their strength for when the visiting company was gone.

In the summer of 1718 John Thurmond skipped off to Drury Lane, where he had the satisfaction of being his own master where dancing and mime were concerned. In December 1719 he turned *A Duke and no Duke* into a pantomime and himself danced the Duke of Florence, but it was not successful and the following season Drury Lane devoted only half of one night to pantomime. Thurmond found himself restricted to interval dances. However he was on hand later when the pantomime flood swept through London. He created five pantomimes in five years, two of them very successful and none of them failures. Yet it must be symptomatic of public preference for Rich's pantomimes that so much music from them survives, whereas from Thurmond's at Drury Lane I can find very little.

With one exception, no music at all survives from the pantomimes devised before the flood began in 1723. The exception is *The Magician, or Harlequin Director* (LIF 16.3.21), Rich's only new pantomime in four seasons. For once he devised it himself, and it was usually known by its alternative title. The British Museum has a cantata of 1723 by the Bermondsey organist, George Hayden, 'Sung by Mr. Platt to the Harlequin Director at Sadler's Wells', but this cannot have had anything to do with the pantomime of the same name at Lincoln's Inn Fields. We know all too little about what went on at the Sadler's Wells 'Musick-House' at this early period. Any other songs catalogued under *Harlequin Director* were almost certainly written for Rich. They include 'A New South Sea Ballad made and sung by Mr. Anthony Aston', one of Rich's actors for a short time, and two other songs that look like Comic Tunes with words added.

2 THE GOLDEN AGE AT LINCOLN'S INN FIELDS, 1723–1728

Few pages of stage history are so confusing as the Pantomime Era when, in the words of Colley Cibber, there

> sprung forth that Succession of monstrous Medlies, that have so long infested the Stage, and which rose upon one another, alternately, at both Houses, outvying, in Expense, like contending Bribes on both sides at an Election, to secure a Majority of the Multitude.

With similar titles advertised at both playhouses, it is no wonder that modern writers have sometimes confused one pantomime with another. The following lists cover the period of pantomime's greatest success. The titles in the first list were to be the basis of Rich's prosperity right up to his death in 1761; the money they made financed many a high-flown blank verse tragedy that nobody much wanted to see. With fewer successes Drury Lane was driven into staging many more new productions in its search for a lasting repertoire. In the titles below 'H' stands for Harlequin. 'I' shows that the harlequinade was integrated with the main story, 'S' that the comic and serious plots were kept separate. The number of performances is an indication of popularity.

LINCOLN'S INN FIELDS

	Author		Composer	1722–3	23–4	24–5	25–6	26–7	27–8	Total
Jupiter & Europa or The Intrigues of H. 23.3.23	? (unpub.)	I	Various	12	10	7	7	4	2	42
The Necromancer or H. Dr. Faustus 20.12.23	Theobald?	I	Galliard		48	11	11	7	12	89
H. Sorcerer with The Loves of Pluto & Proserpine 21.1.25	Theobald	S	Galliard?			32	9	12	4	57
Apollo & Daphne or The Burgomaster trick'd 14.1.26	Theobald	S	Galliard				45	12	9	66
The Rape of Proserpine with The Birth of H. 13.2.27	Theobald	S	Galliard					31	23	54
Others				17	12	7	6	1	7	50
TOTAL PANTOMIME PERFORMANCES:				29	70	57	78	67	57	358

One slightly later but equally lasting success needs to be listed:

Perseus & Andromeda Theobald? S Galliard?
29.1.30

Considering that in the 1727–8 season *The Beggar's Opera* virtually monopolized Lincoln's Inn Fields from 29 January onwards, it is remarkable that there were as many as fifty-seven pantomime performances. (*The Beggar's Opera* was too long to be played with an afterpiece, and thus curtailed pantomime performances very considerably.)

DRURY LANE

	Author		Composer	1723–4	24–5	25–6	26–7	27–8	Total
H. Dr. Faustus 26.11.23	Thurmond & Booth	I	Carey	40	31	14	22	11	118
H. Sheppard 28.11.24	Thurmond	I	Carey?		7				7
Apollo & Daphne or H. Mercury 20.2.25	Thurmond	S	Jones and Carey		17	26	10	1	54
The Miser or Wagner & Abericock 30.12.26	Thurmond	I	Jones				19		19
Harlequin's Triumph 27.2.27	Thurmond	I	?				17		17
Others				10	0	2	0	10	22
TOTAL PANTOMIME PERFORMANCES:				50	55	42	68	22	237

At this theatre too a lasting success on the Perseus story was staged a little later:

Perseus & Andromeda   Weaver   S Pepusch
  with The Rape of
  Columbine 15.11.28

Descriptions were published for all the pantomimes in both lists, with the possible exception of *Jupiter and Europa*; some of them are extremely rare. Drury Lane's *Apollo and Daphne* was revised after one season and renamed *Apollo and Daphne, or Harlequin's Metamorphosis*. In this form it was published in a single volume with *Harlequin Dr. Faustus* and *Harlequin's Triumph*. There was thus three pantomimes called *Apollo and Daphne*; none of them had any musical connection with the masque of that name by Pepusch and Hughes.[1]

In several books on pantomime (none of which bothers about the music) it is suggested that in England the form arose from attempts to popularize the masque, the harlequin scenes starting as improvised interludes between the sung scenes. This theory derives from Tom Davies, who in 1780 wrote the first biography of the recently-dead Garrick and included a famous but not wholly accurate description of pantomime:

> To retrieve the credit of his theatre, Rich created a species of dramatic composition, unknown to this, and, I believe, to any other country, which he called Pantomime. It consisted of two parts, one serious, the other comic; by the help of gay scenes, fine habits, grand dances, appropriate music, and other decorations, he exhibited a story from Ovid's *Metamorphoses*, or some other fabulous history. Between the pauses of the acts, he interwove a comic fable, consisting chiefly of the courtship of Harlequin and Columbine, with a variety of surprising adventures and tricks, which were produced by the magic wand of Harlequin; such as the sudden transformation of palaces and temples to huts and cottages; of men and women into wheelbarrows and joint stools; of trees turned to houses; colonades to beds of tulips; and mechanics' shops into serpents and ostriches.

Davies is obviously describing a type of pantomime unknown to most of his readers; in the 1780s it was taken for granted that Harlequin was identified with the hero of the 'outside' story, and Davies is saying that this was not originally the case. But in fact there was just as much integration in most of Thurmond's pantomimes and in some of Rich's earlier ones as there was in 1780. Furthermore Davies makes no mention of the fact that there were several different ways of treating a pantomime in which the two stories were kept separate. For instance in Drury Lane's *Harlequin Dr. Faustus* the 'grotesque characters' were in sole command until quite near the end; there was then an all-sung 'Masque of the Deities' in which the harlequinade characters took no part. On the other hand in *Harlequin Sorcerer* and the Drury Lane

---

[1] Comic Tunes for one of the *Apollo and Daphne* pantomimes are advertised in *Hasse's Comic Tunes*, Vol. I (c. 1741), but I have not traced a copy.

Perseus, the comic interludes separated what we today would call ballet scenes in which the mythological story was danced quite seriously on the lines of Weaver's *Loves of Mars and Venus*. For Davies's alternation of masque and harlequinade we can cite *The Rape of Proserpine* and the Lincoln's Inn Fields *Perseus*. Because two of the most successful pantomimes in which John Rich took part had double plots, and because they stuck in people's minds more vividly than most of the others, there arose the illusion that all pantomimes of the period had double plots in alternation.

Not that the double plots appealed to everyone. As Fielding put it in *Tom Jones*:[1]

> The serious (portion) exhibited a certain number of heathen gods and heroes, which were certainly the worst and dullest company into which an audience was ever introduced; and—which was a secret known to few— were actually intended so to be, in order to contrast the comic part of the entertainment, and to display the tricks of Harlequin to the better advantage.

On Christmas Day 1732 Aaron Hill found time to write on the subject to Booth, one of the Drury Lane managers:

> There ought to be a *purpose* and a *point*. It is impossible, that any man should laugh, with less pleasure, only because he had *reason*, as well as *humour*, for laughing; and were the tricks of *Harlequin* connected into a *thread*, and the consequence of some story and design, they might, un- doubtedly, be more lively, more various, more extravagant, and sur- prizing; and, yet, give *pleasure* without *shame*; both of which we now receive, together.

In point of fact Drury Lane did attempt a connecting thread. Rich seldom bothered, and it can hardly have been of much use writing to him on the subject. Audiences flocked to see his own mesmeric performances and the ingenious stage tricks that his theatre staff devised. Why should he change anything?

As already mentioned, Rich's most successful pantomimes were devised by Theobald. Lewis Theobald (1688–1744) was the son of an attorney in Sittingbourne, Kent, and he had had literary longings from the first. He began, as did so many in the eighteenth century, with some unwanted blank verse tragedies, and had his first mild success with *Pan and Syrinx*, the masque for which Galliard wrote the music. This may have prompted Rich, some years later, to engage Theobald and Galliard to help him create his pantomime repertory. Success in this field did not bring unalloyed pleasure to Theobald, who felt that life had intended him for something better. When dedicating *The Rape of Proserpine* he wrote of pantomimes in general:

[1] Book V, ch. 1.

> Thus much, however, may be said in their Favour, that this Theatre has
> of late ow'd its Support in great measure to them . . . Whenever the
> Public Taste shall be disposed to return to the Works of the Drama, no
> one shall rejoice more sincerely than myself.

While doing his annual stint for Rich, Theobald was labouring at higher things
on his own account, and in 1726 produced a book called *Shakespeare Restored*.
Five years earlier Pope had published the first critical edition of Shakespeare's
plays, that is, the first edition that made some attempt to restore sense to the
more mangled parts of the text. Theobald's book had the prime purpose of
pointing out 'the many Errors as well committed as unamended by Mr. Pope',
and Pope was furious. As Dr. Johnson put it, he 'was so much offended, when
he was found to have left anything for others to do, that he passed the latter
part of his life in a state of hostility with verbal criticism'. Johnson called Theobald 'a man of heavy diligence, with very slender powers', but he did throw light
on a large number of passages which Pope had left in the dark. For instance
Mistress Quickly's famous 'and 'a babbled of green fields' (when describing the
death of Falstaff) is a Theobald emendation. Later Shakespearean editors have
usually preferred his edition of 1733 to Pope's. But long before this came out,
Pope was gunning for him with all the hostility at his command.

In 1728 Pope published *The Dunciad* with the prime aim of discrediting
Theobald. It was the largest cudgel that ever belaboured an unfortunate mouse,
and it would be no concern of ours here were it not that Pope touched on
Theobald's pantomime activities. In this he was somewhat handicapped by his
friendship with Rich. The relevant section in Book III begins with the line

> See now, what Dulness and her Sons admire!

What follows (line 233 onwards) is worth quoting at some length as it contains
one of the earliest descriptions of the mimed sections in pantomimes. In his
edition of Pope (1776) Warburton suggests that the first four lines refer to *The
Necromancer or Harlequin Dr. Faustus*, the rest to The *Rape of Proserpine*, and
this identification seems confirmed by what can be gleaned from the published
Descriptions.

> [He] look'd, and saw a sable Sorc'rer rise,
> Swift to whose hand a winged volume flies:
> All sudden, Gorgons hiss, and Dragons glare,
> And ten horn'd Fiends and Giants rush to war.
> Hell rises, Heav'n descends, and dance on Earth:
> Gods, imps, and monsters, music, rage, and mirth,
> A fire, a jig, a battle, and a ball,
> 'Till one wide Conflagration swallows all.
> Thence a new world, to Nature's laws unknown,
> Breaks out refulgent, with a heav'n its own:

> Another Cynthia her new journey runs,
> And other planets circle other suns.
> The forests dance, the rivers upwards rise,
> Whales sport in woods, dolphins in the skies;
> And last, to give the whole creation grace,
> Lo! one vast Egg produces human race.

Shortly before his death, Pope, driven by a waspishness that was almost hysterical, went to the trouble of rewriting *The Dunciad* in order to install Cibber as leading Dunce. (Because of the superb new material in the Fourth Book, this is the version to be found in most modern editions.) In Dr. Johnson's words, Theobald was 'degraded from his painful pre-eminence'; as one of Pope's enemies, he had been in quite good company, and may well by this time have preferred painful pre-eminence to being unnoticed.

Theobald may have had a hand in *Jupiter and Europa*, but he did not devise it all, for the words of at least one song were by Leveridge. This was 'Europa fair', set to a charming minuet tune by Galliard. Walsh published this and three other songs, describing the work as a masque on the title page. Two were composed by Leveridge; a long and interesting Italianate aria, 'What Scenes of approaching Delight', is described as by 'the late Mr. Cobston', a composer otherwise unknown. One song was sung by 'Legar' (Laguerre), who played Mercury, but it is not clear who sang the others. Leveridge does not seem to have taken part in the pantomime. Newspaper advertisements show that Harlequin was identified with Jupiter, Scaramouch with Pan, and Punch with Apollo. Europa and Columbine were two different people. We shall meet this pantomime later on, revised and renamed *The Royal Chace*.

We know rather more about *The Necromancer, or Harlequin Dr. Faustus*, which was first staged nearly four weeks after Thurmond's *Harlequin Dr. Faustus* at Drury Lane. Both versions of the story were extremely popular for several decades, mainly because they allowed for the introduction of an imposing devil at the start and a whole horde of hellish inhabitants at the end. In the darkened theatres such spectral creatures made the flesh creep agreeably, and the stage trickery, the very spice of all pantomimes, could be effectively motivated by daemonic intervention. It will be enough to say something of what went on in the Drury Lane version, some pages ahead. An important difference was that Drury Lane showed Helen of Troy as beautiful but unvocal, whereas Lincoln's Inn Fields presented her as vocal but less visually striking. Two of the five songs by Galliard that Walsh published were sung by Mrs. Chambers in the part of Helen, and two by Leveridge in the part of Charon. Of the former, 'Cupid, God of pleasing Anguish' is of interest, for in Bickham's lavish song collection *The Musical Entertainer* (ii, p. 44) it appears as 'Helen charms Dr. Faustus'; there is an engraving of her doing so, watched by Mephistopheles and a winged Cupid. One of Leveridge's songs has a fine Demon King flavour, and there is no need to give the bass for, except where shown, it is in unison with the voice:

Years later in 1752, six Comic Tunes and a long 'Chacone' described as from *Dr. Faustus* were published as a supplement to the Comic Tunes in *Harlequin Sorcerer*; both pantomimes had just been revived with great success at Covent Garden.[1] The Comic Tunes are all binary in form, and the second is identical with Air 4 in the ballad opera *Momus turn'd Fabulist* (1729), where it is described as 'Haymakers Dance in Faustus'. It seems likely that the other pieces also come from the original version of 1723, given at Covent Garden's predecessor, Lincoln's Inn Fields. It would be rash to insist that Galliard com-

---

[1] The British Museum Catalogue attributes the *Dr. Faustus* pieces to Samuel Arnold, who cannot possibly have written them.

posed them, but he may well have done. No doubt the Chaconne accompanied a stage procession, as it would have in Purcell's day. These would seem to be the earliest Comic Tunes to survive.

Early in 1725 Rich planned a Pluto-Proserpine pantomime on a lavish scale, and though his plans went awry, he did manage to stage *Harlequin Sorcerer, with the Loves of Pluto and Proserpine*. In the Description Theobald revealed that Lincoln's Inn Fields had been 'disappointed of some very necessary persons from abroad, on whom we depended'. However, as 'several of the principal Scenes, Machines, and other Parts of the Decoration are finished', he hoped that 'the following Entertainment . . . will contribute as effectively to the Satisfaction of the Town'. (The hope was realized; the pantomime was extremely popular.) The Description starts with plenty of detail and then tails off. We read first of 'dark rocky Caverns, by the side of a Wood, illumin'd by the Moon; Birds of Omen promiscuously flying, Flashes of Lightning faintly striking'. There is a Witches' Chorus, and some stage flying, Harlequin himself being carried in aerially. Later, demons take him down to Hades, singing a song of triumph as they do so, and we hear no more of him. The final scene is in Pluto's Palace. Pluto and Proserpine descend in a Machine and there is a great deal of singing and no action worth mentioning. Presumably Theobald devised only the serious part of the entertainment while Rich worked out the comic relief. There must have been a great deal of vocal music at the end but none of it survives. Leveridge doubled Pluto and First Witch, and Mrs. Barbier was Proserpine.

The Rape of Proserpine, postponed because of the alleged non-arrival of performers from abroad, was eventually staged two years later, yet the only newcomer was Philip Rochetti, who as Jupiter sang only one of the fourteen songs. (He was a tenor, and in 1731 sang Acis for Handel.) Either the foreign performers never did turn up or they were imaginary. I must emphasize that, in spite of statements to the contrary in *Grove* and elsewhere, this pantomime is quite distinct from *Harlequin Sorcerer, or The Loves of Pluto and Proserpine*. Both continued to be performed for several decades. Also, as we have seen, they were quite different in design, *Harlequin Sorcerer* being akin to ballet and *The Rape of Proserpine* more of a masque. The latter is of unusual interest in that nearly all the music survives, and much of it is of good quality. An overture and fourteen songs by Galliard were published in full score, and in addition the Royal College of Music and London's Guildhall Library have MS scores containing the recitatives and final chorus as well. Also there is a copy of the Comic Tunes, apparently unique, in the Mitchell Library, Glasgow (they were published with some of those in *Perseus and Andromeda*), and an anonymous song, 'The Raree Show' which was sung in one of the grotesque scenes and is therefore not to be found in Galliard's score. It makes ribald reference to the contemporary Drury Lane pantomime, *Wagner and Abericock*.

The opening scene shows 'The Gardens of Ceres, with the Palace in the

Distance'. Ceres (Mrs. Barbier) has two agreeable songs, the first of them accompanied by 'octave flutes' for the usual birdsong effects. Mercury arrives to summon Ceres to Phrygia, where the crops are in desperate plight.

After this scene there is an uncommunicative stage direction:

scene: *A Farm-Yard; The Grotesque Part begins.*

Details are resumed for Scene ii, which is in Ceres's Palace. Proserpine (Mrs. Chambers) and her Nymphs are sad, but Ceres soon returns by air 'in her Chariot, drawn by Dragons'. Just when you think nothing will ever happen,

> *An Earthquake is felt, and part of the Building falls; and, through the Ruins of the fall'n Palace, Mount* Aetna *appears, and emits Flames. Beneath a Giant is seen to rise, but is dash'd to pieces by a Thunderbolt hurl'd from* Jupiter.

Few theatres today would venture on anything so difficult. Jupiter appears and sings a short admonitory recitative, after which the 'Grotesque Part' is resumed in a Country House. Again we are allowed no details. Scene iii represents a cornfield, round which Pluto (Leveridge) and his Infernals are roaming. He sings a too-mellifluous song and hides behind a tree when Proserpine appears. She too has a song. Pluto reveals himself, and there is a good deal of recitative punctuated by brief orchestral passages. One of these is for Proserpine's unfortunate maid who, because she expostulates over Pluto's wicked designs, is turned into a brook. Pluto forces Proserpine into his chariot, which sinks into the ground.

Ceres arrives just too late, and sings a rousing if somewhat conventional 'revenge' aria, 'Rise, ye Flames, and blaze around me'. This causes consternation among the local villagers; they even have a few bars of recitative in the middle of her aria. At the end of it, the Gods of the Woods help her

> *break the Trees. The People of Sicily enter and oppose them . . . Ceres snatches flaming branches from her train, and sets the Corn etc. on fire.*

After which irresponsible display of fury, 'The Actions of Harlequin are continued'. In the Elysian Fields, Proserpine sings a slow, sad and very Handelian song, accompanied by two 'German flutes':

Pluto grows magnanimous, as he can well afford to seeing that he is getting his own way. After a fourth and last 'grotesque part', Ceres, in 'A Solitude', has a lovely Invocation to Sleep:

Jupiter arrives to console her with one of Galliard's charmingly simple minuet songs, and the pantomime ends with the wedding of Pluto and Proserpine, and a short final chorus, given only in the MSS.

The only copy of the Comic Tunes that I have traced was not published until about 1763,[1] but fears that they might have been written for a late revival are largely dispelled by the first of them, 'The Birth of Harlequin', which was published (with a different bass) in *The Devil of a Duke*, a ballad opera of 1732. There is no stylistic reason to suppose that the others are any later. We have already had a hint of the way Harlequin was born of an egg in *The Dunciad*. A more detailed description of Lun's performance runs as follows:[2]

> From the first chipping of the egg, his receiving of motion, his feeling of the ground, his standing upright, to his quick harlequin trip round the empty shell, through the whole progression, every limn had its tongue, and every motion a voice.

The 'quick harlequin trip' may well have been the often-admired three hundred tiny steps in a rapid advance of only ten yards. The music for 'The Birth of Harlequin', though very simple, has great charm:

[1] BUCEM wrongly suggests 1740.
[2] *A History of the Scottish Stage* (1793) by John Jackson, quoted in John Doran's *His Majesty's Servants* ii, p. 58.

The snap rhythm in the second bar and elsewhere, so different from the snap rhythm of 'Scotch Songs', is a characteristic of innumerable Comic Tunes in the next fifty years, and was always associated with Harlequin himself. The time signature is invariably six-four, and the tempo mark, if any, is 'Slow'. Thus the first Comic Tune in *Perseus and Andromeda* at the start of this same volume is marked 'Slow', has this same rather gentle snap rhythm in six-four, and is called 'Harlequin Despairing'. A few pages later there is a similar tune called 'Harlequin and Columbine part'. It would seem that the rhythm was associated with some particular gesture by Harlequin that was a convention for sadness. Such tunes continue to be a feature of pantomime until quite late in the century.

There isn't a chord or an inner part in this volume from start to finish; right up to the middle of the century, all Comic Tunes consisted merely of a tune and a bass (and nearly all of them were in binary form). Usually we can assume that the violins played the top line and the other strings the bottom one, but occasionally a tune seems to cry out for inner harmonies, and then we must suppose that there is something missing. I have not found wind parts before 1750, but it is quite possible that occasional tunes were played as oboe or flute solos. One can never be sure that all the tunes have been printed; usually one can be sure that they haven't. Only ten tunes from *The Rape of Proserpine* are given, and these are not nearly enough for four 'grotesque' scenes. I would guess that the engraver was told to include all or nearly all those in *Perseus and Andromeda* and then to fill in up to sixteen pages with whatever he could find room for from *The Rape of Proserpine*.[1] All early Comic Tunes seem to run to sixteen or twenty-four pages.

The Comic Tunes in *Perseus and Andromeda*,[2] as well as being more numerous, seem to me of a higher quality, and the titles are more revealing. As with *The Rape of Proserpine*, the Description offers no information at all about the 'grotesque' scenes. The fourth piece is called 'The Polonese', and though the triple time and dotted rhythm suggest the dance of that name, it is more likely that the title refers to a character, for later on there is a piece called 'Polonese and his Daughter Reconcil'd'. After which they celebrate with a 'Polonese Dance'.

---

[1] Similarly in the 1752 volume described on p. 238, I take the *Harlequin Sorcerer* tunes to be more or less complete, and the *Dr. Faustus* ones to be a selection.

[2] Their early date is proved by the fact that three of them are used in the ballad opera *The Decoy* (1733); one of these also occurs in *The Lottery* (1732).

[D.C.]

This spirited music is followed by successive pieces in related keys entitled 'The Duel', 'Harlequin Stab'd', 'Harlequin Recovers', 'Harlequin Escapes', 'The Lyon'. As in all early Comic Tunes, not much attempt is made to suit the music to the action, but it is interesting that there should be any attempt at all. 'The Duel' is in a quick, vigorous dotted rhythm with the bass imitating the tune in alternate bars, and this does suggest the alternate thrusts of two swordsmen. In 'Harlequin Stab'd' there is nothing to show when the stabbing takes place, but the slow melancholy of the music exactly catches the miniature emotion of the event. As usual Harlequin's progress is from frying-pan to fire, and he recovers from his stabbing to be chased by a lion. The tempo mark is *Hurry*, and the rushing semiquavers remind one of the similarly intentioned Hurry Music of the silent films. Most sets of Comic Tunes have a piece called 'Hurry', and it can be assumed that if Harlequin is not being chased by Pantaloon, he is being chased by an animal. Earlier on, there is a naïve little piece called 'The Dog'; both this animal and the lion would have consisted of a skin with a man inside it. In the course of the century almost every animal one can think of was represented in a pantomime, and a large number of birds and insects too. Ostriches were strangely popular, as also were elephants. On one occasion Rich wanted to employ a real elephant, but he was warned that his stage would not support such a creature. As printed, the last Comic Tune in *Perseus and Andromeda* takes only a single system, but its folk-song style and three-bar rhythm give it a touch of the unusual. In *The Musical Miscellany* vi (1731) this same tune (but in G minor) is described as 'The Sailor's Ballad, Sung by Mr. Legar, in Perseus and Andromeda', and from this source I have added the first of the six verses:

How pleas - ant a Sai - lor's Life pas - ses, Who roams o'er the wa - ter - y main! No Treas - ure he ev - er a - mas - ses, But chear - ful - ly spends all his Gain.

Laguerre was Mercury, which suggests that he took part only in the masque scenes, but the Description, though it gives the words of a dozen or so songs, does not give the words of this one; perhaps it was sung in one of the two 'grotesque' scenes, about which we are given no information. The song can hardly be by Pepusch, as stated in B U C E M; almost certainly Galliard wrote all the music for the Lincoln's Inn Fields *Perseus and Andromeda*, and it is strange that no songs from the three masque scenes should survive. The Description includes a good deal of blank verse between the masque songs, and this was presumably sung in recitative. Improbably, Mrs. Barbier and Mrs. Chambers took the title roles.

Some twenty years later Tate Wilkinson saw a performance of this panto-mime and remembered a near-catastrophe that took place:

Perseus, like a flaming god, suspended by a wheel of large circumference, was whirled with great velocity around the theatric clouds, and struck with his mighty sword the frightful Gorgon, who midst raging billows was ready to seize the chained Andromeda, his wished-for prey: One fateful evening the wheel and pullies broke, and down fell Perseus on the harmless stuffed dragon, and instantly the curtain was dropped.[1]

[1] *Memoirs* ii, p. 118.

Let *The Dunciad* make the transition from the pantomimes of Lincoln's Inn
Fields to those of Drury Lane:

> Immortal Rich! how calm he sits at ease
> 'Midst snows of paper, and fierce hail of pease;
> And proud his Mistress' orders to perform,
> Rides in the whirlwind, and directs the storm.
> But lo! to dark encounter in mid air
> New wizards rise; here Booth and Cibber there!
> Booth in his cloudy tabernacle shrin'd,
> On grinning dragons Cibber mounts the wind:
> Dire is the conflict, dismal is the din,
> Here shouts all Drury, there all Lincoln's Inn;
> Contending Theatres our empire raise,
> Alike their labours and alike their praise.

3 DRURY LANE PANTOMIMES, 1723–1728

In the above passage Pope was presumably thinking of Colley Cibber, for he
linked him with the other Drury Lane manager, Barton Booth; in which case
his being placed on grinning dragons is figurative. But Pope may have been
referring more literally to one of Cibber's sons, for Drury Lane's Harlequin was
usually advertised as 'Cibber jun.'. Cibber had several children. The only one
known to have made a living in the theatre was Theophilus, later notable as
both actor and dramatist. It thus seems likely that he began on the boards as a
Harlequin. Strangely enough Thurmond never attempted the part, though he
continued to dance all the years he was devising pantomimes for Drury Lane.

As already stated, not much music survives from Thurmond's pantomimes.
What there is was largely the work of Henry Carey, a butterfly figure of charm
but little substance, who left his mark on the London theatres in surprisingly
varied ways. It has often been said that he was the illegitimate son of George
Savile, Marquis of Halifax, the Whig politician who was largely responsible for
ousting James II and putting William and Mary on the throne. Frederick T.
Wood, who edited Carey's poems in 1930, advanced the alternative theory that
he was the Marquis's grandson, that his father was the Henry Savile who died
young in 1688, and that he was born posthumously. Wood also suggested that
he took the name of Carey only when he came to London about 1711. On
4 April 1708 at Rothwell near Rotherham one Henry Savile married one
Sarah Dobson; it is known that Carey's wife's name was Sarah, his own writings
show a keen interest in Yorkshire and its dialect, and no other Henry Savile of a
marriageable age can be traced.

In London Henry Carey was taken up in Whig circles and became a member
of Button's, and an admirer of Addison. Unfortunately he seems to have had no

musical tuition until he was too old to profit from it in full. Hawkins called him 'a man of facetious temper, resembling Leveridge in many respects . . . a musician by profession, and one of the lower order of poets'. When Carey published his poems in 1729,[1] he excused their imperfections on the grounds that Poetry 'is my Amusement, not my Profession'. The trouble was that his music was even less professional than his verse.

Among Carey's poems is a panegyric to 'Mr. Olaus Westeinson Linnert, commonly called Westen, who gave him his first notion of Composition'. Nothing seems to be known of this musician except that he was working at Cannons about 1720. Pepusch made a list of the musicians employed there for the Duke of Chandos; opposite each name he wrote the instrument or instruments the man played, but opposite the name of Olaus Westeinson Linnert there is a blank. Carey also had a few lessons from Roseingrave and Geminiani, but he must have been grown-up at the time, for Geminiani did not come to England until 1714 (when Carey was about twenty-five), and Roseingrave, who was about the same age as Carey, spent most of his twenties in Italy. It may well be that Carey saw the necessity of lessons only after his two successes in 1715. In that year Drury Lane accepted his short play, *The Contrivances*, and a publisher accepted his delightful song, 'Sally in our Alley', of which he wrote both words and melody.

Of all the girls that are so smart, there's none like pret - ty Sal-ly.

By nineteenth-century standards the end of this phrase is 'incorrect', and William Chappell was so worried by the rhythm that he moved the notes for 'Sally' into the following bar. (In general the Victorians preferred to sing the words to a different and more orthodox tune.) Carey's melody is just the sort that a poet with no very strong rhythmic sense might make up, and it is unlikely that at the time he could either write it down or harmonize it. According to Hawkins he was 'just able to set a bass' by the 1720s, and though counterpoint and varied orchestration remained beyond his powers, he turned out a large number of songs with agreeable words and catchy tunes. His amateurishness may even have been an asset, for there is sometimes a freshness about his lyrics and music that professionalism might have destroyed. The tune of 'Sally' has this freshness, and it is not surprising that it found a place in *The Beggar's Opera* (Air 59) and in *The Devil to Pay*.

Carey's first important musical publication was his *Works* of 1726, a beautifully engraved and extremely rare volume that has attracted little attention. Besides single songs and some solo cantatas, it includes a recitative and two

[1] Some of these had appeared in 1713, rather more in 1720.

arias 'In Harlequin Dr. Faustus, the Words by Mr. Booth'. The music, confined to two staves, is surprisingly Italianate. The introduction to 'Beauteous Queen of Night' is played by flutes, and this is the only occasion I have found Carey writing for wind instruments. The Comic Tunes in Drury Lane's *Dr. Faustus* may also have been by Carey, but they do not seem to have been published. One of them may be 'Dr. Fausters Tumbler', which got into Vol. 3 of *The Dancing Master* (*c.* 1727). Another is quite certainly 'Dicky's Walk in Dr. Faustus' for which Gay wrote words in his ballad opera *Achilles*. Henry Norris a diminutive and elderly comedian, was popularly known as 'Jubilee Dicky' from his performance of this character in Farquhar's *The Constant Couple*, and in Drury Lane's *Dr. Faustus* he played the usurer. Here is the tune that accompanied his 'walk':

Comic Tunes must often have been written very quickly, and perhaps to save time this one was filched from a minor-key tune in *The Dancing Master*, Vol. 3, where it is ascribed to Weaver's *Mars and Venus*. In its turn it was borrowed for the first tune in the first Medley Overture (see page 161), a tribute to its wide popularity. By the middle of the century the borrowing and lending of Comic Tunes between one pantomime and another was a commonplace, but it seems to have been unusual in the 1720s.

We know more about the 'grotesque' action in *Harlequin Dr. Faustus* than in any other pantomime of the period. The Description is unusually detailed, and there are contemporary accounts as well. To us it may all seem rather foolish, as indeed it did to intellectuals of the time. It probably appealed to the same kind of people as horror films do today, and for much the same reasons. Thurmond (or Booth?) began conventionally with Faustus in his study signing in his own blood a contract presented to him by a subsidiary devil. Then comes thunder and lightning; '*Mephistophelus* flies down upon a Dragon, vomiting Fire: Faustus seems surpriz'd'. Given a magic wand, Faustus conjures into his study the wives of two 'Countrymen', and for their entertainment he makes 'a supper ready dress'd' rise from nowhere. The Countrymen arrive and 'catch their wives making merry with the Doctor . . . immediately, upon both the Countrymen's Foreheads, sprout out a pair of large Horns'. When Faustus goes, he beckons to the table, which runs out after him. A usurer (Jubilee Dicky) lends Faustus money in return for Faustus's right leg, which he cuts off. When he offers Faustus a selection of false legs, Faustus chooses a woman's, which immediately fixes itself onto his stump. At about this point in the Description he begins to be referred to as Harlequin, and he is joined by Scaramouche, Punch and Pierrot. Among other adventures, he escapes an enemy by changing himself into a bear, escapes justice by flying up through the ceiling, escapes a mob by coming down a chimney. So far the music has consisted of nothing but Comic Tunes, but in Faustus's study at 1.0 a.m. (why not midnight?) there are songs for Time and Death. Faustus pays the conventional price for his misdemeanours, four devils attacking him and each flying out with one of his limbs.

In the final scene buffoonery gave way to music and spectacle. An onlooker described it as 'the most magnificent that ever appeared on the English stage' and it showed 'a Poetical Heaven with Gods and Godesses rang'd in order' and celebrating Faustus's 'Enchanted Death'. There are no song words in Thurmond's Description, no doubt because they were written by Barton Booth (see above). There was probably dancing as well as singing, for Thurmond himself took the part of Mars and there is no evidence that he had a voice. It was of course for this final scene that Carey wrote the recitative and two songs that he published in his *Works*.

Thurmond's next pantomime, *Harlequin Sheppard*, offered a modern hero, the notorious house-breaker Jack Sheppard, who had that very year escaped from Newgate on no less than two occasions. He was much idolized for these exploits, but the Harlequin version of him was less admired and some performances were hissed.

We may guess that Carey wrote the music for *Harlequin Sheppard* (though none survives), and we know that he wrote songs for Thurmond's next pantomime, *Apollo and Daphne*. There was a scene which showed 'a Stag running across follow'd by a Pack of Hounds', after which the 'hunters' carried in a dead deer and sang 'Away, away, we've crown'd the Day'. The music was published separately as Carey's, and it can also be found in *The Musical Miscellany* ii, and in Bickham's *Musical Entertainer* i. The one Comic Scene in this pantomime is not particularized. Much of it was in the nature of a ballet. But the first scene of all, unusually, was fully operatic, with Night and Aurora singing a succession of recitatives and arias; the words survive in the Description but the music is lost. It was probably by Richard Jones, leader of the Drury Lane orchestra. In August 1723 Drury Lane had put on a masque on the Apollo and Daphne story with music by 'Mr. Jones', and it seems likely that this was drawn on for the first scene in the pantomime.

Jones certainly wrote most or all of the music for Thurmond's next pantomime, *The Miser, or Wagner and Abericock*. This was a sequel to *Dr. Faustus*, Wagner being described as 'Faustus heir, in Character of Harlequin', and Abericock as a 'Spirit left him by Faustus'. In the first volume of *The Ladys Banquet*, an anthology of harpsichord pieces, there is a 'Symphony or Overture in Wagner and Abericock', and the index ascribes it to 'Mr. Jones'. It consists unconventionally of a short spirited Handelian Allegro leading into seven bars in three-four time; this section ends in the dominant and is followed by a short Adagio in the tonic. Some or all of the pieces on the next nine pages are probably Comic Tunes from the same pantomime. The volume consists mainly of dance movements; it is credible that Jones's overture might have been thrown in with his dances, most improbable that it would have been chosen on its own. Also one of the pieces is called 'Statue Dance', and this is quite certainly a Comic Tune; the coming-alive of statues was a common pantomime trick.

Jones published some interesting violin sonatas and harpsichord pieces in the 1730s, and his last activity seems to have been to write the music for *Hymen's Triumph* (LIF 1.2.37), a pantomime put on by Giffard's company after its transfer from Goodman's Field's.[1] Neither the description nor the music survives.

For their next pantomime, *Perseus and Andromeda*, Drury Lane persuaded Pepusch to write the music, his fame the greater for the recent success of *The Beggar's Opera* at Lincoln's Inn Fields. The managers pushed Thurmond into the unflattering part of Medusa, and re-engaged Weaver to revise what he had created, without notable success, in 1717. In fact Weaver revised only the 'grotesque' scenes, leaving the serious ones to 'Mons. Roger'; however, Roger took the part of Pierrot in Weaver's half of the entertainment. Most of the mythological scenes were danced rather than sung, but Pepusch composed (and published) a number of songs for subsidiary characters. One of these was Minerva, a part sung by Miss Rafter at the age of seventeen; it was one of her first parts, and she later was famous as Kitty Clive. John Devoto painted the scenery for *Perseus and Andromeda*, and there were three 'Serious' Interludes and two 'Comic'. The two sides of the entertainment were unrelated.

An alternative title for the Drury Lane *Perseus* was *The Flying Lovers*, but though Lally and Mrs. Booth played and sang the title roles, it was not necessarily they who were suspended in mid-air at the well-known climax of the story. In October 1737 Covent Garden was staging *The Necromancer, or Harlequin Dr. Faustus* (the production originally put on at Lincoln's Inn Fields), and when Harlequin, the Miller, the Miller's Wife, and his Man were all suspended high above the stage in a 'machine' the wires broke. As a result two of them died. But it turned out that those in the machine were stand-ins, and not Rich, Nivelon, Mrs. Moreau, and Salway, the portrayers of the roles. At forty-five Rich may well have felt disinclined to attempt such stunts, but it may be that there was always a substitution, concealed so far as possible from the audience. (On the occasion of the crash, Thomas Gray was in the audience, and wrote about it to Horace Walpole.) These machines were often made to look like dragons or clouds, and they were used for both exits and entrances. Great use was also made of trap-doors for disappearance tricks, and here too there must have been an element of danger, with stunt-men perhaps on call for the most difficult moments.

[1] See p. 144.

It was realized from the first that stunts and magical effects would be the chief attraction of pantomime. On 6 April 1723 *The Weekly Journal or Saturday Post* devoted the whole of its front-page story to a puff of Rich's first lasting success, *Jupiter and Europa*:

> The Transformation of *Jupiter* into a Bull, is done in Sight of the Audience; the Contrivance and Deception is so excellent that we cannot account for it.

A great deal of money was spent on trick scenery that could be changed in an instant. Scene-changing was always much quicker in the eighteenth century than at any time since, and the way this was done will be described later.[1] Carefully rehearsed stage hands could give the illusion of a palace being changed into a prison at a single wave of Harlequin's wand.

The most ingenious pantomime tricks depended on clockwork, and Rich employed a well-known watch-maker and his son, Samuel and John Hoole, to make what was required. By no means all pantomime animals had men inside them. *The Scots Magazine* for March 1740 carries a good description of the serpent then attracting Londoners to Covent Garden's *Orpheus and Euridice*. It was

> wholly a piece of machinery, that enters, performs its exercise of head, body, and tail in a most surprising manner, and makes behind the curtain with a velocity scarcely credible. It is about a foot and a half in circumference at the thickest part, and far exceeds the former custom of stuffing a bag into such a likeness. It is believed to have cost more than £200 pounds, and when the multitude of wings, springs etc., whereof it consists are considered, the charge will not appear extravagant.

This particular serpent was said to be found very frightening by the ladies, which no doubt made them the more ready to see it.

The extra expense involved in the construction of such animals, as also the numerous sets and props, gave the managers an excuse for charging higher prices for pantomimes than for other entertainments, and this, coupled with the crowded houses, made them money-spinners on an unprecedented scale. According to Colley Cibber,[2] Drury Lane 'generally made use of these Pantomimes, but as Crutches to our weekest Plays: Nor were we so lost to all Sense of what was valuable, as to dishonour our best Authors, in such bad Company'. In other words Drury Lane tried to avoid playing pantomime as an afterpiece when a Shakespeare play was the mainpiece, and they would have done without

---

[1] See p. 254. The eighteenth-century theatre at Drottningsholm near Stockholm is one of the few still equipped for such scene-changing. There is a surprising number of engravings of eighteenth-century English theatre personages in the foyers.

[2] *Apology*, ch. 15.

pantomime altogether if they could have afforded to. Cibber complained that the trouble arose from having two theatres in rivalry; with only one theatre, standards would have been higher. (Similar arguments greeted the arrival of commercial television in Britain.) Rich never bothered his head over the ethics of playing pantomime. Where was the harm in putting on shows for which he had more flair than his rival and which people flocked to see? In any case he was also prepared to welcome Handel operas, which is more than Drury Lane ever did. For several decades his theatre was in much better financial shape than Drury Lane, and it must have been doubly galling for the latter when they found Rich initially reaping a far more profitable harvest from the next theatrical innovation.

3
Ballad Opera
1728–1736

1 'THE BEGGAR'S OPERA'

The Beggar's Opera was first performed at Lincoln's Inn Fields on 29 January 1728, and it was the greatest theatrical success of the century. John Gay originally offered it to Drury Lane, but Cibber turned it down; Gay's previous plays had not been very profitable, and Cibber probably felt suspicious of the bizarre qualities of the new one.

Gay was born in Barnstaple in the same year as Bach and Handel. He was a tubby, low-temperatured, easy-going man with a surprisingly venomous pen and a great capacity for making people like him provided that they were not Whigs. Thus he had few dealings with Addison and his followers, but enjoyed a deep and lifelong friendship with Pope and Swift. His poems are little read today. They tend to have barbed meanings hidden under pastoral trappings. But in 1716 he broke new ground with *Trivia, or The Art of Walking the Streets of London*. This is a poem of some thirteen hundred lines divided into three books, and much of it is straight reporting of a Defoe-like realism. Gay gives us vignettes of the muddy streets, the crossing-sweepers and shoe-shine boys, football in the snow outside Covent Garden's church, the frozen Thames with booths and carts on it. Dr. Johnson complained with some reason of the unnecessary dragging-in of classical deities, but most of the poem is readable and vivid. Only in Book iii, 'Of walking the Streets by Night', does Gay touch on the themes of his *Beggar's Opera*. He ignores prisons, but there is plenty about pickpockets, as also about more frightening thugs.

> Where Lincoln's Inn's wide space is rail'd around,
> Cross not with vent'rous steps; there oft is found
> The lurking Thief, who while the day-light shone,
> Made the walls eccho with his begging tone;
> That Crutch which late compassion mov'd, shall wound
> Thy bleeding Head, and fell thee to the Ground.

The prostitutes 'Of Drury's many Courts and dark abode' are treated with realism and moral undertones not apparent in *The Beggar's Opera*:

> 'Tis she who nightly strowls with saunt'ring pace,
> No stubborn Stays her yielding Shape embrace;
> Beneath the Lamp her tawdry ribbons glare,
> The new-scower'd manteau, and the slattern air;
> . . . With flatt'ring sounds she sooths the cred'lous ear,
> My noble Captain! Charmer! Love! My dear!

Gay already saw literary possibilities in London's riff-raff.

Perhaps it was after reading *Trivia* in Dublin that Swift wrote to Pope suggesting a set of Quaker Pastorals for 'our friend Gay', and he went on:

> I believe, further, the Pastoral Ridicule is not exhausted; and that a Porter, a Footman, or Chairman's Pastoral might do well. Or what think you of a Newgate Pastoral, among the Whores and Thieves there?

The first eight words of the last sentence have been endlessly quoted as the supposed source of Gay's inspiration, but, if they influenced him at all, they did not do so for nearly twelve years, and it should be remembered that *The Beggar's Opera* is in no sense a Pastoral. On the other hand Swift's suggestion of a Quaker Pastoral drew an almost immediate response. Gay also wrote at about this time his Pastoral Masque, *Acis and Galatea*, which provided Handel with the best dramatic libretto he ever set.

In an age when Literature and Politics were expected to walk together, Gay went for some years in expectation of being given an easy government position. Sinecures often followed the publication of poems, and Gay had excellent friends; for instance Mrs. Howard, the mistress of the future George II. But, as he himself wrote in a notable sentence, 'They wonder at each other for not providing for me, and I wonder at them all'. A poet who dabbles in political satire can hardly expect preferment unless the right party be in power, and for Gay it seldom was. The resentment he came to feel towards those in high places, especially Walpole, was increasingly reflected in what he wrote, and his acerbity was the greater when he lost all he had made from the sale of his poems in the South Sea Bubble. He never had any business sense, and until he wrote *The Beggar's Opera* he was nearly always in want. In 1727 he published his most successful poems, the fifty *Fables*, ostensibly written for one of the young princes. The last of them, 'The Hare and Many Friends', has unusual strength and bitterness. Gay himself is the Hare, worn out from being hunted and imploring the other fleeing animals for assistance. They all have excellent reasons for not giving him any. It was probably this poem that roused Mrs. Howard to plead his cause, and as a result Gay was offered the post of Gentleman Usher to the two-year-old Princess Louise. Feeling that so humble a position was no sort of reward for his labours, Gay turned the offer down, and it was at this point, in a mood of anger and humiliation, that he started to write *The Beggar's Opera*.

In 1724 two notable rogues had been brought to book and hanged at Tyburn. One, Jack Sheppard, we have already met. The other was a highwayman named Joseph Blake, but more usually known as 'Blueskin'. Both men were arrested as a result of information laid by the notorious Jonathan Wild. In court Blueskin was so enraged by what Wild said of him that he leapt out of the dock and assaulted Wild with a knife, without doing him any great harm. The incident was much talked about, and the next year Gay published a 'new ballad' on the subject called 'Newgate's Garland, to be sung to the tune of Cutpurse'. It can be found with the tune (better known as 'Packington's Pound') in Vol. V of *The Musical Miscellany*. Gay had a reason for choosing this particular tune. *Pills*, iv, p. 20, reveals that 'Cutpurse' was Nightingale's song from Ben Jonson's *Bartholomew Fair*, every verse ending with the refrain:

> Youth, Youth, thou had'st better been starv'd at Nurse,
> Than for to be hang'd for cutting a Purse.

The beginning of Jonson's last verse is strikingly similar in mood to some of the lyrics Gay was to write for *The Beggar's Opera*:

> But oh you vile Nation of Cut-Purses all,
>   Relent and Repent, and amend, and be sound,
> And know that you ought not by honest Men's Fall,
>   To advance your own Fortunes, to die above Ground,
>   And tho' you go Gay,
>   In Silks as you may,
> It is not the High-way to *Heaven* (they say) . . .

Thus Gay wrote his 'Newgate Garland' to the tune of 'Cutpurse' because he could count on people associating it with Jonson's words and appreciating its relevance. When he came to write the lyrics for *The Beggar's Opera* he several times found tunes whose original words were on much the same subject as his own.

'Newgate's Garland' assumes that Blueskin's attack on Wild was successful,[1] and that the informer's death would make things easier for the 'fraternity'.

> Ye Gallants of *Newgate* whose Fingers are nice,
> In diving in Pockets, or cogging of Dice;
> Ye Sharpers so rich, who can buy off the Noose,
> Ye honester poor Rogues, who die in your Shoes,
>   Attend, and draw near,
>   Good News ye shall hear,

---

[1] Wild had in fact been hanged by the time the poem appeared.

How *Jonathan's* Throat was cut from Ear to Ear;
How *Blueskin's* sharp Penknife hath set you at Ease,
And ev'ry Man round me may Rob, if he please.

Later verses take a swipe at the 'Courtiers of highest Renown, Who steal the King's Gold, and leave him but a Crown', and at Customs men, and even at Church-Wardens, who 'as yet only venture to steal from the Altar'. All of them are 'set at Ease' by Jonathan's death, and the same two lines end every verse. (Two final verses, less felicitous, were added by Swift).

There can be no doubt that Peachum in *The Beggar's Opera* was a portrait of Jonathan Wild, but Gay was not as consistently satiric as his critics have made out. It is often said that he had two targets, Walpole and Italian Opera, and this view was first stated by Swift in a puff he wrote for a Dublin paper just before the first performance there:

> The author takes the occasion of comparing the common robbers of the public and their several stratagems for betraying, undermining and hanging each other, to the several arts of the politicians in time of trouble. This comedy likewise exposes, with great justice, that taste for Italian music among us, which is wholly unsuitable to a Northern climate and the genius of the people, whereby we are overrun with Italian effeminacy and Italian manners.

But the satire is haphazard rather than all-pervading. No character consistently represents Walpole or anyone in the world of Italian Opera. Knowing that Gay disliked him, Walpole attended the first night, curious as to what might be said of him, and he had the sense to smile at Lockit's song (Air 30) warning everyone against offending those at Court:

> When you censure the Age,
> Be cautious and sage,
> Lest the Courtiers offended should be:
> If you mention Vice or Bribe,
> 'Tis so pat to all the Tribe;
> Each cries that was levell'd at me.

At these words every eye in the theatre was turned towards Walpole's box, for bribery was a sore subject with the government. Furthermore the part of Lockit was taken by Hall, an actor with a stomach as vast as Walpole's own.

Thus the Prime Minister of Newgate sometimes represents the Prime Minister of Great Britain. But elsewhere it is Macheath and his gang who reflect the more dubious activities of Walpole and his government, and certainly Polly and Lucy, Macheath's two 'wives', were seen as an allusion to Walpole's wife and Molly Skerrit, his mistress. But in their quarrelling duet (Air 38) Polly and Lucy represented Faustina and Cuzzoni, who had recently quarrelled on stage in a Bononcini opera, though the plot would surely have insisted on such a squabble had these singers never existed. In short we must guard against reading too much into the words. First and formost Gay was writing a play about the riff-raff of London. Though he worked in haphazard digs at Walpole as opportunity offered, he was equally concerned with chastising the Court as a whole for not giving him preferment.[1] When Macheath remarks that, rather than tear Polly from him, 'you might sooner tear a Pension from the Hands of a Courtier', he is Gay rather than Walpole. As also when he sings

> The Modes of the Court so common have grown
> That a true friend can hardly be met.

At the end of the scene in 'the condemn'd Hold' he is virtually Everyman, singing of the unfairness of the world (to a version of 'Greensleeves') with all the bitterness of a modern 'folk singer':

> Since Laws were made for ev'ry degree,
> To curb Vice in others as well as in me,
> I wonder we ha'n' better company
> 　Upon Tyburn Tree!
> But Gold from Law can take out the sting;
> And if rich men like us were to swing,
> 'Twould thin the Land, such numbers to string
> 　Upon Tyburn Tree![2]

Gay's title seems irrelevant. As may be remembered, it arises from the Introduction, in which the Beggar supposed to have written the opera talks about it to one of the actors. That other play of low life in London, *Bartholomew Fair*, has a similar prologue for the prompter, house manager, and copyist, and, as has already been implied, Gay was influenced by *Bartholomew Far*. But Jonson did not allow his preliminary matter to beget his title. Perhaps the beggar is dragged in because Gay is cadging again, he himself being the beggar. And perhaps the curious claim that the piece was written for the marriage of two ballad singers is intended to account for the highly unusual prevalance of ballads among the sixty-nine airs.

We have already seen that D'Urfey's *Wonders in the Sun* included a few popular song tunes, as also did one or two plays of the previous century. But the vast number in *The Beggar's Opera* must have seemed its most original feature. People associated opera with a succession of long arias whose music was hard to grasp and whose words were incomprehensible, and it was piquant, perhaps even

---

[1] For a more bitter and consistent attack on Walpole, see another ballad opera *The Patron, or The Statesman's Opera* (1729) by Thomas Odell, who, a few months later, was the first manager of Goodman's Fields. It had only one performance.

[2] This lyric may be by Pope; see Henry Angelo's *Reminiscences*, i, pp. 25–6.

funny, to have an opera whose tunes were short and familiar, and whose words made good sense. The plot too was as far removed as might be imagined from those used by Handel, Bononcini, and Ariosti. Instead of cardboard heroes of antiquity, Gay offered very real modern Londoners; instead of noble sentiments, every crime in the calendar. In fact he satirized Italian opera in the main by upending both its musical style and its moral flavour.

There are also some incidental digs. In the Introduction the Beggar remarks that he has provided the two ladies with parts of equal weight, and it was well known that Faustina and Cuzzoni had recently insisted on just this. He also mentions with pride that he has 'introduc'd the Similies that are in all your celebrated Operas; The Swallow, The Moth, The Ship, The Bee, The Flower', and these can in fact be found in Airs 34, 4, 10, 15, and 6 respectively. The Simile Aria was a great feature of Italian opera at this period, and the airs in which Polly compares herself to a ship and a swallow are not so much skits as copies of the real thing. But Air 6 is based on a simile that would not have appealed to Handel's librettists. The comparison is too real and too clever, the pay-off at the end too squalid.

> POLLY. Virgins are like the fair Flow'r in its lustre,
>   Which in the Garden enamels the Ground;
> Near it the Bees in play flutter and cluster,
>   And gaudy Butterflies frolic around.
> But, when once pluck'd, 'tis no longer alluring,
>   To Covent Garden 'tis sent (as yet sweet),
> There fades, and shrinks, and grows past all enduring,
>   Rots, stinks, and dies, and is trod under feet.

Somehow the effect of these words is enhanced by their being sung to one of Purcell's most sublimely beautiful song-tunes.

Gay's final slap at Italian Opera comes at the end, when realism is suddenly abandoned, and the actors step outside their roles in order to contrive a wholly incredible happy ending. The effect is hard to bring off today, for few people know enough about what is being satirized. But in 1728 Macheath's absurd reprieve, totally unprepared for by anything said or done earlier, must have seemed a brilliant stroke to an audience familiar with the endings of Handel and Bononcini operas, in which men consistently evil for two acts and three-quarters suddenly reformed their whole mode of life and found love for a more convenient woman so that everyone should live happily ever after. As the Beggar puts it, 'In this kind of drama, 'tis no matter how absurdly things are brought about', and the Player soon realizes that 'All this we must do, to comply with the taste of the town.'[1]

---

[1] There is an equally absurd last-second reprieve for a man about to be hanged in Gay's *The What d'ye call it* (1715).

Of the sixty-nine airs in *The Beggar's Opera*, forty can be found in *Pills*. Gay probably learned many of them in the course of rowdy coffee-house sing-songs, but he had the advantage of playing the recorder, and some slight knowledge of notation must have helped him fit his words to the tunes. Among the *Pills* borrowings there are songs by Purcell, Eccles, Clarke, Barrett, and Ramondon, but as many as thirty are 'anon', and there are eighteen anonymous songs from sources other than *Pills*, making fifty-eight in all. Gay was inevitably influenced by the recently-developed vogue for the Scotch Song. In 1724 Allan Ramsay, the Edinburgh poet and father of the artist of the same name, began publishing his collection of Scottish song lyrics, *The Tea-Table Miscellany*, the music being issued separately. Two years later, William Thomson, an Edinburgh singer, drew largely on Ramsay for his London publication, *Orpheus Caledonius*. This contained fifty Scotch Songs with basses presumably by Thomson himself, and he gained great popularity by singing them at London concerts and parties. In 1733 he issued a two-volume edition containing a hundred songs. Airs 17, 18, 40, 49, and 52 in *The Beggar's Opera* can be found in Ramsay's book or Thomson's or both. Gay also worked in two song-tunes written several years earlier for words of his own. His famous 'Black-eyed Susan' had been set by Carey, Hayden, Leveridge, and the Italian Sandoni, Cuzzoni's husband; surprisingly it was the latter's tune that Gay chose for Air 34. When his farce *The What d'ye call it* was revived in 1725, he added the lyric ''Twas when the Sea was roaring', and it seems almost certain that Handel composed the setting. The tune turns up in *The Beggar's Opera* as Air 28.

As has been mentioned, Gay sometimes chose tunes whose original words were relevant to his purpose, the presumption being that the audience would be aware of this relevance. Thus for Lockit's song about the infamies of 'gamesters' (Air 43) he chose 'Packington's Pound', because in his own 'Newgate's Garland' this had been associated with words about the 'cogging of dice', that is, the fraudulent control of the way they fell. For the 'Hanging Trio' (Air 68) he chose a strangely moving song by Lewis Ramondon called 'A Hymn upon the Execution of Two Criminals' (*Pills* vi. p. 327); I give the beginning of it with both the original words and Gay's:

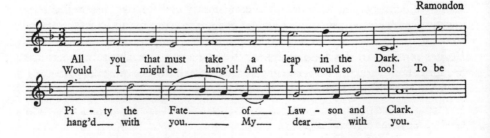

There is some late and rather suspect evidence that Gay originally intended the airs to be sung unaccompanied. Rich, so the story goes, suggested accompaniments 'at the second last rehearsal', but this was resisted until, at the last rehearsal of all, Gay's patroness, the Duchess of Queensberry, converted everyone to Rich's view. The story assumes that there was then time for Pepusch to arrange the airs, for the parts to be copied, and for the results to be rehearsed; this seems to me improbable. It must be admitted that the basses to the airs look as though they might have been composed in a hurry, but Pepusch took plenty of trouble over the overture, which has one touch of remarkable originality. For the fugue subject in the main *allegro* section, he used a disguised version of Air 47 (from *The Dancing Master*, where it is called 'The Happy Clown').[1] It only becomes clear what he is up to when he bases the episodes between the fugal entries on the second half of the tune. The result is a delightful and provocative piece that must have had the audience on its toes from the start.

Soon after the first night, *The Beggar's Opera* was published with the song tunes at the end as a supplement. In the spring a second edition appeared with the addition of the overture in score on four staves, with cues for oboes. About this time the song tunes were published in an arrangement for solo flute. A third edition of the libretto, together with that of *Polly*, followed at the end of the year, and this gave the overture on six staves, two of them for the oboes, and added basses to all the songs. As we shall see later, it was virtually a full score.

No one expected *The Beggar's Opera* to succeed. James Quin turned down the part of Macheath, which had to be given to Thomas Walker who was not then much esteemed as either actor or singer. Polly was played by an unknown actress, Lavinia Fenton, who, the cantankerous whispered, had been born and bred in 'The Mint', and was thus type-cast. This did not stop London ringing with her praises as *The Beggar's Opera* achieved in what was left of the season the unprecedented number of sixty-two performances.[2] The Duke of Bolton seemed so infatuated with the opera that he attended nearly every performance, sitting with the privileged on the side of the stage—where he can be seen in Hogarth's famous picture. But when the season ended, it turned out that it was not the opera that infatuated him so much as Miss Fenton. He made her his Duchess. Her defection from the company cut down the number of performances in the following season, for it took Rich some time to find a suitable replacement. For his benefit in March Quinn swallowed his pride and played Macheath.

From the first it was thought that *The Beggar's Opera* might have a bad effect on public morals, and Dr. Herring, who later became Archbishop of Canterbury, attacked it from the pulpit for making a hero of a highwayman and

[1] In his *Music in the Baroque Era* Manfred Bukofzer suggests that Pepusch chose this air because its alternative title was 'Walpole'.

[2] Not sixty-three, as sometimes stated.

leaving him unpunished at the end. Many years later Dr. Johnson showed more sense when pronouncing it

> not likely to do good; nor . . . to be productive of much evil. High-waymen and housebreakers seldom frequent the playhouse, or mingle with any elegant diversion; nor is it possible for anyone to imagine that he may rob with safety, because he sees Macheath reprieved upon the stage.

Yet every night, at the moment of the reprieve, the gallery cheered hysterically. It looked as though the Common People enjoyed seeing Wrong triumph over Right, and with crime on the increase it was easy enough to be disturbed by the implications.

But some of the parodies of *The Beggar's Opera* were much more worthy of censure than the original. On 1 January 1729 Rich put on what he called his Lilliputian version, in imitation of similar performances in Dublin produced by Madame Violante.[1] The entire cast consisted of children. Macheath was played by a girl, Filch by Henry Woodward who was later famous as a straight actor and as Drury Lane's Harlequin. The prostitute scenes can hardly have been in the best of taste. On 11 March 1730 the Little Theatre put on one performance of *The Metamorphosis of The Beggar's Opera*, in which all the male parts were played by women and all the female by men. Again it is the prostitute scenes that exercise the imagination. No comment seems to have been aroused, though there was plenty in 1780 when George Colman repeated the experiment in the same theatre. In 1734 The Little Theatre tried *The Beggar's Opera* as a tragedy, with 'All the Characters play'd in Roman Dresses'. Macheath was taken by Mrs. Charke, one of Colley Cibber's daughters, but there were no other travesty roles. The following year Covent Garden turned it into a 'Serio-Comi-Farcical-Elysian Ballad Opera' of two acts called *Macheath in the Shades*. Macheath, Polly, and some of the tarts are in Hades where they meet as improbable a collection of notables as one could devise: Alexander the Great, Cleopatra, Helen of Troy, Horace, Cardinal Wolsey, and Ben Jonson. It had one performance, which no doubt was as many as it deserved. Much more successful was *The Beggar's Pantomime, or The Contending Columbines* (LIF 7.12.36) 'intermix'd with Ballad Songs in the Characters of Polly and Lucy'. Woodward played Harlequin Macheath, and billed himself as 'Lun jun.'.

These parodies reflect an ennui behind the curtain that was not at all apparent in front of it. Indeed audiences became increasingly fascinated by the original as a result of a change of emphasis in Drury Lane performances. As Gay's Introduction to *Polly* makes clear, *The Beggar's Opera* had originally

---

[1] She was a French (or Italian) tight-rope artiste 'celebrated for Strength and Agility', says Chetwood, but for his taste too apt to show her 'masculinely indelicate Legs'. The Mayor of Dublin closed her theatre because she had no licence. Her Macheath was Peg Woffington, aged ten.

been staged without a single notable singer in the cast. When Drury Lane first put it on, which was in July 1732, Polly was played by Miss Raftor, soon to become Mrs. Clive. Burney says her voice was intolerable in serious songs, but in ballad operas even he found her singing enchanting. Without any doubt she set new vocal standards. But higher standards still were to come. In the autumn of 1736 Mrs. Clive found, to her indignation, that Polly was to be played by Mrs. Cibber. The row that followed was extremely scratchy, but the results were far-reaching. Mrs. Cibber was one of the best English sopranos in the country, and it was for this reason that the managers preferred her to Mrs. Clive.[1] In the same production England's first great tenor, John Beard, sang Macheath, and for the rest of the century all our best tenors were heard in the part. Some of them were very indifferent actors, but this seems to have worried no one. Whether we today approve or not, for most of its long life *The Beggar's Opera* has been popular not because of the dialogue and the acting but because of the songs and the singing.

2 LATER BALLAD OPERAS

Fortunately for Drury Lane, they too had a success while *The Beggar's Opera* was running non-stop at Lincoln's Inn Fields. When Vanbrugh died, he left a half-finished comedy which Colley Cibber completed and named *The Provok'd Husband*. It ran for twenty-eight nights without interruption, and stayed in the repertoire for the rest of the century. The success of these two pieces led to a boom in the theatre world. With the money he made from his pantomimes and *The Beggar's Opera*, Rich planned and built a new theatre in Covent Garden; the architect was Edward Shepherd. At the other end of London in October 1729 Thomas Odell opened a makeshift theatre in Goodman's Fields. Two years later it was taken over by one of his actors, Henry Giffard, who was also an astute and efficient business man. Giffard started a subscription to build a proper theatre on the same site, and countered accusations by the local clergy that it would lower morals by averring that it would have an educational effect on all the sailors in the neighbourhood. The 'New Theatre' in Goodman's Fields was also designed by Edward Shepherd, and it was open from October 1732 for four seasons.[2] Its internal arrangements are known in unique detail. It contained what is thought to have been the first fan-shaped auditorium, and, as in so many European theatres of the century, the stage was twice as deep as it was broad—

---

[1] Later, when her acting distracted some of her attention from her singing, Mrs. Cibber became what we would call a mezzo-soprano.

[2] And briefly in 1740–2 when Garrick first played in London. Later it became a chapel and then a warehouse. It stood just south of today's Aldgate Station. For plans of it see *The London Stage*, Part 3, Vol. 1. Another theatre in Goodman's Fields, the 'New Wells', was run by William Hallam from 1739 to 1751. See T.N., July 1946, article by Sybil Rosenfeld.

47 feet by 20 feet. The house held only 700 and encouraged an intimate style of acting. Two months after the opening of Goodman's Fields, Covent Garden opened too (7.12.32), but for the time being Rich continued to own Lincoln's Inn Fields, which he sometimes hired out for special performances, most of them musical. With the Little Theatre unusually active, Londoners had more theatres to choose from than at any other time in the century. The patent theatres frequently complained that their monopoly was being infringed, and it was largely in an attempt to snuff out the rival theatres that the Licensing Act of 1737 was introduced.

The boom in ballad operas caused the boom in theatres, and was equally short-lived. In Appendix D[1] I have listed the forty-one I have found that were published with their airs during the first eight seasons; at least as many more were published without music. Thereafter new ballad operas, in the true sense of the term, were a rarity. It will be noticed that in the first half of the boom most ballad operas were full-length, while in the latter half most were after-pieces. Apart from *The Beggar's Opera*, not a single full-length example was a lasting success, though several which failed in full-length form succeeded as afterpieces. Eight short ballad operas hung on into the second half of the century, and most of these still had at least a provincial popularity after 1800. Rich showed surprisingly little interest in the form, and, making few attempts, had only two successes: *The Beggar's Opera* and *Flora*. In the 1730s he con-tinued to rely mainly on his pantomimes. Drury Lane on the other hand made repeated attempts to find profitable new ballad operas; of the last twenty in my appendix, thirteen were staged at Drury Lane, and the proportion would not be much different if ballad operas published without tunes were taken into con-sideration. Goodman's Fields was not at first able to find enough singers, but in 1732 they put on more ballad operas than any theatre, filching most of them from their rivals; at no time were they equipped for pantomimes on any scale.

One might expect that the most widely imitated aspects of *The Beggar's Opera* would be the use of popular tunes and the scenes of low life in London. In fact very few ballad operas were set in London, apart from the earliest.[2] *The Cobler's Opera* takes place in Billingsgate Fish Market, *The Quaker's Opera* in and around Newgate. The latter was much the closest imitation of *The Beggar's Opera* that I have found, with Jack Sheppard as its hero and a cast largely of robbers and prostitutes. As *Penelope* takes place in a London pub, all the 1728 ballad operas seem to be linked by a common theme. Thereafter quite different subjects prevailed. For the first Drury Lane ballad opera, *Love in a Riddle*, Colley Cibber went back to Arcadia, and wrote all the dialogue in blank verse.

---

[1] This appendix also gives the date of the first performances.

[2] *The Decoy, or The Harlot's Progress* (1733) takes place in a London brothel, and is not without interest; it has a highly moral end with the bawds and more elderly tarts locked up in Brideswell. Hogarth's famous engravings had come out the previous year. *The Lover his own Rival* (1736) is also set in London, but makes nothing of it.

It was quickly hissed into failure, but as all Drury Lane's early ballad operas suffered this fate one suspects a claque of catcallers hired by Rich. Cibber fooled them all by making an afterpiece of his failure and putting it on anonymously at the Little Theatre under the title of *Damon and Phillida*. This was surprisingly popular. Perhaps it was Damon's preference for free love as opposed to marriage that appealed, though when he finds Phillida prepared to do without him he accepts marriage with a good grace. *Momus turn'd Fabulist* was also set in the mythological past, but was more satiric. Drury Lane did not find a successful ballad opera until *The Jovial Crew* of February 1731; this was the theatre's tenth attempt.

The commonest subject for ballad opera was English village life. Throughout the eighteenth century townsfolk were easily diverted by the stupidity of the countryman, and they flocked to *Flora*, an extremely naïve piece, because they enjoyed seeing Hob tumble down a well, and his mother pull him up in a bucket and mistake him for a monster. Theatre-goers were also fascinated by servants. *The Livery Rake* is peopled entirely by servants and country girls. *The Village Opera*, which failed in spite of some amusing scenes, is about a young man who disguises himself as a gardener and a girl who disguises herself as a lady's-maid in order to further their respective love-affairs. In Fielding's *The Intriguing Chambermaid*, as also in *The Lover his own Rival*, it is the maid who motivates all the action by her scheming. In the same author's *An Old Man taught Wisdom* the middle-class country-girl, Lucy, rejects the suitors her father suggests and marries the footman.

Beggars were seen as figures of romance rather than of squalor. In *The Jovial Crew* middle-class girls escape from their homes and find freedom wandering through the countryside in beggars' disguise. Unlike *The Beggar's Opera*, *The Beggar's Wedding* is about beggars. Chaunter, their 'king', expresses the new attitude thus:

> I would not change my condition with the greatest Prince in Europe; for there is not one of 'em all but envies the freedom of us Beggars . . . As for our Dirt and Uncleanness they are without us, and signify nothing at all to true happiness; and for our Rags 'tis to them we chiefly owe our Felicity.

Many songs of the period treat begging with sympathy, for instance *Pills* iii, pp. 100 and 265, and iv, p. 142. Two of these may have been sung in *The Jovial Crew* before it was turned into a ballad opera. (The original was a play by Richard Brome dating from 1641.) 'The Jovial Beggars' was especially popular. The tune turns up in numerous ballad operas including *The Quaker's Opera*, *The Beggar's Wedding*, and *Polly*; also in the much later burletto, *Midas*. The second phrase has a curious likeness to 'Blow away the Morning Dew'. I quote two significant verses as given in *Pills*, whose version cannot be very early as it refers to Jonathan Wild.

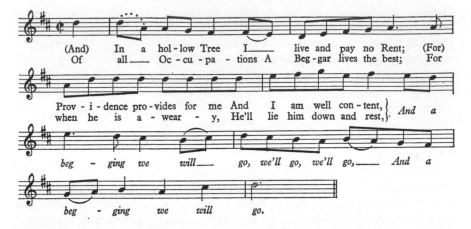

Fielding introduced a more sophisticated note into ballad opera with his adaptations from the French, notably *The Mock Doctor*[1] from Molière's *Le Médecin malgré lui*. His *Lottery*, though rather dully written, had a novel plot about a confidence trick. Chloe (Mrs. Clive) is pretty, apparently rich, apparently innocent, and thus fair game for the two rogues who try to relieve her of her money. One of them disguises himself as a lord and offers matrimony. But it turns out that she is not rich. She has merely bought a lottery ticket, assumed she would win, and boasted of non-existent wealth. Needless to say, she does not win.

Only the earliest imitators of *The Beggar's Opera* imitated Gay's title. *The Cobler's Opera* is not about a cobbler, and *The Quaker's Opera* is not about a quaker. But from 1729 onwards titles tell you what a ballad opera is about, and not who is alleged to have written it. Introductions featuring the supposed author and one or more actors are common throughout the period, though seldom much to the point. Fielding, in the years when he ran the Little Theatre (1735–7), developed these introductions into an amusing framework. His very popular *Pasquin*, which gave Sheridan the basis of *The Critic* (it is not a ballad opera), presents two authors; one has written a tragedy, and one a comedy, and we watch them rehearsing their ridiculous effusions. In this, as in its short sequel *Tumble-down Dick, or Phaeton in the Suds* (which *is* a ballad opera of sorts), the framework is more interesting than what it frames.

A few ballad operas deserve somewhat more detailed treatment, either for their own sake or for what they led to. *Penelope* was mostly written before *The Beggar's Opera* as a skit on the classical masque, the author being John Mottley, son of a prominent Jacobite colonel. Penelope keeps the Royal Oak Ale-House in London and is plagued by suitors (a butcher, a tailor, and a parish-clerk), her

---

[1] Sizergh Castle in Westmorland has a large oil of a scene from this ballad opera by Francis Hayman, who painted scenery for the playhouses in the 1730s and 1740s. The painting is said to have been 'formerly in the Alcoves at Vauxhall Gardens', and it is badly in need of cleaning.

husband, Ulysses, having been away at the wars for twenty years. Penelope is told that, like other soldiers in the Marlborough Wars, he has been lingering at Rotterdam, where

> One Circe there, a Witch that deals in Gin,
> By magic Spells has drawn the Serjeant in.

All the dialogue is in heroic couplets of this flavour. The classical scholar Thomas Cooke helped Mottley finish the piece and turn it into a ballad opera with the addition of songs. As a sample here is the maid tempting Penelope with a description of her suitor the butcher:

> He'll love Thee truely,
> And pay Thee duely
> What you from Uly
> Expect in vain.

This is exactly in the vein of the English 'Burletta', the all-sung masque with a cod mythological plot and outrageous double rhymes, so popular in the 1760s and later. *Penelope* is not itself a Burletta for it has spoken dialogue, but it prepared the way.

Of the fourteen airs, the first, 'Gimmiani's Minuet', and the last, 'Hark the Cock crows', merit brief discussion. The Italian violinist Geminiani lived mostly in London or Dublin from 1714 until his death in 1762, but he made little impact on our theatres because, as Hawkins revealed, he never had any idea how to deal with singers or any interest in writing for them. But his first two sets of Concerti Grossi (op. 2 and 3, 1732) were known to all theatre-goers as they were constantly used for interval music. The *Allegro* Finale of op. 2 no. 1 was one of two tunes that became famous as 'Geminiani's Minuet':

This found its way into several operas, including Arne's *Love in a Village* (1762). The other 'Geminiani's Minuet', in a major key and of unknown origin, was even more popular. About 1725 it was given words by one M. A. Bradley, 'Gently touch the warbling Lyre', but it does not occur in the only music of Geminiani's then in print, the op. 1 violin sonatas. Here is the tune, as given, slightly decorated, in *Achilles* (Air 48):

Penelope was the first of many ballad operas to make use of this, and it can be found in so late a work as Sheridan's *The Duenna*. The last air in *Penelope*, 'Hark the Cock crows', was taken from a jovial farmer's song by Jeremiah Clarke (*Pills* i, p. 310). Surprisingly, both the last-mentioned airs are employed in the overture to *Penelope*, a sprightly and delightful imitation of Pepusch's overture to *The Beggar's Opera*. 'Hark the cock crows' supplies the theme of the fugal *Allegro*, the second half of the air being used for the episodes. The Geminiani minuet, harmonized for strings in four parts, forms the third movement, and then reappears immediately as the first song.

Penelope is said to have failed because the Little Theatre had not yet managed to collect and train an adequate company of performers. It earned Cooke one line of abuse in *The Dunciad* because Pope thought he was getting at his Homer translation.

The success of *The Beggar's Opera* revolutionized the entertainments offered at London's Fairs. In theory Bartholemew Fair was held for three days in the latter half of August, but in practice it was often kept going, illegally, for anything up to a fortnight. There was always at least one theatrical booth, and in 1731 as many as four, at which short ballad operas and farces were given; in some years there were performances every hour from two o'clock in the afternoon till eleven o'clock at night. As the patent theatres were usually closed at this time, the fairgrounds were able to call on reputable actors and actresses, as also on surprisingly lavish orchestral resources. In 1733, Theophilus Cibber's mixture of masque, ballad opera and pantomime, *The Harlot's Progress*, was given with a band that included oboes, bassoons, horns, trumpets, drums, and strings. (The music is lost, the composer unknown.) Prices were about half those prevailing in the patent theatres, boxes costing 2s. 6d, the pit 1s. 6d, and the galleries 1s. and 6d. After Bartholemew Fair, much the same entertainments, stalls, and sideshows were offered south of the Thames at Southwark Fair, which was held in September. On a number of occasions Bartholemew Fair commissioned works, for instance *The Quaker's Opera* by the original Macheath, Thomas Walker.

It was to be expected that Thomas Walker would closely imitate *The Beggar's Opera*. Another writer one might expect to do this was Gay himself, but he never did. For the first months of his success he lived in luxury, being taken round England and Scotland by the Duke and Duchess of Queensberry. In the summer they were all in Bath, where Gay helped with the rehearsals of the first provincial production of *The Beggar's Opera*, and wrote its sequel, *Polly*. This takes place entirely in the West Indies, to which Macheath has been transported. Escaping from his plantation, he has disguised himself as a negro, 'Morano', and with Jenny Diver as his 'wife' he runs a band of pirates. Polly, crossing the Atlantic in search of him, is robbed of all her money and sold as a slave to a lascivious planter named Ducat. But Mrs. Ducat, told by Polly of her husband's intentions, is only too glad to release her. The pirates invade the island in the hope of seizing the Indian King's treasure, and they capture Polly, who by now is disguised as a boy. She and 'Morano' do not recognize each other. Jenny Diver tries to seduce Polly and, affronted at getting no response, accuses Polly publicly of raping her. 'Morano' puts Polly in prison with Cawwawkee, the son of the Indian King, who has just been captured too; he is a Noble Savage, with exemplary English. After Polly has bribed the guards, they escape together to the Indian stronghold. In battle the Indians beat the pirates, and Polly captures 'Morano'. Too late to save him from execution, Jenny Diver reveals that he is really Macheath. Polly, realizing that a high-principled husband is best, agrees to marry Cawwawkee.

The main point of *Polly* is to show the Indians as far superior in morals to the Europeans, and there is a good deal of satire directed against the corruption of London society. 'I married a man only because I lov'd him,' says Polly, 'and for this I was look'd upon as a fool by all my acquaintance.' Macheath, dumbfounded by the honesty of the Indians, decides it must result from their lack of education, and Jenny offers the opinion that 'since they are made like us, to be sure, were they in England they might be taught'. Of satire against the Court there is scarcely a trace.

In the autumn Rich put *Polly* into rehearsal, but stopped when the Lord Chamberlain told him he wished to read the play before things went any further; he did this on the secret advice, so it is thought, of Walpole, who was feeling both apprehensive and vindictive. Gay, conscious of innocence, offered to read the play himself to the Lord Chamberlain, but was given no chance of so doing, and in December, to his astonishment and indignation, a total ban was laid on *Polly* without any reasons being given. There is nothing in the text to account for this treatment. It has been suggested that Gay's reputation suffered from the misattribution to him of certain virulent pamphlets by Swift; rightly or wrongly Walpole thought him a troublesome scourge who should be taught a lesson. *Polly* was not staged until 1777.

Financially the ban was a godsend to Gay. Published by subscription, *Polly* enjoyed enormous sales, though readers must have been disappointed at finding nothing in it to offend. The Duchess of Marlborough paid £100 for her copy. The Duchess of Queensberry, a young woman admirable in both appearance and character, went so far as to solicit subscriptions at Court and even from the King himself, knowing that if she went too far, she would be flung out. She did go too far, and as she left for the last time she enjoyed telling the Court what she thought of it. It may well be that her belief in honesty and sincerity, unusual among the aristocracy of her day, inspired much of the substance of *Polly*, and it is pleasant to read of her as an old lady attending such performances as there were in 1777.

Gay seems to have written the dramatized Introduction after the ban. It begins poorly, but ends with a heart-felt credo:

The stage, Sir, hath the privilege of the pulpit, to attack vice however dignified or distinguished; and preachers and poets should not be too well bred upon these occasions: nobody can overdo it when he attacks the vice and not the person.

A few months later Gay developed one implication of this in a short farce, apparently never performed, called *The Rehearsal at Goatham*. This is about an innocent puppet-show in a small country town whose inhabitants take every remark as a personal insult. Shocked indignation is generated by references to Paris ('All the World must apply it to me . . . I had a relation once there who was bubbled'), and even to neighbours ('Ay, there he is at us all. For you know all of us are Neighbours to somebody or other'). All of which suggests there are no references to real people in *Polly*.

Like most sequels, *Polly* is rather hum-drum, and it has never had any real success. Macheath has dwindled into a charmless bore; not even Polly minds much when he dies. The dialogue is more pointed than that of most ballad operas, and there is plot in plenty, but the vivacity of *The Beggar's Opera* is lacking. Gay knew a lot about London, and nothing at all about the West Indies, and Cawwawkee, however much we may admire the sentiments that prompted his creation, is a lifeless stick.

For reality in the West Indies we can turn to a curiously apposite account in Chetwood of a troupe of actors who visited Jamaica in 1733.

> They receiv'd 370 Pistoles the first Night to the *Beggars Opera*, but within the Space of two Months they bury'd their 3rd *Polly*, and two of their Men. The Gentlemen of the Island for some time took their Turns upon the Stage to keep up the Diversion; but this did not hold long, for in two Months more, there were but one old Man, a Boy, and a Woman of the Company left, the rest died either with the Country Distemper, or the Common Beverage of the Place, the noble Spirit of Rum-Punch, which is generally fatal to new Comers.

It was, of course, Rousseau who popularized the Noble Savage theme in the middle of the eighteenth century,[1] but it began seeping into men's consciousness years earlier. Montaigne's essay 'Of Cannibals' has been cited as its first expression in literature. It first appears in the English theatre in Southerne's *Oroonoko* (1696), a tragedy based on a story of the same name by Mrs. Aphra Behn. Steele devoted *Spectator* No. 11 to the Noble Savage, and Cawwawkee was his first appearance in English opera. We shall meet further examples later in the century, by which time the subject was being much more closely associated with the evils of slavery.

As mentioned earlier, *Polly* was published in the same volume as the third edition of *The Beggar's Opera*, and all the airs have basses by Pepusch. The

[1] For a good discussion of the subject, see Basil Willey's *The Eighteenth-Century Background*, pp. 19–21.

overture, though mentioned in the libretto, is missing, and was probably never written. Gay took his airs from much the same sources as before, three of them from Handel. Two of the Handel examples are based on minuets in *The Water Music* which had not then been published except in innacurate song-arrangements. Airs 23 and 47 and the un-numbered Recitativo were by Handel's rival Ariosti, usually known by his first name, Attilio. Some of the loveliest airs come from Scotch Songs recently popularized by Allan Ramsay.

Ramsay himself, it has been claimed, planned a ballad opera before Gay thought of the idea. The success of his *Tea-Table Miscellany* of Scotch Songs (1724–7) led to his writing a Pastoral in 1725 in which four of these songs were included. It has been suggested, without much evidence or likelihood, that this was performed in Edinburgh in 1726. In October 1728 an English company gave *The Beggar's Opera* in Edinburgh, and rather improbably the boys of Haddington Grammar School were taken to see it. They were delighted, and for their annual play they asked Ramsay to develop his Pastoral, *The Gentle Shepherd*, into a full ballad opera. With great speed he brought the songs up to twenty-two, all his words being written to fit traditional Scotch tunes, and the boys gave the first performance in the Taylors' Hall, Edinburgh, on 22 January 1729. Gay had been in Edinburgh the previous spring, and had met Ramsay, who wrote a poem to celebrate the occasion. They are said to have liked each other, and the possibility of a Scottish ballad opera must surely have come up in their conversation.

In some ways Ramsay's treatment of old songs was similar to Burns's at the end of the century. When, as was often the case, he thought the original words inferior or indecent, he rewrote them, usually keeping the opening lines. Sometimes he preserved the original words unaltered or scarcely altered. But these could not be his methods in *The Gentle Shepherd* because he had a plot of sorts to pursue and characters to develop. For his ballad opera he wrote entirely new lyrics for the tunes he borrowed, and thus occasionally he produced two quite different lyrics for the same tune, the one new and the other a rewriting of traditional words. For *The Tea-Table Miscellany* he had persuaded various Scottish writers to contribute lyrics to supplement his own, and some of these are in the English pastoral tradition. Mainly for this reason those who in later years made a fortune out of Burns and a rather different brand of Scotch Song were at some pains to discredit Ramsay, but in fact his lyrics are often appealing, and a high proportion of the tunes he made famous are extremely beautiful.

The plot of *The Gentle Shepherd* is uneventful and innocent. The basic situation is like the one in *Giselle*, with the nobleman's son, Patie, disguised as a shepherd so that he can court the simple country girl, Peggy. In the end Peggy turns out to be well-born too. There is a parallel and semi-comic courtship between two yokels, Roger and Jenny, and there are several parts for non-singers. The dialogue is in heroic couplets, and even the stage directions are in verse, which suggests that Ramsay wrote for the study rather than the theatre.

At this period he could not hope for much encouragement as a playwright in Edinburgh. *The Gentle Shepherd* received its first professional performance at Drury Lane in 1730, shortened, anglicized, and mutilated by Theophilus Cibber. He kept eleven of the original Scottish tunes, introduced eleven new ones, completely rewrote most of the lyrics, and changed the title to *Patie and Peggy*. It failed. But in the third quarter of the century it was given one or two performances almost every season at the Little Theatre, an obscure actor called Lauder being very popular as Patie's father, Sir William Worthy. There were performances in Scotland too, and about 1758 a Glasgow publisher brought out the words with the airs for the first time.

Drury Lane's attempt at a full-length Scottish ballad opera, *The Highland Fair*, lasted only four nights. Most of the tunes derived from Ramsay's collection. The characters have Scottish names, but there was no attempt at a Scottish flavour in the dialogue, which is uninteresting.

In the summer of 1731 *The Devil to pay* was casually presented with an inexperienced cast, the experienced being on holiday, and it proved the second most successful ballad opera of the century and a great stand-by at Drury Lane. By 1750 it had averaged twenty-five performances a year, and throughout the century it scarcely missed a season at one theatre or another. As late as 1814 Jane Austen expressed herself in a letter as 'highly amused' by it, and it might well find favour today. The words were mainly the work of Charles Coffey, a hunchbacked little Irishman who had also written *The Beggar's Wedding*. He was helped by John Mottley, and they got most of the plot from *The Devil of a Wife* by Thomas Jevon, an actor and dancing-master who flourished briefly in the 1680s. To complicate matters still further, Jevon is said to have been helped by his brother-in-law, the dramatist Thomas Shadwell. The first night was a disaster, the audience being strangely offended by Lady Loverule's nonconformist chaplain, Ananias, who has a mind for nothing but eating. To a modern reader Ananias may well seem the funniest character in the opera, but the original audience found him in gross taste, and after the one performance Theophilus Cibber reduced *The Devil to pay* to an afterpiece, and cut Ananias out altogether. Of the forty-eight airs, only sixteen were left.

The plot revolves round two married couples of very different social status. The part of Nell Jobson, the heroine, was written for Mrs. Clive, and Burney thought it her best role. She is the wife of the village cobbler, a desperately jealous man. Up at the Hall, Lady Loverule makes herself powerfully disliked by the servants, and she henpecks her husband, Sir John, whenever he tries to remonstrate with her. Late at night a mysterious doctor comes to the Hall in search of lodging. Lady Loverule turns him rudely away; Sir John advises him to try Jobson in the village. But Jobson turns him away too, for fear of being cuckolded. The irate doctor, alone in the countryside at midnight, conjures up spirits and orders them to exchange Lady Loverule and Mrs. Jobson in their beds. Jobson, suddenly confronted with Lady Loverule, beats her, but Sir John is courteous to Nell, and the servants are overjoyed by her kindness and consideration. No one is cuckolded, and all ends happily, with useful lessons learned.

The production was evidently enjoyed by the Prussian ambassador in London, C.W. von Borcke. He had just produced the first German translation of Shakespeare's *Julius Caesar*, and he now performed a like service for *The Devil to pay*. His *Der Teufel ist los* was given in Berlin in 1743 without much success, but four years later in Hamburg it was liked, and it was soon being enjoyed all over Germany. At what stage the English tunes were jettisoned is uncertain. The version given in Leipzig in 1764 as *Die verwandelten Weiber* had entirely new music by J. A. Hiller, most of it in the *galante* style. Loewenberg and others have claimed that *The Devil to pay* was a major influence on German Singspiel; Hiller was Mozart's chief predecessor in the field. As late as 1845 Adolphe Adam wrote music for a ballet version, *Le Diable à quatre*.

After Gay's death, Rich staged his third and last ballad opera, *Achilles*. The plot is much the same as that of Handel's last opera, *Deidamia*, as indeed of later operas by Naumann and Paisiello. Achilles is left on Scyros by his mother disguised as a girl in the hope that he may escape the Trojan War. He is known as Pyrrha. The attempts by the King to seduce Pyrrha are the converse of the 'love scene' in *Polly* between the two girls, and gave a certain amount of offence. The one person on the island with good reason to know Pyrrha's real sex is the King's daughter, Deidamia, who is pregnant by 'her'.[1] Searching for Achilles, Ulysses comes to Scyros disguised as a trader, and suspecting Pyrrha (who does most things very gauchely) he leaves a suit of armour lying around. Achilles is discovered because he takes too much interest in the armour. He marries Deidamia and leaves for Troy.

The situation may seem promising, but Gay's dialogue makes little of it. This is a dull piece, uneventful and poorly constructed. Deidamia does not speak until near the end of Act II. Of satire there is next to none. Occasional lines show Gay's personal touch; as for instance when one of Deidamia's friends, looking at the clothes laid out by the trader, remarks hopefully: 'There must be something pretty in everything that is foreign.' Some of the airs have points of interest. 'Dicky's Walk from Dr. Faustus' has already been mentioned. Air 37 is called 'The Clarinette', and this is the earliest known use of the word in English by several years, but the origin of the tune and the reason for the title are obscure. The first reference to the instrument being played that I have come on occurs in an advertisement for a concert on 11 March 1737, when a Mr. Charles played solos in the Stationer's Hall on 'the French Horn, Clarinette, and Sharlarno'. No less than four tunes in *Achilles* are attributed to Corelli. Airs 44 and 53 are from his 9th and 10th Concerti Grossi, Airs 49 and 54 from his Trio Sonatas op. 4 no. 5 and op. 2 no. 5. It is unexpected that Gay should have

---

[1] In the original legend all twenty-four of the King's daughters are aware of Pyrrha's sex for the same reason.

known this music. Air 34 is called 'Beggar's Opera. Hornpipe', and it is strange that it should have been overlooked, for it must be 'The Dance of the Prisoners in Chains' just before the scene near the end in the 'condemn'd Hold'. Presumably it was composed by Pepusch, and there is no reason why it should not be used in modern productions of *The Beggar's Opera*; indeed there is every reason why it should. Here is the tune:

Pepusch (?)

Though *Achilles* has a dull libretto, the general run of ballad opera librettos is duller still. They got by, if at all, on their song tunes. Perhaps it was at this time that the belief arose that if you are writing words for music it does not very much matter what words you write. Before the ballad opera craze, England's leading literary men were eager to be associated with her composers. Afterwards they were more wary.

3 THE MUSIC, ITS PERFORMERS AND ARRANGERS

There has been a conspiracy of silence as to how ballad operas were performed and scored. The few writers who have given the subject a single thought have excused themselves from a second one by alleging that the original orchestrations are all lost. Even if this were true, we would need to enquire what these original orchestrations were like, and to what extent the songs as printed are incomplete.

Four ballad opera overtures survive. All were printed in score in the librettos, and all are for two oboes and strings:

The Beggar's Opera (LIF 1728) by Pepusch; two movements, the second a fugue on one of the airs.

The Cobler's Opera (LIF 1728); anon but perhaps by Pepusch; two movements, the second based on 'Nobody's Jig', which is not one of the airs. (It is in the *Fitzwilliam Virginal Book*, No. 149, and in many editions of *The Dancing Master*.)

Penelope (LT 1728); anon; three movements, the second a fugue on Air 14, the third an arrangement of Air 1 (see p. 107).

The Wedding (LIF 1729) by Pepusch; three movements, not based on any of the airs.

The first three of the above were the first three ballad operas to be staged. Thereafter we must suppose that either publishers preferred to avoid the expense of printing overtures or theatres saved money by using music already in print.

In early days ballad opera airs usually formed an appendix at the end of the libretto, but later, if printed at all, they were inserted in the text in their proper place. They never have introductions. In only five cases were the airs published with their basses:

The Beggar's Opera (LIF 1728), 3rd edition; basses by Pepusch.

Polly (unperformed), published with the above; basses by Pepusch.

Flora (LIF 1729); early editions give melodies only, but one of about 1737 has 'a new base, & thro' base to each Song'. There is a copy (unique?) in the Royal College of Music; above each song there is a picture of an incident in the plot 'design'd by the Celebrated Mr. Gravelot, and Engrav'd by G. Bickham jun^r.'. Original title: *Hob's Opera*.

The Devil to pay (DL 1731); Almost all editions give melodies only. One 'with a new Bass to the Whole' was advertized in the *London Daily Post* for 20.10.40 'with the Score engrav'd [by Bickham] in Picture Work, on the top of each Song, as represented at the Old Play-house', and there is a copy (unique?) in the Mitchell Library, Glasgow. The original basses were probably by Seedo, who contributed an original song to this ballad opera.

The Devil of a Duke (DL 1732); basses by Seedo, whose name is given not on the libretto but in advertisements in other librettos. London Library has a copy.

In addition four songs from *The Beggar's Wedding* were published with basses in *The Musical Miscellany* Vol. V and another in Vol. VI. Vol V of *The Musical Miscellany* also contains six songs with basses from *The Honest Yorkshireman* by Carey.

We have now to decide whether or not the songs in the above publications were printed in their entirety. For the moment let us assume that they were. In which case they had no introductions to set the tempo and give the singer his note. In which case they surely had no more than a continuo accompaniment, for without introductions only continuo songs would have been practicable. The singer would be given his note during the last speech, and the harpsichordist and cellist would follow his tempo as best they might. Ensemble would probably be shaky for a bar or two, but not nearly so shaky as if a conductorless orchestra tried to follow the singer. Purcell was aware of a distinction here, for all his songs *without* introductions have continuo accompaniment. He clearly thought that with an orchestra you needed an introduction to establish tempo and tonality, and he apparently thought that without an orchestra you could dispense with an introduction.

But it is only an assumption that continuo songs were performed as they were printed. There is, perhaps, a parallel in church hymns, which have no printed introduction though in fact organists extemporize one for practical reasons. It may well be that in continuo songs harpsichordists also extemporized an introduction. One was surely needed more than ever in the theatre, with the singer and the continuo instruments at some distance from each other.

Where ballad opera songs are concerned, we can reach the same conclusion with less guesswork if we assume that the airs were *not* printed in their entirety. As has been shown earlier, publishers normally cut introductions when printing popular songs; for instance in that fountain-head of ballad opera tunes, *Pills to purge Melancholy*, as also in such operas as D'Urfey's *Wonders in the Sun*. We can be certain that if the airs in *The Beggar's Opera* had had introductions the publisher would have left them out, and such evidence as survives suggests that ballad opera airs were performed in fact not only with a few instrumental bars at the start but with some at the end as well.

The Royal Music Library in the British Museum has a set of part books (RM 21.c.43–5), both vocal and instrumental, for three ballad operas: *Damon and Phillida*, *The Devil to pay*, and *The Lottery*. The same part books contain more elaborate music for *Macbeth* (Leveridge), *Henry VIII*, and *Theodosius*. All this music was copied by one E. R. Simpson, and almost certainly for one particular theatre. No composers are named. *Theodosius* was a Restoration play by Nathaniel Lee, and it was normally performed with Purcell's music until 26 April 1744, when Thomas Arne's incidental music was performed for the first time in Dublin. I cannot trace that Arne's music was ever used in London, except possibly in 1768, but at this period *Henry VIII* was in no theatre's repertoire. It thus seems possible that the Simpson part books were made for Dublin in or about 1744.

Harder to date is MS 2232 in London's Royal College of Music. As well as music for other plays and operas, this contains a rather different selection of songs for *The Devil to pay*, most of them on two staves. (But No. 8 from Leveridge's *Macbeth* and an intruder, Galliard's 'The early Horn' from *The Royal Chace*, are scored for four-part strings with a horn solo in the latter.) The MS cannot be earlier than 1740 for it includes music for Garrick's *Lethe* of that year.

All the ballad opera songs in both these MSS have instrumental introductions and codas. The introductions consist of the opening bars of the 'vocal', usually the first four, and the codas consist of the closing bars, usually the last two. The MSS seem to me early enough for the conclusion that ballad opera airs were always so performed from the first. There is confirmatory evidence in *The Village Opera* (1729), one of whose stage directions reads: *They talk while the Symphony plays, and turn as Colin sings*. Then follows Air 36, which, needless to say, is printed without a 'symphony' (introduction). In *The Welsh Opera* (1731), one of those published without any music, there occurs the following stage direction before Air 10: *While the Symphony is playing, Robin pulls out an Handkerchief, blows his Nose, and drops a Letter*. Here is the start of Air 14 in *The Devil to pay*, as given in RM 21.c.43–5:

The above tune, a derivative of "Twas within a Furlong of Edinburgh Town' in Purcell's *The Mock Marriage*, is much closer to Purcell in the Royal College of Music manuscript, and in E minor. Also the bass is quite different. It will be remembered that, apart from a late and extremely rare edition, the airs in *The Devil to pay* were published without basses. Provincial theatres presumably made their own arrangements of the published melodies, and we would therefore expect different bass lines in different MSS. We would also expect that the instrumental introductions might differ in length in some of the airs, and this again is the case.

The Royal Music Library manuscript includes parts for first and second violins, and these are different in the music for *Macbeth*, *Henry VIII*, and *Theodosius*, for which works violas and other instruments were also required. But in the three ballad operas the first and second violin parts are identical, and there is no viola part. In these ballad operas, and probably in all, the violins doubled the vocal line, the violas (if any) doubled the bass, and the harpsichord alone filled in the harmonies. Some ballad operas have an air in which the voice stops for a bar or two in the middle of the verse, leaving the strings playing on their own; such interludes were marked 'Sym' (symphony), and there is an example in the last air in *The Beggar's Opera*.

I have come upon only four references to instruments other than strings. In Act II of *The Beggar's Opera* Macheath, in the tavern with the street women, hears 'the harper at the door'; he calls him in and asks him to play 'The French Tune that Mrs. Slammekin was so fond of'. Then follows 'A Dance à la ronde in the French Manner', which leads into Air 22, the French Cotillon, 'Youth's the Season made for Joys'. The tune must have been played first by the harper on his own for the dance, and then repeated as a song with the usual string accompaniment. (Later in the century the harper was always cut.) Near the end of *Achilles*, Air 47 is preceded by the stage direction 'Agyrtes takes a Trumpet which lay amongst the Armour, and sounds'. Ulysses, Diomedes, Achilles, and Agyrtes then sing a bellicose quartet beginning:

> Thy Fate then, O Troy, is decreed.
> How I pant! How I burn for the Fight!

The tune, 'My Dame hath a lame, tame Crane', is playable on the natural trumpet except for one unimportant passing note near the end. This can hardly be a coincidence. The probability is that the introduction to this quartet consisted of the first half of the tune played as a trumpet solo. (The quartet is formally interesting, for it is followed immediately by Air 48 in which Achilles contemplates abandoning the sword for love, after which Air 47 is repeated 'as a Catch'. The result is a Da Capo item of some length.) In *Robin Hood* (1730)[1] 'March on, brave Hearts' (Air 6) is identified as 'Scots Guards March. French Horns', and the entire tune is playable on natural horns, which it no doubt was.

At the end of *The Author's Farce* (LT 30.3.30) by Fielding, Luckless, the author, calls out 'Strike up, kettle drums and trumpets', and there is then a dance, but we do not know what they danced to because this ballad opera was published without any music.

It might be thought that when ballad operas made use of Italian opera arias by Handel and others, something more than unison violins and a continuo bass would be required. But in fact Pepusch, when arranging the March from *Rinaldo* for *The Beggar's Opera* (Air 20, 'Let us take the Road'), made no attempt at correct harmonies, let alone a correct orchestration, and he even got the tune wrong. The libretto describes this air as 'March in Rinaldo, with Drums and Trumpets', but the last four words are an identification and not a description of Pepusch's arrangement. The tune as printed in *The Beggar's*

---

[1] *The London Stage* describes it as a droll, but in fact it was an ordinary ballad opera, commissioned for Bartholomew Fair, with nineteen airs, and dialogue in blank verse.

Opera is in B flat, a key trumpets and drums could not then manage. Perhaps Pepusch's dislike of Handel made him scornful of accuracy.

A much more respectful treatment of Handel can be found in *The Lottery*, whose music was arranged and in part composed by Seedo. Originally Air 18 was 'Si, caro', from *Admeto*, but this was cut before the Royal Music Library parts were made. However 'Sono confusa' from Handel's *Poro* (1731) held its place, and the parts allow it all eighteen bars of the introduction, and the correct bass throughout. Handel's unimportant flute part disappears, as also his parts for second violins and violas, but in fact these are independent in only a few bars. For most of the time Handel's violins all double the voice, and the version in *The Lottery* is scarcely distinguishable from the original. The standard ballad opera accompaniment described above may seem primitive and uninteresting, but it occurs in most Italian operas of the period, even in Handel's.

The string parts in the Royal Music Library MS have brief verbal cues before each song to show the band when to come in. They are so brief that a deduction can be made from them. Today it is usual in productions of *The Beggar's Opera*, as also in modern 'Musicals', for introductions to be played behind the preceding dialogue to achieve what producers like to call 'a natural transition' from speaking to singing. But the 'transition' denies the audience the pleasure of listening to the introductions, which were never so played before the end of the eighteenth century. Air 4 in *The Lottery* is a slow minuet song. The Royal Music Library manuscript gives it an eight-bar introduction that would last nearly twenty seconds. The cue on the parts consists of no more than the last four words of the preceding soliloquy: 'Sticks in her Side'. The soliloquy could not possibly have overlapped the introduction; indeed there must have been a small gap before the strings could begin.

It is almost unknown for ballad opera airs to have tempo marks, but in *Polly* there are eight. Five airs are marked 'Not too fast', two are marked 'Slow', and one 'Very Slow'. This last is a special case, for a normally cheerful tune, 'Buff Coat', is being used as a dirge after Macheath's death. The others suggest that either Pepusch or Gay thought there had been a tendency in *The Beggar's Opera* to sing some of the airs too quickly, and that this should be guarded against in the sequel.

Almost all ballad opera airs seem intended for high voices, the top note is seldom lower than F, and often it is G or even A. Yet singing actors with untrained voices can have been no more inclined to sing tenor in the 1730s than they are today. In modern productions of *The Beggar's Opera* nearly all the airs are transposed down, some of them by as much as a fourth or fifth. The explanation has been touched on already, and the subject is discussed at length in the section on Singers in Chapter 7. Male singers expected to have to sing their top notes falsetto, these falsetto notes being a hang-over from the days when the counter-tenor voice was widely cultivated. Because of this, baritones and even basses could manage notes which today look possible only for tenors. When the castrati became the rage, baritones continued to toy with falsetto because men had so sung for generations, either occasionally or regularly. It does also seem that the key in which ballad opera airs were printed was sometimes of the publisher's choosing, for it is suspicious that the tunes should so often be in whatever key results in the fewest leger lines. In any case there was nothing sacrosanct about keys. The first song in *The Devil to pay* is in C minor in the libretto, in B minor in the Royal Music Library MS, and in A minor in RCM 2232. By the middle 1730s publishers often used blocks from earlier ballad operas when, as often happened, the same tune was wanted again, and in at least some cases this must show an indifference to the key requirements of particular singers.

The question of key is especially teasing when there is a succession of airs with no intervening dialogue. One would expect conventional key relationships between one air and the next for the sake of both listeners and performers, but no such relationship is to be found in the succession of airs Macheath sings in the 'Condemn'd Hold' (Airs 58–67). The first nine are incomplete fragments, the last a complete version of 'Greensleeves', and the sudden and frequent switches of key, time signature and tempo in the course of uninterrupted music must have made this scene of the greatest practical difficulty. In our own century much ingenuity has been exercised on it by Dent and Britten; as I shall show in a later chapter, the same problems exercised Thomas Linley in the 1770s. With the addition of intervening bars for the orchestra, and a few changes in note values and keys, it can be made wonderfully effective. But how did Thomas Walker manage in 1728? He must have made a good job of it, for the scene was much imitated, and in general these imitations pay some attention to key sequence. Thus in *Love in a Riddle* Airs 4 to 6 in Act II were sung without a break, the keys being A, F and C, while in *The Village Opera* Airs 41–6 were sung consecutively, and here too the key relationship seems to have been thought out. In the full-length version of *The Devil to pay* the scene at midnight in which the spirits are conjured up is entirely sung. *The Beggar's Wedding* has three pairs of songs, in each case the second being in the same key as the first, or a closely related one, and having the same time signature. One suspects a *Da Capo* plan, with the first song repeated after the second, and we have met an example of this in *Achilles*. The long aria from Handel's *Poro* that has already been mentioned as coming in *The Lottery* is immediately followed by an almost equally long aria in the same key by Seedo. All such sequences resulted from attempts to make ballad opera music less scrappy and more truly operatic.

It does seem that *The Beggar's Opera* is a little out of step with its successors in the matter of key, and this is further suggested by the fact that as many as four airs (Nos. 7, 16, 18, and 39) end in keys other than those of the start. Modern ears find these tonal quirks attractive, but even we might be a little surprised by the end of Air 18, which is also the end of Act I, for it provides no sense of finality whatever:

There is a tantalizing hint as to what may have happened at the ends of acts in *The Prisoner's Opera*, a work quite unlike any so far mentioned, and of extreme rarity.[1] According to the title page it was published in 1730 and

> perform'd at Sadler's Wells, During the Summer Season. Where also the best of Wines, excellent Ale, brew'd of the Well Water, and all other Liquors may be had in perfection.

It is clear from *The Prisoner's Opera* that speaking on the stage there was illegal, for there is no dialogue. The tunes, which are not named, are printed together at the end, and the text consists of lyrics and stage directions. The work begins with 'the Prisoners begging in Song, thro' a Grate', and after a song by the Head-Turnkey 'the Musick plays a short Lesson in the same Key of the following Song'. This direction, which recurs later, may mean that the next song tune is played through by the orchestra as an introduction. A new prisoner arrives, a debtor, and 'the Constable of the Prison' sings to him of the 'Garnish' he must pay him. Then comes a Prisoners' Dance, of which the tune is not given, and later a woman prisoner sings of her downfall, each of the four verses being followed by a chorus to a different tune in the same key. 'The Harlequin' dances with the woman prisoner, and as everyone goes out 'the Musick continues playing as at the end of an Act'. (Thus we know that something was conventionally played, but what it was we can only guess.) There are two songs for the Basket Man, who was allowed out of the prison to beg for food for the prisoners, and during a chorus the prisoners pull some rather unappetizing rib-bones from his basket. In all there are eleven ballad tunes, among them 'Jamaica', 'Hey Boys and up we go', and finally 'The bonny grey-eyed Morn'.[2] Apart from the absence of dialogue, the work is unlike a normal ballad opera in that

[1] BUCEM gives only one copy, and this is bound up in the first of three MS note books on eighteenth-century drama made in the early nineteenth century by Francis Place, the well-known trade unionist and agitator (BM Add. 27,831).

[2] The libretto also contains other songs sung at Sadler's Wells.

there are several verses to every tune. *The Prisoner's Opera* would play for about half-an-hour, and it was just one item in a variety programme that also included dances and acrobatics. In fact it was the fore-runner of the Dialogues Charles Dibdin was to write for Sadler's Wells in the 1770s. According to Baker, the author was Edward Ward, a famous London pub-keeper who wrote *The London Spy* and a surprising number of other works. By 1730 he was in his sixties.

Not enough is known of the musicians who made the ballad opera arrangements. Each theatre must have had a composer on hand to supply whatever was needed, and at Drury Lane Henry Carey worked on the early ballad operas, to be succeeded in 1731 by Seedo. We have already found Carey writing pantomime music for this theatre, and for its first ballad opera, *Love in a Riddle*, he produced a novelty in the form of a sung Epilogue, the tune being his own 'Sally in our Alley'.[1] No doubt he provided basses for the airs as well. In the summer of 1729 he turned his fourteen-year-old farce *The Contrivances* into what he described as a ballad opera by adding a dozen airs, but the result was not a ballad opera in the strict sense for all the music was by Carey himself. Significantly the songs were published not only with basses but with introductions as well. In its new form *The Contrivances* (DL 20.6.29) was enormously successful; by the middle of the century there must have been several hundred performances, and in the provinces it was still being played as late as 1820. The plot is the familiar one of the gay hero, Rovewell, duping the foolish father in order to elope with his daughter, but the amusing disguises distinguish it from many of its fellows. In one scene Rovewell appears as a simple country girl, while his servant Robin turns himself successively into a garrulous yokel, a lawyer, and a constable. The dialogue is lively, the tunes catchy.

The following year Carey had another success with his pantomime masque *Cephalus and Procris* (DL 28.10.30), which had seventy-two performances the first season. Again Carey wrote all the music, but he lacked the calibre for a serious masque and the songs are undistinguished. We know from advertisements that the Comic Tunes for the pantomime interlude, sometimes known as *Harlequin Volgi*, were also published, but I have not found a copy. In the ballad opera *The Lover his own Rival* Air 8 is identified as 'Millers Dance in Cephalus', and the tune is a good one. Carey would have been more in his element in this part of the entertainment.

In spite of these successes Carey left Drury Lane in 1731, perhaps because of a quarrel with Cibber, perhaps to turn his attention to higher things; the following year he was closely associated with the attempts to restore English Opera. He had already worked for the fairgrounds, composing songs and perhaps arranging all the music for both *The Quaker's Opera* and *The Generous Freemason*. The latter was the work of William Chetwood, Drury Lane's prompter, so loyalties will have been involved. Thereafter Carey worked for

[1] Purcell's *The Indian Queen* (1695) had had a sung Prologue.

whatever theatre would have him. In 1734 he wrote the words and about half the music for another ballad opera, *The Honest Yorkshireman* (LT 15.7.35); the other songs are partly traditional and partly by such composers as Porpora,[1] Handel, and Greene. Charles Fleetwood, now manager of Drury Lane, kept the MS for nine months before turning it down, and the subsequent rumpus is vividly described by Carey in the preface to his libretto. He announced performances at Lincoln's Inn Fields, which he proposed to rent from Rich, but they never took place. Eventually in the summer of 1735 the Little Theatre put it on, and the result was another of Carey's lasting successes.

The plot of *The Honest Yorkshireman* is much the same as that of *The Contrivances*. The duping of the heroine's father or guardian by a series of preposterous disguises was to be the standard situation in *galante* comic operas, as also in some by such nineteenth century composers as Rossini and Donizetti. In Carey's day it was not yet hackneyed. An essential character in all such operas is the man chosen by the father-guardian for the heroine's husband. Usually he is senile, and almost invariably he is silly. In *The Honest Yorkshireman* he is neither, and this is a pleasingly original touch. It is indeed the Yorkshireman himself who has been chosen as Arbella's husband, but before he has set eyes on her he is waylaid on his arrival in London by Arbella's lover, Gaylove, who persuades him that he is inadequately clothed for the metropolis. This allows Gaylove to purloin the discarded countrified clothes, put them on, and intrude into Arbella's house disguised as the Yorkshireman. But the latter, though taken in by the trick, is bluff and likable, and we do not despise him. Carey has taken unusual trouble to give his speeches a North Country flavour; one cannot but imagine them spoken with the appropriate accent.

> Wuns-lent! What a mortal big place this same *London* is? Ye mun ne'er see End on't, for sure;—Housen upon Housen, Folk upon Folk—one would admire where they did grow all of 'em.

Burney thought well of *The Honest Yorkshireman*, comparing it to Rousseau's *Le devin du village*, a work he himself translated, and the tribute stresses Carey's modernity. The music of *The Honest Yorkshireman* may not be remarkable, but the words are well above average for eighteenth century comic opera. Carey would have written well for Galuppi or Piccini or their English contemporaries. Like so many men associated with English opera, he lived at the wrong time— in his case too early.

One song in *The Honest Yorkshireman* has words 'taken from Mr. Worsdale's *Cure for the Scold*' and sung to Charles Young's tune 'When the bright God of day'. James Worsdale was just such another butterfly charmer as Carey himself, flitting happily from one profession to another without reaching the top in any of them. He began as an artist, studying with Kneller until he secretly

[1] Porpora had been composing Italian operas in London since the end of 1733; see p. 129.

married his master's niece and thereby fell from favour. Horace Walpole thought poorly of his paintings, but his portrait of Carey, of which there is an engraving in Carey's Poems, looks competent enough. Worsdale also tried his hand at singing, and in his own farce *The Assembly* revealed his powers of mimicry by taking the part of Old Lady Scandal. His *Cure for a Scold*, a ballad opera version of *The Taming of the Shrew*, was staged at Drury Lane in 1735 without much success. He and Carey were close friends.

Carey's successor at Drury Lane was the mysterious Seedo. Loewenberg suggested that he was a Prussian named Sidow or Sydow, and he spent about ten years in London from 1726. He had an Italian wife who had arrived at the Queen's Theatre back in 1711 as Maria Manina. About 1715 she became Mrs. Fletcher and started singing small parts at Lincoln's Inn Fields. Her first husband dying, she married Seedo in 1727.[1] Perhaps handicapped by her accent she never appeared in ballad operas, singing at Drury Lane for the first time in her husband's masque *Venus, Cupid and Hymen* (21.5.33); the music is lost. Seedo had a gift for composing songs in the English ballad style, and he contributed to the following Drury Lane ballad operas, and no doubt others as well:

The Devil to pay (1731)	1 song
The Lottery (1732)	10 songs (out of 19)
The Mock Doctor (1732)	3 songs (out of 10)
The Devil of a Duke (1732)	1 song

Seedo probably arranged all the music for the above ballad operas, as also for the 1734 revision of *The Author's Farce* by Fielding, with whom he was often associated. In Act III, just before the presentation of the puppet show, Luckless, the supposed author of it, actually addresses Seedo in the orchestral pit.

LUCKLESS: Let us begin immediately: I think we will have an overture played on this occasion. Mr. Seedo, have you not provided a new overture on this occasion?
SEEDO: I have composed one.
LUCKLESS: Then pray let us have it.

Fielding does not appear to have taken Seedo with him to the Little Theatre. In 1736 he and his wife were deep in debt, and they made off for Potsdam where Seedo became director of the Royal Band. He died about 1754.

Drury Lane also provided intermittent work of a surprisingly varied kind for Richard Charke, who allowed himself the advantage of marrying Colley Cibber's youngest daughter, Charlotte. He was primarily a violinist, and accord-

---

[1] See Edgar V. Roberts's 'Mr Seedo's London Career' in *The Philological Quarterly*, Jan. 1966. He suggests that some of Seedo's songs in *The Lottery* had previously been sung in Fielding's *Grub Street Opera* (LT 1731).

ing to Hawkins he succeeded 'Dicky Jones'[1] as leader of the Drury Lane orchestra. He often played violin solos and concertos in the intervals. He also aspired to be a singing-actor, playing Rovewell in Carey's *The Contrivances*, and Damon in *Damon and Phillida* as well as leading roles in *The Beggar's Wedding* and *The Wedding*. He even tried his hand at composition, contributing songs to *The Lover's Opera* and *The Generous Freemason*. All these activities were crowded into the years 1729–30. A year or two later he composed the first Medley Overture, which will be discussed in the next chapter. Burney tells us that Charke had also been a dancing-master, and he describes him as a man of humour. He was also a profligate, gambling and whoring continually. His marriage in 1730 was a disaster. Charlotte, only seventeen at the time, was a very strong-minded girl, and Burney remarks that 'there was nothing in which this ingenious pair exercised their talents more successfully than in mutually plaguing each other'. In the ebullient though not quite reliable *Life of Mrs. Charke by Herself* (1755) Charlotte was more charitable: 'We ought rather to have been sent to School than to Church in Regard to any Qualifications on either Side towards rendering the Marriage-State comfortable towards one another'. By 1735 Charke was so deeply in debt that he made off to the West Indies, where he died two years later. Mrs. Charke took part in a number of ballad operas, and at the Little Theatre she sometimes played Macheath. In 1735 she cooked her goose at Drury Lane by attacking the new manager, Fleetwood, in a scurrilous play, *The Art of Management*, and she spent most of the next twenty years struggling for a living in the provinces, part of the time in man's clothes. She even played Hamlet.

Apart from Pepusch, no composer is known to have worked on ballad operas for Rich. In the early days at Goodman's Fields the music was directed by George Monroe, who played the harpsichord there. Monroe, a Scot, had been a pageboy at Cannons, and the Duke had been so impressed by his promise that he had had him taught by Pepusch and (briefly) by Handel. Today he is known only for his exquisite song 'My lovely Celia'.[2] Unfortunately he died young, and in 1731 or soon after he was succeeded by Peter Prelleur. According to Hawkins, Prelleur was a Spitalfields writing-master of French extraction, who turned to music comparatively late in life. He became both a city organist and a singing-teacher, and he wrote an important educational work, *The Modern Musick-Master* (1731), which was published anonymously, and aimed to teach singing, the flute, the oboe and the violin. Prelleur's pantomime masque *Jupiter and Io* (24.1.35) has not survived, but his opera *Baucis and Philemon* (New Wells, G.F. 7.4.40)[3] was published with the overture in full score. He apparently

---

[1] Jones in turn had succeeded Carbonelli; we have already met him as the composer of the pantomime *Wagner and Abericock* (see p. 90).

[2] So-called by its Victorian arranger, Lane Wilson; the real title is 'My Goddess Celia'. The song can be found in *The Musical Miscellany*, Vol. 4.

[3] The date is from Allardyce Nicoll; this opera is not mentioned in LS or Baker.

arranged ballad operas both for Goodman's Fields and later for the near-by New Wells Theatre. In one of these, *The Lover his own Rival* (1736), there is a song by a fellow city organist, John Stanley, who was blind at the time and only thirteen.

No composer is known to have worked regularly for the Little Theatre at this period, but John Frederick Lampe and the harpsichordist John Sheeles must surely have been given occasional work by some theatre or other. The latter contributed two songs to the fairground opera *The Generous Freemason*, apart from a large number to *The Musical Miscellany*.

Pepusch, the man who so casually helped the ballad opera to its success, did not assert himself again. He lived on in strange retirement, developing a love for the music of the past which he managed to communicate to Hawkins. At the time it seemed to most people inexplicable. In music, novelty was thought to be almost everything. On one occasion John Wesley called on Pepusch, and wrote in his *Journal* (Vol. VII p. 22):

> I spent an hour or two with Dr. Pepusch. He asserted, that the art of music is lost; that the ancients only understood it to perfection . . . Purcell made some attempts to restore it: but that ever since, the true, ancient art, depending on nature, and mathematical principles, had gained no ground, present masters having no fixed principles.

Handel was the 'present master' Pepusch had constantly in mind, and Charles Avison was jealous of him too. In his *Essay on Musical Expression* (1751) Avison looked at the past with feelings of nostalgia, and allowed especial merit to 'Palestina', Tallis, and Corelli. It was to be Hawkins's love of Elizabethan music that so infuriated Burney, who took the much more usual view that music had been steadily improving since ancient times, to reach perfection in 'modern' Italian opera. Pepusch, ineffectual though he was, can be counted among the very first of our musical antiquarians.

4

'English Opera' and Burlesque
1732–1745

1 ITALIAN OPERA IN LONDON: HANDEL'S LATER OPERAS

FOR two chapters we have been concerned with theatre music of very humble pretensions. In the three that follow we are to consider some short-lived attempts to give Londoners something more substantial than pantomimes and ballad operas. These attempts were spread over a quarter of a century, but separated by periods of theatrical stagnation when whole seasons would go by without a single new production, musical or otherwise. In 1732–3 there was an interesting attempt to establish full-length all-sung English opera, and this was followed by experiments in burlesque opera. In 1738–42 Thomas Arne returned to the masque with some success, and about 1750 Garrick prodded more than one composer into promising activity. None of these moves was wholly ineffectual, yet none made a lasting impression, and thus these twenty-five years lack purpose and direction. Yet a small store of good music resulted, and at least it will be shown that English composers more than held their own with naturalized foreigners working in the same field.

Though most society people, Mrs. Delany for instance, gave all their musical attention to Italian opera, there were always a few to deplore its supremacy. In the 1729 edition of Carey's poems we meet the sort of opera snob who perhaps can still be found in the wilds of Sussex today. In 'Blundrella', a sort of sequel to 'The Rape of the Lock', there is a tea-party presided over by Belinda at which Blundrella chatters away, pulling names from her small store of knowledge with irritating superficiality.

> She talk'd of Singers and Composers,
> Of their Admirers and Opposers,
> Of the *Cuzzoni* and *Faustini*,
> Of *Handel* and of *Bononcini*;

> One was too rough, t'other too smooth,
> *Attilio* only hit her Tooth;
> And Tamo tanto[1] was a Song
> Would give her pleasure all day long.

She then asks Belinda to sing a particular song which, as she is quick to mention, she has just heard marvellously performed by one of the great Italians. But even the Italians come in for a few back-handers.

> She next of Masters 'gan to preach;
> The English were not fit to teach,
> Italians were the only Men,
> And ev'n of those not one in ten;
> For she had heard a Lady say,
> Scarce two in Town could sing or play.

The second line is the more bitter for the fact that Carey himself, when not employed by the theatres, lived by private teaching. Eventually Blundrella is put down by Eugenio, who asks what she would like him to play on his flute.

> *Si caro*, if you please, said she:
> He played the Tune of *Children Three*.
> She was in Raptures, and intreated
> The self-same Tune might be repeated.[2]

Carey's antipathy to Italian Opera comes out more strongly in his 'Satyr on the Luxury and Effeminacy of the Age'.

> I hate this Singing in an unknown Tongue,
> It does our Reason and our Senses wrong;
> When Words instruct, and Music cheers the Mind,
> Then is the Art of Service to Mankind:
> But when a Castrate Wretch, of monstrous size,
> Squeaks out a Treble, shrill as Infant cries,
> I curse the unintelligible Ass,
> Who may, for ought I know, be saying Mass.

He notes a national characteristic with the couplet:

> But, such is the Good Nature of the Town,
> 'Tis now the Mode to cry the English down.

In fact it had been the Mode since Purcell's day, and it did not stop in Carey's.

---

[1] 'T'amo tanto' was a simple and very popular minuet song in *Artaserse* (1724) by Attilio Ariosti.

[2] 'Si, caro' is from Handel's *Admeto* (1727); 'Children Three' was a nursery rhyme.

Carey's satire refers solely to Handel's time with the Royal Academy of Music, which terminated in 1728. For a whole season Italian opera was unheard in this country. But Handel was so bitten with the opera germ that he soon went into partnership with Heidegger, manager of the King's Theatre, each of them putting up money towards further opera seasons. In the cold weather of January 1729 Handel set off for Rome to find more singers, and when he got back in June he had contracted a fine soprano in Anna Strada; a little later Senesino returned, until replaced in the autumn of 1733 by another alto castrato, Giovanni Carestini. In four years Handel staged six new operas of his own,[1] and revived as many more that he had written earlier. Then followed a time of confusion, over-work, and rising doubts. A rival company, the Nobility Opera, took Lincoln's Inn Fields for the 1733–4 season, and then moved into the King's Theatre for three further seasons. During this time John Rich generously gave up two days a week at Covent Garden so that Handel could stage his own operas there.

But the Nobility Opera had much more sensational singers. Not only did they lure Senesino away from Handel and bring back Cuzzoni, but a year later they were presenting the greatest castrato of all time, Farinelli. Farinelli's début was in a version of *Artaserse* (KT 29.10.34) composed jointly by his own brother, Riccardo Broschi, and by Hasse; there were twenty-eight performances that season and eight more the next. No opera by Handel was repeated so often. 'It is impossible to sing better', wrote the Abbé Prevost of Farinelli, and that was what everyone thought. For part of the time that he sang in London, the official composer to the Nobility Opera was Porpora, and Veracini was also on hand to supply some of the music. When Farinelli left the country for good in June 1737, the Nobility Opera went out of business.

Meanwhile Handel had to struggle. With singers counting for much more than usual and the music for much less, his chief advantage over his rivals was of little account. Now that he was at Covent Garden, it occurred to him that he might be able to attract some of the usual playhouse audience by presenting English singers that they already knew and liked; accordingly he engaged John Beard and Cecilia Young, and they appeared in *Ariodante* (CG 8.1.35) and *Alcina* (CG 16.4.35). Handel still had Strada for his heroines. He composed with feverish energy; during his three seasons at Covent Garden he wrote six operas, completing three in succession during the closing months of 1736.[2] As a result of these desperate efforts, he had a mild stroke which paralysed his right arm, and he had to spend the summer of 1737 abroad taking the waters at Aachen. He made a remarkable recovery.

Failing finances coupled with the stroke must have made Handel wonder if all the effort was worth his while. Also he was giving increasing thought to another form of composition, oratorio. With Farinelli out of the way, he did

[1] *Lotario, Partenope, Poro, Ezio, Sosarme,* and *Orlando.*
[2] *Arminio, Giustino,* and *Berenice.*

try his hand at two more operas early in 1738 (*Serse*, like *Flavio*, had effective comedy scenes), but doubts were still in his mind, and that summer, after beginning an opera called *Imeneo*, he uncharacteristically laid it aside and wrote *Saul* and *Israel in Egypt* instead. As we shall see, he was influenced by the success of a burlesque English opera, *The Dragon of Wantley*, which so turned people against Italian opera that there was none at all in London for two of the next three seasons. Handel preferred to offer oratorios and odes, to the great advantage of his bank balance. His final fling in the world of opera was in 1740–1. He finished *Imeneo* and wrote his last opera, *Deidamia* (LIF 10.1.41). They were not greatly liked, and he spent the rest of his career composing profitable oratorios.

2 THE 'ENGLISH OPERAS' OF LAMPE, SMITH, AND ARNE

If Handel could not make serious opera pay, it was not much to be expected that untried English composers should do so. Nevertheless the experiments of 1732–3 were praiseworthy. One of the prime movers in these experiments was Henry Carey, whose gentle satire at the expense of Italian opera lovers and Italian castrati was quoted a few pages back. He was no more than a minor poet, but on musical subjects, his favourite, he was very readable. In spite of his ambitions to restore English Opera at the expense of the Italian, he never attacked Handel and he was never jealous of him. Indeed he subscribed to most of the Handel operas published in the late 1720s, perhaps for purposes of self-education, and the eulogy of Handel among his poems sounds wholly sincere. He also wrote brief verse commendations about Pepusch (a shade unenthusiastic), Geminiani, Galliard, Roseingrave, Shuttleworth, Lampe, Stanley, Dubourg, Hayden ('the late'), and 'Linnert, commonly called Westen'. He liked his fellow men, and his wit is almost always directed at institutions and classes of people rather than at individuals. He was much more genial than Gay.

The commendation of Lampe dates from 1726,[1] and it is strange that Carey should call him 'my learned friend' at a time when Lampe is not known to have composed anything. Indeed he can only recently have arrived from his native Germany. Still in his early twenties, he joined the orchestra at the King's Theatre as a bassoon player, and he remained in Britain for the rest of his life.

Thomas Arne, also involved in the 'English Opera' experiment, was even younger than Lampe. His father was an upholsterer in Covent Garden, and he claimed to have been educated at Eton, though there is doubt about this. He was a pupil of Geminiani, as Burney reveals in his unpublished reminiscences.[2] He and Lampe became brothers-in-law, for each later married a daughter of the London organist, Charles Young. Both girls were famous for their singing, as

[1] See the dedication in Carey's *The Dragon of Wantley*.
[2] BM Add. 48345, f. 4.

were several other Miss Youngs later in the century. With Arne's sister yet
another notable singer, confusion can best be checked with a family tree.

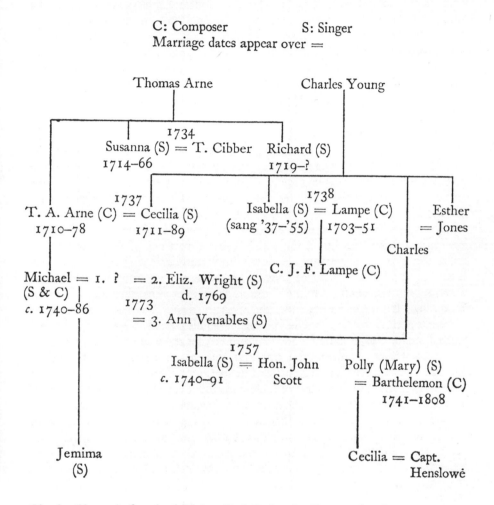

C: Composer   S: Singer
Marriage dates appear over =

Charles Young's fourth child is called Esther by Burney, but her name may
have been Mary. The confusion of the Miss Youngs is the less in that they all
usually sang under their married names after the dates indicated. Richard and
Michael were both called 'Master Arne' when young. Burney says Michael
was illegitimate.[1]

The other foreign composer besides Lampe was John Christopher Smith,
and it may be that he did not regard himself as a foreigner. In 1720 when he was
eight he was brought from Germany to England by his similarly-named father,

---

[1] For much of this information I am indebted to various writings by Mollie Sands.

Handel's friend and assistant, and with brief intervals he remained in England for the rest of his long life; he did not die until 1795. The elder Smith, who died in 1763, is remembered as Handel's indefatigable copyist, and as his amanuensis during the final years of blindness. The son had ambitions as a composer, studying the rudiments of music with Handel himself from his thirteenth year, and later composition with Roseingrave, with whom he lived in his late teens. His teachers gave him a professionalism denied to most English composers of the time, but they could not give him sufficient individuality. His music is best when it is most Handelian, whereas Arne's is best when it is least Handelian.

In less than fifteen months London was given no less than seven new full-length fully-composed English operas—almost as many as were staged there in all the remaining years of the century put together. The previous example was Galliard's *Circe* of 1719, and because of the failure of the venture no more were put on afterwards at the playhouses for a quarter of a century. The failure was predictable, with Italian opera still mesmerizing the moneyed classes; contributory causes were the shabby unfashionable theatres at which the English operas had to be staged, and the youth and inexperience of those who wrote them. In 1732 Lampe was 29, Arne 22, and Smith 20. Carey was older, but it seems to have been recognized that he lacked sufficient status as a composer, and his work was confined to the librettos. Today Arne has far more of a reputation than Lampe or Smith, and rightly, but it must be stressed that his merits were not noticed until 1738 when he composed his *Comus*. It was so many years since England had produced a good composer that the event was not expected.

Arne's father organized and financed this season and a half of 'English Opera', which began at the Little Theatre, and then, when Rich opened Covent Garden in November 1732, blossomed out at the now vacant Lincoln's Inn Fields as well. It has been suggested, for instance by Deutsch in *Handel, a Documentary Biography*,[1] that the two theatres presented English opera in rivalry, but there is no evidence for this. In one and the same season the composer Arne was involved at both houses, as were the singers Cecilia Young, Miss Jones, Waltz, and 'Master Arne'. Lincoln's Inn Fields was empty, and Rich was always willing to hire it out. The probability is that it was used when the proprietor of the Little Theatre felt unable to make his stage available.

Besides the seven new works, one old one was staged, Handel's *Acis and Galatea*. As mentioned earlier, this had been written for an unrecorded performance at Cannons about 1718, and it was given a concert performance, the first in London, on 26 March 1731. The elder Arne had the excellent idea of having it acted, with his son directing the performance from the harpsichord and his daughter singing the part of Galatea. Handel so little approved of the idea that he hurriedly put on four rival concert performances at the King's Theatre, sung in a mixture of English and Italian in front of a backcloth depicting

[1] p. 297.

a Rural Prospect, with Rocks, Groves, Fountains, and Grotto's; amongst which will be disposed a Chorus of Nymphs and Shepherds, the Habits and every other Decoration suited to the Subject.

It is tantalizing that, having gone so far, he should have added 'There will be no Action on the Stage'. He had in fact been driven into denying the work's obvious suitability for the stage by what he regarded as an act of piracy.

At this point it may be helpful to list the English Operas under discussion, with the librettist's name first:

Amelia (LT 13.3.32); Carey and Lampe; 10 perfs., and 2 the next season.
Acis and Galatea (LT 17.5.32); Gay and Handel; 2 perfs.
Britannia (LT 16.11.32); Lediard and Lampe; 4 perfs.
Teraminta (LIF 20.11.32); Carey and Smith; 3 perfs.
Dione (LT 23.2.33); Gay and Lampe; 3 perfs.
Rosamond (LIF 7.3.33); Addison and Arne; 6 perfs.[1]
Ulysses (LIF 16.4.33); Humphreys and Smith; 1 perf.
The Opera of Operas (LT 31.5.33); Fielding (*et al.*) and Arne; 11 perfs.

The first and last of these can be counted successes, but the rest all had disappointing receptions. It will be noticed that the venture began at the tail-end of one season at the Little Theatre, and in the following season spread to two theatres with three productions at each. *The Opera of Operas*, the first burlesque opera, will be considered in the next section. The others require attention here, though not at any length, for so little of the music survives. Hardly any of it got into print.

Carey seems to have been so over-awed by the task of writing the libretto of *Amelia*, that his sense of humour deserted him. The plot has all the improbability of those set by Handel and the Italians. Casimir, a Hungarian prince, is captured by the Turks. Amelia, his faithful wife, sets out in Turkish disguise to rescue him, innocently accompanied by a friend, Rodolpho. They succeed, but Casimir, too easily persuaded of a guilty liaison between the rescuers, sentences both of them to death. The opera ends with the situation mocked by Gay, the last-minute reprieve. Amelia sings her final aria on the scaffold, 'The Executioner prepares to strike', and in the nick of time Casimir changes his mind and all ends happily. Carey was hardly the man to inject any life into such stuff, though it may well have seemed to him that no other kind of opera was possible. We with our hind-sight may condemn him for not writing a genuinely tragic libretto or a full-scale comic one, but at the time such librettos were unknown. The age was inimical to tragedy, and scarcely any eighteenth-century opera in any country tries to deal realistically with tragic emotions or ends unhappily. As for full-length comic opera, even the Italians had scarcely begun on it, and

---

[1] Cummings incorrectly gave the production eleven performances and described it as a great success; it was a moderate one.

though we can instance Carey's *The Contrivances* as ideal material for the sort of comic operas that were written in the latter half of the century, we cannot blame him for leaving it as a spoken play with incidental songs at the time when he wrote it.

Of Lampe's music for *Amelia* only two songs survive, and according to BUCEM these are to be found only in the Mitchell Library, Glasgow. As with most of the operas listed above, the music was advertised as being in the Italian manner, and it was offered as an attraction that the performers had 'never yet appeared in Public'. Arne's sister, Susanna, was eighteen at the time of her début as Amelia.

No music at all survives from Lampe's next opera, *Britannia*. Arne's future wife, Cecilia Young, made her début in the title role, Mrs. Seedo doubled Victory, Concord and Peace, while Gustav Waltz, previously the Turkish commander in *Amelia* and Polyphemus in *Acis*, doubled Mars and Honour. The names of such characters can offer little hope of enjoyment to us today, and the libretto is unlikely to be admired except by those who have read later and worse ones about Britannia. But it is in fact of some interest, as is its author, and together they were the subjects of a series of articles in *Theatre Notebook* in 1948, to which I am largely indebted for what follows.

Thomas Lediard, London-born in 1684, had been on the Duke of Marlborough's staff in Saxony during the 1707 negotiations with Charles XII of Sweden, and from 1724 he was secretary to the British envoy in Hamburg, by which time he had fluent German. It happened that the British envoy was one of the proprietors of the Hamburg opera house, and for six years Lediard, who seems to have had some training as an architect, designed much of the scenery there. In 1725 he made the first German translation of Handel's *Giulio Cesare*, and his settings for the Hamburg production were published, as also his representations for other dramatic occasions of London's river-front and Oxford's gleaming spires. Lediard's speciality was what he called 'The Transparent Theatre', first attempted in 1727 for a Hamburg production in honour of George I's birthday. It was in Lampe's *Britannia* that he introduced this innovation to London, and the lavishly-produced libretto has a large pull-out of the architectural setting, as well as a long Prefatory Argument which describes his methods with no sort of clarity, and explains at great length the allegorical purpose of every character and detail.

The 'transparency' consisted, it seems, of a drop curtain of arches, the spaces between them being cut out so that the back-cloth could be seen between them. Nothing like this had been tried before on the London stage. The pull-out frontispiece shows what the audience saw when the curtain rose, with Public Virtue (Susanna Mason) on the right as a beautiful nymph, Honour (Waltz) on the left as a Roman hero, an equestrian statue of George II 'gilt in the Habit of a Roman Emperor' at the back (with Fame hovering overhead), and at the foot of the statue Britannia (Miss Young) on a throne, with Europe, Asia,

Africa, and America beside her. The figures on each side at the back were Victory (Mrs. Seedo) and Valour (Baker). The numerous painted figures high up and at the sides all had their significance. Lediard apologizes because Liberty, 'design'd for a Woman as usual', had to be given to a man, and moans understandably because the stage of the Little Theatre was too small to do his Transparent Scenery justice.

The chief, indeed the only event in the 'plot' comes at the start of Act II, when, during 'a Furious Symphony' and much thunder and lightning on the darkened stage, 'Discord arises as a hideous Fury', and calls on the inhabitants of Hell to upset Great Britain's flourishing tranquillity. At the end of the third act no less than five machines lower various characters from the heavens, while Discord and Neptune rise from under the stage in yet another, this one being drawn by sea-horses. Perhaps part of the pleasure lay in waiting for something to go wrong, and in such a production one would not expect to have to wait long.

It should be added that Lediard's lyrics are not without merit. His recitatives are written in free verse without rhyme, as were Carey's in *Amelia*.

Carey originally wrote the *Teraminta* recitatives in free verse too, but in his Collected Works (1743) the lines have been tidied into regular blank verse. It is these blank verse recitatives that are set in the Royal College of Music's MS score of *Teraminta*, and Mollie Sands has suggested[1] that for this reason the score could not be by Smith, who must have set the free-verse recitatives of the published libretto. No other composer is known to have worked on this libretto, but, supported by John Stanley's bookplate on the MS and the opinion to some extent shared by Gerald Finzi that the music was too good for Smith, Miss Sands hazarded that the MS was a previously unrecorded composition by Stanley himself. She also pointed out that Xarino's air, 'Laugh, ye Valleys', has the same tune as a minuet in Stanley's op. 1 'Solos for a German Flute', published in 1740, and she added that Stanley was not known to have borrowed from any composer other than himself.

This ingenious argument, which needs to be read in full, is almost convincing. Yet it is still possible to advance Smith's claims to the score of *Teraminta* with some confidence. There seems only one possible reason for Carey's rewriting of the recitatives, a singularly thankless task. I suggest that after he had sent the libretto to the printers, Smith (who would naturally leave composing the recitatives until last) implored him to make the words more rhythmic. Having done so, Carey preferred the blank verse version for his *Collected Works*. Against the view that the music is too good for Smith I would put my own conviction that in fact it is less mature and interesting than the music of *Ulysses*, Smith's second opera. Furthermore Stanley did borrow from other composers. He took Handel's Hunting Song, 'The Morning is charming', for *Arcadia, or The Shepherds Wedding* (1761), and he might well have taken a tune by Smith for

[1] M&L, July 1952.

his Flute Solos, for he and Smith were always friendly. There is nothing in the bookplate evidence. Stanley liked collecting music by his friends; the British Museum scores of Greene's *The Song of Deborah and Barak, Love's Revenge,* and *Phoebe* all have Stanley's bookplate at the start, with his signature across the bottom of it. (He cannot have been completely blind.) Stanley had been a pupil of Greene's, and in old age he worked with Smith on the London oratorio seasons. The great weakness of Miss Sands' theory, as she herself admitted, is that it involves the disappearance of a score known to have existed and the appearance of one for which there is no accounting. It is simpler to believe that the *Teraminta* score is by Smith.

There are, however some straws in the wind which may seem to point in the opposite direction. When Smith's *Teraminta* was performed in 1732, the hero, Xarino, was played by Mrs. Barbier, who also played the hero in *Ulysses* the following year. In *Ulysses* she is taken up to F, and the part is clearly meant for a woman. But Xarino is only taken up to D, and the part looks as though it had been written for a counter-tenor. Furthermore the surviving score of *Teraminta* makes Cratander a tenor, but in 1732 the part was sung by Miss Jones. On the other hand so young a composer as Smith might well have written his first opera without knowing who would be singing in it, and it was a commonplace for tenor roles to be sung an octave up by a woman if no tenor was to be found. It can hardly be a coincidence that the final choruses of the two operas are so alike. Each has only three vocal lines (Treble, Tenor, and Basso), each has trumpets for the only time in the opera, and each is in the same style, tempo, and rhythm.

In general the scoring of *Teraminta* is more primitive and uncertain than that of *Ulysses*. Violas are found in only one air, whereas in *Ulysses* there are violas in the overture as well as in half the songs. Perhaps a larger orchestra was assembled for the second season of the 'English Opera' venture. Many of the airs in *Teraminta* are charming, but one wearies of the lack of middle harmonies. One for Xarino is unusual in having a cello obbligato independent of the bass line; here is the introduction:

A brief account of the rise of cello playing in London is relevant at this point.

Although cellos were being made in England 'soon after the Restoration by such well-known men as Urquhart, Pamphilon, Rayman, and Barak Norman',[1] we lagged behind our continental neighbours in their orchestral use. Long after violins replaced treble viols, the bass viol lingered on, especially for continuo work, and I have not found mention of a cello solo in London before an advertisement of 22 December 1718. This states that the cello would be played the following day at the Stationer's Hall by 'Signior Pipo'. This was Filippo Mattei Amadei, who worked at the King's Theatre from about 1718 to 1724 and who composed an act of *Muzio Scevola*, the others being by Handel and Bononcini.[2] But I have found no cello solos in London theatre music before 1730, when Handel wrote one in an aria he added for a revival of *Scipione*. Cellos are also named in his *Deborah* and *Athalia* of 1733; 'Gentle airs, melodious strains' in the latter has a cello obbligato of real interest. In *Alexander's Feast* (1736) Handel even had a cellist playing the continuo, as well as an aria with cello obbligato, and the player he had in mind was Andrea Caporale, who ten years later published in London a set of cello sonatas in collaboration with Galliard. But Caporale does not seem to have arrived in London until 1735.

From all this, it will be clear that Smith's use of the cello in *Teraminta* (1732) was very unusual. He must have liked the sound, for the following year in *Ulysses* he marked the bass line below flutes in an Accompanied Recitative 'violoncelli soli'. Such writing presupposes a particular cellist in the orchestra, and it may well have been Cervetto, an Italian Jew whose real name was Basevi or Bassevi. The date of his arrival in England is uncertain, but *Grove* (all editions) favours 1728. In London he produced a natural son, James, who played the cello better than he did, and when he died in 1783 he was, by his own estimate, 101 years old .

The story of *Teraminta* is the familiar one of the prince, Xarino, who disguises himself as a shepherd in order to court the shepherdess, Teraminta. He unwisely takes with him his friend Cratander, who falls in love with Teraminta too. A happy solution is achieved by turning Cratander's thoughts towards Ardelia, who has followed them into the country in disguise. It all happens in Cuba. *Teraminta* was broadcast on the BBC's Third Programme in the early 1950s.

Little is known of Lampe's *Dione*. It was based on a 'Pastoral Tragedy' by Gay, published in 1720, and the five long acts, written entirely in heroic couplets, can be read only by the most persevering. Dione loves Evander who loves Parthenia. Accordingly Dione disguises herself as a boy to be near her beloved. Evander catches the 'boy' apparently threatening Parthenia, and stabs 'him'. As Dione dies, they are reconciled; Evander stabs himself. Someone must have shortened the work and added lyrics for the airs, but neither libretto nor music survives. It is unlikely in an opera of this period that the hero and

---

[1] Galpin, p. 71. But were they well known?

[2] Deutsch (pp. 146 and 168) has other references to 'Pippo's' cello-playing.

heroine died; the end was probably altered. Cecilia Young sang the title role. Gay's work is not otherwise known to have been staged.

Arne's re-setting of Addison's *Rosamond* was more successful than *Teraminta* and *Dione* but not by much. Again Mrs. Barbier played the hero, King Henry; his queen and mistress were taken by Miss Jones and Miss Arne. Leveridge was Sir Trusty, as he had been in Clayton's setting twenty-six years earlier. A newcomer to the stage was 'Master Arne', who doubled the Page and the First Angel. Old Thomas Arne had given his children a splendid opportunity to acquit themselves, but he did not live to see his eldest son succeed. *Rosamond* was little thought of until 1740, when the composer cut it down to an afterpiece and rewrote half the score. However one song from the original version, the only item to be published, became the hit of the season; on countless occasions Susanna Arne sang 'Was ever Nymph like Rosamond' as an interval song between the acts of various plays. Here is the song-sheet version; it can be compared with Clayton's setting of the same words on page 48.

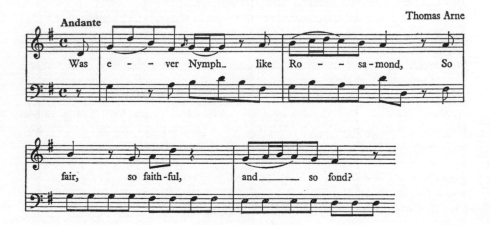

In 1740 Arne slightly improved both the melody and the accompaniment.

We have already noted that Addison's libretto for *Rosamond* lacked incident. That for *Ulysses* by Samuel Humphreys is equally uneventful, and much less pleasing as literature. In Act I Ulysses, returning home unexpectedly, tells his son Telemachus that he will conceal himself to test his wife's virtue. In Act II he conceals himself. In Act III he reveals himself; the suitors are routed off-stage, and we see them only as a chorus of ghosts. Humphreys also wrote the librettos of *Athalia* and *Deborah* for Handel, and it is hard to decide whether *Ulysses* or *Deborah* is his worst performance. Fortunately composers are less handicapped by dreadful words than is sometimes supposed, and Smith achieved his most vital aria to a lyric which at first glance has no meaning at all:

Eight bars later Ulysses joins in to the words:

> To view thee thus blooming,
> The Hero assuming,
> What Transports my Bosom will fire.

The fine tune and the spirited horn writing give this song a lift in performance
that one does not expect of a composer with so modest a reputation as Smith.
Elsewhere he confines himself almost entirely to string accompaniments, though
the final chorus has trumpet parts as well as oboes, horns, and strings. There are
as many as six choruses, all of them rather short and with only three vocal lines.

Nearly all the arias are in *Da Capo* form with very short middle sections. One in the first act for Antinous, a bass, is accompanied throughout at the unison, an unexpectedly effective device which Handel sometimes used when the singer was a bass and the tempo quick. 'Col raggio placido' in *Agrippina* (1709) is one example, and 'Presuming Slave' in *Samson* (1741) is another. But Smith would more probably have learnt the trick from the pantomime song given on page 80.

Most of the first act is rather uninteresting, and there is little to commend in the overture, but the second act is good all through, and at its best very good indeed. Penelope has two excellent songs, one of them a lovely Siciliano, 'O God of Sleep'. The act also includes Ulysses's aria with the horn parts, and it ends with a remarkable Trio for Penelope, Telemachus, and Antinous that catches the melancholy of the situation wonderfully well. Here is a passage from the middle of the main section:

Act III is less even, but Penelope again has two good songs. The first, 'Say I to his Commands resign', has curiosity value on account of the double sharps in the middle section, while the second, a 'suicide' aria, is the one song in the opera that has only continuo accompaniment. Inevitably the score shows the influence of Handel, though Smith had much less sense of the dramatic. But he was, after all, still learning the job, and the merits of the music are much more noteworthy than its failings.

Ulysses survives in manuscript full score in the Staats-und-Universitats-bibliothek in Hamburg, along with the scores of four oratorios Smith wrote in the 1760s, an unfinished opera of the same decade called *Medea*[1] and some minor works. They have been listed by Andrew D. McCredie in *Music & Letters* January 1964; the article reveals that two of the choruses in *Ulysses* were taken from Smith's earliest known composition, the Funeral Ode of 1729

[1] An aria from *Medea* is given in Coxe's *Anecdotes* (1799).

called *The Mourning Muse of Alexis*. Those who saw the 1963 production of *Ulysses* in London under Charles Farncombe will read with astonishment that their eighteenth-century predecessors thought the opera worth no more than a single performance. For a composer of twenty-one the music was of high promise. Yet it brought Smith no encouragement whatever from the London theatres. Indeed it was another twenty-two years before he got anything published, apart from some harpsichord suites. It looks as though he had no talent for advancing his own cause, and no luck in finding someone to advance it for him. One would expect Handel to have bestirred himself a little on his pupil's behalf, but he seems to have done nothing.[1]

It is unlikely that shortcomings in the music caused the English Opera venture to fail. The fact was that it fell between two stools. Those who worshipped at the shrine of Italian Opera saw no reason to desert their idols, while those besotted with the easy attractions of ballad opera found the all-sung variety tedious. At the time the rage for ballad opera was undiminished. *Amelia* was staged two months after *The Lottery*, *Rosamond* one month after *Achilles*. Ballad operas needed much less concentration and gave the audience something to laugh at. Silly stories might be tolerable in a language you did not understand, but sung in English they were recognizable as silly stories. Furthermore it was ballad operas on which the reputable patent theatres put their money. Covent Garden was opened right in the middle of the English Opera season. It was a brand-new theatre with fresh clean paint-work, and everyone wanted to see it. Lincoln's Inn Fields was old and faded, and most people had seen it all too often,[2] while the Little Theatre was too small for the grand effects serious opera needed.

It will be remembered that Aaron Hill had made efforts on behalf of English Opera soon after the Italian invasion began. In 1732 it occurred to him that the attempted revival would be much more likely to succeed if it enjoyed the collaboration of Handel, and it was probably after seeing *Britannia*, *Teraminta*, or both, that he wrote his famous letter to Handel on 5 December.

> Having this occasion of troubling you with a letter, I cannot forbear to tell you the earnestness of my wishes, that, as you have made such con-

---

[1] In his Will Handel left the elder Smith the breath-taking bequest of all his MSS as well as his harpsichord, his bust, and a portrait. The younger Smith eventually gave all the MSS to George III, which is why they are in the Royal Music Library (at the British Museum) today.

[2] Yet it seems that fops still found reasons for liking Lincoln's Inn Fields, as Fielding suggested in *The Historical Register* of 1736.

Lord Dapper (looking round the Little Theatre): Really, this is a very bad house.
Sourwit: It is not indeed so large as the others, but I think one hears better in it.
Lord Dapper: Pox of hearing, one can't see—one's self I mean; here are no looking glasses; I love Lincoln's Inn Fields for that reason better than any house in town.

siderable steps towards it, already, you would let us owe to your inimitable genius, the establishment of *musick*, upon a foundation of good poetry;
where the excellence of the *sound* should be no longer dishonour'd, by the
poorness of the *sense* it is chain'd to.

My meaning is, that you would be resolute enough, to deliver us from
our *Italian bondage*; and demonstrate, that *English* is soft enough for
Opera, when compos'd by poets, who know how to distinguish the
sweetness of our tongue, from the *strength* of it, where the last is less
necessary.

I am of opinion, that male and female voices may be found in this kingdom, capable of every thing, that is requisite; and, I am sure, a species of
dramatic Opera might be invented, that, by reconciling reason and dignity,
with musick and fine machinery, would charm the *ear*, and hold fast the
heart, together.

Such an improvement must, at once, be lasting, and profitable, to a
very great degree; and would, infallibly, attract an universal regard, and
encouragement.[1]

Handel's reply to this sensible letter is lost, but must have been negative. He
would not yet have forgiven the unauthorized staging of *Acis and Galatea*;
indeed Hill's letter arrived the day after one of the concert performances of this
work that he put on as a riposte. About this time he did knock up incidental
music for a production of *The Alchemist*,[2] in circumstances that are still obscure,
but he saved himself trouble by taking all or nearly all the music from his
Italian operas. He was not prepared to bestir himself for the English variety.
Rich might have talked him into an experiment, but by the 1730s Rich was
showing little interest in English opera, and indeed in novelties of any kind; as
we shall see, he passed the last thirty years of his long reign battening on endless
repetitions of tried favourites. What one would most have welcomed would have
been some English comic operas by Handel. There are enough hints in *Serse*
and *Deidamia* to suggest that he had it in him to write enchantingly in the *buffo*
style.

Hill would have preferred the serious approach. About this time he wrote a
long and complex synopsis for an opera to be called *Hengist and Horsa, or The
Origin of England*,[3] in which Vortigern, King of Britain, loses his enthusiasm
for resisting the Saxon invaders through falling in love with Hengist's daughter,
Matilda; he had previously been engaged to Merlin's daughter, Godiva. The
opera ends with Merlin giving Hengist a preview of later English royalty[4] from
Ethelred to Charles I, and finally

[1] Hill's *Works* (1753) i.
[2] BM Add. 31576.
[3] Hill's *Works* ii.
[4] The device was borrowed from Addison's *Rosamond*.

the back scene breaks away, and discovers, in effigy (as lately done to a great perfection) the whole present Royal Family, surrounded above, with angels, smiling, and pointing thro' the clouds; from the midst of which a beam of light shoots down, over the head of the king, in the centre.

This frightful piece of invention may serve to remind us that patriotism was becoming increasingly fashionable, especially in musical entertainments.

In December 1735 a full-length English opera set in the same remote period and similarly patriotic in substance met with surprising success at Goodman's Fields. Giffard's revival of the Dryden–Purcell *King Arthur*, renamed *Merlin or the British Enchanter*, enjoyed thirty-five consecutive performances. Giffard himself played Oswald, and published the libretto as his own revision of the original, but in fact it is very hard to find any alterations, and the text of the sung sections seems unchanged. Thomas Gray was especially impressed by the Frost Scene, and gave a long and vivid description of the lavish staging in a letter to Horace Walpole dated 3 January 1736. A great many other people must have enjoyed the opera too, and one wonders if waning interest in ballad opera explains its success. It is tragic that Giffard was never able to follow it up. In the summer of 1736 he moved to the larger Lincoln's Inn Fields, closing his East End theatre and selling up most of its contents; he opened with *Merlin* which received another half dozen performances, but his hopes of higher profits from more seats were disappointed. Lincoln's Inn Fields had lost its attraction for theatre-goers, and the move proved an expensive mistake.

We may here jump on a few years and pick up Smith's next all-sung opera, *Rosalinda* (4.1.40), which was specially written for performances at Hickford's Rooms,[1] where it was played half a dozen times in the early part of 1740. In a concert-hall such as this elaborate staging was impossible. *Rosalinda* has only one scene, and only three soloists, and the evening was filled out with a number of concertos. The plot is excusably uneventful. In John Lockman's libretto the 'Argument' looks impressive, but in fact it tells you not what happens in the opera but what happened before it began, the information being mostly irrelevant. All that occurs can be told in a sentence: Rosalinda, thinking her lover Garcia has been slain in battle, retires to a 'solitude'; Garcia turns up. The only other characters are Rosalinda's attendant and a chorus. Much more interesting than the libretto is the long, rambling, intelligent preface, 'An Enquiry into the Rise and Progress of Operas and Oratorios'.

Lockman, a prolific writer who combined an interest in the arts with being Secretary of the British Herring Fishery, starts his enquiry by tracing the sad course of English opera in the eighteenth century through the Italian invasion and Addison's *Rosamond* to *The Beggar's Opera*. He then goes back to Italy and the year 1600, shows off some knowledge of Lully and Quinault to prove the importance of a good librettist, and tackles the much-discussed question of the

---

[1] In Brewer Street near what is now Piccadilly Circus.

suitability of English for musical setting. Though Italian is sweeter, English, in the hands of a poet such as Waller, can be just as 'soft and harmonious'. In any case opera words do not always need to be sweet; for 'the rougher Passions' English, with its harsher consonants, is positively superior to Italian. Then, after unexpected support for descriptive orchestral music, in particular the operatic 'storm' (beloved of Rameau), Lockman shows surprising subtlety about the type of lyric a poet should write for a composer. He had sounded a number of composers on this subject, and they all wanted the 'most flowing' words possible, 'smooth Verses of six or eight Syllables that run in Iambicks.' 'In short, they are for such Verses as are most wanting in the true Spirit of Poetry.' Lockman himself was well aware that the very best, what he calls 'the Flame of Poetry', was not suited to music, and he quotes Addison's 'Behold the glorious Pile ascending'[1] as an example of words that defy the composer. As an example of poorer words that are much better suited to music, he then quotes another lyric from *Rosamond*:

> My *Henry* is my Soul's Delight,
> My Wish by Day, my Dream by Night;
> 'Tis not in Language to impart
> The secret meltings of my Heart,
> While I my Conqueror survey,
> And look my very Soul away.

Not everyone today would agree that these are the poorer words, but they are certainly the more 'soft and harmonious'. The alleged lack of softness or sweetness in the English language is constantly remarked on by eighteenth-century writers on music.

In *Rosalinda* Lockman had no difficulty in avoiding the 'Flame of Poetry', but the softness of his lyrics is too often spoilt by insipidity. Cecilia Young, now Mrs. Arne, sang the title role, and Beard was Garcia. Smith's music is not to be found.

According to Andrew D. McCredie there is a score in Hamburg of another Lockman–Smith work of 1740, the 'Serenade Opera' *The Seasons*, but I have traced neither a performance, nor a libretto. Smith had set Lockman's short oratorio *David's Lamentation over Saul and Jonathan* in 1738, and this too was done at Hickford's Rooms in 1740.

3 BURLESQUES BY ARNE, LAMPE, AND CAREY

In his book *The Burlesque Tradition in the English Theatre*, V. C. Clinton-Baddeley suggests that whereas satire is 'violent and angry . . . burlesque is never angry, because its criticism is directed not against faults of virtue, but

[1] See p. 47.

against faults of style'. Thus Buckingham's *The Rehearsal* (1671), though a burlesque in conception (and the first 'rehearsal' play), had 'too much of personal enmity' for true burlesque. On the other hand Thomas Duffet's *Psyche Debauch'd*, a skit on the Shadwell–Locke opera *Psyche* (1675), was a burlesque because it ridiculed a particular entertainment without going into personalities. (Duffet lugged in no less than five ghosts, and was the first to see their comic possibilities.) Similarly Gay's *The What d'ye call it* of 1715 is a burlesque, whereas *The Beggar's Opera* is satiric.

The fashion for burlesque in the 1730s derived mainly from an extra-ordinary piece called *Hurlothrumbo* (LT 29.3.29), for which 'Samuel Johnson of Cheshire' wrote both words and music. The ten songs were published in simple full score; Johnson had been a dancing-master, and he had some notion of how to write for the violin, but his basses are incompetent. However it was not the music that attracted audiences that spring for 29 performances; it was the mad fustian of the dialogue, the unmotivated plot, Johnson himself as the craziest character of all, Lord Flame, with a fiddle in his hands and stilts on his feet. 'See, see', he cries to a couple of girls, 'those two glow-worms how they glitter; these are Cleopatra's radiant eyes, just scrall'd up from her body, ambitious to vie against the stars: how vain is woman! Veil thy bosom: those heaving monsters fire me; oh that I was a child again, that I might suck.' And out he rushes, for no more reason than he has just rushed in. Is it total nonsense, or is there a fascinatingly original mind behind it all? No one was sure then, and it is hard to decide today. Johnson was probably unhinged, but that need not debar him from some degree of inspiration. Fielding and Carey were intrigued not only by the new brand of rubbish, but also by the polysyllabic names—King Soaretherial, Dologodelmo, Hurlothrumbo himself.

A year later the same theatre staged a more enduring burlesque, Fielding's *The Tragedy of Tragedies, or The Life and Death of Tom Thumb the Great*; originally an afterpiece, it was enlarged to three acts in 1731. It has been described as 'a dance on the grave of heroic tragedy'. As well as the text, Fielding provided for his full-length version an *apparatus criticus* in which he offered absurd alternative readings, and parallels between his own lines and the most pompous and ridiculous he could find in the tragedies of such writers as Dryden and Lee. The result must always be funnier to read than to see. Never-theless the occasional modern revival confirms the eighteenth-century view that in the theatre the text on its own can be very funny indeed. The bombast is at its most absurd in the mouth of the pigmy hero, and the wild improbability of everything that is done, felt, and said, has an almost surrealist quality.

It was soon appreciated that the piece could be very comfortably adapted as a burlesque of opera, whose vices were so like those of heroic tragedy as to be scarcely distinguishable. *The Opera of Operas, or Tom Thumb the Great* was first performed at the Little Theatre in May 1733 as the final offering in the season of full-length all-sung English opera. The diminutive 'Master Arne', the composer's brother Richard, played Tom Thumb, Susanna Mason was Huncamunca, Miss Jones Queen Dollalolla, and Waltz doubled Grizzle and the Ghost. Thomas Arne wrote the music, and the lyrics were added by William Hatchett and the notorious Eliza Haywood.[1]

The subsequent history of *The Opera of Operas* has caused some confusion. No fewer than three different versions were staged in 1733, and there was another in 1780 to which Arne contributed posthumously. The original Little Theatre version described above received eleven performances at the tail-end of the 1732–3 season, and these by no means exhausted people's interest in it. But its revival the following season was complicated by a row at Drury Lane of such dimensions that half the company walked out and offered their services to the Little Theatre. In desperation, Drury Lane, which had no effective manager until Fleetwood took over the following March, lured from the Little Theatre such actors and actresses as were edged out by the distinguished newcomers. Thus the October revival of *The Opera of Operas* at the Little had to be recast. Master Arne and Miss Jones retained their old parts, but Huncamunca was now taken by Susanna Arne, and Grizzle and the Ghost by Charke. All the smaller parts were differently cast. The opera was cut to an afterpiece, and in its new form it enjoyed another eighteen performances and rather widely spaced revivals every decade for the rest of the century. It was Arne's first success, and though it brought him only a modest degree of fame, it established the burlesque opera as a viable form of entertainment.

Meanwhile Drury Lane, though having no rights in Arne's music, found itself with a number of performers who had taken part in the original production. Accordingly Lampe was commissioned to write a new score for the full-length version. Another boy was found for Thumb, and Mrs. Clive, who had remained faithful to the theatre, sang Queen Dollalolla. Mrs. Mason, Waltz, and several others now in the company had to set about learning new music to the familiar words. The result lasted three nights, and Lampe's music does not survive.[2] He had now created four full-length operas, of which we have not a note, apart from two songs in *Amelia* that apparently can be found in only one library.

According to Baker the Hatchett–Haywood libretto of *The Opera of Operas* was published in 1733, and he describes it as 'no more than Fielding's *Tragedy of Tragedies* . . . transformed into an opera, by converting some passages of it into songs, and setting the whole to music'. Allardyce Nicoll mentions two librettos of this year, one of which he certainly saw for he comments on Lampe as the composer. I have failed to find a copy of either of them. It seems certain that Arne and Lampe set the same text, and the lyrics can be found in Arne's

---

[1] In *The Dunciad* Miss Haywood is handled with contempt (Book II from line 157); Pope describes her as 'of majestic size, With cow-like udders, and with oxlike eyes', hints at two illegitimate babies, and makes her the prize in a memorably indecent contest, one of several held in honour of the King of Dulness.

[2] First performance 7.11.33.

vocal score. Like Lampe's music, Arne's was advertised as being 'after the Italian Manner', and the sixteen short songs were published anonymously in sheet form. They are not in their correct order. Usually it is a simple matter to find blank verse lines in Fielding which a particular lyric paraphrases, but in some cases guess work is required. Thus the King's minuet song

> A Monarch when his People's gone
> Wou'd look but awk'ard on a Throne . . .
> What signifies it to survive
> When only thou art left alive?

must come last of all, though there are no corresponding words in Fielding, and the song is placed in the very middle of the vocal score.

It is hard to uncover any trace of burlesque in Arne's undistinguished music other than the presence in many songs of a coloratura passage, sometimes to an absurd word. We should not expect too much of the musical contribution to an eighteenth-century burlesque. The best of all, *The Dragon of Wantley*, was admired by the young Lord Wentworth because the music was 'excessive pretty'; in other words, he took it seriously.[1] Yet Carey in his preface praises Lampe for making it 'as grand and pompous as possible'. If a reasonably intelligent listener in the 1730s could miss the burlesque intention, we today, unfamiliar with the musical climate of the time, are even less likely to notice such touches of parody as there were. In the main the laughs must have come from the silly words and from the way in which they were sung; there is evidence that individual Italian singers were sometimes aped. An aria with absurd words sung in exaggerated style might be funny not so much in spite of a 'straight' setting as because of it.

Carey must have welcomed the new taste for burlesque, for it suited his talents admirably. Just before writing his 'ballad opera' *The Honest Yorkshireman*, he enjoyed concocting the words and music of *Chrononhotonthologos* (LT 22.2.34), described as 'the most Tragical Tragedy that ever was Tragediz'd by any Company of Tragedians'. There are even more murders and sudden deaths at the end than in *Hamlet*. In spite of its great success the music was never published,[2] no doubt because so much of it was already well known. Thus in Scene ii a 'Fidler' enters and says to the Queen in a suitably highbrow voice:

> *Fidler*: Thus to your Majesty, says the suppliant Muse:
> Wou'd you a S O L O or S O N A T A chuse;
> Or bold *Concerto* or soft *Siciliano*,
> *Alla Francese overo in Gusto Romano*?
> When you command, 'tis done as soon as spoke.
> *Queen*: A civil Fellow!—play us the *Black Joak*.

[1] Deutsch, p. 449.
[2] Some editions of the text include four 'traditional' tunes given on a single page; for instance the first edition, which was published as by 'Benjamin Bounce'.

The Whole court then starts capering to the lowbrow little tune that had been used as an interval dance for years.[1] For a burlesque of the traditional *scène de sommeil* we may turn to a scene not given in all editions in which the king, Chrononhotonthologos, lies asleep.

> *Rough Musick. viz.: Salt-boxes and Rolling-pins, Grid-irons and Tongs; Sow-Gelders Horns, Marrow-Bones and Cleavers etc. etc. He wakes.*
> *Chron*: What heav'nly Sounds are these that charm my Ears!
> Sure 'tis the Musick of the tuneful Spheres.

A cleaver is a butcher's chopper, and it also makes absurd music on marrow-bones in the last act of Fielding's *The Author's Farce*. Carey made fun of both pantomimes and operas—notably of the operatic Prison Scene. Queen Dollalolla has fallen furiously in love with the King of the Antipodes, who spends most of the opera in prison and upside down; he walks on his hands with his crown balanced on his feet (as shown in the frontispiece to some librettos), and he answers all the Queen's endearments with an unintelligible roar. Inevitably this prison scene has its vision and its machine, Venus descending to sing not the usual high-faluting aria but the silly pop song 'My Dilding, my Dolding' (Air 31 in *Achilles*). Carey's burlesque leans heavily on bathos.

Chrononhotonthologos is only marginally qualified for inclusion in this book for it depends in the main on the spoken word; though forgotten today, it is probably Carey's masterpiece. On the other hand his last two burlesques were sung throughout, and the first of these was a riotous success. *The Dragon of Wantley* was publicly rehearsed at the Little Theatre on 10 May 1737, and given its official first performance six nights later. As the preface to the libretto[2] reveals, it had been written some two years earlier and offered to 'Squire What-d'ye call-him, Master of Drury Lane', who kept it for months before turning it down. Fleetwood was known as the Squire because of his passion for race-meetings and gaming-tables, and he had also delayed for years his rejection of *The Honest Yorkshireman*. The reason for his dislike of Carey is unexplained. His rejection of *The Dragon of Wantley* was an expensive mistake, for in the following October Rich took it over for Covent Garden, and there it earned sixty-nine performances in its first season, seven more than *The Beggar's Opera*; it was given on fifty-six of the first fifty-seven possible nights.[3]

Rich's unexpected encouragement of all-sung English opera was due not so much to a change of heart as to the activities of the Lord Chamberlain. In the summer of 1737 the Licensing Act came into operation, and for a time put the

---

[1] See *Achilles* Air 12.

[2] There is a good modern edition of both *The Dragon of Wantley* and *Chrononhotonthologos* in *Burlesque Plays of the Eighteenth Century* (Oxford Paperback 1969).

[3] For six weeks in the middle of this run all theatres were closed because of the Queen's death. The first night at Covent Garden has sometimes been mistaken for the première.

Little and all other fringe theatres out of business. Rich found that the entire production of *The Dragon* could be had, fully rehearsed, for the asking. From now on the Little Theatre could present spoken plays only by the subterfuge of advertising a concert during which a play was offered 'free' as an extra item. Lincoln's Inn Fields soon sank into oblivion. Little more was to be seen there apart from Handel's season of Oratorios, Odes, and Serenatas in 1739–40—they were laced with his new op. 6 Concerti Grossi—and in the following year his last operas, *Imeneo* and *Deidamia*. For all practical purposes the two patent theatres had regained their monopoly. As we shall see, the security thus engendered had the result of making them much less adventurous over new productions.

The libretto of *The Dragon of Wantley* went into fourteen editions within a year. It claimed to be written 'after the Italian manner by Sig. Carini', a pseudonym Carey also used for some spoof cantatas he published in 1740. The prefatory material begins with a dedication to Lampe, who is addressed as 'Dear Jack' and who apparently thought up the idea in the first place; it was he who wrote the music. 'Many joyous Hours have we shared during its Composition', wrote Carey, 'chopping and changing, lopping, eking out, and coining of Words, Syllables, and Jingles, to display in *English* the Beauty of Nonsense, so prevailing in the *Italian Operas*.' Then comes the poem from which Carey derived his plot, 'A true Relation of the dreadful Combate between More of More-Hall, and the Dragon of Wantley'. I give the first verse and tune as they occur in *Pills* iii, p. 10; the tune has interesting folk-song characteristics.

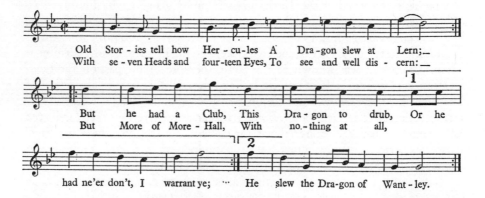

Pills gives nineteen verses. The scene is 'In *Yorkshire*, near fair *Rotherham*,' and the locals plead with More to save them from the dragon. More refuses their offer of 'goods'; all he wants by way of return is 'a fair Maid of Sixteen that's brisk, And smiles about the Mouth' to anoint him at night and dress him in the mornings. He buys a new suit of armour in Sheffield, drinks 'Six Pots of Ale, And a Quart of *Aqua-vitae*', and creeps into a well

> Where he did think
> This Dragon would drink,
> And so he did in Truth,
> And as he stoop'd low,
> He rose up and cry'd boe,
> And hit him in the Mouth.

The Dragon retaliates by excreting over him. The subsequent fight lasts two days and a night, and at the end of it More kills the Dragon with a kick in the backside (Carey's word; *Pills* has the four-letter equivalent). Carey's introductory matter ends with a poker-faced puff exhorting 'all Fathers and Mothers, Godfathers etc.' to give this far from suitable libretto to their children as a reading manual.

Carey did in fact clean the story up a little, but he had chosen his subject well. Men would have read of it with the sort of grin with which, in the 1930s, they might have welcomed an opera called *Mademoiselle from Armentières*. He developed the 'fair Maid of sixteen' into an extremely tatty heroine named Margery; it is Margery's father, Gubbins, who calls on Moore to save her. There is also a cast-off mistress of Moore's named Mauxalinda, and she is quite as eager to kill the heroine as is the Dragon. Most of the lyrics have a pleasing inanity. Monstrous double rhymes abound. The characters, though sillier than the silliest to be found in Italian opera, clearly inhabit the same world, and it was Carey's good fortune that a particularly absurd monster was currently to be seen at Covent Garden in Handel's opera *Giustino*.

The first advertisements for *The Dragon* made it clear that Italian Opera was to be pilloried. After the patently untrue cliché that the work would be sung 'by a Company of Singers just imported', there was an appeal to

> any Chronologer, in what University so ever presiding, if he will communicate the precise Century Moore of Moore-Hall liv'd in so that the Hero may be dress'd in Character; but if the Recherche shou'd prove too laborious, it is resolv'd he shall come as near the Figure of the Divine Farinello as possible.

Salway, who played the Hero, was dressed like Farinelli from the first, though the point of this must have been blunted when the great castrato left London that summer, never to return. The Dragon was said to be played by 'Sig. Furioso (his other Name to be conceal'd)'. His other name was in fact Reinhold, the bass for whom Handel wrote so regularly; Reinhold actually sang the Dragon one night in the public rehearsal at the Little, and the following night Polidarte in *Giustino* at Covent Garden. When *The Dragon* was transferred to this latter theatre, Margery and Mauxalinda were sung by Isabella and Esther Young respectively.

As has already been mentioned, much of the music is unashamedly charming.

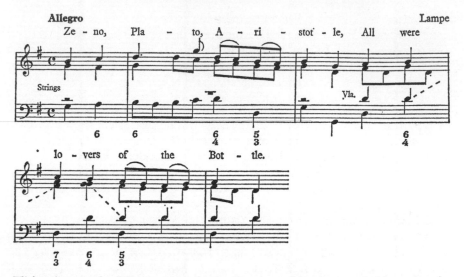

This aria, sung by Moore, comes in the first act and is accompanied by strings in four parts. Lampe must have realized that words such as the following would make their effect best when sung to perfectly serious music:

> *Moore* Let my dearest be near me;
> *Margery* I'll ever be near thee;
> *Moore* To warm me, to chear me;
> *Margery* To warm thee, to chear thee;
> *Moore* To fire me, inspire me;
> *Margery* To fire thee, inspire thee;
> *Moore* With kisses and Ale;
> *Margery* With kisses and Ale.

It need hardly be said that these eight lines are repeated a great many times. Little more than solemnity was needed for the Dragon's one and only aria:

But Lampe saw clearly enough which word needed coloratura treatment:

Lampe

After this, there is 'The Battle Piece', a March for trumpets, oboes, and strings, during which 'Moore gets out of the Well, encounters the Dragon, and kills him' as already described. There are however several points in Lampe's score at which we can detect satiric attempts of a more obvious kind. The Overture has an Adagio and Fugue whose inanities are surely intended. Margery's aria, 'Sure my Stays will burst with sobbing' makes one grin by its endless sequences, while 'Dragon, Dragon, thus I dare' has an interminable introduction which is funny because you keep thinking it must be ending and then it goes on again.

The music of *The Dragon of Wantley* was published in two books, one containing the songs and duets, the other the overture and choruses, all of them in full score. In addition the Royal College of Music in London has a MS full score which includes the recitatives as well; it gives some of the songs, notably Mauxalinda's, in keys quite different from those in the published version. Most of the songs are scored for strings alone; one has the addition of flutes and two the addition of oboes; more than half are in *Da Capo* form. One of the choruses, 'Or else this cursed Dragon will plunder our Houses', takes the form of a fugue of unexpected drive and solidity. Some of the choruses require horns, trumpets, and drums.

So popular was *The Dragon* that it enjoyed the rare distinction of being pirated by the rival house. Drury Lane put it on in May 1738 acted 'by Lilliputians', as did Bartholomew Fair that summer. In 1747 the same theatre staged a successful adult production with Mrs. Clive as Margery and Lowe as Moore, but in general revivals were commoner at Covent Garden, where they can be traced up to the end of the century. Praise for the burlesque came from unexpected quarters. Burney much enjoyed it, and Lord Wentworth reported that 'Mr. Handel owns he thinks the tunes very well composed'.[1]

[1] Deutsch, p. 449.

Handel might have been less enthusiastic had he known how soon his own opera projects would crumble. There can be no doubt that the marked decline in the popularity of Italian Opera was partly due to the ridicule with which it was treated in *The Dragon of Wantley*. At the King's Theatre for three seasons from the summer of 1738 there were no Italian operas at all. It is scarcely an exaggeration to claim that *opera seria* as written by Handel and Bononcini was finished; it took the arrival of Galuppi and the *galante* style to renew interest in it. Carey must have realized that no lasting victory had been won, as is shown by his poem 'The Beau's Lament for the Loss of Farinelli'.

> Come, never lament for a Singer, said I,
> Can't English performers his absence supply?
> There's Beard, and there's Salway, and smart Kitty Clive,
> The pleasantest, merriest mortal alive.
> Let's go to *The Dragon*, good company's there,
> There's Marg'ry and Mauxy and Signor Laguerre.[1]
> O talk not of horrible English, said he,
> I tell you Italian's the language for me.
> 'Tis better than Latin, 'tis better than Greek,
> 'Tis what all our nobles and gentry should speak;
> Plain English may serve for the cit or the clown,
> But not at the elegant end of the town.

With praise for *The Dragon* ringing perhaps over-loudly in their ears, Lampe and Carey found the idea of a sequel irresistible. *Margery, or a Worse Plague than the Dragon* (CG 9.12.38) had three short acts, and the same singers in the same roles, though in the meantime Isabella Young had become Mrs. Lampe. The plot of *The Dragoness*, as it came to be called, follows hard on the heels of its predecessor. It seems to Margery that her bridegroom spends far too much time at their wedding bothering about the absence of his old flame, Mauxalinda. To escape her incessant verbal onslaughts, he runs away on his wedding-night to 'a Desart near Rotherham', where he is so fortunate as to find Mauxalinda. They renew their love. Needless to say Lady Moore arrives in furious pursuit, and only the selflessness of her father, Gubbins, who undertakes to get Mauxalinda out of the way by marrying her, allows the opera to 'conclude happily, according to the custom of all operas, no matter how improbable, absurd, or ridiculous'.

There were a couple of dozen performances of *Margery*, and by normal standards it was a success, but there were no revivals in subsequent seasons. The Dragoness was an inadequate substitute for the Dragon, and the satire seems less pointed. The music was published in full score, again with one volume for the airs and duetto, and a smaller one for the overture, ensembles and choruses.

[1] He played Gubbins.

There appears to be no surviving MS score to supply the recitatives. Lady Moore
has some fine raging arias, and Mauxalinda's 'Then come to my arms, old Dad,
old Dad' has a charming sincerity that was presumably intended. Two of
Gubbin's songs deserve mention. One is a hunting song with two horn parts
notated *loco* in D major; the parts include a number of high Ds. There had been
a spate of hunting songs in the late 1730s, of which Galliard's 'With early Horn'
was the most popular,[1] and the intention was probably to parody them. Perhaps
the high Ds were a form of calculated risk, the expectation being that they would
'break' with diverting effect. Gubbins also has a song with only continuo accompaniment, but it is far from conventional, for the bass line, marked 'violoncello',
ranges with a freedom seldom or never found in earlier English examples intended for the viola da gamba. Lampe's score is of interest in other ways than
those mentioned here.

Carey's strange career was nearly over. His masques will be briefly mentioned
in a later section; two short unpretentious pieces can be more conveniently
discussed here. For *The Coffee-House* (DL 26.1.38) he wrote four of the six
songs, the others being composed by the theatre's harpsichordist, Henry Burgess.[2]
Perhaps they shared the work because the songs had to be set in a hurry. Although there was only one performance, the songs, complete with introductions
and basses, were published in the libretto, which had been printed in advance in
expectation of a success. Burgess's are the more elaborate and professional. The
libretto was by the Rev. James Miller, who later wrote two similar afterpieces
for which Arne wrote the music, *The Hospital for Fools*, and *The Picture*. All
three were howled down; only one of them got as far as a second performance.
As Miller also thought up Handel's worst oratorio libretto, *Joseph*, it might be
expected that *The Coffee-House* got the reception it deserved. In fact it is
amusing and original, and offers a vivid picture of coffee-house life, with gamesters playing backgammon, know-alls talking ignorantly of politics, effeminate
beaux deploring Farinelli's departure,[3] and a poet waiting to read his new
tragedy to Cibber. This last is the main theme, and, a novel touch, Cibber
played the part of himself. Unfortunately the audience took the scene to represent Dick's Coffee-House near Temple Bar, and their howls were in defence of
its popular proprietress and habitués.

Of much more importance musically was Carey's last work for the theatre,
Nancy, or The Parting-Lovers, later known as *True Blue, or The Press Gang*.

---

[1] Introduced into the pantomime, *The Royal Chace* (1736).

[2] Burney says he used to play concertos at Drury Lane 'generally of his own, as
clear and unmeaning as if set on a barrel' (i.e. of a barrel organ).

[3] A theme people seemed incapable of leaving alone. One of the beaux has a
song, set by Burgess, which ends:

> O cruel Spain! will nought surfice?
> Will nought redeam this lovely Prize?
> Take all our Ships, take all our Men,
> So we enjoy but him again.

He described it, not very accurately, as an imitation of an Italian intermezzo. The only examples he can have seen were the 'Comic Interludes' given by the Nobility Opera at the King's Theatre in Farinelli's last season, 1737–8. Three of the four were composed by Orlandini, the other by Domenico Sani; none seems to survive. No other Italian comic operas, long or short, were staged in London until 1749; though Pergolesi was already dead, *La Serva Padrona* did not reach London until 1758.

Carey wrote both words and music of *Nancy*. There is no spoken dialogue, and the action is so simple that one suspects the piece was intended for concert rather than dramatic performance. Indeed it started life as several linked songs in one of the intervals at Covent Garden (1.12.39). The following March Carey gave the heroine a father and added a song and a chorus. The result was a very short afterpiece. The sheet-songs were published together in April. All that happens is that True Blue, in love with Nancy, is 'pressed' by Dreadnought, a lieutenant from a man-of-war. Nancy's father tries to comfort her, and there is a brief chorus at the end for the press-gang. The implied moral smacks of propaganda: press-gangs are a necessary evil, and loyal citizens accept their actions with a good grace. Carey claimed that the plot was founded on an incident he had witnessed.

The work was a break-through for operatic realism. Never before in England had a modern situation involving ordinary people been treated entirely in music. The situation was sentimentalized, but that was inevitable. *Nancy* succeeded partly because it was 'different', partly because Carey's tunes have his particular brand of fresh simple charm, a quality that deserted him when he set his sights too high. Of the four solo songs, two are strophic, as are also the oddly-named 'Dialogue after the manner of Horace' for the lovers and the final chorus. The plot is so simple that only Dreadnought needs any recitative. A vocal score published about 1765 has an additional chorus at the start which may or may not be by Carey; references to the Spanish War of 1739 are cut.

In 1740 Salway and Mrs. Lampe were the lovers, Laguerre the press-gang officer, and Leveridge the father. Under one title or another the piece had a humble but lasting success, notably in the 1770s when Mr. and Mrs. Mattocks gave it more than fifty times; perhaps it is significant that this was the period when Dibdin was writing his short all-sung 'Dialogues' about ordinary Londoners for Sadler's Wells. No overture survives. There is no evidence that Carey wrote overtures for any of his pieces, or that he was capable of so doing.

Carey's last years are a blank. In spite of his numerous playhouse successes he lacked work and sank into poverty. Almost certainly his death in October 1743 was by his own hand. In the last two theatrical seasons of his lifetime there were hardly any new productions at the playhouses, and in the three that followed no new plays at all at Covent Garden. Authors as well as composers were out of work, and it was typical of Arne's native shrewdness that he spent much of this period in Ireland.

Lampe suffered less from the drought than Carey, for his wife was a successful singer and he himself could always pick up money playing the bassoon in the theatres. Encouraged by his previous successes, Rich accepted *The Sham Conjuror* (CG 18.4.41), but when it failed he fought shy of Lampe for several seasons. The libretto of *The Sham Conjuror* was never published, and it is not known who wrote it, but much of the music from this 'Comic Masque of Speaking, Singing and Dancing' appeared in full score, and included a 'Grand Concerto' for oboes, horns and strings which apparently served as overture. It is of no great interest. The most attractive item is a trio, 'Love me—no, no, love *me*' in which Dingle and Dangle charmingly press their rival claims on the heroine. The conjurer was played by Leveridge, now very old. If he risked any tricks, he forestalled the conjuror in Menotti's *The Consul* by two centuries.

Early in 1744 Lampe composed two works for the Little Theatre, and though neither words nor music survive, it can be assumed that they were all-sung. There was no possibility of either enjoying a long run. At this period the Little Theatre was closed for most of the year. In the 1741–2 season it had been opened on only three nights, the following season on only five, always for concerts. Early in 1744 there was some increase in activity with both Lampe and Macklin interesting themselves in the house, presumably in some form of partnership. Anxious to play Iago, Macklin put on several performances of *Othello*, advertised as 'A Concert of Musick after which will be acted Gratis the Tragedy'. Othello was played by 'a young Gentleman, first time on any Stage', and this was Samuel Foote, later to devote his career to freeing the Little Theatre from the restrictions that beset it. Lampe's *The Queen of Spain* (LT 19.1.44) opened the season, though this is an imprecise word for some twenty isolated performances of plays and operas spread over several months. The subtitle, unsurprisingly, was *Farinelli at Madrid*, and according to the *Daily Advertiser* it was 'receiv'd by a numerous Audience with great Approbation'. Baker thought the libretto was by Carey's friend Worsdale, but the author may have been James Ayres, who certainly wrote *The Kiss accepted and returned* (LT 16.4.44). This is the first work I have come upon that was categorized as an operetta. On two occasions it was staged on the same night as *The Queen of Spain*. Mrs. Lampe, her sister, and Waltz sang in both works.

From September 1744 the Little Theatre embarked on the legally risky policy of presenting plays in larger numbers. Lampe preferred to offer what turned out to be his last opera to Rich, and because, apart from pantomimes, he seemed able to succeed only with burlesques, it was a burlesque that he offered. *Pyramus and Thisbe* (CG 25.1.45) received nineteen performances that season and fourteen the next. It will be remembered that Leveridge had composed a similar burlesque based on the last act of *A Midsummer Night's Dream* nearly thirty years earlier. Lampe, or whoever wrote the libretto for him, took a little from Leveridge's version but not very much, cutting the equivalent of Shakespeare's I, ii, but keeping Mr. Semibreve as the alleged composer of the spoof opera.

There is a brief introduction for the Master and the Prompter, and then Semibreve comes in with two friends he is anxious to impress, and remarks

> One of these Gentlemen having made the *Tour* of *Italy*, has but little Taste for our home spun, *English* Entertainments . . . I don't doubt I shall bring him over to our Opinion; and let him see, the *English* Tongue is as fit for Musick, as any Foreign Language of 'em all.

To which the Master replies, referring to Handel, 'One of our greatest Composers has been of that Mind'. Quince's Prologue, somewhat cut, is spoken,[1] and then follows the opera of *Pyramus and Thisbe*, beginning with an overture of four short movements. The opera is all-sung, but it is interrupted by spoken ruderies from the two gentlemen, much as in Shakespeare; they are not in fact converted to 'our homespun, *English* Entertainments'. In the opera itself Shakespeare's words needed little alteration. Sometimes a new lyric had to be invented for aria treatment, but often Lampe found what he wanted in the original; for instance Thisbe's last aria begins 'These lily Lips, This cherry Nose'. Because an opera could not end tragically, Pyramus and Thisbe are revived at the end of it, and this allows them to sing the Epilogue, a charmingly gay duet with horns added to the accompaniment.

The published full score is for oboes, horns and strings; besides the overture, it contains fourteen arias and duets, but not the recitatives.[2] The title-page describes it as 'A Mock Opera', and many more signs of musical burlesque can be found than in *The Dragon of Wantley*. The first aria is for Wall, and it ends with senile futility:

---

[1] With Shakespeare's punctuation; Leveridge, incredibly, had 'corrected' it.

[2] The British Museum copy of the score includes an accompanied recitative not given in other copies that I have seen.

Pyramus has a tempestuous aria addressed to Wall which delightfully parodies one of Handel's favourite tricks. The long orchestral introduction ends:

After Thisbe's supposed death, Pyramus has a splendid suicide Aria based entirely on clichés to the words 'O fates, come, come, Cut thread and thrum'. Not all the songs are so spirited; for modern ears too many are spoilt by an excess of the then fashionable Scotch Snap rhythm.

In the summer of 1748 Thomas Sheridan, manager of Smock Alley Theatre, Dublin, decided to devote more money and attention to music. He raised the orchestra to twenty-two,[1] and among those he engaged were two composers, Nicolo Pasquali and Lampe. No doubt Lampe was the more eager to try his luck in Dublin because of the prodigious success there of his brother-in-law, Arne. He gave several performances of *The Dragon of Wantley* and its sequel, with his wife as Margery, and he also put on with success his *Tom Thumb*, cut to an afterpiece, and *Pyramus and Thisbe*; in these his wife sang the male title roles. Lampe's *Tom Thumb* was popular for a decade and more, though it had found little favour in London.

Lampe's contract was for two years. In the summer of 1750 he and his wife left Dublin for Edinburgh, and Lampe died there the following year. In their later years they had become friendly with Charles Wesley, and Lampe had set some of his hymns to music. On 7 October 1748 Wesley wrote in his *Journal*: 'At two Lampe and his wife called, and were overjoyed to see me. I cannot yet give up hope, that they are designed for better things than feeding swine; that is, entertaining the gay world.' The Lampes were just off to Dublin, and they

---

[1] Sheldon, p. 130.

probably never saw him again. They may well have been converted to Methodism by John Rich's wife, Priscilla. When Lampe died, Wesley wrote a hymn as a memorial to him in which he again deplored his theatrical career:

> He hymns the glorious Lamb *alone*;
> No more constrain'd to make his moan
> In this sad wilderness,
> To toil for sublunary pay,
> And cast his sacred strains away,
> And stoop the world to please.

The Wesleys did much to weave the mantle of respectability that enveloped our nineteenth-century theatre.

4 PANTOMIME AND THE MEDLEY OVERTURE

At the same period as the burlesque opera, there arose a taste for burlesque overtures, and most of them were associated with Drury Lane pantomimes. Six Medley Overtures were published in parts in 1763; all had been written, and some published separately, many years before. The composers of the first four are named as Arne, Lampe, Charke, and Howard. No composer is given for the last two, but in the British Museum Catalogue Barclay Squire suggested that they were by Peter Prelleur. Only one overture is allowed a title—*The Amorous Goddess* by Samuel Howard, and this was a Drury Lane pantomime of 1744. Alone of the six it is not in medley form. Perhaps the publisher thought of the set as consisting of pantomime overtures rather than medleys. Lampe's example was certainly written for a pantomime; the music is identical with the overture to his *Cupid and Psyche* (DL 4.2.34), more usually known as *Columbine Courtezan*, of which a keyboard arrangement was published in 1735. This is the earliest medley overture whose performance can be proved, but it was almost certainly not the first. It is not easy to establish the occasions for which the others were written.

Hawkins tells us that the first medley overture was the one by Charke. This was advertised for performance at Drury Lane on 30 March 1734, just eight weeks after Lampe's, but it was not described as 'new', and I suggest an earlier date below. One by Prelleur, advertised as 'new', was given before the pantomime *The Emperor of the Moon* (GF 15.10.35), and three nights later one by Arne was played before the Drury Lane pantomime, *Harlequin Restor'd*. The Arne was thought such an attraction that it was advertised with every performance of this pantomime for several weeks. This was not the first version of *Harlequin Restor'd*. I believe that Charke also wrote a medley overture for this pantomime, as also some Comic Tunes, but he could not be called on for the revision because he had just fled to the West Indies to escape his debts.

The following is an attempt to unravel the history of this pantomime from information given in *The London Stage*. No Descriptions survive, and very little music.

1. *The Country Revels* (DL 17.11.32), 'A Grotesque Entertainment'.
2. *Harlequin Restor'd* (DL 14.12.32); every performance followed one of *The Country Revels*, but no character was common to both. A near-failure. Charke wrote some or all of the Comic Tunes and probably his Medley Overture for this version.
3. *Harlequin Restor'd, or The Country Revels* (DL 7.10.35); the advertised characters are an amalgam of those in 1 and 2. 31 perfs. by the end of the year and then no more. Arne's Medley Overture advertised from the sixth night onwards.
4. *Harlequin Restor'd, or Taste à la Mode* (DL 12.1.36); characters from 1 mostly dropped; a success for several seasons. 'The Comic Tunes in Taste à la Mode' were published, but the unique BM copy is imperfect; the only named composer is Charke. (This pantomime had no connection with *The Fall of Phaeton*, as stated by Baker.)

If the right conclusions have been drawn from the facts and implications, then the following is the order and context of the Medley Overtures, with one omission:

Charke	*Harlequin Restor'd*	1732	Medley Overture No. 3	DL
Lampe	*Columbine Courtezan*	1734	Medley Overture No. 2	DL
Arne	*Harlequin Restor'd*	1735	Medley Overture No. 1	DL
Prelleur	*Emperor of the Moon*	1735	Medley Overture No. 5 or 6	GF
Howard	*The Amorous Goddess*	1744	(Medley) Overture No. 4	DL

None of these pantomimes was in the repertoire of any theatre from 1745 onwards; the fact that the Medley Overtures were published many years later suggests that they were often played in front of quite different pantomimes.

Their music is surprisingly sophisticated, and quite different from the Musical Switch overtures that came in later. The Medley Overture of the 1730s was no inane succession of tunes, but a piece of ingenuity that called for quick wits on the part of the audience. Though all the tunes were well known at the time, they occur only in fragments, often in the bass or middle parts, and sometimes two are being played at once. Charke's overture, the prototype, begins with 'Dicky's Walk from Dr. Faustus',[1] and almost at once fragments of this are being mixed with fragments of the famous March in Handel's *Scipione*. This is by way of introduction; the main section is a quick six-eight. I have not

[1] See p. 89.

identified all the fragments quoted, but the following extract is based on tunes that are still well known:

(I have adjusted the bass at the start because it seems to be one bar out in the parts.) The tunes are: 'The Happy Clown' as used in *The Beggar's Opera* overture and as Air 47; 'We've cheated the Parson' from Purcell's *King Arthur*; 'Lilliburlero'. After this six-eight Allegro there is a short Adagio, and then the six-eight music is repeated. The Adagio is so remarkable that it must be quoted in full:

The tempo must be very slow, and rubato is probably called for. If this is a borrowed tune, I have not identified it. One wonders how the reprobate Charke came to think of marrying a three-four melody to a six-eight accompaniment in this beautiful way.

Lampe's Medley Overture is mostly based on more highbrow tunes. It draws on Handel's *Rodelinda*, *Giulio Cesare*, *Admeto*, *Ottone*, *Siroe*, and other operas too. But Lampe does also find time to combine 'Over the Hills and Far away' and 'Butter'd Peas' in double counterpoint of a sort:

Similarly he has 'La Folia' and 'Caro vieni' in double counterpoint. I take the latter identification from the keyboard arrangement, but the information it gives is seldom very helpful; 'Caro vieni' is not the aria of that name in *Riccardo Primo*.

Arne's Medley Overture quotes from the finale of Handel's Organ Concerto, op. 4, no. 2, in B flat, which was not published until 1738. But, according to Burney, Handel had been playing his organ concertos between the acts of his oratorios since 1733, in which year Arne probably heard the B flat at Oxford during a performance of *Esther*;[1] he told Burney years later that he had never

---

[1] Deutsch, p. 323.

heard such playing. Either he memorized the tune of the finale, or had access to a manuscript copy.

Arne's first pantomime, *The Burgomaster Trick'd* (12.1.34) had been written for the Little Theatre during the secession of half the Drury Lane company. Two years later he had a modest success with a pantomime for Drury Lane, *The Fall of Phaeton* (28.2.36), and from then on he wrote exclusively for that theatre for some fifteen years, producing, as we shall see, an astonishing number of failures.

The Fall of Phaeton had the advantage of scenery by Hayman, and the libretto, so far as it existed, was by Pritchard, of whom not even the christian name is recorded. The libretto shows three serious scenes of a masque-like nature, and two 'Comic Interludes' whose action is left undescribed; these latter were sometimes referred to as *Harlequin Captive*. It must have made an agreeable change to have the hero in a masque played by a man, but the hero's father, Phoebus, was given to Mrs. Cantrell. The only song to survive was published in 1741 among some of Arne's Shakespeare songs.

Fielding's burlesque of this entertainment must have been a good deal more lively. *Tumble-Down Dick, or Phaeton in the Suds* appeared two months later at the Little, and was described as 'A Dramatick Entertainment in Walking, in Serious and Foolish Characters . . . being ('tis hop'd) the last Entertainment that will ever be exhibited on any Stage'. Though in some respects a ballad opera—there are five songs sung to well-known tunes—this is primarily a 'rehearsal' burlesque, and it was invariably played as an afterpiece to Fielding's most famous 'rehearsal' play, *Pasquin*, with which it shares several characters. Mr. Machine, the author of the pantomime we are to see rehearsed, is earnest in his insistence that the first and last acts of *Othello* should be cut so that there will be due time for his afterpiece. The following rather ham-fisted dialogue refers to both *The Fall of Phaeton* at Drury Lane and *Harlequin Sorcerer* at Covent Garden.

> JUPITER: Hark'ee, you Phoebus, will you take up your lanthorn, and set out, Sir, or no? For, by Styx, I'll put someone else in your place, if you do not . . . I would not have you think I want Suns, for there were two very fine ones that shone at Drury Lane playhouse; I myself saw 'em, for I was in the same entertainment.
>
> PHOEBUS: I saw 'em too, but they were more like Moons than Suns; and as like anything else as either. You had better send for the Sun from Covent Garden house, there's a sun that hatches an egg there, and produces a Harlequin.
>
> JUPITER: Yes, I remember that; but do you know what animal laid that egg?
>
> PHOEBUS: Not I.
>
> JUPITER: Sir, that egg was laid by an ass.
>
> NEPTUNE: Faith that Sun of the egg of the ass is a most prodigious animal.

A pantomime that Giffard staged at Goodman's Fields in December 1734 and later brought to Lincoln's Inn Fields deserves a sentence or two, for it is one of the few early examples of which the Comic Tunes were published. It has the somewhat charmless title of *Harlequin turn'd Wormdoctor* (later it was known as *The Worm Doctor, or Harlequin Female Bone Setter*), and it is possible that Prelleur's remaining Medley Overture was composed for this piece, and that he also wrote the very feeble Comic Tunes. No Description survives.

Covent Garden rested so long on its pantomime laurels that it had some difficulty in getting off them. Year after year Rich relied on the pantomimes created in the 1720s by Theobald and Galliard, but when they offered him another, *Merlin, or the Devil of Stonehenge,* he saw no reason to go to the expense of a new production, and he turned it down. Accordingly they took it to Drury Lane where, having little of Rich's flair for such things, the company did poorly by it and there were only five performances. Harlequin was Faustus's son, and Salway sang the part of Faustus himself, a ghost; the piece was in fact another sequel to *Harlequin Dr. Faustus.* A Description survives but not the music. Rich, as so often, observed what his rivals were up to, and planned to go one better. With an operatic *Merlin* drawing large crowds to Goodman's Fields, he put on *The Royal Chace, or Merlin's Cave* (23.1.36) and, as always when he exerted himself over a pantomime, the result was a vastly profitable success. The material was by no means all new, a fact which must have kept down production costs. The Description, rather oddly published as a sort of supplement to Giffard's *Merlin*,[1] offers on the title-page the information that 'This *New-Entertainment* is Introduced in the *Old-One* of *Jupiter* and *Europa*'. A Frontispiece shows 'Merlin's Cave in the Royal Gardens at Richmond', a small 'Eastern' palace with thatched roofs and a duckpond in front. Near the start, John Beard, representing a Royal huntsman—it was one of his very first parts—sang the hit-song of the show, 'With early Horn'. Galliard, who had probably written the music for *Jupiter and Europa* in 1723, also wrote the new music for *The Royal Chace.* The reader may well wonder how the story of Jupiter ferrying Europa over the Hellespont is tied up with junketings in Richmond Park, and he will not be told by the Description. Once again Rich played Jupiter-Harlequin, but there is no indication of any comedy interludes and no obvious signs of plot. The entertainment ends with a laughing chorus for the Gods. The Comic Tunes were published, but only the first page seems to survive; the copy listed in the British Museum Catalogue consists almost entirely of pages from *Columbine Courtezan.*

Rich's last pantomime success, *Orpheus and Euridice, with the Metamorphoses of Harlequin* (CG 12.2.40) had music by Lampe, and easily outlasted an Orpheus pantomime Drury Lane had introduced in 1735. It landed Rich in some legal trouble, for John Hill, a voluminous and always cantankerous writer, accused

---

[1] Dryden's *King Arthur* scarcely altered; see p. 144.

him of pirating an opera libretto on the same theme that he had submitted a year or two earlier. Full details are given in the Preface to Hill's libretto, which does not make out as good a case for its author as one might expect. The climax was a public reading before a picked audience of extracts read alternately from the two librettos; the audience pronounced in favour of Rich. The truth was that all his life Rich had been filching ideas for pantomimes from rivals and enemies, but he was much too confident of his own flair to filch the details. With great frankness Hill lists Rich's objections to his opera libretto, one of them being that Orpheus's song to Pluto and Proserpine 'would take up to six weeks in the performing'. In all solemnity Hill took the trouble to ask 'a Judge in Musick' if this estimate was correct, and as a result he was able to inform his readers with an air of triumph that in fact the song would take only nine minutes. Baker devotes twelve ill-deserved columns to Hill's career.

The libretto Rich did accept was also described as an opera. According to Baker the author was Theobald, though his name does not appear on the published version. This reveals that the famous clockwork snake,[1] seventeen feet long according to Hill, bites and kills Euridice at the command of Rhodope, a witch whose love Orpheus has spurned. After he has finally lost Euridice, Rhodope courts him again, and being spurned a second time she stabs herself. In a final scene Apollo honours Orpheus for his courage. In other respects the plot runs on expected lines. Of Lampe's songs only the words survive. The Comic Tunes were published, but they are mostly very poor. They may or may not be Lampe's. There is no indication in the libretto of what the grotesque characters did. This was the last pantomime of any importance in which Harlequin was *not* identified with the hero, and it is probably no coincidence that it was also the last with which John Rich was closely associated. In 1741 he ceased to be Covent Garden's regular Harlequin, a part he had sustained for a quarter of a century, and, occasional performances apart, he handed the role over to Woodward, whom he had lured over from Drury Lane for this purpose. Woodward had the added attraction of being an excellent straight actor as well. As for the serious scenes, Salway and Esther Young took the title roles, Mrs. Lampe was Rhodope, and Leveridge Pluto.

Two Drury Lane pantomimes of the 1740s merit attention, and the first of these is *The Amorous Goddess, or Harlequin Married* (DL 1.2.44). It is not known who devised the action and wrote the words of the songs, but the music was by Samuel Howard (*c.* 1710–82). 'This honest Englishman', says Burney, 'brought up in the Chapel Royal, preferred the style of his own country to that of any other so much, that he never staggered his belief of its being the best in the world, by listening to foreign artists or their productions.' Howard must have counted Handel as an English composer, for his music at its best is Handelian in the extreme, and it is an indication of his high ability that he was able to imitate him so well. He had started his career as a tenor, but found himself more

[1] For a description see p. 92.

at home in the organ-lofts of St. Clement's Dane and St. Bride's, Fleet Street; later he assisted Boyce in the compilation of his *Cathedral Music*. Yet his compositions seem to be almost entirely secular. He seldom put himself to the strain of writing anything longer than the simple ballad, and it is strange that he should have given up theatre music so young, when his first attempts had been so auspicious. Of his pantomime *Robin Goodfellow, or The Rival Sisters* (DL 30.10.38) only one song survives, and three Comic Tunes published with those of *Orpheus*. (The cast consisted mainly of children.) But we have a quantity of excellent music from *The Amorous Goddess*. The overture has already been mentioned. Long before its inclusion in the set of Medley Overtures, it was published in parts on its own (1744), the first English overture to be so honoured for more than thirty-five years. It is, in my view, quite as entertaining as the best of Handel's.

In the first two movements Howard's model seems to have been Handel's Concerto Grosso, op. 3, no. 4, in F. The introduction is solid and noble, the fugue alive, its texture and interest sustained to the end.

Then come two binary-form dances, a delicate Musette and a vigorous Minuet, and they are among the most tuneful and captivating of their kind. The musette begins thus:

Each had more than one set of words written for it, so that they could be heard as songs. Besides the overture, the published score contains a number of good Comic Tunes on two staves, and two delightful songs in full score, one of them preceded by an accompanied recitative in G minor. This latter is very dramatic, and leads into a charming gavotte song whose only fault is that it seems rather too mellifluous for Hecate, the character who appears to sing it.

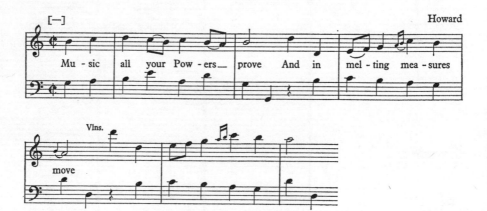

There is no indication in any of this music of parts for wind instruments, but these may have been cut by the publisher in order to save money.

In the 1780s the firm of Harrison & Co. republished a quantity of theatrical music from the past that was no longer available, often converting full scores into keyboard arrangements. It is hard to find a parallel for this in any European country, and perhaps we can thank the rather low state of music in eighteenth-century London for the mainly English discovery that old music is often more interesting than new. Harrison reprinted Howard's *The Amorous Goddess*, even though it had not been performed for forty years and there was no likelihood of a revival. Perhaps the overture and songs were still popular in concert programmes. There are many examples of eighteenth century pantomimes that ran for years without anyone taking much notice of the music. *The Amorous Goddess* is a unique example of the music outliving the pantomime.

A curiosity is *Harlequin Incendiary, or Columbine Cameron* (DL 3.3.46). The libretto says the music was by Arne, but none of it seems to have been published. As might be expected, the Young Pretender's invasion of England caused a good deal of disturbance in London theatres, and partly accounts for the lack of new productions, but when the danger was over it stimulated at least one novelty. *Harlequin Incendiary* manages to be grossly insulting to Scotsmen and Catholics alike. It begins by showing the Pope teaming up with the Devil (Harlequin) to destroy 'Old England', and telling him in recitative (or was it an aria?):

> And to delude all mortal Eyes
> Assume the Form of Harlequin . . .
> To Scotland's frozen Mountains haste,
> All cover'd with eternal Snow,
> And in that dreary barren Waste
> Bid Faction and Rebellion grow.

Columbine represents Jenny Cameron, a girl who was alleged to have helped Bonnie Prince Charlie, and Harlequin finds her in Edinburgh, where there is the usual trickery and chasing around. When a beau makes love to Columbine, Harlequin turns her bedroom into a sty and the beau into a yokel feeding the pigs. Bonnie Prince Charlie himself makes an appearance. At the end all is confusion, with a battle scene and the expected expressions of patriotism in honour of 'George our King'.

By this time those who felt pantomimes were an absurdity that should be stopped were becoming more vociferous, and, as we shall see later, when Garrick began his reign at Drury Lane in 1747 he tried at first to manage without any pantomimes at all. Even Rich, now that he was no longer the Harlequin, was pushing them with less enthusiasm. We may suitably end this section with what seems to be the first attack on pantomime in the theatres themselves, though it was not perhaps wholly sincere, for the manager was presenting and making money out of the very thing he was affecting to condemn. Our newspapers today are often similarly indignant, much to their profit, about sex.

Harlequin Student, or The Fall of Pantomime was presented by Giffard at Goodman's Fields on 3 March 1741. The scenery was painted by John Devoto, and the music (which is lost) was composed by Peter Prelleur. The chasing around described in the libretto seems even more futile than usual, but when at the end we are shown the usual concourse of gods and expect the usual masque-like conclusion, the entertainment suddenly changes direction. Mercury inter-rupts the action (a strong word for what is going on) by crying out:

> Forbear the Rites, mistaken God of Love;
> Such is the Mandate of your Father, Jove . . .
> Genius and Taste to *Britain* he'll restore,
> And Farce and Harlequin shall be no more.

When Jupiter arrives, he uses language that must have somewhat confused the original East End audience; the patent theatres might employ foreign dancers, but not their own Goodman's Fields.

> Too long, *Britannia*, hast thou blindly err'd,
> And foreign Mimes to *English* Wit preferr'd!
> Eunuchs to Sloth your Senses have betray'd,
> And British Spirits (as they sung) decay'd.

The solution, says Jupiter unexpectedly, is more Shakespeare, and the scene changes to a Monument to him designed by William Kent which had just been erected in Westminster Abbey at the instigation of Lord Burlington and others.[1] By the end Jupiter has rather forgotten that it was pantomime he started by condemning:

> Banish Foreign Songsters hence,
> Doat on *Shakespeare's* manly Sense,
> Send th'invading Triflers Home,
> To lull the Fools of *France* and *Rome*!

The audience may have applauded this advice, but could hardly have been expected to follow it. That season there were not in fact any Foreign Songsters in England to banish.

Nearly twenty years later we shall find Garrick staging a pantomime that extolled Shakespeare at the expense of itself.

---

[1] The expenses were defrayed by performances of *Julius Caesar* at Drury Lane, and of *Hamlet* at Covent Garden, for which the actors gave their services.

5
Masques and Pastorals
1734–1748

1 THE OCCASIONAL MASQUE

MUCH the best theatre music in the second quarter of the century occurs in the masques of Arne and the pastorals of Greene, and at this point a definition must be attempted of the categories into which Londoners put such entertainments.

The full-length all-sung works performed under the elder Arne's management in 1732–3 were called 'English Operas' because they were meant to be in rivalry with the Italian variety. Arne used the same term in 1762 for *Artaxerxes*, which was also full-length and all-sung. But the word opera without national qualification invariably implied spoken dialogue between the musical items; it was never used on its own in the modern sense. The proportion of speech to music varied considerably, and was at its most surprising in Theobald's *Orestes* (LIF 1731), which looks like a blank verse tragedy, but the title page calls it an opera on the strength of its having an average of one vocal item an act.[1] In spite of such examples, it is generally true to say that an opera was a stage piece in which the music was the main attraction.

In this book I use the term Ballad Opera only for entertainments whose songs were already familiar and mainly 'traditional'. No such consistency will be found in eighteenth-century usage. To take random examples, *The Generous Freemason* is called a Ballad Opera on its title page, but *Achilles*, a precisely similar work, describes itself as an Opera. After 1760 the term Comic Opera was often used for a musical entertainment with spoken dialogue.

Other terms had to be found when the entertainment was all-sung but only half-length, and for the first thirty years of the century such entertainments were so similar that all could be described as masques. These, as we have seen, began as interpolations in plays, but soon became self-sufficient, with or without pantomime interludes. By the middle of the century the pastoral and burletta were also established. The burletta was a skit on the masque, and mocked

---

[1] From Breval's ballad opera *The Rape of Helen*, Air 25, we can deduce that the music was by Pepusch, but none of it survives.

mythological personages. The distinction between masque and pastoral was somewhat narrow. In a masque classical deities played a major part and elaborate scenic effects were expected, usually with machines descending from the sky or ascending through traps. In a pastoral the staging was very much simpler, and the characters were mainly shepherds living in Arcadia. In 1704 Alexander Pope, when still in his 'teens, wrote four short pastorals, one for each season of the year, and prefaced them with 'A Discourse on Pastoral Poetry'. He suggested that 'as the keeping of flocks seems to have been the first employment of mankind, the most ancient sort of poetry was probably *pastoral*'. Since then poets have gone on writing pastorals because,

> by giving us an esteem for the virtues of a former age, (they) might recommend them to the present. . . . A Pastoral is an imitation of the action of a shepherd, or one considered under that character. The form of this imitation is dramatic, or narrative, or mixed of both.[1] . . . The complete character of this Poem consists in simplicity, brevity, and delicacy . . . (it) is an image of what they call the Golden Age. So that we are not to describe our shepherds as shepherds at this day really are, but as they may be conceived then to have been; when the best of men followed the employment.

Though both masques and pastorals were supposed to take place in the Golden Age, they offered opportunities for quite different degrees of invention. In a masque the characters and the story, if any, were familiar to all with a knowledge of classical mythology. In a pastoral the characters and story were newly created.

It may surprise the modern reader that either form of entertainment should have been so long-lived, but our modern enthusiasm for change, whatever the cost, was not shared in the early eighteenth century. It was a 'classical' age, an age in which assumptions were seldom challenged, and people believed that their way of life and artistic tastes were not a passing phase but

> permanent habitations, the final outcome of reason and experience. Such an age does not aspire to progress though it may in fact be progressing; it regards itself not as setting out but as having arrived. . . . And therefore the men of this 'classical' age looked back with a sense of kinship to the far-off ancient world. The upper class regarded the Greeks and Romans as honorary Englishmen, their precursors in liberty and culture.[2]

---

[1] Of Pope's pastorals, *Spring* and *Winter* are in dialogue form. The latter, subtitled *Daphne*, has two characters, Lycidas and Thyrsis, and it was set in January 1744 by J. C. Smith for concert performance; the MS is in Hamburg. For a good historical account of the pastoral in European literature see Cuthbert Girdlestone's *Rameau*, pp. 376–85.

[2] G. M. Trevelyan, *Illustrated English Social History: 3* (The Eighteenth Century), Pelican ed., pp. 85–6.

Innovations were acceptable only if they were widely spaced and mild in character. Sometimes they were barely intentional. Thus Arne transformed English opera in 1762 with two of his finest works, *Artaxerxes* and *Love in a Village*, but he was scarcely conscious of originality, being more bent on recapturing the past in a new way than in sallying out into the future. In his other great period, 1738–42, he composed two masques, *Comus* and *Alfred*, each of which has the apparent innovation of spoken dialogue and one of which has a faintly historical plot. It was felt at the time that 'masque' was not quite the category for *Alfred*, and it was later advertised as a serenata, as an opera, and even as an oratorio. As for the introduction of speech, *Comus* may have been forestalled by a batch of masques of which we know all too little, because, with one exception, none of the librettos were published.

On 15 March 1734 Princess Anne, the Princess Royal, married the Prince of Orange. The wedding, first announced for the end of the previous year, was more than once postponed, and two theatres jumped the gun. Of *The Festival, or The Impromptu Revels Masque* (LT 24.11.33) nothing is known except that the music was by Carey. Carey also wrote the Goodman's Fields contribution to the festivities, *The Happy Nuptials* (12.11.33), extensively revised on 11 February 1734 as *Britannia, or The Royal Lovers*, but still too early. The other three theatres managed to time their offerings more happily. The King's put on Handel's *Il Parnasso in Festa* (13.3.34), a serenata 'sung in costume but without action'; most of the music was taken from *Athalia*. Covent Garden staged *The Nuptial Masque* (16.3.34) with music by Galliard that does not survive; there were six performances. Least successful was Drury Lane's *Love and Glory* (21.3.34), given only three times. Arne's music is lost. The libretto by Thomas Phillips calls itself a masque, but advertisements prefer the word serenata, which probably means it was sung 'in costume but without action' like Handel's. There was certainly no temptation to act it, for the mixed assembly of gods and shepherds do nothing but sing the praises of Britannia and each other. It is typical of the age that all this adulatory fuss was about a plump pock-marked princess who, in order to get away from home, was prepared to marry a singularly ugly prince she did not love at all.

Britannia, or The Royal Lovers by Carey was much the most successful of these wedding masques. *The London Stage* can suggest no author, but in fact Carey wrote the words as well as the music; extracts are given in *The Gentleman's Magazine* for November 1733. These words, of course, belong to the first version, *The Happy Nuptials*, and some of them only to that, for there are forty lines of dialogue in heroic couplets between Geron and Daphnis, characters who seem to have been dropped in the revision. Forty lines seem too many for one recitative, and it may be that this rather than *Comus* was the first eighteenth-century masque with spoken dialogue. Carey published some of the music in his two-volume anthology, *The Musical Century*; more can be found in the first two editions than in the third of 1744. Besides a song 'sung by

Master Osbourne' in *The Happy Nuptials*, there are eight from *Britannia*, four of them rather primitive duets. None are of much musical interest; they aspire no higher than the ballad style and thus lack the expected quality of masque music. Nevertheless some of the tunes are rousing, and no doubt this masque succeeded where the others failed precisely because the music was simple and obvious. There were forty performances of *Britannia* in the first season, and twenty more the next, when pantomime scenes with new music by Seedo were interpolated; this was probably the last music Seedo wrote before going back to Germany. The pantomime scenes were known as *Harlequin in the City*.

2 GREENE'S 'FLORIMEL'

It is sad that Maurice Greene was not asked to write for the playhouses on this or indeed on any other occasion. Today he is remembered mainly as a church musician. His *Forty Select Anthems* (1743) have touches of genius, and the collection of Cathedral Music that he started in comfortable retirement (it was completed mainly by Boyce) is an enduring monument. Yet Greene did also compose operas, and though none were performed in a London theatre or published, more MS scores of them survive than of all the operas by Arne, Dibdin, Shield and Storace put together. Much of the music they contain is astonishingly good.

The son of a London vicar, Greene was small and somewhat deformed. He was born on 12 August 1696 and thus belonged to an older generation than Arne and Boyce. Musicians died conveniently for him. He succeeded Daniel Purcell as organist at St. Andrew's Holborn in 1718, Croft as organist and composer to the Chapel Royal in 1727, Tudway as Cambridge Professor of Music in 1730, and Eccles as Master of the King's Musick[1] in 1735. He held all these jobs except the first at least until he retired, and from 1718 he played the organ at St. Paul's as well. This sounds like a success story, yet Greene was never sought after by either the playhouses or the publishers. Initially he was handicapped by being a late starter. Though he probably helped with the compilation of *The Musical Miscellany* (1729–31), six pocket-size volumes that included some of his own songs, he had even then not quite reached maturity as a composer. Furthermore his career was fatally clouded by his quarrel with Handel.

It has sometimes been suggested that Greene was so imprudent as to support Bononcini when he and Handel were being set up as rivals in the late 1720s, but a much more likely cause of the quarrel has recently been suggested. Early in 1727 William Croft, organist and composer to the Chapel Royal, was known to be seriously ill, and in February Handel went to the trouble of having himself declared a naturalized Englishman. The likelihood is that he thought this

---

[1] He composed thirty-five Court Odes, of which about a dozen survive in MS. I am indebted to Dr. H. Diack Johnstone for this information, as also for the date of Greene's birth, and the suggestion as to why Handel disliked him.

would make it easier for him to inherit Croft's position. He must have known of the numerous princelings in Germany who patronized composers, and it was natural for him to seek a similar post near the King, the only man in England who was likely to finance his efforts in the German way. Croft died that August, but no replacement was made, or rather none was announced, because two months earlier the King himself had died. The new King, George II, was always a Handel supporter, and on 9 September[1] he invited his favourite to compose the Coronation music. This was only possible because of very unusual circumstances. The Master of the King's Musick, John Eccles, was elderly, and had composed little or nothing in recent years. Furthermore there appeared to be nobody in charge of the Chapel Royal. The choice of Handel for the occasion can scarcely have been open to criticism. But on some unknown date that autumn Handel must have discovered that Croft had been replaced at the Chapel Royal by Maurice Greene. This may well have been arranged by the Duke of Newcastle before George II had been crowned and without the new king's knowledge. There can be no doubt that Handel never forgave Greene for something or other, and this was almost certainly his offence. To stand in Handel's disfavour was to stand in the disfavour of his admirers as well, and that meant most of London's musical elite. Hence the neglect of Greene's music in the capital.

Even the new Academy of Ancient Music was pro-Handel. In self-defence Greene and the violinist Michael Festing[2] formed a similar concert-giving society, and like the Academy of Ancient Music they gave weekly concerts in a London tavern—the Devil's Tavern near Temple Bar. Because the room they used was called the Apollo, they became the Society of Apollo. The room must have been large, for it could accommodate a band of twenty or more, solo singers, a chorus, and an audience. The chorus consisted of Greene's choir from St. Paul's. We know little or nothing as to what was performed because the concerts were 'private' and were hardly ever advertised in the press, but there can be no doubt that major works by both Greene and by his pupil Boyce were given on numerous occasions over a period of some twenty years. These circumstances account for the large number of Greene manuscripts that survive, a number that seems at odds with the almost total lack of recorded performances.

Apart from his Odes Greene wrote six major vocal works, three of them dramatic. They are listed here with their librettists and the number of manuscripts that I have found. The dates are those shown on the earliest-known published libretto.

1732 *The Song of Deborah and Barak* (librettist unknown)	3 MSS
1734 *Florimel, or Love's Revenge* (John Hoadly)	5
1737 *Jephtha* (Burnet)	1
1740 *The Judgment of Hercules* (Hoadly)	

---

[1] Deutsch, p. 213.
[2] Greene's daughter married Festing's son.

1744 *The Force of Truth* (Hoadly)
1747 *Phoebe* (Hoadly)   2

The first work on this list is the only one that has ever been published at any time, and that was not until 1956.[1] Winton Dean himself has pronounced that 'Greene's *Deborah*, words and music together, is a better work than Handel's',[2] and the more one looks at the music of the above works the more one is astonished at the discrimination that has operated against Greene in his own lifetime and ever since. The music in his *Deborah* is remarkable for a quality hardly ever found in Arne or Boyce, though it is constantly evident in Handel. It is pre-eminently a dramatic quality. In the tenor aria 'Kishon, that ancient brook o'erflown', the entire accompaniment suggests the rushing of swollen waters. Towards the end of this short oratorio grief is expressed in music of unusual intensity, and the whole score suggests a composer ideally qualified for the theatre.

In his *Essay on Musical Expression* of 1753[3] Charles Avison discusses music's 'very confined powers' of imitation at length and with good sense, and it is noticeable that although he disliked Handel and avoids mentioning him where possible, he mentions him continually on the subject of imitation because 'no one has exercised this Talent more universally'. Avison distinguishes between Imitation (of ascent, descent, flying, laughter, etc.) and Expression, which is much more general. The former is intended rather to 'excite a reflex Act of the Understanding than to affect the Heart and raise the Passions of the Soul', and it almost certainly involves a neglect of Air and Harmony. The latter is an altogether higher thing.

Avison thought imitations of natural sounds should be confined to the accompaniment so that the voice could concentrate on Expression, and he holds up for admiration 'Hush, ye pretty warbling Quire' from *Acis and Galatea*. On the other hand imitations of movement are likely to involve voice and instruments equally; they are much the more hazardous kind. Avison cannot excuse Handel for 'condescending to amuse the vulgar Part of his Audience, by letting them *hear the Sun stand still*' in *Joshua*, and he dislikes 'Alexander's Nod' in *Alexander's Feast* (No. 7) because the music has been reduced 'so much below the Dignity of the Words':

---

[1] Edited by Frank Dawes for Schott & Co.
[2] Dean, p. 228; he quotes two extracts from Greene's *Deborah*.
[3] pp. 60–3.

In our own century this air must in general have been sung without anyone being aware that any imitation was intended, yet to Avison it was obvious and vulgar. We can profitably brood on the fact that, our susceptibilities coarsened by the excesses of Romantic tone-poems, we miss a great many imitative touches in eighteenth century music. Avison ends with a warning:

> The Composer, who catches at every particular Epithet or Metaphor that the Part affords him, to show his imitative Power, will never fail to hurt the true Aim of his Composition.

Such were the views of one musician in 1753, and it has seemed worth while to dwell on them here even though they do not account for the neglect of imitation by Arne and Boyce in their theatre music. Only Greene, of our English composers, saw its value.

Greene's first dramatic work was also the first in which he collaborated with his friend John Hoadly. Hoadly was the son of a famous Bishop of Winchester, and he himself was ordained in 1735 when he became Chaplain to the Prince of Wales. Like Greene, he was an unashamed pluralist, and he seems to have been more interested in amateur theatricals than in his many benefices. He is thought to have helped his brother Benjamin write *The Suspicious Husband* (1747), one of the most successful comedies of the century; Ranger was Garrick's most popular comedy role.

Hoadly was twenty-three when he published his 'Dramatic Pastoral' *Love's Revenge*, called *Florimel* on the MS scores. There are two 'interludes' or acts, and Allardyce Nicoll coupled the libretto with that of *Comus*, by way of praise. According to a note in the Sale Catalogue of Boyce's Music, the work had been written for private performance in the house of Hoadly's father at Winchester, and it may therefore date from a little earlier than when the first libretto was printed. The British Museum has a MS of Act II written by Boyce, no doubt at the time when he was Greene's pupil; it includes emendations by the composer. In this version Myrtillo, the hero, was sung by a counter-tenor; no doubt good counter-tenors were easy to come by in Winchester.[1] But two other MSS of *Florimel* make Myrtillo a breeches part for a soprano, and they naturally give Myrtillo's songs in a different key.[2] Both were copied by Martin Smith, Greene's pupil from 1737 to 1740, and they too have emendations by the composer. Greene must have approved of both versions, and it is impossible to be

---

[1] BM Add. 1598; similarly in the much later BM Add. 5325.
[2] RM 22 d.14 (in the BM) and RCM 226 (at the Royal College of Music).

certain which version was the original or which his final choice. The MSS that make Myrtillo a soprano may seem to be the later, but they were probably taken from a lost original, for they give violin obbligati in a much more violinistic key. For this reason they are slightly to be preferred.

The Royal College of Music has a copy of a 1737 libretto in which someone has written in the casts heard at two different performances. The first cast is remarkable for the fact that Greene himself sang the part of the Satyr, the second for the fact that all four singers were men. None of the surviving scores reflects this extraordinary situation, but we shall later come on one by Boyce that does; in the only surviving score of Boyce's *Secular Ode* all the soloists were male, even Diana and Venus. We must suppose that for some strange reason either the Society of Apollo or the Three Choirs Festival sometimes favoured concert performances with all-male soloists; it is known that *Florimel* was performed at the Three Choirs Festival of 1745.[1]

As in all pastorals the plot is very simple. Myrtillo hangs on a tree a song he has written in praise of Florimel in the hope that she will find it.[2] Cupid sees him doing so, and out of jealousy alters the name. Florimel finds the song and is mortified; she and Myrtillo meet and quarrel. In Act II a Satyr (bass) finds Florimel asleep, and pricks her with a dart whose effect will be that she loves the first man she sees on waking. But when she wakes she first sees Myrtillo, and all ends happily with a chorus of shepherds and shepherdesses.

The overture is undistinguished. The first movement is a kind of Allemande in binary form, the second has only seven bars, and the third is a brisk minuet. All three movements are scored for strings alone, as are most of the airs. But the Satyr has two good arias, the one with horns and strings in the accompaniment and the other with oboes, bassoon and strings. Elsewhere flutes appear briefly, and the violin writing is of unusual interest throughout. Eighteen of the twenty-two songs are in *Da Capo* form, which Greene had avoided completely in his earlier *Song of Deborah and Barak*. The fact is symptomatic of a difference in approach. In *Deborah* he aimed to arrest attention; in *Florimel* he was more inclined to lull it. The Old Testament situation had for him more reality and intensity than the pastoral one, in which artificiality was to be expected. In sylvan surroundings unhappiness should be only a dimmed reflection of genuine human misery and, except at the end of the first Interlude, Greene is content to understate it. We today may think that the music of operas should be more dramatically 'felt' than the music of oratorios, but neither Handel nor Greene would have understood this view, and in their own output the reverse is usually the case.

But though for the most part *Florimel* lacks the intensity of *Deborah*, the music frequently shows a sympathy for words, an ability to express them in

---

[1] Lysons, p. 169. The performance was in the 'Boothall', Gloucester.
[2] A mere five bars long, it can be found in *The Musical Entertainer* i, p. 2, *The Muses Delight*, p. 58, and other collections.

dramatically appropriate music, that is almost impossible to parallel in English music of the first half of the century, Handel's excepted. Here for instance is part of an aria Florimel sings near the end of the first Interlude, when she thinks Myrtillo loves some other girl.

Most of the music expresses indignation, but whenever Florimel sings 'on her believing Bosom die', the mood of the music switches to melting languor, as though the singer envisages what she describes. Handel set words in this essentially dramatic way on countless occasions, but Arne and Boyce hardly ever did. In their songs the mood is constant throughout, and there is only a generalized relationship between words and music. Thus *Florimel* is essentially operatic in spite of its pretty artificiality. After her 'indignation' aria, the heroine flounces out, leaving Myrtillo to end the act with a long Da Capo lament that achieves an almost Bach-like vein of deep melancholy, 'Blow, Winds, and bear me to some Grove'. It is typical of Greene's unusual approach that there is a 'wind' motive in triplet semiquavers, but that is a mere incident in music of rare beauty that could lift up its head in any company.

Each of the two acts would play for about an hour; *Florimel* is virtually a full-length opera.

3 ARNE'S 'COMUS'

Arne must surely have attempted emotional depths in his masque *Dido and Aeneas* (LT 12.1.34), but though it was successful it was never published, and not a note survives. It was a resetting of a libretto by Barton Booth for which Pepusch had written music in 1716; never again did Arne have to find music for a genuinely tragic situation. Indeed he seems deliberately to have turned his back on opportunities for dramatic music. The enormous success of *Comus*

(DL 4.3.38) was due partly to the lyrical charm of the songs and partly to the current admiration for Milton. Inevitably the music is undramatic, for in the original production the leading characters, The Lady, her two Brothers, and Comus, were nowhere called on to sing a note. The songs were all given to subsidiary characters and are thus irrelevant to the action. The same can be said of the songs in Purcell's operatic masques, and it does seem that in both *Comus* and *Alfred* (1740) Arne was looking back to the Purcellian masque with spoken dialogue. He may well have wanted to excuse himself from any obligation to write dramatic music, for he must have realized that his gifts were mainly lyrical. He seems also to have been anxious to raise the literary level of the masque. In James Thomson he found the only active English poet of accepted merit, and *Alfred* was the result of their collaboration. But for *Comus* and *The Judgment of Paris* (1742) he preferred to resurrect librettos by poets long dead because it was only in the past that he could find words of the quality he wanted.

There was a vogue for looking back at this period, and it was more pronounced in Britain than in other European countries. In part it must have been caused by the inadequacy of the present. During the second quarter of the century, as Pope and Swift approached death, it was generally felt that poetry was in a decline, and there was to be no clear-cut revival until Wordsworth and Coleridge published their *Lyrical Ballads* at the end of the century. The decline was felt at the time to be connected with the growing rift between poets and politicians. Early in the century Addison had been Secretary of State, and Matthew Prior had held a number of important diplomatic positions. Poets and politicians, when they did not trifle with each other's jobs, courted each other's company. They were no longer doing so by 1740. Sir Robert Walpole had been endlessly abused by writers of all kinds, and the rift was due to his influence as much as anyone's. Socially poets were sinking very nearly to the level of musicians.

The new fashion for delving in the past for librettos is well illustrated by the odes that were so often performed in November on St. Cecilia's day. In the 1730s Greene set the one Pope had published back in 1708, Festing one Addison had written in the 1690s, and Handel two of Dryden's from the same far-off period. In the seventeenth century all such odes had had new words as well as new music. Even concert-givers were beginning to look back. Little is known of the programmes given in the 1730s by the Academy of Ancient Musick, but by the following decade they were performing madrigals by such composers as Morley and Marenzio, anthems by Byrd, Vittoria and Lassus, and a good deal of Purcell that had been forgotten in the playhouses; for instance an act of *The Indian Queen.*

It was in this climate that Arne looked back to Milton for his first big success, *Comus.* In 1634 the songs had been set by Henry Lawes for the performance in Ludlow Castle. For Drury Lane in 1738 John Dalton, a young clergyman, rewrote the libretto to allow for a much higher proportion of music;

it was to be his only dramatic attempt, and on the whole he made a good job of it. *Comus* was the first full-length three-act masque of the century, and at the first performance Quin and Mrs. Cibber spoke the leading parts, Comus and The Lady, while the singing was done by Beard (Bacchanal and Attendant Spirit), Mrs. Clive (Euphrosyne) and Mrs. Arne (Pastoral Nymph and Sabrina). It is a tribute to Mrs. Cibber's remarkable improvement as a straight actress that she should have been given the leading non-vocal part, and extraordinary that she should not have been allowed to sing 'Sweet Eccho', which had been allotted to The Lady by Milton himself. Instead, the song was sung off-stage by Mrs. Arne, while The Lady mimed the sentiments of the lyric. At a much later date this tradition allowed Mrs. Siddons, who never sang, to make a success of the part. As might be expected, Arne's songs for Mrs. Clive are comparatively simple and never go above G, while those for his wife are harder, as well as higher in tessitura.

The music of *Comus* was published in full score but without the two choruses (one of which comes twice), without the choral ending to 'Now Phoebus sinketh in the West', and without the recitatives. The three dances are placed together at the end, and this practice was occasionally followed in later scores of Arne's, for instance *The Fairy Prince*. The publisher's intention no doubt was to engrave only such dance movements as there was room for without starting a fresh set of four or eight pages, and there is thus the possibility of omissions. However, judging by the librettos, all the dances in *Comus* seem to have been included. The missing choruses and recitatives are to be found in the British Museum's Add. 11518. This manuscript belonged to Samuel Arnold and someone has inserted three items from Handel's *L'Allegro* at the beginning of Act III. In the Musica Britannica edition of *Comus* (1951) Julian Herbage dates this manuscript '*c.* 1785'. Its existence means that *Comus* survives virtually complete, and surprisingly it is the only major theatrical work by Arne of which this can be said.[1] It is also the only one available in a trustworthy modern edition.

The success of *Comus* seemed at first to be ephemeral. There were eleven performances the first season, none the second (1738–9). Thereafter its popularity was constant, and by 1760 Drury Lane had given nearly eighty performances. There were others at Covent Garden from 1744 onwards. In October 1772 Covent Garden staged an afterpiece version contracted into two acts by George Colman, and three years later Drury Lane followed suit. A great deal of the dialogue was cut, but very little of the music, and London supported this much less Miltonic version with enthusiasm until the end of the century.

The relationship between *Comus* and Handel is complex, and to some extent conjectural. Cummings[2] thought that 'Arne did not compose the chorus music, but adapted several pieces from Handel', and he was probably led into this error

---

[1] A line and a half of recitative is missing; see Herbage's note on his p. 114.
[2] *Dr. Arne and Rule, Britannia*, p. 13.

by the likeness between the beginning of the chorus in *Comus* that occurs twice, 'Away, away, to Comus' Court repair', and the hunting chorus in Handel's *Il Parnasso in Festa* (1734); Handel himself had already used the theme in the first chorus of *Athalia*. But the likeness is close only in the first four bars, and Arne cannot have made use of choruses from *L'Allegro*, as Cummings may also have thought, because it was not yet written.

There is no doubt that Handel was led to set Milton's *L'Allegro* and *Il Penseroso* by the success of *Comus*, and in some of the items he aimed at an English flavour resembling Arne's. He wrote the music at the beginning of 1740, just when it had become apparent that *Comus* was to be a lasting success. Back in 1738 John Dalton, as a happy means of lengthening the original, had made Comus speak the first twenty-six lines of *L'Allegro* at the beginning of Act III, and in 1740 this passage was set by Handel in four sections:

Hence, loathed Melancholy	Accompanied recit for tenor
Come, thou Goddess fair and free	Air for soprano
Haste thee, Nymph	Air for tenor with chorus
Come and trip it as you go	Air for tenor with chorus

The last three of these Handel items are the ones inserted into the British Museum MS of *Comus*, and they are inserted at the point where Dalton originally intended the words to be spoken. It will be remembered that Beard sang the tenor songs in *Comus*. He was also the tenor soloist in the first performance of *L'Allegro*, and in subsequent performances of Arne's masque it must have been almost more than he could bear that the words of two of the most delightful songs ever written for him should be spoken. It was surely at Beard's suggestion that on 1 April 1742 Drury Lane advertised a performance 'with some additional Songs of Milton's, compos'd by Handel'. They must have included the third and fourth of those listed above, and possibly the second as well. It looks as though Arne complained, for 'Additional Songs omitted' was announced at the next performance. Had they been included subsequently, they would almost certainly have been advertized, but I can find no trace of them.

However, 'Come and trip it as you go' was being inserted in the rather widely spaced Covent Garden performances of the 1760s, as also in the successful revival of 1772, and the vocal score published by Thorowgood of 1764–5 shows that it replaced the Act I Dance (Mus. Brit. ed., p. 33). Later vocal scores put it in the same position. However the 1772 libretto has it in Act III when Comus calls on the 'sedge-crown'd Naiades' to appear. The song was always sung by Comus himself, played at this period by Mattocks. There is no evidence that any of the other Handel songs were inserted in the second half of the century, and it may be that the British Museum MS which includes them is earlier than has been thought and was made for the performance in April 1742.

The Bell's Theatre librettos of 1777 and later do not give 'Come and trip it', perhaps because it was never sung at Drury Lane, but they include another interpolation that is unexpected. After the air 'Nor on Beds of fading Flowers' there is a lyric sung by 'A Man' that begins 'Mortals, learn your lives to measure'. The words are those of a rondo song by Motteux for which Eccles provided the music; the ABACA structure has been reduced to ACA. The Song can be found in *Pills* VI, 160. It does not appear in any score of *Comus*, and there is no way of knowing whether or not Eccles's music was used; it seems unlikely.

New information about Handel and *Comus* turned up recently among letters written to the Fourth Earl of Shaftesbury.[1] The Earl was an ardent Handelian, and encouraged his friends to write to him about his favourite's activities. Two people took the trouble to tell him of some open-air performances of *Comus* given in the summers of 1745 and 1748 at Exton in Rutland, the seat of Lord Gainsborough. On the first occasion Handel was staying at Exton, being in need of 'Quiet and Retirement'. In consequence, says the writer,

> we were very loath to lay any task of Composition on him. Selfishness however prevailed . . . what should have been an act of Compliance, he made a voluntary Deed. . . . We likewise intermix'd the Poem with several of his former compositions.

In other words Handel reset some of the lyrics in *Comus* because Arne's settings were despised by the Italian opera enthusiasts of Exton. It is sad that what he wrote appears not to survive. 'Two or three songs of Arne's' were included in the 1748 performance, and no doubt had been sung in 1745 as well. In the latter performance (and perhaps in the earlier as well) Lord Gainsborough himself took the part of Comus, and 'sang the three songs made by Handel for the entertainment with the Chorus at the end of each of them'. Two of these were probably 'Haste thee, Nymph' and 'Come and trip it'; the third must have been one of those specially composed in 1745. One of the writers offers some interesting details about country-house productions, and it is strange to find Exton anticipating a famous effect in Chekhov's *The Seagull*. The performance took place 'a little before Sunset' in a 'grove'. At one end there was

> a Box with four rows of benches raised above one another and 20 feet in front. The intermediate Space between that and the stage was bounded on the sides by high trees. . . . When Comus and the Revels begin, the Back Scene was drawn up and behind it was another space of the same bigness as that where the Box and Theatre were, with a high Tree in the middle filled with lights . . . the most Romantick Fairy Scene imaginable.

Arne's music for *Comus* varies a good deal in both quality and style. The overture is of the 'French' variety favoured by Handel, and the fugue can be

[1] 'Unpublished Letters concerning Handel' by Betty Matthews, M&L, July 1959; to be read in conjunction with Winton Dean's letter in the next issue.

forgiven for being rather loosely written in the usual Handelian way. The counterpoint is completely professional, and in 1738 there was no recent precedent for a really competent orchestral fugue by an English theatre composer, but the piece suffers a little from a subject without much character or direction. The third movement, a hornpipe, is dull and charmless. Act I, though lacking any music of real distinction, contains some pretty songs in a style that seemed new at the time. Burney found in them 'a light, airy, original and pleasing melody, wholly different from that of Purcell or Handel'. It was a style Arne was to cultivate in the 1740s when making his delightful Shakespeare settings for Drury Lane productions, and it might be described as a sublimation of the 'traditional' ballad opera air, the melody longer and more sophisticated but the English quality still preserved. A few items in *Comus* are consciously Italanate, but, as Burney pointed out, Arne was liable to drift into an Italian cliché even when writing in his English style. Thus 'Now Phoebus sinketh in the West', the first song in *Comus*, begins charmingly in the new style Arne had virtually invented:

But later in this song Burney found what he calls a 'battered passage' that had been repeated in countless Italian operas ever since *Thomyris*:

The most ambitious item in the first act of *Comus* is an almost total failure.

The music of 'Sweet Eccho' does not begin to match Milton's marvellous words; the melody lacks character, and the echoes on the flute soon become tedious. It is extraordinary that this song should have no orchestral introduction to set the tempo and give the singer her note.[1] The chorus that ends Act I is ebullient.

There is not much music in Act II. The best item is another echo song, this time with words by Dalton, and it is strikingly individual with its quick movement. It was one of the very few musical items to be cut in the afterpiece version of *Comus*; no doubt it lost favour because it is so difficult to sing. More popular was 'Would you taste the noontide air', for which in 1766 Arne wrote special graces for his pupil Miss Brent.[2]

The best and most nearly operatic music is in Act III, in which a majority of the songs are given to a new character borrowed from *L'Allegro*, Euphrosyne or Mirth. There are several stretches of continuous music, some of real quality. After Euphrosyne's first song, Comus summons the Naiads who perform 'a slow Dance expressive of the Passion of Love', and as usual at this period the flute is chosen as the most amorous of instruments; it doubles the first violins throughout. The dance is immediately followed by an excellent accompanied Recitative and 'Ballad' in which the Pastoral Nymph sings conventionally of her love for Damon, while Euphrosyne 'by her Gestures expresses to the Audience her different sentiments of the Subject of her Complaint, suitable to the Character of their several Songs'. The Ballad has one of those slow suave minuet tunes that Arne helped to make so popular in the middle of the century.[3] The melody is unusually long and well organized for such songs, and of assured beauty. This Recitative and Ballad is immediately followed by a similar pair of movements in which Euphrosyne treats love in a more light-hearted manner.

In Comus's Palace the Lady has been silent all this time 'in an enchanted Chair'. Comus announces a feast in her honour, but is interrupted by the arrival of an ally for the beleaguered Lady in the form of an Attendant Spirit (male), who 'descends gradually in a splendid Machine' to some of the noblest music Arne ever wrote. (The score is easily available, and there is no need to quote.) He then sings a long and excellent Accompanied Recitative about the Good Life in 'the Realms of Peace' above; a trumpet joins in with marvellous effect when he lauds 'Patient Virtue's Triumph'. This must be one of the first Accompanied Recitatives in English theatre music. Then comes the finest aria in the masque, 'Nor on Beds of fading Flowers,' for which the previously-heard 'descent' music provides the introduction and main theme. Here Arne touches greatness. There has not so far been a syllable of Milton in this act, but there now follows

[1] Towards the end of the century Parke, according to his *Reminiscences*, always played the flute obbligato on the oboe.

[2] See p. 277.

[3] The librettos give four verses both for this and for Euphrosyne's song, but only two appear in the Musica Britannica edition.

what Dr. Johnson called 'the most animated and affecting scene of the drama'—
the quarrel between Comus and the Lady. A later composer would have seen it
as a musical challenge and the climax of the opera, but Dalton and Arne had no
option but to leave it as spoken dialogue. Then follows Euphrosyne's 'Preach
me not your musty Rules', from which Michael Tippett quotes in his *Diverti-
mento on Sellinger's Round*, and this leads into an unusual sequence akin to ballet.

The dancers in *Comus* were felt to be of such importance that their names
were almost always advertised in the press. In 1737 Desnoyer had succeeded
Thurmond as Drury Lane's Dancing-Master, and he spent three seasons at this
theatre followed by two at Covent Garden.[1] Besides being the leading dancer in
Comus, Desnoyer must also have been the choreographer. Furthermore it was
his job to arrange the dances so often given between the acts of this and other
theatrical pieces of the period. Foreign dancers were becoming one of the leading
playhouse attractions.

In the middle of Euphrosyne's 'Ye Fawns and ye Dryads', there is a stage
direction at the change of key and tempo (not given on p. 126 of the Musica
Britannica edition) asking the dancing Fawns and Dryads to 'attend to the following Directions', clearly those about to be sung by the singer:

> Now lighter and gayer, ye tinkling Strings sound;
> Light, light in the Air, ye nimble Nymphs, bound.
>   Now, now with quick feet
>   The ground beat, beat, beat.

It must be confessed that Dalton scarcely captures the tones of Milton's deep
diapason, but all this part of the masque provides fascinating glimpses of an unexpected form of opera-ballet. After the 'Dance Tambourin', which follows
without a break, the dancers remain on the stage to attend to some more sung
directions which this time invite the miming of contrasted moods.

I said earlier that *Comus* consists in the main of pretty songs that, being
incidental to the plot, inevitably lack dramatic feeling. Arne's setting of the
following words by Dalton is an exception:

> Now cold and denying,
> Now kind and complying,
>   Consenting,
>   Repenting,
>   Disdaining,
>   Complaining,
> Indiff'rence now feigning,
> Again with quick Feet
> The Ground beat, beat, beat.

[1] Later he was employed by the Prince of Wales, and it is said that he was playing
the fiddle in the royal bedroom when Frederick died.

It looks as though Arne made two versions of this unusual number. The first, given in all eighteenth-century published versions, is in three-four (apart from the two final lines) and has a two-bar echo of the voice part for the strings after lines one, two and seven. Otherwise the words 'run on' as in a normal song. But in the MS version, though the voice part is the same, the echoes are cut, and each of the first seven lines is followed by four or eight bars for the strings intended to express in sound the mood of what has just been sung. Some of these interpolations are in common time; thus the time signature changes frequently, and presumably the tempo changes too, though the MS version is almost completely devoid of expression marks. It cannot be pretended that Arne distinguished between the various moods very successfully; the task would have taxed a much more dramatically-minded composer than he. But it is interesting that he should have made the attempt, and if great care were taken to find the right tempo and degree of volume and phrasing, and with dancers to interpret the mood, the effect might be very striking. Throughout this piece the accompaniment is scored merely for two-part strings, the violins being in unison throughout. (I must add that though it is likely that Arne was responsible for this second version, it is not certain.)

The last passage of extended music in *Comus* is also the longest, and it occurs after The Lady's brothers have arrived to rescue her. Comus and his crew are driven off, and Sabrina, nymph of the Severn, 'arises attended by Water-Nymphs'. The words to be sung are all Milton's. After more dialogue, a chorus, again much too short and undeveloped, ends the masque. Two trumpets help to give a bright effect.

Arne's scoring is competent though not striking; it was to become much more imaginative in later life. As in almost all English works of this period, the flutes and oboes were played by the same two players. In the first two movements of the overture, only oboes are asked for, in the third only flutes. Towards the end of 'Sweet Eccho' the flute is given seven and a half bars rest during which the player was expected to switch to the oboe. When *Comus* was staged in Dublin in 1743, the flautist was advertised as 'Mr. Neal, from England, who perform'd it originally'. But Neal's speciality was playing oboe concertos. It is very probable that the trumpets and horns were also blown by the same two players, for they are never called for in the same piece. Timpani appear only in the first movement of the overture, and then only in the MS score, but they probably played later on whenever the trumpets did. No doubt Arne wrote out a drum part for the player without bothering to incorporate it in the score, as Haydn sometimes did for his symphonies. But we must also face the probability that in published full scores the less important instruments were sometimes omitted to save space and expense. Such full scores were aimed in the main at the provincial market, and sometimes one suspects that the intention was to provide just enough to make sense, and no more. In *Comus* the trio in Act II, 'Live and Love', is accompanied by strings alone in the published full score, but in the MS there are oboes as well, and it is quite likely that for the published version some-one made an amalgam of the violin and oboe parts to save staves.

The bassoon player has some very short passages divorced from the string basses in the fugal movement of the overture and in the choral close to the first air, 'Now Phoebus sinketh in the west'. Elsewhere he doubled the string basses, or kept silent. Nearly all the airs appear to be accompanied by strings and continuo alone, and several have ballad-opera-type accompaniments, with the violins in unison doubling the voice part and nothing else going on but the bass.

Arne's way of writing for horns was curious. Like other English composers, Boyce and Greene for instance, he wrote for the trumpets *loco*, giving the parts a key signature when, as was almost always the case, they were in D. But for the horns he devised or adopted a system whereby the parts could be thought of as either transposing or *loco*. He notated them in C major in the way that was normal then and still is, and thus gave the players what they wanted. But he added a clef and a key signature (which the players had to ignore) in order to provide the score reader with the actual sound. This familiar cadence

can be made to sound in D, in F, in E flat, and in G as follows:

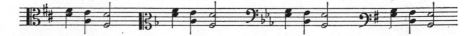

When there is a bass clef, the score reader has to hear the notes an octave higher. Examples of the curious bass clef needed for music in G can be found in *Artaxerxes* (in three numbers) and in *The May Day*. I have not found any examples by Arne of horns in B flat, though the tenor clef would have accommodated them easily enough. Perhaps Arne thought B flat basso too dull and B flat alto too difficult.[1] So far as I am aware, the only English composers who followed Arne's method were Philip Hayes, Lampe, and his warm admirer Dibdin.

4 ARNE'S 'ALFRED' AND 'THE JUDGMENT OF PARIS'

Early in 1740 Arne salvaged what he could from his youthful 'English Opera'. On 8 March *Rosamond* was revived at Drury Lane 'new set to Musick by Mr. Arne, reserving 2 or 3 Favourite Songs out of his former Opera'. In his preface

---

[1] Handel wrote for horns in the same keys as Arne plus B flat and A, but he used these latter keys only before 1740 and never in oratorios (see Dean, p. 78). He did not trifle with Arne's clefs.

to *Rosalinda* of the same year, John Lockman mentions a rumour that 'Mr. Arne has reduced his Opera into one Act, and set the whole scene anew, and so manag'd Matters, that Rosamond appears throughout the whole Drama'. Beard was the King, Mrs. Arne the Queen; Mrs. Clive took the title role. As an afterpiece *Rosamond* had a modest success, especially in 1744–5 when there were thirteen performances, but after Garrick's arrival at Drury Lane two seasons later it was virtually forgotten.

About 1745 Arne published his first two sets of Vauxhall songs under the title of *Lyric Harmony*, and at the foot of the title-page he told his public that

> The Opera of ROSAMOND written by Mr. Addison as contracted and perform'd at the Theatre Royal in Drury Lane is now publishing at a Subscription of Eight Shillings.

This was two shillings more than *Comus*. Subscriptions were originally taken at Arne's house in Great Queen Street near Lincoln's Inn Fields, but when Volume II appeared a year later he had moved to 'Marble Hall near Vaux-hall'. No doubt he moved after he was put in charge of the music at Vauxhall Gardens in the spring of 1745. No copy of *Rosamond* is known, and it may be that no copies ever appeared because not enough people subscribed. There is a MS score in the British Museum (Add. 29370),[1] but in the absence of a libretto of the revised version it is impossible to assess its degree of completeness. It begins and ends with scenes for Sir Trusty and his wife Grideline. In all there are five airs, three duets, and three recitatives, of which two are accompanied. Especially notable is the King's 'Rise, Glory, rise', a long Italianate Da Capo aria running to thirty-six pages and scored for oboes, trumpet, drums, and strings. It was much admired by Burney, and about 1770 it was published on its own.

Arne's next masque, though not so long as *Comus*, also had spoken dialogue, and its first performance was at Cliveden House on the Thames near Maiden-head. In the eighteenth century people found the name hard to spell, and of several variants Cliefden was the most usual. From 1739 onwards it was rented by George II's eldest son, Frederick, Prince of Wales, who was to die in 1751 before he could come to the throne. Few deaths have been so little regretted.

Frederick carried reaction against his parents to unusual lengths, and gave much of his mind to the task of making them look foolish. His extreme dislike of them has been described as 'the scandal of the reign'. In the famous quarrel between Handel and Bononcini, he favoured Bononcini mainly because Handel was patronized by his father. When Bononcini fled the country, he picked on Giuseppe Sammartini, the King's Theatre oboist, as his favourite musician. Though never a persistent patron of the arts, Frederick had some appreciation of music, as had all the Hanoverian royal family. Hawkins says Sammartini 'was received upon the footing of a domestic, and appointed master or director of the

---

[1] Someone has written 1733 on the MS, but the more elaborate items cannot have been written so early.

chamber music to his royal highness'. It will be remembered that when Frederick's sister was married in 1735, the occasion inspired a number of masques, but when Frederick himself was married in the following year the playhouses took little or no notice of the occasion (though it was the cause of Handel's writing *Atalanta*). When his wife became pregnant, Frederick concealed the fact from his parents. At the last moment the Princess of Wales was rushed to St. James's Palace, where no preparations had been made, and gave birth to a daughter almost as soon as the King and Queen knew that a baby was on the way. Frederick was adept at hurting their feelings.

The little girl was known as Augusta, Princess of Brunswick, and for her third birthday, or rather one day after it (1 August 1740) her father arranged a grand entertainment in the garden of Cliveden consisting of two masques and some pantomime scenes, all of them performed by the best London professionals money could buy. The Princess may have enjoyed Rich as Harlequin, but she can have made nothing of the masques. However they were enjoyed by a large throng of society guests, of whom there were so many that the entertainment had to be repeated on the following night—when a rainstorm drove everyone indoors, and *Alfred* had to be finished in the hall.

At the north-west corner of the Cliveden estate there is what the Guide Book calls a Rustic Theatre, cut into the side of the steep descent to the Thames in such a way that the view provided the backcloth. No doubt it was often used for unpretentious plays. A notice-board claims that *Alfred* and 'Rule Britannia' were first performed there, but this cannot be so. The tiny circular stage could not possibly have accommodated the actors, singers, chorus and orchestra; there is a precipice behind, and no room at the sides. *Alfred*, by far the grandest entertainment ever put on at Cliveden, must have been given in front of the house; that is, to the south of it. Probably the area round John of Bologna's statue was the stage. Here again there would have been a superb natural backcloth; also plenty of room.

The words of *Alfred* were written for the occasion by James Thomson, author of *The Seasons*. At the time he was receiving a much-needed allowance from Frederick; shortly before he had been languishing in a debtor's prison, but had been bailed out with a £100 note by the actor Quin. Thomson's libretto was suitably patriotic, and dealt rather distantly with the routing of the Danes, none of whom appeared. For Alfred's edification a Hermit raised the unborn spirits of Edward III, the Black Prince, Queen Elizabeth, and William III, all of whom, he prophesied, would carry on Alfred's good work in founding the Navy. The masque ended with 'Rule Britannia', a prayer that our shores be protected from foreign invasion. In modern times the lyric has been accused of vainglory, of claims to control all the oceans, but in fact it has been misunderstood; the sentiments are not unreasonable for a constantly-invaded island in the ninth century, and they had topical relevance in 1740. Arne's setting was brilliantly scored for oboes, bassoon, trumpets, drums, and strings, and overnight the song was a sensation, firing the imagination of all who heard it. It was soon being sung everywhere, and in 1742 the full score was published as an appendix to Arne's *The Judgment of Paris*.

Alfred and his wife Eltruda were non-singing parts, as was the Hermit (played by Quin). The songs were sung by the two shepherds, Corin and his wife Emma (Salway and Mrs. Clive), and by the Spirit (Mrs. Arne). Thomas Lowe, who had just begun his career as a tenor, represented the Bard and thus was the first to sing 'Rule Britannia'.

Though *Alfred* was never as popular as *Comus*, it was performed in a bewildering number of different versions, and textually this is the most confused of all eighteenth-century English operas. But, apart from 'Rule Britannia', none of the music was published for more than a decade, and then only in much altered form. The probable reason can be deduced from a study of the other masque given at Cliveden that summer. This was *The Judgment of Paris* by Frederick's employee, Giuseppe Sammartini;[1] it is a setting of the Congreve libretto of 1701. Three MS full scores can be found in the British Museum, and they show that instrumentalists had been assembled regardless of cost. Flutes and oboes play at the same time, and so do horns and trumpets. *Alfred* was surely scored with similar lavishness. It follows that the original version was written for a larger orchestra than could be accommodated in the London playhouses, and thus *Alfred* could not be performed there until it had been given an economizing revision. This, as it happened, was not until 1745.

Originally the music consisted of an overture, a march and eight vocal items. As the relevant librettos show, six of the songs recur among the twenty-seven items published in 1753; the other two do not survive. It is impossible to say to what extent, if any, Arne cut down on the scoring of these six songs; he may even have had to re-set some of the lyrics. There is a hint of his problems in the overture, which begins as follows:

The above is taken from the earliest source, the 1753 full score. When, at bars 15–16, the substance of the first two bars is repeated, there is no equivalent of

[1] Reference books, accepting an erroneous statement by W. H. Cummings, give Arne as the composer of this masque too. But see my article in M&L, April 1966.

the oboe phrases, and the last beat of each bar is silent. At no other point in the movement is this oboe phrase omitted, and the likelihood is that at bar 15 it was played by the flutes, and that when on revision Arne cut the flute parts, transferring whatever of importance they played to other instruments, he forgot to do so this time.

The start of the overture is also of interest for its anticipations of 'Rule, Britannia' in bars 3 and 5, and for the presence in bar 6 of one of those appoggiaturas whose most obvious resolution produces a succession of consecutive fifths. Of more importance than such details is the fact that this is an 'Italian' overture, among the first of its kind by an English composer.[1] It has some of the characteristics of the *galante* symphony of ten years later, and it is of good quality. The minor-key slow movement is outstanding. But all the music that survives of the Cliveden *Alfred* is of interest, except perhaps for yet another of Arne's echo songs. 'Sweet Valley' is as poor as 'Sweet Echo' in *Comus*. But 'The Shepherd's plain Life' with its exuberant horn parts is a joy, 'If those who live in Shepherd's Bower' has a splendidly English tune, and 'O Peace' is a beautiful song by any standards. The first vocal phrase is *not* a repetition of what the orchestra plays in the introduction, and though Handel had allowed his singer to surprise in this way ever since 'Cara sposa' in *Rinaldo*, the effect was still unsuual in music by English-born composers. The scoring is for unison violins and bass, and the song begins:

At bar 16 the singer comes in:

[1] It was anticipated by Boyce's overture to *Peleus and Thetis*; see p. 210.

It has sometimes been suggested that in baroque music the violas played from the bass part if nothing else was provided for them. There is a clear evidence for this in the middle section of the *Da Capo* air, 'A Youth adorn'd with every Art'. Where the bass line rose well above middle C the composer wrote 'Violoncellos and Tenors soli e pia'. Yet elsewhere in this aria there is no stave for the tenors (as violas were then called), and no other indication that they were expected to play. (The purpose of Arne's direction was of course to silence the double basses.) This middle section is also of interest in that it is dramatically conceived; bars 4–6 are the most obviously descriptive in the whole of *Alfred*:

Sammartini's *The Judgment of Paris* had far more music in it than there was in the original version of *Alfred*, and it is for the most part of good quality. Congreve's libretto, which is unchanged, is divided into two acts each beginning with an overture notable for an excellent fugue. The first of these has the sort of strong pithy subject Bach often employed. Mercury is a bass, Paris a soprano. Mercury's second air, 'This radiant fruit', is probably the first in English music with a bassoon obbligato.[1] There is also one near the end with a cello obbligato,

---

[1] Later examples can be found in Boyce's *Solomon* (1741) and Festing's Miltonic Ode 'On May Morning' (*c.* 1745).

and Arne, who must have been listening, produced a very similar air two years later in his own *Judgment of Paris*. Two fines air for Pallas are scored with unusual fullness for oboes, horns, trumpets, drums, and strings. Sammartini perhaps felt insecure about English accentuation in the recitatives, for in the first of them he took over John Eccles's setting of the same words, confident that no one would notice.[1] In an earlier chapter we saw how Eccles, Daniel Purcell and Weldon reacted to the words Paris sings when he first sees the three goddesses. It may be of interest to show also how Sammartini and Arne treated them. Sammartini allows the goddesses much longer to arrive than any of the other composers, and it may well be that they had to traverse a spacious lawn while this agreeable music was played:

---

[1] I owe this fact to Veronica Pritchard; see M&L, Jan. 1967, pp. 101–2.

Arne took almost no time about their arrival, and no trouble either. Clearly he was writing for a playhouse performance in which the three ladies descended rather briskly from the sky:

It is sad that Sammartini's masque has never been performed in recent times, or in London at any time.

A strange sequel to the Cliveden venture can be found in Horace Walpole's *Memoirs of the Reign of King George II* (i, p. 452), in which an Appendix offers a song by Frederick himself, written in French. It begins

Venez, mes cheres Deesses

(there are no accents), and it is 'addressed to Lady Catherine Harmer, Lady Falconberg, and Lady Middlesex, who were to act the three goddesses with Frederick Prince of Wales, in the Judgment of Paris, whom he was to represent, and Prince Lobkowitz Mercury'. It is unlikely that they were singing Sammartini's far-from-easy music. What in fact they were playing at we shall probably never know.

Arne's third masque, *The Judgment of Paris*, must have been written in emulation of Sammartini. It was first performed on 12 March 1742 at Drury Lane, when it was described in the advertisements as 'new set'. The advertisements also speak of the 'extraordinary expense' the composer has been put to 'for copying all the Music, building the stage, additional instrumental performers, chorus singers, and erecting an Organ'. In fact Drury Lane must have had shamefully limited orchestral resources if extras had to be hired, for the scoring is very modest in comparison with Sammartini's. Beard sang the part of Paris, and Lowe was Mercury, the goddesses being Mrs. Arne (Venus), Mrs. Clive (Pallas), and Mrs. Edwards (Juno).[1] The music seems to have been recognized as well above Arne's usual level, but it never enjoyed much success. Covent Garden gave a performance on 3 April 1759 advertised as having 'new Additions' but it is not known what these were. By 1767 there had been no more than eleven scattered performances in London.

As usual the score provides only the overture, the airs, and the accompanied recitatives, and the first vocal item is the recitative for Paris quoted above. Either Arne had a long *secco* recitative for the preceding dialogue between Paris and Mercury (in Sammartini's setting it includes two airs for Mercury and one for Paris) or he cut it. He certainly cut the opening airs for Juno and Pallas. Nevertheless, what we have of the masque would sound complete in performance if there were an ending. In the libretto the final chorus runs to nine lines. Arne's brief setting of lines 8 and 9 can be found in British Museum Add. MS 29370. The rest of the chorus is lost.

The four-movement French overture is a great improvement on the one in *Comus*, and the 'Giga' at the end is a delightful piece of humour. The airs are again of good quality, and there is some excellent writing for the trumpet in Pallas's 'Hark, the glorious Voice of War', a full-scale *Da Capo* aria, elaborate

[1] Mrs. Edwards had recently sung the part of Achilles in Handel's last opera, *Deidamia*.

and professionally Italianate. Easier to illustrate in a book such as this is the Italian-influenced air with cello obbligato, 'Gentle Swain'. The singer is Venus.

With one exception, Arne was not to write another theatre score of such solid worth for another twenty years.

It was earlier mentioned that French dancers were popular at the play-houses.[1] Their music can be found in *The Comic Tunes etc. to the Celebrated Dances Perform'd at Both Theatres*, and the eight volumes are usually cata-logued under 'Hasse' because his is the only name given on the title-page. In fact most of the music is anonymous. Vol. I contains eighteen short ballets and single dances performed in 1740–41, including (pp. 70–79) *The Peasant's Triumph on the Death of the Wild Boar* (DL 12.2.41) by Arne. He wrote it for the two Fausans and Mlle Chateauneuf,[2] and it was his only ballet. There is no indication of the action. The six dances are given on two staves with cues for oboes, and the music is surprisingly *galante* in style.

Just a month after the first performance of Arne's *The Judgment of Paris*, the concert-goers of Dublin were listening to the first performance of *Messiah*, given under Handel's direction and with Arne's sister, Mrs. Cibber, singing some of the contralto arias. Probably it was at her suggestion that Arne and his wife crossed the Irish Sea in June to spy out the land, and in July he gave a benefit concert at Fishamble Street which included a scene from *Rosamond* and 'O Peace' from *Alfred*. It was quickly apparent to Arne that Dublin held out far more exciting possibilities than London, where the theatres were stagnating, and after a repeat of the concert he hurried back to London to make arrange-ments for a more prolonged absence and to collect orchestral scores and parts. By the end of September he was back in Dublin, where he stayed for two seasons, no doubt all the happier that Handel had left the country. Dublin was especially

---

[1] In Fielding's *Pasquin* someone says: 'If I'm not better used, I'll go to France; for now we have got all their dancers away, perhaps they may be glad of some of ours'.

[2] Mlle Chateauneuf began her stage career as a dancer, but acquired good English and turned to acting. When she retired to Bordeaux, says Chetwood, she frequently regaled her compatriots with English songs, in particular Euphrosyne's 'Song of Rosie Wine' from *Comus*.

eager to welcome celebrities at this time, and even to make them, for earlier that year the worth of Garrick and Peg Woffington had been first recognized. All Arne's major stage works were enthusiastically acclaimed. *Comus, Rosamund, Tom Thumb, Love and Glory*, and *The Judgment of Paris* were all performed several times, with Arne directing from the harpsichord. *Alfred* ('as perform'd at Cliefden') and *The Judgment of Paris* ('as perform'd at Drury Lane') were given four times as a double bill, but apparently not acted; *Alfred* was always announced as a Serenata. Arne also directed performances of *The Beggar's Opera*; Lowe was Macheath and Mlle Chateauneuf was Polly.

Early in 1744 Mrs. Arne made what was advertised as her first appearance in a comic character—Margery in *The Dragon of Wantley*. She never attempted comedy roles in London. Mlle Chateauneuf was Mauxalinda, and Lowe the dragon. Again Arne presided at the harpsichord; it was rare for him to direct the music of other composers. His only major composition in Dublin was the first of his two oratorios, *The Death of Abel*. As already mentioned, he also set the songs and choruses in Lee's *Theodosius*, perhaps because Purcell's music was not available in Dublin; in 1749 Lampe seems to have set them again.[1] In June 1744 the Arnes and Lowe returned to London, where they found success harder to come by than in Dublin. Arne earned a reasonable living by teaching and by running the music at Vauxhall Gardens, but his theatrical ambitions had to be curbed, especially when Garrick took over Drury Lane.

5 WILLIAM HAYES, GREENE, AND PASQUALI

Full scores of English masques are not so common that any can be ignored, and *Circe* by William Hayes (1707–77) must be mentioned even though little light can be thrown on it. The music was published in 1742, the year Hayes became Professor of Music at Oxford University; he had been organist at Magdalen since 1734. I have not traced a performance, but *Circe* was probably given at one or more of the Three Choirs Festivals of the time, for the Musical Societies of Gloucester, Worcester, and Hereford all subscribed to the publication. The volume was calculated to impress the university with the prowess of its new professor. It was in three parts, the second consisting of a trio sonata and vocal music, and the third of selections from the ode Hayes had submitted for his degree of Bachelor of Music. *Circe*, given pride of place in Part I, was probably the most recent composition.

I have not found a libretto or even the name of its author. None of the words in the score make any reference to the Circe legend, and it follows that, as in Arne's *Alfred*, the singers were not concerned with the plot. This must have been another masque with spoken dialogue. Those who sang are named as 'Shepherd', 'Virtue', and 'Pleasure'; there is also a Siciliana sung by Circe herself. The airs, as also the three-movement overture, are competent, dull, and

[1] Sheldon, p. 338.

more Handelian than Arne's music of this period. Much the most individual item is an aria for Virtue that colours the gloomier words with sudden minor chords and strange modulations; at times it alternates between $\frac{3}{4}$ and $\frac{2}{4}$. Handel had experimented with such irregularities in 'Bel piacere a godere' from *Agrippina* (1709), and liked the result so well that he transferred it to *Rinaldo* two years later; Hayes cannot equal Handel's bright glow of newness, but his song deserves revival.

Virtue is also a character, a rather unappealing one, in Greene's short masque *The Judgment of Hercules*; the libretto appeared in 1740, but no score seems to survive though *Grove* invents one in the British Museum. The plot is without interest. In 'a wild uninhabited Wood' Hercules has to choose between Virtue and Pleasure. Virtue, allowed three songs to Pleasure's one, wins easily.

The popularity in the 1740s of this triangular theme was astonishing; it is adequately discussed, with some omissions, by Dean (pp. 580–1). It appealed perhaps as a substitute for a Christian Morality of the *Everyman* type. The source was Xenophon's *Memorabilia*, in which Socrates summarized an earlier Greek poem on the theme. In eighteenth-century England, I tentatively suggest the following order of events:

1. 1740: The libretto of Greene's *The Judgment of Hercules* published anonymously in *The Miscellany of Lyric Poems* (mostly) *performed in the Academy of Music held in the Apollo*. Probably by John Hoadly, who wrote most of Greene's other librettos. The only version certainly in dramatic form. It may have been performed at any time in the previous eight years, but coming late in the volume it may be recent.

2. 1740: William Shenstone published *The Judgment of Hercules*, a poem in some 500 lines of heroic couplets. Dr. Johnson, who dates it 1741, found the 'numbers smooth, the diction elegant, and the thoughts just; but something of vigour is still to be wished, which it might have had by brevity and compression'. In short it's rather dull. The most likely work to have popularized the subject, though it was only later that Shenstone won fame through *The Schoolmistress*. Perhaps earlier than 1, which in any case Shenstone, stuck in the country, would probably not have heard.

3. 1713: 'A Student of Oxford' published *The Judgment of Hercules* in Glasgow (copy in Bodleian); 27 ten-line stanzas. Reprinted in two later volumes cited by Dean. The author was Robert Lowth, Professor of Hebrew Poetry at Oxford since 1741, and later Bishop of London.

4. (Unknown date.) *The Choice of Hercules*, an unpublished and perhaps un-performed cantata by John Stanley. The recitatives being narration, it could never be staged. Short, with only one air for each of the three characters and one duet. Possibly later than 5, with which Allardyce Nicoll confuses it. It is presumably this score (BM Add. MS 5328) which *Grove* wrongly attributes to Greene. Though mostly in octosyllabics, the libretto

shows slight affinity with 2. There is another score, lacking the overture, in the Rowe Library at King's College, Cambridge.

5. 1751: Handel performed his 'interlude' *The Choice of Hercules* (CG 1.3.51) with *Alexander's Feast*. The libretto freely adapted from 3, the first recitative being a complete stanza. It could be acted, but never was in Handel's day, and Hercules is not allowed a note till two-thirds of the way through. Dean suggests Handel wrote it to spite his old enemy Greene. He borrowed most of the music from what he had written in 1749 for the unperformed *Alceste* by Smollett.

Alceste came to nought; Rich, who had commissioned it, turned it down. It seems an incredible decision, for though Smollett was virtually unknown, Handel's drawing power was immense. The libretto is lost. All writers have assumed it was a tragedy, but on one of his autographs (BM Add. 30310) Handel wrote 'Songs in a Farce composed for Mr. Rich', and the music seems much too cheerful for tragedy.[1] It ends with ballet music, the 'Ultimo Ballo' being a delightful gavotte that Handel does not seem to have used elsewhere. None of the principal characters were to have sung, and the vocal items, uniformly charming, were probably concentrated in masque-like sections at the ends of each act, for they were clearly linked in groups. By 'farce' Handel implied an afterpiece, so there must have been two acts. Smollett presumably adapted that version of the story in which Hercules brings Alceste back from the dead and all ends happily. Winton Dean has shown that Handel quickly transferred three items to a revision of *Alexander Balus*, a chorus to a revision of *Hercules*, and the main part of the score to *The Choice of Hercules*, which he concocted in the summer of 1750. Perhaps it was the notion of Hercules that led him to write it rather than malice towards Greene.

Greene's *Phoebe* was his last major work; it is a full-length, three-act Pastoral, every note of which survives. Like *The Judgment of Hercules*, it was written for the Society of Apollo, and never reached the playhouses though there was a performance at 'Mr. Ogle's Great Room, Dean St., Soho' on 16 January 1755. Act I introduces two shepherds, Amyntas and Sylvio, whom we hear in 'a Champain Country' singing very cheerfully of their escape from the worries of love-making. But in at least one case this indifference is a pretence. 'Sylvio' is Phoebe in male disguise, come to this remote place after being spurned by Amyntas in order to be near her lover. The situation seems copied from Gay's *Dione*, but Hoadly handles it with far more charm and skill. As might be predicted, 'Sylvio' is embarrassed by the amorous attentions of another girl, Celia, who is Amyntas's sister. The fourth and last character is Linco, a jovially boorish and at first mildly inebriated peasant who loves Celia. Act I ends with

---

[1] But Smollett thought it was 'a sort of Tragedy'; see Deutsch, p. 657. Can it be that Rich cancelled the production because Handel had misunderstood the nature of the entertainment?

Celia, in despair at 'Sylvio's' indifference, singing a moving suicide air. The quotation begins at bar 9 of the introduction:

Act II starts with Celia still alive but asleep. 'Sylvio' is hiding in a thicket, ready to protect her from herself. Celia wakes and sings a short echo song, a great improvement on Arne's, aided by the inevitable flautist, but the subsequent recitative, in which 'Sylvio' supplies the echoes vocally, is original as well as delightful. Eventually 'Sylvio', to divert Celia's thoughts into more profitable channels, reveals that she is Phoebe. It takes Celia several arias to get the point, and she still rebuffs the wretched Linco; he, however, tosses off a splendidly vigorous song:

The above is part of a *Da capo* aria that has no instrumental introduction.

In Act III Amyntas finds his sister wearing a bracelet he had long ago given to Phoebe. She says she got it from 'Sylvio', who in turn stretches the truth by maintaining that 'he' got it from Phoebe. In a furious and excellent *presto* aria Amyntas gives away that he is still in love with Phoebe. He challenges 'Sylvio', who replies with a lovely pleading song in which at long last she reveals herself to her lover.

The libretto of *Phoebe* was published in 1748, perhaps the year of its first performance.[1] A little later, encouraged by a small legacy, Greene retired from active music-making to compile his vast anthology of Cathedral Music through the ages. Some of his own cathedral music is still remembered; his reputation today would be the higher if *Phoebe* were remembered as well. Its neglect in the composer's lifetime was as strange as is its neglect today. Apart from the well-shaped singable vocal lines, the airs are remarkable for the strongly individual violin parts; previous English composers had been all too apt to let the violins double the vocal line as a matter of course. *Phoebe* has a good French overture with one of Greene's long rangey fugue subjects. Some of the episodes are un-contrapuntal to a point of inanity, but in performance the vigour and ingenuity of the rest would probably carry the day. The final minuet is built on five-bar phrases, a device Greene often resorted to in his *Amoretti* when solving the

---

[1] The music had been composed the year before, as is revealed by Hayman's portrait of Greene and Hoadly; see Plate V.

problems of Spenser's long lines. A curious feature of the scoring is that the horns are notated 'loco' with a key signature.

John Mainwaring, who wrote the first biography of Handel in 1760, describes his *Semele* (CG 10.2.44) as 'an English Opera, but called an oratorio, and performed as such'. Modern Handelians are all agreed that both this work and *Hercules* (KT 5.1.45) cry out for stage presentation, though neither of them got it until 1925. The immaculate and comprehensive treatment of their music by Winton Dean must excuse my not dealing with them here.

As was mentioned earlier, the Italian violinist and composer Nicolo Pasquali was engaged by Thomas Sheridan at Smock Alley Theatre, Dublin, in the autumn of 1748. He quickly made himself more popular than Lampe, who was engaged at the same time, and Sheridan allowed him a surprising number of benefits. In his first season he composed or contrived masques called *The Triumphs of Hibernia* (SA 4.11.48) and *The Temple of Peace* (SA 9.2.49), the latter to celebrate the Peace of Aix-la-Chapelle. The published libretto reveals that *The Temple of Peace* was put together in a great hurry, for Pasquali borrowed not only the music of a number of songs but the words as well. The score included 'Your Hay it is mown' from Purcell's *King Arthur* (which was about to be brought into the repertoire), 'O Peace' from Arne's *Alfred*, 'Let the deep Bowl' from Handel's *Belshazzar*, and 'With Hounds and with Horns' from Boyce's *The Secular Masque*. Pasquali wrote about half the music, and 'Signor Pasquali Junior' painted the scenery. Two months later Pasquali set John Hughes's *Apollo and Daphne* (SA 14.4.49), which was presented with pantomime interludes.

None of Pasquali's masques was published, but a surprising amount of the music survives orchestrally. In 1750 a lavish collection of his songs appeared in full score, and a few years later twelve of his overtures were issued in parts. Thus we have in full five songs and the overture from *The Triumphs of Hibernia*, four songs and the overture from *Apollo and Daphne*. The overture in *The Triumphs of Hibernia* is one of five in the set of which the composer curiously says 'The Ripieno parts may be performed by Two Trumpets, Two French Horns and Kettle Drums'. Much the most *galante* of the overtures is the one called *The Nymphs of the Spring*; it is among the few in the new three-movement Italian form, and it must date from before 1750 because a song from this work appears in Pasquali's song collection of that year. As the spring of the title is the one in Bath, it may be that Pasquali had worked there briefly before going to Dublin. In the early 1740s he had also worked in Edinburgh.

Pasquali wrote much better for instruments than he did for voices. The song collection includes a wretched setting of 'Where the Bee sucks'. He was in London in 1752 for a benefit performance of *The Triumphs of Hibernia* (CG 18.4.52), and he died in Edinburgh in 1757. According to Burney, he was 'an excellent performer on the violin . . . and lived much respected as a professor, and beloved as a man'.

Italian musicians were a commonplace in Dublin at this time. We shall see later that Stephen Storace the elder was there at least by March 1749, for he was in dispute with Sheridan about borrowing the Smock Alley orchestra for the New Gardens where he was Music Director.[1] He may have been engaged as double bass in the theatre band when the orchestra was enlarged the previous autumn; the two positions were not necessarily incompatible. He spent at least five years in Dublin.

[1] Sheldon, p. 145.

6

Garrick's Influence
1747–1760

I GARRICK AND ARNE

THE interest Garrick felt in music has been consistently underplayed by a succession of biographers who happened to feel even less. Certainly he made no pretensions to technical knowledge. But he was well aware that it was a playhouse's business to provide a proportion of entertainments in which music predominated. It is sad that he never found the composer he deserved. Nevertheless he worked far harder in the cause of English opera than Rich in the fourteen years they were rivals, and when Covent Garden, under Beard, suddenly made English operas an artistic and financial success, Garrick stepped up Drury Lane's operatic repertoire and was for ever searching for successes of his own in this field. He also believed that quiet background music could heighten the emotion of such scenes as the one in *King Lear* in which the King and Cordelia are reunited; the background music he commissioned from Boyce for 'animating the statue' of Hermione in *The Winter's Tale* is in the Bodleian. (Shakespeare himself had asked for music in these scenes; Garrick was reviving a neglected tradition.)

In 1747 Garrick became joint patentee of Drury Lane with James Lacy. Lacy, for many years prompter at Covent Garden, had replaced Fleetwood as Drury Lane's manager three years earlier, but after Garrick's arrival he was content to take a back seat. Garrick remained in undisputed power for twenty-nine glorious years.

It might be expected that Garrick would have found in Arne the composer he wanted. For more than a decade Arne had written almost all Drury Lane's music, and he felt himself to be England's leading composer. Yet, as Garrick must have noticed, he had had no full-scale success in the theatre since *Comus* nine years before. He had in fact spent two of the intervening seasons in Dublin, and since 1745 he had given his summer energies to the music in Vauxhall Gardens. Even so, Garrick had reason to think less well of him than he thought of himself.

Almost certainly they had worked together before. In April 1740 Garrick's first play, the satirical afterpiece *Lethe*, had been produced at Drury Lane. It had scarcely any plot. With Pluto's permission, some London society creatures come to drink the waters of forgetfulness, and tell Aesop, the Lethe barman, of their desires and indirectly of their foibles. *Lethe* was no opera, but it included several quite elaborate songs sung by Beard as Mercury and Mrs. Clive as Mrs. Riot. Apart from songsheet publications, the music seems to survive only in a very curious volume in the Royal College of Music. This contains three anonymous items in full score, partly in print and partly in MS. 'The Card invites' (it is an Invitation card), sung by Mrs. Clive, is elaborately scored for oboes, horns, and strings, and this particular song turns up in *Clio and Euterpe* (Vol. 3, 1762), where it is ascribed to Arne. If this is to be believed, Arne no doubt wrote all the music, though he seems to have kept quiet about it in 1740. *Lethe* continued to be given throughout Garrick's reign at Drury Lane, and in the middle fifties Mrs. Clive was enlivening her performance of some song or other (probably 'The Card invites') with a parody of the grossly-overpaid Mingotti, then the shining light of the Italian Opera season.[1]

Garrick's policy on arriving at Drury Lane shows that he was already in truculent mood where Arne's music was concerned. Back in January 1746 Lacy had staged *The Tempest* at Drury Lane—astonishingly, it was announced as never acted there before—and the advertisements make it clear that Arne set both Shakespeare's masque in IV. i. about Ceres, Iris, and Juno, and also the Dryden–Shadwell masque in the last act about Neptune and Amphitrite. He also wrote at least three songs for Ariel, of which 'Where the Bee sucks' was to prove his most durable success. The music of two other Ariel songs, 'Come unto these yellow Sands' and 'E'er you can say come and go', survive in MS in the British Museum, together with almost the whole of the Shakespeare masque.[2] Arne's music for the Act V masque is lost. But what we have is of splendid quality, and Arne had good reason to hope that Garrick would keep the production in his repertoire for many years to come. Garrick did not in fact ever revive it. Adding insult to injury, he reverted to the Purcell–Weldon music in his very first season, staged a fully operatic version by Smith in 1756, and in the following year commissioned Boyce to reset Shakespeare's masque in truncated form.[3] He did allow Ariel to sing Arne's 'Where the Bee sucks'.

I shall have harsh things to say of Arne in the pages that follow, but there can be no doubt that his music for *The Tempest* deserved a very different fate, and he had every reason to feel aggrieved. Furthermore, for a whole season and a half Garrick did not ask him for a note of new music, and when at last he was once more allowed inside Drury Lane, he found himself, to his indignation,

[1] See Gwendolyn B. Needham in TN (Winter 1960–1), quoting an article on the subject by Frances Brooke (who later wrote opera librettos for Shield).

[2] Add. 29370; the copyist never finished two of the items.

[3] See O Mus. d. 14 and LCM MS 92.

working in rivalry with Boyce. He managed to keep his indignation on the boil for several years.

Yet Garrick can be forgiven for thinking Arne a poor investment. As Burney put it, 'the number of his unfortunate pieces for the stage was prodigious', and a composer so prone to failure as Arne was unlikely to be encouraged however eminent in theory. Here is a list of his 'unfortunate pieces' up to this time, with brief notes on each; all were afterpieces, and there were to be more failures later.

Britannia, or Love and Glory (DL 21.3.34); Serenata by Thomas Phillips; 3 perfs.

An Hospital for Fools (DL 15.11.39); 'Ballad Opera' by James Miller; 2 perfs. Not really a ballad opera; the four songs (given in the libretto with their basses) are all by Arne, but they are in ballad opera style. The audience disliked Miller and were continuously rowdy.

The Blind Beggar of Bethnal Green (DL 3.4.41); 'Ballad Opera' by Robert Dodsley; 1 perf., but more later in the provinces and at Bartholemew Fair in 1749. The libretto, based on a 17th century play by John Day, is interesting. Some of the nine songs were published with those Arne wrote for *The Merchant of Venice*.

The Temple of Dullness (DL 17.1.45); burlesque by Theobald; 7 perfs. The libretto is from interludes written for Galliard's unsuccessful opera, *The Happy Captive* (LT 16.4.41); it is an amusing satire on Italian Opera, and had Waltz as 'An Opera Director' and Mrs. Arne as 'A Virtuosa'. As someone rhetorically asks,

> What Transports can that Musick make
> That wants the *Demisemiquaver* and the *Shake*?

The piece ended with an opera rehearsal, complete with simile arias and silly lyrics. It was entirely sung. None of the music survives.

The Picture, or The Cuckold in Conceit (DL 11.2.45); 'Ballad Opera' by Miller; 1 perf. The libretto (from Molière) was published, but not the five songs.

King Pepin's Campaign (DL 15.4.45); burlesque by William Shirley; 3 perfs.; probably all sung, but no music survives. The libretto, in short rhyming couplets, amusingly describes the adventures of a feckless monarch among some highly amorous nuns.

Henry and Emma (CG 31.3.49); 'Musical Drama' based on Matthew Prior's poem 'The Nut-Brown Maid'; 1 perf., for Lowe's benefit. All sung, but no music survives.

Don Saverio (DL 15.2.50); Comic Opera; all sung, but no music survives; see below.

At first Garrick avoided opera through lack of singers. Lowe, his only tenor, was so bad an actor that after one season Garrick replaced him with Beard from Covent Garden. The next autumn he opened with Beard and Mrs. Clive in

The Lottery. In general he did not care for ballad operas, which to his generation must have seemed old-fashioned. Of the nine new operatic works he staged in the next eight seasons, only one had spoken dialogue. But Beard alone could not sustain all-sung operas, and in the summer of 1749 Garrick enticed over from Covent Garden a young lyric soprano called Miss Norris. It also occurred to him that a boy treble might have sentimental value, and he engaged 'Master Mattocks', who, strange though it seems to us, was given as often as not the role of a young lover. The turn-over in trebles is inevitably rapid, and by 1751 Mattocks was being replaced by 'Master Vernon'. Both were to make their mark in English Opera as adults. Garrick also encouraged 'Master Arne', the composer's natural son Michael, to play keyboard concertos in the theatre intervals.[1] The boy performer was to be an attraction at Drury Lane off and on for the rest of the century.

Perhaps against his inclinations, Garrick invited Thomas Arne to write a masque to celebrate the Peace of Aix-la-Chapelle in February 1749, and though the result could hardly be compared with Handel's *Fireworks Music*, written for the same happy occasion, Arne's *The Triumph of Peace* (DL 21.2.49) enjoyed ten performances, which for a masque was tolerable. The music does not survive. The libretto, by Robert Dodsley, is the usual mixture of war-loving gods and peace-loving shepherds, and includes such unappealing stage directions as the following:

> *The Goddess of Peace descends in a triumphal Car borne upon the Clouds, which breaking, she is discover'd in her Temple, attended by Justice, Liberty, Commerce and Science. War with his hands fetter'd, stands in a dejected Posture before her; Power, Ambition and Contention attending.*

Arne had set much the same libretto several times before; the most novel feature this time was the absence of Britannia.

It is unlikely that Garrick was impressed by *The Triumph of Peace*, for the following season he engaged Boyce, a move that could hardly fail to irritate Arne. Later in the 1750s Garrick experimented with other composers, notably Charles Burney and John Christopher Smith, and to each of these, as well as Boyce, I shall devote a section. Garrick's pantomimes will demand another. He had started his reign with the laudable intention of doing without the silly things, but soon realized that this resulted in his takings being lower than Rich's at Covent Garden. There might be nothing to be said for them aesthetically,

---

[1] Michael Arne must have been born about 1740, but nothing is known of the circumstances. He was our first child prodigy in music. His song collection *The Floweret* (c. 1750) included a charming setting of the 'Highland Laddie' words, and it caught on immediately. The Belgian composer Maldère was then playing the violin in Dublin, where the Arnes were always popular, and he later incorporated the entire tune in his Symphony in A, op. 5, No. 1. Later Sheridan wrote one of his *Duenna* lyrics to fit it.

V

Henry Carey by Worsdale (1729).

Mrs. Cibber by Hudson.

Maurice Greene and John Hoadly by Francis Hayman (1747);
The score on the left is Phoebe.

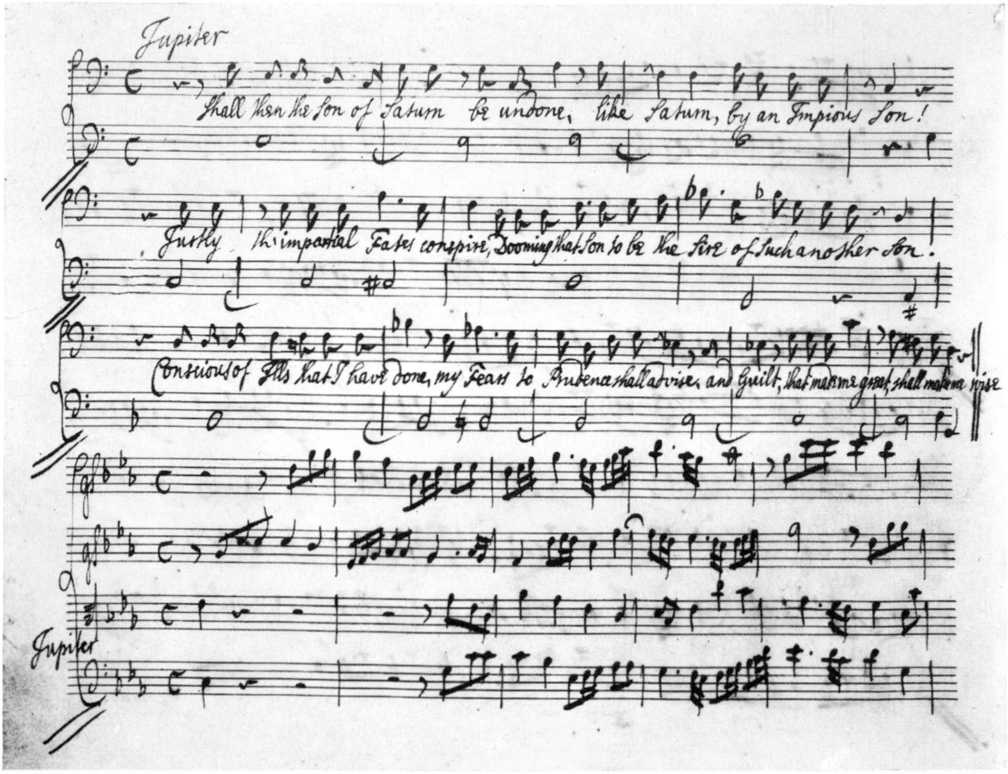

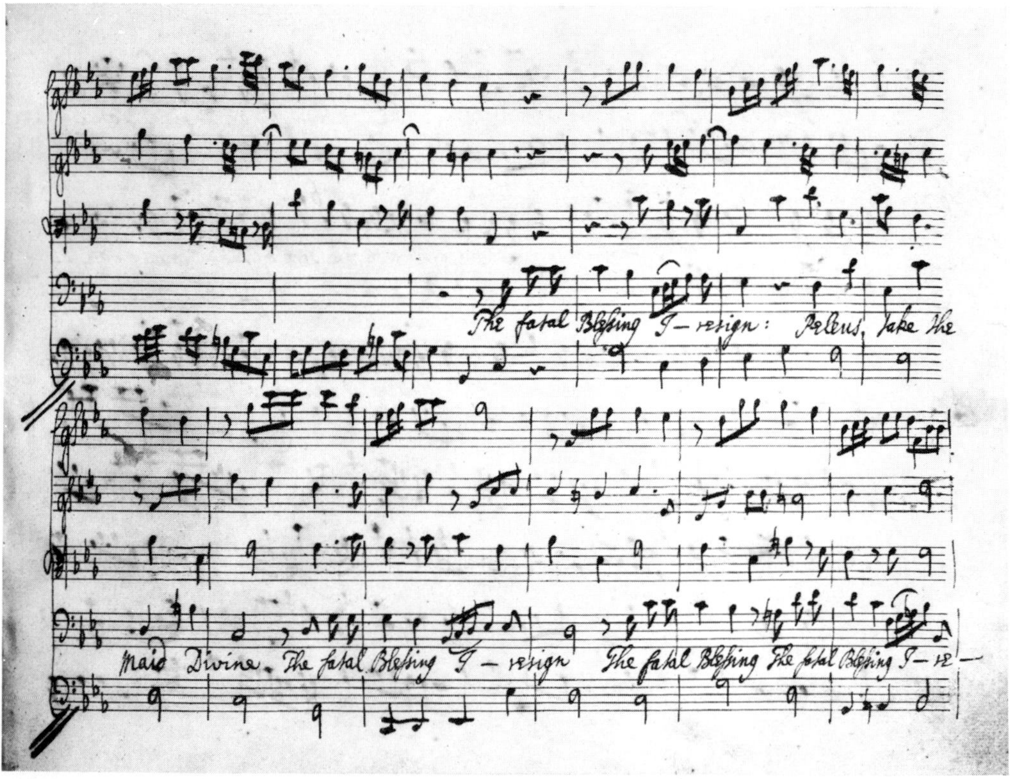

Autograph of *Peleus and Thetis* by Boyce.

but financially there was everything. On Boxing Day 1750 Garrick launched the first of several extremely successful examples.

In June 1749 Garrick married a Viennese girl who had recently been dancing in operas at the King's Theatre; he was always predisposed in favour of stage dancing and indeed of what we should call ballet. A striking and hitherto overlooked example was his ballet version of *Acis and Galatea*, staged as an afterpiece without any actors or singers on 27 November 1749. There were only three performances, and, as so often at this period, the music does not survive, but we know from the Treasurer's Accounts[1] that it was newly composed and entailed the hiring of four horns as extras.

2 BOYCE AND THE PASTORAL

William Boyce (1711–79), the son of a London cabinet-maker, was a choirboy at St. Paul's, and later the articled pupil and close friend of its organist, Maurice Greene. He also had lessons from Dr. Pepusch, who inspired him with a liking, unusual at the time, for such composers as Palestrina, Tallis, and Byrd. As a young man Boyce became hard of hearing, and although he seems never to have become totally deaf the affliction must have affected his music. In 1737 he succeeded Weldon as Composer to the Chapel Royal, and his work brought him close to the Royal Family for the rest of his days. At the same time he was made Director of the Three Choirs Festival,[2] a post he held for a number of years. Clearly he had enough to do without bothering his head with theatre music. Early on he wrote songs for, and sometimes about, Vauxhall Gardens,[3] but nothing substantial that he composed in his twenties reached print, and we must search the vast MS collection of his music in the Bodleian for his short oratorio, *David's Lament over Saul and Jonathan* (1736), and the two St. Cecilia's Day Odes (before 1740). The first of his large-scale works to be published was the serenata *Solomon*, which was probably first performed in Dublin in 1741.[4] This is a near-masterpiece. The sensual words from *The Song of Solomon* understandably put the music outside the Victorian pale, but they should not have put it outside ours.

Unlike Arne, Boyce was a popular man, and almost alone among English composers of his generation he showed no jealousy of Handel. He seems to have been happily married and 'of considerable property',[5] at least in later life. By the 1790s one of his sons, a very big man, was playing the double bass in the King's Theatre band.

Before Garrick engaged him in 1749, Boyce had made two important

---

[1] *LS* Part 4 i, p. 157.
[2] Lysons, p. 167.
[3] See Bickham's *Musical Entertainer* i, 21 and 49.
[4] Deutsch, p. 525.
[5] See Busby iii, 166, and Gardiner i, 70.

attempts at theatre music, and we are not fully informed about either. In or about 1736 he reset Lord Lansdowne's masque, *Peleus and Thetis*, written in 1701 for his Shakespearean travesty *The Jew of Venice*. Boyce must have expected his setting to stand on its own, for by his day *The Jew of Venice* had lost its popularity. The action of the masque takes place in the Caucasus Mountains where Prometheus is chained to a rock. He is famous for his knowledge of astrology, and for this reason Peleus comes to consult him about a problem: he, a mortal, loves Thetis, a nymph, and such love is forbidden; what does the future hold for them? The position is the more desperate in that Jupiter has designs on Thetis. But Prometheus tells Jupiter that he must curb his desires, for the young lovers are destined to beget a world-hero, Achilles.

This Wagnerian situation drew from Boyce some surprisingly dramatic music, with as many ensembles as arias. The overture[1] is among Boyce's best, and also the earliest fast-slow-fast 'Italian' example I have found by an English composer; it forestalls the one Arne wrote for *Alfred* by some four years.[2] The gavotte at the end has charmingly individual cadences, and an unusual slow trio section for two solo violins on their own. The 'trembling' chorus that accompanies Jupiter's slow descent from the heavens has astonishing tension and strength, as has the trio in which he storms at the young lovers; their desperate defiance is beautifully characterized. It is hard to believe that Boyce was genuinely moved by Jupiter's enforced abstinence, but he gave him a magnificent aria near the end, full of tragic feeling and contrapuntal mastery (see Plate VI). The finale has trumpets and is exuberant.[3]

We have already seen that at this period Arne was turning to the past for librettos of quality. Boyce's other early flirtation with opera also has a libretto written before he was born. Dryden's *Secular Masque*, his last work, originally had music by Daniel Purcell and Finger, and as already mentioned it was performed in 1700 at the very end of Fletcher's *The Pilgrim*. 'Secular' is to be understood in its literal sense of 'occurring once a century'; Dryden in fact was celebrating the end of one century and the beginning of another, and the theme had no relevance when Boyce tackled it. We do not know when this was. The first recorded performance was at Cambridge in 1749, but three of the songs were published in Vol. 1 of his *Lyra Britannica* (1747). Perhaps Boyce wrote the work for a Three Choirs Festival in the early 1740s; records of the Festivals are scanty at this period, but it is known that dramatic works were given as well as sacred ones.

Boyce's music is so good that one is astonished that it should never have been

---

[1] See Musica Britannica's *William Boyce Overtures*, p. 131.

[2] Earlier still was the one Handel wrote for *Athalia* (1733).

[3] The Bodleian Library has a complete set of MS vocal and instrumental parts both for this masque and for William Hayes's setting of the same libretto. I have not traced a performance of the latter, which is worthy but unenterprising; one of the two scores is dated 1749. See Appendix A for further details.

published in full. The overture is the first of a series he wrote on an unusual pattern of his own; the middle movement of the three is both quick and marked 'Piano all through', and in these respects the overtures to *The Chaplet* and *The Shepherds' Lottery* are similar. The scoring gives more individual work to the wind than Boyce usually allowed himself. The curtain rises on Janus (bass) who, in an accompanied recitative (Boyce always preferred the accompanied to the *secco* recitative) calls on Chronos to keep going now that the end of the century is in sight. Chronos (tenor, but only up to F) sets down the great World he has had on his back to sing an aria whose music is as weary and heavy as the words. Then follow no less than seven arias, sometimes separated by recitatives (*secco* or accompanied), each of which leads into a chorus on the same musical theme. Momus (tenor) has a laughing aria at the expense of Chronos, who, asked to report on World Improvement, can do no more than extol the past in a jovial hunting song that introduces Diana. But, as the gods comment in a quartet *à la gavotte*,

> Then our Age was in its Prime;
> Free from Rage, and free from Crime.
> A very Merry, Dancing, Drinking,
> Laughing, Quaffing and unthinking Time.

So far from things improving since then, they have gone downhill. In a striking recitative accompanied by trumpet, oboes, and strings (an imitation, perhaps, of the one in *Comus*), Mars (bass) shows that once the world was 'past its Infant Age', war became the thing, and in two well-contrasted arias he boasts of its influence on mankind. In the best-known song in the masque, Momus sheds the light of reason on these monstrous sentiments.

> Thy Sword within the Scabbard keep,
> And let Mankind agree;

> Better the World were fast asleep,
> Than kept awake by Thee.

Venus suggests that Love can solve all problems, and in a song of serene beauty she is conventionally supported by the flutes. Finally Momus, Janus, and Chronos, their trio capped by a splendidly vigorous chorus, review the century that was just ended in words we might equally well apply to our own.

Momus	All, all of a piece throughout:
(*to Diana*)	Thy Chace had a Beast in View;
(*To Mars*)	Thy Wars brought nothing about;
(*To Venus*)	Thy Lovers were all untrue.
Janus	'Tis well an Old Age is out.
Chronos	And time to begin a New.

Both music and words have a bitter sincerity far removed from the conventional lip-service to peace found in the average occasional masque.

With so undramatic a libretto, *The Secular Masque* is a dubious candidate for stage performance today. Yet the music demands attention. The choruses are unusually good for an English composer, and the arias are long and well sustained; only Chronos's 'The World was then so light' attempts the fashionable 'English' quality Arne exhibited in *Comus*. An extraordinary feature of the score in the Royal College of Music, the only one to survive, is that it could be performed by an all-male cast. The choruses are A.T.B., and the arias for the two goddesses never go above c″ and seldom above b′. The female contralto soloist did not then exist, and the conclusion is inescapable that on one occasion at least Boyce expected Diana and Venus to be sung by male altos. Perhaps the early Three Choirs Festivals were men-only affairs.[1] However a male Diana cannot have been to everyone's taste, let alone a male Venus, and there must at one time have been another score in which both parts were sung by sopranos. In the surviving score Diana's 'With Horns and with Hounds' is in F, and this results in improbably difficult horn parts—up to written c′. In *Lyra Britannica* the song is a sixth higher in D, a more reasonable key for the horns. Similarly Venus's 'Calms appear' is given by *Lyra Britannica* a seventh higher in D, a much more likely key for flutes than the E of the surviving full score. These must surely have been the keys in which Mrs. Clive and Miss Norris sang the parts at Drury Lane in 1750; also the keys in which unknown soloists sang at Cambridge the previous July.

Boyce's Cambridge Ode, hastily written and rehearsed in the very short time of ten days,[2] was performed in celebration of the installation of the Duke of Newcastle as the University's Chancellor. On this same occasion Boyce was made a Doctor of Music, and to honour him the more someone organized a four-

---

[1] See p. 178 for an all-male performance of Greene's *Florimel*.
[2] Lonsdale, p. 77.

day festival of his music. Besides the Ode, *The Secular Masque,* and some shorter works, *Peleus and Thetis* and *Solomon* were also given; all the librettos that were published for the festival survive in the Royal College of Music. No English composer had been honoured with a one-man festival before, unless Oxford's Handel Festival of 1733 be admitted. News of it may well have reached Garrick's ears and led to his inviting Boyce to compose for Drury Lane the following season.

According to Burney, in the 1749–50 season Arne and Boyce 'were frequently concurrents at the theatre and in each other's way'. The fact that Boyce was now a Doctor of Music when he wasn't must have added to Arne's irritation. Though they were much the same age, Arne had had virtually sixteen years' start in the theatre. He, surely, was a professional, Boyce little more than an untried amateur. Garrick, however, was more weighed by personal considerations than musical ones, and he knew Arne to be unreliable about appointments and completion dates, and notoriously slippery over evading his contracts.

> Garrick, ignorant what his musical merit may have been, had such an utter contempt for his vanity, and general Character, that he hardly ever qualified him with any other title in Private, than the Rabscalion,[1]

wrote Burney in his private Memoranda, and he added that though Arne 'was selfish, mean & rapacious after money, he spent it when acquired like a Child in gratifying his Vanity and incontinence'. At a time when his moral standards were low, Arne had become a slapdash composer, too easily satisfied with what he scribbled in haste. At best his inspiration was loftier, his scoring more imaginative than Boyce's, but too often he wrote below his capabilities. Boyce on the other hand was conscientious and consistent, and made the most of his talents. His quick music is often more virile than Arne's, his counterpoint stronger and less conventional. Perhaps he lacked a little of Arne's ease and individuality when it came to sublimating the English ballad, but he had his own vein of lyricism, and at its best it was infinitely pleasing.

Garrick asked both men for an all-sung afterpiece, and we can assume that their future at Drury Lane hung on the relative success of these operas. In the event Boyce's was liked and Arne's was not. *The Chaplet* (DL 2.12.49) had over a hundred performances in its first eight seasons, and it was soon being played all over Britain. According to Loewenberg it reached Philadelphia in 1767 and New York the following year. The words were by Moses Mendez, a popular and very wealthy young Jewish stockbroker whose grandfather had come over from Portugal as medical attendant to Queen Catherine of Braganza. Mendez had recently been to Ireland, and written an amusing poem about the trip. He had also dashed off a ballad opera, *The Double Disappointment* (DL

---

[1] Lonsdale, p. 18; and see p. 14 for Arne's womanizing, shocking even in those days.

18.3.46), whose stage Irishman, Phelim O'Blunder, brought the house down.[1] This was the most profitable success that Garrick inherited on his arrival, and it was to be expected that he would turn to Mendez again. He got something very different.

The Chaplet is a conventional Pastoral of the type John Hoadly wrote for Greene, but relieved by a few tongue-in-the-cheek touches. Laura (Miss Norris) is a virtuous and innocent shepherdess, Pastora (Mrs. Clive) an over-experienced one. Both love the world-weary Damon (Beard), who believes in love without marriage; the character is borrowed from Cibber's *Damon and Phillida*. He agrees to marry Laura in the end because he cannot get her in any other way. The only remaining character is Palaemon (Master Mattocks), who is spurned by Pastora, though it later transpires that they have been cavorting in the woods together. The title of the work is unexplained.

The music of *The Chaplet* was published in full score, complete with all the recitatives. There is also a MS full score in the Royal Music Library which clarifies what instruments play the bass line at various points in the overture. The work is scored for flute, oboes, bassoons, and strings; unusually, the flute and the oboes play at the same time. Of the thirteen songs, twelve are strophic, and in the main Boyce is imitating the sublimated ballad style evolved by Arne. The music has far less substance than that of *Peleus and Thetis* or *The Secular Masque*. There is, however, one superb song, given to Laura when she is most miserable; it is the only song that is not strophic. Poignant suspensions and ninths are kept going all through, and much of the writing for flute and strings is in five real parts.

A characteristic of Boyce's scoring is that he liked using the bassoon in the tenor range as a melodic instrument doubling the violins. Examples can be found in the Musica Britannica volume on pages 70, 82, and 126; also, rather briefly, in the middle movement of the overture to *The Shepherds' Lottery*. So far as I know, Boyce first used this delightful effect in the middle movement of the Overture to *The Chaplet*:

---

[1] The only published song, 'Balin a mona', has a delightful Irish tune that alternates between C major and D major; Mendez probably found it in Thurmoth's *Twelve Scotch and Twelve Irish Airs* (1745).

The score indicates that in the music given above the tenors (violas) are required to double the violins. In the final movement of the overture, a charming minuet, they again have no written-out part to play, but here they are specifically required to double the bass line. One final point of convention; the score shows that in all the strophic songs the instrumental introduction is played before the first verse but not before subsequent verses. In many eighteenth century strophic songs it is not made clear if the introduction is to be repeated or not; all available evidence suggests that it was never repeated.

Act II of *The Chaplet* is consistently good, but there are longueurs in Act I, so many as to suggest that the work was fortunate to enjoy the acclaim it received. No doubt people liked the music because it was the sort of music they had liked before. On the other hand Arne's *Don Saverio* (DL 15.2.50) was not in the least like any previous English opera. We do not know why the audience hissed all three performances, but it was probably because they disliked seeing men and women in modern dress singing non-stop. All-sung operas about Arcadian shepherds of the past might be tolerable, but all-sung operas about ordinary people of the present were not. The previous season the King's Theatre had presented the first full-length Italian comic operas to be seen in London, and some or all of these 'burlettas' must have had modern plots, but the new trend may well have had little appeal for playhouse audiences. It seems likely that the unfortunate Arne suffered for being ahead of his time.

No music survives for *Don Saverio*, and the libretto is a rarity. Arne is credited with the music only, but almost certainly he wrote the words as well. For reasons to be suggested later, he was beginning to prefer himself to any other librettist, and there were those who thought he might have found more success as a composer if he had been less vain as an author. The libretto includes an interesting though ill-written paragraph about the purpose of this so-called 'Musical Drama'.

> The Intention of this Piece is to display different Kinds of Expression in Music; florid Epithets and forc'd Conceits are avoided, and the Songs and Recitative are endeavour'd to be written (as nearly as possible) in such a Dialect as the Character concern'd would naturally make use of on such an Occasion, it being a standing Rule in Musical Productions, that, where the Meaning of the Poet is the least intricate,[1] the Song is unattended to, and the Music lost.

The plot is set in Naples, where Alonzo (Master Mattocks), forgetful of the fiancée he has left behind in Rome, is flirting with Clarice (Mrs. Clive). However, the lovely Turkish lady whom Clarice has befriended is really the fiancée in disguise (Miss Norris). There is another element in the story. Clarice's brother, Don Saverio[2] (Beard), has just returned after four years at Padua

[1] Arne meant 'the least bit intricate'.
[2] Saverio was Geminiani's middle name.

University. He is described as 'an affected Imitator of foreign Customs', and is the conventional fop, singing one song in French, another in praise of his own dancing, another about Italian Opera. He does in fact sing five songs in all, which is two more than anyone else, yet he has virtually nothing to do with the plot. One would dearly like to know to what extent Arne was able to distinguish his songs musically.

The new Italian comic operas at the King's Theatre also made their mark on *The Rehearsal* (DL 15.3.50) by Mrs. Clive herself, which had a dozen or more performances in three seasons. Mrs. Hazard (Mrs. Clive) has written a Burletta which is about to have its Dress Rehearsal ('I have taken great care to be delicate; I may be dull, but I'm delicate'). She wanders round her room practising a recitative from it ('Oh if that dear Garrick cou'd but sing'). Her lover asks what a Burletta is.

> Haven't you seen one at the Haymarket,
> Yes, but I don't know what it is for all that.
> Dont you, Why then, let me die if I can tell you, but I
>   believe it is a kind of poor Relation to an Opera.

A strange 'Miss' arrives asking for a part in the burletta. She has a cockney accent.

> Are you qualified?
> O yer, Mame; I have very good Friends.

She turns out to know nothing of music.

> I have a very good Ear—that is, when I sing by myself; but the
> Music always puts me out.

She then renders 'Powerful Guardians' from Handel's *Alexander Balus*, and is told her words are too clear and lack the requisite Italian accent without which success will elude her. (Which English singers, one wonders, cultivated an Italian accent for business reasons?)

The first act of *The Rehearsal* throws light on a number of aspects of the contemporary musical scene. The second is much less interesting. It takes place on the stage of Drury Lane, and ends with the performance of Mrs. Hazard's piece, which turns out to be not a Burletta but a Pastoral. The music of this, as also of one or two earlier songs, was written by Boyce, and the only surviving song, like the words, appears to be quite serious. The humour lay in the style of performance rather than the material, and in fact Mrs. Clive gave a far-from-good-humoured imitation of what she herself once described as 'Mingotti, and a set of Italian squalling devils who come over to England to get our bread from us; and I say curse them all for a parcel of Italian bitches'.[1]

[1] Tate Wilkinson, *Memoirs* ii, 29.

At the end of the season Arne transferred to Covent Garden; either Garrick had thrown him out after the failure of *Don Saverio* or he was driven to leave on his own account. The following season found him engaged in a strange form of rivalry with Boyce. On 28 September 1750 both playhouses staged a new production of *Romeo and Juliet*, and for a fortnight or so each persevered with this tragedy in the hope of outlasting the other.[1] Eventually Mrs. Cibber refused to act Juliet again without a respite. It might be thought that the performance as Romeo of Garrick and Barry would be the chief talking-point, but what fascinated the audience more was the funeral procession introduced near the end, with Juliet's supposedly dead body being carried in state across the stage. Covent Garden thought of the idea first, and Arne provided a processional Dirge whose unusual scoring included 'muffled' trumpets and drums, as also a tolling bell; it ended with a three-part chorus, 'Ah, hapless Maid', accompanied by flute and strings. Later the music was published in full score, and though it is dull as regards invention the scoring must have made it impressive.

Garrick was so alarmed at the sensation caused by Covent Garden's funeral procession that he ordered a similar one for Drury Lane; it was actually staged by the third night. Boyce's music was never published, but it survives in the Bodleian. Garrick's words began 'Rise, rise, Heart-breaking Sighs', and the scoring was very like Arne's, but the music had far more substance and genuine feeling. This processional scene was included in all productions of *Romeo and Juliet* until quite late in the nineteenth century. When Berlioz saw Harriet Smithson as Juliet in Paris, he was so impressed by it that he introduced a similarly-intentioned movement in his *Romeo and Juliet* symphony. But it is unlikely that Boyce's Dirge was performed by Kemble's company in Paris. Writing in 1878,[2] Fanny Kemble was glad that by Victorian times this 'dreadful piece of stage pageantry' had been suppressed.

> But even in my time (*c.* 1830) it was still performed, and an exact representation of a funeral procession, such as one meets every day in Rome, with torch-bearing priests, and bier covered with its black velvet pall, embroidered with skull cross-bones, with a corpse-like figure stretched upon it, marched round the stage, chanting some portion of the fine Roman Catholic requiem music.

Fanny was a good musician, and would not have mistaken Boyce for plainsong.

Later that same season (1750–1) Drury Lane gave four performances of *The Secular Masque*,[3] but they were not much liked.

As we shall see in the next section, Garrick was giving more encouragement at this period to Burney than to Boyce. However in the following season Boyce

[1] See Garrick Letters nos. 93 and 95–6.
[2] *Records of a Girlhood* i, 33.
[3] It was not performed again until 1971 when Opera da Camera presented it in London with James Bowman as Venus.

and Mendez collaborated in yet another all-sung Pastoral; it proved to be Boyce's last major work for the stage.

There is some doubt as to the placing of the apostrophe in *The Shepherds' Lottery*. Early librettos and the published full score shirk the problem by leaving it out. It was Baker who decided that only one shepherd was involved, and all subsequent reference books have followed him. But in fact everyone in the cast takes part in the lottery, and the apostrophe should surely come at the end of the word. *The Shepherds' Lottery* (DL 19.11.51), though very similar in style and quality to *The Chaplet,* was much less successful. It enjoyed some twenty-seven performances in three seasons, and was then laid aside.[1] The plot depends on the improbable and wretched convention that on May-Day shepherds choose their wives by drawing names out of an urn. Phyllis (Miss Norris) is terrified that Thyrsis (Master Vernon), who loves her as much as she loves him, will *not* draw her name. On the other hand Daphne (Mrs. Clive,) who has been slighted more than once, is cynically indifferent as to who gets her; she is indeed against the whole male sex, and at the start of Act II makes an assignation with a young shepherd for the pleasure of not keeping it. Colin (Beard) is the world-weary Damon of *The Chaplet* under another name. In the end he refuses to draw any name at all, to Daphne's indignation. Needless to say, Thyrsis draws Phyllis.

Not much is to be expected of any Pastoral plot, and not much can be said in favour of this one. The music, however, has enough vitality to make the work a viable proposition on the stage even today. The overture is a joy. In spite of a fundamentally contrapuntal texture, it is full of *galante* influence. The first movement is a buoyant Allegro in binary form, with a partial recapitulation in the second part. The delightfully original middle movement, though quick, is marked to be played quietly throughout. It begins:

[1] There was also a performance at Hereford in 1753 during the Three Choirs Festival.

The horns, silent in the first four bars, join in for the repeat. The last movement is as charming a gavotte as can be found anywhere, and it would be universally known if Bach or Handel had put his name to it.

In 1760 Boyce published some of his overtures in parts under the title of
Eight Symphonies, and these were discovered by Constant Lambert in the 1930s
and published in full score. More recently there has been a Philharmonia
miniature score of them, and this offers a much more reliable text. Neither of
these editions identifies the 'symphonies'; in fact they were all overtures that
Boyce had written much earlier. No. 3 is the overture to *The Chaplet,* No. 4
the overture to *The Shepherds' Lottery.*

Like those in *The Chaplet,* the songs in *The Shepherds' Lottery* are nearly all
strophic and in the sublimated ballad style. Again there is a superb exception,
written for Miss Norris, 'Goddess of the dimpling Smile'. It begins in the
grand manner:

Had he been encouraged, Boyce could have written an *Artaxerxes*. Unfortunately he seems to have felt that playhouse audiences were incapable of stomaching much music of this nature, and before he has done full justice to his material, he switches to an *Allegro assai* for contrast. Nevertheless this is one of his best songs.

Colin's song 'The Drum is unbrac'd and the Trumpet no more Shall rouse the fierce Soldier to fight' has in places a sort of military band accompaniment in which two horns and 'A Common 4th Flute' are prominent. For most of the century ordinary flutes, whether of the recorder type or *traversi*, were seldom expected to play above D, and various kinds of small flute were employed for higher notes. The modern piccolo, transposing an octave up, was seldom used in England in the eighteenth century; most of these small instruments seem to have been notated a fourth below the actual sounds, and their compass was thus a fifth higher than that of ordinary flutes. The subject will be dealt with in more detail later in this book (see page 281) when the use of such instruments is much more common. Boyce clearly asks for a treble sopranino recorder, and it will be recalled that in *Venus and Adonis* (1715) Pepusch asked for a 'flageletto', which must have been a *traverso* instrument. Dean cites evidence which suggests composers did not always mind which was used so long as the compass was right; in one of the *Rinaldo* arias the autograph asks for a 'flageolett', the conductor's score for a 'flauto piccolo'.[1]

The Shepherds' Lottery was the first English opera to have a finale of the type later known as 'vaudeville' (because of its prevalence in popular French opera). This consisted of a song, usually strophic, with ensemble or choral refrains in which each of the main characters was allowed one verse. It may be presumed that vaudevilles were always sung with the company lined up across the stage and facing the audience. Later on they were always in six-eight time.

Several eighteenth-century full scores show evidence that the engraver was sometimes content to leave out wind parts in order to save space. The song on page 9, 'What Beauties does my Nymph disclose', appears to be accompanied by strings alone, but in bars 15–16 and twice later there are signs of an oboe part, which we obviously do not have complete. Similarly the Finale seems to be accompanied by horns and strings, but close inspection uncovers parts for two flutes, of which only two bars were engraved. By cutting staves a publisher could cut pages and reduce his costs.

A curiosity in *The Shepherds' Lottery* is a *secco* recitative mainly in F sharp major. Boyce shows his usual tendency to prefer accompanied recitatives at the more emotional moments.

After the summer of 1752 Garrick asked Boyce for no more than the occasional song. But they must have remained on friendly terms, for when Greene died in 1755 Garrick took the trouble of writing to the Duke of Devonshire to recommend Boyce as the next Master of the King's Musick. Boyce was given the appointment, and for the rest of his life had to write two elaborate odes every year, one for the King's birthday and the other for the New Year celebrations. He also gave a great deal of time to the completion of Greene's

[1] Dean, p. 77.

great collection of Cathedral Music. For a deaf man such activities were surely more satisfying and less worrying than theatre work with its constant hurry and bustle.

3 'THE TEMPLE OF APOLLO' AND 'ALFRED'

Since about 1740 a Scottish musician called James Oswald (*c.* 1710–69) had been making a varied living in London. He had been a Dancing Master in Dunfermline and Edinburgh, and he was a good cellist. According to Burney, he 'kept a Music-shop on the pavement of St. Martin's church-yard',[1] and he published many collections of Scotch song tunes, notably *The Caledonian Pocket Companion* in twelve books. He was not above making up some of the tunes himself.

In the summer of 1750 Oswald told Garrick about the Society of the Temple of Apollo. It consisted of a number of 'gentlemen of taste and talents' who wrote music and met regularly to vet each other's work. They wished to remain anonymous. If, said Oswald, Garrick was dissatisfied with the music at Drury Lane (and it was known that he was), why should he not commission the Society for new music; he, Oswald, would act as go-between.

Garrick was certainly not deceived for long by this subterfuge, and he may not have been deceived at all, but with Arne's dismissal in his mind he had good reason to humour Oswald. Three musical novelties in the 1750–1 season were all ascribed to the Society of the Temple of Apollo, and one at least was enormously successful. Not until another twenty years had passed was it publicly revealed that in each case the composer was Charles Burney, then aged twenty-five. The Society was in fact a myth.

A great deal is known and readily available about Burney's later life, but his early years did not arouse much attention until Roger Lonsdale worked on the unpublished biographical Memoirs and letters in the British Museum and in America for his excellent 'Literary Biography' (1965). Burney was a godson of Charles Fleetwood, whose reign as manager at Drury Lane had been much unadmired. At school in Chester, he aroused the interest of Arne, who in the late summer of 1744 was returning from his two years in Dublin. Burney could play both violin and viola as well as keyboard instruments, and Arne was anxious to set himself up once more in London with an articled pupil who would do his hack work for him. Burney signed on for seven years.

In London he found himself so busy on music copying, preliminary rehearsals of singers, and playing the violin and viola at Vauxhall Gardens, that he had no time to study. Anything he earned went straight into Arne's pocket, and it soon occurred to Arne that if he locked up Burney's books and music his young pupil would waste less time in study and spend more to his master's profit. Burney maintained that he learned more from accompanying Mrs. Arne, whom

[1] BM Add. 48345, f. 12.

he liked, than from his master, whom he loathed. By 1746 he had a regular place in the Drury Lane orchestra. However, in the summer of that year he was to enjoy a few months' respite.

Fulke Greville, one of many aristocrats who put musicians very low indeed in the social scale, challenged a friend to produce an example 'who had mind and cultivation, as well as finger and ear'. As a result he was confronted with Burney, and was so impressed that he took him to Bath and elsewhere for the summer as a member of his entourage. He had to pay Arne for the privilege. Two years later Greville, now married, bought the rest of Burney's indenture from Arne, who by this time was feeling the pinch from Garrick's neglect. Burney had even helped Greville elope, and he gave the girl away at the wedding. For a time he abandoned all his London work and lived at Greville's country house near Andover, providing music whenever he was asked. After nine months Greville proposed a trip abroad, but by then Burney was in no position to leave the country; he had just decided to marry a girl who, a month earlier, had presented him with his first offspring. Greville generously released him.

Burney set himself up in London as a city organist and singing teacher, and he began writing song accompaniments for Oswald. There was no use in his pressing theatre music on Rich, who by now had no mind for novelties, and it was embarrassing for him to press music on Garrick, for this would be under-cutting Arne. Oswald and Burney must have cooked up the Society of the Temple of Apollo partly, and perhaps mainly, to deceive Arne. In view of what writers other than Lonsdale have said on the subject, it is important to stress that *all* the theatre music attributed to the Society was in fact composed by Burney alone. Burney stated this quite clearly in his unpublished Reminiscences.[1]

Burney's first work for Garrick was an all-sung 'burletta' called *Robin Hood*. (DL 13.12.50). Three songs were published anonymously, but the rest of the music is lost. The libretto by Moses Mendez attributes the music to the Society of the Temple of Apollo. The plot is more interesting than those Mendez concocted for Boyce. Robin Hood (Beard) gets into Nottingham heavily dis-guised, saves Clarinda (Miss Norris) from the fop her father wants her to marry, and gives her to Leander (Master Mattocks), the husband of her own choice. Clarinda's maid (Mrs. Clive) sings a recitative couplet that echoes opinions expressed ten months earlier of Don Saverio:

> Of all the Wretches Fate could hither bring,
> Your travell'd coxcomb is the vilest Thing.

There must have been a lot of them about at the time. When *Robin Hood* had run for a week or two, Beard became ill; for some reason the piece was never revived.

Burney's most successful work for Garrick was the pantomime *Queen Mab*, which will be considered in the next section. His third and last stage work this season brought him willy-nilly into competition with his master, Arne.

[1] BM Add. 40345, f. 12.

It will be remembered that back in 1740 Arne had set the songs in *Alfred*, a mainly-spoken masque with words by James Thomson. Arne had revised the music for Dublin, adding more songs to new lyrics presumably by himself, and there were isolated and financially unprofitable London performances in 1745 either for his wife's benefit or his own. Cummings describes a libretto issued for one of these performances, which seem to have been acted, but I have not traced a copy. It gives twenty items, more than double the number performed at Cliveden; in eight cases no setting survives.[1] By 1751 the music had still not been published, apart from 'Rule Britannia', and though Arne must have known that *Alfred* was among his best achievements, it had had no perceptible success. Among the many irritations he suffered at Garrick's hands, none can have irritated him more than the way Garrick now produced a new version of the masque without consulting him.

The man who talked Garrick into an interest in *Alfred* was David Mallet, and he is said to have done so by offering to work him, improbably, into his Life of Marlborough. This was the most notorious non-book of the century. Mallet was paid £1,000 in advance, had copious help from the family, and was for ever talking of his progress. At his death not a word of the book could be found. Needless to say, it was part of the arrangement with Garrick that Mallet should rewrite *Alfred*. And who better, for by this time, with Thomson safely dead, he was claiming to have written much of the original. He may indeed have given Thomson a few suggestions, for he had been a hanger-on of the Prince of Wales at Cliveden in 1740, but the *London Daily Post* of the time names only Thomson as author, and it is significant that in his Life of Mallet, Dr. Johnson stresses his habit of passing off other people's work as his own.

Mallet must, however, have boasted of his authorship to Aaron Hill, who in 1741 wrote to him about *Alfred* in mainly laudatory words, adding

> The *business* will, I fear, be thought too *thin* for the occasion. The masque, though sweetly full of things divinely *thought* and *said*, yet languishes for *want* of what the stage calls with reason *action*.

Hill complained that Alfred himself never does anything. The criticism is just, and it was mainly for this reason that Garrick, who wanted to play the title role himself, got Mallet to rewrite. Garrick also wanted the work lengthened into a mainpiece. Mallet's three-act libretto makes Alfred a much more meaty character, cuts the preview of sea-minded kings and queens of the future, adds some Danes, limits the singing to subsidiary characters and introduces some stage dancing. The result, though less poetic, is a little more dramatic.

Garrick must have known of Arne's all-sung version of *Alfred*; almost certainly he had already turned it down. By now Arne would have been interested only in a version that stressed the music, whereas Garrick was interested

---

[1] Burney made a new score and set of vocal parts at Arne's request; see Lonsdale, p. 10.

Love in a Village I vi by Zoffany. Hawthorn (Beard, centre) is eager to go to the village fair; his host, Woodcock (Shuter, left): 'I wish I could teach you to be a little more sedate.'

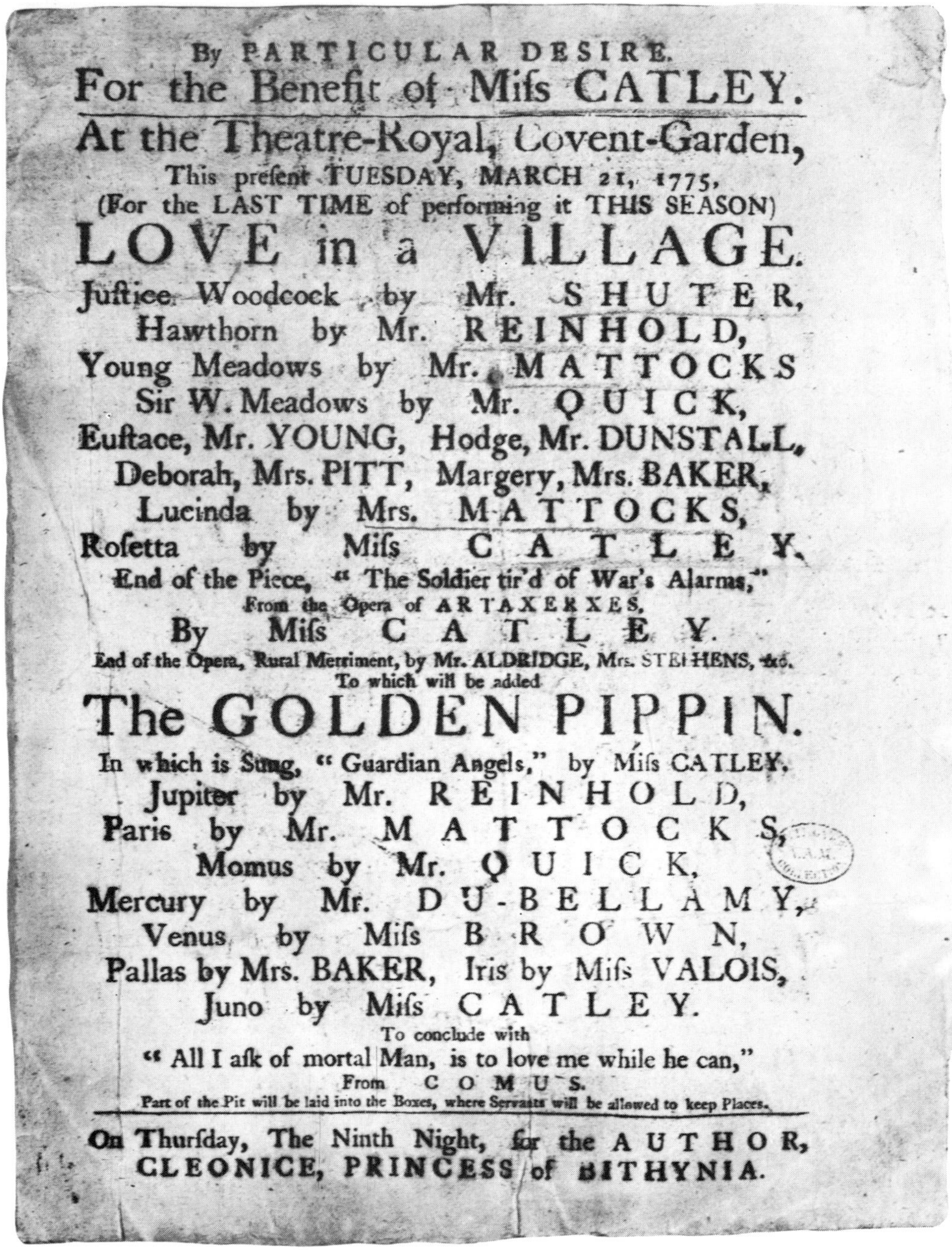

By PARTICULAR DESIRE.

For the Benefit of Miss CATLEY.

At the Theatre-Royal, Covent-Garden,

This present TUESDAY, MARCH 21, 1775,

(For the LAST TIME of performing it THIS SEASON)

LOVE in a VILLAGE.

Justice Woodcock by Mr. SHUTER,

Hawthorn by Mr. REINHOLD,

Young Meadows by Mr. MATTOCKS

Sir W. Meadows by Mr. QUICK,

Euftace, Mr. YOUNG, Hodge, Mr. DUNSTALL,

Deborah, Mrs. PITT, Margery, Mrs. BAKER,

Lucinda by Mrs. MATTOCKS,

Rofetta by Miss CATLEY.

End of the Piece, " The Soldier tir'd of War's Alarms,"

From the Opera of ARTAXERXES,

By Miss CATLEY.

End of the Opera, Rural Merriment, by Mr. ALDRIDGE, Mrs. STEPHENS, &c.

To which will be added

The GOLDEN PIPPIN.

In which is Sung, " Guardian Angels," by Miss CATLEY.

Jupiter by Mr. REINHOLD,

Paris by Mr. MATTOCKS,

Momus by Mr. QUICK,

Mercury by Mr. DU-BELLAMY,

Venus by Miss BROWN,

Pallas by Mrs. BAKER, Iris by Miss VALOIS,

Juno by Miss CATLEY.

To conclude with

" All I afk of mortal Man, is to love me while he can,"

From COMUS.

Part of the Pit will be laid into the Boxes, where Servants will be allowed to keep Places.

On Thursday, The Ninth Night, for the AUTHOR,

CLEONICE, PRINCESS of BITHYNIA.

Playbill.

only in one that stressed the speaking role of Alfred himself. Garrick may well have waited till Arne was safely out of the way before launching this production. He suggested to Mallet that the music should be commissioned from the Society of the Temple of Apollo.

Mallet, himself a Scotsman, welcomed collaborating with his fellow-countryman Oswald because he had a theory that *Alfred* needed the most ancient music available. As Burney wrote, Mallet

> wanted all the songs to be adapted to old Scotch tunes . . . I indulged him in 2 or 3; but as Alfred was not a Scotsman, I thought it wd. be ridiculous to confine all the songs to Scotish melody. I therefore new set all the rest except 'Rule Britannia', wch. had been so happily set by my Master Arne. . . .[1]

In two respects Burney is not quite accurate. Though he set 'Peace, thou fairest child of Heav'n', Arne's version was preferred; one suspects divided loyalties among the singers, and Beard at least always recognized Arne's merit. Also Burney did attempt a patriotic Finale intended to replace 'Rule, Britannia'. There is nothing to be said in favour of the vainglorious words, but the tune is rather good:

[1] Lonsdale, p. 34.

On 23 February 1751 the Mallet–Burney version of *Alfred* had its first performance, and it was thought to be sufficiently new to be advertised as 'never acted before'. Three days later *The General Advertiser* carried the following:

> To the Public: As Mr. Arne originally composed the Music in the Masque of Alfred, and the Town may probably on that account imagine the Music, as now perform'd, to be all his production, he is advised by his friends to inform the Publick that but two of his songs are in that performance, viz.: the first song beginning *O Peace thou fairest Child of Heaven*; and the Ode in Honour of Great Britain . . . *Rule Britannia, Rule the Waves* etc., which Songs he submitted to be mix'd with the production of others, to oblige the Author of the Poem. Tho.Aug.Arne.

The plural 'others' near the end suggests that Arne did not know that the rest of the music was all by Burney. *Alfred* had nine performances. The singing was mainly done by Beard, Reinhold, Master Vernon, and Mrs. Clive; Madame Camargo, sister of the famous Camargo, was among the dancers. According to the prompter Cross, *Alfred* 'was play'd with great Applause, only some of the Dances, being too long were dislik'd, & some of the Songs had the same reception'.

The score is a rarity not to be found in the British Museum, though there are copies in Cambridge, Glasgow, and London's Royal College of Music. It does not include the dance music, and it omits three lyrics to be found in Mallet's libretto probably because they ended with a chorus. Apart from 'O Peace', only two of Thomson's lyrics were thought worth keeping, one being 'Hear, Alfred, father' of which Arne's setting does not survive because he himself later cut the song. Mallet even took the trouble to rewrite the last four verses of 'Rule, Britannia', not to its advantage. Scots tunes include 'Pinkie House', and a note in the score says 'the above Melody is Old, & suppos'd to be David Rizzio's.' The absurd myth that Mary Queen of Scots' Italian secretary composed the best of the old Scottish tunes was started by William Thomson in the first edition of his *Orpheus Caledonius* of 1726, though he withdrew the ascription in his second edition. Oswald thought it worth perpetrating for publicity reasons, though he can hardly have believed in it, and Geminiani lent it support in two of his theoretical works because he wanted to think that a fellow country-man created these lovely tunes. The theory was eventually exploded by Hawkins.

Two of Burney's songs are in the grand manner, notably 'Swell the Trum-pet's boldest Note', scored for trumpet, drums, and strings with good indepen-dent parts for the violins. But some of the music is of poor quality, notably Burney's naïve unsung setting of 'O Peace'. A month or so after the first night Burney became very ill; in the summer he left London for nine years for the sake of his health, to become organist in King's Lynn.

The only published score of Arne's *Alfred* has often been associated with Garrick's production of 1751, but it cannot be earlier than 1753.[1] It corres-ponds with the libretto issued for a performance at the King's Theatre on 12 May of that year, given for the benefit of 'the Charitable Hospital for Lying-in Women in Jermyn St., St. James'. There had been no Italian Opera that season, and thus Arne was able to make use of a theatre usually denied to him, as also of three excellent Italian singers who were in the country and short of work. Alfred and his wife were sung by Beard and Frasi, two shepherds by Baker and Galli. Mrs. Arne was the Spirit, and her niece, Isabella Young, made her début as the second shepherdess, Edith. A new character, Alfred's son Edward, was taken by Guadagni, the castrato who later sung Orfeo in the first performance of Gluck's opera. For the first time in his career, Arne had an all-star cast.

Cummings deduced from a note in the libretto that it had been adapted from the one by Mallet of two years earlier, but the deduction is unwarranted; the likelihood is that Arne adapted his own libretto of 1745. Certainly the work is full-length and all-sung, but it was not invariably staged. In Dublin in 1744 the work was described as a serenata, and at Drury Lane in 1754 and Dublin in 1756 as an oratorio; these must have been concert performances. But at Drury Lane in 1745 and 1753 it was a Music Drama and as such must have been acted. (The published score still calls the work a Masque.) The story is much

[1] It is misdated in the British Museum Catalogue and in BUCEM.

more static than in Mallet's version. The Danes have disappeared, and with them goes what tension Mallet was able to achieve. Very little happens. Unexpected stress is laid on choral singing, and for the chorus that ends Act II Arne borrowed the well-known lyric 'How sleep the Brave who sink to rest', which had been written some seven years earlier by William Collins.

Newspaper advertisements of 1753 describe the music as 'New-Composed', which can have been true only in part; they add that, as a special attraction, there will be introduced 'a *Solemn Dirge* in Honour of the Heroes who died in the Service of their Country'. This imaginative piece was sung by Mrs. Arne, and is notable for the imitations of weeping on the oboe. This instrument is in counterpoint with the voice throughout.

Later the wailing phrase is sung to the words 'to dwell a weeping hermit there'. The published score omits all *secco* recitatives and choruses;[1] also 'Rule, Britannia', which was already available in *The Judgment of Paris*. It was howeveer included in a second edition which appeared a year or two later, probably at the time of the Drury Lane performances of 1754 or 1755.

The scoring seems unadventurous, though it must be remembered that we can seldom tell to what extent, if any, wind parts have been omitted by the engraver. As in *Comus*, about two-thirds of the arias and duets are scored for

[1] Those with access to the 1753 score may be interested in the following statistics:

a. Choruses should follow pp. 34, 49, 67, 70, 73, 77, and 79, as is often predictable from the incompleteness of the preceeding aria. The one following p. 70 ends Act II and Act III begins with another also not given; thus eight choruses in all are omitted, and presumably lost for ever.

b. Some scores have no consecutive pagination between pp. 10 and 41. This is because Walsh first issued pp. 33–41 as 'Songs in the Masque of Alfred' and then pp. 10–32 as a second set; he used the original plates for the 'complete' score and left the original pagination.

c. Besides 'Rule, Britannia', Arne took from his Cliveden score items on pp. 12–14, 21, 30, 37, 40, 76, and no doubt the overture and march.

strings alone; in *Eliza* and *Artaxeres* the proportion is only a little over one-third. The new music is for the most part elaborate. The three simple strophic songs all date from 1740. In 1753, with such excellent singers on hand, Arne was setting his sights higher. Beard, Frasi, and Guadagni all have long and lavishly accompanied *Da Capo* arias of great technical difficulty. Guadagni's, a 'revenge' aria, is the best. In general Arne tends to lose his individuality when attempting quick vigorous music. Much of *Alfred* is rather slow-moving and melancholy, especially in the first act.

The score is deceptive about who sings what. The publishers used the old plates for 'Rule, Britannia' and these incorrectly showed one singer and six verses. The 1753 libretto cut verses 3 and 5, and had the remainder sung alternately by Alfred and his wife Eltruda. As was then usual, the engraver labelled each song with the name of the singer and not with the name of the character, and often he got the singer's name wrong. The MS from which he worked probably had a number of songs labelled 'Ed', for he confuses the shepherdess Edith with Alfred's son, Prince Edward. Thus the libretto shows that 'Come, calm Content' (p. 18) and 'See Liberty' (p. 80), much criticized for resembling 'Love sounds the Alarm' in *Acis and Galatea*, were sung by Guadagni as Edward and not by Miss Young as Edith. Edith is also confused with another shepherdess, Emma; Signora Galli as the latter should sing 'If those who live in Shepherds Bower' (p. 30) and 'Love's the Tyrant of the Heart' (p. 35), and not Miss Young, who, as a newcomer, could not possibly have had as many songs as the score allows her. Again the libretto is to be believed.

It may be helpful to list at this point all the main versions of *Alfred*, including two that have not yet been mentioned.

First Perf.		Librettist	Composer
1. Cliveden 1740	mainly spoken	Thomson	Arne
2. DL 1745	all sung	mainly Arne	Arne
3. DL 1751	mainly spoken	mainly Mallet	mainly Burney
4. KT 1753	all sung	mainly Arne	Arne
5. CG 1759	all sung	mainly Arne	Arne
6. DL 1773	mainly spoken	Mallet-Garrick	mainly T. Smith

No. 6 is discussed on page 366. Of No. 5 there were three concert performances 'with several new Songs composed by Mr. Arne', and their words can be found in a handsome libretto of the 'Oratorio' published by T. Lowndes, but none of the new music seems to survive. Printed scores can be found for versions 3, 4, and 6, but in no case are they complete.

4 PANTOMIME IN THE 1750s

Garrick's reputation was immense even before his arrival at Drury Lane. He and Macklin had introduced a new realism of both gesture and costume, and

Garrick actually appeared to be listening when other people on the stage were talking. Old-fashioned pantomime could hardly have a place in the modern realistic theatre, and no one was surprised when Garrick announced he would do without it. For the first night of his first season at Drury Lane, he got Samuel Johnson to write a special prologue, which traced the decline of Tragedy from Shakespeare's day onwards; Virtue had hung on for as long as possible, 'though Nature fled', but eventually

> Forc'd, at length, her ancient reign to quit,
> She saw great Faustus lay the ghost of wit;
> Exulting Folly hail'd the joyous day,
> And Pantomime and Song confirm'd her sway.

(Faustus, needless to say, was not Marlowe's hero.) Finally Johnson appealed rather obscurely to the audience to show better sense in the future.

> Then prompt no more the follies you decry,
> As tyrants doom their tools of guilt to die;
> 'Tis yours, this night, to bid the reign commence
> Of rescued Nature, and reviving Sense.

No doubt everyone applauded these fine sentiments, and hoped a new day had dawned. The trouble was that they went on flocking to Covent Garden pantomimes, old and faded though they were. Genest reckoned that when a pantomime was running a theatre could take about £1,000 a week; without one it was lucky to average £500. By 1750 Garrick had to sink his pride. 'If you wont come to Lear and Hamlet, I must give you Harlequin.' At least it should not be difficult to improve on Drury Lane's previous efforts in this line, or indeed on those still given up the road at Covent Garden. It so happened that Garrick had in his company the second best Harlequin of the century.

Henry Woodward (1714–77) had attracted Rich's attention while still a boy at Merchant Taylors School; he was Peachum in the Lilliputian production of *The Beggar's Opera*. Soon he was playing small pantomime parts for Rich, 'from a frog to a hedgehog, an ape and a bear, till he arrived at the summit of his ambition, Harlequin'.[1] He was then billed as 'Lun jun.'. Unlike Rich, Woodward could use his voice, though according to *The Theatrical Examiner* (1757) it was 'weak, or rather odd, from a peculiar drawl in his delivery'. But he was very successful in such Shakespearean parts as Sir Andrew Aguecheek, Touchstone, Mercutio, Petruchio, and Parolles. We learn also that he was 'a good size, and tolerably easy made, a countenance most happily droll'. In 1747 he was lured by an offer of £500 for the season to Smock Alley Theatre, Dublin, the luring being done by Thomas Sheridan, but the next season he was back at Drury Lane with Garrick and having one of his greatest successes as Captain Bobadil in Jonson's *Every Man in his Humour*.

[1] Baker, article on Woodward.

At first Woodward must have regretted Garrick's opposition to pantomime, for Harlequin was the breath of life to this curious man. To meet he was reserved and rather uncouth, but the moment pantomime was in the wind he became a dictator of the most energetic and vital kind. He devised six pantomimes for Garrick, playing Harlequin in them all, and the first four were to be the mainstay of Drury Lane's pantomime repertoire for a quarter of a century:

Queen Mab (26.12.50).
Harlequin Ranger (26.12.51).
The Genie, an Arabian Nights Entertainment (26.12.52).
Fortunatus (later *Harlequin Fortunatus*) (26.12.53).
Proteus, or Harlequin in China (4.1.55).
Harlequin Mercury (or *Mercury Harlequin*) (27.12.56).

No Description of a Woodward pantomime seems to survive, and only one song (Arne's 'The beer drinking Briton') survives of the last-named, which was not very successful. Oswald published the Comic Tunes of the first four, as also a few songs, without once giving away the name of the composer. He attributes *Queen Mab* to the mythical Society of the Temple of Apollo, but Burney cannot have written the others for he was no longer in London. Perhaps Oswald himself was their composer. Walsh published the Comic Tunes and three songs sung by Beard in *Proteus*; BUCEM gives only the British Museum copy.

Five of the six Woodward pantomimes were first performed on Boxing Day; Garrick was starting a trend that later grew into a convention. But for most of the century the playhouses were liable to stage new pantomimes as late as the spring, while the summer theatres such as Sadler's Wells often put them on in the hottest weather.

Queen Mab came at a worrying time for Garrick; Barry, Macklin, and Mrs. Cibber had all gone over to Covent Garden. Its immediate success must have been some compensation, if only a financial one. It was the first slickly-produced pantomime ever seen at Drury Lane, and Woodward as Harlequin was a sensation. There were forty-five almost consecutive performances the first season, and hundreds more later. A contemporary cartoon shows Garrick in excellent spirits weighing down one side of a pair of scales; on what might be called the Covent Garden side, too light to balance him, are Peg Woffington, Mrs. Cibber, Barry, and Quin, while Rich in Harlequin costume lies weeping in the dust.

According to Burney, Woodward had

> delivered to Oswald, in writing, subjects for the tunes that were to paint the several scenes & events of the piece; in which Puck the Fairy had several Songs that were written by Garrick, and sent to Oswald for the Society to set, who delivered them to me.[1]

[1] Lonsdale, p. 33.

Puck was played by Master Vernon, and his songs, a rarity, can be found in the British Museum. Of the twenty-one published Comic Tunes, seven are given on three staves and the rest on two. This is not a keyboard reduction; strings playing in two or sometimes three parts were all that could be expected of such music. Oswald's publication is virtually a full-score, however meagre it may look. However one suspects the use of brass in the very first piece, 'The Watchman':

The main tune, though naïve, has plenty of charm; the last two bars clearly represent the watchman's horn, and this rhythm is effectively worked into the accompaniment several times later on, always on a note that could be played by a horn in G. More of the music is designed to match specific movements than in any previously-published Comic Tunes. A piece called 'The Animating Harlequin', though without merit as music, has seven dynamic markings in four bars, including 'pianis', 'pia', 'for', and 'fortis'. One called 'The Whip' has strong accents on the fourth beats which clearly represent whip-cracks. An unusual piece keeps contrasting two conflicting emotions.

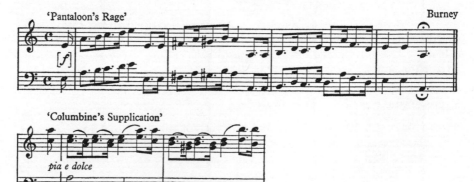

Several pieces have a country-dance flavour, while 'The Last Dance' anticipates a Scottish convention that one associates with a much later period, and was surely played by oboes and bassoons as well as strings:

The Comic Tunes in *Harlequin Ranger* have much less to commend them. One is called 'Covent Garden', and no doubt while the music was played the audience was regaled with a chase seen against a backcloth depicting the streets only a few yards from where they were sitting. We today are fascinated in the cinema if we recognize something as dull and familiar as the local High Street, and in the second half of the eighteenth century pantomimes nearly always indulged the audience's taste for this kind of recognition.[1]

The Genie was the first of many pantomimes to derive from *The Arabian Nights*, but the connection cannot have been very close, for nearly all the Comic Tunes have thoroughly English titles. A curiosity is 'The Fishmonger's Shop', which incorporates two London street-cries; here is the first half:

[1] There had already been a 'Covent Garden' scene in *Harlequin Student*, and there was to be another, of the Piazza, in *The Choice of Harlequin*. Ludgate Circus and Charing Cross were represented in *Pigmy Revels*, Whitehall in *The Touchstone* and *Harlequin's Chaplet* (the latter also offered 'The Chelsea Waterworks'), Cornhill and Westminster Bridge in *The Triumph of Mirth*, St. James's Place in *Harlequin's Museum*, and so on. In each case the title of one of the Comic Tunes provides the information.

An unusually expressive piece is called 'The parting of Harlequin and Columbine'; the style looks forward rather than backwards.

The second part of this binary-form piece is very much longer. Two pieces are scored for flutes and bass. Baker found the production as a whole 'a splendid spectacle'.

The story on which *Fortunatus* is based was much more familiar in the eighteenth century than it is today. Fortunatus, a Cypriot, was the hero of a medieval chap-book. The goddess of Fortune gave him a purse which could never be emptied, and not content with this he stole from the Sultan of Egypt a magic hat which would transport the wearer wherever he wished to go. But on his death his two sons quarrelled over the purse and hat, and came to an untimely end. The story had previously been written up by Hans Sachs and Thomas Dekker, and in eighteenth-century England *The Right pleasant and variable tragical History of Fortunatus* went through as many as twenty editions. But after Henry Bishop had written an opera on the subject in 1819, Fortunatus dropped out of folklore so completely that today it is hard to find anyone who has heard of him.[1] The possibilities for stage trickery that the story offers made it ideal for pantomime.

Apart from some Greek mythology, there is nothing in the tune titles to suggest the Mediterranean. Hercules and Venus were dragged in, to be danced by M. Devise and Mme Auretti; both were very popular at Drury Lane. There were four Chinese Dances, but there is nothing exotic in their music. Much of the pantomime takes place on a farm, and there is an amusing 'Hen's March', printed on a single stave and presumably played by a violin; it bears

---

[1] Wordsworth had; see *The Prelude* v, 342.

some resemblance to the hen tune in *Le Carnaval des Animaux* by Saint-Saëns.[1]

A piece called 'The Laundry' is probably the original of the well-known nursery song, 'The Old Woman and the Pettycoat'. *Fortunatus* remained popular for several decades, and for a revival in 1780 Thomas Linley wrote two new songs which both survive.

Garrick had lured Devise over from Paris in 1750 for Woodward's first pantomime. He always aimed at a more balletic type of pantomime than Rich, and realized that he must search abroad for dancers of the more graceful kind. In the summer of 1751 he was in Paris with his ex-dancer wife, and the trip was not entirely a holiday. Devise was there too. The plan seems to have been that whenever the Garricks saw a dancer they liked in one of the theatres, Devise tried to bribe him or her to join the Drury Lane company. Unfortunately Devise was caught doing so, and arrested for infringing French theatre regulations, and indeed royal edicts. He was back in London in time for Woodward's third pantomime, *The Genie*, and seems to have brought Mme Auretti with him.

The Chinese Dances in *Fortunatus* were symptomatic of a craze for *chinoiserie* already apparent in contemporary furniture. Drury Lane's 1755 pantomime, *Proteus*, was set entirely in China, and about this time Garrick planned the most notorious Chinese entertainment of the century. At the Opéra Comique in Paris a ballet called *Les Fêtes Chinoises* had just had a resounding success, and Garrick set about the unprecedented task of bringing the entire production to London. He began by signing on the ballet's creator, a young Swiss called Jean-Georges Noverre. Noverre was *maître de ballet* at the Opéra Comique, and advocated a much closer relationship between movement and music than had been usual before. Today he is credited with the invention of the *ballet d'action*, but in fact he got many of his ideas on mime from Drury Lane pantomimes.

Arrangements to transport the scenery and cast from Paris took so long that by the time *The Chinese Festival* was due to open at Drury Lane war had been declared between England and France. In a cast of a hundred, only fifteen were said to be continentals, and most of these seem to have been Swiss relatives of Noverre himself, but Garrick was naturally playing down the French

[1] There is a rather more accurate imitation of hens in the accompaniment of a song Arne wrote for *The Guardian Outwitted* (1764).

elements in the production. Unfortunately the audience did just the opposite. This was the nearest thing to a modern ballet that London had yet seen, and London did not at all want to see it. The fact that the scenery and some of the cast were French, while those who said they were Swiss were thought to be equivocating, caused a surge of nationalist resentment, and on the second night the presence of the king did little to quell the clamour. In subsequent performances free fights among the audience attracted more attention than what was happening on the stage, and on the sixth and last night there was a full-scale riot during which much damage was done to the theatre. The mob even threatened to wreck Garrick's house in Southampton Street. Garrick in turn threatened to retire, and this brought people to their senses, but he had to agree to withdraw *The Chinese Festival* and send the company back to Paris. Drury Lane lost £4,000 over the venture, and London got no nearer modern ballet until Noverre returned some thirty years later. But it would be surprising if Drury Lane pantomimes did not turn a few new corners as a result of his first visit.

In 1757 Woodward suddenly went off to Dublin with Barry to set up a new theatre in rivalry with Thomas Sheridan's. With Rooker as his new Harlequin, Garrick scored another success with *Harlequin's Invasion* (DL 31.12.59). By now the Seven Years War was at its height, and the big hit of the pantomime was Boyce's patriotic sea song, 'Heart of Oak', the tune differing a good deal from the Victorianized version known today. Aylward and Michael Arne also contributed songs and probably Comic Tunes, but the latter were never published. No Description survives even though the pantomime stayed in the repertoire nearly to the end of the century. Surprisingly it was not France that Harlequin invaded, but the 'frontiers and domain of Shakespeare', and the climax was Shakespeare's restoration as king. In fact Garrick, who devised the plot and the song words (there must also have been recitatives), had rewritten *Harlequin Student, or the Fall of Pantomime*.[1]

The scenery designer at Drury Lane was a solid dull man named French. Feeling that something original was called for, Garrick engaged Henry Angelo to supervise the decor for *Harlequin's Invasion*. Angelo had recently seen what he calls 'Les tableaux vivants' in Venice, and he described these in his Reminiscences as transparencies against (behind?) which figures designed by Canaletto flitted in silhouette. Garrick wanted a similar scene in which Harlequin was pursued through an enchanted wood, and Angelo got French to

> cause screens to be placed diagonally, which were covered with scarlet crimson and bright moreen, which, having a powerful light behind them, and by turning them towards the scenery, reflected these various colours alternately, with a success that astonished and delighted the audience. Indeed the whole stage appeared on fire.

[1] See p. 169.

There is little to report on the Covent Garden front. According to *The London Stage*,[1] between 1747 and 1761, the last fifteen years of his reign, Rich revived his old successes as follows:

Harlequin Sorcerer	210
Harlequin Skeleton (i.e. *The Royal Chace*)	183
Perseus and Andromeda	129
Apollo and Daphne	123
The Fair (1750)	101
Orpheus and Euridice	90
The Rape of Proserpine	63
The Necromancer (*Harlequin Dr. Faustus*)	38
Harlequin Statue (1739)	23

Thus there were 960 performances of nine pantomimes in fifteen years, an average of sixty-four performances a year; in other words there was a pantomime afterpiece on roughly one night in three. Only the two dated pantomimes were instituted after 1730, and neither of these is of much interest. Rich himself devised *The Fair*, and even appeared himself in a few performances; it is not known who wrote the music, none of which survives. However three songs sung by Beard in a revival of 1759 were published, and may be by Arne.

Harlequin Sorcerer was Covent Garden's chief success in the 1750s. It had not been performed for many years when, in February 1752, Rich revived it with elaborate new music by Arne. According to an account quoted in *The London Stage*,[2] 'The Music is most of it new, and compos'd by Mr. Arne, who himself played the Harpsichord; the songs are excellently well set and adapted to the characters.' We know more about this than any previous pantomime production. The Bodleian has a libretto, and though this follows Theobald's original in saying nothing of the Harlequin episodes ('The Scene changes and the Actions of Harlequin go on'), these are detailed in the contemporary account quoted in *The London Stage*. Arne published five vocal items in full score, and Walsh's anonymous collection of Comic Tunes must contain a good deal of his new music, together with dances from the original production of 1725.

The libretto is called *The Sorcerer* on its first page, and *Harlequin Sorcerer, with the Loves of Pluto and Proserpine* on its second. It follows closely the one described on p. 81, but includes the words of additional recitatives, airs, and choruses, and there are in all twelve major vocal items. Four of these can be found in Arne's *Vocal Melody* Vol. 4, and a fifth item, a Pastoral Dialogue called 'Damon and Florella' (which is not in the libretto) can be found in Vol. 5.[3] All these songs are operatic in scale, and, except for the rather dull

---

[1] LS Part 4, i, p. lxv.

[2] Part 4, i, p. cxlix. It comes from 'Have at ye all; or, The Drury Lane Journal' for 13.2.53.

[3] For this fifth annual song collection Arne changed his general title from *Vocal Melody* to *The Agreeable Musical Choice*.

Revenge Aria for bass, 'Powerful Daughters of the Night', all are well written and delightful. The scoring is for strings alone except for the first of these songs, 'Harvest Home', which was sung in the farmyard scene by Lowe and a chorus of farm-hands; for the chorus oboes and horns were added. No songs for the masque scene at the end between Pluto and Proserpine survive, and here the original settings by Galliard were no doubt used.

The contemporary account of the action starts with Harlequin flying in between two witches on a pole. He serenades Columbine until her father, Pantaloon, chases him away and up onto the scaffolding of a half-built house. This collapses under their weight. Harlequin disguises himself successively as an old woman working on a farm (this is where 'Harvest Home' came in), as an ostrich, and as a washerwoman who throws suds at Pantaloon. His attempt to evade detection motionless on a statue of a horse fails when he sneezes, and it turns out that the horse is alive too. The stage darkens for more witchery and flying stunts, and the pantomime ends with the Pluto-Proserpine masque.

The new libretto, unlike the old one, mentions an overture. In his edition of the Comic Tunes Walsh included the minuet from the overture and it is a charming piece, no doubt by Arne. Then follow some two dozen Comic Tunes, together with seven from *Harlequin Dr. Faustus* which was also popular that season. As we have seen, all of the latter and some of the former are probably from the original productions, and the work of Galliard.[1] Very few have titles, but there is an ungainly piece in nine-eight called 'The Ostrich Tune', and pieces called 'The Witches Dance', 'Hurry', and 'Wash-house Tune'. One with no title is a good example of the typical snap rhythm so often associated with Harlequin.[2] Here is the first half:

Two are of symphonic length and must be Arne's; one of these is unmistakably *galante*:

[1] See p. 80.
[2] See p. 84.

The other alternates between short pleading *Adagios* and short raging *Allegros*, and no doubt accompanied a mimed dialogue between Columbine and Pantaloon.

5 ARNE'S 'ELIZA'

Disliked at Drury Lane and discouraged at Covent Garden, Arne took unusual pains to write an almost full-length all-sung opera called *Eliza*, and for want of a better theatre he put it on at the Little (29.5.54). The words were by Richard Rolt, an amiable hack who often turned out words for Vauxhall songs and cantatas; he also worked with Christopher Smart on various flippant periodicals. Musically *Eliza* is a fine achievement, but the boredom of the libretto would preclude all possibility of a stage performance today. Eliza is Queen Elizabeth, who never appears. Britannia and the usual personifications and shepherds make some pretence of discussing the subjects of Peace and War, and finally there is a representation of the Armada with model ships. One wonders if Sheridan had this opera in mind when writing the end of *The Critic*. Somehow the piece is dragged out into three acts.

The overture is Arne's masterpiece in the French form, with a noble if rather Handelian introduction, a splendid fugue on two subjects that are eventually combined, and a serene minuet. It is as good as any of Handel's, and better than many. Although the action is said to lie in Kent and Essex, the curtain rises on 'A mountainous Country, with a Prospect of the Sea; and Britannia discovered under a Rock, in a melancholy Posture'. It was hardly a novel opening. Britannia's first song calls for music to soften the pain caused, we eventually discover, by the threatening behaviour of the Spanish Armada, and very lovely music Arne gives her:

For 1754 this is old-fashioned and Handelian, and it must be said that the work as a whole shows scarcely a trace of *galante* influence. Its comparative failure was probably due to the fact that audiences were growing weary of this sort of music and this sort of libretto. Britannia's 'With Swords on their Thighs' even goes back to Purcell's style for its patriotic fervour, and in other European countries the trumpet part in the Sailor's 'Come, my Lads! Form a Ring' would have seemed so out of date that it might have been hard to find anyone able to play it:

In London virtuoso trumpet-playing could still be counted on.

But though the substance of *Eliza*'s music was old-fashioned, its scoring was very advanced. Orchestrally this was much the most ambitious work Arne had attempted. There are no fewer than three full-scale arias accompanied by strings, oboes, bassoon, trumpet, and drums. Horns are used in five vocal items, and in Britannia's 'Gentle Breezes' both horns and strings are muted. The March that accompanies the sea-fight has parts for horns, trumpets, and side-drum as well as strings and woodwind. As in *The Judgment of Paris* there is an aria with cello obbligato. The duet 'With Roses be our Temples bound' is accompanied solely by two cross flutes and violins, the latter supplying the bass. Two different kinds of octave flute are required, both a comparative rarity at the time. An 'Octave German Flute' is called for in the middle of Britannia's 'The Lark her lowly Nest defends', and it provides an effective imitation of a lark soaring. Later in the second act the Shepherd has another lark song, this time in siciliano rhythm with the imitations played by a 'Little Flute'; this also transposes an octave, and it must be a descant recorder. Neptune has an adventurous aria in the main section of which the strings (except for the double basses) imitate ocean waves with continuous rushing semiquavers in octaves:

Eight vocal items out of twenty-eight are strophic, four of them in Act I; another is the Finale, a vaudeville with a fine patriotic swagger to it. But in general the arias are more extended than in Arne's previous surviving operas and masques.

Two seasons later (1755–6) Arne was in Dublin with his wife and a very promising young pupil called Charlotte Brent. *Eliza* was given three times with acclaim, and it received several more performances at Drury Lane on Arne's return; the first of these, on 20 December 1756, has sometimes been mistaken for the first night. Mrs. Arne stayed on in Dublin, sickened by her husband's too intimate relationship with Miss Brent. In her absence Britannia was sung at Drury Lane by Frasi, with Miss Brent as Liberty. Isabella Young and Miss Poitier (who now called herself Mrs. Vernon) kept their old parts, and Beard doubled the Shepherd and the Sailor. The published full score omits the *secco* recitatives, two dance movements, and the choruses that should follow on pages 36, 52, 61, 77, and 105. These choruses were not separate movements but final verses to the preceding songs.

In 1784 Michael Arne revised *Eliza* for the Little Theatre, adding choruses from other works by his father. Though the opera made no impression, Harrisons published the first and only vocal score about this time; it did not include Michael Arne's additions.

Shortly before the Arnes left for Dublin in 1755, there was a change of policy at Drury Lane. For years it had been felt that plays were unsuitable on Wednesdays and Fridays in Lent, and Covent Garden had regularly presented oratorios on those days, most of them Handel's. But Drury Lane had lacked the vocal resources for oratorios, and the theatre had had to close. However in the Lent of 1755 Arne's *The Death of Abel* was given its first London performance at Drury Lane, and from then on the theatre rivalled Covent Garden with its own oratorio seasons.

Arne probably risked his own money on *The Death of Abel*, hiring the theatre from the managers. But a month or two later Garrick must have given him positive encouragement, for the theatre staged his patriotic masque, *Britannia* (DL 9.5.55). Though Mallet's libretto is dreary in the extreme, there were a dozen performances spread over four seasons and bolstered by the atmosphere of the Seven Years War. Some of the songs can be found in Arne's *Vocal Melody*, Vol. 10. The libretto resembles that of *Eliza*, but there is a greater emphasis on recruiting, now a burning issue. The music is rather dull, as it usually was when Arne was writing for Garrick. Garrick himself spoke the Prologue 'in the character of a sailor fuddled and talking to himself', but there was an undertow of solid patriotism behind the drunken words. The curtain rose on Britannia 'reclining against a cliff in a pensive posture', and anyone who had seen *Eliza* must have suspected he was seeing it again. Mercifully, Arne was flirting with Britannia for the last time.

6 SMITH'S RETURN TO THE THEATRE

Garrick never let Arne think he was Drury Lane's only available composer, and in the early part of 1755 he found himself in rivalry with John Christopher Smith, who had been lost to the playhouses ever since the failure of his *Ulysses* more than twenty years earlier. A clue to this strange man's behaviour was given by his stepson, the Rev. William Coxe of Bemerton, who wrote: 'It was Mr. Smith's peculiar turn of disposition, not to live much with the professors of music, Pepusch, Roseingrave and Handel excepted; and the friendships he formed in life were with men of a different profession.' Six years of marriage had been ended with his wife's death, and about 1745 he went abroad for several years as tutor and companion to a rich young invalid. At Aix-en-Provence and later at Geneva he amused himself writing a couple of Italian operas, *Dario* and *Artaserse*,[1] and getting to know such *literati* as Benjamin Stillingfleet. In later years Stillingfleet wrote oratorio librettos for Smith to set, and the blue stockings that he habitually wore at the club he ran for intellectual women provided the English language with a term that is still in use. Smith was back in London in the 1750s, and helped Handel with his Foundling Hospital Concerts. His activities at this period have often been confused with those of his similarly-named father. In his book on Handel's *Messiah* J. P. Larsen has shown that the younger Smith did little or no copying for Handel, in spite of many statements to the contrary.

---

[1] I have not traced any performances of Smith's Italian operas.

After Handel's death, the younger Smith married a widow called Mrs. Coxe 'in order to be a father to her children', and his conversations with one of the Coxe boys were the basis of *Anecdotes of G. F. Handel and J. C. Smith* (1799) by the clergyman named above. We are told that Smith was a short man of great integrity, very devout, and unusually kind to his servants.

> As a professional man, he was unobtrusive . . . of a tranquil disposition, little calculated to struggle against the intrigues which modest men must encounter. Though he loved the art, he found himself unequal to the trade, and had not courage to encounter obstacles, or patience to reconcile contending interests.

Such a man was even less likely to move with the times than Arne, and it may well be that his originality was curbed by family veneration for Handel. The three all-sung operas he wrote for Garrick are even more Handelian than *Eliza*; they are also much less interesting. Smith's many years away from the theatre seem to have robbed him of the vitality and dramatic feeling that illuminate so much of his *Ulysses*.

It is impossible to imagine his soliciting work from Garrick. In fact they met by chance at the house of a mutual friend, a wine-merchant, and the result of their conversation was *The Fairies* (DL 3.2.55); there were eleven performances in two seasons, and a few more in New York as late as 1786. The libretto was an adaptation of *A Midsummer Night's Dream* without the comic scenes. Lyrics from other Shakespeare plays were introduced; for instance 'Where the Bee sucks' was sung by Puck, 'Sigh no more, Ladies' by Oberon, and 'Orpheus with his Lute' by Titania. Oberon's 'When that gay Season did us lead' was very freely adapted from Milton's *L'Allegro*, and lyrics by such poets as Dryden and Waller were also dragged in. Garrick was commonly thought to have been responsible for the libretto, but he was at pains to deny the accusation.[1] Perhaps he and Smith patched it up together.

Garrick certainly wrote the Prologue, in which he touched predictably on the snobbish belief that only Italian operas were worth hearing. He carefully distinguished between the writing and the composing, and accepted Smith as indisputably English:

> Excuse us first, for foolishly supposing,
> Your *countryman* could please you in composing;
> An *op'ra* too!—play'd by an *English* band,
> Wrote in a language which you understand—
> I dare not say, WHO wrote it—I could tell ye,
> To soften matters—Signor Shakespearelli:[2]

---

[1] Letter 178—in which he also denied turning *The Tempest* into an opera.

[2] *Gentleman's Magazine* Feb. 1755. No Prologue is given in the copy of the libretto that I have seen.

Garrick then inquires why 'this rash fool, this *Englishman*' should attempt an opera, and the answer is that he hopes he may have caught 'some glimm'ring rays' from his great master, Handel. Garrick is careful to refer only to Handel's oratorios; by 1754 his operas were forgotten.

Smith borrowed the overture from his Pastoral, *Daphne* (1744), adding a very Handelian March which was probably played after the rise of the curtain to accompany the entrance of Theseus and Hippolyta. All the arias are in *Da Capo* form except those written for the two boys who played Oberon (Master Reinhold) and Puck (Master Moore). Guadagni and Passerini sang Lysander and Hermia, and it was a confession of weakness that Italians should have been called on for such parts. Vernon played Demetrius, but was allowed no arias; Helena was taken by Miss Poitier whom he had 'married' in fascinating circumstances only a month before.[1] Beard was Theseus, Isabella Young Titania.

The published score omits the recitatives and dances; also Theseus's 'Joy alone shall employ us', because it leads into a chorus. However the final chorus is given complete. Hermia's 'Farewel, ungrateful Traitor' is replaced in the score by another aria for the same character, 'Come pride, love disdaining'. The songs for the boys are odd in that much of the accompaniment consists of violins doubling the vocal line and nothing else. Smith must have thought that this would help to keep them on the note. In general the word setting is not very good; 'Sigh no more, ladies' is notably poor in this respect, especially when compared with the glee setting by R. J. S. Stevens. 'You spotted snakes', a solo, is mildly charming and Theseus has a big rumbustious hunting song, but in general one can say little more for the music than that it is in a rather tepid good taste.

As Garrick's Prologue implies, *The Fairies* was the first all-sung full-length opera at either playhouse for many years. (*Eliza* had so far been performed only at the Little Theatre.) Though it had not been very successful, Garrick decided to persevere with what was a completely new kind of English Opera, and he or some commissioned hack made an operatic adaptation of *The Tempest* (DL 11.2.56). This time there were only six performances. Years later Smith told William Coxe that it failed 'probably because of the negligent manner in which it was staged . . . the decorations were indifferent'. When Smith complained of this, Garrick countered with a brand-new objection to English Opera, alleging that 'his principal actors threatened to leave him, if these musical pieces, in which they had no concern, were so frequently performed'.

Again lyrics were freely borrowed from other sources, all previous versions of *The Tempest* being drawn on. Thus Ariel (Isabella Young) sang 'Arise ye subterranean Winds', a vast and effective song with thirty-eight bars of introduction representing the storm. One suspects Smith of putting his foot down over Garrick's tendency to cast boys for such parts. This time the comic roles are included, though Caliban's conspiracy is replaced by an irrelevant subplot. Stephano and Trinculo are identified with Shakespeare's Master and Boatswain.

[1] See Appendix F, p. 638.

Surprisingly, Beard doubled Prospero and Trinculo. Ferdinand was played by a woman, Rosa Curioni, who at one time had been intended for Lysander in *The Fairies*. She was the only Italian in the cast, and, with Ariel and Miranda ('Mrs. Vernon'), did most of the singing.

The libretto of *The Tempest* makes sad reading, and falls from grace far more often than that to *The Fairies*. The music however is superior. It is somewhat lighter in style, and it looks as though Garrick tried to persuade Smith to find a more British type of melody and accompaniment. Handelian fingerprints still abound, but the songs are shorter and more obviously tuneful, and only a third of them are in *Da Capo* (or rather *Dal Segno*) form. Prospero, among some big songs, even has one with the fashionable 'Scotch snap'; also an accompanied recitative (a form Smith used much less than Boyce and Arne) full of descriptive touches in the accompaniment. As in Haydn's *Creation*, the musical description optimistically precedes the words that tell you what is being described. 'Full fathom five' is delightfully set. Smith borrowed the overture from his own *Il Ciro riconosciuto* (1745), and the score also includes a hornpipe for wind instruments alone, but none of the *secco* recitatives or choruses. The following season Garrick reverted to a much more Shakespearean *Tempest*, most of it spoken, with music mainly by Boyce.

While Smith's *Tempest* was playing at Drury Lane, Arne was enjoying his long and successful season in Dublin, where he was usually more admired than in London. He announced a performance of *The Fairies*, but it seems not to have taken place. He also put on *The Chaplet*, with Miss Brent as Laura, but understandably he concentrated mainly on his own *Eliza, Rosamond, Comus*, and *Alfred*. The performances of *The Tempest* in which Miss Brent was Ariel and Arne presided at the harpsichord presumably included both of Arne's masques; it is unlikely that they have ever been performed since. Miss Brent also sang Polly in *The Beggar's Opera* for the first time, and Arne produced a new 'farce' called *The Pincushion* (17.3.56), 'the Songs adapted to favourite Ballad Airs of Mr. Arne's', though some of them were said to be new. The words were improbably described as being 'a MS of the celebrated Mr. Gay's', and the whole entertainment as 'never acted before'. It does not appear to have been acted since. I have found neither music nor words. Perhaps the latter were really by Arne too.

Back in London Arne tried to persuade Garrick that Charlotte Brent was the singer his theatre so badly needed, and, as we have seen, during the winter of 1756–7 she did sing at Drury Lane in some performances of *Eliza*. Garrick was unimpressed. In a famous letter he told Arne that all his geese were swans, and he wanted nothing to do with Miss Brent. The letter is known only from its quotation in Tom Davies's *Memoirs of Garrick* (ii. 63–5), and Davies put the rejection of Miss Brent in 1762. But this cannot be right. By then both Arne and Miss Brent were enjoying full recognition at Covent Garden, and had no need to solicit employment from Garrick. Furthermore Garrick could not possibly have spurned Miss Brent after the furore occasioned by her Polly at Covent Garden (10.10.59). This was one of the most sensational débuts of the century. Thereafter her peerless singing made a fortune for that theatre.

Two other events in 1759 improved Arne's prospects. Oxford University made him a Doctor of Music; and Beard married Rich's daughter Charlotte. At first sight this marriage may not appear to have anything to do with Arne, but in fact it led directly to the greatest successes of his career. In part at least the union was a business arrangement. Rich knew that he must soon retire, and wanted Beard as his successor; when he died two years later, Beard took over the running of the theatre. His influence on the repertoire was immense, and as early as 1759 he was surely responsible for Miss Brent's appearances as Polly to his own Macheath. Unlike Garrick, Beard was able to work with Arne and always appreciated his potentialities.

Garrick had made two irreparable mistakes in rejecting Miss Brent and in letting Beard leave his company. For several seasons he had ignored opera, apart from the inevitable ballad operas and trifles by Carey, but in the 1760–1 season he accepted operatic works from both Stanley and Smith. Stanley's, occasioned by the death of George II, was a masque called *The Tears and Triumphs of Parnassus* (DL 17.11.60) with words by Robert Lloyd and Arthur Murphy, and it managed to temper the sentiments proper to a royal funeral with cheerful compliments to the new king. The music seems not to survive.

Smith's contribution, an all-sung afterpiece called *The Enchanter* (DL 13.12.60), was his greatest theatrical success, for there were more than twenty performances in two seasons. The libretto was published anonymously, but there is no doubt that Garrick wrote it, and it would be interesting to know the source of his 'Turkish' plot. A note at the start of the libretto is significant:

> As the Recitative commonly appears the most tedious part of a Musical Entertainment, the Writer of the following little Piece has avoided it as much as possible; and has endeavoured to carry on what fable there is, chiefly by the Songs.

The Enchanter, Moroc, is the opera's villain, bent on upsetting the romance between Zoreb and Zaida because he lusts after Zaida. Indeed he appears to have killed Zoreb, whom we first see as a corpse being carried in procession to the strains of a Dead March. But Moroc's diminutive attendant, Kaliel, saves the day by purloining his master's magic wand and reviving Zoreb. The latter is even allowed a song at the end of the opera.

As before, the score omits recitatives, dances, and choruses, though it does include the Dead March. Smith has gone ever further towards lightening his style than he went in *The Tempest*. Only one of the songs is in *Da Capo* form, and in general they are short, simple, and reasonably tuneful; but they are not very interesting. There is less than half the quantity of music to be found in *The Fairies* and *The Tempest*. Clearly the success of the piece lay mainly in its

Eastern story, so much more fascinating than that of any previous all-sung English opera.

According to Baker, 'the piece was written to exhibit to advantage the fine voice of Leoni, a Jew boy, who long after continued a favourite with the public'. Leoni, needless to say, sang the part of Kaliel; Lowe and Mrs. Vincent were the lovers.

In 1760 Smith turned from opera to oratorio, and from now on he organized the oratorio seasons in Lent at Covent Garden, and later at Drury Lane, with John Stanley. We shall not hear of him again. Stanley, a cheerful man in spite of his blindness, contributed one more occasional masque to the Drury Lane repertoire, and then he too abandoned the theatre for good.[1] He had never felt much interest in it, and his music shows no dramatic instinct. His *Arcadia or The Shepherd's Wedding* (26.10.61) was an all-sung 'Dramatic Pastoral', though in fact it is undramatic in the extreme, with hardly any plot. The words by Robert Lloyd celebrate the marriage of George III, who is represented as the shepherd Thyrsis but not permitted to sing or indeed to do anything. The MS full score borrows Handel's little hunting song, 'Hark, the lively tuned Horn', but in curious form. There are three verses, and in each case the first four bars of Handel's 'vocal' serve as instrumental introduction; Stanley's 'vocal' thus begins with the second half of the tune. The composer must have been in a hurry. But Stanley's charming individuality is never submerged for long, and the minuet at the end of the Boyce-like overture has vitality to a memorable degree. Here is the main section:

Minuet: affettuoso — Stanley

---

[1] In the Rowe Library at King's College Cambridge, there is a MS volume containing Stanley's *The Choice of Hercules*, *The Power of Music*, and *Pan and Syrinx*. For the first of these see p. 199. Lambert published the overtures of the others as by Boyce, but Finzi showed they were Stanley's. They are mentioned here because they look operatic; they are not. All three are short odes, with recitative that tells the story without ever giving dialogue.

7 ITALIAN OPERA IN LONDON: GALUPPI

Handel's last opera, *Deidamia*, had been produced early in 1741. During the next twenty years more than seventy different Italian operas were staged at the King's Theatre, of which at least twenty must be classed as pastiches; many of the others included additional arias by composers other than the main one. The most represented, as also the most influential composer of this period was Baldassare Galuppi (1706–85), a Venetian from the island of Burano, who was engaged by the Earl of Middlesex as official composer for two seasons from the autumn of 1741. His music already smacked of the *galante*. As Burney put it, he 'copied the hasty, light, and flimsy style which reigned in Italy at this time, and which Handel's solidity and science had taught the English to despise'. Galuppi's *Enrico* (KT 1.1.43) was especially popular;[1] almost alone among operas of this period, it was frequently revived. During the twenty years a round dozen of Galuppi's operas were presented in London.

Galuppi's earlier operas were all serious, but there must have been comedy elements in *Rosalinda* (KT 31.1.44), which was distantly based on *As you like it*. The composer was Veracini, who was again leading the orchestra, but he did not compose to the satisfaction of Burney, who found his music 'wild, aukward, and unpleasant'. He also complained that Veracini tried to court popularity by introducing 'The Lass of Patie's Mill', but in fact only the first few notes of the aria Burney refers to bear any resemblance to the popular Scotch tune.

In 1745 there were no Italian operas because of the rebellion. On 7 January 1746 *La caduta de' giganti* was, says Burney, 'performed before the Duke of Cumberland in compliment to whom the whole was written and composed'. The music was by Gluck, official composer for the season, and it is strange to think of his honouring the victor of Culloden.[2] Among the dancers was the future Mrs. Garrick. Gluck's music was undistinguished, being written in unashamed imitation of all other *opera seria* of the time. He contributed a second opera that season called *Artamene*, and then left for Vienna where he composed a number of French-style comic operas with spoken dialogue. His first masterpiece, *Orfeo*, was not produced until 1762.

---

[1] Giulia Frasi (soprano) and Galli (mezzo-soprano) both made their London débuts in *Enrico*.

[2] The date of Culloden was 16 April 1746.

The new Italian comic operas made slow headway in London. They derived from the short intermezzi performed as interval music between the acts of serious operas, and we have seen that four intermezzi had been so performed for the Nobility Opera during Farinelli's last London season, 1736–7. The experiment found so little favour that nothing else in this line was attempted until the autumn of 1748, when a whole season of full-length comic opera was begun by a company brought over especially for this purpose. *La comedia in comedia* [*sic*], with music mainly by Rinaldo da Capua, was advertised as 'a Burletta[1] or Comic Opera . . . being the first of this species ever exhibited in England', but Burney doubted the truth of this claim. Earlier that same year an *ad hoc* company at the Little Theatre had presented a pastiche comic opera called *L'ingratitudine punita* with music mainly by Hasse; there had been only two performances. The season at the King's Theatre also included productions of *La finta frascatana* by Leo and *Gli tre cicisbei ridicoli* mainly by Ciampi, the season's composer, but the manager, Croza, had no flair for keeping his company contented, and break-away productions at the Little Theatre continued. These included serious operas in which the young castrato Guadagni took part, as also Frasi and Galli.[2]

In Italy it was already recognized that the same singers were unlikely to excel in both serious and comic operas, and opera houses were beginning to run two companies, one for each kind. Castrati continued to sing in serious operas for the rest of the century, but almost from the first they were excluded from comic operas because most of them were incapable of acting realistically. One of the chief attractions of comic opera was that the characters, instead of being cardboard figures from a past that had never happened, were as life-like as the characters in spoken comedies of the time. Castrati made little or no attempt to act. They usually had more than their share of conceit, and few of them would tolerate being ordered about. They stood where and how they chose, and thought it enough to sing beautifully. But this was not enough in comic operas, which needed a great deal of stage business, with singers reacting to each other in a way that could only be achieved by careful rehearsal. In any case castrati could hardly be expected to act like ordinary people, for they were not ordinary people.

In the spring of 1750 Croza found his company so unruly that he skipped off to the Continent with the theatre's takings, such as they were, and for nearly three seasons there was no Italian opera in London. In 1753–4 there was a return to *opera seria*, the other kind having found so little favour, and the new manager was Vaneschi (or Vanneschi).[3] Yet another revival of Galluppi's

---

[1] I have preferred this term to the more correct Burletto because it was preferred in eighteenth-century London.

[2] As we have seen, these singers were also performing for Arne at this period; see p. 227.

[3] Back in 1732 he had written the libretto of *Enrico*, though not then for Galuppi.

Enrico had some success, but opera-goers found little else to enjoy. *Admeto*, the last of Handel's operas to be staged during his lifetime (it was revived in 1754), was received, says Burney, 'with great indifference'. It is extraordinary that his operas should have been so ignored at a time when his oratorios were so popular.

In December 1753 a small travelling opera company arrived in England, and its manager, Carmine Giordani, persuaded John Rich to let them stage four burlettas in Italian at Covent Garden. Much the most successful was *Gli amanti gelosi* by Gioacchino Cocchi, a Neapolitan soon to be resident in London. Several members of the company were also members of the Giordani family, and one of the youngest, Tommaso Giordani, was to spend most of his adult life working in London and Dublin.

The King's Theatre aroused more interest when Vaneschi engaged Regina Mingotti and Colomba Mattei as his leading sopranos, and orchestral playing improved when Felice de Giardini became leader of the band. Giardini had been invited to England some years earlier by Frederick, Prince of Wales; he probably replaced the Prince's music director, Giuseppe Sammartini, who died about 1748. 'He introduced new discipline', says Burney, 'and a new style of playing, much superior . . . than [*sic*] the languid manner of his predecessor Festing.' Michael Festing had led the violins off and on from 1737 until his death in 1752.

Mingotti was strong-minded and temperamental even by prima donna standards. Burney, who admired both her singing and her acting, thought her best in male parts, for she did not have enough 'female grace and softness' as a heroine. She and Vaneschi quarrelled incessantly, and for this and other reasons the latter soon found himself a bankrupt lodged in the Fleet. Mingotti herself tried a spell of management aided by Giardini; she refused to have a resident composer. Eventually the theatre proprietors could stand her caprices no longer, and in 1757 she left the country, though not for long. Vaneschi returned to management, and Cocchi was the official composer for five seasons, until replaced by J. C. Bach in 1762. Burney found his music much too 'languid', but some of his operas were popular, notably *Zenobia* (KT 10.1.58), *Il ciro riconosciuto* (KT 16.1.59), and *La clemenza di Tito* (KT 15.1.60). In the second of these operas a young castrato called Tenducci first attracted attention.

In the autumn of 1759 Vaneschi was replaced as manager by the soprano, Mattei, and in her second season comic operas were tried once again, and at last became really popular. This was mainly because they had more interesting music than before and funnier plots. The two that turned the scales were *Il mondo nella luna* (KT 22.11.60) and *Il filosofo di campagna* (KT 6.1.61); both had librettos by Goldoni and music by Galuppi. Audiences were captivated both by the pretty *galante* arias and by the new-style ensembles in several sections. *Il filosofo di campagna*, first performed in Venice in 1754, had become popular in a number of countries, and its influence was considerable, for it established the main characteristics of comic opera for the rest of the century. It is still some-times performed today.[1]

Throughout this period Walsh published the 'Favourite Songs' from nearly every opera that was not a failure. These slim volumes contained some five or six arias in full score, and when an opera was especially liked there might be two such volumes. In addition, or as an alternative, there was what might be called a pastiche series entitled *Le Delizie dell' Opere*; fourteen volumes came out at irregular intervals between the 1740s and the 1770s, and each contained items from several different operas. It is hard to believe that sales were large, for English words were not usually included, and there were no keyboard accompaniments. Unless an opera survives in MS full score—and not many do in this country from this period—it is difficult to judge its quality, and it would be impossible to stage today. Even when nearly all the arias survive, ensembles and recitatives are almost certain to be lost.

We have now reached a watershed, and the landscape before us is very different. For the remainder of the century English opera plots switch from the past to the present, and, in musical style, from the baroque to the *galante*. More important still, perhaps, the proportion of operas at the playhouses increased tenfold. At such a moment we can profitably pause to consider generalities.

---

[1] BM MS Add. 16141 was copied in London about 1761, perhaps for the King's Theatre production.

7
Interlude

I THE LONDON PLAYHOUSES

DRURY LANE and Covent Garden retained their monopoly, in all important senses, until the end of the century. In the 1760s Drury Lane was still a small theatre in which subtleties of facial expression could be enjoyed by the whole audience. In 1775 it was slightly enlarged and sumptuously redecorated in crimson and gilt by the Adam Brothers, and it now held 1,800 tightly-packed people. But the stage was still small; only 45 feet wide and 30 feet deep. In 1776 Garrick retired, and for the rest of the century Richard Brinsley Sheridan was in charge. In 1791 he pulled down Old Drury and in its place built an enormous new theatre which held 3,600. In the comparatively dim lighting that prevailed facial expression counted for nothing, and many production problems resulted from the enlargement.

Before this rebuilding Covent Garden had always been a little bigger than Drury Lane, and in the 1760s its capacity was 2,100. Under Beard's management it increased its operatic repertoire out of recognition, with the unexpected result that for some years the theatre attracted larger audiences than Drury Lane. In 1767 Beard began both to go deaf and to lose his voice; accordingly he sold his share in the theatre and persuaded his wife, John Rich's daughter, to do so too. They retired on a fortune. The syndicate which bought Covent Garden included a businessman named Thomas Harris, William Powell, and the dramatist George Colman who had been briefly at Drury Lane with Garrick. After much squabbling Harris got effective control in 1774 and held it for the rest of the century.

Since the Licensing Act of 1737 the Little Theatre in the Haymarket had seldom been open for more than the occasional concert and all-sung opera. In 1762 Samuel Foote began to offer on two or three days a week what he artfully called his Lectures. These were 'illustrated' with spoken plays, often full-length, and somehow he escaped prosecution. Throughout this period he was trying to obtain a licence for spoken drama, and at last his ambition was satisfied as a result of a painful accident. In February 1766, in the presence of the Duke of York, he fell from his horse and had to have a leg amputated. Out of sympathy for his distress the Duke exerted himself, and that summer the Little Theatre at last got its patent from the Crown and became a Theatre Royal.

The patent allowed Foote to open his theatre only in those summer months when, in theory, Drury Lane and Covent Garden were closed; to be precise, from May 15 to September 1, though in practice Foote usually started his seasons a fortnight or so later. The more affluent were then out of town, but there were plenty of people left in the middle and lower income groups, and by catering for a slightly lower-browed audience Foote was able to fill his house. Two factors worked in his favour. First there was no rival theatre open in the middle of London. Secondly he could draw on actors, singers, and orchestral players from the winter playhouses, who would otherwise have been unemployed in the summer. He could not normally afford the big names, who in any case were increasingly tending to spend their summers in such centres as Dublin and Edinburgh, but from just below the best he could pick and choose.

In his first authorized season, 1767, Foote staged such tried favourites as *The Beggar's Opera* and *Romeo and Juliet*, but he realized that with his limited stage resources he could seldom compete with the winter playhouses on their own ground, and the Little Theatre soon built up its own sizable repertoire of plays and operas that could not be seen at the larger theatres. For pantomime the house was poorly equipped, and few attempts were made in this field.

In 1777 Foote handed over his theatre to George Colman. Colman came of a good family,[1] and at Westminster School had become friendly with Charles Churchill, author of *The Rosciad*. He was a prolific playwright, and as a young man collaborated with Garrick in a comedy that is still enjoyed today, *The Clandestine Marriage,* but sharing Churchill's waspish views of the playhouses he had never enjoyed his subservient work at Drury Lane, and he was glad of the chance of setting up on his own. He had far more interest in music than Foote, and soon increased the proportion of opera at the Little Theatre by engaging his friend Samuel Arnold as resident composer. From this time until the end of the century all three patent theatres relied in the main on 'house' composers; the elder Linley and Storace held this position successively at Drury Lane, and Shield at Covent Garden from 1782. By the late eighties Colman was mentally unstable, and the running of the Little Theatre was taken over by his son, George Colman the younger, who was also a prolific playwright.

Several fringe theatres gave summer encouragement to composers, being pushed into all-sung opera by their lack of a licence to present spoken dialogue. Very short operas on contemporary cockney themes were regularly given at Sadler's Wells throughout the latter half of the century, and no doubt earlier.

---

[1] His father, Francis Colman, kept an 'Opera Register' (a list of performances) from 1712 for about twenty years; Deutsch quotes from it frequently. By 1730 Colman was Envoy Extraordinary in Florence, and Handel sometimes wrote to him there about engaging singers. He is thought to have arranged for Handel the libretto of *Arianna.*

At Marylebone Gardens Italian intermezzos in translation and English imitations of them were presented from 1768 until 1776, when the gardens were closed and the ground built over; there had been earlier operatic performances from 1758 to 1760. The Royal Circus south of the Thames was opened in 1783, and by the end of the century was making important advances in ballet.

But the strength of the playhouse monopoly was demonstrated in 1787, when the actor John Palmer spent all his savings and other people's money as well on building the Royalty Theatre near the Tower of London. Mistakenly he thought the site was outside the jurisdiction of the Crown. The managers of Drury Lane and Covent Garden went to law, and Palmer found himself limited to precisely those forms of entertainment for which he had no talent: short operas, miming, dancing, and acrobatics. London's theatres were not able to proliferate until the following century.

2 STAGING AN OPERA

Rehearsals began at 10 a.m., and both actors and orchestral players were fined if they were late. There was no producer specially selected. An actor-manager such as Garrick 'produced' in the film and television sense, deciding on the repertoire, casting plays and operas, and commissioning scenery when necessary. He would 'direct' as well if he himself were performing. But most of the work of the modern director fell on the prompter. Needless to say, he prompted, and considering the enormous repertoire he must have done so frequently,[1] but this was among the least of his responsibilities. Successive Drury Lane prompters, Richard Cross and William Hopkins, kept diaries in which they commented on each night's performance, and these diaries are a valuable source of information for the Garrick period.

Pantomimes were nearly always staged with lavish new scenery, but plays were often put on with stock scenery that had been used before; this was the case with Goldsmith's *She stoops to conquer*. By contrast Storace's opera *The Siege of Belgrade* had as many as fourteen different sets, all of them new. Scenery consisted in the main of flats or a backcloth and wings. It is obvious that a new backcloth could be lowered or revealed in a couple of seconds, less obvious that a set of flats at the back and wings at the side could be changed equally quickly. They were placed in grooves, in which they could be made to slide suddenly out of sight by means of ropes, one set of ropes for each set of flats and wings. To an eighteenth-century audience a change of scene appeared to take place almost instantaneously, and the ingenuity with which it was achieved was part of the enjoyment. Scott adds a detail in *Rob Roy*[2] when writing of someone's un-

---

[1] 'The Performers—in friendly sympathy—had totally forgotten their parts—and passed the evening in a conversation with the prompter, (the *Public Advertiser* reviewing Shield's *The Nunnery*).

[2] Chapter 14; the period is the 1720s.

usually rapid change of expression: 'I can compare it to nothing but the sudden shifting of a scene in the theatre, where, at the whistle of the prompter, a cavern disappears, and a grove arises'. A 'property plot' survives for Covent Garden's *Love in a Village*, and it shows in which of the five sets of grooves each scene was placed.[1] The most notable scene designer of the sixties and seventies was Philip de Loutherbourg at Drury Lane. Both he and Richards at Covent Garden were beginning to make cardboard models of sets as opposed to sketches on paper; this is said to have been done first by Richards for Arnold's opera, *The Banditti*.[2] In the 1730s and 1740s playhouse scenery had been painted by John Devoto,[3] George Lambert (our first landscape painter), and Francis Hayman.

For many decades the same costumes had been used for all plays set in the past, regardless of their period and country. Garrick was among the first to seek a degree of historical realism in the theatre, and in 1773, instead of dressing Macbeth like any other 'ancient' in the usual wig with a scarlet and gold tunic, he played him in Scottish costume. How insensitive theatres and their audiences could be to period atmosphere is shown by the pictures in Plate no. IX. The scene from Arne's *Artaxerxes* shows a room with wall-paper, wood-panelling, a modern window, and a modern sofa. In *Achilles in Pettycoats*, an adaptation of John Gay's *Achilles*, the hero when disguised as a girl assumed a costume that hardly accords with our own concept of Homeric times.

But by the end of the century people were becoming much more conscious of historical falsity in the playhouses, and some of them took the trouble to write to the managers about anachronisms. In 1784 audiences at the Little Theatre had found nothing to question in O'Keeffe's short opera *Peeping Tom of Coventry*, but by 1799 someone was pointing out that in the days of Edward the Confessor there was no Cross in Coventry and there were no corporals in the army; people did not use knives and forks, or smoke tobacco, or (if they were female) ride side-saddle.[4] By this time John Philip Kemble was so eager for historical accuracy that he often invited comments from antiquarians.

The stage was lit by candles. At least until the 1760s there were between four and six chandeliers hanging above the stage, and these could be raised for dimming effects or lowered for extra brightness. People in the top gallery some-times complained when the lowering obstructed their view. It was Garrick who introduced footlights and, from about 1765, candles one above the other on a wooden batten behind each wing. These battens could be pulled up a few inches by means of a thin rope so that each candle-flame became hidden behind a small metal shield; this was another dimming device. The footlights consisted of candles floating in a metal trough filled with oil and screened from the audience;

[1] *LS* Part 5, i, p. lviii.
[2] O'Keeffe ii, pp. 38–9.
[3] See pamphlet by Edward Croft-Murray (Society for Theatre Research).
[4] Boaden's *Mrs Jordan* ii, pp. 31–2.

the entire trough could be lowered to darken the stage.[1] But a completely dark stage was an impossibility, for the house lights were always left burning; at some period the chandeliers above the audience began to be raised during performance but the candles could not be extinguished. Chandeliers over the stage ceased to be used once footlights and side lights had become established.

3 THE AUDIENCE

Londoners normally had no means of discovering more than a day or two in advance what plays or operas were to be given. Between the mainpiece and the afterpiece the two items for the following night were given out, and these were advertised in the press the following morning. From the sixties onwards advertisements usually gave the plays for that evening and for the following evening as well. Two newspapers, whose names varied from one period to another, shared the right to print these advertisements, and they paid the theatres for the privilege.

There were no matinées. Performances usually began at six o'clock; from 1774 onwards fifteen or thirty minutes later. Doors opened an hour before the curtain rose, and there was then a wild scrimmage for seats, with frequently-shouted warnings of pickpockets. The wealthier members of the audience sent their footmen to keep their seats, for these were not numbered and could not be reserved in any other way.[2] On interesting first-nights the doors were sometimes opened as much as two or three hours in advance.

Until near the end of the century prices ranged from 1*s.* and 2*s.* in the upper and lower galleries to 3*s.* in the pit and 5*s.* in the boxes. The pit was then the entire floor of the house, and the haunt of fashionable young men. Between the mainpiece and the afterpiece some of the audience went home, and others waiting outside were allowed in at half-price. Sometimes half-prices began before the last act of the main-piece. The privilege was especially valued by shopkeepers and artisans who did not finish work until eight or nine o'clock. In January 1763 Garrick tried to withdraw half-prices, with the result that one 'Fribble' Fitzpatrick, who had been quarrelling with him for years, induced the audience to riot. Garrick had to give way, and half-prices continued. A month later, for a Covent Garden performance of Arne's *Artaxerxes*, Beard announced that 'Nothing under Full Price can be taken', and this caused the worst theatre riot of the century. The entire auditorium was wrecked, and £2,000 worth of damage done. Covent Garden was out of action for a week, and Beard had to publish an apology in the *Public Advertiser*.[3]

To a greater extent than today, divisions in the house corresponded to divi-

[1] Boaden's *Mrs Jordan* i, p. 248.
[2] But late in the century seats in the boxes could be reserved.
[3] For a good account of the Half-Price Riots, see TN Autumn 1969; the article is by John C. Whitty.

sions in the social classes. Goldsmith's fictitious Chinese described the position thus:

> It was they [in the top gallery] who called for the music, indulging every noisy freedom, and testifying all the insolence of beggary in exaltation. They who held the middle region seemed not so riotous as those above them, nor yet so tame as those below . . . They were chiefly employed during this period of expectation in eating oranges, reading the story of the play, or making assignations. Those who sat in . . . the pit seemed to consider themselves as judges of the merit of the poet and the performers . . . Those who sat in the boxes appeared in the most unhappy situation of all. The rest of the house came merely for their own amusement; these rather to furnish out a part of the entertainment themselves . . . Gentlemen and ladies ogled each other through spectacles.[1]

In his Epilogue to Murphy's *All in the Wrong* (1761) Garrick wrote:

> What shall we do your different tastes to hit?
> You relish satire (*to the pit*), you ragouts of wit (*to the boxes*).
> Your taste is humour and high-season'd joke (*to the 1st gallery*);
> You call for hornpipe, and for hearts of oak (*to the 2nd gallery*).

There was another song the top gallery was constantly yelling for, as Arne mentions in his anonymous *Elegy on the Death of the Guardian Outwitted* (1765), in which he lamented the failure of his own opera in a parody of Gray's *Elegy*.

> Now strike the glimmering Lamps upon the sight
> And all the House a solemn stillness holds;
> Save where the Seaman from the Gallery's Height
> For Roast Beef bawling, the cue'd Fidler scolds.

Members of the orchestra had to endure a good many ribaldries. Cervetto, the Italian Jew who for years played the cello or double bass at Drury Lane, was invariably greeted on entrance with affectionate cries of 'Nosey'.

Though the lower boxes were filled with gentry, the top ones were virtually reserved for prostitutes, who did much of their soliciting in the theatres. They seem to have been especially troublesome at the Little Theatre, where Thomas Holcroft found the auditorium 'half-filled with prostitutes and their paramours: they disturb the rest of the audience; and the author and common sense are the sport of their caprice and profligacy'.[2] Dorothy Wordsworth, with William in the unlikely surroundings of La Scala, Milan, remarked in her Journal not on the performance—we do not even know what they saw—but on the welcome

---

[1] *The Citizen of the World* XXI (Spring 1760).
[2] Holcroft's diary for 26.4.98; quoted in Hazlitt's Memoirs ii, p. 245.

absence of prostitutes in the theatre passages.[1] The word 'actress' was itself almost synonymous with a lady of easy virtue, as Evelina made clear when running from a persecutor in Vauxhall Gardens: ' "No,—no,—no", I *panted* out, "I am no actress,—pray let me go,—pray let me pass".'[2]

We have already noted that some members of the audience sat on the sides of the stage itself, paying 10s. a night for the privilege. The custom was much disliked by the actors, but for years no manager dared do anything about it. Tate Wilkinson remembered Mrs. Cibber playing Juliet in the Tomb Scene with an audience of at least two hundred in the tomb with her.[3] At a performance of Boyce's *The Chaplet* in 1749 the Drury Lane prompter Hopkins noted that the gentry

> crouding behind the scenes, the audience resented it & the Farce was stop'd for half an hour—I drew lines with chalk but Miss Norris applying publicly to Capt. Johnson, desiring he would retire, he did, & the Farce went on with great applause.

Farce was a common synonym for afterpiece.

In 1762 Garrick felt strong enough to insist that no one but the cast should be allowed on stage, and Covent Garden followed suit. But the young men of the pit continued to get as close as they could to the female performers. Here is William Gardiner, writing of the King's Theatre in 1791:

> Between the acts it was a common practice for many fashionable young men to leave the pit, and, by a secret door, gain admission to the stage. I joined the throng, and was well repaid by seeing the dancers practise their evolutions just before commencing the divertissement . . . When the curtain was suddenly drawn up, you frequently saw shoals of these *petits maitres* on the stage scampering in all directions to avoid the hisses of the audience.

Young men in the playhouse pits behaved in the same way, but to a less objectionable extent.[4]

The more staid theatre-goers spent the period before the curtain rose, as also the intervals, in reading the booklets they could buy from the 'Fruit Woman' as they came in.[5] Texts of plays and opera librettos always gave the names of the cast, for they were the equivalent of the modern programme. They could not be counted on at early performances, but the song words of an opera were always on sale from the first night, and these too included the cast. Critics

---

[1] *The Journals of Dorothy Wordsworth* ed. de Selincourt ii, p. 236.

[2] Fanny Burney's *Evelina*, Letter XLVI.

[3] His *Memoirs* (iv, pp. 113–21) have further information about this abuse.

[4] Smith (p. 8) quotes the *Morning Post* for 4.7.89 on this subject.

[5] O'Keeffe ii, p. 141; she also sold the oranges—see O'Keeffe ii, p. 901, and p. 257 above.

quoted extensively from the opera song-words to pad out their reviews. The booklets often failed to take account of last-minute changes in rehearsal. When the entertainment was all-sung, many people followed the words during the actual performance, and in *Amelia* Fielding revealed how they did so. His heroine has been taken to a Handel oratorio by an old gentleman whose intentions later prove far from honourable. 'He procured her a book and a wax candle, and held the candle for her himself during the whole entertainment'.[1]

In 1767 John Brownsmith, newly-appointed prompter at the Little Theatre, published *The Dramatic Timepiece*, a strange book whose object was to let the audience know the exact time performances would end. It gave the length in minutes of each act of each familiar play or opera, whether full-length or afterpiece. Brownsmith told his readers to add seven minutes for each interval, and thus the four intervals in a five-act play would amount to about half an hour. At this period Shakespeare was always heavily cut. Even so it is a surprise to find that *The Beggar's Opera* at three hours three minutes was the longest mainpiece of the day. (It was the only standard work that was normally given without an afterpiece.) *The Dramatic Timepiece* had a moral purpose, for it enabled the gentry to tell their footmen exactly when to leave home in order to pick them up when the show finished. They would thus be kept out of mischief 'instead of assembling in the *Public Houses*, or Houses of *ill Fame*, to the Destruction of their *Morals, Properties* and *Constitutions*'.

4 INTERVAL MUSIC

Half an hour before the curtain rose, whether the mainpiece was a play or an opera, the orchestra started to entertain those who were waiting. Purcell had sometimes composed 'waiting' music specially for the occasion, using for it the theatre terms 'First Musick' and 'Second Musick'. Examples can be found in *The Fairy Queen*, but not after 1700 by which time there was enough suitable music in print to supply the need. For most of the eighteenth century there was a 'Third Musick' as well, for in half an hour there was ample time to play three overtures, concertos, or early symphonies. Because someone was ill, Mrs. Charke at the very last moment created the role of Lucy in Lillo's *George Barnwell* (1731); 'I was at the Second Musick sent for' she explained in her autobiography, and thus made precise for her readers the problem she faced. During the 'half-price' riots of 1763 at Drury Lane, the *London Chronicle* reported that 'when the third musick began . . . the audience insisted on Britons, Strike Home and the Roast Beef of Old England; which were played accordingly'.[2]

In the 1730s, though in no other decade, interval music was regularly specified in newspaper advertisements. Thus at Covent Garden on 8 May 1735 the waiting audience was entertained with the following:

[1] *Amelia*, Book IV, Chapter IX.
[2] By Purcell (*Bonduca*) and Leveridge respectively.

First Musick: A Concerto for Hautboys etc.
Second Musick: A Concerto of Geminiani
Third Musick: Overture to Ariadne

In the four intervals of the mainpiece that night there were songs, one being 'Roast Beef' sung by Leveridge himself. Before the afterpiece Handel's *Water Music* was played. Though it was not so on this occasion, some of the intervals in the second quarter of the century were usually filled with short dances.

The concerti grossi of Corelli, Geminiani[1], and Handel were performed so often in the playhouses that everyone knew them. In the alehouse scene in *She stoops to conquer* one of the 'rough fellows' shows familiarity with the minuet from Handel's *Ariadne*[2] overture, a minuet very few indeed would claim to know today. Goldsmith had heard it constantly in the theatres, and not only in the intervals; it was also much used as quiet background music. 'Here they are—inconsolable to the minuet in Ariadne', cries Mr. Puff in *The Critic* as Tilburina and her Confidant come in. 'Soft music' says the stage direction, and the pianissimo ending of this minuet is memorable. Another very popular Handel overture was the one Burney and the composer called *Alessandro* and everyone else *Alexander*. Even less probable music was played repeatedly in the playhouses. Busby, following a hint in Burney, says of Boyce's Trio Sonatas (published in 1747):

> Till the tumid extravaganzas of Stamitz and Lord Kelly were adopted, the elegant and well-conducted fugues of these sonatas continued to contribute to the bill-of-fare of every public concert, and, as inter-act pieces, to be listened to with attention at the theatres.[3]

As we shall see later, 'the tumid extravaganzas of Stamitz and Lord Kelly' were adopted about 1762, so the Boyce Trio Sonatas must have enjoyed a vogue of some fifteen years. Today we find a distinction between orchestral and chamber music that was seldom apparent in Baroque times. There is no difference in appearance between Handel's score of the *Messiah* overture and Boyce's of his trio sonatas except that the latter has no viola part; you could play it either as chamber music, or, doubling the strings, as orchestral music.

When Baroque music began to go out of fashion, steps were sometimes taken to modernize it. In the 1770s Corelli's Concerto Grosso No. 4 was being played at Marylebone Gardens with 'additional parts for Trumpets, French Horns, and Kettle Drums . . . by the late ingenious Sg. Pasquali'. Pasquali had died in 1757, so this early example of the Additional Accompaniments menace must have been available for twenty years.

---

[1] The op. 2 and op. 3 sets, says Burney, never the op. 7 concertos which were too 'laboured, difficult and fantastical'.

[2] More correctly *Arianna*. Handel's opera titles were regularly anglicized.

[3] Busby iii, p. 170.

At all periods concertos by well-known solo performers were sometimes advertised as part of the evening's attractions, and it was thus that the clarinet was first introduced to playhouse audiences. On 3 March 1768 the intervals between the acts of Barthelemon's opera *Oithona* were filled with a concerto on the 'Viole d'Amour' played by Barthelemon himself, and one for the mandolin played by Signor Gervasia.[1]

5 COMPOSER AND LIBRETTIST

It has been mentioned that each playhouse usually had one particular composer on contract to provide whatever music was required. We know little about the financial arrangements involved except in the case of Charles Dibdin who always wrote avidly of money matters. 'I made my article for seven years, immediately after the *Jubilee*,' he says, and he was thus under contract to Drury Lane from September 1769 to May 1776. For the first three years he got £6 a week, for the other four £7.[2] Being Dibdin, he thought this inadequate, especially as it prevented his sharing in the profits of a long run. But this was by no means his only source of income. In the summer months he was free to sing at Ranelagh or Sadler's Wells; also he often did well from the sale of his librettos and vocal scores. Comparisons with the wages of other theatre people are hard to make. Actors and singers were paid by the night. Dibdin himself had started at Covent Garden at 10s. a performance and later rose to 20s. Mrs. Pinto got £1. 13s. 6d. a night, which was more than any other singing actor or actress of the 1760s, though less than the famous Harlequin Woodward received; by the 1790s Mrs. Pinto would have been paid at least twice as much. Orchestral players received only two or three guineas a week. It would seem that Dibdin was not treated so badly as he made out. Garrick did not mind his composing summer trifles for Sadler's Wells, but he did jib at his writing *The Waterman* for the Little Theatre, especially as it was very successful, for there was a moral obligation on Dibdin to offer all works of this calibre to Drury Lane. He made £80 from the sale of the librettos and scores of *The Waterman*, and another £35 from his benefit night at the Little Theatre.

By writing his own libretto for *The Waterman* Dibdin had control over both the substance and the profits. In most operas the librettist saw himself as the senior partner, and it was not until Storace's day that this position was reversed. The position is reflected in the way new operas were submitted to the theatres. Managers always had piles of unread manuscript plays in their offices, but composers did not normally submit music to them; indeed Dibdin was furious when asked to do so by Harris.[3] Managers could not read music, and if they

---

[1] For much earlier instances of interval or 'Act' music than any mentioned here, see J. S. Manifold, ch. 2, and the stage directions of Marston's *Sophonisba* (c. 1605).
[2] *Musical Tour*, pp. 206 and 291.
[3] *Musical Tour*, p. 253.

appealed to their house composer they would be likely to receive a biased and unfavourable opinion. The freelance composer's best hope lay in being taken up by a playwright interested in music. If the libretto were accepted, then the music would be accepted as a matter of course, probably without its being looked at. The freelance composer was the hireling of the librettist, and seldom had direct dealings with theatre managements.[1]

By custom, the author was given the takings of the third, sixth, and ninth nights, and out of them he usually had to pay the performers and orchestra as well as his composer. If he was let off all or most of the house expenses, he could hope for a clear profit of about £100 a night. O'Keeffe got £600 from the full-length opera *Fontainbleau* (1784), out of which he paid his composer, Shield, a mere £120.[2] When *Love in the City* failed, Dibdin, in his own words, 'made Mr. Bickerstaff a present of the music'; that is, he did not demand his cut. When Thomas Carter found himself unpaid for composing *The Fair American* he sued not Drury Lane but his librettist, Frederick Pilon. We shall see that in the 1790s composers' earnings improved out of all recognition, mainly because there was much more demand for their published scores.

Freelance composers sometimes appealed to their singer friends rather than to librettists. Late in the season, mainly in April and May, actors were allowed occasional benefit nights. Normally they paid all the wages and kept all the profits.[3] It was usual for either the mainpiece or the afterpiece to be a new work by some struggling writer, and if the actor were also a singer the new work would be operatic. Often the result was no more than a single performance at the tired end of the season, but there was always a chance the piece would be well received, in which case it might be 'adopted' by the theatre and go into the repertoire. Storace's *No Song No Supper* was originally turned down by Sheridan, who doubtless saw only Prince Hoare's naïve libretto, but the tenor Michael Kelly put it on for his benefit, and because the music was much liked it was 'adopted'.

Because most operas after 1762 had spoken dialogue, the librettist usually felt that the music was no more than a decoration, and that the success or failure of the evening depended on the words. Newspaper critics, being mostly playwrights manqués, had the same notion. Often they would damn an opera because the words were insipid and boring, and then admit grudgingly that with the help of attractive music the performance was better received than it deserved. The same might be said as irrelevantly of *Il Trovatore*. In the eighteenth century, as in any other, operas succeeded or failed mainly on the quality of their music, but authors were not conditioned to accept this view. All through his *Recol-*

---

[1] Often he had to set the lyrics without knowing what the dialogue was about. See O'Keeffe ii, p. 15.

[2] See also O'Keeffe's *Reminiscences* ii, p. 12. *Fontainbleau* was always so spelt.

[3] There were a confusing number of different arrangements for benefits; see Troubridge's *The Benefit System in the British Theatre* (STR 1967).

lect.   sublimely unaware that the popularity of his best operas owec   .. deal to Shield's music, in some cases almost everything. He scarcely mentions his composer, and often writes of his many opera librettos as though they were straight plays. Yet such few plays as he wrote mostly failed. It was not vanity that led Arne and Dibdin to write their own librettos but a desire for a fairer share in the profits and in the glory.

Authors had a vested interest in the demise of the all-sung opera, for to them it emphasized the music to excess and deprived them of their pre-eminence. In his *Dissertation on Poetry and Music* (1763), a large and beautifully produced volume, Dr. John Brown found that although songs and odes could provide a satisfying union of words and music, all-sung operas and oratorios could not, for it was unnatural that characters supposed to be taking part in a story should sing.

> To hear Kings, Warriours, Statesmen, Philosophers, Patriarchs, Saints, and Martyrs, holding long conversations in musical Recitative, is a circumstance so out of Nature, that the Imagination immediately revolts, and rejects the Representation as absurd and incredible. The Recitative . . . which prevails in both, being thus unalterably at Variance with the *dramatic Form*, the *one* or the *other* must be *destroyed* ere *Probability* and *Pathos* can arise.

A similar point is made by General John Burgoyne in the preface to *The Lord of the Manor*, set by William Jackson in 1780:

> In a representation which is to hold 'a mirror up to nature', and which ought to draw its chief applause from reason, vocal music should be confined to express the feelings and passions, but never to express the exercising of them. Song, in any action in which reason tells us it would be unnatural to sing, must be preposterous . . . The idea of five or six fellows with fusils presented at a gentleman's head, and their fingers upon the triggers, threatening his life in bass notes, he resisting in tenor, and a wife or daughter throwing herself between them in treble, while the spectator is kept in suspense, from what in reality must be a momentary event, till the composer has run his air through all its different branches, and to a great length, always gave me disgust to a great degree. Music . . . must not only be restrained from having part in the exercise or action of the passions; care must also be taken, that it does not interrupt or delay events for the issue of which the mind is become eager. It should always be the *accessory*, and not the *principal* subject of the drama.

In other words an opera that was reasonable in part, that is, partly spoken, was preferable to one that was not reasonable at all, that is, entirely sung. The example Burgoyne gives to prove the absurdity of all-sung opera would not of course be an 'air' but an ensemble finale of the new Italian kind, with several linked movements and plenty of action. We shall find that Arne, Linley, and Shield were usually of the General's mind and avoided action finales, while Dibdin and Storace frequently welcomed the musical opportunities they afforded.

Burgoyne agreed with Dr. Brown and earlier writers in finding recitative to English words intolerable. He even disliked it in Handel oratorios, and thought the words would be more effective if spoken by an actress such as Mrs. Yates. Few among the playhouse audiences would have disagreed. 'The lower orders of people', wrote Goldsmith in *The Bee* (24.11.59.), 'sleep amidst all the agony of recitative.' Yet in 1762 Arne's all-sung *Artaxerxes* was a prodigious success, and Burgoyne could only explain it as the exception that proved the rule. In his *Memoirs of the Musical Drama* (1838)[1] George Hogarth, who was Dickens's father-in-law, skilfully summarized views that had been expressed before and added some new ones:

> The Italian language is in itself so musical, that recitative is very little more than the natural inflections and modulations of speech, heightened and reduced to determinate musical intervals . . . But no other language has accents and inflections belonging to it which, in the ordinary dialogue of the drama, can be heightened into recitative. Hence, when Arne and others have attempted to introduce this sort of musical dialogue into our opera, they have not had recourse to . . . the accent and inflections of English speech, but have imitated the recitative of the Italian composers: and the consequence is, that, in listening to the dialogue of Artaxerxes, the actors all appear to be Italians, speaking broken English . . .

It is curious that Arne, writing anonymously in the preface to his own libretto of *The Guardian Outwitted*, came out against recitative in English opera— curious because *The Guardian Outwitted* was composed three years after *Artaxerxes*. By the end of the century playhouse audiences, never anxious to hear recitative, must have got quite out of the way of giving it their attention. When Storace's all-sung serious opera *Dido, Queen of Carthage* was produced in 1792, all the critics found the recitatives far too long and very boring. As the *Morning Chronicle* put it, 'The English ear is too much familiarized to the variety of air and dialogue to relish the sameness of Recitative'.

Composers who agreed to forgo recitatives and ensembles could be still further humiliated. Dr. Brown averred that songs and choruses in any opera should be as few as possible, and he advised poets to write their lyrics in whatever style they chose and then search for previously-composed music that would fit them. This, he believed, was easier than trying to write lyrics to fit a given vocal line. In practice poets found either method very difficult, especially in the *galante* period when vocal lines became longer and more complex; a number of librettists said so, notably Isaac Bickerstaffe in the preface to *Love in the City* (1767). The matter was of extreme importance, for the composer's livelihood was at stake.

[1] ii, p. 88.

If all operas were to consist of previously-composed music, all theatre composers would go out of business. In the middle sixties it seemed that this might happen, for a new brand of pastiche opera enjoyed a startling success. *Love in a Village* (1762) and *The Maid of the Mill* (1765) were the most famous, together with Kane O'Hara's popular burlettas, *Midas* (1764) and *The Golden Pippin* (1773). All were full-length, and, taken in conjunction with less successful operas of the same kind, they show an increasing tendency to abjure new music altogether. Mercifully they also show an increasing tendency to borrow *galante* arias rather than traditional ballads, and the difficulty of finding words for arias or arias for words proved their downfall. After *The Duenna* (1775) no new example of the mainly pastiche opera had much success.

A small element of pastiche survived in most operas until the end of the century, but in general after about 1770 the composer slowly regained his authority. This was largely due to the successful collaboration of Bickerstaffe and Dibdin. In his preface to *Love in the City* Bickerstaffe combated the views of Dr. Brown and others with urbane good sense:

> The absurdity attach'd to the musical Drama is so glaring, that there seems no great penetration to discover it; and consequently anyone who will cry out sing-song or tweedle-dee, is capable of turning it into ridicule . . . Yet however preposterous it may appear for people to carry out their most serious affairs in song, we find the mind accommodates itself to those sort of illusions in the Theatre, with so much ease, that it is little better than impertinence and pedantry to enquire into their propriety.

Bickerstaffe had had some assistance from Dibdin in *Love in the City* (1767), which was a pastiche, and in the following season he collaborated with him in *Lionel and Clarissa*. We shall see Dibdin turning from an unknown composer forced to accept the pastiche convention into a known composer who would have nothing to do with it. Bickerstaffe aided and abetted Dibdin because he realized that good opera could be achieved only if the composer and the librettist collaborated on terms of equality.

In the 1790s Stephen Storace was prepared to go even further. As the *Thespian Dictionary* put it (in the article on Storace):

> Mr. Storace openly declared in a music-seller's shop in Cheapside (then Longman and Broderip's) 'that it was impossible for any author to produce a good opera without previously consulting his intended composer; for, added he, the songs must be introduced as *he* pleases, and the words (which are a secondary consideration) be written agreeable to *his* directions'. This is the modern mode of writing operas . . . but formerly the music was provided for the words, not the words for the music.

Storace was the first English opera composer to have the whip-hand of his librettist.

Yet no golden age of opera resulted, partly on account of Storace's early death, partly on account of a firmly entrenched opposition that continued to snipe at all English composers right up to Elgar's time. In his *Dramatic Censor* for 5 June 1800, Thomas Dutton wrote petulantly of a performance of Storace's *The Siege of Belgrade* that

> the composer and the scene painter furnish the principal attractions of Mr. Cobb's Operas.

Not 'Storace's operas', it will be noticed, though this one contains nearly two hours of music.

> It affords a damning proof of the frivolity and vitiated taste of the age that such writers are tolerated; but music when carried to excess and made the object of *primary*, instead of *secondary* concern, has an infallible tendency to enervate and debauch the mind. Hence the importance of late years attached to *music-men*, and *ballad-mongers*; especially if the *music-men* happen to be of foreign extraction, with a *damn'd crabbed* name, which staggers a plain man to pronounce, and almost distorts the *mazard*[1] of honest *John Bulls*.

Another 'honest John Bull', John Dennis, had written similar nonsense about the demoralizing effect of music back in 1706.[2] With Dr. Burney preaching that no opera music could be good unless it were Italian, our composers had the wise men against them as well as the fools.

6 OPERA PLOTS

The subject-matter of English operas changed markedly in the 1760s. It was still believed that all-sung opera should be about the classical gods, shepherds of the Golden Age, or characters allegedly from Ancient History, and 'historical' operas flourished briefly as a result of the success of *Artaxerxes*. But by the last quarter of the century all-sung opera had sunk with scarcely a trace. Even in the sixties the classical Masque survived only to be mocked, as in *Midas*, while the Pastoral can scarcely be said to have survived at all. The changes came in the modernizing of comic opera with spoken dialogue.

In London, as in Paris, Galuppi's *Il filosofo di campagna* (1754) and Piccini's *La buona figliuola* (1760) were welcomed in the main because Goldoni's librettos had at last brought realism and vitality into Italian opera. Audiences enjoyed the contemporary plots, the Italian-style *galante* music, and the absence of castrati singers. But in neither capital did these operas lead to all-sung imitations in the vernacular. Outside Italy, there was a general belief that such operas would be the better for spoken dialogue. Galuppi's masterpiece reached London

---

[1] A punning reference to Mazzinghi?
[2] See p. 49.

in January 1761, Piccini's in November 1766, and the plots of these and similar operas undoubtedly influenced those given at the playhouses. In an incredibly short time *La buona figliuola* was translated by Edward Toms and staged with most of its original music as *The Accomplish'd Maid* (CG 3.12.66.). A few years later Dibdin made an afterpiece version of *Il filosofo di campagna* and called it *The Wedding Ring*. Both these revisions had spoken dialogue, as did the many operas with contemporary plots that these originals fathered; for instance *Lionel and Clarissa* and *The Duenna*.

The village setting found in so many ballad operas managed to survive the changes of the sixties. Indeed the first of our new-style comic operas, *Love in a Village*, was founded on *The Village Opera* which Charles Johnson had written thirty years earlier. These country operas tended to become increasingly sentimental and insipid. The mood is that of Victorian engravings showing girls in white muslin outside honeysuckled cottages. Shield's *Rosina* (1782) was perhaps the most popular of such operas.

Village girls often turn out to have aristocratic blood in the last scene. Disguise had been the basis of Carey's short pieces, and it continued to be a stand-by in operas of many kinds, both English and continental, until well into the next century. The reason why someone takes to disguise often seems insufficient, and sometimes incomprehensible. An extreme example can be found in *Edgar and Emmeline* (DL 31.1.61.), a piece set in Windsor Forest with uninteresting music by Michael Arne. Edgar disguised as a woman meets Emmeline disguised as a man; there is no humorous intention. Disguise is especially prominent in the many harem operas of the sixties and seventies. These will be discussed in relation to Dibdin's *The Captive*, *The Sultan*, and *The Seraglio*.

In the last twenty years of the century there arose a taste for serious though never tragic romances. Melodramatic tales of the kind we find in early Verdi operas come in profusion, their villains spouting stage fustian in remote castles, their heroes consorting with bandits in dense forests, their heroines captured and rescued defending their virtue to the last. A sub-category was the 'Siege' opera, which was well established by the 1780s. It had a predictable but powerful situation, with the hero outside the besieged castle and the heroine inside; or vice versa.[1] Many such plots qualify as 'Escape' operas, and they were popular in England as early as in any country. In the 1790s there was also an emphasis on horror operas, and it is noticeable that the ghosts always haunt castles rather than more mundane dwellings.

There are no grounds for supposing that opera plots had a silliness of their own. They were precisely the same in kind as the plots of contemporary plays. Sheridan's *The Duenna* differs in style from *The Rivals* and *The School for Scandal* only in that it contains a large number of lyrics. In 1811 Baker was able to list

[1] Among the best of many examples was the opera Verdi might have called *The Siege of Castellar*, but in fact called *Il Trovatore*.

thirty-five items whose titles began with the words 'The Siege of', but plays outnumber operas by four to one.

7 THE SINGERS

The Dance you have led me over Hedge and Ditch . . . might be good Sport to a slender, well-breath'd Stripling of a Lover; but to your Adorer, who is somewhat corpulent, it is actually intolerable.

These words were spoken near the start of Cumberland's opera libretto, *The Summer's Tale* (1765), and it is obvious that the author knew his hero would be played by the ageing Beard. All librettists and composers wrote with particular singers in mind, and it is easy to tell from a study of the words and the music which had the best voices and which were the best actors. In *The Duenna* Clara and Don Carlos have a great deal of singing to do but very little to say. So far as the plot is concerned Don Carlos is superfluous, but so far as the music is concerned he is one of the two chief characters. Clara was played by Miss Brown, later Mrs. Cargill, Don Carlos by Leoni, both professional singers without much acting experience. Each of the patent theatres engaged three or four good singers and did what they could to teach them to act; conversely they tried to teach their actors to sing, and many of them could. Garrick and Mrs. Siddons were unusual in the avoidance of operatic roles.[1] Sometimes a theatre was lucky enough to find someone with real ability in both fields. Mrs. Mattocks at Covent Garden and Mrs. Crouch at Drury Lane were outstanding examples, and John Bannister was another who could be safely entrusted with a big Shakespearean role as well as an operatic lead.

As on the Continent, solo singers were mostly sopranos and tenors. There were a few baritones, scarcely any contraltos. The contralto voice, when referred to at all, was sometimes called a counter-tenor.[2] Singers learnt their trade not as today from other singers but from composers. In the third quarter of the century the leading teachers were Thomas Arne in London and Thomas Linley in Bath. When Linley moved to London in 1776 his position in Bath was taken over by the castrato Rauzzini, composer of some goodish operas; Nancy Storace was among his pupils. In the 1780s Charles Dibdin taught Mrs. Mountain, Mrs. Bland, and Miss De Camp, and though his views may not be typical they are of interest. 'I took care', he wrote, 'they should be taught nothing more than correct expression, and an unaffected pronunciation of the words; the infallible and only way to perfect a singer . . . The force and meaning of the words'[3] should be stressed as in speaking them. Mara and Mrs. Sheridan (Elizabeth

---

[1] Mrs. Siddons sang Nell in *The Devil to pay* in the 1770s, but never sang after she came to Drury Lane in 1782.

[2] See Kelly ii, p. 193, 2nd ed.

[3] *Professional Life* ii, pp. 113–14.

Linley) were the best singers of Dibdin's day 'because they were taught on this principle'.[1] There was a sad lack of good textbooks on either the rudiments of music or on vocal technique. Tosi's *Observations on the Florid Song* was still in use—it had been well translated by Galliard in 1743—but as on the Continent the most effective teaching was done by precept and example.

A young singer was apprenticed to his or her teacher for some four or five years, and throughout this period any money earned, or a large proportion of it, had to be handed over to the teacher. Arne did very well indeed out of Miss Brent. It was in the teacher's interest that pupils should make their début as early as possible, and sopranos often began their careers at an age when today they would be about to have their first lesson. Mrs. Crouch first sang Mandane in *Artaxerxes*, a very difficult role, when she was eighteen. Nancy Storace sang a solo at the Three Choirs Festival in Hereford Cathedral when she was only twelve, though this was no more than an isolated stunt. More astonishing was the début at the end of the century of Miss Leake, a pupil of Samuel Arnold's. On the vast stage of the new Drury Lane she appeared as Rosetta, the heroine of *Love in a Village*, when she was just fourteen. At such an age English girls of today do not have enough voice to fill a small school hall. Modern teachers will not be surprised to learn that Miss Leake's voice gave out while she was still in her teens, and she had to retire.

It is hard to find any explanation for these prodigies other than that standards in the late eighteenth century were lower than has been supposed. The explanation that English singers were inferior to those on the Continent, though it would have appealed to Burney, will not hold water. Lord Mount-Edgcumbe in his reminiscences of fifty years of opera-going (1825) went out of his way to stress that much of the singing he heard in Italy in the 1780s would not have been tolerated in the London playhouses. Débuts at too tender an age were just as common abroad as in Britain. Nancy Storace was singing leading roles in Italian opera houses at seventeen, and at eighteen she was Vienna's prima donna. It is significant that, like Cecilia Davies,[2] she was always more admired on the Continent than in London, where many people found it impossible to believe that an English-born singer could be any good.

In all European countries soprano tessitura rose steadily in the latter half of the eighteenth century. Before 1750 English sopranos never or almost never sang above A. In the late fifties and in the sixties Miss Brent and Mrs. Vincent were given plenty of Bs and an occasional C. By 1770 Mrs. Wrighten was tossing off Cs in profusion and an occasional D. In Shield's *Robin Hood* (1784) Miss Harper sang a number of high Ds, and in the nineties Mrs. Billington and Mrs. Crouch were achieving a tone higher still and sometimes a high F, the top note Mozart wrote at about the same time for the Queen of the Night. According to

[1] So for that matter were the pupils of Plunket Greene.

[2] Cecilia Davies sang in Paris, Vienna, and Italy from 1768 to 1773 and again briefly in the 1780s.

Parke,[1] Miss George 'sang up to B in alto perfectly clear, and in tune; this being three notes higher than any singer I ever heard'.

William Jackson complained that instead of developing their voices so as to be soft at the top and full at the bottom, singers were achieving the opposite effect.[2] Leigh Hunt commented in his Autobiography on an unappealing habit of John Braham's:

> what may be call the loud-and-soft style. There was admirable execution; but the expression consisted in being very soft on the words *love*, *peace*, etc., and then bursting into roars of triumph on the words *hate*, *war*, and *glory*.

The history of music was approaching the moment when someone, editing *Hymns Ancient and Modern*, would achieve the memorable line

(*f*) In life, (*p*) in death, O Lord, (*cr*) abide with me.

Michael Kelly, in London after several years of singing in Italy and Vienna, astonished Drury Lane with a big aria in Storace's *The Haunted Tower* (1789):

In his *Life of Kemble* Boaden commented on these actual bars:

> His compass was extraordinary. In vigorous passages he never cheated the ear with feeble wailings of falsetto, but sprung upon the ascending fifth with a sustained energy that electrified the audience.[3]

The implication is that all previous English tenors sang their high notes falsetto, and there is abundant evidence that this was the case. About 1771 a minor singer named Robert Owenson (1744–1812) was told by Arne that he had 'one of the finest baritones he ever heard, and particularly susceptible of that quality of intonation then so much admired and now so out of fashion, the falsetto'.[4] Thus baritones sang their high notes falsetto as well as tenors. At the turn of the century Dibdin wrote of 'Leveridge and Beard having given way to the use of effeminacy and falcetto', and though the remark is the less valuable for the fact that Dibdin can never have heard Leveridge, it is of interest for its pejorative undertones. But until the 1790s people found falsetto singing something to admire rather than condemn.

Both tenors and baritones usually changed gear at about the D or E above

---

[1] i, p. 128; and see p. 468 for a high G sung by Mrs. Billington.

[2] *Observations on the Present State of Music in London* (1791).

[3] See also *The General Magazine* for 1790, p. 33, for another reference to Kelly's singing of this song.

[4] Lady Morgan, Vol. 1 (1862); she was Owenson's daughter.

Middle C, and in baritone songs the voice part was often kept below this pitch in order to avoid falsetto. Above D or E the tenor became a counter-tenor, and as such his range could be extended by nearly an octave. Shield wrote high Cs and Ds for both Incledon and Johnstone, the leading Covent Garden tenors towards the end of the century. Examples can be found in *Fontainbleau* and *The Woodman*. In *The Choleric Fathers* (1785) Johnstone even had a high E. His falsetto was praised by both Kelly[1] and O'Keeffe. *The Thespian* for September 1793 found it 'pleasingly expressive', though the writer was worried by the jerk between his natural and counter-tenor qualities. Most people seem to have accepted the jerk as inevitable. An article on Incledon in *The Musical Quarterly* for 1818 says

> He had a voice of uncommon power, both in the natural and the falsetto. The former was from A to G, a compass of about fourteen notes; the latter he could use from D to E or F, or about ten notes . . . His falsetto was rich, sweet and brilliant, but totally unlike the other. He took it without preparation, according to circumstances, either about D, E, or F, or ascending an octave, which was his most frequent custom.

It seems that neither Johnstone nor Incledon saw any reason to shade the one quality off into the other. We today accept falsetto notes from some of our tenors when these notes are both high and soft, but we expect the singer to conceal the change in quality so far as his skill allows, and in theory we regard it as a small weakness that he should resort to falsetto at all. This is not a viewpoint of any antiquity. Shakespeare for one admired the man 'that can sing both high and low', that is, both falsetto and naturally, and we have already seen that Drake sang falsetto. Incledon too had been a sailor on the West Indies station; modern readers may need reminding that such men were not effeminate.

The falsetto range of a baritone was naturally lower and smaller than that of a tenor. Yet of Charles Bannister *The Thespian Dictionary* says 'His voice was a strong clear bass, with one of the most extensive falsettos ever heard'. In his Memoirs of Charles's son, John Bannister, Adolphus makes the same point: 'His voice united in extraordinary perfection the extremes of deep bass and high-toned falsetto'. In point of fact his earlier parts offered no opportunities for falsetto; in *The Flitch of Bacon* (1778) and *The Lord of the Manor* (1780) he had scarcely a note above E flat. But Charles Bannister was famous for his amusing imitations of well-known castrato singers, and in *Rosina* (1782) Shield decided to exploit these higher notes up to A. Today we give such parts to a tenor, as was done on the recording of *Rosina* conducted by Richard Bonynge. Indeed whenever such operas are performed, all the male parts are allotted to tenors and there is thus no variety in quality. Yet a contrast between tenors and basses was just as important in our eighteenth-century operas as it is today. The only solution is for our singers to cultivate falsetto once more.

[1] i, p. 293, 2nd ed.

I am not informed about falsetto singing on the Continent. There must surely, be significance in Mozart's choice of male voices. In his Singspiel for German singers, *Die Entführung aus dem Serail,* he preferred tenors, but in his later Italian operas for Italian-trained singers he preferred baritones. In *Don Giovanni* the Don himself, Leporello, and the Commendatore are all baritones with E as the top note, and Masetto has nothing higher than D. In the original version Don Ottavio, the only tenor, had only one aria. One might guess that Mozart accepted falsetto singing in a Singspiel, but not in Italianate opera. It certainly seems that Vienna found 'robusti' tenors hard to find, for in *Figaro* all the male singers were baritones except for Michael Kelly, who doubled Don Basilio and the lawyer Don Curzio.

The probability is that throughout eighteenth-century Europe falsetto singing was commoner than has been realized, and that it began to die out everywhere at much the same time. In England it began to die out when audiences thrilled to the high notes of Michael Kelly, and more especially to those of John Braham,[1] a tenor with a European reputation by the turn of the century.

There was another reason as well. The castrato voice no longer intrigued an English audience; it shocked. Counter-tenor singing, though different in quality, was like enough to be frowned on. In December 1824 Rossini was invited to the Brighton Pavilion by George IV. Asked to entertain the other guests with something of his own, he unaccountably obliged with the 'Salce' from his *Otello,* and because it was a soprano air he sang it falsetto. The King no doubt took this in his stride, but newspaper reports the following day show that many people were profoundly shocked by this apparent aping of a brand of singer by then considered unmentionable.

There is some evidence, though not nearly enough, as to how singers behaved while singing. Colman wrote of an opera singer taking 'a genteel turn or two on the stage during the symphony'[2] which is what often happens today. Algarotti thought it absurd that 'in an air expressive of wrath, an actor should calmly wait with his hand stuck in his sword belt, until the ritornello be over, to give vent to a passion that is supposed to be boiling in his breast',[3] and the implication is that this was normal practice in the eighteenth century. There is no evidence before the late nineties that spoken dialogue was ever superimposed on the orchestral introductions.

Gesticulation during a song seems to have been frowned on. Goldsmith refers in *The Bee* (13.10.59.) to Sadler's Wells singers stretching out their hands alternately and then drawing them in again, and implies that playhouse singers were above this behaviour. One suspects that they came down to the footlights, faced

---

[1] But Lord Mount-Edgcumbe (p. 95) says he did sometimes 'quit the natural register of his voice by raising it to an unpleasant falsetto'.

[2] Quoted by Genest v, p. 345.

[3] *Saggio sopra l'opera in musica* (1755), published in English as *Essay on Opera* (1768).

the audience squarely until the introduction was finished, and then let fly. Boaden describes an innovation in the Storace operas of the 1790s: he is writing of Nancy Storace and Michael Kelly at Drury Lane after their return from Vienna:

> The foreign habits of these accomplished singers enabled them to sing steadily while moving about the stage (a difficulty of no mean rank) and infused a life, and a bustle into our opera, which before had hardly trusted itself with action.

The foreign habits must have been those of Vienna; London knew as much about Italian habits as any European capital. We shall see later that Storace's ensembles insisted on stage action.

The word Chorus, in either a vocal score or in a libretto, often meant no more than that the soloists all sang together. Occasionally the playhouses would engage extras for elaborate choruses, but for reasons of economy they preferred to press into service all those members of the company who were not otherwise employed. Even orchestral players, Burney says, were sometimes dressed up and flung onto the stage to swell the sound.[1] Some idea of how choruses behaved can be gleaned from Baker's article on *Macbeth*, which refers to the witches as 'the score, or more, of vocal performers who are brought on in russet cloaks, and drawn up in rank for full ten minutes in front of the stage'.

> The men are mostly comedians, as well as singers; and, whatever they may intend, their countenances, as soon as they are recognised, throw an air of burlesque upon the whole. The women, who are generally pretty enough to *be-witch* us in a sense very different from Shakespeare's, are often employed in laughing with each other, and sometimes with the audience, at their dresses, which they think frightful, but which, in fact, conceal neither their bright eyes, nor rosy lips, nor, scarcely, their neat silk stockings.

The effect led Baker to ask not that the Leveridge music should be cut—that was still unthinkable—but that the chorus should be placed out of sight.

In the last twenty years of the century singers spent more and more of their summer months touring, and even in the winter they sometimes asked for leave of absence, to the annoyance of the management.[2] They often endured extreme discomfort for the sake of their art. Miss Leake once sang a role in *My Grandmother* at Drury Lane, and on the following night one in *The Children in the Wood* in Birmingham. By the 1790s all-night coach travel before a performance had become an occupational hazard.

[1] BM Add. 48345, f. 7.
[2] See Betsy Sheridan's Journal for 20.8.89.

8 OPERA SONGS AND 'BORROWINGS'

The music of the songs can be left until the discussion of individual operas in later chapters. Their *galante* style came not only from such Italian models as Galuppi and Piccini, but also from J. C. Bach (a leading influence from 1762 until his death) and, a little later, from the French opera composers Monsigny, Philidor, and Grétry. Often an English quality was superimposed on the borrowed style.

Vocal items varied from full-scale arias to strophic ballads, and there were several intermediate types. The *Da Capo* aria lingered on at the King's Theatre in such operas as *Orione* (1763) by J. C. Bach, but was seldom heard in the playhouses. There are no examples in *Artaxerxes* or in the all-sung operas that imitated it. Nevertheless English opera can show a large number of arias of great length and difficulty.

Borrowed music can be found in about three out of four operas after 1762, and it includes both fully-composed arias by known composers and simple traditional ballads by 'anon'. Ballad operas had been based mainly on the latter, and even on the rare occasions when more elaborate songs had been borrowed, the orchestration had been simplified, with the harpsichord supplying the harmonies. But the onset of the *galante* style drove the continuo accompaniment out of existence; by 1762 the typical ballad opera song sounded old-fashioned. In *Love in a Village*, produced that very year, the only ballads are sung either by servants or by an old gentleman whose views are represented as antediluvian. No ballads at all are to be found in most pastiche operas of the next thirteen years; for instance *The Maid of the Mill* and *Lionel and Clarissa*. It looked as though their day was over.

However in *The Duenna* (1775) Thomas Linley junior showed that these old and much-loved tunes could be harmonized and orchestrated in the *galante* style, and this discovery led to a reprieve; for the rest of the century nearly all operas included two or three examples. In *The Duenna* the traditional tunes are Scotch, and thereafter Scotch Songs turn up in a great many operas. In the eighties, influenced by his Irish librettist O'Keeffe, Shield began to introduce Irish songs as well, while Arnold was showing an unexpected flair for finding English folk tunes of the type Cecil Sharp was later to 'discover'. In Shield's *The Poor Soldier* traditional ballads predominate, but this was unusual. In general there is a clear distinction between these later operas and those earlier ones inspired by *The Beggar's Opera*, and the term 'ballad opera' should be used only for the latter. A ballad is a simple popular song which can be given length only by strophic repetition and which owes nothing to orchestral elaboration. A Ballad Opera is one mostly made up of such songs. With rare exceptions, English operas after 1762 are not of this type. Yet Dibdin's *Lionel and Clarissa* has often been called a Ballad Opera, and so has his all-sung *The Recruiting*

Sergeant—in a National Theatre programme of all places. Neither work has any strophic songs nor traditional-type tunes at all; *The Magic Flute*, with its four strophic songs, is more of a Ballad Opera than either.

There was nothing underhand about borrowings. Vocal scores usually named the composer or, in the case of Scotch Songs, gave the opening words of the original. Often the latest Italian opera at the King's Theatre was drawn on, and it was thought educational that playhouse audiences should be able to hear such music in proportions they were willing to tolerate. Composers hardly ever delved into the more distant past. I have identified only one borrowing from a Handel opera after 1760—'Verdi prati' from *Alcina* turns up in Arnold's *The Castle of Andalusia* (1782). No Handel opera was staged in the eighteenth century after the 1754 production of *Admeto*. His oratorios were much better remembered, but even in this field borrowings were rare. *Love in a Village* made use of songs from *L'Allegro* and *Susanna*, and Shield drew on *Athalia* and *Judas Macabbaeus* for songs in *Marian* and *The Highland Reel* respectively. Handel's style had no influence whatever. As antiquarian interest grew, compilers occasionally went back to Elizabethan times. The finale of *The Duenna* is based on the tune, though not the harmonies, of Morley's 'Now is the Month of Maying', and Shield borrowed a three-part madrigal by Michael East for *The Flitch of Bacon*. Purcell was better remembered than Handel. Astonishingly, the finale of *The Golden Pippin* consists of the first movement of Vivaldi's Concerto Grosso op. 3 no. 5 with complex voice parts superimposed. I have found no borrowings from Rameau, though his theoretical works were sometimes studied. The many Haydn and Mozart borrowings can be left to the final chapters.

Such borrowings should be kept in perspective. They predominated over the new music in the pastiche operas from *Love in a Village* to *The Duenna*, but even at this period there were a number of operas by Arne and others with no borrowings at all, and after 1775 new items usually constituted at least three-quarters of the whole. Arne, Dibdin, the elder Linley, and Thomas Carter all preferred to compose their operas entire and to borrow nothing.

9 VOCAL DECORATIONS

Most solo singers added what they called cadences (cadenzas) at the pause marks in the bigger arias, and brief 'graces' in songs of all kinds, but the extent of these decorations has often been exaggerated in modern performances. Tosi, in his influential textbook for singers, constantly impressed on his readers the need for moderation. Of the *Da Capo* aria he wrote:

> Generally speaking, the Study of the Singers of the present Times consists in terminating the *Cadence* of the first Part with an overflowing of *Passages* and *Divisions* at Pleasure, and the *Orchestre* waits; in that of the second the Dose is encreased, and the *Orchestre* grows tired; but on the last

> *Cadence*, the Throat is set a going like a Weather-cock in a Whirlwind, and the *Orchestre* yawns . . . Good Taste does not consist in a continual Velocity of the Voice, which goes thus rambling on, without a Guide, and without Foundation; but rather . . . in the true Notion of Graces, going from one Note to another with singular and unexpected Surprizes, and stealing the Time exactly on the true Motion of the Bass.[1]

In other words it was vital that the rhythm of the bass line should be preserved, for it was only at the pause marks that the conductor-less orchestra was capable of both waiting and of knowing when to resume.

Dr. Brown thought that all florid singing should be done away with on the grounds that it made nonsense of the words, and he was against the *Da Capo* aria for the same reason. Many singers were disposed to agree with him. The leading Covent Garden sopranos between 1760 and the end of the century were, successively, Miss Brent (Mrs. Pinto), Miss Catley, Miss Harper (Mrs. Bannister), and Mrs. Billington, and it is clear that Miss Brent decorated with moderation, Miss Catley and Miss Harper scarcely at all, and Mrs. Billington a great deal.

> The great Catley thought one cadence enough in each verse; and Mrs. Bannister, who long after her, led the van in opera, and who was the original Rosina, scarcely ever used any ornament whatever, her style being purely that of ballad singing. Mrs. Billington's singing, therefore, was caviarre to the million . . . though the pit yawned and the galleries gaped in amazement, the music world were [*sic*] enraptured by her beautiful cadences.[2]

John Braham who sang from 1796 onwards was also said to 'italianize our simple songs'. He 'so revelled in his powers of variety', says Mrs. Oxberry, 'that an accurate ear could scarcely follow the air through his multifarious modulations'. There were those who admired such singing. Miss Harper, says *The Thespian Dictionary*, lacked 'ingenuity in her cadences', and did not display Mrs. Billington's 'beautiful *exuberance of fancy*'. On the other hand O'Keeffe approved of Miss Harper's reticence. 'She sung the notes, all the notes, and nothing but the notes'.[3] The men too were sometimes praised for restraint. Boaden, in his *Life of John Philip Kemble*, wrote that Johnstone had 'a plain and pleasing style, without the slightest affectation or mixture of the foreign graces'. But his Covent Garden rival Incledon was remembered very differently by Thackeray, no doubt because his roles called for a more italianate style. In the first chapter of *The Newcomes*, Colonel Newcome sings a ballad, 'Wapping Old Stairs', 'with flourishes and roulades in the old Incledon manner, which has

---

[1] *Observation on the Florid Song* translated by Galliard (1743), pp. 128–9.
[2] Oxberry iii, article on Mrs. Billington.
[3] ii, pp. 71–2.

pretty nearly passed away'. There are other references to Incledon in this chapter; the period is supposed to be about 1830.

It is clear that in English opera decorations were in general restrained until the advent of Mrs. Billington and Braham in the 1790s, and some positive evidence for this statement can be given. About 1767 'Would you taste the Noontide Air' from *Comus* was published with the addition of the graces Arne had specially written for his pupil Miss Brent.[1] In the example that follows, these graces are added in small notes to the original vocal line:

The last two bars are as follows:

There is probably more decoration here than Miss Catley liked; the degree can be described as moderate. For examples of more reticent decoration, as favoured by Miss Catley and Miss Harper, we can turn to Corri's three-volume *Select Collection* (1779), which includes a large number of songs from English operas, all of them lightly graced. In ballads the additions amount to no more than a few appoggiaturas.

Because Mrs. Billington had a voice of exceptional brilliance and agility, she luxuriated in decorations of the most fulsome kind. She was a good musician, proficient on the harpsichord, and a passable composer, but she had no gift for improvisation and for this reason had to work out all her additions on paper. In 1801 Thomas Busby published her songs in three operas, *Artaxerxes*, *Love in a Village*, and *The Duenna* as she actually sang them. It thus happens that in some cases we can compare the simple style of gracing given by Corri with the lavish style favoured by Mrs. Billington. The example given below is one of Clara's

---

[1] A decade later this song was reprinted from the same plates, but this time the graces were said to have been written for Miss Catley; an enterprising publisher was modernizing his title. The key was G; the original had been in *A*.

songs in *The Duenna*, 'By him we love offended'; it was borrowed from Rauzzini's opera *Piramo e Tisbe*. I have omitted the first four bars because Mrs.
Billington did not alter them; they are almost the same as the first four printed
below. The top stave shows the original vocal line with Corri's additions in small
notes.

Mrs. Billington's most elaborate cadenza came at the end, where Corri, short of
space at the end of a page, added nothing at all.

It must be repeated that only Mrs. Billington and Braham added flourishes on this scale. The evidence is overwhelming that in most English operas most English singers added nothing more than the occasional appoggiatura and a brief flourish if there were a pause mark.

10 THE ORCHESTRA

Both in Britain and on the continent orchestras were 'conducted' in two different ways. If the composer were present, he directed from the harpsichord. If not, the leader of the violins directed. There was no regular baton conducting in London until the 1820s. At the Handel Festival of 1784 in Westminster Abbey Dr. Philip Hayes, rightly feeling that with over five hundred performers good ensemble could not otherwise be achieved, started to beat time during rehearsal with a role of parchment, but Cramer, who was leading the orchestra, decided that his time-honoured privileges were being usurped and he refused to play.[1] All over Europe leaders were growing anxious about their rights, and with reason, for it was becoming increasingly apparent that direction by the leader was inefficient.

Nevertheless it must have worked fairly well in the playhouses, and I shall now list such leaders as I have identified.

At Covent Garden the band was led by the following:

c. 1769–78   John Abraham Fisher (1744–1806), who about 1770 prudently married the widow of William Powell, one of the managers; Powell had died in 1769 after catching cold watching a cricket-match. In the 1770s Fisher composed operas and pantomimes for the theatre. For his subsequent career, see p. 382.

1780–94   Karl Friedrich Baumgarten (*c.* 1740–1824), who had settled in London in his teens. He was leading the King's Theatre Band in 1762. He composed a little. Though tall and athletic in appearance, and a voracious eater, he is said to have been nervous and timid. Haydn thought he lacked energy and produced 'a sleepy orchestra'.

1794–?   John Mountain, who was Irish. He had previously led the Liverpool orchestra and, from 1792, the one in Vauxhall Gardens. His wife was a Covent Garden singer. Parke has an amusing but undated story of their both being dismissed at once by Harris.[2]

It is even less easy to establish the dates of the Drury Lane leaders.

1760s   Thomas Pinto, who married Miss Brent in 1766. A brilliant

[1] See Parke i, p. 39, for an amusing account of this battle of wills.
[2] I, p. 109.

player, he was unreliable as a man, and after leading at Marylebone Gardens 1769–70 he fled to Ireland deep in debt and soon died there.

c. 1775   Stayner (see Parke i, p. 3).

1776–8   Thomas Linley junior.

1780s   Richards, who led in the 1784–5 season (Dibdin's *Professional Life* ii, p. 167) but not subsequently.

1785–1800+   Thomas Shaw, who published a violin concerto and some keyboard sonatas as well as theatre music. Dibdin thought him a much better leader than Baumgarten (*Musical Tour* p. 182). He taught Kemble his only song in *Richard Coeur de Lion* (Parke i, p. 72). He was probably the Mr. Shaw who gave Haydn lunch (14.9.91); Haydn thought his wife the most beautiful woman he had ever seen. He was still leading at Drury Lane in 1796 (Boaden's *Mrs. Jordan* i, p. 315). In 1821 he seems to have been one of the proprietors of Drury Lane (Parke ii, p. 157), but if so he must soon have lost his money, for a little later he was teaching music in Paris at the school Fanny Kemble attended (*Records of a Girlhood* i, p. 97). He is not mentioned in any reference book.

At Covent Garden the harpsichord continuo was played by Jonathan Battishill from 1761 to 1764, and presumably by Samuel Arnold for the following five years. In the 1780s Griffith Jones was the harpsichordist; he published a keyboard tutor about 1800. At Drury Lane it can be presumed that Dibdin, the elder Linley, and Storace often officiated in this position during the time they were the house composer; I have found no other names. It is not clear when the harpsichord was superseded by the piano; it cannot have been before the 1790s.

There were nineteen orchestral players on the Covent Garden payroll in 1760,[1] plus a harpsichordist and copyist. We do not know precisely what instrument each played; there was certainly a great deal of doubling, and we can be sure that as in most European orchestras of the time the same two players alternated on flutes and oboes.[2] William Parke, whose Reminiscences are so often quoted in these pages, played not only the flute and the oboe but in his early days the viola as well; significantly he was a good enough violist for a playhouse orchestra after only three months practice. Burney mentions that at Drury Lane in the 1740s 'Hebden, a Yorkshireman, was first Bassoon and second Violoncello'. A theatre band of nineteen may seem small, but Garrick reported about this time that Paris theatre bands were smaller still. The splendid eighteenth-century theatre that survives at Drottningsholm near Stockholm may have a

---

[1] LS Part IV ii, p. 815.

[2] This was still the case at Vauxhall Gardens in the 1790s; see Cudworth's 'The Vauxhall Lists', Galpin Soc. Journal XX, p. 27.

much larger stage than Old Drury, but its orchestral pit will accommodate only sixteen players and a harpsichord, and must therefore be smaller.

After the restoration of Drury Lane in 1775 the band numbered twenty-four, and we know in some detail what they played:

Strings: 16 (5-4-3-4-0); one or more of the cellists played bass; two violinists doubled on the clarinet, one violist on the trumpet.

Woodwind: 4 (0-2-0-2); the oboists doubled on the flutes; with the clarinets there could be six woodwind at once.

Brass: 2 horns. With the trumpet there could be three brass.

Harpsichord

These figures show only the regular members of the orchestra. For certain operas the playing space could be enlarged. Of *The Royal Shepherd* (DL 1764) Hopkins wrote:

> On this Occasion the Stage was cut near two Feet and a Half to enlarge the Orchestra, to make it contain the additional performers who belong to the Opera-House, on whose account the Opera cannot be performed Tuesdays, & Saturdays.

The playhouses quite often had to engage extras, especially trumpets and drums. When Covent Garden put on its anglicized version of *La buona figliuola*, the band cost £8 17s. a night, which was over £1 more than usual.[1] It was not until New Drury was opened in 1792 that a playhouse could accommodate a full Haydn–Mozart orchestra with eight woodwind, four brass, drums, and strings. Numerous vocal scores give cues for all these instruments, but it must be stressed that they could not all play at once until 1792, and then only at Drury Lane.

By 1760 flutes were normally of the *traversi* type. Until about 1780 their range was no more than two octaves from the D above Middle C. Exceptionally Michael Arne took the flutes up to F sharp in a song he wrote for *The Belle's Stratagem* (1780) which was published in full score. Even after 1780 notes in the fifth above high D, notes which a modern flautist can easily play without changing his instrument, were normally given to one of the smaller flutes. There were a bewildering number in use. The octave piccolo was sometimes used; there are cues for '8th flute' in Arne's *Eliza*, Shield's *The Farmer*, and elsewhere. For military effects another small cross flute, the fife, was sometimes asked for, and in Shield's *Fontainbleau* there is a song with cues for both fife and 'flagelet'. The latter must have been a type of recorder, as was the 'common 4th flute' found in Boyce's *The Shepherd's Lottery*. Music for the latter was written a fourth below the sound, as was the music for the 'small flute' so often used by Shield; for instance in the finale of the overture to *Rosina*. It is sometimes not

[1] Rank-and-file players received 5s. a night.

clear if the 'small flute' was a recorder or a piccolo. The piccolo in E flat (but really in F[1]) was much used on the continent, for instance in Beethoven's military marches. This perhaps was Shield's 'small flute'; on the other hand he used it mainly for bird-song imitations, and earlier in the century these had usually been given to a recorder. We shall meet some even more difficult flute problems in the full score of Jackson's *The Lord of the Manor*.[2]

Handel wrote so often for the oboe that one might thank standards of performance in London were good, but William Parke says that in the early sixties it was 'not in a high state of cultivation, the two principal oboe players, Vincent and Simpson, using the old English Oboe, an instrument which in shape and tone bore some resemblance to that yclept a *post-horn*'. Standards were raised about 1767 by the arrival of Johann Christian Fischer, who had been in Frederick the Great's band at Potsdam and who later married Gainsborough's daughter. His tone, says Parke, 'was soft and sweet, his style expressive, and his execution was at once neat and brilliant'. The operative word here is 'soft'. The oboe's tone was changing from a blare to a bitter-sweet murmur, and the Parke brothers, John and William, were the first native-born players to cultivate the new quality. At first the range was only two octaves from D to D, but by the middle eighties Shield was writing high Es for William Parke and even sometimes a high F. At a Salomon concert of 1796 Parke introduced 'some of my newly-discovered high notes (up to G in alto)'.[3]

Though clarinet solos had been played at Drury Lane as early as 1737, little more is heard of this instrument until Arne wrote for it in *Thomas and Sally* (1760). Early clarinettists were oboe players with a taste for experiment,[4] and the sound was so much liked that after 1760 it was introduced into nearly all operas, though usually in only one or two items. At first composers treated it like a horn, as in *Thomas and Sally*, where clarinets and horns either double each other or play similar music antiphonally. But in 'Water parted', one of the most popular arias in *Artaxerxes* (1762), Arne took the instrument down into the chalumeau register. Clarinet tone was more penetrating than it is today, and this made the instrument especially suitable for outdoor music. Advertisements in 1762 for a concert at Ranelagh Gardens promised that in the intervals 'The French Horns and Clarinets will play favourite pieces in the Garden'. Military Bands soon became standardized with two clarinets, two bassoons and two horns, flutes being added about 1780 and a trumpet and a serpent a little later. The clarinettist John Mahon was playing clarinet concertos by 1773, some written by himself; one survives in Manchester's Public Library. At first clarinets were always in C. Jackson has them in B flat in *The Lord of the Manor* (1780); I have not found an earlier example, but it must be remembered that a clarinet cue in a

[1] See p. 221.
[2] See p. 445.
[3] Parke i, pp. 215 and 335.
[4] See p. 304.

vocal score does not reveal the key of the instrument. I have found no clarinets in A, but an additional song written for Arnold's *Inkle and Yarico* (1788) shows them in B major.[1] This unusual and short-lived instrument also appears in the score of Mozart's *Idomeneo* (1780).

Bassoon solos are very common, especially in overtures, and they are often difficult. In Storace's *The Doctor and the Apothecary* (1788) there is an aria with a concertante bassoon part, complete with a cadenza shared with the soprano. In Scotch songs, both real and imitated, the two bassoons were often asked to hold bass octaves in imitation of a bagpipe drone; Parke has a story about a Covent Garden bassoonist called Schubert who ran out of breath of one on these long pedal notes. In vocal scores bassoon solos are often printed an octave up.

Horn writing was as unadventurous as it was abroad. The first movement of Abel's overture to *Love in a Village* (1762) asks the second horn for a note that was usually regarded as unplayable; in fact it can be found in contemporary horn tutors and in Haydn's Symphony No. 61:

Abel

The low Fs are not a misprint; only F will fit the harmony. In the song already mentioned that Michael Arne wrote for *The Belle's Stratagem* (1780) the horns are in D, but at the start of the allegro section they have four bars rest and are told to 'Change quick to G'. I have not found an earlier example of a change in the middle of a piece.

Difficult trumpet solos are fairly common. Technique was preserved because of the continuing popularity of Handel's *Messiah* with its famous 'The Trumpet shall sound', as also of 'Rule, Britannia'. Shield often wrote similar trumpet parts for Sarjeant (whose name is spelt in a variety of ways), and it has been suggested that he played them on a slide trumpet. Such trumpet parts scarcely exist in contemporary Viennese music. They were nearly always in D.

Though trombones were often used in Restoration times for funeral music by Locke, Blow, Purcell, and others, they suddenly fell out of use, and I do not find them in eighteenth-century theatre music until Kelly's *Blue Beard* (1798), where long-held single notes are intended to produce a spine-chilling effect. There are 'bugle-horns' in Shield's *The Noble Peasant* and *The Woodman*, and bagpipes in his *Marian*, Reeve's *Oscar and Malvina*, and other pieces of the 1790s with a Scottish flavour. The harp also came to the fore in this decade, usually to give local colour to operas set in medieval times and earlier. Examples are numsrous, the most striking being Arnold's *Cambro-Britons* (1798), our earliest opera on a Welsh subject.

[1] See p. 471 for a clarinet in D (Shield's *Friar Bacon*).

Percussion instruments were common and varied, and they sometimes seem to have been played in stage by the singers. Shield's *Fontainbleau* includes what might be called a music-hall song, with cymbals, marrow-bones, and cleavers cued in.[1] *Omai*, a pantomime by the same composer, is set partly in Tahiti, and there are cues for native instruments described as nassas and pagges. There is 'Turkish Music' in *The Crusade* with cymbal crashes cued in, and this was another of Shield's operas. He was our most adventurous composer when it came to scoring. As early as 1771 Arne's *The Fairy Prince* called for what seems to have been a keyed glockenspiel, and there was a vogue for this, or perhaps a related instrument, in the 1790s, a vogue initiated by Storace's *The Haunted Tower* and *No Song No Supper*. It may be that the composer brought the instrument back from Vienna, and that it resembled the one Mozart wrote for in *The Magic Flute*. (See also Shield's *Lock and Key*.) Storace also wrote for the tambourine in *Gli Equivoci* (Vienna 1786) and elsewhere.

Drumming was unadventurous. Until near the end of the century timpani were always tuned to the notes D and A, D being the standard key for trumpets. Presumably it was the difficulty of tuning timpani that was the limiting factor.[2] The side-drum was seldom used. In Arne's *Eliza* (1754) there is a 'March with Side Drum', and the part is notated on a stave, but sometimes in other operas the player was expected to tap on the main beats and did not require any music. This certainly happened when military marches were played by a band on the stage.

In general, the orchestration of English operas was more adventurous than it was in most of the countries of Europe.

London's three most famous violinists seldom or never led the playhouse orchestras, but two of them had a good deal of influence on our theatre music, and as they will be frequently mentioned in the pages that follow some account of their careers will now be gien.

Of Wilhelm Cramer (1745–99), the youngest of the three, little need be said. He led the band at the King's Theatre for most of the last quarter of the century. His more famous son, Johann Baptist Cramer, was English by upbringing and wrote some famous piano studies.

Felice de Giardini (1716–96) worked at the King's Theatre from 1755 off and on for ten years, leading the band and composing or adapting several Italian operas. Later he composed violin concertos, string quartets, and an English oratorio, *Ruth* (1773), which was frequently revived; it was his most successful achievement. For some years he was a Governor of the Foundling Hospital and ran the concerts there. He and Burney planned to found a Music Academy on the premises, but the idea fell through. As he grew elderly, Giardini became unhappy and quarrelsome, 'spoke well of few', and developed dropsy. He took increasingly to the viola because its music was less taxing. In 1784 he went to

---

[1] See p. 5.
[2] See p. 426.

Naples where he was patronized by Sir William Hamilton. After an unsuccessful return to London (1789–92) he tried his fortunes in Moscow where he died in poverty. He was never wealthy, as Boswell recorded in 1773:

> GOLDSMITH. 'The greatest musical performers have but small emoluments. Giardini, I am told, does not get above seven hundred a year.'
> JOHNSON. 'That is, indeed, but little for a man to get, who does best that which so many endeavour to do.'

Francis Hippolyte Barthelemon (1741–1808) was born in Bordeaux of a French father and an Irish mother. After a spell as an officer in the Irish Brigade (Parke has him a midshipman in the Spanish Navy) he took to music on the joint advice of his Colonel and the Earl of Kellie. In 1765 he succeeded Giardini as leader at the King's Theatre, where he composed *Pelopida* to an Italian text. For Paris in 1768 he composed *Le Fleuve Scamandre* to a French one, and between the two he contributed an amusing burletta to Garrick's *A Peep behind the Curtain* (DL 23.10.67.); this established him in the London playhouses at the cost of annoying Burney, who thought that he had been asked to compose the burletta.

In 1766 Barthelemon married Mary (Polly) Young, who for some months had been the only English singer at the King's Theatre. She was Mrs. Arne's niece. It was a happy marriage, and they looked after Mrs. Arne in her old age. In 1770 Barthelemon succeeded Pinto as leader at Marylebone Gardens, and we shall find him composing English burlettas for the little theatre there and several operas for Drury Lane, but by 1779 he was disgruntled with the playhouses, and apart from ballet music for the King's Theatre he devoted himself to string quartets and violin sonatas. Because he was friendly with the Chaplain, he wrote hymn tunes for the Asylum for Female Orphans in St. George's Fields; his 'Awake my soul' is popular still, and deservedly. When Robert Hindmarsh organized the first Swedenborgian Society in London in 1782 the Barthelemons were founder members. According to his daughter, Mrs. Henslowe, he was a very small man, very handsome, and very good at fencing.[1] In middle life he dropped the accents on his surname.

11 ORCHESTRAL DECORATION

Burney has the following anecdote about Giardini, an anecdote that must date from the 1740s.[2]

> He went to . . . Naples, where, having obtained a place among *Ripienos* in the opera orchestra, he used to flourish and change passages much more frequently than he ought to have done. 'However', says Giardini, of whom

[1] Cradock iv, p. 131 ff.
[2] Near the end of Book IV, ch. 6, of *A General History of Music*.

I had this account, 'I acquired great reputation among the ignorant for my impertinence; yet one night, during the opera, Jomelli, who had composed it, came into the orchestra, and seating himself close by me, I determined to give the Maestro di Capella a touch of my taste and execution; and in the symphony of the next song, which was in a pathetic style, I gave loose to my fingers and fancy; for which I was rewarded by the composer with a violent slap in the face; which', adds Giardini, 'was the best lesson I ever received from a great master in my life.'

To savour the story in full, one needs to know that both participants were young men, Jomelli being only two years older than Giardini.

By the 1760s Giardini was by far the most respected violinist in Britain, and his dislike of orchestral decoration must have reduced such enthusiasm as there was for it at the playhouses. There had certainly been a vogue for decorating a little earlier, for in 1763 John Potter complained of 'some errors, which many *young* musicians in particular are guilty of'; he himself thought that

> The parts should be played simply as they are, without any additions, or graces, which are almost generally improperly applied . . . It is almost certain, that the different graces and additions by the players, will destroy the harmony; one is flourishing his part one way, and one another, a quite different way; and as these things are done *extempore*, there is not the least probability they can accord . . . If an author has taste in his compositions, it is very difficult to add anything that will render it [sic] more beautiful.[1]

Potter ended by advising orchestral players to play exactly what was printed. We may hopefully conclude that the combined influence of Giardini and Potter led to more restraint.

This conclusion is supported by a common discrepancy in vocal scores and full scores alike. When a violin part doubles a vocal line, the former will often include an appoggiatura which is not given in the voice part. The assumption seems to be that the singer would inevitably add the appoggiatura, but because violinists played what was put in front of them it was prudent to include the appoggiatura in their part.

When an orchestral instrument was featured in an aria, the player was expected to add a cadenza at any pause mark, and perhaps to play with a good deal of freedom in other respects. We shall find Shield writing a number of big soprano arias with a concertante part for oboe, and these usually provide opportunity for an oboe cadenza in the long introduction. Parke also added cadenzas at pauses in ballads. 'Had I a heart for falsehood fram'd' in *The Duenna* makes use of the Irish tune Tom Moore later immortalized as 'The harp that once through Tara's halls', and Parke says his cadenza in the eight-bar introduc-

---

[1] *Observations of the Present State of Music and Musicians* (1763), pp. 79–80.

tion was always greeted with a round of applause.[1] In fact there are two pause marks, so perhaps there were two cadenzas.

12 THE OVERTURE

By the 1750s more and more English opera overtures were being written in the Italian form, their first and last movements fast and the middle one slow. We have already seen that some of Boyce's show *galante* influence. But the fully *galante* symphony-overture did not reach England, and was not composed here, until 1762. For the rest of the century the English used the word overture both for the music that preceded an opera and for what we today would call a symphony. At first there was virtually no difference, either in form or in length. But the opera overture was never allowed a repeat of the first movement exposition or a minuet and trio; the movements numbered three rather than four, and sometimes only two. Haydn's symphonies were billed as overtures as late as the 1790s, but by then their length and density were demanding the modern term.

The symphony-overture was the chief vehicle for a special brand of *galante* influence imported from Mannheim, and it was soon transforming the English opera overture. The Mannheim orchestra had been the first in Europe to achieve virtuoso precision. Its leader was the Czech violinist Johann Stamitz. By careful rehearsal he trained the orchestra to make sudden constrasts between *forte* and *piano* passages, to emphasise sudden *sforzando* chords, and to make crescendos and diminuendos. According to Schubart, 'its *forte* was a thunder-roll, its *crescendo* a cataract, its *diminuendo* a dying ripple of sound, its *piano* the murmur of spring'.[2] We today may think *galante* music lacks emotional feeling, but to those for whom it was written it appeared to have a great deal. The dynamic contrasts were of a kind that had scarcely ever been attempted before; they were now a primary objective, occurring in every work. The Mannheim Crescendo became the talk of Europe, and those whom it excited neither knew nor cared that the musical substance of what they were hearing was often negligible. Because no music existed in which the band could show off its special skills, Stamitz and some of the other players composed their own repertoire. These Mannheim Symphonies were published in batches of six in several European capitals, with the important result that orchestras for the first time became standardized. From now on they all had to have oboes and horns, as well as strings; also a bassoon or two to double on the bass line even when not indicated in the score. Orchestras without these resources could not play the new symphonies and concertos.[3]

---

[1] ii, p. 14.

[2] Quoted in Terry's *J. C. Bach*, p. 126.

[3] It is curious that Mannheim concertos were much less 'modern' than Mannheim Symphonies; they have far fewer dynamic contrasts and virtually none of the famous crescendos.

Mannheim Symphonies were not published in London until 1763, when Robert Bremner started bringing out both his Periodical Overtures and his sets of Stamitz symphonies. There were slightly earlier channels along which the new influence flowed, or something very like it. Johann Christian Bach had recently arrived in London to become our most admired foreign composer. He had acquired the *galante* style in the opera-houses of Italy rather than at Mannheim. But he published no music in London until 1763, when his op. 1 keyboard concertos appeared.[1] Mannheim influence can be identified a year earlier in the overture to *Love in a Village* by Bach's friend Abel, and in the music of a Scotsman inaccurately known as the Earl of Kelly.

'The Scots are all musicians', wrote Jery Melfont in Smollett's *Humphry Clinker*;[2] 'every man you meet plays the flute, the violin, or violoncello; and there is one nobleman whose compositions are universally admired.' This was Thomas Alexander Erskine (1732–81). His father had been imprisoned for his activities in the '45', and it may have been for political reasons that the son was sent to Mannheim when he was about eighteen to further his abilities on the violin. He played in the orchestra there, studied with Stamitz, and composed symphonies and chamber works. Boswell, a close friend of his brother, heard one of these symphonies in Kassel in 1764. Long before then, in 1756, Thomas Erskine's father had died, and Thomas returned to Fife to become the Sixth Earl of Kellie. Six of his symphonies, some of them modelled directly on those of Stamitz, were published in London in 1762, and they were the first such symphonies to appear in this country. A seventh was written as overture for *The Maid of the Mill* (1765), and this became known everywhere. Burney praised 'Kelly's' knowledge of composing and his skill on the violin, but he ruined his chances of a lasting fame by indulging in all the fashionable vices. 'A bon vivant with a very rich face' wrote Parke, and Foote advised him to put his nose in his greenhouse to ripen his cucumbers. He seemed an old man when he died, though he was only 49.[3]

Carl Friedrich Abel (1725–87) may have been brought up under J. S. Bach at the Thomasschule, Leipzig; his father certainly played under Bach at Cöthen. He made a name for himself as a viola da gamba player at a time when everyone else had abandoned the instrument. In his twenties he worked in Dresden where the Italian style was dominant, and like J. C. Bach he came to London and was employed by Queen Charlotte. For some years Bach and Abel shared a house in Soho Square, and they numbered Gainsborough among their friends. It is not known why Abel was asked to write the overture to *Love in a Village*, but it was probably due to the success of the six symphonies he had just published. These

[1] A Bach symphony was issued as No. 1 in the Periodical Overture series (1763).
[2] Letter of 'Aug. 8'; *Humphry Clinker* was published in 1771.
[3] Kellie Castle near Pittenweem, Fife, was opened to the public, beautifully restored, in 1971, but the composer-earl had had to sell it before he died, and there is no trace of him there now.

may be slightly earlier than Kelly's set, but they show less Mannheim influence.

Abel's overture to *Love in a Village* was first performed on 8 December 1762, and it can be taken as the prototype English opera overture in the fully *galante* style. It was usual to begin with a loud tune in octaves that arrested the attention without offering much to the mind; there is a late example in Mozart's 'Jupiter' Symphony. Abel began:

In most *galante* symphonies an important feature was the contrast between two themes within a single movement. Usually the first had masculine strength, the second feminine lyricism. Abel's second subject is as follows:

A pedal bass in repeated quavers is very common in *galante* music, and is found at the beginning of such symphonies as do not begin with an octave theme. It is an invariable feature of the Mannheim Crescendo, which starts low down and builds up through four bars to a repetition an octave higher:

Abel's example shows two more *galante* fingerprints: the snap rhythms, and the trick of building a climax out of quickly repeated semiquavers high on the violins with a tune of sorts below. As in most early symphonies, scarcely anything is developed in the 'development section'.

Abel's slow movement aims at charm; the gloomy intense slow movement was still several decades in the future. A pedal point of repeated quavers is again a feature of the second subject. For his third movement Abel followed English rather than *galante* convention and wrote a gavotte. Two years earlier the 'Scotch Gavotte' that ended Arne's overture to *Thomas and Sally* had been made into the 'hit' song of the year. Arne tried another gavotte finale in his *Artaxerxes* overture of 1762; luckily for him its banality passed unnoticed in the furore this opera created.[1]

The conventional ending for a Mannheim Symphony was a quick binary movement in three-eight. Our earliest operatic example occurs in the overture to *Midas* (1764), which was borrowed from a set of recently-published 'Symphonies or Overtures' by John Collet.[2] Better three-eight finales can be found in *The Royal Shepherd* and *The Capricious Lovers* by Rush, in Chalon's *Daphne and Amintor*, and in Dibdin's *The Padlock*; all date from before 1768.

All the overtures mentioned above, except for *The Capricious Lovers*, have typical Mannheim Crescendos in their first movement, as do the overtures to *Pharnaces* by Bates and *The Maid of the Mill* by Kellie. After 1770 examples are rare. A very late one can be found in Mozart's *Figaro* overture, starting at bar 236. The earliest English example occurs in the overture to Arne's oratorio *Judith* (1761).

In *galante* first movements the treatment of the second subject was far from standardized either in Mannheim or in London. Sometimes it fails to reappear in the recapitulation, as in *The Royal Shepherd*; sometimes it precedes the first subject as in *Pharnaces* (and occasional works by Mozart). There is a tendency for the second subject to be in canon, as in the first movements of the *Midas* and *Maid of the Mill* overtures; a late example of this can be found in Beethoven's Fourth Symphony. In no country did the development become the tight-packed, logical but exciting discussion we associate with classical masterpieces until Haydn wrote such symphonies as 'La Chasse', but from the first composers were prepared to branch off into remote keys in this section. A striking example can be found in Shalon's *Daphne and Amintor* (1765), which, like most of these overtures, survives only in vocal score. At the start of the extract below a phrase from the end of the exposition is being developed; at the asterisk the recapitulation begins; in between there is, I would guess, the first enharmonic modulation playhouse audiences had ever heard:[3]

---

[1] There is an even worse 'Scotch Gavotte' in Hook's early pantomime overture, *The Sacrifice of Iphigenia*.

[2] BUC's 'c.1760' is too early; Bremner, Collet's publisher, did not move from Edinburgh to London till 1762. Not much is known of Collet except that for years he had been a violinist at Vauxhall Gardens and the Foundling Hospital. Parke says he was eccentric and lame. Burney (who calls him Richard Collet) thought him an 'inelegant player', though 'his tone was full, clear, and smooth, and his hand strong'.

[3] In his *George Frideric Handel* (p. 598) P. H. Lang quotes a much earlier example from Handel's opera *Imeneo* (1741).

By the 1780s the elder Linley was beginning to develop the first movement themes of his overtures in what we think of as the classical way (see p. 450).

In the last quarter of the century English opera composers showed a marked liking for basing one movement of the overture, nearly always the last, on a tune that was later to be sung, nearly always in the finale. The trick was of French origin, for the earliest playhouse example of it occurs in *The Deserter* (1773), a rewriting by Dibdin of an opera by Monsigny[1]. Dibdin himself tried the idea out in his *Poor Vulcan* and *Liberty Hall*; Shield and Arnold did so frequently. Besides being labour-saving, the trick helped to 'plug' the tunes in a way audiences found agreeable, and it seems to have been commoner in England than anywhere else in Europe.

In *Peeping Tom* (1784) Arnold went further. Of the two movements of the overture, the second is a 'Medley of Tunes used in the Opera'. Arnold wrote

[1] Monsigny and his contemporaries may have been influenced by Rameau's *Castor et Pollux* (1737), whose overture includes themes that are later sung. An earlier example, though non-operatic, can be found in Handel's *Deborah* (1733); the second and fourth movements of the overture are based on choruses in the body of the oratorio.

similar overtures later, and so did Shield, but the device does not seem to have become common in our theatres much before the time of Gilbert and Sullivan.

The classical one-movement overture had superseded the symphony kind on the continent by 1780, but it never got much of a foothold in the eighteenth-century playhouse. There is an isolated and fortuitous example by Arnold in *The Spanish Barber* (1777), and Storace tried to accustom his public to the continental fashion in *The Doctor and the Apothecary* (1788) and *No Song No Supper*. He then lost heart for some reason, and turned to multi-movement overtures.

Count Algarotti complained that all overtures seemed to consist of 'two allegros with one grave, and to be as noisy as possible', and so far as I am aware he was the first to suggest (in 1755) that every overture should be specially devised to prepare the audience for what followed it. The same music, he said, could not be right for an opera about the death of Dido and one about the nuptials of Demetrius and Cleonice. An overture 'should announce the business of the drama, and consequently prepare the audience to receive those affecting impressions, that are to result from the whole performance'. This view was echoed by Gluck in his well-known dedication of *Alceste* (1767):

> I have felt that the overture ought to apprise the spectators of the nature of the action that is to be represented, and to form, so to speak, its argument.

Gluck's own overtures do not always seem very obvious examples of this theory in action, but the one in *Iphigenie en Tauride* (1779) is well worth noting. It is short, and in two parts labelled 'The Calm' and 'The Storm', and it was played with the curtain up so that the audience could see the priestesses of Diana reacting to the tempestuous elements. We shall find Storace writing a somewhat similar but more 'classical' storm overture to *Gli equivoci* (1786), an overture he thought well enough of to put into *The Haunted Tower*. There is another goodish storm overture in *The Shipwreck* (1796) by Arnold, and we shall find other traces of a desire to make overtures appropriate. But for the full flowering of the descriptive overture as envisaged by Count Algarotti we must wait for those Beethoven wrote early in the next century for two plays, *Coriolan* and *Egmont*. Like most of those on the continent, English composers of the eighteenth century were no more than fumbling towards dramatic truth. Even Rossini as late as 1818 could write a trivial comic opera overture for his wholly serious *Mose in Egitto*.

13 PUBLISHERS AND SCORES

The sudden increase in the number of English operas was accompanied by new methods of publishing them. As we have seen, before 1762 operas sometimes appeared in full score without their recitatives and choruses, and this made it easy for their overtures and arias to be performed at provincial concerts. The more popular songs were published singly on two staves for the music-lover at home, and early in the century these sheet songs were sometimes bound together as a vocal score selection with no pretensions to completeness. The last of these casual compilations was Arne's *The Opera of Operas* 1733; Carey's *Nancy* (1740), though published complete, also consisted of an assembly of sheet songs. With two exceptions, the operatic vocal score was unknown in Britain until 1763. The exceptions were William Smith's vocal scores of Arne's *Comus* (1745)[1] and Lampe's *The Dragon of Wantley* (1752). They omitted the overture and choruses, but they allowed the amateur at home to play the accompaniments of all the songs for any relative or friend who sang, and it was thus possible for the first time to get to know an English opera as a whole at the keyboard.

After 1762 full scores were no longer published. Oblong vocal scores became standard, and by the late sixties they usually appeared complete, choruses and all. This important change of policy can be made clearer with some statistics embracing the twenty years before and after 1763:

	Full Scores	Vocal Scores
1743–62	11	2
1763–82	2	80 at least

The 80 includes a dozen or so pantomimes, but not the short Sadler's Wells Dialogues and not musical interludes such as Barthelemon's short burletto about Orpheus. The published full scores after 1763 are Dibdin's *The Recruiting Sergeant* and Jackson's *The Lord of the Manor*. There would be no more to add if the period were extended to 1800. The possibilities of modern performance are reduced even further by the fact that hardly any MS full scores survive after 1763, though they are fairly numerous earlier in the century.

Publishers turned away from the full score for economic reasons. The *galante* style is much more loquacious than the baroque, more prodigal of notes. Not only are there far more quick bustling pieces of considerable length, but the increasing use of wind instruments demands more staves. Anyone who counts the pages in a full score of *The Marriage of Figaro* and of any Handel opera will appreciate the point. The former would take at least four times as long to engrave and thus be four times as expensive to publish, even though the two works would play for about the same length of time.

The new vocal scores were not at first engraved complete for it was not yet certain that there would be a demand for them. Between 1763 and 1765 Walsh offered *Love in a Village*, *Midas*, and *The Summer's Tale* each in three volumes, one for each act, and Michael Arne's *Cymon* was published in the same way.[2] All except *The Summer's Tale* sold so well that one-volume editions were soon on the market, their double pagination revealing the publisher's second thoughts. In 1764 Peter Welcker initiated what was to become normal procedure by issuing one-volume scores from the first, starting with *The Royal Shepherd* by Rush, but he left out the choruses.

---

[1] About 1752 John Cox brought out an edition using the same plates.
[2] The full score of *Artaxerxes* was originally issued act by act.

The engraving of these scores was carried out much more quickly than would be the case today, but it was never completed until a month or two after the first night,[1] and it sometimes happened that an opera failed before the score was ready. In such cases engraving was stopped, and what was finished was offered as though it were the whole. Thus *Love in a City* folded after six performances, *Amintas* after only two. In each case the published vocal score contains only the first act songs, though there is nothing on the title-page to indicate this.

The risks of publishing were not necessarily borne by the publisher. Unless he was already established, the composer paid for the engraving, printing, binding and paper,[2] and on top of that he had to pay the publisher 5s. in the £1 for selling the end product. That is why composers often sold their scores in their own homes during the initial 'rush'. They saved the publisher's rake-off when the music was most in demand, after which they were content that sales should be in the hands of the musicshops, with their more effective means of promotion. *Thomas and Sally* and *Cymon* were among many scores sold in this way; early editions of the latter are described on the title page as 'sold by the Author at Mr. O'Keeffe's, Coach Maker, at the Gold Unicorn near Hanover Street, Long Acre, and at the Music Shops', but later editions were sold exclusively by John Johnston at his shop in the Strand. Dibdin found the publisher's share an especial irritation. Yet of *The Recruiting Sergeant* he wrote 'I published the music on my own account, and found it unsuccessful'. His *Musical Tour* is full of details about the profits he made from his various operas.

When the full score of *Comus* was published in 1738, music copyists must soon have been at work in Bath, York, Edinburgh, and elsewhere, producing sets of orchestral parts so that local singers could perform the music in whole or in part. But what happened when the even more successful *Love in a Village* was published in vocal score alone? This and many later operas were performed up and down the country on countless occasions, and there must have been many sets of manuscripts parts to make such performances possible. If they were made on the spot from the two-stave vocal score, every item must have been reduced to continuo-song proportions, and it is all too likely that this sometimes happened. There can hardly have been much of an orchestra in 1766 at Castle Cary, Somerset, when Parson Woodforde saw *Love in a Village*. In the 1770s Thomas Holcroft, later well known as a playwright, was acting in Stanton's company at such places as Kendal and Cockermouth, and because he could play the violin a little he sometimes found that 'he was to be the *music*, that is, literally the sole accompaniment to all the songs, etc., on his fiddle in the orchestra'. No doubt he had a vocal score in front of him and played the top line throughout, presumably with the support of a harpsichord. But the larger provincial centres had the same

[1] Examples: *Daphne and Amintor* (8.10.65), an afterpiece, was advertised for sale on November 8; *The Woodman* (26.2.91), a mainpiece, was advertised for sale on May 4.

[2] See indignant letter signed 'Appolo', Humphries and Smith, p. 33.

orchestral resources as London, and if they wanted authentic parts for their operas they must have hired manuscript sets from the London publisher, yet I have found no evidence that this ever happened.

Though vocal scores were of little help in the preparation of orchestral parts, they were welcomed by the amateur musician. Dibdin tells that the vocal score of *The Padlock* was so sought after that in twenty years three sets of plates were worn out. He reckoned that each set of plates could be used for about 3,500 impressions, so at least 10,000 copies must have been sold, as against 28,000 of the libretto.[1]

Composers surely regretted that the beauties of their orchestration were no longer visible, and this was the more irksome in that orchestration was becoming increasingly colourful. Rather faltering steps were sometimes taken to offset the absence of full scores. Occasional songs were published on three staves or even more in order to show details of instrumentation, and this was done at the composer's request, for the publisher had nothing to gain by it. Today all vocal scores give arias on three staves, the top one being the vocal line and the other two the piano arrangement, but this was never the case before 1788. With two staves as the norm, the top one could be used for orchestral music only when the singer was silent. When a third stave was added it usually gave the second violin part, and it was put at the top and ignored by the amateur keyboard player. Thus the voice part was in the middle, and because it was assumed that the first violin part would be doubling the voice, the first violin part was printed *below* the second whenever the voice was silent.

Whether there were two staves or three, orchestral details could sometimes be added in small notes; their size allowed the keyboard player to omit them with a clear conscience. The more there were of these cues, the better use could be made of the score by provincial copyists. The vocal scores of Arne's later operas and of Shield's first, *The Flitch of Bacon* (1778), are especially helpful. The title-page of the last-named carried a foot-note: 'Mr. Napier (the publisher) to render this Work more useful to the Public in general has Printed the Second Violin with the Harpsichord Part.' And not only the Second Violin. Here is an extract from the overture as Napier printed it:

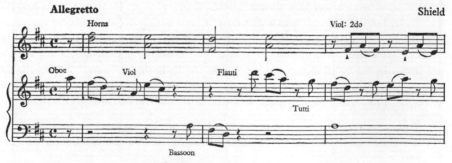

[1] *Professional Life*, i, p. 71.

Any intelligent musician could produce a passable approximation to the original full score from the above. More than any other composer of his time Shield enlivened his vocal scores with extra staves, verbal indications of scoring, and orchestral counter-themes in small notes.

Composers who did not take such steps often gave an impression of inanity. The 1768 vocal score of *Lionel and Clarissa* shows one of Dibdin's songs on two staves, and the 'vocal' begins:

The music appears to have no quality whatever. Two years later Dibdin drastically rewrote this opera, and it so happened that the engraver, patching together a new vocal score, found himself with a whole page to spare for the first seventeen bars of this song, bars which had previously been fitted on to half a page. Accordingly he added the violin part on a third stave:[1]

The song leaps to life. It becomes apparent that Lionel is in a rage, and that the orchestra is expressing this rage with unexpected fire. So often in these operas

---

[1] BUC entries for this opera are wrong. The third 'as perform'd at Covent Garden' is the earliest, 1768. Any edition given at Drury Lane or 'The Theatres Royal' or with the alternative title *The School for Fathers* in large letters must date from 1770 or later.

the music looks inept because only the skeleton got printed and none of the flesh.

The modern-style vocal score on three staves with the voice at the top came in gradually. The two biggest songs in Shield's *The Highland Reel* (1788) are so printed, and examples can be found in most of his subsequent operas. The first score I have found that is entirely printed in the modern way is Kelly's *Blue Beard* (1798). Unfortunately these improvements coincide with two retrogressive steps: in the 1790s publishers no longer bothered to name the composer of a borrowed item or the instrument that played a solo. The title-page may say that the music has been 'selected and composed', but there is no way of telling which are the selected items, let alone who wrote them. Almost all eighteenth-century scores, whether full or vocal, tell you who sang each song at the first performance; they are much less conscientious about telling you the name of the character being represented.

On the Longman and Broderip vocal score of Storace's *The Haunted Tower* (1789) there is a fine engraving of the Act III set, and in the years that followed publishers quite often decorated their title pages in this interesting way. Perhaps the most magnificent of all such engravings is the set depicted on the title page of *Blue Beard*, with the two ladies waving from the castle walls at distantly approaching horse-riders. In the last years of the century the upright vocal score started to come in, and because stage-sets were oblong they no longer fitted the title-page as effectively.

Before 1762 pantomime music, if published at all, appeared in a haphazard way, with a few songs in sheet form and a selection of Comic Tunes on their own. As we have seen, the vocal and the instrumental items were the work of two different composers, and this is the case with so late a pantomime as *The Rites of Hecate* (1763), which has sophisticated vocal *scenas* by Battishill and naïve Comic Tunes by John Potter. Thereafter it became usual for one man to write all the music, and it was then practicable for it to be published complete in a single volume resembling a vocal score. The first pantomime to be so published was Arnold's *Harlequin Dr. Faustus* (1766), and the number of such scores averaged more than two a year in the last quarter of the century.

Though very few operas appeared in full score in this later period, far more opera overtures appeared in parts. We saw earlier that at the beginning of the century a large number of theatre overtures had been published in parts together with dance movements and 'Act Tunes', but the spate had dried up by 1708, and for many years only Handel's overtures were thought to be marketable. In the 1740s two pantomime overtures appeared on their own in parts, Lampe's for *Columbine Courtezan* and Howard's for *The Amorous Goddess*. In the fifties Arne and Boyce published sets of symphony-overtures for concert use, and each set included two opera overtures, Arne's *Comus* and *The Judgment of Paris*, and Boyce's *The Chaplet* and *The Shepherds' Lottery*. But the great spate of such publications occurred between 1764 and 1778 during the rage for symphony-overtures in the *galante* idiom, and it dried up when Haydn's symphonies began to be popular. From 1779 to the end of the century only one English opera overture survives in parts, *Ramah Droog*, and that was by Mazzinghi, a composer of rather dubious anglicism. No overture by Arnold, Linley, Shield, or Storace was thought worthy of publication, though these composers dominated the playhouses in the last quarter of the century and often showed more aptitude for orchestral writing than those who got into print so easily between 1764 and 1778. In the last sixty years of the century at least forty theatre overtures appeared in parts,[1] and at least thirty more can be recovered from published full scores and MS sources.

As might be expected, London publishers increased greatly in numbers and activity in the 1760s. The younger Walsh died in 1766 and his successors, Randall and Abell, made little attempt to increase their catalogue. More adventurous were John Johnson and Robert Bremner. The latter was a Scotsman from Edinburgh, and he took over Johnson's catalogue in 1777, and Welcker's two years later. He died in 1789 a rich man, with property in South London and Brighton as well as his shop in the Strand opposite Somerset House. Confusingly there was also an active publisher called John Johnston, who was later bought up by Longman and Broderip. These take-overs sometimes resulted in vocal scores of identical appearance apparently being published by two different houses.

The vocal score of a full-length opera usually sold for 10s. 6d. Afterpieces cost about 6s. It was usual, however, for all music to be sold at less than the marked price. In 1783 James Harrison tried to stimulate the market with bargain prices. He started his *New Musical Magazine*, a publishing landmark which appeared at weekly or fortnightly intervals and included as a supplement a sixteen-page vocal score, oblong in shape, for a mere 1s. 6d. If you bought five consecutive instalments you had as a bonus a complete vocal score of *Messiah*. Harrison even resurrected theatre music of a bygone age, much of it no longer in the repertoire, offering the first-ever vocal scores of 'Purcell's' *The Tempest* (three instalments), Howard's *The Amorous Goddess*, Boyce's *The Chaplet*, and Arne's *Eliza*.

This firm's successor made an even more ambitious attempt to cut prices at the end of the century. From 1797 to 1802 Harrison, Cluse & Co.[2] issued their *Pianoforte Magazine*, each number of which cost 2s. 6d. and included as supplement a complete vocal score or other music. The magazine was to appear weekly, and those who bought every issue were to be presented with a free piano as a final instalment. However, it would seem that only about two-thirds of the projected 250 numbers ever appeared. The first supplement was

---

[1] See Appendix C.

[2] They were still Harrison & Co. for the first numbers; see Humphreys and Smith p. 31 for further details, but they give the publisher's intention rather than what happened. The subject needs further investigation.

Arnold's *The Agreeable Surprise*; Arnold had been associated with Harrison for years, and he probably advised on the series. All the more popular operas from *Artaxerxes* to those of the late 1780s were reissued; also *Comus*, some Handel oratorios, and various kinds of instrumental music. There were no recent operas because of the fourteen-year copyright law that now had some teeth in it.[1] Vocal scores in this series make no mention of their association with *The Pianoforte Magazine* but their upright shape and rather small size make them easy to identify. They appear fairly often in second-hand lists and are usually cheaper than other editions.

Towards the end of the century a new generation of publishers came to the fore. Thomas Preston had bought up Bremner's stock and plates in 1789, and Longman & Broderip set new standards of engraving. At the peak of its success the last-named firm had shops in Brighton and Margate as well as in the City and London's West End, and a van with Longman & Broderip in large letters on each side was driven continuously round the streets 'to persuade the public that they were driving what is called a roaring trade'; in point of fact it was usually empty.[2] John Longman treated his composers with unprecedented generosity. In the 1790s he paid Shield a thousand guineas for the music of *The Woodman*, and Storace five hundred guineas for most of his operas. Such fees were much higher than those Arne and Dibdin had received, and they probably contributed to the firm's bancruptcy in 1798. Longman later went into partnership with Clementi.

The Walshes had often advertised a handful of works at the foot of the title-page, but from the 1770s it became more usual to include in a vocal score a catalogue of from one to four closely-printed pages of titles and prices; the composer's name was omitted as being of little importance. Very occasionally these lists reveal an opera we would not otherwise know had been published.

14 LIBRETTOS AND PIRACY

In the third quarter of the century a great many librettos were published anonymously. The motive was in part the fashionable one of false modesty, and in part a desire to escape censure if the opera should fail.

In the fourth quarter many librettos were not published at all. In England this practice was begun by Sheridan, who withheld *The Duenna* and *The School for Scandal* for twenty years to stop rival theatres putting them on. A number of the librettos O'Keeffe wrote for Shield to set were not printed in London at the

---

[1] The original law of 1709 gave authors and their publishers (then called book-sellers) the sole right to print new books for fourteen years; if the author were still alive at the end of this period, the right was extended for another fourteen years. The law was ill-worded and frequently broken; legal disputes proliferated until a House of Lords decision of 1774 brought some order to copyright.

[2] Busby i, pp. 82 and 127.

time of their greatest success. However, they were published piratically in Dublin; also more legally in his Collected Works of 1798.

In Paris Beaumarchais sometimes withheld his librettos as Sheridan did in London. Because *Le Barbier de Seville* had been performed all over Europe with no benefit to himself, he decided not to publish *Le Marriage de Figaro*. A pirated *Spanish Barber*, turned into an opera by Arnold in 1779, had been very successful in London, and when Holcroft got wind of the fact that its successor was to be withheld he was so enterprising as to go over to Paris in September 1784 and persuade a French friend to come to every performance for a week or ten days. In the daytime they tidied up what they had scribbled the night before in the theatre. This was an unusually difficult act of piracy because of the language problem, but the result is surprisingly close to what Beaumarchais wrote. Besides the one given in Holcroft's *Memoirs* there are other accounts of the pirating of a libretto. Tate Wilkinson describes how he pirated *The Duenna* for performances at his theatre in York; he was much helped by the published vocal score. When Ryder pirated the same opera for Dublin, Sheridan sued him but lost his case. Thomas Snagg tells how five men commissioned to pirate *The School for Scandal* for Dublin managed it by each concentrating on one character.[1] The partially-lit auditoriums must have made the task easier than it would be today. Whenever the playhouses put on a promising opera in the 1780s, there must always have been one or more Irishmen in the house scribbling away night after night.

After the 1737 Licensing Act, everything staged at the playhouses had to be approved by the censor. A few days before the first night a carefully-written copy of the words was submitted, and these MS copies were filed and for the most part preserved. They are now in the Huntington Library in California, and they are known as the Larpent Collection. It thus happens that even if a libretto appears never to have been published at all, a photostat of it in MS form is usually obtainable. So far as I have checked, alterations in the final rehearsals are not shown in the Larpent copy.

[1] *Recollections of Occurrences* (London 1951), p. 99.

8

Arne's 'Artaxerxes' and 'Love in a Village'
1760–1770

I 'ARTAXERXES'

WHEN John Beard married Charlotte Rich in 1759, there must have been an understanding that he would inherit Covent Garden from his father-in-law. For years John Rich had felt no urge to experiment, and the theatre's repertoire had been moribund. Knowing Beard's interest in opera, he may well have had misgivings, but in fact under Beard Covent Garden flourished as it had not done for years. Success flowered in full only after Rich's death in 1761, but there were good omens in the previous two seasons when Beard was taking over.

The first omen was the production of *The Beggar's Opera* with Miss Brent as Polly and Beard as Macheath. The occasion established Miss Brent as the leading English soprano for a decade, and Londoners flocked to see a ballad opera they had seen countless times before just for the sake of the new Polly. There were thirty-seven performances in the first thirty-eight nights; such popularity in a revival had no precedent, and there were many more performances later. In addition Miss Brent was brought forward as Venus in Arne's *The Judgment of Paris*, and as Zayda in a new masque by Arne called *The Sultan* (CG 29.11.59). This was the first of our 'Eastern' operas, preceding by a year Smith's *The Enchanter* in which the heroine is similarly named. It is especially regrettable that neither music nor libretto survives.

It took Arne some months to realize that, with a sympathetic manager and a superlative singer on the premises, Covent Garden would repay the most careful work of which he was capable. His first opera under the new regime was small in scale, but it proved more successful than anything he had written for over twenty years. *Thomas and Sally* (CG 28.11.60), delayed a few weeks by the death of George II, received more performances in the Garrick era than any other afterpiece, musical or otherwise, and it continued to be repeated at all the patent theatres until the end of the century. Its simplicity must have been intentional. The songs are short, the plot slight. One sentence tells all: Sally, pursued by the wicked squire, is saved at the last moment by the return of her sailor lover. Londoners were just as willing to be fascinated by guileless country innocence as they were when *Flora* was first staged, and no doubt they were just as smugly aware of their own sophisticated and licentious ways. Shield's *Rosina* and Storace's *No Song No Supper* have a similar and almost self-conscious naïveté, quite at odds with the spirit of most other operas by these composers.

But in one respect *Thomas and Sally* was unusual: it was an all-sung opera on a recognizably modern theme. To some extent Carey's *Nancy* was a precedent, and still popular. But *Nancy* consisted of little more than a short sequence of songs, whereas *Thomas and Sally* had recitatives between the airs. Arne himself, it will be remembered, had written an earlier all-sung opera on a modern theme, *Don Saverio*, and it had failed miserably. *Thomas and Sally* succeeded.

The overture began with a tiny and undistinguished Allegro, and concluded with the most popular item in the opera, the 'Scotch Gavotte':

This was soon having words written for it, and as 'To ease his Heart' it became the hit song of the season. People liked the Gavotte not only for the charming tune, but also for its unusual placing in the tenor register; it comes three times on cellos and bassoons, with only double basses and harpsichord for accompaniment. Later the music was borrowed for two pastiche operas, *Tom Jones* and *Summer Amusement*.

When the curtain rose after the overture, the audience was surprised by a bare stage representing a 'Country Seat' and the unfamiliar sound of horns and clarinets coming from the wings. 'Then the Horns & Clarinets come on Sounding the Crest of the Symphony (i.e. Introduction), several Huntsmen follow & last of all the Squire.'

Later in this introduction the clarinets double the horns. They had never before been heard in a London opera, and as might be expected they were played by oboists. Karl Barbandt was established in London by 1755, Karl Weichsel by 1757; both were German oboists who also played the clarinet. When Barbandt's oratorio based on Book I of *Paradise Regained* was given at the Little Theatre in March 1756, one of the intervals was filled with 'A Great Concerto with Clarinets, French Horns and Kettle Drums, composed by Mr. Barbant'. By the 1760–1 season Covent Garden had an oboist described in the accounts as Mr. Wrexell, and this no doubt was Karl Weichsel. He received the usual rate of 5s. a night, but for each performance of *Thomas and Sally* he was paid a special fee of 10s. 6d. for doubling on the clarinet.[1] The horns and oboes had played in the first movement of the overture; during the 'Scotch Gavotte' the four players left the orchestra pit and made their way on to the stage. After the opening song they had plenty of time to get back again.

Weichsel deserves a further word. In the early sixties he was employed as an oboist at the King's Theatre, though he returned to Covent Garden on those nights when there was no Italian opera, for the clarinet continued to be in demand there. By 1763 he was playing the clarinet at the King's Theatre as well in J. C. Bach's *Orione*. In 1765 he seems to have married a Miss Weirman, who had had one season at Covent Garden singing mainly in pantomime. In the autumn she appeared for two months as Mrs. Weichsel and then left the company, perhaps because she was pregnant. A pupil of J. C. Bach's, she was later popular at Vauxhall Gardens, where she sang Bach's songs. The Weichsels were the parents of Mrs. Billington.

The libretto of *Thomas and Sally* was printed in advance to be ready for the first night, and it took no account of the considerable alterations made in rehearsal. The stage music at the rise of the curtain was an afterthought; the Squire's song originally came later. Thomas's song at the start of Act II was given new words. Some copies of the first edition of the libretto carried a Postscript detailing these and other changes, but the many editions brought out later in the century ignore this postscript and thus carry a version that was presumably never performed. The Postscript reveals that verses were cut in most or all of the strophic songs.

<hr />

[1] *LS* Part IV ii, pp. 815 and 827.

The first edition of the music appeared in full score. To fill up some blank pages at the end the engraver padded out with the short dances Arne had written for the interval between the acts, and an isolated song for the comedy *The Way to keep him*. None of this music had anything to do with *Thomas and Sally*, yet it was conscientiously included in all the vocal score editions that appeared later. We should be grateful that a full score exists; none of Arne's other afterpieces is capable of performance today in its original orchestral dress. The little songs have such charm that the opera well deserves the occasional revivals that it still receives, while the duets[1] that end each act have an endearing humanity and warmth.

The anonymously-published libretto was the first of many by Isaac Bickerstaffe, an Irishman born about 1735. At the age of eleven he had been page to Lord Chesterfield, the then Lord Lieutenant of Ireland, and later he became an officer in the Marines. In 1772 Bickerstaffe was detected in a sexual crime described by Baker as 'unmentionable', and he fled to St. Malo. The result of this wretched affair was that those who would have mentioned him in their reminiscences and kept his letters and published his Collected Works went out of their way to do no such thing. References to Bickerstaffe are extraordinarily hard to come by. Yet he was the most successful opera librettist of the century, with a style of humour that had considerable influence on Sheridan. In 1769 when Boswell first entertained Dr. Johnson to dinner in his lodgings, he assembled his most interesting friends as fellow guests: 'Sir Joshua Reynolds, Mr. Garrick, Dr. Goldsmith, Mr. Murphy, Mr. Bickerstaffe, and Mr. Thomas Davies'. But Boswell made no reference to Bickerstaffe's disgrace three years later.

In the winter of 1760–1 Arne wrote his fine but neglected oratorio *Judith* for performance at Drury Lane in Lent, and the following autumn he composed his masterpiece, *Artaxerxes* (CG 2.2.62). He has sometimes been criticized for translating and setting a libretto Metastasio had written as long ago as 1730 on the grounds that such operas were outmoded, but this is to do him an injustice. Metastasio was still writing, and still considered a major European poet. John Hoole, son of the maker of watches and pantomime machinery mentioned earlier, published six translations of his librettos in 1767 (including *Artaserse* and *L'Olimpiade*), and another dozen as late as 1800. Burney, whose admiration was boundless, met Metastasio in Vienna in 1772, and published a book about him in 1796. By then his reputation had waned, but it was bright enough in 1762.

Like most Metastasio librettos, this one was set by a number of different composers; for instance by J. C. Bach for Turin in 1761. London opera-goers were acquainted with a version mainly by Hasse, given at the King's Theatre in 1754 and revived there in 1766. In any language the plot is confusing because the

---

[1] The last duet in the score, for the squire and Dorcas, seems always to have been cut.

names of the chief male characters all begin with the same two letters. A family tree will help

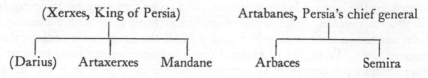

(Xerxes, King of Persia)　　　　　Artabanes, Persia's chief general

(Darius)　Artaxerxes　Mandane　　Arbaces　　Semira

We never see Xerxes or Darius. The other children of Xerxes and those of Artabanes are in love. Arbaces is the hero, his father Artabanes the villain, prepared to go to any lengths to get the crown. The opera opens with Arbaces telling Mandane that Xerxes has banished him for aspiring to her hand. His father, partly in fury at this injustice, unobtrusively murders Xerxes 'off'. When Darius is suspected of the murder, Artabanes, assuming self-righteousness, murders him too, openly. Because Arbaces is caught quietly leaving the city, he is suspected of killing Xerxes, and in the 'Trial Scene' the new king, Artaxerxes, declares that his friend must be tried by his own father. Artabanes condemns Arbaces to death. Because he doubts the justice of this, Artaxerxes visits Arbaces in prison and shows him how to escape. After escaping, Arbaces meets a band of rebels and saves the state by killing their leader. This is reported by Semira. Artaxerxes says he can no longer believe in Arbaces's guilt, and it becomes apparent that Artabanes is trying to poison him. All comes out. In the usual act of clemency, Artabanes is forgiven his many crimes; unwisely, one might think.

Beard and Miss Brent sang Artabanes and Mandane; Artaxerxes and Arbaces were given to the castrati Peretti and Tenducci. When castrati became unavailable, Arbaces was always played as a breeches part by a soprano. Tenducci was famous, Peretti much less so; this was his first appearance on the English stage. Clearly he was a lyrical singer rather than a coloratura. Later he taught Michael Kelly in Dublin.

The success of *Artaxerxes* was steady rather than spectacular. For four seasons it averaged ten performances, and then for three seasons it was dropped. Revivals at both playhouses in 1767–8 were followed by performances at one or other every season until the end of the century. As late as 1827 it was being given at both Covent Garden and Drury Lane; the last performance at Covent Garden was in 1839. Since then the only performances seem to have been the enjoyable ones at St. Pancras Town Hall, London, in March 1962, with Heather Harper as Arbaces.

Burney thought that Arne

> crouded the airs, particularly in the part of Mandane for Miss Brent, with most of the Italian divisions and difficulties which had ever been heard at the opera . . . Though the melody is less original than that of *Comus*, Arne had the merit of first adapting many of the best passages of Italy,

which all Europe admired, to our own language, and of incorporating them with his own property, and with what was still in favour of former English composers.[1]

In *The Rosciad* Charles Churchill made a similar point more bluntly:

> Let T[ommy] A[rne], with usual pomp of stile,
> Whose chief, whose only merit's to compile,
> Who, meanly pilf'ring here and there a bit,
> Deals music out as MURPHY deals out wit.[2]

Churchill also moaned about Arne's use of castrati:

> But never shall a TRULY BRITISH Age
> Bear a vile race of EUNUCHS on the stage.
> The boasted work's called NATIONAL in vain,
> If one ITALIAN voice pollutes the strain.

For a singers' opera such as *Artaxerxes* Arne had no choice but to call on castrati, and he was surely right to attempt an amalgam of the Italian and English styles; the result has much more character than most Italian operas of the time, and was likely to have more appeal for playhouse audiences.

The most 'national' and for that reason the most popular of the songs were 'In Infancy' and 'Water parted from the Sea'. Their tunes were reproduced, with added graces, on numerous barrel-organ rolls. The former is in simple binary form, with a vocal flourish at the end of each half to give it an Italianate veneer. For some reason the voice part is printed an octave too high in all scores, though this was not the case with Peretti's other songs. Like 'In Infancy', 'Water parted' is scored for clarinets and horns as well as strings, and the scoring is unusually thick.

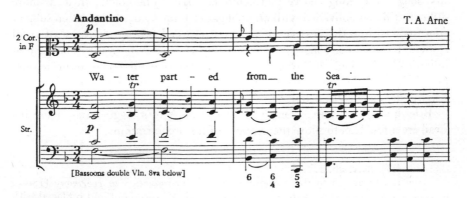

---

[1] Book IV, ch. 12.
[2] Added in 5th ed., 1762, at line 713.

The Introduction starts much as above, but with the clarinets doubling the violins. The form is more or less ternary. This song still falls very sweetly on the ear. To Leigh Hunt 'it winds about the feelings with an earnest and graceful tenderness of regret',[1] and though one can say of it, as of other items in this opera, that it is yet another of Arne's minuet songs, it must be added that he wrote such songs better than anyone else.

These simple airs give no idea of the elaboration of *Artaxerxes* as a whole. Arne took unprecedented trouble over the scoring. After the curtain first rises, the strings (double basses apart) are held back for twenty-four bars while oboes, bassoons, and horns give a charming open-air impression of dawn. Miss Brent's first song is very long and very difficult. Her last, 'The Soldier tir'd', is more difficult still and enlivened with an obbligato trumpet part. It was often sung at concerts well into the next century, being regarded as a standard test of vocal agility.[2] In scale such songs are at least as big as those Arne was to some extent imitating, and though to Burney's ears his models were all too apparent, to ours his music seems less imitative than is that of his Italian contemporaries. The English flavour makes it individual.

Brief quotations cannot convey the scope of Arne's bigger arias. Here instead are a few bars to show the subtlety of his orchestration:

[1] *Autobiography*, ch. 2.

[2] Shield had access to the autograph. In his *Introduction to Harmony* (1800), p. 120, he gives an excerpt with Arne's first thoughts crossed out and replaced with improvements. No doubt the autograph was in the Covent Garden library until the fire of 1808.

This comes from the slow section at the start of a tripartite aria with a raging Presto in the middle and a minuet-style conclusion, 'Behold on Lethe's dismal Strand'. It was sung by Beard as Artabanes. As elsewhere in this opera, Arne showed a technical ability and an emotional depth he seldom bothered to reveal in his other works.

The published full and vocal scores omit all recitatives, as also the one and only chorus which came at the end. The latter is probably lost for ever, but most of the recitatives are recoverable. The Royal College of Music has a MS volume of theatre music that Henry Bishop wrote for Covent Garden in 1814 (RCM 60), and it begins with 'The Recitative of Artaxerxes as compressed into Two Acts & Arranged for a Full Orchestra by Henry R. Bishop'. Oxberry's shortened libretto of 1828 accords with this MS in the main. All the recitatives are accompanied by string band, and it is possible that they are entirely Bishop's invention, but this is unlikely on two counts. First, he is careful in the rest of the volume to distinguish between what he has composed, arranged, and borrowed; and with one exception he does not claim these recitatives as his. Secondly, where recitative has been cut in compressing the opera into two acts, key relationships sometimes cease to make sense. Thus Mandane's 'Adieu, thou lovely Youth' is in A; the three lines of recitative that originally came next are omitted, and what follows in Bishop's MS starts in G. Had Bishop composed this section he would have started it in a more nearly related key. Thus the likelihood is that the vocal line and the bass are Arne's. Bishop's MS is of interest for its emphasis on expression. Volume indications are extraordinarily numerous in the string parts, and there are many changes of tempo which cannot possibly have been in the original. Bishop indicates what follows each section of recitative, and in two cases indicates a transposition; Peretti's 'In Infancy' and 'Fair Semira' were put down a third and a fourth respectively, no doubt so that they could be sung by a tenor. Mandane's accompanied recitative, 'Dear and beloved shade', is marked as by Bishop himself, which is easy to believe on the evidence of its style. He seems also to have composed a quartet in the Trial Scene and a duet in the Prison Scene, for the words are not in the original scores and librettos. The duet must have had a short life, for it does not appear in the 1828 libretto.

When Miss Catley sang Mandane, Arne wrote for her a new setting of 'Fly, soft Ideas', perhaps because the original one was too long and difficult. The new setting has never been published except in Shield's *Rudiments of Thoroughbass* (1815), p. 61, where it is given in short score. In his last Song Collection, *The Syren* of 1777, Arne included a song he wrote specially for his pupil, Mrs. Farrel, who was then singing the part of Artaxerxes. It consists of an Accompanied Recitative and Aria, 'Can salt tears and loud Lamenting', which enabled her to show off her coloratura; the music Arne had written for her predecessor, Peretti, had been mainly lyrical. The new song begins well, but is too short and underdeveloped.

Artaxerxes was the subject of Charles Lamb's essay, 'My First Play'. Being 'not past six years old', he made no comment on the music.

> All feeling was absorbed in vision. Gorgeous vests, gardens, palaces, princesses, passed before me. I knew not players. I was in Persepolis for the time, and the burning idol of their devotion almost converted me into a worshipper . . . It was all enchantment and a dream.

In its first sixty years of life almost every notable person in London must have seen this opera. In 1763 Boswell 'relished the music'. In 1791 Haydn 'was delighted with *Artaxerxes*', and told Mrs. Barthelemon that 'he had no idea we had such an opera in the English language'; he thought especially well of the duet 'For thee I live, my dearest'. By 1814 Jane Austen was 'very tired' of *Artaxerxes*.[1] No one today can be tired of it, though there must be many people who do not know that we have such an opera.

It is sad that Arne never followed up *Artaxerxes* with another 'English Opera'. For the marriage of Princess Augusta and the Prince of Brunswick he wrote an all-sung masque, *The Arcadian Nuptials* (CG 20.1.64), which was inserted as the climax of the old pantomime, *Perseus and Andromeda*. There were twenty-four consecutive performances, and a duet from it appeared in Arne's *Vocal Melody* xiv. Drury Lane celebrated the same occasion with an 'Occassional Interlude' called *Hymen* by Arne's son Michael; not much of that survives either.[2] Next year, on the strength of *Artaxerxes*, Thomas Arne talked the directors of the King's Theatre into accepting an all-Italian opera from his pen, *L'Olimpiade* (KT 27.4.65), and again the words were by Metastasio. There were only two performances. The Italians in London believed passionately in a Closed Shop, and they would have taken care that an opera by a non-

---

[1] The Haydn references are from Cradock iv, pp. 127 and 133, the Jane Austen from a letter of 5 March 1814. See also Boswell's *London Journal* for 9 April 1763.

[2] Three songs and two duets shared a volume with some of Michael Arne's music for *A Fairy Tale*. They are uninteresting.

Italian would have failed whatever its merits. Burney made little attempt to conceal his glee over the failure. Arne had

> written for vulgar singers and hearers too long to be able to comport himself properly at the Opera-house, in the first circle of taste and fashion . . . The common playhouse and ballad passages, which occurred in almost every air in his opera, made the audience wonder how they got there . . . A different language, different singers, and a different audience, and style of Music from his own, carried him out of his usual element, where he mangled the Italian poetry, energies, and accents, nearly as much as a native of Italy just arrived in London, would English, in a similar situation.

Arne's music has disappeared.

This was not a happy time for him. In June he was being pilloried at the Little Theatre as Dr. Catgut in Foote's *The Commissary*. He would not, perhaps, have minded the gentle fun poked at him for deserting music in favour of bad poetry, but he cannot have relished hearing himself described in public as 'that meagre musician, that sick monkey-faced maker of crotchets, that eternal trotter after all the little draggle-tailed girls of town'.[1] For one reason and another he wrote hardly any music during the next four years.

2 IMITATIONS OF 'ARTAXERXES'

It did not at first occur to Garrick that *Artaxerxes* had come to stay. When it did, he tried to find a similar success for Drury Lane. In less than twelve months he staged no fewer than three full-length all-sung 'English Operas', each based on a translated Italian libretto. In no case did the result prove more than mildly popular.

The Royal Shepherd (24.2.64) by George Rush; libretto by Richard Rolt based on Metastasio's *Il re pastore*; ten performances that season and then no more.

Almena (2.11.64) by Michael Arne and Battishill; libretto by Rolt; six performances, and two more the following season 'with additions and alterations'.

Pharnaces (15.2.65) by William Bates; libretto by Thomas Hull based on Lucchini's *Farnace* (1731); six performances that season and then no more.

George Rush has evaded all the reference books, and his dates are unknown. Apart from three operas he wrote four concertos 'for harpsichord or pianoforte', and his first published work was a set of sonatas for beginners on the harpsichord, an instrument which he probably taught. *The Royal Shepherd* was his second

---

[1] *Eighteenth-Century Drama: Afterpieces* (Oxford Paperback ed. R. W. Bevis), p. 258.

publication. A setting by Hasse had been seen in London in 1757, and Metastasio's libretto was later set by Mozart. The plot is less interesting than that of *Artaxerxes*. Alexander the Great, on the rampage round Sidon, deposes the king (whom we never see) and then unthinkingly upsets the love affairs of two couples. Amintas, a shepherd, is revealed as heir to the Sidonian throne as early as Act I, but is appalled by Alexander's attempt to marry him off to the ex-king's daughter, Thamiris; both are in love with other people. When Amintas tells Alexander that he would rather remain a shepherd and marry Eliza, Alexander bows to the inevitable. Metastasio wrote the libretto in 1751 and thought it his best, perhaps because it contains less action and villainy than the others and more moral sentiments.

Joseph Vernon, who for some years had been an actor allowed only the occasional song, found himself pushed into the leading role of this as also of Drury Lane's other 'English Operas'. Thamiris was sung by Polly Young, Eliza by an Italian, Clementina Cremonini, who was in the middle of a three-season spell at the King's Theatre. Hopkins reported that 'she sings very fine—very graceful Deportment,—and is a great support to the Opera,—some Hisses,—Many of the Songs encored,—Upon the whole was well liked'.

Only the overture of *The Royal Shepherd* survives orchestrally, and it continued to be popular as a concert piece until the end of the century. The middle movement is that rarity, an English minuet of quality; the influence of J. C. Bach can be detected. But though the music of this opera is more modern in style than that of *Artaxerxes*, it is much less attractive. Rush was to write better music in *The Capricious Lovers*. His attempts at short binary-form songs with an English flavour lack charm, and the big Italianate numbers are mechanical and dull. The vocal score omits the recitatives and three choruses, one of these being the Finale of the opera, but it includes the Quartet that ends Act II.

Five years later the rival playhouse staged a revised two-act version of Rush's opera under the title of *Amintas* (CG 15.12.69). Tenducci, who had adapted *The Royal Shepherd* for Dublin in July 1765, made this adaptation too, replacing half the arias with Italian ones or with new settings by Arnold or by Rush himself. The new overture by Thomas Carter has a well-developed first movement, but the middle one in the Scotch style is poor. Only the Act I music was published; the opera failed after three performances.

Almena has a Persian plot and begins in a seraglio garden. The Sultan has been deposed and killed by Mohammed, the villain, and this results in two political factions. As so often in opera, people tend to fall in love with those in the opposing faction. Thus Mohammed espouses Aspatia, the ex-Sultan's widow, and his Vizier loves her too. Aspatia's problem is whether or not to rebuff Mohammed, bearing in mind that her own daughter, Almena, is being pursued by Mirza, the hero, nephew to the late Sultan; he in turn is being pursued by Zara, the villain's sister. As by now will be realized, the plot is not among those that can be taken in at a glance. There are similarities to the story of *Artaxerxes*, among them a Prison Scene in which Mirza is rescued by Zara heavily disguised; he gives her few thanks, preferring to stress his love for Almena. All ends in improbable amity.

Two Italians strengthened the singing. The castrato Giustinelli was Mirza and Clementina Cremonini Aspatia; Vernon was the villain and Miss Wright sang the title role. The six performances all took place between November 2nd and 23rd; on the 24th the Italian Opera season opened at the King's Theatre with Signora Cremonini taking one of the leads in a pastiche called *Ezio*. It would seem that Drury Lane dropped *Almena* because they could no longer count on her services. A little later there were performances in Dublin.

It would be interesting to know why the composition of *Almena* was shared by two composers. Neither Michael Arne nor Jonathan Battishill had had much experience in the theatre. They published their contributions in separate vocal scores, and if comparison of these is made with the libretto it will be seen that the music is complete to the middle of Act II but from then on only a few items by Battishill survive. It may well be that all Battishill's music was printed except for the two choruses in the last act.[1] Presumably Arne's publication was less forward, and when the opera seemed likely to have no further performances the publisher issued only as much as had then been engraved.

Arne's music is flowery and full of coloratura passages, no doubt because he wrote all the arias for the hero and the heroine. (Battishill set Mohammed's and Zara's songs, and the two composers shared Aspatia.) Much his most curious contribution was one with a concertante part for the mandolin: 'No fears alarm.' The strings (presumably) play the main theme which is then repeated as follows by the mandolin on its own:

During the vocal parts the mandolin often has strikingly idiomatic writing, such as the following:

We have already noted a mandolin concerto at the Little Theatre in 1768, and it is likely that the same player, Giovanni Battista Gervasia, was employed by

---

[1] Busby (iii, p. 71), says Battishill wrote all the choruses.

Drury Lane for *Almena*. A few years later he published 'Airs for the mando-line, guitar, violin or Ger. flute, Opera III'.

Some of Battishill's songs are given in full score, two of these being marked 'Omitted in the Performance'. It is not surprising that the Vizier jibbed at the last one, an elaborate coloratura aria for bass; Champness, who played the part, would hardly have had the necessary technique. The music, like Michael Arne's, is far from being despicable, but it lacks character.

We know scarcely any more of William Bates than we do of George Rush. Both wrote concertos and sonatas, and in a later chapter we shall find Bates modernizing ballad operas with some success. *Pharnaces* was much his most ambitious work. The libretto was familiar to the cognoscenti because in 1759 the King's Theatre had staged a version mainly by Perez under the title *Farnace*. It was translated by Thomas Hull, a Drury Lane actor, and the result is not worse than most of its kind. Everyone is obsessed by desire for revenge. Phar-naces, King of Sinope, because he has just been defeated by Pompey, wants to be revenged on the entire Roman nation. But the Romans, because they think he has seduced the daughter of Athridates, one of their generals, want to be revenged on Pharnaces. They capture his sister, Selinda, and it goes without saying that Pompey falls in love with her. But Athridates is still raging for satisfaction. His attempts to capture Pharnaces's small daughter are foiled by her mother, Tamiris, who hides her in a tomb. When the Romans start destroy-ing every tomb in sight, the little girl runs out, but Athridates's delight at capturing her is dissipated by his almost immediate discovery that her mother is his own long-lost daughter. At this point everyone forgives everyone else.

Vernon played the title-role, and Mrs. Vincent his wife. Their small daughter, who has some simple and rather charming songs, was taken by Miss Rogers. The castrato Giustinelli was Pompey and Reinhold Athridates. As Giustinelli was not engaged at the King's Theatre this season, the fate of the opera presumably depended on its merits. In fact its merits are considerable. This is the most competently written and the most inventive of the three Drury Lane 'English Operas'. Again some of the arias are very long and very hard, and there is little attempt to tickle the ears of the gallery with catchy English-style melody. As well as the recitatives, the vocal score leaves out four choruses, one of these being the Finale of the opera, but it includes some good ensembles.

One other full-length all-sung work merits attention, not for its music which does not survive, but for its strangeness. In 1760 James Macpherson had pub-lished his *Fragments of Ancient Poetry collected in the Highlands and translated from the Gaelic or Erse*. In his preface he hinted that the fragments were part of a long epic about the wars of Fingal written by Fingal's son, Ossian. Money was raised to enable Macpherson to tour the Western Highlands and Outer Islands in search of this epic, and in 1762 *Fingal*, 'composed by Ossian', was published in Macpherson's prose translation. The result had an influence on European romantic literature, especially on the poetry of Goethe, that is seldom realized in this country, where 'Ossian' is virtually forgotten. Dr. Johnson was the most influential of those who thought Macpherson guilty of forgery; he was never able to supply sources for his translations. Nevertheless he certainly had oral sources for at least a part of what he wrote, and it may be that he deserves more attention today.

It was Barthelemon who wrote the first Ossianic opera, *Oithona* (LT 3.3.68); there were to be many others by continental composers later on. To us with our hindsight their plots seem strikingly Wagnerian. *Oithona* is based on a poem from the 1760 volume, and is presumed to occur around the second century A.D. While Gaul is away fighting, his wife, Oithona, is carried off by Dunrommath, raped, and concealed in a Hebridean cave. Gaul and his men come to the island for revenge, but during the fight Oithona arms herself, rushes into the fray, and is killed. Perhaps it was his Irish blood that suggested the theme to Barthelemon. But his performers were unequal to his demands. Only two of the three acts were ready in time, and though the whole work was promised for a second performance, this never took place.

The anonymous libretto is a curiosity. The blank verse recitative was sung either by a 'Chorus in Harmony' or a 'Chorus, single voice'; antiphonal effects were indicated by the words 'Strophe' and 'Antistrophe'. In fact Barthelemon and his librettist were attempting Greek Tragedy. It is not certain that the piece was acted. In Act I only Gaul and chorus appear, and the recitatives are such as to suggest an oratorio. But in the other acts the recitative looks operatic, and the work was described in advertisements and on the libretto as a 'Dramatic Poem'.

The influence of *Oithona* was nil. We shall notice an Ossianic pantomime, *Oscar and Malvina* (1791), but the main mass of Ossianic music was to be written not by British but by continental composers; for instance Méhul, Schubert, Gade, and Brahms. After *Oithona* there was to be only one full-length all-sung English opera before the end of the century, Storace's *Dido, Queen of Carthage* (1792).[1] However, there were a number of half-length all-sung operas, and those of the 1760s will now be considered.

Telemachus was the only dramatic work by Philip Hayes (1738–97), who in 1777 was to succeed his father, William Hayes, as Professor of Music in Oxford. It was performed at the Oxford Music School (10.5.63) when its composer was twenty-five, and the MS, which lacks the last few pages, is in the Bodleian. The libretto by George Graham, a master at Eton, has much the same plot as Galliard's *Calypso and Telemachus*, and though unlikely to appeal today, it was well reviewed by Dr. Johnson, who, years later (18.2.77), even asked Boswell to get him another copy. The music is surprisingly modern. The *galante* overture has a good Mannheim crescendo near the start, and a movement in the middle for 'clarionets', bassoons, and horns on their own. In this respect it anticipates the overture to *The Duenna* by Thomas Linley the

[1] Perhaps *Orpheus and Euridice* of the same year should count as another; see p. 547.

younger. I have not found an earlier example of the mis-spelling 'clarionet', so common in the nineteenth century. The instrument turns up in a surprising number of arias, and Hayes is quite prepared to write for it in the chalumeau register. The score is not in other respects of much interest.

Such currency as the all-sung Masque and Pastoral[1] still had was due mainly to a rather lack-lustre desire to honour the Royal Family, and three examples can be conveniently grouped together. William Shirley wrote his *Birth of Hercules* 'in Honour of the auspicious Birth of his Royal Highness, the Prince of Wales', and it would have been given at Covent Garden in 1763 but for the half-price riots. By the time the theatre had been restored, the piece had lost its topicality and it was never staged. The title-page of the libretto attributes the music to Arne, but it is not to be found and he probably never finished it. In Act I Jupiter, Minerva, Apollo, Mars, and Venus are eagerly awaiting news of the Happy Event. In Act II Mercury announces that

> The chaste Alcmena to immortal Jove
> Has born a son—the infant Hercules.

The piece was to have been all-sung, with blank verse recitatives, and it ended with some fulsome prophesying, not much of it borne out by subsequent events. In the original legend Hercules was illegitimate; it was a strange analogy to have chosen.

A very poor Masque, *The Choice of Apollo* (LT 11.3.65), received but one performance, yet it cannot be wholly ignored for it survives complete in MS full score. The rather amateurish music was by William Yates, and the libretto, a collector's piece, was by John Potter, whose activities were multifarious. The masque begins with Britannia on the banks of the Thames making, one hopes, positively her last appearance on the English stage.

> Grant that my Sons in Arts and Arms may rise
> And fill each distant Nation with Surprise,

she sings, and soon 'the sister Arts of Poetry, Painting and Music' hurry in to seek her advice on how best to effect this Surprise. Britannia is delighted to be asked ('My Bosom beats with Extacy divine'), and recommends that all three should go to Parnassus and find out what Apollo thinks. Apollo does not hesitate.

> Prefer your Wishes to the Throne with speed,
> Nor will the Queen disdain to intercede.

Unfortunately the Masque stops at this point, and we never see the Sister Arts in Windsor Castle getting useful suggestions from Charlotte.

However, George III and his wife were represented in *The Royal Pastoral* by James Nares—disguised as the shepherds Damon and Delia who have been happily married for six years. Probably the only performance was in Windsor

---

[1] For English Pastorals by J. C. Bach and Dibdin, see pp. 324 and 338.

Castle, but with virtually no plot there can have been virtually no acting. The full score was published in 1769. Nares (1715–83) was organist at the Chapel Royal and among our better church musicians; his masque may be undramatic, but the music has a mildly interesting solidity.

Every year of this decade saw at least one new all-sung afterpiece with English words, and for one of them Charles Burney was responsible. In 1760 he had returned from self-imposed exile in King's Lynn, and eventually Garrick entrusted him with the music for what, incredibly, was the only eighteenth-century production of *A Midsummer Night's Dream* (DL 23.11.63). Even then, most of the last act was thought too 'low' for contemporary taste. According to Hopkins, the first night was calamitous, the young lovers being very bad indeed. The audience suffered the entertainment for only the one performance. However the singing of Miss Wright as a fairy gave pleasure, and George Colman, left in charge of the production because the Garricks had gone to Paris, cut the play to an afterpiece in which only the fairies appeared. *A Fairy Tale* (DL 26.11.63) was unexpectedly successful, a fact that gave no pleasure to Burney, for most of his music had been replaced by items from Smith's *The Fairies*, and (this was not to be borne) by new settings of Michael Arne's. Four of Arne's songs, all sung by Miss Wright and Master Rawworth (First Fairy and Puck), shared a vocal score with the same composer's *Hymen* (see p. 310). They show scarcely a trace of Shakespeare. Three years later Michael Arne married Miss Wright.

After the total failure of his most ambitious theatre music, Burney was tempted to wash his hands of the playhouses, and indeed the catastrophe must have been a major cause of his turning to musical literature. However he was always on friendly terms with Garrick, and when he found that in Paris Garrick had seen and enjoyed Rousseau's *Le Devin du Village* (1752), he mentioned that he himself had translated the libretto. Partly because Rousseau was then in England and being much talked about, Garrick asked Burney to prepare a version for Drury Lane, and Burney called it *The Cunning Man*[1] (DL 21.11.66). Though not described as a pastoral, it is hard to think of any other name for it. The fortune-teller advises Phoebe (Colette in the original) to pretend to love someone else in order to win the reluctant hand of Colin. The simple ruse works. Burney's translation flows easily, but the music is not very interesting, and it is surprising that the opera was so popular in Paris. Burney's vocal score omits the recitatives and a chorus, and appears to include some arias by Burney himself. He took the liberty of filling out some of Rousseau's flimsier accompaniments. The opera ends with an intolerable quantity of 'villaging', quite unconnected with the plot. Burney assembled these dances in a separate publication which he called 'The Comic Tunes'. In view of his dislike of French music, it is curious that he bothered himself with the undertaking.

[1] Thomas Hardy used this term for the 'white wizard' in his short story, 'The Withered Arm'.

Years later he met Rousseau in Paris and presented him with a copy of his translation.

The Cunning Man was an early example of a trend that will become increasingly apparent in the 1770s—the fashion for borrowing the plots of English operas, and much less often some of the music, from French ones of the period, most of them by Monsigny, Philidor, and Grétry.

Samuel Arnold (1740–1802) made his bow in the playhouses with his contribution to *The Maid of the Mill* (1765), which will be considered later in this chapter. It is sad that no scores survive for his two all-sung afterpieces of this period, for his early music tends to be more interesting than his later. *Rosamond* (CG 21.4.67) was got up for Miss Poitier's benefit (she had now become Mrs. Thompson), and it had only the one performance. The published libretto may well be the same as that of Arne's afterpiece version, which had itself been revived at Drury Lane in 1765. *The Royal Garland* (CG 10.10.68) had a dreary-looking libretto by Bickerstaffe, written to honour the state visit of the young king of Denmark.

3 'MIDAS' AND THE ALL-SUNG BURLETTA

Associated with the decline of the masque, and perhaps one of its causes, was the rise of the burlesque masque exemplified by Kane O'Hara's *Midas*. Classical myths had been satirized in *Penelope* (1728),[1] but *Midas* is more significant, in that it was much more successful and much funnier. It spawned a number of imitations, one of them by O'Hara himself, and the genre can be seen flourishing in such Offenbach operettas as *La Belle Hélène* and *Orphée aux enfers*.

Kane O'Hara (c. 1713–82) was a very tall and very short-sighted Irishman from Sligo, with a keen interest in music and painting. The famous harper Carolan had written a fine drinking song for his father, 'O'Hara's Cup'.[2] *Midas* was his first, as also his most successful work for the theatre, and its origins are not so well documented as one would wish. An Italian company in Dublin had been playing Italian burlettas with great success in the late fifties, and Lord Mornington, the father of the Duke of Wellington and himself a composer, commissioned O'Hara to create a somewhat similar burletta for private performance in April 1760; it was given at the home of an MP called William Brownlow, who lived at Lurgan near Belfast and played the harpsichord. The Irish playwright John O'Keeffe claimed to have been present at a preliminary conference in Dublin, when Lord Mornington, O'Hara, and Brownlow all discussed the project, and 'were settling the music for Midas'.[3] All three must have been good amateur musicians, and Lord Mornington even had semi-

---

[1] See p. 106. Also earlier still in Dryden's *Amphitryon*.
[2] See Donal O'Sullivan's *Songs of the Irish* (1960), in which the name is spelt Kean O'Hara.
[3] O'Keeffe I, p. 53.

professional status as a composer, for his glees were among the most popular of the day. Victor states that O'Hara chose all the music himself; no doubt all three made suggestions. According to the libretto later published in London, six of the sixty-six songs had newly-composed music, but we know neither who wrote them nor for which of three productions they were written.

Midas was first given professionally at the Crow Street Theatre, Dublin, on 22 January 1762[1] and it reached Covent Garden two years later (CG 22.2.64). But Collet's overture, published in the vocal score of 1764, was almost certainly not available in time for the Dublin production of 1762, and it is quite likely that the six new songs were not performed on that occasion either. They share common *galante* characteristics for a very good reason, and they were not as new as was pretended. Those on pages 7, 10, and 62 derive from songs in Vol. 2 of 'Venetian Ballads Compos'd by Sigr. Hasse and all the celebrated Italian masters' (1742); in the third instance only the first two bars are the same, in the second nearly all the song. In addition the first few bars of the 'new' song on page 12 is taken from one of the Hasse Comic Tunes (Vol. 1, p. 16). Further search would probably reveal origins for the other two 'new' items. The conclusion is inescapable that someone, commissioned to provide new music, drew on two volumes he happened to possess, at least to get himself started, and palmed the results off as his own.

Midas is different in method from any other pastiche of the century, for a number of the originals are rewritten with extreme freedom. In the last act Apollo's 'Fine Times' and Mysis's 'Mark what I say' both start with solemn bustling Italianate introductions which lead bathetically into trivial Scotch song tunes with amusing effect, and in Pan's 'Strip him, whip him' a frivolous Comic Tune from *Fortunatus* is provided with operatic 'symphonies' between the sung sections. There must have been a guiding hand throughout the compilation, certainly at the stage when the items had to be orchestrated. It must have been someone with an affection for the rather outmoded pieces published as Hasse's, someone vain enough to stoop to a little deceit, and someone competent enough to get all this music into shape. Lord Mornington (still in his middle twenties) is a possible candidate.

The success of O'Hara's libretto depends less on plot than on felicities in the lyrics. Jupiter detects Apollo in an amour and drums him out of Olympus. Heavily disguised as the shepherd Pol, Apollo takes refuge on earth in the cottage of a farmer, Sileno, and in no time is making advances to Sileno's daughters, Nysa and Daphne. The girls already have lovers, Nysa being pursued by Midas, and Daphne by Damaetas, but it is about 'Pol' that they squabble. Midas tries to outface 'Pol' by organizing a singing contest between him and Pan and giving the prize to the latter; Pol in a fury reveals his identity and claps asses' ears on the wretched Midas.

[1] The National Library of Ireland in Dublin has librettos used in this production (MSS 9429 and 9250), but I have not seen them.

O'Hara's lyrics show a flair for the very short line.

> All around the maypole how they trot,
>> Hot
>> Pot,
> And good ale have got;
>> Routing,
>> Shouting,
> At you flouting,
>> Fleering,
>> Jeering,
> And what not.

This is sung to the pantomime tune now known as 'The Old Woman and the Pettycoat'. O'Hara's recitatives are in heroic couplets all with feminine endings and double rhymes. A typical example comes from the scene when Apollo, after his expulsion from heaven, finds himself landed on earth.

> Zooks! what a crush! a pretty decent tumble!
> Kind usage, Mr. Jove—sweet sir, your humble.
> Well, down I am;—no bones broke—tho' sore pepper'd!
> Here doom'd to stay.—What can I do?—turn shepherd.
>> *(Puts on cloak, etc.)*
> A lucky thought—In this disguise, Apollo
> No more, but Pol the swain, some flock I'll follow.
> Nor doubt I, with my voice, guittar, and person,
> Among the nymphs to kick up some diversion.

The music for these recitatives was never printed and is not now to be found in manuscript. The opera survives in curious form, due to the fact that, after nine performances, it was dropped 'on Account of the Indisposition of a Principal Performer', and the postponement lasted two years. When *Midas* was revived, it was as a two-act afterpiece. Early three-act librettos, the only ones that identify the music, are rare; most give the afterpiece version. But the vocal score contains the music of all three acts, even though *Midas* can never have been performed in this form after its publication.

As might be expected of a burlesque, the borrowings are often flippant. Nearly half are traditional tunes, Irish and French as well as English. Most of them are very hard to identify. Often the humour lies in outrageous words to a familiar tune, as in this song of Juno's near the beginning:

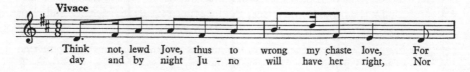

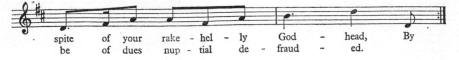

spite   of your   rake - hel - ly   God - head,   By

be   of dues   nup - tial   de - fraud - ed.

There are at least five borrowings from pantomime music, most of them from Drury Lane examples of the 1750s. Burney's feelings must have been mixed when he heard two of his own compositions from *Queen Mab* sung to mocking words. One of Burney's contributions comes in the Finale, where it is sparked off by Apollo rounding on the assembled company with a tirade that begins:

> Thou a Billingsgate Queen,
> Thou a pander obscene . . .

The wretched mortals ask his forgiveness, to the strains of Burney's 'Watchman' quoted on page 232. I have found three items by Arne and Boyce, two by Handel and Worgan; also two borrowings from Italian opera, one being by Pescetti and one by an unnamed and untraced composer. The use of Joseph Vernon's 'When that I was and a little tiny Boy' is curious, for this song is supposed not to have been published until 1770. The vocal score omits the opening chorus of gods and goddesses in Olympus, but Dr. Kitchener inserted a MS copy into his own vocal score, now in the British Museum; also it was later published on its own.

The two-act version of *Midas* was given some seventy-five performances in its first four seasons, and there were numerous revivals at least until 1825. The last known production was in Cambridge in 1923.

The best of the *Midas* imitations were *The Golden Pippin*, compiled by O'Hara himself in 1773, and Dibdin's *Poor Vulcan* (1778). But at this point we shall notice only some earlier afterpiece burlettas. With one exception their music is lost, but they helped to establish the view that the classical gods and goddesses could no longer be taken seriously. Barthelemon's *The Judgment of Paris* (LT 24.8.68) had a singularly un-funny libretto, far inferior to that of *The Golden Pippin* on the same plot, but together they sank Arne's serious *The Judgment of Paris* without trace.

J. A. Fisher's *The Court of Alexander* (CG 5.1.70) had a libretto by G. A. Stevens which Baker found 'very low', but there are amusing moments. *The London Stage* wrongly describes it as 'a roaring burlesque of Lee's *The Rival Queens*'; had this been the intention, it would not have been all-sung. In fact *The Court of Alexander* is a burlesque of the 'historical' opera created, in their different ways, by Handel and Metastasio. It begins with Alexander's court waking up with a communal hang-over, to alleviate which Alexander orders coffee and Thais tea.

The following year James Hook set a wretched libretto perhaps by Thomas Bridges called *Dido and Aeneas* (LT 24.7.71); as usual in these burlesqus, the story is presented in modern slang, and it ends with Dido hanging herself in her own garters. The tenets of Italian *opera seria* were being questioned with much more vigour than in the past. Perhaps the Seven Years War bred a satiric view of the arts. Even Dr. Burney sank to a burlesque *Ode on St. Cecilia's Day* in 1763.[1]

A burletta of a different kind was Samuel Arnold's *The Portrait* (CG 22.11.70). Colman's witty and well-written libretto was based on that of Grétry's *Le Tableau parlant*, which had been staged the previous year in Paris at the Théâtre des Italiens. The plot hinges on the situation Shakespeare treated seriously in *The Winter's Tale*. Fat old Pantaloon loves his ward Isabella, and in order to spy on her he cuts out the head of his own portrait in the dining-room, and stands behind it with his head poking through the hole. Needless to say, he catches Isabella flirting with Leander. The score describes Arnold's music as 'entirely new', and it is full of charm. Unfortunately the recitatives are omitted. Isabella was played by the vivacious Miss Catley, and there were fourteen performances the first season.

It is convenient at this point to trace briefly the progress of all-sung Italian opera in London, more especially because our dialogue operas so often borrow items sung at the King's Theatre.

4 ITALIAN OPERA IN LONDON: J. C. BACH AND SACCHINI

Italian opera is often said to have dominated eighteenth-century music, yet the best examples were not composed by Italians. Early in the century Handel reigned supreme, and in the last quarter of it Mozart. In between, the most interesting opera music was written by J. C. Bach and (though not in the Italian style) by Gluck. Needless to say, these are modern judgements, and few musicians at the time would have accepted them. True Italians resented any attempt to demote the vocal line and its singer. But history has supported the German view that inventive harmony and orchestration and the rich interplay of ensembles are essential qualities in a good opera.

To give Burney his due, he recognized these very qualities in J. C. Bach. Of his first London opera, *Orione*, Burney wrote:

> Every judge of Music perceived the emanations of genius throughout the whole performance; but were chiefly struck with the richness of har-mony, the ingenious texture of the parts, and, above all, with the new and happy use he had made of wind-instruments: this being the first time that *clarinets* had admission in our opera orchestra.[2]

---

[1] Lonsdale, pp. 485–90.

[2] But they had had admission in playhouse orchestras since Arne's *Thomas* and *Sally* of 1760. Bach probably noticed them in *Artaxerxes* and liked the effect; see p. 304.

But the Italians at the King's Theatre were seldom willing to allow success to non-Italians, and Bach's activities there were much curtailed by prejudice.

John Christian Bach (1735–82), known in his own day as the English Bach, spent most of his career in England. The youngest son of Johann Sebastian, he probably came to London in the summer of 1762 when he was twenty-seven, and at least by the following July he had been appointed Music Master to the young Queen Charlotte. The date of his arrival is doubtful. The Royal Music Library in the British Museum has a short *Ode on the auspicious Arrival and Nuptials of . . . Queen Charlotte, by John Lockman. Set to Music by Mr. Bach.* Charlotte had come over from Strelitz at the time of her marriage to George III in September 1761, at which time the Ode must surely have been written and performed. But Bach was so busy in Italy that there seems no time for him to have come to London. Three of his operas were staged in Italy within twelve months: *Artaserse* (Turin 1761), *Catone in Utica* (Naples 4.11.61), and *Alessandro nell'Indie* (Naples 20.1.62). With acclaim in Italy and patronage at court as his credentials, Bach was appointed music director at the King's Theatre for the 1762–3 season.

He began by contributing new overtures (and one or two arias) to four pastiche operas. The overture he wrote for *La calamita de' Cuori* (KT 3.2.63) is of interest because the central slow movement begins with four beautiful bars that Mozart later borrowed for the slow movement of his Piano Concerto in A, K.414.[1] Here is Bach's version of them:

The music well illustrates 'the ingenious texture of the parts' that impressed Burney. The D sharp in bar 2 and the chord progression in bar 3 are typical of Bach's style, and because this style had so much influence on Mozart they seem typical of his music as well. The two operas that Bach composed for his first London season show both this very personal quality of warmth and the trivial *galante* style he had picked up in Italy.

Bach was a progressive mainly in his lyrical melodies and in his harmonic progressions, and these had some influence on English composers. In other respects he could be oddly conservative, resetting the most elderly opera librettos

---

[1] Mozart probably wrote this movement just after hearing of Bach's death.

to the end of his life and having no truck with the new comic operas. Nearly all his operas include a good many old-fashioned *Da Capo* arias.[1]

Although *Orione* had been the most popular opera of the season,[2] Bach was not re-engaged for 1763–4. Mingotti had again been made manager in harness with Giardini, and they preferred an Italian as their composer, Matteo Vento (*c.* 1735–76).[3] Bach gave his time to Court music, and the long series of public concerts that he began in London with his friend Abel. But he was back at the King's Theatre in the following season when Peter Crawford was manager for the first of several seasons. However it was not a good time for non-Italian composers. Bach's *Adriana in Siria* (KT 26.1.65) was not liked much, and Arne's *Olimpiade* was not liked at all. Bach found some compensation in befriending the boy Mozart during his time in London. In a pastiche opera of the time called *Ezio* he inserted an aria from his Neapolitan opera, *Alessandro nell'Indie*, and Mozart was so much moved by it, perhaps as a boy in London and certainly as a man in Paris, that he told his father that it was his 'favorit Sache'.[4] It was a *Da Capo* aria of enormous length and memorable beauty called 'Non so d'onde viene', and Mozart himself composed ravishing decorations for it.

Bach was quite prepared to write for English singers. In the summer of 1764 he directed a Pastoral called *Manalcas* at the Salisbury Festival.[5] The words were by James Harris, the festival's originator and later the Queen's Secretary. He wrote lyrics to fit arias from *Orione* and *Zanaida*, as well as music by other composers, and he persuaded Bach to compose two choruses. The music was not published, but Terry saw a MS score in private hands in Germany.[6] The following summer Bach felt sufficiently at home with the English language to write a set of Vauxhall songs for his talented pupil Mrs. Weichsel, and it was also in 1765 that he wrote songs for two pastiche operas at Covent Garden, *The Maid of the Mill* and *The Summer's Tale*.

Such borrowings were easily made, for the 'Favourite Songs' in Bach's operas were published in full score in the usual way; we have eight arias from *Orione* and *Zanaida*, rather more from *Adriana in Siria*—perhaps a third of the whole. Manuscripts at the British Museum and St. Michael's Tenbury can provide some additional items of *Orione*, but several items are missing, and no recitatives seem to survive for any of these three operas. None of them could easily be revived today.

In his fourth London opera, *Carattaco* (KT 14.2.67), Bach courted popularity with a story about Ancient Britons, but it was not much liked, and in the remaining fourteen years of his life he was asked to write only one more opera for

---

[1] See 'J. C. Bach's Operas', by Ernest Warburton, RMA 1965–6.
[2] Incredibly, it alone of his London operas was revived in his lifetime.
[3] Vento was a Neapolitan who lived in London from 1763 until he died there.
[4] Letter of 12 June 1778.
[5] See 'J. C. Bach in the West Country', by Betty Matthews, M.T. Aug. 1967.
[6] Terry, p. 244.

London[1]—*La clemenza di Scipione* (KT 4.4.78). Burney did not bother to mention it, but it was sufficiently popular for Welcker to publish it in full score complete except for the recitatives (which do not survive) and the choruses. Bach's pupil Mrs. Billington felt affection for it, and revived it for her benefit in 1805; it was the only one of Bach's operas to be staged after his death. Perhaps the most remarkable aria in the score is one for soprano called 'Infelice, in van m'affanno' with elaborate concertante parts for flute, oboe, violin, and cello. It was probably in the same year that Bach wrote his fine Sinfonia Concertante for the same four solo instruments,[2] and it is no coincidence that Mozart chose these very instruments for the famous soprano aria in *Die Entführung aus dem Serail*, 'Martern aller Arten'. He and Bach met each other in Paris in the summer of 1778 just four months after the production of *La clemenza di Scipione*. This was the only Bach opera with an overture in one movement, and the only one in which themes from the overture are used later.

Throughout Bach's time in London anything from six to a dozen operas were being given at the King's Theatre each season. In 1766–7 Crawford engaged two companies so that he could present both serious and comic operas, and there were often three performances a week, on Tuesdays, Thursdays, and Saturdays. Much the most successful opera of the time was a comic one, Piccini's *La buona figliuola* (KT 25.11.66). There were twenty-seven performances that season, an unprecedented number, and the opera was frequently revived later on. Goldoni's libretto derived from Richardson's famous novel about an inviolable servant-girl, *Pamela*, which had been published in 1740 and quickly translated into other languages. Burney says the music made Galuppi's *Il filosofo di campagna* sound old-fashioned, and Piccini's long action finales certainly seem one stage closer to Mozart's. Vento's operas were also very popular at this time, especially *Demofoonte* (1765) and *Sofonisba* (1766). Another Italian who seemed happy to live in Britain was Tommaso Giordani (*c.* 1733–1806). He had worked in Dublin[3] from the early 1760s, but from the autumn of 1769 he spent several seasons at the King's Theatre directing the music from the harpsichord and composing such operas as *Artaserse* (1772) and *Antigono* (1774). He was replaced in 1776–7 by a Neapolitan, Traetta, and returned to Dublin.

All other composers at the King's Theatre at this time were eclipsed by Antonio Sacchini (1730–86), yet another Neapolitan. In nine seasons starting in the autumn of 1772 he composed as many as seventeen operas for the King's

---

[1] Yet he wrote three more for the Continent: *Temistocle* (Mannheim 1772), *Lucio Silla* (Mannheim 1776), and *Amadis de Gaule* (Paris 1779).

[2] Eulenburg Miniature Score No. 1236.

[3] See p. 250. His brother Giuseppe, who also composed, was with him in Dublin, but soon returned to Italy. Tommaso is best known today for his song 'Caro mio ben', always sung with a heavily Victorianized accompaniment. The piano quintets he published in London about 1770 would be much more worth performing; they are among the first of their kind.

Theatre, almost two a year, and the serious ones were outstandingly successful.[1]
'His operas of the *Cid* and *Tamerlano*', said Burney ecstatically, 'were equal, if
not superior, to any musical dramas I have heard in any part of Europe', and
writing of the *Cid* he even praised the composer's 'knowledge of stage effects'.
Sacchini was not, of course, the supreme genius that Burney supposed, but his
music has substance and style, and for an Italian he took unusual care over
orchestration. His quick arias are rather like those in Mozart's *Idomeneo* but
without the fire and character; he certainly influenced Mozart's *opera seria*.
Much earlier in his History Burney added a curious footnote (when writing of
Handel's *Teseo*):

> The late exquisite composer Sacchini, finding how fond the English were
> of Handel's oratorio choruses, introduced solemn and elaborate choruses in
> some of his operas; but though excellent in their kind, they never had a
> good effect; the mixture of the English singers with the Italian, as well as
> the aukward figure they cut, as actors, joined to the difficulty of getting
> their parts by heart, rendered these compositions ridiculous, which in still
> life would have been admirable.

I have not come on any choruses Sacchini wrote for London; they are not
included in the 'Favourite Songs', which are the only music that survives from
some of his operas.

Burney is so selective about Italian operas towards the end of the 1770s and
omits so many that Sacchini wrote for London that a complete list is given below;
so far as I know all but *Rinaldo* were first performed at the King's.

Il Cid (19.1.73)	*Erifile* (7.2.78)
Tamerlano (6.5.73)	*L'amore soldato* (5.5.78)
Lucio vero (20.11.73)	*L'avaro deluso* (24.11.78)
Perseo (29.1.74)	*Enea e Lavinia* (25.3.79)
Nitteti (19.4.74)	*La contadina in corte* (14.12.79)
Montezuma (7.2.75)	*Rinaldo* (22.4.80)
Didone abbandonata (11.11.75)	*Mitridate* (23.1.81)
L'isola d'amore (12.3.76)	*Euriso* (23.6.81)
Creso (8.11.77)	

The later operas were less successful than the earlier, and the later comic operas
were near-failures. Burney thought Sacchini had stayed in London too long for
his reputation. But he was not written out. The last of several operas he com-

---

[1] In Venice in 1770 Sacchini told Burney that up to then he had written 'nearly
forty serious and ten comic operas'; though his morals aroused comment, he was
not lazy.

posed in Paris, *Oedipe à Colone* (1786), is usually regarded as his masterpiece. It shows the influence of Gluck.[1]

Little need be said of the singers so reverenced at this time. After a spell in prison for debt, Tenducci sang at the King's Theatre from 1763 to 1766, suffered a further financial crisis, thought it prudent to live in Dublin, and got back to London in 1769; after which time he became a close friend of Bach and sang regularly in the Bach–Abel concerts. Polly Young was the only English singer tolerated in the 1760s. In the early seventies Cecilia Davies, who had been greatly admired abroad, sang the leads in several Sacchini operas with acclaim. Venanzio Rauzzini (1746–1810) was described by Burney as 'a beautiful and animated young man . . . as able to set an opera as to sing it', and his skill as both composer and harpsichordist was very unusual in a castrato. Mozart's cantata 'Exultate jubilate' had been written for him in 1773, and the vocal line shows Rauzzini was a soprano. The following year he came to England and stayed for the rest of his life. As well as singing at the King's Theatre he wrote two operas; one of them, *Piramo e Tisbe*, started life as a cantata, but was later given full dramatic treatment. Much the most eminent castrato of the period was another soprano, Gasparo Pacchierotti (1740–1821), who could sing sweetly up to C in alt, which was a third higher than Rauzzini could manage. Invited to London for the 1778–9 season, Pacchierotti brought with him the ageing Venetian composer Ferdinando Bertoni (1725–1813), who composed four operas for him; they can hardly have all been new. Much the most popular was yet another setting of *Demofoonte*, but it was Pacchierotti's singing rather than Bertoni's music that made the audience sigh with ecstasy. According to Lord Mount-Edgcumbe he 'could not sing a tune twice in exactly the same way; yet never did he introduce an ornament that was not judicious'.[2]

In February 1779 there were performances of Grétry's so-called *Zemira ed Azore*, sung in Italian. It would be interesting to know whose idea it was to stage the first French opera ever given at the King's Theatre.

5 'LOVE IN A VILLAGE' AND THE PASTICHE

Love in a Village (CG 8.12.62) appeared in the same year as *Artaxerxes* but in the following season, and it proved even more successful and influential. Arne and his librettist, Isaac Bickerstaffe, must have planned it together. As we shall see in the later chapter on Ballad Opera, *The Jovial Crew* had just been modernized by William Bates, and the result had been well received. Arne and Bickerstaffe determined to attempt a much more radical revision of a ballad opera, and the one they chose was *The Village Opera* (1729) by Charles Johnson. This had

---

[1] Sir Joshua Reynolds painted Sacchini's portrait for the Duke of Dorset. Fanny Burney saw it, thought it ' charming', and reported in her diary for 27 February 1775: 'Sir Joshua himself said that Sacchini was the highest type of manly beauty.'

[2] Lord Mount-Edgcumbe's *Musical Reminiscences*, p. 13.

not been a success, but Bickerstaffe was probably attracted by the modern touches in the dialogue. Thus Sir Nicholas Wiseacre, country gentleman and father of Rosetta, keeps snubbing his silly wife with a sort of curmudgeonly charm : 'Well, well, thou art an innocent Stupe, a poor tame Bird, and mean'st no harm.' A young man disguised as a gardener wants to marry a young woman disguised as a maid, and Rosetta also has a secret lover (who never appears). The plot depends very largely on the confidence tricks practised on the girls by two villainous footmen. Bickerstaffe cut the footmen, and identified Rosetta with the disguised maid, and her lover (Young Meadows) with the disguised gardener. He changed all the names except that of the heroine, and he changed all the lyrics and dialogue as well. As none of the original tunes were kept either, it was virtually a new work.

The libretto, though quite amusing, is not Bickerstaffe's best. The opening scene in the garden reveals Lucinda and her supposed maid Rosetta giving each other information which both know already about their respective amours; it is, of course, the audience that needs to be informed. This giving of information in a natural way is a frequent problem to playwrights; Bickerstaffe had not yet learnt to solve it. However Justice Woodcock, Lucinda's father, is splendidly done. Played by Shuter, who was no singer, the old man has only one song, and that a ballad. But his crony Hawthorn, who has very little to do with the plot, has plenty to sing, the part being written for Beard. Young Meadows and Rosetta were played by Mattocks and Miss Brent, while Miss Hallam (soon to be Mrs. Mattocks) was Lucinda. There is also a bucolic courtship between two genuine servants, Hodge and Margery. Nothing striking occurs, but the libretto has a pleasing amiability. Nearly all the singing is done by the two girls, Hawthorn, and Young Meadows; Miss Brent had as many as eleven songs.

Love in a Village started a vogue for a type of entertainment that was essentially different from ballad opera. Its originality lay partly in the kind of song that was borrowed and partly in the way the songs were orchestrated. It was a transitional work, in that a few of the songs were still of the traditional ballad type, but thirty-six of the forty-two items were fully composed, with introductions and postludes for orchestra, many of them demanding a wide range of wind instruments. There is a manuscript full score in the Royal College of Music, part of which is said to be in Arne's hand. Where one song should be, 'In Love should there meet a fond Pair' by Barnard, there are blank pages, and a reason for this will be suggested later. Of the forty-one songs that are included, six are for full orchestra of oboes (or flutes), bassoons, horns, and strings, and fifteen others demand wind as well as strings. Just under half are for strings alone. Such scoring was unknown in the ballad opera proper, and in any case most of the songs were in no sense ballads.

Early editions of the libretto indicate those songs which had new music; six by Arne and one by Samuel Howard.[1] Also Abel's overture was advertised as new.

[1] Over one song the librettos are wrong. Howard's 'How much superior' is

Thus the new items amount to less than a fifth of the whole. Of the borrowed items, twelve were by Arne himself, and he was thus the composer of just under half the entire opera. The borrowings are highly unusual in two respects. First, very few are taken form other operas, and secondly very few are taken from recent publications. All the Arne and Boyce borrowings are from songs written for Vauxhall Gardens.[1] Four items were taken from Italian operas given at the King's Theatre, and these are listed in my Appendix on borrowings. Their sources are *Tito Manlio* by Abos (1756), *La forza d'amore* by Paradies (1757), and two very popular operas by Galuppi: *Enrico* (1743) and *Il filosofo di campagna* (1761).[2] The last-named is among the few contemporary sources; others include two Italian songs by Giardini, one of which, 'Quanto mai felici sieti innocenti', had been published as recently as April 1762. (Arne added wind parts to the original string accompaniment.) The Arne and Boyce sources are spread over the preceding twenty years, and songs from two Handel works of the 1740s are also drawn on: *L'Allegro* and *Susanna*. Arne also borrowed the minuet theme in the finale of Geminiani's Concerto Grosso op. 2/1 (1732), adding a flute part, and for the opening duet wrote a full accompaniment for 'Let Ambition fire the Mind' from Weldon's *The Judgment of Paris*; the song had never been published with more accompaniment than a bass line. The vocal score of *Love in a Village* gives little of the orchestral detail to be found in the full score.

Arne must also have harmonized and scored the five items that use 'traditional' tunes. There is significance in the characters to whom they are allotted. Two are sung by the bovine Hodge, and another is described as a 'Servants' Medley'. As mentioned earlier, Justice Woodcock sings only one song, a ballad which he introduces as follows:

> I had once a little notion of music myself, and learned upon the fiddle; I could play the Trumpet Minuet,[3] and Buttered Peas, and two or three tunes. I remember, when I was in London, about thirty years ago, there was a song, a great favourite at our club at Nando's coffee-house; Jack Pickle used to sing it for us, a droll fish! but 'tis an old thing, I dare swear you have heard of it often.

He then tosses off 'When I followed a Lass', the words from Colley Cibber's

---

marked as new instead of the following song, Arne's 'When we see a Lover languish'. It is the latter that is thought to be in the composer's autograph in the RCM score.

[2] I have failed to trace 'Since Hodge proves ungrateful' by Arne, but it is not likely to be operatic in origin.

[3] The dates are those of the first King's Theatre production. In vocal scores of *Love in a Village* the Abos item, 'Whence can you inherit', is attributed to Arne, but the libretto assigns it correctly. Girolamo Abos (1716–60) was Maltese, and a pupil of Alessandro Scarlatti. He was harpsichordist at the King's Theatre in 1755–6.

[4] From Handel's *Water Music*.

Love in a Riddle, the tune the familiar country dance known as 'Joan's Placket'; the humour of the song probably lay in its old-fashioned boresomeness. Thus, with one exception, the 'traditional' songs are sung by servants or fuddy-duddies, and it is implicit that the ballad was outmoded. The exception is '*The Miller of the Dee*' sung by Hawthorn. Though the tune was old (it occurs in *The Devil to pay* and other ballad operas, where it is called 'The Budgeon is a fine Trade'), the words are presumably Bickerstaffe's. The song became lastingly popular, and even got into the National Song Book. Arne scored all these songs for two violins and bass, and gave them introductions and postludes just like those discussed on page 116.

Act I ends with a fair on the village green, and 'The Servants' Medley' is the Finale. In the Royal College of Music MS no less than ten tunes are strung together at this point, but in the published vocal scores the number is cut to five. The singers are described as the Housemaid, the Footman, the Cookmaid, and the Carter. The tunes include the country-dance named after the still-living Sadler's Wells dancer, Nancy Dawson, and Leveridge's 'Roast Beef'. The final section is no doubt by Arne himself. Every song in this Medley has its own introduction to set the tempo and the new key.

As has been mentioned already, Barnard's 'In Love should there meet a fond pair' is not given in the Royal College of Music full score, though blank pages were left for its later insertion. As the words do not appear in the first two editions of the libretto, it is clear that the song was added a few weeks after the first night. It is a curiosity in several senses. The words do not fit the tune very well; it looks as though the latter was originally intended for a lyric whose odd-numbered lines were two syllables longer:

Bickerstaffe was efficient at fitting words to music, and it is unlikely that he was responsible for this song. Yet there is no composer of the time called Barnard that we can blame. One of this name is mentioned in Bickham's *Musical Entertainer* of 1738,[1] but this Barnard is not known to have written anything else, and it is highly unlikely that twenty-five years later anyone so insignificant would have been drawn on for a last-minute addition. An intriguing explanation can be found in an article by Dr. Busby about George III, who was dead by the time it was written.[2]

[1] ii, p. 48.
[2] ii, p. 199.

Early in life he . . . availed himself of Handel's instructions on the harpsichord, and practised and listened to the best compositions, till he . . . imbibed such correct notions of the principles of the art, as to be qualified to compose. Among the many pleasing offsprings of his Majesty's imagination, is the melody applied to the song 'In Love, should we meet a fond pair', in the opera of *Love in a Village*.

Dr. Busby adds, rightly, that the tune is charming. And why the pseudonym Barnard? As Boswell happens to divulge, at this very time a Mr. Barnard was Librarian at 'The Queen's House', that is, Buckingham House in St. James's Park; his name might well have been borrowed for the purpose. Busby will have got his information from Mrs. Billington, with whom he was friendly, and she in turn from her parents who were prominent in London's musical life at the time. It would be interesting to know who approached whom in arranging the matter.

Their Majesties attended the performance on 30 December 1762, and this may well have been the night when Miss Brent first sang the King's song. The Royal visit coincided with a notorious interval dance by Miss Poitier, described with relish in the *Theatrical Review*.[1] Her low-cut dress allowed her breasts to flab 'like a couple of empty bladders in an oil-shop', one of her shoes came off, and those in the front of the the the pit were able to observe that she was not wearing any drawers. 'The Court turned instantly from the stage—The Pit was astonished.' Miss Poitier's attempts to defend her conduct in print did her little good.

Several songs were specially written for revivals of *Love in a Village* later in the century.[2] Miss Catley when singing Rosetta liked to include 'The Shepherd's Invitation' ('Come live with me and by my Love'); the words, only distantly related to Marlowe's, had been fitted by Arne himself to the 'Scotch' Finale of his own overture to *Achilles in Petticoats*, and he published the song in *The Vocal Grove* (1774). One of Shield's first tasks in London was to write a 'Scotch Song' for Miss Catley to sing in *Love in a Village*; it was called 'Johnny and Mary'.[3] Arne's 'Cease, gay Seducers' near the end of Act II was never much liked. Miss Catley replaced it with an indifferent setting of the same words allegedly by herself. In 1786 Mrs. Billington made her London début as Rosetta, and was soon complaining of the lack of a long bravura aria in which she could show her paces. One was written for her by Tommaso Giordani, and it can be found in the Birchall vocal score of 1796. The words are a paraphrase of the original, and begin 'Shun, ye fair, each gay Deceiver'. It looks dull but a singer who could overcome its appalling difficulties might make it exciting.

[1] Quoted in LS for this date.

[2] And one was cut before the music was published. The earliest librettos have 'Air 41, Duet for Eustace and Lucinda: The Merchant whose Vessel', with music by Arne. Probably this love duet was too hard for Eustace, who was no singer.

[3] The words were by Thomas Holcroft; see his *Memoirs* i, p. 280.

Most of the songs in *Love in a Village* call for lyrical rather than bravura singing. Miss Brent was allowed some coloratura writing in the last act, notably in 'The Traveller benighted', a new and difficult song by Arne himself, but in general the vocal writing is much easier than it is in *Artaxerxes*. The lyrical songs are certainly the most memorable, Arne's being outstanding; he had nothing to fear from foreign competition in this field. It is significant that he borrowed the famous minuet by his master, Geminiani, for it fathered so many similar melodies of his own, the very ones that made this opera so popular.

There were forty consecutive performances. *Love in a Village* reached New York in 1768, and was still being given in London in the 1840s after being played all over Britain for season after season. Like all eighteenth-century operas, it then fell out of the repertoire, and the only productions of recent years have taken unpardonable liberties with the music. It is hard to feel benevolent towards either Alfred Reynolds's version for Nigel Playfair or Arthur Oldham's for Aldeburgh. There may be a case for modernizing *The Beggar's Opera*, but there is none at all for re-harmonizing and re-scoring a work as fully and competently written as *Love in a Village*.

6 IMITATIONS OF 'LOVE IN A VILLAGE'

It can hardly be a coincidence that the sudden fashion for pastiche in playhouse operas was paralleled and slightly preceded by a similar fashion at the King's Theatre. In the 1761–2 season, six out of the ten Italian operas were pastiches, and in 1762–3 five out of seven.[1] There was even an element of pastiche in many plays; critics often drew attention to ideas a dramatist had borrowed from his predecessors. Baker thought that Sheridan had got the plot of *The Duenna* from '*Il Filosofo di Campagna*, from Molière's *Sicilien*, and from *The Wonder* by Mrs. Centilevre', yet there is no vestige of censure in the remark; he is in fact ecstatic in his praise of *The Duenna*. Critics harped on multiple sources not because they disapproved but because they found the subject interesting. The past was wide open for pillage. New plays that were grounded in the past made an audience feel secure, and new operas that reanimated favourite songs of the past were especially nostalgic.

Yet it was some time before imitations of *Love in a Village* began to flow, and when they did, there were some marked differences. The five examples listed below were all full-length, and in four of the five less than a fifth of the music was new. Two, *The Maid of the Mill* and *Lionel and Clarissa*, were lastingly successful.

The Maid of the Mill (CG 31.1.65); Arnold–Bickerstaffe
The Summer's Tale (CG 6.12.65); Arnold–Cumberland
Love in the City (CG 21.2.67); Dibdin–Bickerstaffe

[1] The only original works were Bach's *Orione* and *Zanaida*.

Lionel and Clarissa (CG 25.2.68); Dibdin–Bickerstaffe
Tom Jones (CG 14.1.69); Arne and/or Arnold–Joseph Reed

Drury Lane did not attempt to compete in this field, at least not to much purpose. As we shall see, this theatre preferred operas all by one composer, and their policy eventually paid dividends.

These five pastiche operas borrowed fewer traditional tunes than *Love in a Village*, and the three Bickerstaffe examples borrowed none at all. Borrowings tended to be from recent music, and in the Bickerstaffe examples this was almost wholly operatic, and in the new *galante* idiom. The music is thus more 'modern' than that of *Love in a Village* and more difficult to sing. All five have an important feature not to be found in *Love in a Village*—the extended Finale in several contrasted sections. Londoners had met such Finales in Galuppi's *Il filosofo di Campagna* in 1761, and in 1766 the Covent Garden company had first-hand experience of them when they performed a translated version of Piccini's *La buona Figliuola* under the title *The Accomplished Maid*. The libretto, it will be remembered, was distantly based on Richardson's *Pamela*. The previous year, in 1765, Bickerstaffe had based the libretto of *The Maid of the Mill* on the very same novel. In his Preface Bickerstaffe says: 'Not only the general subject is drawn from Pamela, but almost every circumstance,' and he then mentions some parallels.[1] This is more than a little ingenuous in that the basic situation in *Pamela* is completely left out. At no time do we see Patty (i.e. Pamela) being employed by Lord Aimworth (i.e. 'Mr. B.'), and he never makes any attempt to seduce her. Patty is the local miller's daughter, and her period of working in the Big House occurs before the opera begins. Like Goldoni, Bickerstaffe jibbed at the idea of presenting a stage clergyman in desperation for the girl, and he changes Parson Williams into an innocuous and boresome farmer called Giles. Lord Aimworth and Patty eventually come together because the former is jealous of Giles (who loves Patty) and the latter of Theodosia (who she wrongly thinks loves Lord Aimworth). The result is a somewhat insipid story, or at least it would be if Bickerstaffe did not keep stirring it into life with brisk and amusing dialogue. Theodosia's parents, Sir Harry and Lady Sycamore, are splendidly managed, and though both are prosily loquacious they are well contrasted. Patty's brother Ralph is the nearest thing in the opera to a rogue, and he too is alive and kicking. In spite of obvious faults, most apparent to those who know their Richardson, this is an effective libretto with felicitous lyrics. The hero is a stick, but so are a great many opera heroes.

Mattocks and Miss Brent played the hero and heroine, and Beard was Farmer Giles. The only other characters with much to sing are Ralph (Dibdin) and Theodosia (Miss Hallam). Miss Brent as Patty predictably had the hardest songs.

---

[1] Genest (v, p. 74) thought 'Bickerstaffe, in writing the parts of Fairfield, Patty, and particularly Ralph, seems to have had his eye on the characters of Franio, Florimel, and Bustopha, in Fletcher's Maid in the Mill'.

It might have been expected that Bickerstaffe would collaborate again with Arne, but at this time Arne was deeply involved with his Italian opera, *L'Olimpiade*. Bickerstaffe worked instead with the young Samuel Arnold, an outstandingly industrious musician who later composed voluminously in all forms, played the organ and conducted. In middle life he had the vision and the energy to attempt a Complete Edition of Handel. As a composer he lacked self-criticism, apparently writing down whatever first came into his head, and much of his theatre music is worthless. Nevertheless, both in his overtures and in his songs, he was always liable to light on a happy vein of invention, and this was especially the case in his younger days.

For *The Maid of the Mill* Arnold wrote the Finales to Acts I and II, and two airs. In one of the latter Theodosia is frightened of being caught with her lover, Mervin.

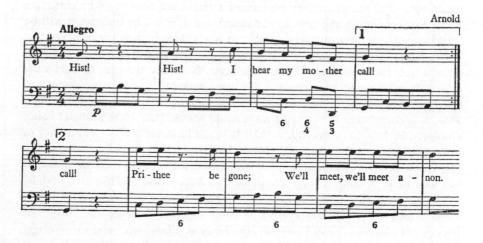

This is charming, and very up to date in style. But there is better to come. In the middle of the lyric Theodosia hesitates, searching in her mind for an excuse to keep Mervin with her. Arnold catches this hesitation to perfection with a switch to the minor key which is the essence of good operatic writing.

stay, a mo-ment stay, a mo-ment stay   Some - thing be - side I

had to say. Well, 'tis for - got, No mat - ter___ what.

Much of the music is pleasing. In Act II Lord Aimworth had a song to music from Cocchi's *Tito Manlio* of 1761 which included a surprisingly Mozartian sequence:

Allegro   Cocchi

And speak to, and hear her, And speak to, and hear her,

Miss Brent sang a particularly lovely aria from Bach's *Orione* which is even more Mozartian. Almost certainly the other Bach contribution, 'My Life, my Joy', was especially written for *The Maid of the Mill*. With the four Arnold pieces and the Earl of Kellie's overture, there were thus six new items in thirty-eight. About two-thirds of the borrowings were from Italian music, nearly all of it operatic; the only instrumental example is the one near the end attributed to Martini, which I take to be a minuet by Giuseppe Sammartini. It is not always easy to decide the nationality of a borrowing; five items were taken from operas by Egidio Duni (1709–75), a Neapolitan who worked almost entirely in Paris.[1] In borrowing also from French operas by Monsigny and Philidor, Arnold was ahead of the fashion, but the Italian and German music that he purloined is of a higher order.

According to Busby, Arnold was paid a mere £12 for composing his four items and compiling the rest.[2] Three months before the first night, the publisher Lowndes paid £23 10s. for an eighth share in the copyright of the words, because he anticipated good sales for the libretto.[3] It was a sound investment, for the

---

[1] One of these, 'Let me fly', is wrongly attributed in the vocal score to Jomelli.

[2] Busby i, p. 91.

[3] BM Add. 38730, f. 104.

opera was the chief London success of the season. That summer the Crow Street Theatre in Dublin planned to put it on, but interest was so great that a rival production was staged at Smock Alley at the same time. The latter theatre had been unable to obtain a set of parts of the music; accordingly they commissioned Tommaso Giordani to provide an entirely new score, and this was composed, copied and rehearsed inside a fortnight. Giordani's music does not survive. The affair provides striking confirmation of the belief then common in some circles that in English operas the words were what mattered.

The Maid of the Mill reached New York in 1769, St. Petersburg in 1772, and Jamaica in 1779. A Covent Garden production of 1814 included new music by Bishop. From 1769 Drury Lane was also staging the opera, using parts that must have been obtained illicitly. A performance of 12 May 1773 was graced by a 'New Occasional Epilogue' written by Oliver Goldsmith.

The Summer's Tale was a much closer imitation of *Love in a Village*, with its country setting and its disguised heroines. As Amelia Hartley puts it, 'Persecuted by my Family, who wou'd have driven me into the Arms of a Man, who is my mortal Aversion, I have taken refuge here, under the Disguise that you now see me wear.' Such situations turn up rather often in playhouse operas at this time; for that matter they turned up rather often in everyday life. Miss Hallam presumably eloped in disguise with Mattocks to avoid marrying someone else, and certainly Elizabeth Carr did so with the poet Charles Churchill; in the latter case the parents wanted the girl to marry just such a rich old horror as we find set up for a husband in so many plays and librettos of the time. The music of *The Summer's Tale* includes three items by J. C. Bach, and of these 'So profound an impression' is specifically described as new in the libretto.[1] The second song in the vocal score is attributed to Lampugnani, but the same music is marked 'Laschi' in *The Maid of the Mill* and 'Galuppi' in *The Golden Pippin* The libretto says the overture was by Abel, but it is not given in the vocal score.

The Summer's Tale lasted only nine nights. It was revived and revised as an afterpiece, *Amelia*, in the 1767–8 season, and, revised yet again, had two performances at Drury Lane in 1771. There is nothing in the libretto or the music to make one regret the failure. A pastiche needs some element to bind the music together. In *Love in a Village* the high proportion of songs by Arne achieved this cohesion. The music of *The Summer's Tale* is just a rag-bag.

On the other hand the failure of *Love in the City* was a tragedy. The libretto, published anonymously, was Bickerstaffe's masterpiece, and it was the originality of the setting that sank the opera. All the main characters are working-class Londoners, the chief of them being a grocer and his son and daughter (Penelope). The grocer's brother-in-law, Mr. Barnacle, is in coal. Priscilla Tomboy,

---

[1] The 1967 revision of Terry's *John Christian Bach* lists the incipits on p. 246, but fails to identify the second as an aria from *Alessandro nell'Indie* (No. 10) and the third from *Zanaida* (No. 1).

described as a Creole[1] from Jamaica, has been placed in the Grocer's house to be educated, and she has a black servant, Quasheba, whom she treats with disdain.

PRISCILLA: I will have you horsewhipped till there is not a bit of flesh on your bones
PENELOPE: Oh poor creature!
PRISCILLA: Psha!—What is she but a Neger? If she was at home at our plantation, she would find the difference; we make no account of them there at all.
PENELOPE: I suppose then you imagine they have no feelings?
PRISCILLA: Oh! we never consider that there.

At this period West Indians were often brought to England as servants; sometimes they came as slaves and were then given their freedom. Many people viewed with horror the fortunes made in Jamaica by absentee landlords such as William Beckford's father. Even so stern a Tory as Dr. Johnson was vehement in his hope that the Jamaicans would rise against their masters and drive them out. Johnson himself had a coloured servant and treated him admirably.

Nevertheless we are not meant to be wholly alienated by Priscilla Tomboy, even though some of her remarks on the colour question are outrageous, as also some of her actions. In the Finale of Act II her high spirits even drive her into a street fight, described by Charles Dibdin as 'The Boxing Trio';[2] the word 'tomboy' derives from this character. Priscilla apart, Bickerstaffe's libretto is full of amusing and keenly-observed Londoners. The plot is intriguing, the dialogue full of life.

Love in the City was the first full-length opera with which Dibdin was associated, though he was allowed to contribute no more than the music for two Finales and an occasional song. The cockney 'Dialogues' he later wrote for Sadler's Wells suggest that such a libretto would have brought out the best in him, had he been given a free hand. In November 1781 someone cut the opera down to an afterpiece called *The Romp*. This version was soon taken up by Daly in Dublin and by Tate Wilkinson in York, and in both cases Priscilla was acted by the then unknown Mrs. Jordan. From 1785 onwards she was playing the part with huge success at Drury Lane. No score of *The Romp* was ever published, and only the Act I songs from *Love in the City* were issued. However a delightful and characteristic song that Dibdin wrote for Priscilla in Act II appeared on its own: 'Dear me, how I long to get married'. It was a very late example of the *Da Capo* aria, and towards the end of the main section Priscilla sings:

---

[1] In the eighteenth century a Creole was a European born in the West Indies, 'the name having no connotation of colour' (O.E.D.).
[2] *The Musical Tour*, p. 286.

How charming 'twill be
Beside me to see
   My husband and maybe
   A sweet little baby
As pretty as he.

Then follows:

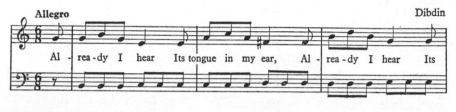

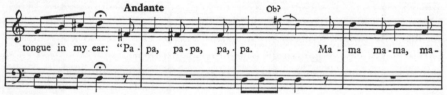

As abstract music that is abysmal, but as a vehicle for an ebullient singing-actress it is superb. Dibdin's music often reveals a quality in performance that is hard to discover on paper. His best songs are an expression of character or situation, and they show much more sense of the theatre than the better-written songs of Arne and Boyce.

Charles Dibdin (1745–1814) was born in Southampton, the eighteenth child of a sorely-tried mother who was fifty at the time. His father was a silversmith. Dibdin's claim to have been educated at Winchester College is not supported by any records, but he did have lessons from the cathedral organist. He taught himself to compose mainly by keeping his eyes and ears open at Covent Garden, and he started singing in the chorus of *Comus* at this theatre when he was only fifteen. At the same time he did casual work for the music publisher Johnson. By 1762 he was adding to the general noise in pantomimes. His promise was noted by Beard, who was so encouraging as to subscribe to his op. 1 *Collection of English Songs*. At nineteen Dibdin was allowed to write and compose an all-sung Pastoral, *The Shepherd's Artifice* (CG 21.5.64), and to sing the lead in it.[1] The piece failed, but the following year Dibdin became suddenly famous for his performance as Ralph, the farmer's son in *The Maid of the Mill*. He was already rather plump, and his bovine appearance and flair for accents— no doubt he played Ralph with a Hampshire accent—had much to do with the opera's success. Three years later he was a sensation as Mungo, the coloured servant in his own short opera, *The Padlock*. He was among the first to attempt 'coon' English,[2] and in later life his one-man variety shows often included 'darkie' songs, the forerunners of those sung by the Christie Minstrels. He was always a character actor, and had no success in straight parts.

Stage experience gave Dibdin an easy style for dialogue. In his earlier and better operas Bickerstaffe wrote the words for him, but after the latter's disgrace in 1772 Dibdin wrote his own librettos; indeed he wrote a very large number. He was careless and hasty in everything, but his dialogue was much more natural than Arne's, and his lyrics more felicitous. In *The Duenna* Sheridan sometimes began his lyrics with inversions that make them incomprehensible when sung, and even when first read.

> What Bard, O Time, discover,
> With wings first made thee move?

Dibdin, with more inside knowledge of the theatre, would never have written so opaquely. Being himself a singer he knew that words must be simple in construction to be intelligible, and we have already noted that he counted intelligibility the first requirement in the singers he taught. In *The Sheperd's Artifice* he wrote with total simplicity:

> Turn, O turn, relentless fair;
> Pity hapless Strephon's pain,—
> Raise him from the last despair;
> Smile and bid him live again.

The words have no poetic merit, but they have the virtue, so vital in the theatre, that they can be instantly comprehended when sung. In his later 'music-hall' days Dibdin turned out lyrics by the dozen, balancing patriotic sea-songs against satirical attacks on Italian Opera and almost Dickensian accounts of some cockney debacle. His success in the 1790s when he ran his own one-man theatre is outside the scope of this book, but it is worth mentioning that in George Hogarth's *The Songs of Charles Dibdin* the lyrics from the early operas and from the late variety shows fill more than three hundred two-column pages of small print. Many well-known poets wrote much less.

If it was Beard's restraining hand that limited Dibdin's contribution to *Love*

---

[1] The words survive but not the music. The Artifice, not an original one, consisted of Strephon pretending to love another shepherdess in order to win Caelia.

[2] Tony Aston had advertised 'Negroe Songs' at Goodman's Fields in the winter of 1743–4.

in the City, the hand was no longer there when Bickerstaffe and Dibdin set about *Lionel and Clarissa*. In the summer of 1767 Beard retired, and the four patentees who took over were too busy squabbling to pay any attention to the repertoire. Bickerstaffe had learnt his lesson. The characters in *Lionel and Clarissa* are country gentry, and thus much more to the liking of the playhouse audience than the tradesmen of *Love in the City*. Bickerstaffe boasted that he had not borrowed a single incident.[1] The action centres round the family of Colonel Oldboy, a bluff outspoken landowner who chases every girl in sight. His wife is a hypochondriac, terrified of draughts and for ever wanting to try out new medicines. Of their two children, Jessamy has been brought up in London by an uncle, and this has turned him into an aggressive fop with French manners and a French servant. His more likeable sister, Diana, has some of her father's outspokenness. Jessamy has come down to the country because his father is trying to arrange his marriage with Clarissa, the daughter of a neighbour. In fact Clarissa is becoming increasingly in love with Lionel, a university student studying for the church in her father's house. Diana also has a secret lover. In the end the two fathers learn that the only way with daughters is to let them marry the man of their choice. The sub-title of the opera was *The School for Fathers*.

> With regard to what is called sentiment, it is not because I dislike it in its place that I have neglected it . . . I could have got together, not only all the moral, but all the cardinal virtues, and half an hour's reading in the Oeconomy of Human Life, would have enabled me to ring the changes on them through my three acts.

So wrote Bickerstaffe in the Preface to *Love in the City*, and it is clear that he had doubts about 'sentiment' in the theatre, the quality that modern writers on *The Rivals* find boring in the Julia-Faulkland scenes. Nevertheless in Bickerstaffe's next opera the scenes between Lionel and Clarissa are open to the same objection, even though he manages them a little more naturally than Sheridan. But it is easy to forgive Bickerstaffe, for the Oldboy family is as vigorous and amusing as any in eighteenth-century drama. Jessamy is, perhaps, his most original creation.

Dibdin composed just under half the score, the rest of it being taken from the operas of such composers as Galuppi and Vento. Two years later he rewrote *Lionel and Clarissa* for Drury Lane, raising his own contribution to three-quarters of the whole. This second version will be considered in the next chapter. Even in its first form, Dibdin's music is a great improvement on anything he had written before, the two Finales being outstanding. He must have learnt how to write such Finales from singing the part of Robin, the gardener, in *The Accomplished Maid*, Covent Garden's adaptation of *La buona figliuola*.

---

[1] In the 'Advertisement' (Preface) to the published libretto.

Dibdin's defection from Covent Garden in the summer of 1768 is unexplained. In the following January this theatre put on what turned out to be its last full-length pastiche for several years, *Tom Jones*.[1] Ludicrous as it may seem, Joseph Reed's libretto was an adaptation not of Fielding's novel, but of the French adaptation Poinsinet had written for Philidor's opera of 1765. Reed's Preface is off-putting to a degree. After avowing a veneration for Fielding and a desire to preserve as much of the novel as possible, he goes on.

> I have stripp'd its hero of his libertinism, to render him, as I imagined, more amiable and interesting; and have metamorphos'd Parson Supple into a country 'squire', to avoid giving offence to the *cloth*. The characters of *Western* and *Honour* I have divested of their provinciality, lest the attention of the performers, to the pronunciation of an uncouth and difficult dialect, should produce an *inattention* to the more material business of the drama. I have also endeavour'd to purge Western's character of its coarseness and indelicacy, in conformity to the refined taste of the present age; and of its Jacobitism . . .

Reed claimed that all he had taken from Poinsinet was 'the hint of legitimating Jones', but the dishonesty implicit in this remark was among his lesser failings. Though the dialogue is not without a certain liveliness, the quality of Fielding's invention has been debased beyond recognition. Arne and Arnold each contributed about a quarter of the score, and it is impossible to tell which of them, if either, was in charge of the musical side. The overture was taken from a Piccini opera. The Finale was based on the last movement of Corelli's Concerto Grosso No. 2 in F, a piece well known to the audience as interval music. Shuter was Squire Western, Mrs. Pinto (Miss Brent as was) Sophia.

There was only one pastiche at Drury Lane in the 1760s, and it was an afterpiece called *Daphne and Amintor* (DL 8.10.65). It was a success. The libretto was adapted from one called *L'Oracle* by Saint-Foix, which had been much liked in Paris. Mrs. Cibber had made a translation back in 1752, but this was said to have failed because the character of the Fairy 'threw upon it an air of childishness'. The ubiquitous Bickerstaffe turned the Fairy into a female Magician, and this was felt to be an improvement. There are only three characters and a small chorus. Amintor has been told in childhood by an oracle that he will enjoy life only if his bride thinks him 'deaf, dumb and insensible'—until after they are married. His mother, the Magician, has found a suitable girl, Daphne, and protects her from the world by bringing her up among a set of magically-inspired statues. We see four of these robots on the stage, two men holding flutes and two girls with guitars, and they periodically descend from their plinths to dance. Thus when Daphne first sees Amintor, she thinks he is just another robot. While he stands as still as he can, she strokes him and coos at him

---

[1] Garrick had turned this opera down in 1767: see Letters 465 and 477.

in the most uninhibited way, trying to teach him to say her name; he affects to find this very difficult. The Drury Lane audience enjoyed seeing a young woman being unaffectedly amorous, and a young man struggling to conceal his own feelings in this direction. The title roles were taken by Vernon and Miss Wright, who was speaking on the stage for the first time.

Bickerstaffe's prefaces always contain something of interest. In this one he reveals a predictable dislike of the Scotch Song.

> Some people may possibly be of opinion, that I ought to have chosen old English and Scotch ballads; or got music composed in the same taste. But, in fact, such sort of compositions scarce deserve the name of music at all; at least they can have little or no merit on the stage; where everything ought to be supported by a degree of action and character.

In fact none of the song tunes are English or Scotch. No less than five are by Vento. I have not been able to find an origin for any of the *Daphne and Amintor* songs under his name, and it seems probable that he set Bickerstaffe's lyrics on commission specially for Drury Lane. There are other instances of his setting English words, including a poem by Oliver Goldsmith lamenting the death of George III's mother. The overture to *Daphne and Amintor* is attributed in the score to 'Mr. Shalon', whom I take to be John Chalon. Chalon published some harpsichord sonatinas in London this same year, and was presumably French or of French origin. His overture (see p. 292) has considerable quality; indeed most of the music in this opera is of interest.[1]

7 THE PROPORTION OF OPERAS TO PLAYS IN THE 1760s

In no decade of the eighteenth century did the playhouses stage so many new full-length operas as in the 1760s. These operas have been so persistently ignored by both musical and theatrical historians that it will be salutary to list them here. The composer's name is put first; P. stands for Pastiche. Full-length all-sung operas:

1762	*Artaxerxes* (T. A. Arne–T. A. Arne)	CG
1764	*Midas* (?–O'Hara)	CG
	The Royal Shepherd (Rush–Rolt)	DL
	Almena (M. Arne and Battishill–Rolt)	DL
1765	*Pharnaces* (Bates–Hull)	DL
1768	*Oithona* (Barthelemon–?)	LT

[1] The borrowed items come from Galuppi's *Il mondo della luna*, Cocchi's *La Clemenza di Tito*, Piccini's *Il Tutore e Pupilla*, Monsigny's *Le Maître en droit*, and *On ne s'avise jamais tout*.

Full-length Dialogue Operas:

1762	*Love in a Village* (P. arr. T. A. Arne–Bickerstaffe)	CG
1764	*The Capricious Lovers* (Rush–Lloyd)	DL
	The Guardian Outwitted (T. A. Arne–T. A. Arne)	CG
1765	*The Maid of the Mill* (P. arr. Arnold–Bickerstaffe)	CG
	The Summer's Tale (P. arr. Arnold–Cumberland)	CG
1766	*The Accomplished Maid* (Piccini–Toms)	CG
1767	*Cymon* (M. Arne–Garrick)	DL
	Love in the City (P. arr. Dibdin–Bickerstaffe)	CG
	The Royal Merchant (Linley–various)	CG
1768	*Lionel and Clarissa* (P. arr. Dibdin–Bickerstaffe)	CG
1769	*Tom Jones* (P. arr. Arnold and/or Arne–Reed)	CG

If it be felt that only the all-sung opera is a true test of musical taste, then the remarkable number of all-sung afterpiece operas must also be considered.

1760	*Thomas and Sally* (T. A. Arne–Bickerstaffe)	CG
	Tears and Triumphs of Parnassus (Stanley–Lloyd)	DL
	The Enchanter (Smith–Garrick)	DL
1761	*Arcadia* (Stanley–Lloyd)	DL
1764	*Hymen* (M. Arne–Allen)	DL
	The Shepherd's Artifice (Dibdin–Dibdin)	CG
1765	*The Choice of Apollo* (Yates–Potter)	LT
1766	*The Cunning Man* (Rousseau–Burney)	DL
1767	*Rosamond* (Arnold–Addison)	CG
1768	*The Judgment of Paris* (Barthelemon–Schomberg)	LT
	The Royal Garland (Arnold–Bickerstaffe)	CG
1769	*The Ephesian Matron* (Dibdin–Bickerstaffe)	RG

We have still to add afterpiece operas with dialogue such as Dibdin's *The Padlock* and a number of pantomimes. These lists can be broken down in several ways. There were seventeen full-length operas in the decade, nearly two a year, and eighteen all-sung operas. There were at least forty new operatic works of some kind or other, excluding pantomimes.

It may be objected that a number of these operas were unsuccessful. But this would be equally true of a list of plays first given in this decade. If we consider the total number of performances, the proportion of opera is still striking. *The London Stage* offers very detailed statistics on this subject,[1] and they fully support my point even though some operas have been incorrectly classed as plays. At Covent Garden during the Garrick period (1747–76) the following were the most frequently performed mainpieces:

The Beggar's Opera	255
Romeo and Juliet	188

[1] *LS* Part 4, i, p. clxii ff.

Love in a Village	183
Richard III	113
The Provok'd Husband	102
Comus	94
The Maid of the Mill	94

There are four operas in the first seven. Naturally the proportion at Drury Lane is very different, for this theatre had no Beard or Miss Brent to offer; there is only one musical piece in the first seven—*The Beggar's Opera*, which stands second to *Romeo and Juliet*. However, if we turn to afterpiece operas, Drury Lane shows up better than one would expect:

The Anatomist	157
Lethe	155
The Jubilee	152
The Devil to pay	144
The Padlock	142
High Life below Stairs	140
Miss in her 'Teens	127
The Chaplet	127

If we count *The Jubilee* as an opera, the proportion is four out of eight. At Covent Garden in this period the top two afterpieces were both operatic: *Thomas and Sally* and Henry Carey's *The Contrivances*. At both theatres pantomime performances far outstripped all other afterpieces, Burney's *Queen Mab* leading at Drury Lane with 261, and *Harlequin Sorcerer* (as revised by Arne) at Covent Garden with 337. If pantomimes be included, there were more musical items staged in the Garrick period than straight plays, and even without them the emphasis on opera is very remarkable, especially when it is remembered that there was *no* such emphasis for the first fifteen years of Garrick's reign.

9

The One-composer Dialogue Opera
1764–1776

1 RUSH, MICHAEL ARNE, AND LINLEY

IN spite of the fashion for pastiche operas with spoken dialogue, there were always composers who preferred to write all the music themselves. *The Capricious Lovers* (DL 28.11.64) had music by Rush and a libretto written in the Fleet Prison by Robert Lloyd. Lloyd's father, who was Under-Master at Westminster School, had rescued his one-time pupil Charles Churchill from debt, and accordingly when Lloyd was imprisoned for the same inadequacy Churchill did what he could to help, though with his slender means and wild tastes this was not very much. On 4 November 1764 Churchill died aged only thirty-two. Lloyd, a year younger, found the effort of living too great, and despite the production of *The Capricious Lovers* in the interval, he killed himself in prison on December 15. His friend Colman must have staged *The Capricious Lovers* partly in the hope of arresting Lloyd's melancholy.[1]

The libretto was based on one of the most popular French operas of the century, *Ninette à la Cour*, a setting of Favart's words by Duni. The same libretto was drawn on for Giordani's *Phillis at Court* (Dublin 1767) and Arne's *Phoebe at Court* (LT 1776). None of the adaptors seems to have used Duni's music. The basic situation is rather like that of *Giselle*. A disguised prince tries to wean a country girl, Phoebe, from her country lover, and carries her off to court hoping to make a fine lady of her. He fails. Of some interest is the scene in which Lisetta, one of the Court attendants, tells Phoebe what to expect of Italian opera. The dialogue is verbose and under-pointed, but eventually Lisetta

---

[1] His Poetical Works (2 vols.) were published ten years later. *The Actor* is an interesting source of information about contemporary stage gesture; it quickly led to two similar and more famous poems, Churchill's *The Rosciad* and Hugh Kelly's *Thespis*.

illustrates the confusion of opposite emotions to which she has been referring by singing an aria whose words are an excellent parody of the real thing.

> Tho' thunder in thy accents roll,
> No fear shall shake my daring soul;
> O tyrant, grumble, rant, and rave,
> My spirit scorns to be thy slave.
> But pity lends her soothing aid;
> Can I forsake my tender maid?
> O tyrant, vain is thy decree,
> Her mournful looks are death to me

This perceptive nonsense is not matched by equally perceptive music. Yet in general Rush's score is an improvement on *The Royal Shepherd*. The overture has a short slow movement full of melancholy charm; the tune was surely played by an oboe:

Though the last movement is in the over-used three-eight formula, the main tune has a touch of individuality. The songs vary from the Italianate to the English in style. Three times Rush uses a 'Mozartian' sequence of great beauty which he probably got from J. C. Bach.[1]

The Guardian Outwitted (CG 12.12.64) is a title that could be given to many dozen comic operas of this and the following century. Arne's libretto, though

---

[1] See the songs on pp. 19, 20, and 27 of the vocal score.

praised by Allardyce Nicoll, is rather undistinguished. He always denied having written it, perhaps because of an untruth in the Preface, in which he claimed it as the first he had ever published; he did not care to remember *Don Saverio*. As Victor put it,

> Dr. Arne . . . was the composer of the songs but denies being the Author of this strange medley Performance: His appearing the first night at the Harpsichord to attend to his Music, as usual, brought this Disgrace upon him, and the Minor Critics on this information alone abused him unmercifully.

The disappointment, following on the gratifying success of *Artaxerxes* and *Love in a Village*, must have been extreme, and it may have had something to do with Arne's strange avoidance of the playhouses for the next five years. Brooding on the failure, he wrote an anonymous 'Elegy on the Death of the Guardian Outwitted', parodying Gray's 'Elegy' verse by verse. 'Pensive Arne' stands for 'storied urn', and there are other touches of mild felicity.[1] The published vocal score has a pleasing overture, and a fine song for Miss Brent, 'Oh how great is the Vexation', but much of the music is rather dull.

The music Arne's son wrote for *Cymon* (DL 2.1.67) is duller still, yet this opera was prodigiously successful. One cannot help thinking that Garrick's tongue was in his cheek when he wrote this preposterous five-act libretto on an Arthurian theme. It derived from Dryden's 'Cymon and Iphigenia', and allowed for a great many grand processions and a great deal of armour. Garrick was careful not to include a part for himself. His friend John Hoadly was sufficiently worried to write to him about *Cymon*.

> The character, and the scenery, etc. of the rest may support it through two or three acts at the most; but surely nothing full of Urgandas and Merlins can be drawn out longer, to keep a sensible audience pleased.

Garrick knew that his audience was often not sensible at all, and Drury Lane made a great deal of money from the venture. There were sixty-four performances in seven seasons, and as late as 1827 there was a Covent Garden revival with a new overture by Bishop. The old one had been a shapeless piece of invention. Michael Arne either did not care for sonata form or had not yet noticed it in the overtures of others. The arias, though on a grand scale, lack character and interest. No doubt audiences sat through them and waited for the next procession.

Not much more will be said of Michael Arne. After the success of *Cymon*, he devoted more time to chemistry than music, having the notion that he was destined to discover the Philosophers' Stone; no doubt the early death of his wife in 1769 helped to push him into a morbid way of life. However he roused

---

[1] One of the verses is quoted on p. 257.

himself in 1772, when he took a pupil, Ann Venables, to Hamburg for a performance of *Messiah* that he directed; next year he wrote her a set of Vauxhall songs and married her. But he was soon engaged once more in the transmutation of metals, both in the laboratory he built for himself in Chelsea and later near Dublin. In 1779 he was in the debtors' prison in Dublin, where he composed *The Artifice* for Covent Garden with the help of a piano supplied by Michael Kelly's father,[1] but the music was never published, and his only success in the last nineteen years of his life was the pantomime, *The Choice of Harlequin* (CG 1781), his last work. He died insane in 1786.

A new composer, Thomas Linley of Bath (1733–95), contrived his first opera, *The Royal Merchant* (CG 14.12.67), by adding songs to a popular blank-verse play closely based on *The Beggar's Bush* by Beaumont and Fletcher. The scene is Flanders, and Fletcher's plot was, perhaps, the first that presented a band of beggars in a favourable light[2]. The beggars have five songs in the original,[3] but Thomas Hull replaced most of these lyrics with some by himself. The characters were conscientiously dressed in Flemish costumes of the period, but the diarist Silas Neville found the opera 'trifling and childish, and barren of incident and character'. Certainly the music is rather undistinguished, except perhaps for the overture. As we shall find later, Linley was one of the very few English composers interested in adventurous and freely-modulating development sections, and there is a good example in the first movement of *The Royal Merchant* overture. The key is D major, and the modulations include a brief exploration of C sharp major, a flight of fancy that would not have occurred to Arne. Similarly a song in B flat, 'Hope to me thy aid extend', includes a passage in D flat. But in general the songs are fairly simple in form; as in most Linley operas, roughly half of them are strophic. One sung by Shuter is for a drunk, and the word 'Hicc' is frequently cued into the vocal line. There are hardly any ensembles, and there is no Finale at the end.

At this period Linley seems to have had few ambitions as regards the London playhouses. He always returned with relief to his home in Bath, and he did not resign himself to the theatre world until 1775.

2   DIBDIN AT DRURY LANE

Because of his autobiographical writings, we know more about Charles Dibdin than we do of any other English composer of his century. His *Musical Tour* (1788) and *Professional Life* (1803) are outrageously padded and factually un-reliable, but for the most part they are delightfully readable. Dibdin's disdain for dates is charmingly expressed in *The Musical Tour*.[4]

---

[1] Kelly i, p. 14. 2nd ed.
[2] See page 105.
[3] See *Pills* v, pp. 302 and 330; these settings were for revivals in 1687 and 1706.
[4] p. 15.

Some readers remember nothing but the chronological parts, and it does not signify three-pence by what means this Queen happened to be ravished, or that Emperor flayed alive, so that they can give a faithful account of the time such an event took place.

Dibdin could not accuse himself of so doing; almost all his dates are wrong. Yet he does tell us a great deal about his own music; also about his dislike, at times vitriolic, for Garrick, Sheridan, and Linley at Drury Lane and for Harris at Covent Garden. His inability to get on with other people in the theatre world is important because it wrecked his career.

His career was further impeded by events he inevitably glosses over in his own writings. His marriage about 1764 was the first of his failures; he was already eyeing a Covent Garden pantomime dancer called Harriet Pitt whose mother, Mrs. Pitt, was a well-known actress in elderly parts. At least by 1767 Dibdin had deserted his wife and was living with Harriet. The liaison lasted intermittently for nearly eight years, during which time two sons were born, Charles Isaac Mungo in 1768 and Thomas in 1771. Each was to make a name for himself in the theatre. Garrick is said to have been Thomas's godfather, and he certainly agitated when Dibdin deserted Harriet and took up with another Drury Lane actress, Miss Wilde. Such behaviour seemed bad even by theatre standards, and it was also ruinously expensive. By the summer of 1776 Dibdin was £800 in debt, and when those to whom he owed money became aggressive he fled to France. His two years abroad began when he was thirty-one, and they divide his career into two parts that are unequal in every way. Before he left England, Dibdin wrote all his best theatre music. After his return he was briefly on contract to Covent Garden, but by 1782 all the main playhouses regarded him as unemployable. He had to make his living in other ways.

Dibdin's music is wholly *galante* in style. His knowledge of counterpoint was rudimentary and his harmony unadventurous, but he had all the *galante* tricks of melody and orchestration, as well as one asset that was especially unusual in England. This was his ability to write a vocal line that reflected the dramatic situation. His best airs encourage the singer to act as well as sing, and thus they keep the drama alive instead of freezing it as in most of Arne's opera songs. Dibdin was especially good at blusters and flusters, and though he wrote too many such songs in a quick six-eight and too often repeated immediately a two- or four-bar phrase, his continental contemporaries were doing so too. He was the first of our composers to attempt the Italianate Finale in several sections in which the plot is carried forward, and his dramatically-felt vocal lines give these Finales a buoyancy we find in no other English operas before those of Storace. He was uncertain as to pure melody in arias of sentiment, and at his most casual he often wrote near-nonsense, but in his best years his music is good-humoured, adroit, and alive. By nature, though not by education, he was at least as well fitted to write comic operas as Paisiello or Cimarosa.

Dibdin's best years were all at Drury Lane. He transferred to this theatre in the summer of 1768, with the help of Mrs. Garrick who was so impressed by what he showed her of his latest afterpiece, *The Padlock*, that (as the dedication puts it) she brought him 'out of obscurity . . . to the Notice and Favour of Mr. Garrick'. She even suggested improvements in the music. Dibdin was on contract to Drury Lane for seven years, and he persuaded Bickerstaffe to transfer to this theatre as well. From now on, with unimportant exceptions, Dibdin composed all the music in his operas himself, instead of being submerged in pastiches as at Covent Garden. For the first and only time in his career Garrick had a composer of real promise who brought good money into the theatre. *The Padlock* (DL 3.10.68) should have heralded a highly successful career.

The chief event of Dibdin's first autumn at Drury Lane was the state visit to London of the nineteen-year-old King of Denmark, Christian VII. Two years earlier he had married Caroline Matilda, George III's youngest sister, but to everyone's surprise he did not bring his wife with him. He was very small, mentally unstable, and insatiable as regards mistresses. But it was Caroline Matilda's infidelity that later became notorious. In 1772 she was arrested with her lover, a German doctor called Struensee. In public and with tumultuous publicity, he was beheaded, drawn, and quartered. The young Queen's death three years later may have been due to poison. By this time Christian VII was insane.

However in 1768 he was fully capable of enjoying the London playhouses, and in the course of six visits to Drury Lane he saw *The Padlock* twice, no doubt because Bickerstaffe had dedicated the libretto to him. Bickerstaffe got the plot from Cervantes,[1] and the very first song shows a new spirit in English opera. The curtain rises on Don Diego, the usual old gentleman of comic opera, who is wondering whether or not to marry his ward Leonora.

> Thoughts to council—let me see—
> Hum—to be, or not to be
> A husband, is the question.
> A cuckold! Must that follow?

In verse 2 he decides that if he keeps his house well locked he can risk it; he ends:

> Then horns, horns, I defy you.

Thus in the very first song something happens, the plot moves forward. Dibdin's setting, unimpressive as pure music, follows the changing emotions of the words with delightful aptness, and the word setting is unexpectedly sophisticated.

---

[1] Genest says from 'The Jealous Estremaduran', and adds that Bickerstaffe altered the end.

Dibdin

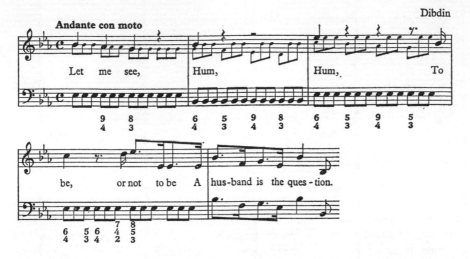

Let me see, Hum, Hum, To be, or not to be A hus-band is the ques-tion.

For the 'cuckold' line the tempo quickens to *Allegro,* and for the agitation of verse 2 there is a switch to a typical Dibdin six-eight *Presto,* with the horns bubbling away to point the last line.

We first see Leonora singing tenderly to a tame bird she has on her finger.

> Say, little, foolish, flutt'ring thing,
> Whither, ah! whither would you wing
> Your airy flight?

A piccolo represents the bird whose situation is so like Leonora's; the song is by implication a Simile Aria, and though uneven the best bits are lovely. After a vigorous song about a man being as old as he feels, Don Diego goes off to tell Leonora's parents that he proposes to wed her the next day. He takes the precaution of giving the elderly maid, Ursula, six keys with which to protect Leonora's virtue, and of telling his negro servant Mungo to keep awake all night in case of any intrusion. Mungo's first entrance carrying a hamper is managed with dialogue that must have sounded delightfully fresh and unusual at the time.

Mungo. Go, get you down, you damn hamper, you carry me now. Curse my old Massa, sending me always here and dere for one something to make me tire like a mule—curse him imperance—and him damn insurance.

Diego. How now.

Mungo. Ah, Massa, bless your heart.

Diego. What's that you're muttering, Sirrah?

Mungo. Noting, Massa, only me say, you very good Massa.

Diego. What do you leave your load down there for?

Mungo. Massa, me lilly tire.

Diego. Take it up, rascal.

Mungo. Yes, bless your heart, Massa.

When at last the old man goes, Mungo has a splendid song some of which anticipates Figaro's in *The Barber of Seville* by Rossini. 'What e'er's to be done,' he
sings, 'Poor Black must run'. And then:

As will be expected, there is a brisk young student at the local university who
has heard about Leonora's beauty from Mungo. Leander appears outside the
house disguised as a one-legged beggar, and Ursula is all for letting him in to
divert them with his guitar songs, but they find that without telling anyone Don
Diego has clapped a great padlock on the front door so that no one can get either
in or out. Ursula is furious at not being trusted, and in the 'action' Finale to Act I
(there are five short contrasted sections) she shows the 'beggar' how to get over the
garden wall.

Act II takes place in the house, and to Ursula's shocked delight, Leander has
removed his disguise. He bribes her with both money and pretended admiration
to unlock Leonora. Ursula becomes amusingly amorous. Mungo has a song
accompanied in part by Leander's guitar, and Leonora a delightful one with words
deranged by agitation. Leander takes her into the garden. The stage empty, Don
Diego returns unexpectedly, to find Mungo emerging from the cellar the worse
for drink. Mungo lets out that Leander is on the premises. However, when confronted with the truth, Don Diego realizes he has been silly, and all ends happily
with a Vaudeville in the now usual six-eight rhythm.

Vernon and Mrs. Michael Arne played the young lovers, but after three
weeks the latter was attacked by the illness from which she died the next year,
and she was replaced by Miss Radley. The part is a high one, with some top Ds.
Charles Bannister was Don Diego. Mungo had been written for Moody, who
had been in the West Indies, and 'knew the dialect of the negroes',[1] but Dibdin
realized he was a poor singer, and made the songs too difficult for him to prevent
his undertaking the role. Dibdin wanted it for himself, but before he got it
Mungo was offered to Dodd, who was expected to play the part only two or
three days before the first night. No doubt he too found he could not sing the
songs. Dibdin made Mungo the talk of London.

There were fifty-four performances of *The Padlock* in the first season, and
more than a hundred in three years; the popularity of the piece lasted well into

---

[1] Dibdin, *Professional Life* i, p. 70.

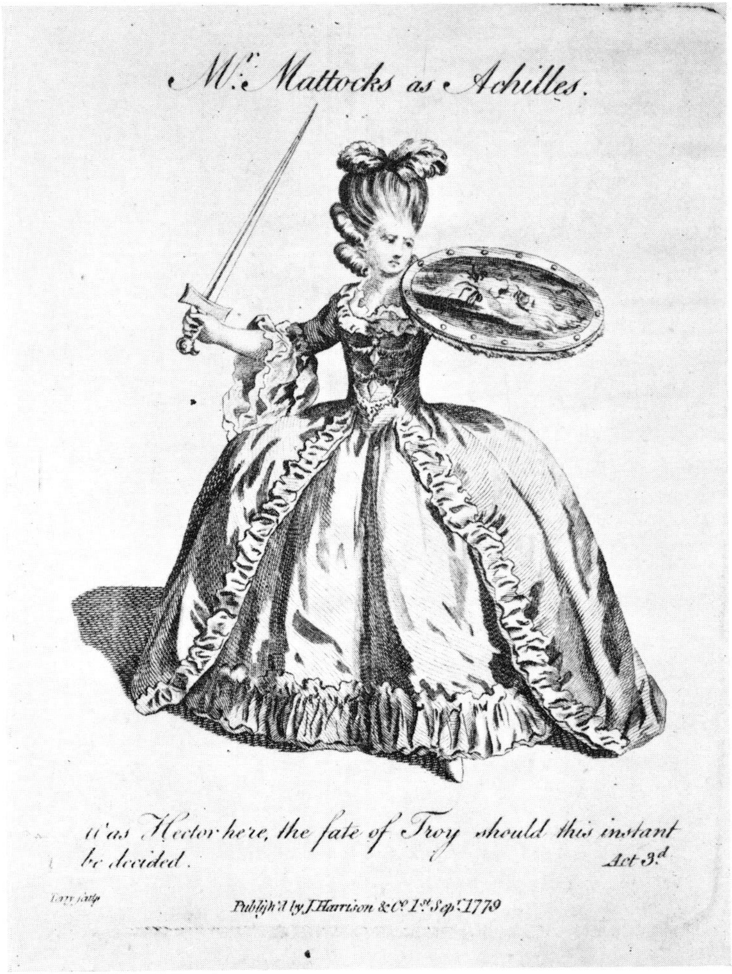

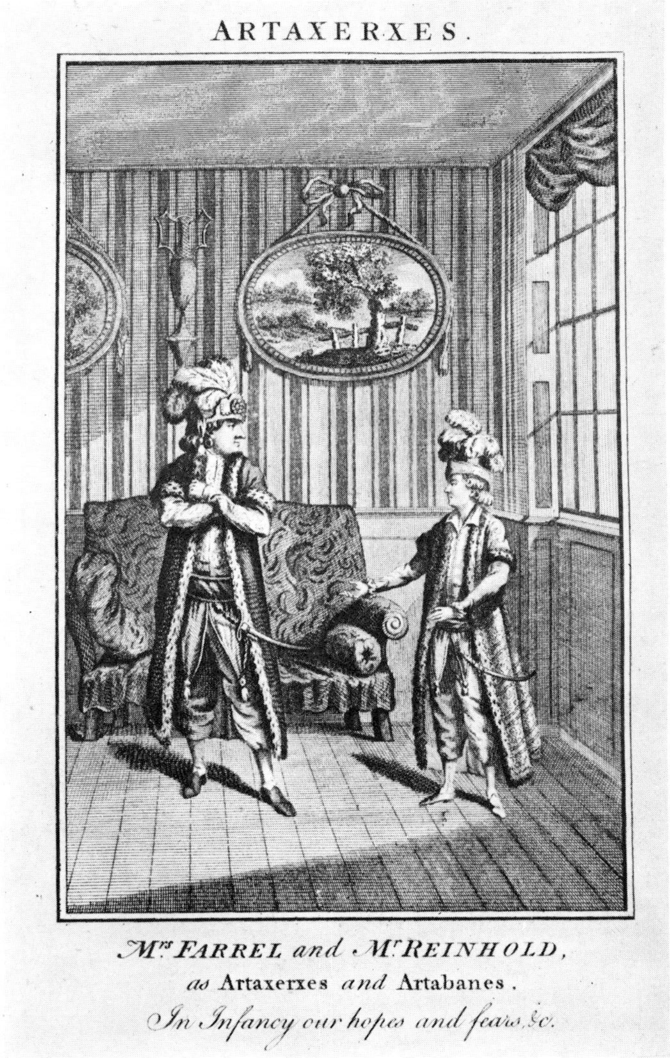

Stage costumes at Covent Garden in the late 1770s.
(See p. 255.)

Dibdin as Mungo in his own *The Padlock* (1768).

the next century. Bickerstaffe's libretto is neatly contrived and well characterized; Mungo and Ursula have especially rewarding parts. Nearly all the music
is well above Dibdin's run-of-the-mill level, and it is sad that none of it should
survive in the original scoring except for the overture.

After wasting his time refurbishing an old ballad opera, *Damon and Phillida*
(DL 21.12.68), Dibdin spent the following spring and summer writing music
for three different types of entertainment to be given in three different places.
The Padlock had made him in demand everywhere.

The first of these entertainments was Garrick's famous Shakespeare Festival
at Stratford, an event that was washed out by torrential rain. It sparked off the
ill-feeling between Garrick and Dibdin that was increasingly to bedevil their
association.

> I was a slave to it for months. I set and reset the songs to it till my patience
> was exhausted, which were received or rejected just as ignorance or
> caprice prevailed . . . at last I was so palpably insulted that I declared I
> would not go to Stratford.[1]

What palpably insulted him was the discovery that Garrick, with his usual
infuriating prudence, had asked Aylward and Boyce to set his verses as well, so
that he could choose the best settings. In fact he chose Dibdin's, and in the end
Dibdin did go to Stratford. The day began with his Serenade being sung at 6 a.m.
in the streets to the accompaniment of flutes and guitars. Other songs of his
were sung both in the streets and in the Great Booth, where the speeches and
the food were also competing for attention. 'The Warwickshire Lad' and 'Sweet
Willy-O' were especially popular; we would not care to honour Shakespeare in
such terms today, but the tributes were sincerely meant. More formal performances were given of a Dibdin cantata with words by Bickerstaffe called
Queen Mab (it was published virtually in full score) and of Arne's *Ode upon
Dedicating a Building to Shakespeare*, parts of which were very good indeed.
Incredibly, nothing by Shakespeare was performed.[2]

The following autumn Garrick devised a dramatic framework for the procession of Shakespeare characters and the music that had been seen and heard at
Stratford, and *The Jubilee* (DL 14.10.69) enjoyed the longest consecutive
London run of the century; there were ninety-one performances in the one
season. It was of course the visual side of the entertainment that was most talked
about, but there was a great deal of music to accompany the processions and the
dancing, and much of it was published. Seven of Dibdin's songs had appeared
before the first night in two slight volumes called *Shakespeare's Garland*, and
sets of his minuets and country dances were also available. When it was realized
that *The Jubilee* would be liked, most of this music, together with an overture
and the *Queen Mab* cantata, appeared in one volume. There was never a libretto,

[1] Dibdin's *Professional Life* i, p. 78.
[2] See Johanne M. Stockholm's *Garrick's Folly* (London 1964).

but the Larpent copy shows that the entertainment began with Stratford residents complaining of the coming celebrations (as indeed they had done), one thinking the Pope was behind it, and another the Young Pretender. What followed consisted mainly of a description of the procession of Shakespeare characters, and the song words. As Hopkins put it 'There was never an Entertainment that gave so much Pleasure to all Degrees, Boxes, Pit and Gallery'.

That summer Dibdin was engaged at Ranelagh Gardens as both composer and singer, and he and Bickerstaffe quickly created *The Ephesian Matron* (RG 12.5.69). According to the libretto preface they were imitating such Italian pieces as *La Serva Padrona*—by which they meant it was all-sung (as by law it had to be at Ranelagh). There can have been no scenery in what was virtually a bandstand, but *The Ephesian Matron* is fully dramatic in intention, and it was later staged at the Little Theatre (31.8.69; 'never acted before') and in 1771 at Drury Lane. According to the libretto,

> The Scene is supposed to lie in a Tomb, near the City of Ephesus. A Lamp burning; on one side a dead Body. The MATRON clasping her Husband's Corps; her Father and her MAID endeavouring to force her away.

In a panting *presto* trio Dibdin ingeniously conveys the Matron's exaggerated grief and basic insincerity. No one can comfort her, and she announces that she will stay in the tomb for ever. To prove that she is inconsolable, she sings a ridiculous 'Mad Song'. That night, however, she cheers up a little when a centurion guarding the bodies on the gibbets outside comes down to investigate the light burning in the tomb. 'What ho, charming Dame, what ho', he sings jovially, and he is soon revealing other attributes besides a good appearance.

> *Centurion:* A flask of wine I've got by stealth—
> 'Tis strong and old—
> Against the cold
> Upon my post this night has fenced me.
> *Matron:* I vow, and swear, it goes against me,
> However, sir, your health!

When the centurion finds that one of the bodies outside has been stolen (by relatives for proper burial), the Matron saves the situation by generously offering her husband's body in its place, and by the end of the opera all her sounds of woe have been converted into Hey nonny, nonny. The plot will be familiar to modern theatre-goers for its use in Christopher Fry's *A Phoenix too Frequent*; it comes from the *Satyricon* by Petronius where it is revealed that the bodies on the gibbets were those of early Christians, strung up as an example to the neighbourhood.

Though never much liked in its own day, *The Ephesian Matron* is a minor masterpiece. Apart from a poor overture and finale, both words and music are irresistible, and the lack of a full score is more than ever a calamity. The Matron was played by the beautiful Mrs. Baddeley, the Centurion by Dibdin himself. For a playhouse revival Dibdin added a second song for the Father; it is bound up with the British Museum vocal score. It is not very interesting, and it would unnecessarily delay the action.

Dibdin spent the autumn rewriting *Lionel and Clarissa*, and it was staged at Drury Lane under its sub-title, *The School for Fathers* (DL 8.2.70), with Vernon and Mrs. Baddeley in the title roles, and Dibdin (sometimes Dodd) and Mrs. Wrighten as Jessamy and Diana. The revision was not only due to Dibdin's natural wish to write most of the music himself. In the anonymous preface to the libretto, Bickerstaffe says the alterations were necessary because Garrick was bringing out a new soprano—Mrs. Wrighten—and because some of the cast had different compasses from those Dibdin had written for originally. Most of the new songs were for Clarissa and Jessamy. Hopkins wrote of Mrs. Wrighten: 'A very fine Voice—Aukward & Clumsy Figure—well faced'. Some of her songs were very hard, with a high tessitura and a great many top B flats.

A new vocal score and libretto were published, and today the Drury Lane version of each is much commoner than the original. In Appendix E I have tried to show in what way they differ. The new engraver, faced with problems that had not previously come his way, confused Covent Garden and Drury Lane singers and made a great muddle of 'The Table of the Songs' on page 1.

For some reason Dibdin wrote a new overture; the outer movements are a decided improvement, but the original slow one is the better. It is not often that one can praise Dibdin's instrumental music, but there is a remarkable episode in the first movement at the point where later composers would have had a development section. It consists of a long and expressive oboe solo with the strings moving below in quaver sixths. There must also have been a simple bass, but the engraver left it out because he could not see how to make it playable by two hands. It can easily be reconstructed. In the body of the opera there are plenty of ebullient songs of the usual type, and though their character cannot be conveyed in short extracts, one of Dibdin's six-eight songs must be represented for the sake of a balanced view. Here is Colonel Oldboy addressing with distaste his own son, Jessamy:

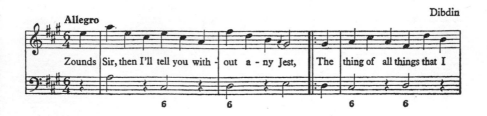

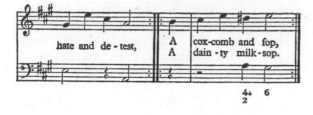

Diana has three large-scale arias of extreme difficulty, the best being 'Ladies, ladies' in Act II, which is almost a cantata in three movements. Elsewhere there is more lyrical writing than usual. Clarissa's 'Immortal Powers', which comes in both versions, is lovely, though much of importance is clearly missing from the accompaniment as given in the vocal score. There are also lyrical sections in the splendid Finales to Acts I and II, each of which is headed 'Quintetto'. The small notes below are editorial, but the original must have had something of the sort.

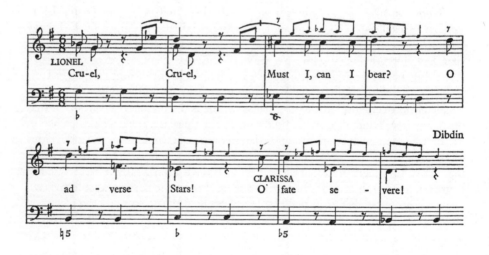

The above episode from the middle of the first Quintetto leads eventually into a quotation from Handel's *Alexander's Feast*, called for by Bickerstaffe's quoting of the Dryden words, 'None but the brave deserve the fair'. The second Quintetto begins well, and also has several well-contrasted sections. Inevitably Dibdin often draws on his predecessors, as did all *galante* composers. For the maid, Jenny, he wrote a jaunty little song to replace a rather poor setting of the same words by Arne, and the new one is none the worse for its use of galante clichés:

Such phrases were common property all over Europe. Dibdin managed a love duet at the end that shows an emotional feeling rare not only for him but for any other opera composer of his day. Not a note of *Lionel and Clarissa* survives in orchestral form, apart from some of the items borrowed from Italian opera. It is incomparably the best of his full-length operas.

Covent Garden made some attempt to combat the Drury Lane production, staging their own *Lionel and Clarissa* with Miss Catley as Clarissa and some new songs by Fisher, and this version was revived in 1777–9. But most of the revivals for the rest of the century were at Drury Lane. At York in 1783 the part of Lionel was played by Mrs. Jordan, who for once gave the part 'sensible utterance', according to her biographer James Boaden. Michael Kelly played Lionel in Dublin as a boy, with O'Keeffe, the future playwright, as Jessamy, and he repeated it often in London on his return from Vienna. In 1814 Bishop wrote or adapted some new songs for the opera, and they can be found in a MS volume at the Royal College of Music. Bickerstaffe would not have approved of his introduction of a Welsh and a Scotch tune, nor Mozart of what was done to Clarissa's 'Hope and Fear'. Bishop did not care for Dibdin's introduction for two clarinets followed by two horns, so he wrote out the first few bars of 'Dove sono' from *Figaro*, and these led straight into Dibdin's vocal section which happens to be in the same key and tempo. In our own century *Lionel and Clarissa* has endured the ministrations of Nigel Playfair and Alfred Reynolds, and it has also received more veracious performances on the Third Programme. If a full score survived, it would surely be in the Sadler's Wells repertoire.

The following summer Dibdin and Bickerstaffe wrote *The Recruiting Sergeant* for Ranelagh Gardens (20.7.70). As in *The Ephesian Matron*, the songs are linked by recitative and the characters are limited to four, two of each sex, but the result is much less interesting. The uneventful plot never comes to life. The score contains two superb songs and a number of poor ones, and it is tragic that this and not its predecessor was published in full score. Nevertheless *The*

Recruiting Sergeant was more successful than *The Ephesian Matron*. It was later given isolated performances at both winter playhouses and more numerous ones at Marylebone Gardens (1776) and Palmer's ill-fated Royalty Theatre (1787). Recruiting Sergeants were familiar and perhaps fascinating figures. In a theatre they had to be shown as necessary evils, yet the Sergeant's *tour de force* song in praise of war is ambivalent with its element of the ridiculous:

> O what a charming thing's a battle!
> Trumpets sounding, drums a-beating:
> Crack, crick, crack, the cannons rattle,
> Every heart with joy elating.
> With what pleasure are we spying
> From the front and from the rear,
> Round us in the smoky air,
> Heads, and limbs, and bullets, flying!
> Then the groans of soldiers dying;
> Just like sparrows, as it were,
> At each pop,
> Hundreds drop . . .

This is a song to bring the house down; Dibdin is here at his most vigorous. But equally good is the rangey individual tune with which the Countryman's young Wife pleads for him not to be recruited: 'O could you bear to view Your little Tom and Sue'.

The full score of *The Recruiting Sergeant* is less full than it pretends. The indifferent overture is given complete, with staves for horns and for oboes alternating with flutes, but there are no wind parts in any of the songs. In fact the engraver was saving space and expense, for in a British Museum MS (Add. 30951) there are oboe and horn parts for two of the songs. The Sergeant's big aria must surely have had trumpet and drum parts as well as woodwind.

The Recruiting Sergeant was the last opera libretto that Bickerstaffe wrote. As Garrick mentioned in a letter written just after the scandal, his friends had been noticing peculiarities in his behaviour for some time; the letter also provides some details of the unfortunate affair that led to his fleeing the country, and Garrick wrote it within a few days of the event:

> My Wife & I have long thought him to be out of his Mind—he has hurry'd away in the midst of Conversation, without any apparent reason for it—the Story they tell, if true, is a most unaccountable one; but the Watch, Seal & Ring are in the Soldier's hands & B—would not claim them, but absconded—this business has hurt me greatly as well as my Wife, the Stage has a great loss.[1]

[1] Letter 688 (19.5.72).

Inevitably it was to France that Bickerstaffe fled. He had been to Paris at least twice,[1] and his French was good enough for him to write about the London theatres for a Paris publisher. It was in French that he wrote to Garrick from St. Malo in June, and Garrick scribbled on it 'from that poor wretch Bickerstaffe —I could not answer it'. However there is some evidence that he did answer later letters Bickerstaffe wrote from abroad, and it is probable that he sent him money for at least one dramatic work that he covertly accepted. Baker and others thought Bickerstaffe the author of *The Spoiled Child* (1790), in which Mrs. Jordan played Little Pickle, and thereby added a word to our language.

3 THOMAS ARNE'S LAST OPERAS

With Dibdin starting a period of inactivity, we can turn to the last theatre works of Thomas Arne, the only contemporary musician for whom Dibdin ever expressed admiration. There is a Cox and Box element about Arne and Dibdin at this time. While one slept the other worked, and it is an indication of Arne's basic instability that his return to theatre music between 1770 and 1772 should have been divided between all three playhouses. Like Dibdin at a later period, he was virtually unemployable. Yet his truculence did not prevent him from writing some of his most delightful music.

In the summer of 1770 Garrick decided that the success of *Cymon* warranted a similarly lavish armour-and-banners production of Purcell's *King Arthur*, and as, through no fault of his own, he was on equally bad terms with both Arne and Dibdin, he had nothing to lose by turning to the more musicianly of the two for a revision of Purcell's score. Arne had written little or nothing for Drury Lane since 1751. Such neglect would have made some composers especially anxious to please: it made Arne more high-handed than ever.[2] After a disdainful perusal of the original, Arne wrote to tell Garrick which numbers should be kept and which re-composed; he had, of course, a vested interest in the proportion. The Sacrifice Scene at the start, he thought, might still be 'solemn and noble', and he condescended to describe 'Come, if you dare' as 'tolerable' (though not as good as what he had written in its place), but

> All the other Solo Songs of Purcell are infamously bad; so very bad, that they are privately the objects of sneer and ridicule to the musicians . . . I wish you would only give me leave to *Doctor* this performance . . .

He wanted to doctor it to a point of castration, but either Garrick or the singers saw to it that nearly all the best Purcell items were preserved. The music as published shows the Purcell items in full score, Arne's in vocal score, and the

[1] Garrick Letters 402 and 413.
[2] Cummings quotes extensively from his correspondence with Garrick, both during the period of neglect and during the *King Arthur* preparations.

former include a number of pieces Arne had not only damned specifically but actually reset. As he put it in a later and more restrained letter (3.9.75):

> Several other things that employed my utmost efforts, were laid aside, in favour of Purcell's music, which (though excellent in its kind) was Cathedral, and not to the taste of a modern theatrical audience.

The new music included an overture with foolish cuckoo effects on the flute in the first movement, some settings of new words by Garrick, and an effective if grandiose Finale on the 'St. George' words. The only example of a well-known Purcell song being replaced is of interest because it must have been Purcell's usually lauded word-setting that condemned it.

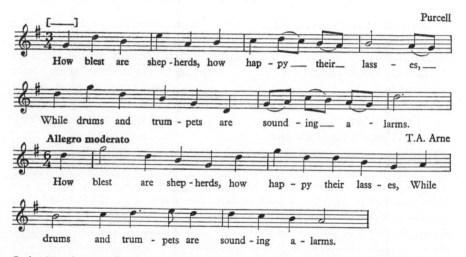

It is Arne's contribution to *King Arthur* that attracts disdain, and it appears from later correspondence that Garrick was a good deal disappointed by it.

Next season Arne was the more anxious for success in that his wife was dunning him for maintenance, and for Covent Garden he composed one of his most delightful afterpieces, *The Fairy Prince* (CG 12.11.71). It was also among his most profitable, for there were thirty-six performances that season, though no revivals subsequently. George Colman, then one of the Covent Garden managers, had got wind of a Drury Lane 'spectacular' called *The Institution of the Garter, or Arthur's Round Table Restored* (DL 28.10.71) which was described as a masque and set at Windsor in the time of Edward III. (A Miss Hopkins played the Black Prince.) Covent Garden must also have its Windsor masque, so Colman rewrote a suitable one by Ben Jonson, introducing references to George III and the eldest of the princes. He was fortunate in arousing Arne's interest; Dibdin, who set *The Institution of the Garter*, had no gift for the choral writing the subject demanded, whereas Arne, as usual at Covent Garden, was in his best form.

Jonson's masques are hard to come by today, but his Collected Works were several times reprinted in the seventeenth and eighteenth centuries. *Oberon, the Fairy Prince* had been first performed in Whitehall Palace on New Year's Day 1611, and Oberon represented and was performed by the young Prince Henry, the ill-fated Prince of Wales. It began with an anti-masque of satyrs before 'a dark Rock, with Trees beyond it, and all wildness, that could be presented'.[1] Then 'the whole scene opened', revealing a palace with transparent walls. Later the palace itself

> open'd, and the Nation of Faies were discover'd . . . and within afar off in perspective, the Knights Masquers sitting in their several Sieges: At the further end of all, OBERON, in a Chariot . . . drawn by two white Bears.

As usual, there was a good deal of speaking as well as songs, dances, and scenic effects.

Colman scarcely altered the first section about the satyrs, and even kept the Stage Direction asking for the First Satyr to 'wind his cornet', though no such instrument can have been available at Drury Lane. When the rock 'opened' it revealed the West Front of St. George's Chapel at Windsor, and Part I ended with a 'vision' of the inside of the chapel 'with the original Knights in their several stalls'. Part 2, which was much shorter, showed the Fairies in the Lower Court of the Castle, the songs being all Jonson and the recitatives all Colman. There is veiled talk of 'solemn rites', and 'the proper Heir.' Finally the Knights process into the Chapel. Part 3, which is very short indeed, shows the fairies in Windsor Park and ends with the installation of the Knights in St. George's Hall and their Dinner there. There is a final chorus about 'great George's name' and 'the Garter's Glory'. Jonson's contribution to this third part is confined to the Fairy duet, 'Nay, nay, you must not stay'.

It will be apparent that the masque did not owe its success to its plot; for that matter it had not done so in 1611. Good music and well presented spectacle were the attractions; also, though decreasingly as the masque went on, Jonson's poetry, which is charmingly light-footed. In 1771 none of it was spoken; the libretto shows that the spoken passages were turned into recitative, and it is sad that the *secco* examples are not given in the published vocal score. Worse still, two choruses are omitted, including the one at the end. The 'Advertisement' that prefaces the libretto reveals that they had words by Gilbert West and Dryden, and in fact the Finale words were adapted from the Finale of *Albion and Albanius*, the all-sung opera Dryden wrote in 1685; the music by Louis Grabu was published in full score. Grabu has been consistently denigrated by those anxious to do their best for Purcell, and it is usually said that *Albion and Albanius* was a total failure. The degree of failure has probably been exaggerated, for BUCEM lists as many as thirteen surviving scores, many more than can be

---

[1] Inigo Jones's imaginative design survives at Chatsworth.

found of any Purcell opera. Grabu was greatly inferior to Purcell in invention, but the Finale of his *Albion and Albanius* might do well enough to end Arne's *Fairy Prince*. The music would sound old-fashioned, but so for that matter would Arne's chorus at the end of Act I.

A glance at Dryden's libretto shows why this lyric came into Colman's mind. Dryden has a stage direction that runs as follows: 'A Vision of the Honours of the Garter; the Knights in Procession, and the King under a Canopy; Beyond this, the upper End of St. George's Hall'. The words Colman borrowed are then sung by Fame and a Chorus, after which there is another Stage direction:

> A full Chorus of all the Voices and Instruments: Trumpets and Ho-boys make Ritornelloes of all Fame sings: and Twenty four Dancers all the time in a Chorus, and Dance to the end of the Opera.

Grabu did not in fact indicate any oboe and trumpet parts; indeed there is nothing in the score that trumpets could play. Had there been Oboe parts, they would have been the earliest in English theatre music. Like Lully, Grabu wrote most of his accompaniments in five parts, presumably for strings, and the middle three are usually dull.

The overture to Arne's *Fairy Prince* was published in parts, and it begins with one of those casually constructed movements that Arne never grew out of, but the second is beautifully lyrical and the last an engaging piece of *galanterie*. The songs are nearly all engraved on three staves, and this allows of more instrumental detail than usual. Arne catches the airy quality of the poetry both with unusual orchestration

T.A. Arne

and with sheer good writing, as in the Wood Nymph's bird song, one of the best of a too-common tribe. There is a rousing Handelian chorus at the end of Part 1,

'God save the King', but the frequent woodwind solos elsewhere show Arne moving with the times. The Fairy Duet, 'Seek you Majesty to strike?' appears to be accompanied solely by clarinets and bassoons.

At the end of the score there is an appendix of dance movements, twelve pieces in all on seven and a half pages. The second piece is marked 'For the entrance of the Sylvans', and it alternates between resolute phrases in D major and plaintive ones in D minor; it then suddenly switches to a 'sprightly' six-eight dance in G, and ends with a four-bar Presto that modulates into B flat. The piece cannot have been intended to stand on its own; it demands a context that makes sense of the opening and closing keys. At first sight this context is provided by the dances that come before and after in the appendix, but a closer study of this appendix shows that the twelve dances cannot have been played consecutively at the end of the opera; they must have come one by one earlier on, and to some extent this is confirmed by the libretto. The trouble is that the titles of the dances in the music are not the same as those in the libretto; Arne must have made up his own titles. All we can claim for them is they do sometimes help to establish a placing. The tonality of the dances should have helped too, but does not in fact help very much because so many of the recitatives that frame the dances are missing. In short the order of the music is not easy to establish. However the attempt is worth making because the music is of high quality; it has been broadcast in the past, and will surely be better broadcast in the future. I have suggested an order in Appendix F. In modern performances the words of the missing recitatives should of course be spoken; indeed Jonson's delightful poetry might make more impact spoken than sung.

Of the performers in *The Fairy Prince* only two need be named. Sylvan was sung by Robert Owenson, a pupil of Arne and the father of Lady Morgan, whose Memoirs are so informative about music in Dublin. The Second Fairy was sung by Miss Brown, the future Mrs. Cargill, making her first stage appearance as a child; four years later her superb singing in *The Duenna* helped that opera towards its prodigious success.

At this period Arne made much of his income from his singing pupils, and he was for ever pushing their alleged merits at the theatre managers so that he could profit from their earnings while they were still his apprentices. To display their virtues he sometimes hired the Little Theatre in the spring for odd nights, putting on a mixed programme of songs stiffened with a short all-sung opera or ode. *Squire Badger* (LT 16.3.72) was such an opera, and it was revived in 1775 as *The Sot*, but none of the playhouses took it up and the music was never published. The libretto was freely based on Fielding's *Don Quixote in England*. On such occasions the entire cast was usually said to be performing in public for the first time, and at one of the 1775 performances this was said of Mrs. Farrel, better known after her second marriage as Mrs. Kennedy.

1772 was a fecund year for Arne. That summer his afterpiece *The Cooper* (LT 10.6.72) had nine performances. The libretto was a translation, presumably by Arne himself, of *Le Tonnelier* (1765), but no use was made of the original music by Gossec. Arne had been giving thought to Dibdin's recent operas, and he went out of his way to advertise the songs as being 'in character'. In fact he was not very adept at such writing, but many of them have his usual brand of lyrical charm. The plot demands five characters and is conventional. Old Martin, the cooper, and young Colin both love Fanny, Martin's ward; Colin gets her. There is a good scene in Act II in the dark, with Fanny waiting alone for her lover. Her accompanied recitative 'He's gone to bed' has some bars of steady crotchets marked 'play to the steps of her feet'. Her song a little later is specially pleasing.

T.A. Arne

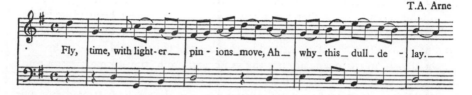

Fly, time, with light-er — pin - ions—move, Ah— why— this— dull— de - lay.—

The Cooper is the only Arne opera of which there is a modern vocal score, and though the Schott edition leaves out two characters (a drunk farmer and Colin's uncle) and needlessly alters countless details, it is better than nothing.

That autumn Arne contributed elaborate music to a production of *Elfrida* (CG 21.11.72), a 'Dramatic Poem' set in Saxon times by William Mason; he had written it in 1751 'on the Model of the Ancient Greek Tragedy', and it had not been intended for the stage. Colman split it into five acts, and the result was not much like the original. 'Little Mr. Colman and old fumbling Dr. Arne', wrote Mason to Lord Nuneham, 'have commited rape on the body of my poor daughter *Friddy* . . . They say she is in very high keeping, & has eight *femmes de chambre* to attend her, & fourteen more to sing her asleep.' To Horace Walpole Mason wrote more angrily: 'Do you not think it somewhat cavalier in Mr. Colman to do what he has done without any previous intimation to me?' He had only heard about the production by chance, and when he got hold of the song-words, he found them 'worse than the productions of Handel's poet, Dr. Morell'. Arne had ruthlessly ironed out Mason's irregular lines by omitting epithets in the longer ones. Mason later made his own stage version, and it was produced in 1779 with music by Giardini that does not survive.

The original was in blank verse, relieved by choruses of 'British Virgins' in which the lines of irregular length occur, and it has considerable merit as literature. Colman arranged for a chorus at the end of each act, and it is at these points that all Arne's music is concentrated. No male singers were required. The vocal music was for three soprano soloists (among them Miss Catley and Mrs. Mattocks) and a two-part women's choir. Some of the acts must have ended with at least fifteen minutes of continuous singing, and the orchestral writing was elaborate. Many pages have so many staves that they are virtually full scores, and the orchestration could easily be reconstructed. An unusual proportion of songs are in a minor key and solidly written. 'Kind Mortals, know', composed for Miss Catley, is long and very difficult, with a high D near the end. There are some good accompanied recitatives, and the score appears to be complete.

The overture is curious in that it starts with seven bars of quiet music in a minor key, and then plunges into the usual loud *galante* clatter in the major:

The minor key theme recurs twice later on. In the Minuet that ends the overture, horns and trumpets play at the same time, and this suggests a larger orchestra than usual. *Elfrida* takes place on 'A Lawn before Athelwold's Castle in Harewood Forest', Athelwold being Elfrida's husband. The only other speaking characters are her father and Edgar, King of England, who falls in love with Elfrida and kills Athelwold. Elfrida thwarts the King by becoming a nun.

Arne's fourth work for the theatre in 1772 was another afterpiece, *The Rose* (DL 2.12.72), and it must be significant that from now on he never had two consecutive operas put on at the same theatre. It is not clear why *The Rose* was ever accepted at Drury Lane, for Hopkins states that 'Mr. Garrick protested against its being performed'; also that it was 'a very dull, insipid Piece—very much hissed, would not suffer it to be given out again'. The music was not printed except for the overture which appeared in parts.[1] The libretto was ostensibly by 'A Gentleman Commoner of Oxford', but Oulton and Baker both thought Arne wrote it himself, the 'Gentleman Commoner' being a form of insurance against failure. It is a very silly libretto. Lord Gainlove is ordered in his father's Will to invite every marriageable girl in the district to his coming-of-age birthday party, and to ask them 'to display the Rose which Time can ne'er decay'. There is some boring speculation as to what this can mean. It turns out that the Rose that never decays is Woman's Virtue, hardly a subject

---

[1] The same overture was used for *The Trip to Portsmouth*. The BM parts both of this and of the *Elfrida* overture lack VI. II and Ob. I.

Arne was competent to praise. The piece is unusual in asking for more women than men. Those who sang in it included a Mrs. Smith, whose husband was about to find himself among Arne's innumerable enemies.

Garrick was never for long able to ignore the Ancient Kings of Britain. As early as 1771 he was planning a revision of *Alfred* with new music,[1] and when the project matured two years later he managed to infuriate both Arne and Dibdin by engaging neither. His methods over the music were as devious as ever. Four days before the first night he became desperate over the lack of one particular song, and sent 'some Gentleman' round to Dibdin's house to ask him to set it. But Dibdin was well aware that, behind his back, most of the new music had been composed by an obscure composer named Theodore Smith, and whatever his real reason for taking offence, the reason he gave was that everyone would think he was trying to set himself up against Smith; he 'would conceive it a most indelicate thing for any Man to introduce a Song of his in a piece which had been given to me'. Garrick was furious, and that same day, 6 October 1773, he wrote Dibdin one of his rudest letters;

> Sir, If I could be surpriz'd at anything Mr. Dibdin does, I should think the inclos'd very Extraordinary . . . you are *our Composer*, and not to do what *you* please; but what the Managers please . . . besides Alfred is not Mr. Smith's Composition but Dr. Arne's etc.. . . I am oblig'd to You for your opinion of what will be of Service or not, but as I have not yet given up the Management, You must excuse me for not following your opinion; As I think the Letter is such a one as I ought not to receive I here send it back.

Garrick had good reason to distrust Dibdin's powers in a piece such as *Alfred*, and good reason too for general annoyance, but, even if it be accepted that a manager should write to his House Composer like this, he should not have bent the truth with regard to Smith's and Arne's contribution. Though Garrick was at pains to advertise the music as 'by Dr. Arne and other Masters', he had not in fact consulted Arne at any point, and Arne later felt constrained to insert a paragraph in the newspapers disclaiming all responsibility for it. The fact was that Smith had written quite enough new music to warrant a credit in the advertisements.

We learn from Mrs. Papendiek that Theodore Smith 'lived by teaching the pianoforte and singing. He had married a most beautiful woman some few years back; an actress whom he taught to sing.'[2] This must have been about 1769, when Smith published some Vauxhall songs 'sung by Mrs. Smith'. Perhaps it was her beauty that persuaded Garrick to employ her husband, for Smith was a mild unforceful person who would hardly have got past Garrick's de-

[1] Letter 656 (16.10.71).
[2] ii, p. 117.

fences on his own. Mrs. Smith had been singing at Drury Lane since the autumn of 1772.

Though Garrick claimed that 'the favourite airs of Dr. Arne' were preserved in his revision of *Alfred*, the libretto shows that, apart from the inevitable 'Rule, Britannia', only three of Arne's songs survived, two of them written for the 1753 production.[1] There were as many songs by Burney from the 1751 production, though neither he nor the mythical 'Temple of Apollo' was mentioned in the new libretto. Smith's contribution consisted of a two-movement overture and five songs, and they show for the first time in English theatre music a new type of lyricism that derived from J. C. Bach and pointed towards Mozart. Smith may well have been a Bach pupil. The first movement of the overture is in impeccable sonata form, with a well contrasted 'feminine' second subject. The only other movement begins:

Of the songs, 'O Joy of Joys' and 'Restore, good Heaven, our gracious King' are especially attractive. The latter was a coloratura air for Mrs. Smith, who played Emma, and the words are presumably by Garrick as they are found in no previous libretto.

Smith does not seem to have written any other theatre music. In the summer that followed, his wife abandoned the London stage, and Mrs. Papendiek provides both a reason and a pathetic coda:

> A Mr. Bishop took her off, and when the first shock had subsided, he prevailed upon Smith to accept a sum of money and be silent, for his wife would never return to him, and he, Bishop, would marry her.

Years later Smith got a job teaching in a Chiswick girls school because the daughter of the Bishop marriage was a pupil there and he could sometimes catch a glimpse of his ex-wife when she came into the schoolroom. He was not a good teacher. In the 1790s William Horsley, later a friend of Mendelssohn's, was articled to Smith for five years and 'received but small instruction and much ill usage'.[2]

Smith was the first English composer to specialize in piano duets, and as some of his music was published in Berlin he may have lived there for a time.

---

[1] 'The Shepherd's plain Life', and 'Arise, sweet Messenger'.
[2] Grove's *Dictionary*, 1st ed., under 'Horsley'.

With *Alfred* annoying him at Drury Lane, Arne switched to Covent Garden for his ballad opera revision, *Achilles in Petticoats*,[1] but he was soon plaguing Garrick again with letters that listed grievances and demanded work for himself and his pupils. Because he knew that Dibdin's contract was ending, he even offered himself as House Composer.[2] Garrick replied on 24 August 1775:

> The Managers of Drury lane have no intention to employ a constant Composer, but to engage with different gentlemen as business may arise in the Theatre.

He added, stressing a truth Arne could hardly have denied:

> In Short, dear Sir, your heart and your genius seem more inclin'd to the Theatre of Covent Garden than that of Drury lane—and when I consider the additional music to King Arthur, and the Music to Elfrida, I trust that I am justified in my Opinion.

To his credit, Garrick was still willing to employ Arne as opportunity offered, and he was soon asking him to set an operatic afterpiece he had just written called *May Day, or the Little Gipsy*. His intention was to introduce a young Jewess called Harriet Abrams ('she is surprizing!', he told Colman) but he was careful to give her as little speaking as possible. Her voice was as small and rounded as her person, and she never enjoyed much success, though she sang Leonora in *The Padlock* a few months later.

May Day (DL 28.10.75) takes place for the most part on a village green with a maypole in the middle of it. The Little Gipsy, who tells fortunes with double meanings, is really a local girl in disguise who cannot marry her William because his father objects. The father gives way in the end. The libretto is hardly distinguished, but the music is full of charm, and as with all Arne's later operas, there are enough extra staves in the published score to provide most of the orchestral detail. The overture is unusually good, and the first movement, with its engaging second subject, is about as near to conventional sonata form as Arne ever got. The Little Gipsy has some entrancing songs, and her friend Dolly has a 'winner' as well. With fifteen performances the opera was a mild success.

1776 was Arne's last year of activity. He wrote two works for his pupils' concerts at the Little Theatre, *Phoebe at Court* (22.2.76) and *Whittington's Feast*, a burlesque ode.[3] The former is a setting of Robert Lloyd's *The Capricious Lovers*. Arne wrote to tell Garrick how bad was the original music by Rush, but Garrick, on the point of retiring, had had enough, and he refused to

---

[1] See p. 399.
[2] So did James Hook, to whom Garrick wrote a kindly refusal (Letter 1310).
[3] The appalling libretto 'by a College Wag' (Arne himself?) is a skit on *Alexander's Feast*. The only surviving published score is in America.

Drury Lane as altered by the Adam brothers in 1775. Note the stage boxes, the new stage doors, the new 'circular painting' on the ceiling; the old chandeliers have been replaced by branches on the pillars holding two candles each.

Boyce by John Russell.

Dibdin by an unknown artist.

Thomas Linley and his son by Gainsborough.

stage the work, which in consequence was never published. That autumn Colman arranged another of William Mason's ancient tragedies, *Caractacus* (CG 6.12.76), and Arne produced for it his last score. Some confusion has been caused by the fact that the British Museum has an anonymous score of music for *Caractacus*, and in spite of its abysmal banality it has been more than once mistaken for Arne's. In fact it was by Charles Wesley. Arne's music is lost, and was lost even in Dr. Busby's day, and it is no consolation that Samuel Arnold told Busby he thought it one of Arne's finest achievements.[1] It may well have been, for Arne is one of the very few English composers who showed no signs of declining powers in old age. In 1784 *The Universal Magazine* announced that Michael Arne was planning to publish such of his father's music as was of high quality and unprinted. The works named were *Caractacus*, the oratorio *The Death of Abel*, the choruses in his other oratorio, *Judith*, and the six keyboard concertos. Only the last-named ever appeared, and then only after Michael Arne's death. No doubt the failure of his mental powers prevented this excellent plan from being completed.

4 DIBDIN LEAVES DRURY LANE

Dibdin resumed activity as a composer in 1773, just after Bickerstaffe's disgrace. *The Wedding Ring* (DL 1.2.73) was an afterpiece, and the libretto derived in part from Goldoni's *Il filosofo di campagna*. At the first night there was a near-riot, because, as Hopkins put it,

> The Town had a Notion that this was one of Mr. Bickerstaffe's productions—they called to know who was the Authour; Mr. Garrick assured them it was not Mr. Bickerstaffe; that did not satisfy them; at last Mr. Dibdin went on, and owned himself the Authour: and then it went on with Applause.

Dibdin later claimed that he had declared himself the author 'without hesitation', but Maria Macklin remembered that 'he was push'd upon the stage ready to drop with fright'.[2] Bannister and Vernon sang the two chief male roles; Mrs. Wrighten and Mrs. Smith were Felicia and her maid, Lissetta. The songs were unremarkable, but at the end of the first act there was a splendidly animated Quartet Finale in several sections and running to as many as 273 bars. *The Wedding Ring* was allowed some twenty performances spread over three seasons.

In the summer that followed, Dibdin had some help from Arne in the writing of an afterpiece for the Little Theatre, *The Trip to Portsmouth* (LT 11.8.73). Arne allowed his overture to *The Rose* to be used, as also a Country Dance

---

[1] i, p. 60.
[2] Quoted by *The London Stage* in its entry for this date.

version of 'Rule Britannia', and he himself scribbled an undistinguished horn-pipe. Dibdin wrote all the vocal music, and the score included his first sea-song. Baker has a long account of the librettist, a failed actor of the most feckless kind named G. A. Stevens.

For the 1773–4 season Dibdin revised a French opera for Drury Lane, *The Deserter* (DL 2.11.73), and set Garrick's full-length *The Christmas Tale* (DL 27.12.73). (With so much work on hand, his complaint that autumn that he had not been asked to compose any of *Alfred* is curious.) *Le Deserteur* (1769) had been a very successful opera with music mainly by Monsigny and a few songs by Philidor. In his preface to the English version Dibdin says he had to reset some of the songs either because of their extreme length in the original or because of 'that sameness which so particularly characterises the French Music'. In fact his songs are among the best, and Jenny's angry 'I'd have you to know, Mr. Simkin' is outstanding. The plot is about a monstrous trick played on a young soldier, Henry. He is about to leave the army to marry Louisa, but, because of malicious rumours spread by his ex-girl-friend, Jenny, it is decided that his sincerity shall be tested by a report that Louisa has just married the oafish Simkin. Soldiers searching for an army deserter overhear Henry murmuring miserably of his 'desertion', mistake his meaning and identity, and put him in prison. Leonora-like activity by Louisa saves him. Mrs. Smith and Mrs. Wrighten played Louisa and Jenny; Vernon and Dibdin himself were Henry and Simkin.

The theme of *The Deserter* was strangely popular for a long time. In 1784 the King's Theatre put on a ballet with the same plot. Some years later Sadler's Wells staged a barely credible performance given entirely by a troupe of dogs, and it should surprise no one that they had full houses.[1]

According to Hopkins, *The Christmas Tale* was

> Written by Mr. Garrick in a Hurry & to show some fine Scenes by M. de Loutherbourg, particularly a burning Palace, which is extreamly fine indeed—it was very well received. The Musick by Dibdin—not very happy in the Composition.

Parke tells us that Loutherbourg introduced 'his newly invented transparent shades, so much admired afterwards in his popular exhibition called "The Eidophusicon".' Unusually for an English opera of this period, there was a chorus, as also a good deal of dancing. The score includes a very poor 'revenge' aria, a duet accompanied by guitars, and Finales which offer the most interesting music, but most of it is dull, and so is the libretto. The plot is about a good and a bad magician, and a heroine who disguises herself as an old woman.

That summer Dibdin reacted to the happier atmosphere of the Little

[1] Reynolds i, pp. 261–4.

Theatre by writing one of his most lasting successes. *The Waterman, or The First of August* (LT 8.8.74) was loved from the first, and it continued to be revived up to the end of Victoria's reign; there was even a Covent Garden performance in 1911. This makes it the more extraordinary that the full score and orchestral parts all seem to have vanished. As we shall discover in the next chapter, Dibdin had spent the last two summers writing short all-sung 'Dialogues' on cockney themes for Sadler's Wells, and it was surely their popularity that led to *The Waterman*. For the Little Theatre he did not need to set the dialogue in recitative. The characters were more artfully chosen than the tradesmen who had given offence in *Love in the City*. The watermen who rowed people from Westminster Steps to Vauxhall Gardens had the popular ebullience of the best modern bus-conductors. Also the first night was timed to follow closely on a popular event that provided the climax of the plot—the race every 1 August by six of London's watermen for Doggett's Coat and Badge.

Doggett the actor has been mentioned already. The race he instituted in 1716 is still with us today, and there is a good description of it in *The Public Advertiser* for 2 August 1775:

> The Coat and Badge given by the will of Doggett the player was rowed for by six watermen, from the Old Swan at London Bridge to the Swan at Chelsea. At twelve o'clock a number of cutters and other boats with flags, streamers, and awnings etc. had assembled on the river, in many of which were drums, fifes, and other music, which had a very agreeable effect . . . The candidates for the prize assembled at twelve, and at five minutes before one started on a signal given by the firing of a pistol. A general shout now cheered the contending parties who rowed against wind and tide . . . some of the rowers without shirts.

Dibdin's excellent libretto concerns the Bundles of Battersea. Mr. Bundle (the name sounds Dickensian) is a philosophical gardener, much hen-pecked by his wife. Their daughter is called Wilhelmina, and the name was not her father's choice. In fact 'Tis such a damn'd, confounded, hard name, that I was a matter of three years before I cou'd pronounce it right'. He does not much like the way she is always off with Robin 'to the two-shilling gallery of one of the play-houses; where they have picked up such a pack of damn'd nonsense about senti-ments and stuff'. But Wilhelmina likes Robin, she says, because 'he can spout Romeo by heart, and he's for ever talking similies to me'. In a Drury Lane play a man with such accomplishments might have been the hero, but not at the Little Theatre, where the more working-class audience distrusted artistic young men. Much more to their liking was Wilhelmina's other admirer, honest Tom Tug the waterman, and partly because he supports Mr. Bundle against his wife Mr. Bundle prefers him too. Wilhelmina herself is in a quandary. 'Which, which', she asks, 'is the man who deserves me the most?'

> Let me ask of my heart,
> Is it Robin, who smirks, and who dresses so smart,
> Or Tom, honest Tom, who makes plainness his plan?
> Which, which is the man?

When she seems to be set on Robin, Tom Tug declares that he will enlist on a man-of-war and go abroad ('Then farewell, my trim-built wherry'). This manly reaction and Robin's intolerably long and high-falutin' sentences fill Wilhelmina with doubts, and at last she says she will marry whoever first does something to deserve her. Tom announces he will row in the forthcoming race, and the Bundles take a room in the Swan Inn, Chelsea, on the fateful afternoon, and provide a running commentary on the race from one of the windows. Needless to say, Tom wins both race and bride.

In the preface to his libretto Dibdin says that he wrote it to make use of 'a number of Ballads which I took great pains with . . . for Ranelagh and the Theatre'. The most popular song in *The Waterman*, Tom's 'And did you not hear of a jolly young waterman',[1] was borrowed from 'There was a fair Maiden, her name it was Gillian' in *The Ballads sung by Mr. Dibdin this evening at Ranelagh* (1769), and Bundle's 'I just as eagerly as thee' comes from the same collection. Mrs. Bundle's 'How can she thus low-minded be?' is taken from the Maid's song near the end of *The Ephesian Matron*. Three of Wilhelmina's four songs (not 'In vain, dear Friends') are borrowed from the unsuccessful *Damon and Phillida*, as is also Tom's 'I row'd for the Prize' and the Overture. Less than half the opera was newly-composed. The music was originally published without the overture, and the twenty-five pages cost four shillings, but it was soon reissued for a shilling more with the addition of both the overture and an extra song for Mrs. Bundle, 'To be modish, genteel, and the true thing, my dear'. (This second edition appears to have twenty-nine pages, but in fact there are more, for the overture was paginated separately.)

The music was simpler and less Italianate than anything Dibdin had previously written for the playhouses. Half the songs were strophic, and there were no ensembles. Inevitably there are *galante* tags, but Dibdin seems to have been aiming at a more English, a more individual style. The tunes are not much like the 'traditional' ones in ballad operas, but they are like those Dibdin was later to write for his one-man theatre, and many could be recognized as his on stylistic grounds. The self-borrowings may seem to invalidate the novelty of the style, but in fact it was because they anticipated the style he now wished to cultivate that Dibdin borrowed these particular songs.

His ability to build up a long melody of beauty and distinction can be illustrated by the end of Tom's ever-popular 'Then farewell, my trim-built Wherry':

---

[1] James Hook wrote variations on the tune for harpsichord.

Dibdin

For generations Tom was the favourite among our opera heroes, and Charles Bannister played him to everyone's satisfaction.

Garrick was furious with Dibdin for writing such a successful afterpiece for someone else,[1] yet when Dibdin attempted a similar opera for Drury Lane, the result was a failure. *The Cobler, or a Wife of Ten Thousand* (DL 9.12.74) is based in part on Sedaine's *Blaise le Savetier*,[2] and takes place mainly in an ale-house. There is a curiously modern scene in the 'Club Room' there, in which eight men, seven of whom take no further part in the opera, all talk at once about unrelated and irrelevant matters, until finally they combine in a glee.

There are some excellent lyrics and one or two goodish songs, but the trouble is that the Cobbler makes an unlovable hero, with his shady past and dishonest leanings. Also the intrigue whereby his wife gets him out of debt is wildly improbable. There were only nine performances, and Dibdin lost interest in what might be called the cockney-based opera. Garrick went further; he lost interest in Dibdin.

The Quaker (DL 3.5.75) had but one performance in the last thirteen months of Garrick's reign, and it is ironic that when Dibdin did offer him a success he failed to recognize it as such. According to himself, Dibdin sold the opera, words and music, for £70 to the actor Brereton because he thought Garrick too hostile ever to accept it. Brereton, though he took no part in it, chose it for his benefit night, and then sold it to Garrick for £100. Garrick put it in a drawer and forgot it,[3] and only after he had retired did Linley recognize its worth. Thus the opera's success occurred while Dibdin was in France. Its

---

[1] In his *Professional Life* (i, p. 135) Dibdin says he first offered *The Waterman* to Garrick, who turned it down. This is almost certainly untrue.

[2] Set by Philidor about 1760.

[3] Dibdin maintains in his *Professional Life* that Garrick filched the 'essence' of *The Quaker* for his *May Day*, set by Arne. In fact there is no discernible likeness. Dibdin's determination to discredit Garrick often led him into falsehoods.

history has been misrepresented more than once. Allardyce Nicol and others give the date of the Linley revival as the date of the first night, and it has also been muddled with a Shadwell play currently in the Drury Lane repertoire, *The Fair Quaker of Deal*; in fact there is no connection.

The hero of the opera is Steady, a middle-aged Quaker who is the father-figure of a village community and the solver of everyone's problems. He has a steward called Easy, and Easy has a pretty daughter called Gillian. The opera begins with Lubin's return to the village. He has been away getting his parent's permission for his marriage to Gillian, and we see him outside Easy's house. But during his absence Easy has agreed that his daughter shall marry the Quaker. When Lubin taxes Gillian with fickle behaviour, she assures him of her love. But how can a girl disobey both her father and the most important man in the neighbourhood? Her friend Floretta, who is herself pursued by a Quaker called Solomon, suggests a plan. The Quaker is known to be the soul of honesty. Lubin, who has never met him, shall petition for leave to marry the girl he loves, giving all the circumstances but none of the names. The Quaker, apparently deceived by the ruse, writes a letter supporting Lubin, which he is to read out to all concerned. When Lubin does so, it turns out that the Quaker has seen through the ruse, and magnanimously named all the parties concerned including himself.

Charles Bannister, burly and honest, was a natural choice for the title role. Lubin was played by Dibdin, and Gillian by 'a young Gentlewoman'—in fact Miss Wilde, the girl with whom Dibdin was now in love. Hopkins found the music 'pretty and novel', but thought the opera very badly performed: 'When the Parts are better cast, the Farce will do very well.' According to one critic, Miss Wilde 'was much frightened, so it would be unfair to decide on her abilities', and Dibdin himself must have been ill-suited as the hero. I cannot trace that he ever performed in the playhouses again.

Both *The Morning Post* and *The Westminster Magazine* noticed that the Finale to Act I was 'in a new style'. In fact a good deal of the opera was experimental. In spite of a plot that sounds insipid, the libretto is very well written, especially the lyrics, which are easy and natural in style. Some of them look much too long on paper. Thus the duet at the start, with Lubin knocking up Gillian's mother Cicely (she appears first at the upper window of her cottage and later at the front door), runs to nearly forty lines. Only four of these lines are ever repeated, and then only when they would have been repeated in spoken dialogue. Indeed the whole duet bustles along like normal conversation; except that the words happen to be sung. It would be pretentious to claim that Dibdin was aiming at *Sprechgesang*, but not wholly wide of the mark. Similarly the Act I Finale runs to three pages in the libretto, though in the vocal score it looks shorter than most Dibdin Finales. Both here and in the duet near the start of Act II the effect is of uninterrupted chatter. Here is an example from the first number in the opera.

The solo songs, though less experimental, are often curious and intriguing. Lubin's 'Women are Will o' the Wisps' is a fascinating patter song, sung half in anger and half in wry compassion, and the vocal line reflects the words with astonishing skill. The Quaker's love song is another moment of high originality. In the main section, 'In verity, Damsel, thou surely wilt find', this dignified incorruptible keeps to his usual Biblical phraseology,[1] but in the contrasting section he lapses into the normal inanities of love-making. Dibdin precisely gauges the moods. This is a lover who is not going to get his girl, so he must not sound too heroic; on the other hand his inanity must be tinged with charm and, in the splendid phrase at the end of this extract, with fundamental honesty:

[1] If Lionel Monckton's *The Quaker Girl* is to be believed, Quakers were still talking like this in Edwardian times.

As nearly always in Dibdin there are some poor songs, and there is the usual absence of inventive instrumental writing. In particular the first movement of the overture is abysmal. Nearly all Dibdin's good qualities lie in his vocal lines. But this is not to condemn him out of hand, for his good qualities are often very good indeed. *The Quaker* is full of original touches of characterization and insight, and would be worth performing today.

In October 1777 Sheridan revived *The Quaker* at Drury Lane with Linley's assistance, and from then on it was a lasting success. Vernon played Lubin and an obscure singer called Miss Walpole played Gillian. Linley added a big coloratura song for Mrs. Wrighten (Floretta), and it is notably different in style from anything else in the opera. Linley had little of Dibdin's dramatic sense; Dibdin on the other hand could not have achieved the remarkable harmonic progressions in the middle of the Linley aria:

the Po-li-ti-cian   for e - ver in a dream

The rewriting of the reprise to fit different words just after the above extract is another moment of subtlety outside Dibdin's reach. Whether the aria improves the opera is another matter. Dibdin would never have written or accepted the incomprehensible words, which begin with just the type of opaque inversion that he abhorred:

> The face which frequently displays an index of the mind
> Dame Nature has her various ways to stamp on human kind.

The words will not of course be found in the first edition of the libretto (1775), but the aria is in the vocal score, which did not appear until after the 1777 revival. When Dibdin got back from France, he added a song for Solomon, originally a non-singing part; it can be found in *The Lyrist*, the collection he brought out in 1781.

From Dibdin's point of view it was tragic that Garrick made no attempt to stage *The Quaker*, for he needed a success more than ever. In the winter of 1774–5 he began cutting rehearsals at Drury Lane because he was afraid of being caught in the theatre and arrested for debt. Garrick mentions a benefit that spring for Dibdin 'who is starving', but Dibdin could not even afford to advertize it.[1] However, he hung on, and though Garrick would not reappoint him as House Composer, he did not entirely desert him.

But Dibdin's last opera for Garrick was a disaster. *The Blackamoor wash'd White* (DL 1.2.76), sometimes known just as *The Blackamoor*, had four performances, none of which were heard by anyone. The house was in an unceasing uproar, and the last performance never got more than half-way. One might think that the hissing and the catcalls were fully justified by the atrocious music and the story's colour prejudice, but these were not the reasons. The truth is that there was uproar even before the curtain rose, for a hostile claque had been organized against Dibdin's librettist because of a recent brawl.[2]

Henry Bate, who later became Sir Henry Bate Dudley, deserves consideration both for his multifarious activities and for his authorship of a number of opera librettos to be considered later. A muscular Christian, he took Holy

[1] Garrick Letter 901; and see footnote to Letter 941.
[2] Garrick Letter 983 (13.2.76).

Orders and then set about founding the *Morning Post*. Later he became a distinguished magistrate, and received the Gold Medal of the Society of Arts for land improvements in Essex. According to Parke, he was a good amateur cellist. In the Birmingham Art Gallery there are large and resplendent portraits of both him and his wife painted by Gainsborough in his latest and finest style.

Shortly before *The Blackamoor* was first staged, Bate had 'chastised' a Mr. Fitzgerald in Vauxhall Gardens for insulting him when with a lady. Fitzgerald set a well-known prize-fighter on him, and Bate chastised the prize-fighter as well. Those who approved referred to him affectionately as the Fighting Parson; those who disapproved or were hard up accepted money from Fitzgerald to go to Drury Lane and hiss his first opera to perdition.

The libretto of *The Blackamoor* was never published, and the vocal score is of the greatest rarity. It is also far from complete, only the earlier songs being given. A long aria for Mrs. Wrighten has an elaborate oboe obbligato of the type Shield was to write later; I have not found another example in Dibdin. *The London Stage* gives the plot, taking it from the Larpent MS. Sir Oliver Oldfish plans to replace all his servants with negroes. This allows Frederick to gain access to the house disguised as a blackamoor, and to elope with Sir Oliver's daughter, Julia. Act I contains some criticism of Londoners' tolerance of negroes, and ends with the comment: 'O that I should ever live to see the day when white Englishmen must give way to foreign blacks.' It is a surprise to discover that Julia was played by Mrs. Siddons. She did not become famous until her return from the provinces several years later. There are no songs for her in what survives of the music.

About the time that Dibdin fled to France, *The Metamorphoses* was presented without success at the Little Theatre (26.8.76). Dibdin's libretto was published, but not his music. He had so far kept on good terms with Foote, but, attributing to him the failure of this opera, he managed to quarrel with yet another manager. With the retirement of Garrick that summer and the arrival of Sheridan and Linley, Dibdin saw that his prospects at Drury Lane were minimal, and he started to work on *The Seraglio* for Covent Garden. The composition was interrupted by his flight, and the opera had to be finished by Arnold. Dibdin later complained that in his absence Harris, the Covent Garden manager, had altered his libretto out of all recognition.

Harem operas are of especial interest because of Mozart's *Zaide* (1779) and *Die Entführung aus dem Serail* (1782). Both of these derive in some measure from French and English predecessors, though it is beyond my powers to construct an accurate genealogical table. Common features of many harem operas are a heroine named Zaide, an overseer or slave-trader named Osmin (who features in both the Mozart works), and one or more English slave girls, for instance Blonde in *Die Entführung*. The owner of the harem appears cruel in the middle of the opera, magnanimous at its end. The name Zaide was given to a slave girl in the 1668 revision of Molière's *Le Sicilien*, and it was popularized by Madame de La Fayette's novel of that name published in 1670; an English translation appeared in 1678. Though set in Spain during the Moorish wars her plot is much more concerned with the desirability of love at first sight than with any Moorish-Christian clash, and Zaide was in fact a self-portrait, the unscrupulous Moorish prince Alamir being Madame de La Fayette's alleged lover, the Duc de Rochefoucauld. Dryden, who was passionately interested in the Moorish-Christian wars, has an Indian slave girl called Zayda in *Aurengzebe* (1765), and much more significantly in his longest and finest tragedy, *Don Sebastian*, he uses the name for the unseen Moorish mother of his heroine; her illicit liaison before the play begins with Don Sebastian's Portuguese father is the mainspring of the action. We have already noted a Zayda in Arne's *Sultan* (1759) and in Smith's *The Enchanter* (1760), and the name reappears in Favart's *Soliman Second* (1761). It had also occurred in *The Arabian Nights*, first published in 1704–17 in a French translation; the steadily increasing popularity of this collection was a major cause of the popularity enjoyed by the type of opera discussed below.

Dibdin and Bickerstaffe first tackled the harem theme in *The Captive* (LT 21.6.69), a not-very-successful pastiche for which Dibdin wrote about half the songs and, according to the libretto preface, some of the dialogue. The plot is distantly based on the scene in *Don Sebastian* in which the Mufti, in his own garden, disguises himself as the young captive Don Antonio, thinking him to be the object of his wife's attentions, and then is horrified at being amorously accosted by his own daughter. Dryden never mentions a harem, but Bickerstaffe gives one to the Cadi (Dryden's Mufti) and makes the two women its inmates rather than relatives of the owner. One is called Zorayda,[1] which might be a derivative of Zayda. Bickerstaffe also makes the Cadi magnanimous at the end, with everyone going free.

In 1775 Garrick staged a similar though less musical piece called *The Sultan*, and thought it prudent to conceal Bickerstaffe's authorship. It seems Bickerstaffe sent him the libretto from abroad, having adapted it from Favart's *Soliman Second*, and it was not published for nearly ten years. There are only three songs, all sung for the entertainment of Solyman, 'great Emperor of the Turks'. Dibdin's settings and the Grand March he wrote for Solyman's entry do not survive. Osmyn is the chief of Solyman's eunuchs, and the heroine is an English slave called Roxalana. The impregnable virginity of the latter leads Solyman to make her his lawful wedded wife and to abandon his harem.

For *The Seraglio* (CG 14.11.76) Dibdin has an English slave called Lydia who again will accept Abdallah's love only if he marries her, but he stretches coincidence with a great many other English characters as well. Polly and her

[1] This name was well-known from *Don Quixote*; Zorayda is the Moorish girl turned Christian that the Captive rescues and takes to Spain. Cervantes had himself been a slave in Algiers, and the story has a reality born of circumstantial detail for which one looks in vain in harem operas.

sailor lover, Tom Reef, come to the same remote Algerian shore to rescue Polly's father, working as harem gardener; and a party of English sailors, among them Frederick and Venture, arrive to rescue Lydia. For good measure Dibdin throws in yet another English couple who are improbably employed as the court fishmongers. In the end all the English are magnanimously set free, and Abdallah makes an honest woman of a discarded Turkish mistress. In all these harem plots the titillation inherent in the subject is nullified by the astonishingly high moral behaviour of everyone concerned.

The best things in Dibdin's score are Tom Reef's 'Blow high, blow low', the first of his really popular sea-songs, and (as so often) the Finale of Act I, which is long, full of action, and well characterized. The overture is dreadful, but the vocal numbers, more Italianate than in any opera since *The Wedding Ring*, have considerable merit, and unusually this is equally true of the slower songs of sentiment. The score omits a chorus sung in the harem garden, and includes two beautiful traditional songs for Frederick; 'Here each morning and every eve' makes use of the Irish tune 'The Banks of Banna'[1] and 'The pious Pilgrim' is based on the Scottish tune 'She rose and let me in'. Dibdin had always set himself against such borrowings, but in his absence Arnold indulged his own love of folk-song; also Leoni, the young singing-actor engaged for Frederick, had recently shown how well he could sing such songs in *The Duenna*. It looks as though the score was knocked up in a hurry, for Arnold farmed one song out to Fisher, writing two others himself. Dibdin's contribution amounts to about two-thirds of the whole. Though he inveighs against what was done to *The Seraglio*[2] in his absence, he can never have seen a performance.

5 BARTHELEMON AND FISHER

Only two other composers besides Dibdin and Arne received much encouragement at the playhouses at this period, Barthelemon and Fisher, and both of them were violinists. In June 1774 the young Earl of Derby (Lord Stanley) married Lady Betty Hamilton, and at his seat, The Oaks, near Epsom, he celebrated the event with an elaborate *fete champêtre* that included a masque by Barthelemon. As they arrived, the guests were 'saluted by French-horns placed in a retreat so obscure as not to be observed by the company'. In somewhat similar fashion Queen Elizabeth had often been welcomed, as also Anne of Denmark at Althorp in 1604, and in similar fashion a few years later William Beckford was to welcome his guests at Fonthill. The adulatory masque, *The Maid of the Oaks*, was the centre-piece of the entertainment; it was given on the back lawn

---

[1] It had recently become popular in the Gardens to words beginning 'Shepherds, I have lost my Love'. Thomas Moore later wrote for it 'When through Life unblest we rove'.

[2] *Musical Tour*, p. 299.

and produced, in the modern sense, by General Burgoyne, the bridegroom's uncle, who also wrote the words.[1] The main singers included such professionals as Vernon and Mrs. Barthelemon, but relations and friends of the family also took part, including some children as Cupids. There were a number of choruses and a great deal of dancing. The Earl of Kellie contributed some minuets, and the whole entertainment cost £12,000.[2]

Garrick had been so impressed by *The Maid of the Oaks* that he asked Burgoyne to expand the original to a full-length entertainment, and it was put on that autumn (DL 5.11.74) with scenery by de Loutherbourg which Hopkins thought 'beyond Description fine, and the whole Performance, tho' the most complicated of any upon the Stage, went off with uncommon applause'. The new libretto in some respects anticipates that of Hofmannsthal's *Ariadne auf Naxos*, for Burgoyne aimed to reproduce the actual preparation of the masque at Epsom, though he renamed all the people involved. Sir Harry Groveby, about to marry Maria, discusses with his Painter and his Architect the entertainment he plans by way of celebration. There is not much music before Act IV, but in Act V it is almost continuous, the scene being 'a representation of the temporary Saloon as designed by Mr. Adams, and erected at Lord Stanley's'. The published score omits a good deal of this music; in particular there are no choruses, ensembles, or recitatives. But it includes no fewer than fifteen pages of music that Garrick cut. Also a pretty one-movement 'Pastoral Overture' that Barthelemon apparently wrote especially for Drury Lane, and a great many pleasant but not at all striking dances. Much of the music looks like what it was—an unobtrusive background for spectacle. There are borrowings from Rousseau and Philidor, and a French flavour all through

That same autumn Barthelemon composed an 'Interlude' for Drury Lane called *The Election* (DL 19.10.74). The libretto by Miles Peter Andrews is virtually a tract against election candidates taking bribes, and for some reason it roused Baker to high invective ('What nauseous potions will not music wash down the throat of the public?'). The overture is unusual in that the movements are linked, the first starting in D but ending in E to prepare for the slow movement in A. Much the most original item is the long Finale for Trusty, the honest but misrepresented candidate, and the Mob.

John Abraham Fisher has already been mentioned as the composer of the burlesque, *The Court of Alexander*, and the leader of the Covent Garden band

---

[1] In the following year he helped to lose the American War of Independence; he is, of course, a leading character in Bernard Shaw's *The Devil's Disciple*.

[2] For a full description, see *The Gentleman's Magazine* for 1774, p. 263. The marriage was not successful. After producing two children Lady Derby ran off with the Duke of Dorset, asked her husband for a divorce, and was refused. When later he asked for one, she refused in turn; by this time she had been deserted by Dorset and was embittered, and by this time Lord Derby was living with the Drury Lane actress, Miss Farren. It was one of the most famous stage romances of all time. They married as soon as Lord Derby's first wife died.

from about 1770. At much the same time he published some violin sonatas and Vauxhall songs, and also a considerable quantity of theatre music. His earliest vocal scores were those of a pantomime, *Harlequin's Jubilee* (CG 27.1.70), which parodied Garrick's Stratford festival, and *Zobeide* (CG 11.12.71), a completion by Joseph Cradock of Voltaire's unfinished *Les Scythes*; *Zobeide* was a play with incidental music. Fisher also composed an all-sung masque based on Ben Jonson called *The Druids* (CG 19.11.74), but it was less liked than Drury Lane's Jonsonian *Fairy Prince* even though it was enlivened with pantomime scenes. There is a libretto in the Library of Congress but not apparently in Britain. Of another all-sung masque, *The Syrens* (CG 26.2.76), no music survives except for the overture which was published in parts. The words were by Captain Edward Thompson, who foolishly blamed Garrick for its failure.[1] We shall later find Thompson working with Fisher on a strange revision of *The Beggar's Opera*.

Fisher's most lasting achievement was the compilation of the music for *The Golden Pippin* (CG 6.2.73), Kane O'Hara's all-sung burlesque on the Judgement of Paris story. Like *Midas*, it began as a rather short mainpiece, and succeeded only when it was cut to an afterpiece. The cutting (after three performances) was done because of rowdy behaviour by the audience, who objected to allegedly low humour in a scene with a dragon. As libretto and music survive only in the shortened form we do not know what gave offence. The burlesque starts with a trio during which the three goddesses are playing cards; Venus has no difficulty in fleecing Juno and Pallas, who accuse her of cheating. (The game, Tredille, would be incomprehensible to a modern audience.) The libretto is deft and amusing, and among the best of its kind.

Fisher himself contributed a competent and pleasing overture which shows a proper grasp of sonata form. He also composed one new song and all the recitatives; the latter do not survive. He dragged in songs by Arne and some Italian opera arias, and it was he who chose for the Finale the first movement of Vivaldi's Concerto Grosso in A, op. 3, no. 5, no doubt playing the difficult solo violin part himself. The adaptation is done with a good deal of skill. Fisher had plenty of technique both as a composer and as a violinist.

About 1778 Fisher left for St. Petersburg, and his later moves are hard to establish. In Berlin he published three astonishingly difficult violin concertos, and by July 1783 he was in Vienna, where he married Nancy Storace, his first wife having died. Nancy was less than half his age, and his treatment of her soon led to the Emperor ordering him out of Vienna. Fisher must also have worked in Italy and France, for about 1790 he published a set of songs 'composed during residence in those countries'. We get our last and clearest glimpse of him in Dublin towards the end of the century, visiting Robert Owenson, who

---

[1] See Garrick Letter 994 (11.3.76). Baker began his article on Thompson with the words 'This meretricious bard'.

had been a Covent Garden singer in Fisher's day. Owenson's daughter, Lady Morgan, did not find Fisher impressive.

> A foreign valet in showy livery, bearing a magnificent violin case, in crimson and gold, was followed by the entrance of the great professor, who stepped on tip-toe, dressed in a brown silk camlet coat lined with scarlet silk, illustrated with brilliant buttons, and a powdered and perfumed *toupée*, so elevated as to divide his little person almost in two. His nether dress was fastened at the knees with diamond buttons, and the atmosphere of the room was filled with the perfume from his person. He kissed my father on either cheek, and my mother's hand with such fervour, that she was left in doubt whether the gallantry were profane or indecent.

He had brought the Owensons lavish presents of foreign lace and embroidery. Suddenly one realizes that characters such as Dibdin's Jessamy were true to life. In the last twenty-eight years of his career Fisher made no attempt to return to London's theatre world. One wonders what he did.

Kane O'Hara's third opera was *The Two Misers* (CG 21.1.75). Unlike its predecessors it was an afterpiece from the first, and it had spoken dialogue. According to the *Morning Post*'s review, O'Hara wrote all his lyrics to fit airs he had himself selected, and there is no new music. This makes the vocal score uninteresting, especially as it has no attributions and no overture. But the libretto is well-written and amusing; it is set in Smyrna, and O'Hara based it on the one Grétry had recently set as *Les deux avares*.

The time-span of the next two chapters corresponds with that of this one. Thereafter circumstances changed. At Drury Lane Sheridan took over from Garrick, and Linley was in charge of the music. At Covent Garden Dibdin returned briefly, but was soon superseded by Shield. At the Little Theatre Colman took over from Foote and made Arnold his composer.

10

The Fringe Theatres
1760–1780

1 MARYLEBONE GARDENS

WITH no licence to present spoken dialogue, the fringe theatres that opened in the summer were often pushed into offering all-sung opera. At Marylebone and Ranelagh Gardens, such operas lasted a little under the hour; at Sadler's Wells some fifteen minutes. They were the main item in a concert or variety programme, and because there were no facilities for scene-changing they had only one set.

Marylebone Gardens was a small but concentrated entertainment centre just over the road from where the Royal Academy of Music now stands. It had existed in Pepys's day, but it did not emphasize music until 1738, when the proprietor erected an 'orchestra', that is, a bandstand. Two years later he followed the example of Vauxhall Gardens and added an organ. In 1751 John Trusler became the proprietor, and though at first he gave most of his attention to fireworks and the bowling-green, he was willing enough to concentrate on opera when his daughter Elizabeth became engaged to a go-ahead Italian musician, Stephen Storace. Storace, who must not be confused with his more famous son, had been born at Torre Annunziata near Naples, and he has already been mentioned as working in Dublin. At least by 1749 he was band director at Dublin's New Gardens,[1] and a year or two later he was in a syndicate with Pasquali that ran Johnson's Music Hall. He had anglicized his name from the first, and judging by a letter he wrote to *The Gentleman's Magazine* in September 1753 he quickly acquired excellent English. A little later he was playing the double bass at the King's Theatre under Giardini.

Elizabeth Trusler was also accomplished. In 1758 Marylebone Gardens were boasting that 'Mr. Trusler's daughter continues to make the Rich Seed and Plumb Cakes, so much admired by the Nobility and Gentry'. A year later she was also making 'almond cheesecakes in a small size at 2s. per dozen. Six or

---

[1] Sheldon, p. 145.

eight make a Dish, and are hot every day one o'clock.' Miss Trusler's cakes were advertised so regularly from 1758 to 1760 that they must have been a major attraction. Storace married her at St. James's Church, Piccadilly, on 16 June 1761.[1]

The first opera ever staged at Marylebone Gardens was also the most successful—*La Serva Padrona* by Pergolesi; it was always given in Storace's English translation, and in 1758 there were as many as seventy performances. The maid was sung by an Italian, Dominica Saratina, her master by Reinhold. Pergolesi had died of consumption in 1736 when he was only twenty-six, and though *La Serva Padrona* is a very early example of *opera buffa*, it is said to be neither the earliest nor the best. Circumstances have conspired to make people think better of this composer than he deserved. *La Serva Padrona* became a *cause célèbre* in Paris during the so-called 'Guerre des Bouffons' of 1752–3. On the one side were the middle-aged conservatives who liked Rameau and traditional French opera; on the other were the young rebels who preferred Italian opera, in particular *opera buffa*. Rousseau was a vociferous supporter of the rebels, going so far as to argue that the French language was quite unsuited to singing, even though he himself had just composed *Le Devin du Village*. Rousseau's praise of *La Serva Padrona* was fulsome in the extreme. Of the duet that ends the first scene, 'Lo conosco a quegli occhietti', he wrote:

> I will fearlessly cite it as a model of agreeable music, of unity of melody, of simple harmony, brilliant and pure, of rhythm, of phrasing and of good taste, to which, when properly executed, nothing is wanting save an audience capable of understanding it.[2]

It is a pretty piece, but not that good.

As in other European countries, the lowbrows who supported the new *galante* style won the day, and Rameau's operas soon lost ground to those of Duni, Monsigny, Philidor, and Grétry. Everyone wanted to hear *La Serva Padrona*. The little songs slipped pleasantly in and out of the mind with nothing to obstruct their passage. The tiny pert phrases were so quickly repeated that you could not help remembering them, and the accompaniments were so light and unobtrusive that there was never any fear of attention being distracted from the vocal line. Indeed the scoring is just like that of English ballad operas of the time, with all the violins playing the voice part and the harpsichord filling in between that and the bass. The orchestral writing seldom runs to three independent parts, and no wind instruments are required. Nevertheless the historical importance of *La Serva Padrona* was immense. It was the Italian intermezzo that Europe knew best, and more than any other one work it influenced the switch to the *galante* style.

[1] I have to thank Mr. R. A. Lynex for this discovery.
[2] Quoted in the anonymous 'Biographical and Critical Sketch' that prefaces the nineteenth-century Ricordi vocal score.

Modern scores of *La Serva Padrona* contain two scenes, and back in Naples in 1733 the first had been presented after Act I of an *opera seria*[1] and the second after Act II. Thus in the literal sense it consists of two intermezzi, and each of these contains two arias, a final duet, and an inordinate amount of recitative. In addition there is an Introduzzione at the start and an alternative duet at the end. There are thus eight 'numbers' in all, though only seven would be sung in any one performance.

La Serva Padrona had been first heard in London at the King's Theatre (27.5.50), when it attracted no attention in a season that has been described as disastrous. It was much easier to enjoy in English as presented at Marylebone Gardens in 1758, by which time news of its prodigious success in Paris had filtered through. The following year James Oswald published the 'Favourite Songs', and he included Storace's translations of them. There are only four songs in the collection, Nos. 3 and 4 being the same as Nos. 3 and 4 in modern scores. But Storace's libretto, published in or about 1760, shows that all the music sung in modern productions was sung at Marylebone Gardens except for the alternative finale, No. 8, in three-eight time, and it shows too that a whole new scene was inserted in the middle; this scene introduced a new character, an old woman. Obviously the two unfamiliar songs that Oswald published came from this additional scene; one of them, 'Una donna come me', was later borrowed for *The Maid of the Mill* where it is attributed to Pergolesi, but it can hardly be his. One of the lyrics in the new scene was taken from Pasquali's *Apollo and Daphne*, and it is quite possible that some of the new music was also taken from this masque. The new scene was first advertised in 1759, by which time Pasquali was dead.

At least two full scores of *La Serva Padrona* were published in the eighteenth century. The Paris one of 1752 accords with modern editions except that, like Storace's version, it omitted the alternative finale, No. 8. On the other hand Robert Bremner's of 1777 keeps the alternative finale and cuts the first one, No. 7.

Storace did not feel equal to making his lyrics rhyme, and he was so unfortunate as to begin with a split infinitive:

> To long expect and want, in vain,
> To be in Bed and not to sleep,
> To slave for ever without profit
> Will break the Heart of anyone.

It is not easy to make this doggerel fit Umberto's Introduzzione; many liberties must have been taken with the rhythms of the vocal line. But in general the translation is idiomatic and singable. In 1759 Storace added two more short operas to the Marylebone Gardens repertoire, and both were translated by himself. *La Cicisbea alla Moda*, later known as *The Coquette*, had words by Goldoni

---

[1] This was also by Pergolesi—*Il prigionier superbo*.

and music by Galuppi; *La Strattaggemma* had music ascribed to Pergolesi, though it is not mentioned in any modern list of his compositions. After Storace and Elizabeth Trusler were married, they ceased to have any more to do with Marylebone Gardens, which abandoned opera for several years. But in the summer of 1761 the same repertoire of intermezzi in English was offered at the Little Theatre, and this time *La Strattaggemma* was attributed to Hasse. Since 1759 Storace had been playing the double bass at the Three Choirs Festivals, and he was regularly advertised as one of the leading artists. Presumably he continued to play at the King's Theatre in the winter. He and his wife produced two notable children in 1762 and 1765: Stephen John Seymour, who composed, and Ann Selina, known as Nancy, who sang.

In 1763 John Trusler sold Marylebone Gardens to the famous tenor, Thomas Lowe, who did not bother himself with opera, preferring to offer mixed concerts with himself and his pupil Ann Catley as the leading singers. The Gardens were finding it difficult to compete with the more fashionable Ranelagh, even though tea and coffee were sometimes thrown in with the price of admission. Concerts were given out of doors, and apparently operas as well, but there was a sizeable hall for when the weather was bad. More and more emphasis was put on the fireworks, which were often extremely spectacular. Those who lived in the neighbourhood began complaining of the noise. Concerts were sometimes tricked out with such catch-penny items as a Trumpet Concerto played by 'a small boy', but often the music was excellent. Fanny Burney, a good judge, took her Evelina there, and was thus able to offer her own opinions disguised as those of her heroine:

> This Garden, as it is called, is neither striking for magnificence nor for beauty; and we were all so dull and languid, that I was extremely glad when we were summoned to the orchestra, upon the opening of a concert; in the course of which I had the pleasure of hearing a concerto on the violin by Mr. Barthelemon, who, to me, seems a player of exquisite fancy, feeling, and variety . . . The firework was really beautiful, and told, with wonderful ingenuity, the story of Orpheus and Euridice; but, at the moment of the fatal look, which separated them for ever, there was such an explosion of fire, and so horrible a noise, that we all, as of one accord, jumped hastily from the form, and ran away some paces . . .[1]

Evelina's visit must have been in the early 1770s. By this time Samuel Arnold was in charge of the Gardens. He had bought them from Lowe in 1769, the money being found by the rich young woman he had just married. Arnold appointed Pinto his leader, and when Pinto fled from his creditors to Ireland he appointed Barthelemon. In the five summers from 1770 to 1774 fourteen different burlettas were staged. Much the most popular was *La Serva Padrona* with fifty-five performances. Also liked was *The Magnet* (1771; 29 perfs.)

[1] *Evelina*, Letter 52.

with music by Arnold himself. Barthelemon's *The Magic Girdle* and Arnold's *Don Quixote* also found favour. Galuppi's *The Coquet* was revived, and Storace's translation of it was published. It is a great improvement on his previous translation, and this time the lyrics rhyme. A few of the other librettos were also published, including *The Magic Girdle* by Henry Carey's posthumous son, George Savile Carey, but apart from *La Serva Padrona* no scores of these Marylebone Gardens burlettas ever appeared. Throughout this second burst of musical activity there, James Hook played organ concertos in the short concerts that led up to the operas. The one with variations on 'Lovely Nancy'[1] is perhaps his most pleasing instrumental work, but three of the four short operas he contributed failed.[2] His one success was *Il Dilettante* (28.8.72), performed in three consecutive summers. In it 'Bannister will introduce the German, French and Italian styles of singing'. A more notable event was the staging of Handel's *Acis and Galatea* (27.5.73).

An opera Marylebone Gardens presumably failed to stage is of more interest than those it did. In April 1770 a phenomenal but unmanageable youth of seventeen arrived in London from Bristol. Thomas Chatterton had already perpetrated his 'Rowley' forgeries; he was now intent on theatrical success. He got an introduction to a 'doctor of music' from someone he met in the pit at Drury Lane, and as a result thought himself all set to write for 'Ranelagh and the Gardens'. It is not clear who this doctor of music can have been; certainly not Arnold, who did not get his degree till 1773. Nevertheless it was for Marylebone Gardens that Chatterton wrote his burletta *The Revenge*, and he knew enough of conditions there to limit it to four characters and to cast it for Mrs. Thompson, Reinhold, Bannister, and Master Cheney. The libretto leans heavily on that of *Midas*, as did most burletta librettos for the rest of the century, but it is competent and amusing. Cupid wants his revenge on both Jupiter and Bacchus, He tells Juno that her husband is courting Maia (a character who never appears) and persuades Bacchus to attempt to seduce Maia disguised as Jupiter. Inevitably Juno catches Bacchus, thinking she has caught Jupiter. As a sample of the writing:

> Ah! I'm quite out here—plaguily mistaken—
> The man's in earnest. I must save my bacon.

It has always been supposed that Arnold intended to set *The Revenge* but never did so; in which case his lack of interest may well have contributed to the despair that caused Chatterton to poison himself in August. But newspaper advertisements are not complete at this period. A song Chatterton wrote for *The Revenge*, 'Away to the Woodlands', was published as 'Sung by Master Cheney at Marylebone Gardens', and it may be that the whole burletta was sung there. Busby

---

[1] This is a song Bates introduced into a revival of *The Jovial Crew*; see p. 397.
[2] One of these was a setting of the *Apollo and Daphne* libretto by John Hughes that Pepusch had set back in 1716.

says it was,[1] and he names Chatterton's Drury Lane contact as Lukey, who was about to go into partnership with Longman, the music publishers. At the time Busby was fifteen, and an articled pupil of Battishill; he might well have known the facts. On 6 July Chatterton was paid £5 for his libretto, and it was virtually the only money he ever earned in London. He was so confident *The Revenge* would be produced that he started another burletta, *The Woman of Spirit*. *The Revenge* was not published until 1795, by which time his tragic story was known all over Western Europe.

By 1775 the Gardens were in decline. Barthelemon and Hook had left, and there were no operas. In 1776 there were ten performances of Dibdin's *The Recruiting Sergeant*, and when the gates closed in the autumn, Arnold sold his property to building speculators.

2 RANELAGH GARDENS

Little space need be given to the music performed at Ranelagh Gardens. Not much of it was operatic, and there is a good book on the subject by Mollie Sands. The Gardens were situated in what are now the grounds of Chelsea Hospital, just to the east of the main building, and they had been opened in 1742. The Rotunda was circular, with a bandstand in the middle and boxes all round the circumference. It was quite unsuited to dramatic entertainments; there can have been no scenery, and very little stage movement. The Rotunda was mostly used for concerts and masquerades. For your 2s. 6d. you got free tea and coffee, and when highwaymen became a nuisance between the Gardens and the rest of civilization, advertisements promised 'an armed Guard on Horseback to patrol the Roads'. The Mozart children played at Ranelagh in 1764, and found some entertainment there in the long months when their father was ill in near-by Ebury Street. If Matthew Bramble is to be believed, the building was bad for sound, though he thought it just as well that some of the singers could not be heard distinctly.[2]

Arne's *The Judgment of Paris* had been given without action in the Rotunda in both 1760 and 1761. Only in 1769 and 1770 did Ranelagh make any real attempt to compete with Marylebone in the matter of opera. As we have seen, Bickerstaffe and Dibdin wrote *The Ephesian Matron* and *The Recruiting Sergeant* for the Rotunda, in each case limiting the cast to four. Dibdin was paid £100 for his work at Ranelagh in 1770, and for this he had to sing as well as compose. That year he and Bickerstaffe tossed off a third work with four characters, but only the words were ever printed. *The Maid the Mistress* (RG 28.5.70) was yet another version of *La Serva Padrona*, and like the one being given in Marylebone Gardens it had an additional scene in the middle in which the old gentleman flirted with an old woman. Dibdin played the old woman.

---

[1] Busby iii, p.118.
[2] Smollett's *Humphry Clinker* (1771), Letter of May 29.

There were four performances, and one more the following year at Drury Lane, when a new title was tried out: *He would if he could, or An Old Fool worse than any.* Opera at Ranelagh Gardens clearly did not pay, and after 1770 the experiment was not repeated.

3 SADLER'S WELLS

Very little was known of the early history of Sadler's Wells until Dennis Arundell combed the documents now at Hardewicke Court, Gloucester,[1] and not enough is known even now. We have already noted a solitary ballad opera that was staged there in 1730, *The Prisoner's Opera.* Mr. Arundell names six short all-sung operas on classical themes that were presented in the late 1740s, but no music survives and it is not known who wrote them. They seem to have been the result of a new policy instigated by Thomas Rosoman, who had become manager in 1745, but he hung most of his expectations on rope-dancing, acrobatics, and popular songs. In 1764 Rosoman pulled down the old building and erected a brick structure whose walls survived until 1928. In 1771 he took pity on the destitute Thomas Lowe, who was now over fifty, and made him his principal vocalist. That winter he sold Sadler's Wells to the Drury Lane actor, Thomas King, and retired to Hampton. When he died, he was found to be worth £40,000.

The Sadler's Wells season usually ran from Easter Monday to October, and the house, though small in appearance, held as many as 2,000. Most of them were of the shopkeeper class, and the entertainment reflected a different kind of audience from that which frequented the playhouses. The stage was only about 28 feet wide under the proscenium arch, but its depth was astonishing—as much as 90 feet. Spectacular effects were possible and popular, though there is hardly any information about them until the turn of the century.

The one meagre musical and literary source for the 1760s is a large volume in the British Musuem, 'The Sadler's Wells Collection, Vol. 8';[2] it consists of material performed there in the last half of the century. There is an almost complete libretto for *Harlequin Deserter*, a pantomime ascribed to the year 1761, and it may have been Bickerstaffe's source for *The Recruiting Sergeant.* Harlequin and 'The Countryman' are recruited, but the latter is bought off by his father. Columbine, the Countryman's sister, goes off to the wars with Harlequin. But Harlequin deserts, and is then chased in the usual way. There is no indication of the trick effects so popular in playhouse pantomimes, but facilities can have been few before Sadler's Wells was rebuilt. The music for *Harlequin Deserter* was by one Pattersal, and an unusual feature of it was that Harlequin sang recitatives—in a Loamshire accent. (Speaking was, of course, forbidden at

---

[1] See Arundell's *The Story of Sadler's Wells* (1965).
[2] BM Crack. I. Tab. 4.b.4/8.

Sadler's Wells.) None of the music of this pantomime survives, but the British Museum volume does include two songs from one ascribed to the following year, *Harlequin Quack*.

After the rebuilding in 1764, many more composers wrote for the theatre, and not all are obscure. Charles Lockhart, Michael Arne, William Yates, John Snow, and Joseph Olive all contributed songs, and probably dialogues and pantomime music as well. In 1771 Olive composed an interlude called *India hoa*. Some of these composers were probably members of the orchestra. James Hook worked at Sadler's Wells off and on from 1767, and even wrote dialogues for the theatre after his appointment at Marylebone Gardens. The only dialogue in the British Museum volume that is complete as to both words and music is *The Mischance* by Dibdin.

When Thomas King took over the management of Sadler's Wells in 1772, he gave special encouragement to Dibdin, with whom he had worked at Drury Lane. In the ten years of King's rule Dibdin composed more than thirty dialogues and pantomimes for the theatre even though he was also employed at one of the winter playhouses for most of this time. Sometimes he tossed off six in one year, and he even sent four from France when he found himself exiled there in 1777. Dibdin got on better with King than with any other manager. King also commissioned a few Dialogues and Pantomimes from Fisher and Arnold. Only a minority of them ever reached print, and some that did do not seem to survive. Vocal scores and librettos of so slight a nature were much more likely to be thrown away than those associated with the playhouses. It is impossible to assess their relative popularity, for they were hardly ever advertised after the first night, and often not even then. There is information in Dibdin's *The Musical Tour* (1788; pp. 292–300), in Hogarth's 700-page *The Songs of Charles Dibdin* (1842; pp. 4–32), and in Dennis Arundell's book, but some of it is contradictory, especially as regards dates.

Nine vocal scores of Sadler's Wells Dialogues and Pantomimes are known to have been printed in the 1770s; six, possibly seven, survive.

Hook: *Trick upon Trick* (?), old Pantomime revived with new music.
          The Country Courtship (?), Dialogue. No vocal score is known, but one was advertised in *The Brickdust Man*. The work may be the same as *The Country Wake* (see below).

Fisher: *The Monster of the Woods* (13.4.72), Pantomime. The only known vocal score is in the British Museum, and contains a one-movement overture, several arias and accompanied recitatives, and twenty-two Comic Tunes.

Dibdin: *The Palace of Mirth* (1772), Prologue. No vocal score is known, but one was advertised in *The Grenadier* and *The Mischance*.
          The Brickdust Man (1772), Dialogue for two characters. Dibdin says it was the first he wrote. Bickerstaffe's libretto was not published,

but it appeared in newspaper reviews. The only known vocal score is in the Royal College of Music.

The Ladle (14.4.73), Dialogue for three characters. Dibdin based his libretto on Matthew Prior's humorous poem of the same name. See Hogarth p. 8.

The Grenadier (19.4.73), Dialogue for three characters. Dibdin says the libretto was by Garrick; it was published anonymously. Lowe sang the title role.

The Mischance (1774?), Dialogue for three characters. Dibdin says he founded the libretto on 'The Barber of Baghdad'. Lowe sang the only male role.

The Vineyard Revels (14.4.77), Pantomime. A vocal score was advertised in *The Grenadier* but seems not to survive.[1] The song words can be found in BM 11779.c.57.

In addition to the above vocal scores, two attractive sea-songs that Dibdin wrote in France for *Yo, Yea, or the Friendly Tars* (18.8.77) were published with their music; they can be found in Hogarth, who also gives two further lyrics from this Dialogue.

It should be explained that Hogarth set out to publish all Dibdin's lyrics; they fill the first half of the book and they are accompanied by informative notes. It was impossible to include all the music, but Hogarth provided a wide selection in the second half of his book, with 'New Piano-Forte Accompaniments by Various Composers'; one of these was himself. He managed to print lyrics from a number of Dialogues that had never been published in conventional ways. He must have found most of them in Dibdin's *Professional Life*; others, perhaps, in newspaper reviews. Here are some details:

England against Italy (1773)—4 lyrics
None so blind as those who won't see (1773)—1 lyric
The Impostor, or All's not Gold that glisters (1776)—2 lyrics
The Razor-Grinder (21.4.77)—2 lyrics
She is mad for a Husband (1777)—5 lyrics (perhaps all there were)
The Old Woman of Eighty (1777)—4 lyrics

Somehow Hogarth managed to give the plot of the last-named, and he may have had access to a libretto. Perhaps there were always librettos on sale inside Sadler's Wells, but if so it is extraordinary that none of them should have been known to Baker in 1812.

An account of one Dialogue will suffice for all, and I have chosen Dibdin's *The Brickdust Man*, the first that he wrote, because it exemplifies the cockney setting which was their most interesting feature. It alone of his Dialogues has

---

[1] The dates don't fit. Either *The Grenadier* was published long after its first performance or my *Vineyard Revels* date is much too late.

an overture, but it is a poor one. The curtain rises on John hawking his brickdust round the streets of London. In the final bars of his first song, the rival
cries of Moll the Milkmaid start to intrude. When they meet, Moll flies into a
rage because it turns out that three months earlier the Brickdust Man jilted
her at the church door. In angry recitatives she cries:

> What bought I this brass ring for, pray?
> You came dress'd out upon the day;
> I too was dress'd, a silly Toad—
> But frighten'd at the Man in black,
> At the Church door you turn'd your back,
> And ran away down Tyburn Road.

She continues storming at him in an air which begins with an eighteen-bar
introduction and then continues as follows:

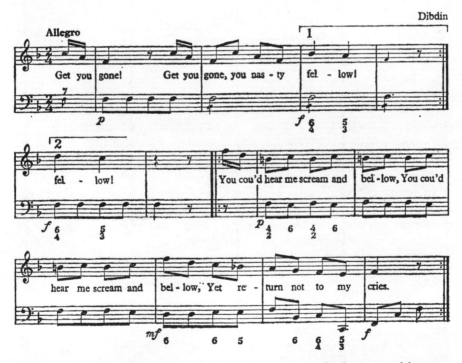

As so often with Dibdin, this is nothing as pure music, but everything as a
theatre song. John explains that he was worried by unsavoury rumours about
Moll's behaviour with other men, but when she retaliates with a few rumours
she has heard about him, they agree to settle their differences and get married
after all.

The vocal score allows John two airs and Moll one; there are two duets. The accompaniments include no instrumental cues, and no middle parts; much has been left out.

No doubt *The Razor-Grinder* had a similar type of plot, and it is a pity it does not survive. Several of the other Dialogues also have cockney settings. In *The Grenadier* we are in a basement kitchen with two servants, Jenny and Ralph, who are 'walking out'. But when Jenny sends Ralph off to the shops, it is revealed that she has a smart young soldier hidden in a cupboard. Ralph returns unexpectedly and catches them, but by now Jenny is prepared to admit that she finds the Grenadier and his uniform irresistible. *The Mischance* is about three street-hawkers, an Egg Man, a Fish Woman, and a Potato Woman, who quarrel incessantly. The 'mischance' occurs when the Egg Man drops all his eggs. In *The Ladle* a 'Conjuror' offers to grant three wishes to a couple who have been kind to him. The wife says that above all things she wants a new ladle. The husband thinks this is a ridiculous wish.

> Your're in the wrong—come, come,—
> Of serious things you made a joke;
> For having in this manner spoke,
> I wish you may be dumb.

The Conjurer takes this unconsidered remark as the second wish, and thus the third one has to be wasted on restoring the lady's tongue.[1] These miniscule plots, naïve though they were, allowed the 'working-class' audience to identify pleasurably, and they were sufficiently popular to be revived quite frequently in the 1780s. I have found only one new vocal score for this decade, but in the last one of the century William Reeve, an uninteresting composer, wrote a number of short all-sung pieces for Sadler's Wells to words by Mark Londsale.

In our own times *The Brickdust Man* and *The Grenadier* were in the repertoire of the Intimate Opera Company between the wars, and still have plenty of entertainment value. *The Mischance* might well be revived as well, for much of it was published in full score, notably the opening trio for the three hawkers, which is scored for oboes and strings.

---

[1] Back in 1704 Matthew Prior had been able to treat the climax rather differently. Jupiter and Mercury visit a farmhouse, and are entertained with such kindness that they offer the farmer and his wife three wishes. The wife at once exclaims:

> A Ladle for our Silver Dish
> Is what I want, is what I wish.—
> A Ladle! cries the Man, a Ladle!
> 'Odzooks, Corisca, You have pray'd ill:
> What should be Great, You turn to Farce:
> I wish the Ladle in your A— . . .
> Our Couple weep Two Wishes past,
> And kindly join to form the last,
> To ease the Woman's aukward Pain,
> And get the Ladle out again.

Some problems arise over the only Sadler's Wells Dialogue that survives by James Hook. This is *The Country Wake*, and judging from its opus number, 36, it was published about 1784. The published score, which is in the British Museum and in no other major British library, reveals that Lowe sang the part of the hero, Damon. But Lowe had died in 1783, and in his last years he is said to have been sunk in poverty and not singing at all. It thus seems likely that this little piece is the same as *The Country Courtship*, the dialogue advertised on *The Brickdust Man*, and that it originated in the middle seventies. Phillis is pursued by both the 'Captain', who claims her by right for he is also the Lord of the Manor, and by the simple countryman, Damon, who arrives just in time to preserve her honour. After some 'villaging' Damon suddenly finds himself recruited for the army; in fact the 'Sarjeant', who has an excellent recruiting song, has taken action at the request of the nefarious 'Captain'. Phillis is suitably pathetic in a pleasing song with clarinet cues, and in the end the 'Captain' relents and the lovers are re-united. It will be seen that both titles suit the plot equally well (or ill). It is likely, however, that *The Country Courtship* is the correct one. *The Country Wake* was the sub-title of the long-popular ballad-opera *Flora*, and the engraver might easily have put these familiar words on the title-page by mistake. The piece is unusual in having a one-movement overture.

4 VAUXHALL GARDENS

In 1775 Hook became music director at Vauxhall Gardens, and remained there for forty-five years. Parke says he played an organ concerto there every night,[1] which works out at about 5,000 performances. He certainly wrote over 2,000 songs. It was well for him that the organ had no pedals, for he was club-footed; he walked only with difficulty. Parke says he 'preferred making an observation to listening to one', but he was well-liked. In winter when the gardens were closed he turned to teaching in schools, and counted on making about £600 a year from this activity. One of his pupils was Miss Mitford.

In the middle eighties, and perhaps at other times as well, Hook experimented at Vauxhall Gardens with operatic pieces. There can have been no scenery or action in the cramped 'orchestra'. Presumably the singers, as at Ranelagh, sang with the music in their hands and made the semi-dramatic gestures we too are familiar with at concert performances of operas. Four of these little Dialogues were published, complete with their recitatives:

The Poll Booth, op. 34; 1784

A Word to Wives, op. 41; c. 1785. Described as a sequel to the 'cantata', *The Cryer*.

The Triumph of Beauty, op. 46; 1786. The singers included Incledon and Mrs. Wrighten.

The Queen of the May; c. 1787.

[1] ii, p. 254.

Each of these is described as 'A Musical Entertainment' and limited to four singers, all there was room for. They may well have been staged later at Sadler's Wells; *The Country Wake* (see above) was certainly given both there and in Vauxhall Gardens. *The Poll Booth* is the best of them, and might merit revival today. (The 'Poll' is taken to decide which singer is the favourite.)

We shall meet Hook again, for his unquenchable industry led him to write operas for both the winter playhouses. But his lack of a dramatic sense and slap-dash methods limited their success; as James Boaden put it, 'he wrote too fast'.[1]

[1] *Mrs. Jordan* ii, p. 63.

II
Ballad Operas and Pantomimes
1760–1780

1 BALLAD OPERAS MODERNIZED

ALL over Europe the rise of the *galante* style led to a diminution in the importance of the continuo. Though the harpsichord was still to be used by composers directing their music, its role became the setting of tempos rather than the filling in of harmonies. The continuo song with only keyboard and cello for its accompaniment began to seem too quiet and unexciting.

The ballad opera had always depended on harpsichord continuo. As we have seen, the violins doubled the vocal line and the harpsichord filled in between this and the bass. If continuo accompaniment was to be down-graded, it would seem that ballad operas had no future. Yet when *The Beggar's Opera* was staged at Covent Garden in October 1759 with Miss Brent as Polly and Beard as Macheath, the production was the talk of London. Whether the accompaniments were modernized is uncertain, but it is likely that they were not. However that may be, Beard was soon asking William Bates to rejuvenate *The Jovial Crew* with at least a proportion of new-style accompaniments, and the result was staged on 14 February 1760, with Miss Brent as Rachel, and Beard, Lowe, and Mattocks in support. This production, much more successful than the one back in 1731, lasted a good twelve years.

Soon after the first night, John Johnson published the music of *The Jovial Crew*, 'The Overture in Score and the Accompaniments to the Airs composed by Mr. Bates'; it is the only publication of its kind. The three-movement overture, which is very poor in quality, is scored for oboes, horns, and strings, the oboes switching to flutes for the minuet movement in the middle. The airs all have introductions and postludes derived from the vocal line, the former being mostly four bars long, the latter two. The majority are just like those already described in the MSS of *The Devil to pay*, and they must have been performed in the same way, with all the violins on the top line and only the harpsichord between that and the bass. In fact there was no rejuvenating at all in most of the airs. However Air 15 and the unnumbered one on page 39 have a second violin part in the introduction; Airs 27 and 42 have a second violin part all through, given on a third stave; Airs 24 and 26 are fully scored, the former[1] for flutes, horns, and three-part strings, the latter presumably for flute and strings. There are also two dances in full score for oboes, horns, and strings. Most of the airs had been in the 1731 version, but all the instrumental pieces were new, as also the two songs in full score and one or two others. Some of the songs are delightful, notably 'Lovely Nancy', but William Bates had not yet learnt how to write instrumental music.

Miss Brent was not satisfied with the simple airs she was given to sing, and six of her ten solos[2] were replaced by newly-composed songs that Arne wrote in order to show off her voice to more advantage; he published them that same year in his Ninth Collection. Three are scored only for two violins and bass, but they have much more musical substance than those they replaced, while the remaining three were quite elaborately orchestrated. In one case Arne merely provided a more interesting accompaniment for an attractive old tune—the tongue-in-the-cheek tear-jerker that Rachel sings when disguised as a beggar-woman:

> My Daddy is gone to his Grave,
>   My Mother lies under a Stone,
> And never a Penny I have—
>   Alas! I am quite undone.

Beard must have thought well of Bates's modernization, for a few months later he accepted from him a similar revision of *Flora*. The published score claimed to give only the principal items, and these included a new overture (but in keyboard arrangement), eight new songs by Bates, and seven of the original airs. But there were at least two retrogressive attempts at ballad opera in the old style: *Love at first Sight* (DL 17.10.63) by Thomas King, and *The Spanish Lady* (CG 2.5.65) by the Covent Garden stage manager, Thomas Hull. Their total lack of success reflected the growing dissatisfaction with old-style ballads; an era in operatic history seemed to be coming to a close. But it was still not clear why a pastiche like *The Maid of the Mill*, based on fully-composed songs, was more popular than the kind based on ballads. Was it the *galante* scoring that did the trick? Arne's new-style additions to *The Jovial Crew* had been well-liked, and it might be that other once-loved ballad operas could be rejuvenated with a few similar songs or even with new music throughout. These further attempts of the kind are listed below:

Damon and Phillida (DL 21.12.68) by Colley Cibber, with all-new music by Dibdin; 'Went off very dull, and some Hisses—The Music was not vastly liked' (Hopkins).

---

[1] Based on 'Lovely Nancy', a song by James Oswald published in his *Caledonian Pocket Companion* ii of c. 1745.
[2] Airs 7, 11, 20, 21, 30, and 33 in Bates's score.

The Ladies' Frolick (DL 7.5.70), a cut version by James Love of *The Jovial Crew* put on at the rival theatre, with a new and better overture and six new songs by Bates, and one or two by Arne; a dozen or so of the original airs were kept.

Achilles in Petticoats (CG 16.12.73), a cut version of Gay's *Achilles* with a good overture and new songs by Arne; none of the original airs was kept.

None of these afterpiece revisions was nearly so successful as the full-length 1760 production of *The Jovial Crew*. Indeed they were not so well liked as *The Devil to pay* and *The Lottery*, which continued to draw audiences throughout the last quarter of the century, though I have found no evidence of their being modernized.

2 'THE BEGGAR'S OPERA' AFTER 1759

It is very hard to establish just what changes were made in *The Beggar's Opera* at this period, even though they were certainly considerable. The chief complicating factor is the arrangement ascribed to Thomas Arne, which was advertised by Straight & Skillern in the *Public Advertiser* for 17 April 1769, at which date it was brand-new. The title page runs: 'The Beggar's Opera/as it is Perform'd at both/Theatres,/with the Additional Alterations by/Dr. Arne,/for the/Voice, Harpsichord & Violin./The Basses entirely New.' The Additional Alterations will be considered first; my numeration is that of the original editions, as also of Dent's (OUP).

1. Arne made very small and unnecessary alterations in the overture.
2. He cut Airs 11, 43, 45, and 56.
3. He added appoggiaturas to some of the vocal lines; for instance in Airs 4 and 6.
4. He transposed fifteen items; in all but one instance, he put the music up, usually by a tone or a tone and a half. Both Mrs. Peachum's airs go up, seven of Polly's and three of Lucy's; also Air 52, a duet for Polly and Lucy.
5. He rounded off Act I (Air 18) with some two-part writing for Polly and Macheath.
6. He wrote a new Hornpipe, and as it is placed between Airs 57 and 58, it must be 'The Dance of the Prisoners in Chains'.
7. He added Tempo Marks to every item.

The tempo marks are of interest, for they must reflect tradition. In general they are unsurprising, but the following examples may lead to some re-thinking:

Air 20 ('Let us take the Road'): *Andante* with unbarred C. Dent's edition of 1941 has *Allegro* and barred C, which makes the minims the marching beats rather than the crotchets. It looks as though we sing this item at double speed.

Air 39 (Polly's 'No Power on Earth'): *Largo*. Dent hovers between *Allegro agitato* and *Andante*.

Air 54 (Polly's 'When my Hero in Court appears'): *Siciliano*.

Air 55 (Lucy's 'When he holds up his Hand'): *Andante*. Dent's *Allegro agitato* cannot be right.

We can accept these tempo marks, and indeed all the other Additional Alterations, as the work of a sound musician. But the New Basses in this same edition are much less musicianly. They are no better, nor indeed very different in style, from those by Pepusch. They show no instrumental introductions, no filling-in of harmonies, and no trace of *galante* orchestration. It is very hard to believe that such a version could have been made after the 1760 revision of *The Jovial Crew*, in which Arne himself had been involved. It is easier, though not much, to believe that he wrote the basses either for the Dublin performances of 1743 when he 'presided at the harpsichord', or for the 1759 production at Covent Garden when Miss Brent sang Polly.

But the 1743 dating does not stand up to scrutiny. Arne would not then have put so many airs into a higher key, for the resulting B flats would have been beyond the reach of almost all sopranos. By 1759 such notes had become fairly common, and Charlotte Brent and Polly Young as Polly and Lucy might well have wanted to show off their B flats. Also the new hornpipe was quite certainly composed for the 1759 production, though not for the first performance of it. It will be remembered that Pepusch had written a hornpipe in three-two time for the 'Prisoners in Chains', and that the tune had become one of the airs in Gay's *Achilles*. By the 1750s it was the custom for it to be danced by a single girl prisoner, and in 1759 the dance was given to Nancy Dawson. But in the following summer Garrick lured Miss Dawson over to Drury Lane for this very dance in a rival production of *The Beggar's Opera*, and it looks as though she brought the orchestral parts with her, for when Covent Garden revived their production (11.10.60), they advertised 'A new Hornpipe compos'd by Dr. Arne perform'd by Mrs. Vernon'. Arne's tune was so well liked that it was made into a song and sung by Tenducci at Ranelagh Gardens. No doubt the orchestration for strings and horns given in his *Winter Amusement Collection* was the same as that of the hornpipe.[1]

But if we accept, on this rather flimsy evidence, that Arne made his revision for Covent Garden in 1759, we must then find a reason for his not publishing it for ten years. Did the basses seem to him so indifferent that he did not wish them to be exposed to the eye? Could he at any time in his career have written this one?

[1] Arne's tune can be found in Frederic Austin's well-known edition of *The Beggar's Opera* on p. 87.

in___ my___ Arms___ em - braced my Lass,

A quite different solution is possible, and it was first put forward about 1827 by John Addison when he was preparing a new vocal score of *The Beggar's Opera*. In his Preface he avers that the edition 'purporting to have new bases composed by Dr. Arne, is a gross imposition, and to receive it as his, would be to libel both his taste and judgment'. Addison had been born in or about 1766 and being a competent musician he must have known what went on in late eighteenth-century productions. Indeed he tells us about them in his Preface:

> Until the year 1777 the orchestral music to the airs consisted of merely the melodies and a base, at which time Mr. Linley brought forward his pupil, Miss Wright, afterwards Mrs. T. Blanchard, in the part of Polly, and composed some very ingenious and effective accompaniments: notwithstanding which, the prejudice in favour of the former continued till within a few years, when Mr. Arnold[1] revived it at the English Opera-House, and (with some exceptions) restored Mr. Linley's accompaniments, which have since been generally adopted, and to which I owe great obligation in the following arrangement.

The Linley version has its own problems, and they will be considered later. Let us first give another glance at Arne's title page with Addison's remarks in mind.

> As it is Perform'd at both Theatres, with the Additional Alterations by Dr. Arne, for the Voice, Harpsichord & Violin. The Basses entirely new.

Surely there is significance in that first full stop? It is not in fact stated that the basses are by Arne; only that they are new. This is, I suggest, an unauthorized edition intended to deceive. Later publishers, less careful in their claims, state positively that Arne wrote the basses, but their title-pages are not evidence. Furthermore it is most unlikely that new basses would have been played at 'both Theatres'. But if the full stop on the title-page be given its full meaning, Straight & Skillern never claimed that they were.

The explanation that best fits the facts is as follows. For the 1759 production Arne suggested some alterations which were eventually adopted at Drury Lane as well. The chief of these was the transposition of the girls' songs so that they could show off their voices to better advantage. On the same occasion someone put new basses to the airs, and judging by their incompetence it may have been

---

[1] Samuel Arnold's son.

Bates. Ten years later Straight & Skillern published the Covent Garden version with an equivocal title page and without Arne's knowledge.

It is clear from Addison's statement that, however much other ballad operas were renovated, prejudice prevented similar treatment being given to *The Beggar's Opera*. Addison says there were no new-style accompaniments until Linley's of 1777, but in fact Covent Garden's musical director, J. A. Fisher, attempted some degree of renovation the year before, as is revealed in a *Morning Post* article of 2 October 1776:

> Mr. Fisher . . . in avoiding one extreme, has run into another equally unjustifiable, in accompanying the airs only with a first and second fiddle, and Merlin's new Forte Piano. By this super delicate pianissimo, the melody and harmony of the matchless airs were filtered down to nothing; but the obbligato flourishings of the first fiddle, and the chord of the new-invented Harpsichord [*sic*] . . . (were) more absurd, if possible, than the old style of overpowering the voice with the full force of a large band.

It follows from this that another innovation in 1759 had been to have all the strings playing in the airs; Fisher reverted to the previous practice of having only one or two players to a part, so that the rather unobtrusive tone of the early piano might be heard. Indeed it seems to follow that solo strings were used, both in 1729 and 1776. Fisher's version does not survive; no doubt his piano accompaniments were improvised.

It was not only the accompaniments that were being changed at this period In 1773 the famous magistrate Sir John Fielding, half-brother to the novelist, had expressed the view that *The Beggar's Opera*, by condoning vice, was a prime cause of the increase in London's crime. Other justices thought so too, and their opinion received much publicity. The playhouses refused to be browbeaten into withdrawing so profitable a piece, but they did react in time. On 10 October 1777 Covent Garden staged a much-discussed production with an additional scene at the end by Captain Edward Thompson, the young naval adventurer who had collaborated with Fisher the previous year in a masque called *The Syrens*. The new scene, a sop to Sir John Fielding, included several additional songs and showed Macheath suffering retribution 'in the hulks near Woolwich Warren'. Both Polly and Lucy visit him, the latter only to upbraid. Polly stays, and when Macheath promises to change his way of life on release, she undertakes to wait for him. The *Morning Post*, as also some of the audience, found the new ending ridiculous, and the more so because, in an attempt to tone down the incitement to vice, Macheath was played by a woman, Mrs. Farrel.

Mrs. Farrel, described by the *Morning Post* as a 'counter-tenor', was one of Arne's last pupils, and it was for her that he wrote his famous song 'A-Hunting we will go', known at the time by its opening words, 'The dusky Night'. It may well have been his last composition. Mrs. Farrel sang it in *The Beggar's Opera*, probably in the final scene when an expectation of eventual happiness might reasonably have been allowed to the wretched Macheath. But it is unlikely that Arne provided the other songs for the new ending. Fisher was still under contract to Covent Garden, and would have been expected to compose most of the additional music.

A month later (8.11.77) Drury Lane also felt impelled to stage a white-washed *Beggar's Opera*, though it was not advertised as new. However the critics got wind of it for they were there in force. Many of what the *Morning Chronicle* called 'the looser parts' of the dialogue had been cut, and the final reprieve of Macheath was given a motive; he was reprieved so that he might be reformed.

> *Player :* Will the Town approve?
> *Beggar :* An act of Mercy will always be acceptable to an English Audience.

But, as the *Morning Chronicle* pointed out, to most people this was 'a pernicious doctrine' for it implied that you could sin as much as you liked if you reformed in the end.

For us today the reformation of the music is of more interest. The same review went on:

> Symphonies were added to several of the airs, and the harmony made more full, by Mr. Linley, which had a very pleasing effect, particularly the accompanyment of the horns in various places.

The *Morning Post* also liked the new 'accompanyments', but added:

> The public ear having been so long accustomed to the simple melody of these celebrated airs, it was a service of danger to attempt any innovation, lest the generality of play-going people should not be able to recognise their favourite tunes, under the disguise of such embellishments.

No doubt it was through fear of antagonizing die-hards that Drury Lane did not at first advertise these innovations, but the music was so well received that the third performance was announced as 'with Alterations', and the fourth as 'With Accompanyments to the Airs by Mr. Linley'.

It is disquieting to learn that 'Symphonies' (i.e. introductions) were added to 'several of the airs'. But not to all? And were there none before? Earlier in this book I have suggested that there were 'symphonies' from the first in all ballad operas. Perhaps in this performance they made more impact on the critic's mind because of the addition of wind instruments, the filling-out of the harmonies, and their extra length. They impressed William Parke as well; he wrote of Linley's

> admired and well-known accompaniments to the original airs . . . several of which elicited strong marks of science and genius, particularly those to 'Cease your Funning', and, 'O ponder well': the elegant and effective oboe

accompaniment to the former, finely played by the elder Parke, and the appropriate and impressive decorations to the latter by the French horns and clarionets, have been justly eulogised by foreign writers, as well as by those of this country.[1]

It happens that Linley's 'O ponder well' is given in Shield's *Introduction to Harmony* (1800) on page 100, and very curious it is.

To save space I have cut the vocal stave as it follows the first violin part. Presumably for the same reason Shield cut the introduction. Clearly there was a vocal cadenza in bar 17, and one for the first violin in bar 21. The tempo must be very slow; the 'Arne' edition marks this song *Largo*. The extraordinary change from three-four to two-four would not be quite so worrying to the ear

---

[1] Parke i, p. 11.

as to the eye, for the three-bar phrases at the start would each sound like a single bar of the original. Nevertheless, it is curious that both Parke and Shield admired so thick and perverse an arrangement. No other of Linley's accompaniments can be identified with certainty, but, if Addison is to be believed, many others are preserved in his edition. George Hogarth, writing in 1839, seems in the main to accept Addison's Preface when he writes 'Linley composed the orchestral accompaniments to the songs in the *Beggar's Opera*, which have been always used since his time'.[1]

Addison's edition is the best before Dent's. It is the earliest in which the songs have two staves for the accompaniment in the modern way, and these accompaniments have enough individuality to be interesting but not so much as to be irritating. Addison's sense of style preserved the wrong-key endings to airs 7, 16, 18, and 39; the two Victorian editors, John Barnett (1858) and J. L. Hatton (1874) found them barbaric and unendurable. It may well be that the violin obbligato that so charmingly reflects the words in Air 21 is by Linley:

Though the Barnett and Hatton editions differ from Addison's in most respects, they follow it in their treatment of the final prison scene in which Macheath sings a continuous series of song snippets. All three editions may be assumed to give Linley's intelligent solution to the problem of linking these snippets into a *scena*.

The tendency for actresses to play Macheath became more pronounced in the last quarter of the century. Mrs. Farrel, widowed in her twenties, became Mrs.

---

[1] ii, p. 436. It is worth noting that Addison did *not* reproduce Linley's 'O ponder well'.

Kennedy in 1779 and under her new name sang Macheath repeatedly. Her large frame and rugged features made her more acceptable in male parts than female. But slim graceful girls like Miss De Camp were also successful Macheaths. Patrick, the hero of Shield's very successful opera *The Poor Soldier*, was regularly played by an actress, notably by Mrs. Jordan, and it is tempting to derive the convention from Handelian opera, but in fact transvestite roles were just as common in plays. In Farquhar's *The Constant Couple*, performed more often this century than any other Restoration comedy, Sir Harry Wildair was frequently given to an actress; Peg Woffington and Mrs. Jordan were especially memorable in this role. About 1780 a very large woman called Mrs. Webb was sometimes entrusted with the part of Falstaff. Thus Colman's experiment of playing *The Beggar's Opera* with *all* the sexes reversed (LT 8.8.81), though meant to be ludicrous, was less perverse than it would seem today

'As truly laughable as it was strange', says Mrs. Crouch's biographer, but the same source reveals that massive Charles Bannister as Polly sang the songs quite seriously, 'in his finest style'. He did not even attempt a consistent falsetto or a mincing gait. However, there was plenty of slapstick. Wilson as Mrs. Peachum used 'to swing too headlessly in his chair' and let the audience see his black plush breeches under the petticoats, and Edwin, the leading low comedian of the day, was a riot as Lucy. But Mrs. Webb as Lockit and Mrs. Cargill as Macheath must have been quite unfunny, for the audience was conditioned to their appearing in male roles. In spite of well-grounded complaints about the prostitute scenes (John Bannister was Jenny Diver), the production was popular, and it was still being revived in 1790, notably at Covent Garden. This theatre also gave *Midas* with the sexes reversed (19.3.85).

However, *The Beggar's Opera* continued to be played conventionally at the winter playhouses, where the best tenors continued to sing Macheath and the best sopranos Polly. In the 1790s Incledon was especially admired as Macheath, and at Drury Lane they even gave Polly to Madame Mara, a plain woman with atrocious English. These defects were of course the subject of comment, but they were offset by her beautiful singing. The fact that she was offered the part shows the extent to which the songs were regarded as the main attraction of the work.

In 1781 Linley arranged *The Gentle Shepherd* for Drury Lane with the help of his son-in-law Richard Tickell. Of the two movements in the *galante* overture, the first is rather incompetent while the second, 'taken from a Violin Concerto by the late Mr. Thos. Linley Junior', is based on one of several tunes known as 'The Highland Laddie'; there are cues for flute, oboe, bassoon, and solo violin. But there are no cues for wind instruments in the songs, though all have introductions and several appear to have second violin parts. Linley changed a few of the original tunes, and introduced two 'composed' songs, one by himself and one by Samuel Howard. The latter is much the more attractive; it replaced the song to the tune of 'The Bush aboon Traquair', which had been sung in *The Duenna* so often that Linley felt it needed a rest. Drury Lane had earlier presented *The Gentle Shepherd* with 'New Accompaniments' (9.5.74) and 'A New Medley Scotch Overture' by Dibdin, who probably wrote the accompaniments too, but not a trace of this version can be found.

3 PANTOMIMES 1760–1775

Pantomime music was in a low state at this time, but there was one example of real interest, and one innovation that led to improved standards in the eighties.

The Witches, or Harlequin Cherokee (DL 23.11.62) was devised by James Dance, who until recently had been manager of the Edinburgh Theatre; he had left the previous summer in shady circumstances, and now called himself James Love. He acted a little, and as his Falstaff was praised he was probably corpulent. A year or two later he started the theatre at Richmond in Surrey. Boswell, who was constantly lending Love money, thought *The Witches* 'but a dull thing', and the *St. James's Chronicle* described the subtitle as 'an absolute misnomer; with so little about Cherokees and so much about witches and cauldrons the pantomime should have been called *Harlequin Macbeth*'. There are certainly no signs of Red Indians in the wretched Comic Tunes by Walter Clagget. Clagget was one of the Drury Lane violinists, and his brother Charles won some fame later for inventing a double trumpet that could play in both D and E flat.[1] In this, as in all other Drury Lane pantomimes of the sixties, Rooker was Harlequin.

In 1771 *The Witches* was revised without the Cherokees and subtitled *Harlequin's Trip to Naples*; the climax was an eruption of Vesuvius. New music was composed by Henry Moze and Joseph Vernon, and Moze's quite worthless overture was published in parts. (He had collaborated with Prelleur in 1758 in the publication of a hymn collection, and he may have been Prelleur's pupil.) Moze probably composed the new Comic Tunes that were published with Vernon's songs. The British Museum has a children's booklet of verses and pull-out plates ('6d. plain, 1s. colour'd') that was published under this pantomime's revised title.[2] Each plate is divided across the middle so that there are flaps above and below the division; when a flap is raised, the reader sees underneath what happens next. For example Plate No. 3 shows Harlequin disguised as a one-legged fiddler; underneath the flaps he is belabouring 'the old man and the clown'. None of the four pairs of pictures shows either Naples or Vesuvius, but the combination of title and date makes it certain that they do represent incidents in the Drury Lane pantomime.

James Love's next pantomime was *The Rites of Hecate, or Harlequin from the Moon* (DL 26.12.63), and this is unique in that the music of the serious scenes survives in MS full score. *The Rites of Hecate* was lucky to succeed as well as it did, for within hours of the curtain rising, the succession of incidents

[1] Busby ii, p. 174, and Galpin p. 157.
[2] BM 11643.aa.55 (1), pub. 1772.

was still undecided. Because Love was ineffectual, Colman took control.[1] According to Hopkins, 'The Pantomime went off very well & with great applause.—I think the Tunes in general very bad.—and a great Want of Business and Incidents.—The scenery very pretty.—The Elephant is excellent'. At later performances the audience found unusual grounds for complaint. Love's seven-year-old son William 'was hiss'd for playing out of tune upon the organ'.[2] They also complained, increasingly, of the Mad Scene in Bedlam at the end, and this was eventually cut on the grounds that 'the unhappiness of human beings is too melancholy for a Diversion'. Yet at this precise moment in time Gluck was holding up to ridicule the madness of a painter in *La Rencontre imprévue*, and Einstein thought that 'the eighteenth century found all evidence of madness extremely funny'.[3] It is to the credit of the Drury Lane audience that they found it no such thing.

It was the Comic Tunes by John Potter to which Hopkins objected in *The Rites of Hecate*, and they are certainly very poor. Potter has been mentioned before, and an attempt must now be made to draw the many strands of his career into a single thread.[4] Baker, our chief source, says that Potter was a doctor in the West of England who studied music as an amateur. In 1762, aged about twenty-eight, he came to London to give the annual Music Lectures at Gresham College, and these were published as *Observations on Music and Musicians*. As well as composing some of the music for *The Rites of Hecate*, he wrote the deplorable libretto of *The Choice of Apollo* which was set by Yates. But his main work in the 1760s and 70s was at Vauxhall Gardens; for the concerts there he wrote the words of several hundred songs as well as the music for a few dozen. In between times he dashed off five novels and a crusty account of one season's activities at the playhouses (1771–2), which he published anonymously as *The Theatrical Review*. Baker lists other literary works, including a bowdlerized *Don Quixote*.

Potter's Comic Tunes for *The Rites of Hecate* appear to survive only in the Pendlebury Library, Cambridge. They are printed in what looks like full score, though there are no parts for wind instruments. The style is old-fashioned. The Elephant plods to a *Largo* that reminds one of the Dead March in *Saul*. The titles suggest that the pantomime ended with Harlequin being tried in Westminster Hall (Potter aptly quotes 'The Charge is prepared' from *The Beggar's Opera*), after which he was flung into Bedlam—represented by a short energetic Handelian *presto* with rushing semiquavers.

The British Museum MS of the vocal music[5] is in the hand of R. J. S.

---

[1] See LS, Part 4, p. xxiv.

[2] Hopkins meant that he got the tune wrong. See Dibdin's *Musical Tour*, p. 272, for a similar use of the phrase.

[3] Einstein's *Mozart*, p. 416. But see also Boaden's *Mrs. Jordan* i, p. 116.

[4] His activities were so various that it may be there were two John Potters; if so, it is beyond my powers to separate them.

[5] Add. 31812.

Stevens, and it was composed by Jonathan Battishill, the harpsichordist at Covent Garden from about 1760 to 1764. In December 1765 he married Elizabeth Davies, the original Madge in *Love in a Village*. He had left Covent Garden to write *Almena* for Drury Lane,[1] and when this failed he turned to church music. Some of his hymns and chants are still sung today. In the seventies his wife ran off with an actor named Webster,[2] and this unhappy event caused him to abandon composition entirely. Battishill became a recluse, pottering endlessly among the many books he had accumulated. He never did justice to his solid talents.

His contribution to *The Rites of Hecate* is operatic in the grand style. It begins with a long *scena* alternating between snatches of chorus, recitative, and arioso. Tempo and rhythm change so often that one wonders how they managed without a baton conductor. The music begins spookily for strings alone.

[Violas double Vcl. or at the 8ve]

---

[1] See p. 313.
[2] Kelly, i, p. 13, 2nd ed.

The scoring is much more elaborate than the above suggests; later there are parts for oboes, bassoon, horns, and trumpets. The chorus keeps calling for Hecate, as also does the First Witch ('Mr. Vernon') whose aria is darkened with bassoon tone. When at last Hecate arrives, Harlequin descends from the moon and all the witches fly off. So far the music has depended very little on melody of the usual theatre kind, the composer being more interested in depicting the words and situations from a purely dramatic point of view. When Columbine has an air of a more conventional kind, it turns out to be based on a lyric Potter set as well; his version comes at the end of his Comic Tunes, and is marked 'Omitted in the Performance'. One suspects bad staff work by Garrick or Colman.

I have written about Battishill's score as though it were unique, and to us it is. But in fact many pantomimes must have had music of this nature, music that is more dramatic in approach than most opera scores of the time. We shall never know just what we have lost.

Drury Lane continued to search for new successes in the pantomime field, and Garrick allowed Love a third attempt. *The Hermit, or Harlequin at Rhodes* (DL 6.1.66) was not much liked. Collet's overture was printed in parts,[1] but none of the other music was published. Tommaso Giordani's overture to *The Elopement* (DL 26.12.67) also appeared in parts, and in keyboard arrangement with the Comic Tunes; the title page of the latter makes it clear that Giordani wrote nothing but the overture. Grimaldi, father of the famous clown, played Pantaloon; he had been a Cherokee in *The Witches*. *The Elopement* was very popular for some ten or twelve years, yet we do not know who devised it, who wrote most of the music, or what it was about.

Meanwhile Covent Garden was saving money and trouble by sticking to such tried favourites as *Perseus and Andromeda* and *Harlequin Sorcerer*. In 1766 Beard got Arnold to refurbish *Harlequin Dr. Faustus*, and the new music was published.[2] *Harlequin's Jubilee* (CG 27.1.70) is the first pantomime whose music was quite certainly all by one composer—John Abraham Fisher. From now on it was customary for one musician to be in overall control, and eventually this meant that more trouble was taken over pantomime music.

There is little to be said for Arnold's *Mother Shipton* (CG 26.12.70). The scenario and the song words were by George Colman, and they were to be much better served by William Shield in a revised version called *Harlequin Museum, or Mother Shipton Triumphant* (1792). Only one of Arnold's Comic Tunes shows a dramatic sense, and that is the curiously named 'Inside of the Coal Pit'. Mother Shipton was a poor man's Nostradamus, alleged to have lived towards the end of the Wars of the Roses at Knaresborough in Yorkshire; her 'cave' is

---

[1] It also survives in MS full score (BM Add. 31576).
[2] Also some of the old. No. 28 in Arnold's score ('Dusty Miller') occurs in Medley Overture No. 6 (Prelleur?) and was probably written for the original *Harlequin Dr. Faustus*.

still a tourist attraction. Her mother was a local woman, her father the devil, and she is said to have fortold the death of Cardinal Wolsey, the Fire of London, and (less successfully) the End of the World in the year 1881. Dibdin's *The Pigmy Revels* (DL 26.12.72) was thrown together so rapidly that Dibdin himself never knew who devised it. A Comic Tune called 'Columbine Drunk' broke new ground, and in a big coloratura song Mrs. Wrighten made mock of Miss Catley's vocal mannerisms. Arne contributed a 'Morris Dance' that must have taken him all of five minutes to compose.

I end this chapter with some thoughts that Garrick had been repeating in one form or another all through his career. In September 1775 Drury Lane was opened for the first time after a resplendent redecoration that summer by the Adam brothers. It was the sort of occasion on which a Prelude was expected; that is, a short topical piece, celebratory and musical. *The Theatrical Candidates* (DL 23.9.75) had music by William Bates, and Garrick wrote the words. The Candidates are Tragedy, Comedy, and Pantomime, the latter represented by a speaking Harlequin. Which of them is to hold sway in the more-or-less new theatre? Harlequin's song makes the predictable point.

> Shou'd Harlequin be banish'd hence,
> Quit the place to wit and sense,
> What wou'd be the consequence?
>   Empty houses;
>   You and spouses
> And your pretty children dear,
>   Ne'er wou'd come,
>   Leave your home,
> Unless that I came after,
>   Frisking here,
>   Whisking there,
> Tripping, skipping ev'ry where,
> To crack your sides with laughter.

The reference to children is interesting. In recent times it has always been taken for granted that pantomimes were ostensibly for children, but this is the first reference I have found to their swelling a pantomime audience in the eighteenth century.

12
Change and Decay
1775–1782

THE popularity of opera in the last quarter of the century is even more striking than in the Garrick period. Lumping the playhouses together and starting in the summer of 1776, *The London Stage* (Part 5) shows that of the twelve most performed main pieces six were operas, four were plays by Shakespeare, and two were modern plays.[1] The list begins:

The School for Scandal	261
The Beggar's Opera (Pepusch)	229
Love in a Village (Arne)	168
Hamlet	
The Duenna (the Linleys)	164
Inkle and Yarico (Arnold)	

If the 1775–6 season were included, *The Duenna* would move up to second place. Astonishingly, the nine most popular afterpieces were all operatic, the leaders at Drury Lane and Covent Garden being:

Comus (Arne)	215
Rosina (Shield)	201
The Poor Soldier (Shield)	165
No Song no Supper (Storace)	151

Also very popular were three Arnold operas given almost exclusively at the Little Theatre: *The Agreeable Surprise* (200), *The Son-in-Law* (197), and *Peeping Tom* (152). Though the number of new operas rose, the number of categories fell. Composers concentrated almost entirely on the comic opera with spoken dialogue. The all-sung opera virtually vanished, as did the burlesque, and there is no more to be said of the ballad opera. Thus it becomes unrewarding at this point to deal with theatre music in categories; from now on each theatre and its dominant composer will be taken in turn.

[1] These statistics make it the more extraordinary that the otherwise excellent 218-page Introduction to *The London Stage* (Part 5) makes virtually no mention of composers, singers, or orchestras; nor indeed of the preponderance of operas in the repertoire.

I THE LINLEYS 1775–1780

Thomas Linley (1733–95) has already been mentioned as a singing teacher in Bath and the composer of one opera, *The Royal Merchant*. There is no need to tell in detail how Richard Brinsley Sheridan, son of the Irish actor-manager Thomas Sheridan, eloped with Linley's eldest daughter, Elizabeth. After their marriage the two families were soon reconciled, and in the autumn of 1775, his reputation made over-night by *The Rivals*, Sheridan persuaded his father-in-law to come to London and supervise the rehearsals for *The Duenna* at Covent Garden. The following year, on Garrick's retirement, Sheridan went over to the rival playhouse, Drury Lane, to become manager, the other patentees being Linley and Dr. Ford. Linley left Bath for good, and from now on he was in charge of all the music at Drury Lane.

The Linley family were uniquely talented and as uniquely ill-starred. Elizabeth, Sheridan's wife, was among the finest sopranos of the century, but there will be little about her in this book partly because she specialized in oratorio and partly because, after her marriage, her husband forbade her to sing professionally. Thomas, the second Linley child, was our most promising composer between Purcell and Elgar, and his accidental death when only twenty-two changed for the worse the whole history of our music. Two other Linley daughters sang with professional brilliance, and at the end of the century the youngest child, William, composed for the London theatres. Furthermore the Linleys were extremely handsome, as the superb Gainsborough portraits at Dulwich reveal.[1] (Gainsborough painted Elizabeth three times, and also made busts of her head which do not survive.) Nothing went right for the Linleys. Of the three singing daughters, two died in their twenties and the third was forced to be mute. Tom's death alone would have made the father's remaining years barely endurable.

Thomas Linley the Younger (1756–78) studied as a very small boy with William Boyce; he used to visit Boyce at his house in Kensington Gore after the Bath season was over. Aged ten he made his only known stage appearance in a masque not so far mentioned, *The Fairy Favour* (CG 31.1.67), which had music by J. C. Bach. It was devised for the first visit to the theatre of the future Prince Regent, aged four, and it was thought that he might make less heavy weather of the occasion if the entire cast consisted of children. Tom Linley represented Puck, a part which had him both dancing a hornpipe and playing the violin on stage. The music does not survive, but Hull's libretto was published, and it tells, boringly, how Titania has lost 'her boy', but finds him away to the west in a castle by the Thames.

[1] Reynolds's portrait of Elizabeth, 'the best picture I ever painted', is at Waddesdon Manor; it makes her look austere and sexless. Reynolds remarked of her 'What reason could they think I had in inviting them to dinner, unless it was to hear her sing?—for she cannot talk'. But she was intelligent about music.

The following year Tom was leading the Bath orchestra, but not for long; his father wisely sent him to Italy to study the violin under Nardini. The date of his leaving can be roughly fixed from a letter Gainsborough wrote to William Jackson on 11 May 1768:

> I have begun a large picture of Tommy Linley and his sister, and cannot come. I suppose you know the Boy is bound for Italy the first opportunity.[1]

In the spring of 1770 Tom Linley had his famous meetings with Mozart in Florence; Mozart was his exact contemporary. By 1773 Tom was back in London leading the Drury Lane orchestra and playing his own violin concertos in the intervals. His sisters Elizabeth and Mary had been singing at the Three Choirs Festivals for two or three years, and Elizabeth was already the leading soprano there, earning £100 a festival even though she was still in her teens. Tom had a splendid anthem with full orchestral accompaniment performed at the Worcester Festival of 1773, and this was the last time that Elizabeth, now married, was allowed to sing.

By the summer of 1775 Tom was nineteen years old, and working on the music for one of the most successful operas ever staged. *The Duenna* (CG 21.11.75) was the second and last full-length work that Sheridan wrote for Covent Garden. There were seventy-five performances in the first season, and it was constantly given all over Britain until the 1840s, when Covent Garden staged it for the last time. Both Hazlitt and Byron thought it had the best opera libretto they knew. The lyrics, wrote Hazlitt, 'have a joyous spirit of intoxication in them, and a strain of the most melting tenderness', and as an example of admirable 'softness' he quoted the lyric near the end of Act I that begins 'Had I a heart for falsehood framed'. Modern readers may well think the plot and the dialogue more interesting than the song-words, but few people seem to have thought so at the time. Leigh Hunt found 'too much jesting upon personal defects, but they are very amusing; and if the poetry has little claim to that most abused term, it is very good town poetry'.[2] Apart from the 'personal defects', which belong mainly to the duenna, Sheridan was also rather too prone to make fun of Mendoza for being a Jew. The fun is mainly good-humoured, for Isaac is likeable and we laugh with him as well as against him, but when he makes love to the heavily-veiled duenna under the impression that she is Louisa, the duenna says to him with a simper, 'So little like a Jew, and so much like a gentleman'; the foolish remark is nicely in character, but Hitler's activities still cloud our attitude to it.

The plot concerns Don Jerome, a Spaniard, who wants to marry off his daughter Louisa to the rich Isaac Mendoza, and has to keep her immured to

---

[1] The picture is now in New York.

[2] 'Biographical and Critical Sketch' of Sheridan that prefaces early nineteenth-century editions of his plays.

stop her running off with Antonio. Don Jerome's son, Ferdinand, is having somewhat similar difficulties over his secret affair with Clara. As has been mentioned, Sheridan borrowed some of the plot from Moliere's *Le Sicilien*. This piece and Molière's *Dom Juan* fathered an immense number of comic operas in the eighteenth century and even later. *Le Sicilien* had begun with a servant in the street at night explaining why the daughter of the house is about to be serenaded, and the scene ended with her father expostulating from an upper window. *The Duenna* begins in the same way, and so, for that matter, does Beaumarchais' *The Barber of Seville*. In Molière the servant's master gets into the house disguised as a portrait painter, and though this does not happen in *The Duenna*, its influence on Beaumarchais is obvious. Eventually Molière's heroine escapes from the house disguised as her own servant; in *The Duenna* Louisa escapes disguised as the very duenna who is supposed to be guarding her. Sheridan develops his characters in more depth than Molière and with more verve. The dialogue is brilliantly witty and inventive, and the fact that the plot is derivative matters no more than the fact that Beaumarchais also took incidents from others.

Sheridan held back the publication of his libretto until 1794 in the hope of preventing it from being pirated. When Thomas Ryder staged performances in Dublin, Sheridan sued him, but lost his case because the Irish judges ruled that 'any person may make memoranda, or write all, if capable, of whatever is publicly exhibited'.[1] The 1794 libretto has always been reproduced in modern editions of Sheridan's Plays, although a glance at the vocal score shows that it leaves out three songs that were originally sung but later omitted because of their difficulty.[2] One of these, 'Sharp is the woe', is among the best songs in the opera, and was only left out because later Ferdinands could not manage the coloratura passages. Also a number of small verbal changes of the type opera composers always make for rhythmic reasons are not reflected in modern editions, though in my view they should be.

The original manuscript of the libretto survives, and was reproduced by W. Fraser Rae in his book on Sheridan of 1902. It differs widely from the published version, and it is a pity that Sheridan later cut the amusing dialogue in II. ii. in which Isaac talks about his mother.

Significantly this manuscript is mainly in Elizabeth's hand. Sheridan could not have undertaken the opera without her help, for he was no musician. Roughly a third of the lyrics were written to fit previously composed music, either arias from Italian operas or songs by such English composers as William Jackson. Five lyrics were written to fit Scotch or Irish tunes of the ballad opera type. The remainder, nearly one half of the whole, was sent to Linley with a request for new music. We know quite a lot about the genesis of some of the

[1] Thespian Dictionary; article on Ryder.
[2] Those at the end of II. i. for Jerome; at the end of III. ii. for Ferdinand; and just before the Maid's entrance in III. iii. for Antonio.

items because, with Sheridan in London and Linley in Bath, the opera had to be compiled by correspondence, and much of this is reproduced in Thomas Moore's *Memoirs of the Life of Sheridan*.[1] For reasons to be explained later, Linley was unenthusiastic about the whole venture, and though he probably composed four or five of the thirty-three items, he pushed most of the work on to his son. Tom composed the overture, the three-section Finale to Act I, and most of the bigger songs, and he harmonized and scored the five traditional tunes. One way and another he was responsible for half the opera, and most of his contribution survives in full. His overture was published in parts, his own songs were copied out in full score after his death as part of a memorial manuscript his father had made (BM Egerton 2493), and his own manuscript of the last act (lacking the Glee and Finale) can be found in the Guildhall Library, London (Gresham MS 376).

Tom's overture has a slow movement for wind instruments alone and a particularly charming Finale. The scoring is for oboes, bassoons, and horns plus strings. Most of the songs are accompanied by strings with one pair of wind instruments for colour contrast. This is the only full-length opera of the period without trumpets and drums, and it is very unusual in apparently having no clarinets. The opening Serenade sung in the street is also Tom's, and as the trio that immediately follows it (pp. 8–11 in the vocal score) is not his and cannot possibly have been borrowed, it must be by the elder Linley. With Louisa at one window, Don Jerome and his blunderbuss at another, and the love-sick Antonio down below, the elder Linley showed unexpected skill in finding musical equivalents for their differing emotions. But the trio is an example of a problem that has already been mentioned, and one that militates against modern performances. Without any doubt Don Jerome was a baritone, but in his excitement he several times achieved a high G, which he sang falsetto. These falsetto notes are an essential element in the trio, and it is no solution for Don Jerome to be sung by a tenor.

A little later Antonio has a lovely song, 'Friendship is the bond of Reason', and this too was composed by the younger Linley; in much of the writing there is a warm, almost Mozartean lyricism. The main substance of the opera is provided by Tom's longer contributions and the three arias borrowed from Italian operas by Giordani, Rauzzini, and Sacchini. These are all beautiful too, and we can thank Sheridan's wife for choosing them and for making sure that his words fitted the music.

Those items that seem most interesting to us were probably not those that seemed most interesting in 1775. There can be no doubt that the four Scotch songs and the Irish 'As down on Banna's Banks' did much to make the opera succeed. Don Jerome's Scotch Song is no more than exuberant, but the other three are among the loveliest of their kind—'De'il tak' the Wars', 'The Bush

---

[1] See my 'A Score for "The Duenna",' M&L, April 1961.

aboon Traquair', and 'The Birks of Endermay'. Audiences had been starved of such songs for years because no one had discovered how to arrange them for *galante* orchestra. This is what Tom Linley made of 'The Birks of Endermay' (Sheridan's 'How oft, Louisa'):

The Act III Finale is a curiosity. The tune is that of Morley's 'Now is the Month of Maying', which had never at that time been printed in score. But the bass bears no resemblance to Morley's, so somebody, one of the Linleys or one of the Sheridans, must have been relying on memory.[1]

[1] John Immyns had started The Madrigal Society in 1741. Antiquarianism in all fields was beginning to burgeon.

Five quite separate but basically similar vocal scores of *The Duenna* had appeared by 1835, and in no case is the composer or arranger named on the title page or above each item. In these respects *The Duenna* is unique for its time, and only peculiar circumstances can account for the omissions. As already mentioned, Linley worked on the score without enthusiasm. For several years he had been negotiating for a share in Drury Lane when Garrick resigned, and with the resignation imminent he did not care to be seen associating with the rival theatre. He felt bound to inform Garrick of the project, and his letter (28.9.75) reveals aesthetic and personal objections as well as political.

> I have promised to assist Sheridan in compiling—I believe is the properest term—an opera . . . I have already set some airs which he has given me, and he intends writing new words to some other tunes of mine. My son has likewise written some tunes for him . . . This is a mode of proceeding I by no means approve of. I think he ought first to have finished his opera with the songs he intends to introduce in it, and have got it entirely new set. No musician can set a song properly unless he understands the character,—and knows the performer who is to exhibit it. For my part, I shall be very unwilling for either my name, or my son's, to appear in this business; and it is my present resolution to forbid it; for I have great reason to be diffident of my own ability and genius; and my son has not had experience in theatrical composition, though I think well of his invention and musical skill.

The correspondence printed by Thomas Moore reveals that Linley at no time was told what the opera was about, and there is more than a possibility that Sheridan concealed from him that it concerned yet another elopement, with the girl's father held up to ridicule.[1] Linley in his turn may well have wished to conceal from his son-in-law how little of the music he had written, and Tom had the less grounds for wanting publicity in that he was leading the orchestra at the rival playhouse. The result was the least informative vocal score of the period. None of the first-night critics guessed who was responsible for the music.

The chief singing roles, Clara and Don Carlos, were taken by Miss Brown and Leoni, who made their reputations in them. Mattocks and his wife played Ferdinand and Louisa. Wilson was Don Jerome and Quick the Jew. When Leoni became unavailable in the 1779–80 season, Covent Garden was driven into letting Mrs. Kennedy sing Don Carlos, and in Dublin the notorious Daly even presented the whole opera with the sexes reversed. For several decades all our leading singers were eager to appear in *The Duenna*, and Mrs. Billington was a notable Clara. It is sad that our singers are less eager today. The operatic settings by Roberto Gerhard and Prokofiev prove the lasting attraction of the

---

[1] I would guess that Mrs. Malaprop had been based in part on Mrs. Linley, a well-meaning but foolish woman (see Betsy Sheridan's *Journal*). If so, Sheridan's motives for secrecy were the stronger.

libretto, but originally the opera owed its success as much to the music as to the words, and a modern stage production that makes use of it cannot be delayed much longer.

In the summer of 1776 Garrick retired, and Drury Lane was taken over by Sheridan and Linley.

For his first opera in his own playhouse Linley naturally took a good deal of trouble; *Selima and Azor* (DL 5.12.76) contains his finest music. It seems to have been planned as a three-act mainpiece, proved rather short, and with two arias and a duet cut from Act II served as an afterpiece. The libretto was by Sir George Collier, a naval officer, and it derives from Grétry's recent success, *Zémire et Azor*. The plot is that of Beauty and the Beast, Selima being Beauty and Azor the Beast, and it is laid in Persia. Linley made no use of Grétry's music. All three movements of the overture have merit, and occasionally the songs capture something of the strange magic of the story. The scene in which Selima's father and his comic servant (Scander and Ali) are suddenly confronted with a dinner-table rising from nowhere, though deriving from pantomime, looks forward to the Tamino-Papageno relationship in *The Magic Flute*. Much the most popular song was 'No Flower that blows is like this Rose', sung at the end of Act I by Selima when her father gives her the flower plucked in Azor's garden. It is a simple rondo and sweetly pretty. In Act II Selima has a fine Adagio song with a concertante violin part that Tom Linley played. This act ends with one of the three-part Elegies Linley had published in 1770, but with new words. It is sung by Selima's family as they bid her a sad farewell. Azor has a melancholy song in the last act with cello obbligato, and the opera ends with a delightful love duet. So far as I know, not a note of the elder Linley's music survives in full score; this is especially to be regretted as regards *Selima and Azor*.

The title roles were sung by Mrs. Baddeley and Vernon, both of whom were past their best. Linley must have been eager to introduce some of his own pupils, but he never encouraged his own daughters, Mary and Maria, to go on the stage; there is evidence that he feared their morals might suffer if they did.

The following spring Drury Lane accepted an afterpiece opera by Thomas Carter, *The Milesian*[1] (20.3.77). Isaac Jackman's libretto about a garrulous Irish sea-captain is rather amusing, but the songs all seem dragged in by the scruff of the neck and the result is hardly operatic. Thomas Carter (c.1734–1804) started his career as a Dublin organist and did not settle in London till 1770. He was never nearer the theatre world than its fringe, but his writing is professional and sometimes individual, as we shall find later.

Belphegor (DL 16.3.78) had music by Barthelemon and a libretto that rehashed the Matthew Prior story recently used by Dibdin in *The Ladle*. The title is the name of a devil who amiably allows Booze and his wife three wishes. Mrs. Booze, who for some reason is called Dame Din, asks for 'a hunting

---

[1] 'Irish(man). (f. *Milesius* fabulous Spanish King whose sons are said to have conquered Ireland)' (OED).

pudding'; Booze wishes she were dumb for choosing so foolishly and then has to use the third and last wish to loosen her tongue. The opera was not quite a failure for it had a dozen or so performances, but the wretched libretto by Miles Peter Andrews was never published. Much the oddest item in the score is a duet in which Dame Din sings and Wheatear, a farmer, speaks. Barthelemon must have wanted this particular effect, for Moody (who played Wheatear) was allowed to sing elsewhere.

About this time composers at all three playhouses were beginning to unify their operas in two different ways. In both *The Milesian* and in *Belphegor* the first movement of the overture ends on the dominant so that it can run without a break into the second. In both *Belphegor* and *The Cady of Bagdad* (which preceded it by a month) a tune in the overture is sung later on in the Finale.

The Cady (or *Cadi*) *of Bagdad* (DL 19.2.78) was Tom Linley's last major work, and it was a failure. Since *The Duenna* he had produced two masterpieces, neither of them dramatic. One was his full-scale *Ode on the Witches and Fairies of Shakespeare*, and the other a short oratorio, *The Song of Moses*. Both were first performed at Drury Lane, and both survive in full score. Tom also wrote some additional music for a revival of *The Tempest* (DL 4.1.77) which included traditional Purcell items and Arne's 'Where the Bee sucks'. Shakespeare's first scene was replaced by a long, exciting, and difficult storm chorus. This and four songs for Ariel can be found with Tom's music for *The Duenna* in the MS the elder Linley had copied after his son's death.[1] The Ariel songs were written for Miss Field, who was making her stage debut. 'O bid your faithful Ariel fly' is much the best, though modern ears would be surprised by the amount of coloratura in it. The words are probably Sheridan's. Tom's storm chorus is one of the most remarkable achievements in English music, and it is tragic that there can be no place for it in modern theatres and concert-halls.

The splendid promise revealed in the works just mentioned makes the quality of *The Cady* hard to understand. The surviving MS[2] looks too hurriedly written, but the main trouble seems to have been the libretto by Abraham Portal, who ran the Drury Lane box-office. It was based on the one set by both Gluck and Monsigny as *Le Cadi dupé*, and it was never published. There are some pleasant songs in the Scotch style as well as arias of considerable elaboration. Clarinets are used in the Act I Finale. Advertisements described the music as 'entirely new'.

That summer Tom was invited by the Duke of Ancaster to his house near Gainsborough in Lincolnshire, presumably to teach music to his daughter and to provide music in the evenings. These at least were the purposes for which Piozzi had been employed there the previous summer; he refused to go again

[1] BM Eg. 2493 and 522d. There are also MSS of the storm chorus at the RCM, one of them attributed to Purcell. It seems to have served as the overture.
[2] BM Add. 29297.

because he had been treated like a servant.[1] On 5 August Tom was drowned while sailing on the lake. He was a competent swimmer, but the water got into his long boots and dragged him down.

The death of his son made it hard for the elder Linley to provide music for the new opera that autumn. This was *The Camp* (DL 15.10 78). In desperation Linley borrowed where possible from his own *The Royal Merchant*, even blowing up a one-page strophic song into the elaborate-looking Finale.[2] The music is of no great interest, apart from a military-style overture with horns, trumpets, and drums featured in its Finale, but the libretto reads well and offers some unexpected details about military life. It was at one time thought to be by Sheridan, and it is included in early editions of his plays, but the greater part of it was quite certainly written by Linley's future son-in-law, Richard Tickell.[3] The occasion was the formation of a vast camp at Coxheath near Maidstone, a camp that drew sightseers from London in huge numbers. There is not much plot. O'Daub, a painter, has come 'to take the camp', that is, to paint it for a production at Drury Lane where, so he says, he works under 'Lanternberg'. (In fact de Loutherbourg must himself have 'taken the camp' for the scenery for this opera.) When some yokels overhear him using this expression, with frequent reference to the OP side of the stage, they think he is referring to the Old Pretender, and they have him arrested as a spy. The incident is borrowed from Dibdin's *The Deserter*, but it is less serious and better contrived. Gage, a camp-follower, has been selling lime to one regiment as hair powder; when contracted to shave a company of grenadiers, he immediately sub-contracts at great profit to himself. There is the inevitable girl disguised as a soldier-boy and searching for her husband. Not least of the attractions were the two Marches played on stage by a 'Regimental Band'. *The Camp* offered lively and topical entertainment, and it was a success.

Linley managed nothing more that season, and in 1779–80 he felt able only to add a couple of songs to *Fortunatus*, the old Garrick pantomime. The one musical novelty was Michael Arne's *The Artifice* (DL 14.4.80), which failed. It was two years before Linley felt sufficiently recovered to resume composing on any scale.[4]

2 DIBDIN AND OTHERS AT COVENT GARDEN
1778–1781

It will be remembered that in the summer of 1776 Dibdin fled the country to

---

[1] Lonsdale, p. 280. Piozzi later married Dr. Johnson's friend, Mrs. Thrale.

[2] The only new songs are those on pp. 11, 13, 17, and 18.

[3] Descended from Addison's secretary (see p.45). He married Mary Linley in 1780.

[4] It was probably Linley's lack of spirits that led Sheridan to ask Giordani to set the 'trios etc.' sung by the Italians in Act I, scene ii, of *The Critic* (1779). For some reason Giordani composed a French trio and an Italian duet. They were published but lack distinction.

escape his creditors. Barred from Drury Lane, he had been searching for an entrée into Covent Garden, but *The Seraglio*, with which he hoped to ingratiate himself with Harris, had to be completed in his absence by Dr. Arnold. Covent Garden music was in the doldrums, with Fisher ineffectual and anxious to leave. The most interesting event of the 1777–8 season was the revision of *The Beggar's Opera* with its new ending (see p. 402). A little later Fisher concocted a pastiche, *Love finds the Way* (CG 18.11.77); the words were adapted by Hull from Murphy's *The School for Guardians*, which was itself adapted from Molière's *L'École des Femmes*. Apart from two songs, nothing was published. *The Morning Chronicle* admired Fisher's overture, and mentioned new songs by Arne and Sacchini. After adding music to Dibdin's *Poor Vulcan* (CG 4.2.78) Fisher left on his continental travels, and Harris was prepared to welcome back Dibdin in his place.

Dibdin spent twenty-one months in France, and is entertaining though unreliable on the subject in his *Professional Life*. 'I had now determined to visit France for two years, in order to expand my ideas, and store myself with theatrical materials.' This is a brazen untruth, as his readers must have suspected when they read of his reiterated hatred for the French and all their ways. He stayed in Calais until December 1776, and found it full of English riff-raff. He then accepted an offer of cheap transport to Nancy for himself and his family. One wonders what family he is referring to. Certainly not Miss Pitt and their sons Charles Isaac Mungo and Thomas. He must have taken Miss Wilde with him, and it is more than likely that by this time she too had presented him with an illegitimate infant. We hear no more of his 'family'. Dibdin knew he could not return to England unless there appeared to be reasonable hopes of his repaying his debts; otherwise he would be imprisoned. He therefore busied himself first with *Poor Vulcan*, which he posted to Harris, then with Dialogues for Sadler's Wells, and then with adaptations of French operas which he may have seen in the Nancy theatre; it was visited, he tells us, 'by the best performers of Paris'. Harris was sufficiently impressed to make Dibdin 'composer to the theatre' as from the autumn of 1778. In any case Dibdin had to leave France in the late spring of that year because war had been declared against Britain and all Englishmen were ordered out of the country. Dibdin had hoped to return via Paris, but had to take the shortest route. He found Rheims Cathedral some compensation.

Poor Vulcan was produced in his absence, and he was horrified when he found out what they had done to it.[1] An all-sung burletta, it was to prove his last playhouse success; it was still being performed in the following century. The libretto apes that of *Midas*. Vulcan and Venus, bundled out of Olympus for their indiscretions, set up as pub-keepers in an English village. The other gods decide to live in England too so that they can mock Vulcan and Venus—who fail to recognize them. Each god has a homespun English pseudonym which suits

[1] *Musical Tour*, p. 300.

his personality; thus Jupiter becomes the local squire, Stud, and Mars the local sergeant, Pike. Adonis is there too, and Dibdin thought it would be a novel touch to satirize him as well. Harris however felt that his audience was conditioned to see Adonis only as a serious lover, and he got Thomas Hull to rewrite the second act accordingly. It was presumably these rewritten sections that were 'graced by the lovely music of Dr. Fisher';[1] needless to say, Dibdin is being sarcastic.

The libretto of *Poor Vulcan* is well written and amusing. The vocal score shows signs of more care than Dibdin usually took, but is far from complete. Some of the first act recitatives are included, though not all; no second act recitatives seem to survive. The various editions of the libretto differ widely, and one cannot be sure just what was sung in the original production. Dibdin started by parodying an anonymous Vauxhall song of 1758, 'Dear Chloe, come give me sweet kisses', and Arne's well-known 'When forced from dear Hebe to go'; he kept the original music. (Neither of his lyrics appears in later editions of the libretto.) When Vulcan suspects he is being cuckolded, there is a brief burst on the horns, after which the flute effectively quotes the cuckoo refrain from Arne's 'When Daisies pied'. A long and splendid action quartet begins characteristically:

The Finale makes use of a tune in the overture.

'I had prepared a great variety of materials during my stay in France', wrote Dibdin, and these included one full-length opera, *The Islanders*, and six very short ones. All were adapted from French operas, but there is no evidence that Dibdin made any use of the original music. He must have bought or borrowed the French librettos in Nancy, and translated them there. Either in Nancy or back in London he wrote the music. In the short operas he aimed at a length of not much more than twenty minutes, on the grounds that French afterpiece operas, having only one plot, lacked incident when compared with English examples. For this reason he thought the playhouses would tolerate them only if they were drastically cut. Harris accepted three of the six: *Rose and Colin* and *The Wives avenged* (both CG 18.9.78) and *Annette and Lubin* (CG 2.10.78). It was necessary to stage two of these short operas in place of the usual afterpiece, and Harris found this awkward and uneconomical. Of the three he rejected, one was never put on anywhere and the other two came in useful later when Dibdin was at the Royal Circus. French publishers were much more helpful to composers than their London counterparts. Monsigny's *Rose et Colas* (1764) and Philidor's *Les Femmes avengées* (1775) were both published in

---

[1] *Professional Life* i, p. 174.

lavish full score, as were many other French operas of the period whether all-sung or not. Dibdin got the plot of *Annette and Lubin* from a Favart libretto based on one of Marmontel's *Contes moraux*. The two main characters are very innocent cousins. They live together on the banks of the Seine in a small cabin made of leaves, preferring a carpet of daisies to the other sort, and birdsong to 'a band of musick'. The local Bailiff informs them that it is a crime for cousins to love each other, a view that astonishes them. However the Lord of the Manor undertakes to get a special dispensation so that they can get married. This is the more urgent in that Annette is pregnant. Genest pointed out that, 'as so much is made of Annette's being in a family way, it was quite absurd for Mrs. Farrell to play Lubin'; on the other hand a male hero in such a story would not have been tolerated.

Dibdin's contract with Harris bound him to write the equivalent of three afterpieces a season in return for £10 a week. Anything extra was to be paid for additionally, and he was forbidden to write for any other theatre. He gave Harris good measure his first season, for he also turned out a much loved panto-mime and a normal-length afterpiece. *The Touchstone or Harlequin Traveller* (CG 4.1.79) was probably the first pantomime to have spoken dialogue. Harle-quin was played by Lee Lewis (who did not sing) and Columbine by Miss Brown. The overture has five tiny movements, the last allegedly a 'Fuga', and the Curtain rose on a scene we today might recognize as pantomimic: 'A Desart Island—a number of barren Rocks, and at a distance is seen an agitated Sea—Harlequin gains the shore upon a Plank.' There is a Storm Chorus sung 'off'. Later scenes are in Vauxhall Gardens and Whitehall, and Pierrot has a song in which he likens himself to a tennis-ball. Dibdin was so proud of his 'Fuga' that he repeated it in the Finale, but he did not like the heavy alterations made to his libretto by Harris, Pilon, Cumberland, and (incredibly) Garrick. In old age Dibdin remembered Garrick at rehearsals burying the hatchet and shyly asking him to call. A characteristic act of kindliness, if true. Garrick died before Dibdin could take advantage of the gesture.

Dibdin wrote both words and music of *The Chelsea Pensioner* (CG 6.5.79), an afterpiece that tried unsuccessfully to repeat the homely success of *The Waterman*. It starts 'near Wandsworth', and there is a trio, of which the music does not survive, with 'Lapstone working in a Stall underneath the Window; Ester is ironing within-side, the window open; and Nancy sits on a Bench at the Door making a Shirt'. Act II is in Chelsea Hospital, where Ester has a song that begins:

> Why, thanks be praised, I'm pretty free
> From sickness though I'm old.
> Indeed an asthma teazes me
> Now that I've got a cold.
> The gout too plays me tricks;
> Then I've the rheumatics . . .

In spite of Dibdin's fecundity, Harris put on operas by other composers too. Hook's *The Lady of the Manor* (CG 23.11.78) was full-length, and had words by that ill-tempered wasp, William Kenrick. It is the most interesting of the not-very-interesting operas Hook wrote at widely-spaced intervals, and it was also the most successful. In 1788 Mrs. Billington chose it for her benefit, and there were revivals in both 1808 and 1818; the additional music Hook wrote for the latter production survives in confused MS in the Cambridge University Library. The plot is based on that of *The Country Lasses* (1715) by Charles Johnson, and it is unexpectedly outspoken. There are two young society bucks and two young society women in a country setting, the women being disguised as farm-girls. They know who the men are, but the men are unaware that the girls are socially their equals. The situation is like that in *She stoops to conquer*. One of the girls is a widow, Mrs. Townley ('Laura'), who does not care for country life, but Lady Lucy ('Flora') is happy to live on the farm, and all the more so when Manly marries her, which he does without discovering her identity. Young Wildman takes longer to hook, and is all too liable to flirt with the dairy-maid, Cicely. However he becomes more serious when told he has a rival for 'Laura's' hand. When 'Laura' turns up in trousers disguised as the rival, they fight a ridiculous duel, and to Hook's credit this is dealt with not in dialogue but in a duet sung in canon. 'Laura' falls as if shot dead, but in fact she has been careful to prime both pistols with blanks, and all ends as expected. This is an amusing scene, with 'Laura' very bold and even bawdy in her male disguise. The part was taken by Miss Brown, Vernon being her lover. Earlier Manly sings to 'Flora':

> In the gentle Laura's stead
> Take me, fair one, to your bed;
> To your arms I'll softly creep
> When your father's fast asleep.

This is quite unlike the veiled circumlocution Sheridan resorted to in *The Duenna*, and audiences must have been surprised to hear anyone singing in simple words of what they really thought.

The vocal score stars nine songs to show they are 'from former collections by the same composer'. Miss Brown has one big-scale aria, and Manly (Mattocks) another; the latter, which is rather good, is printed on three staves and includes some coloratura. None of the songs descends to the level of Dibdin at his most slapdash, but none shows his feeling for situation when at his best. The overture was almost the last this century by an English composer to be published in parts, and I shall return to it later.

Thomas Hamly Butler contributed two full-length operas to the Covent Garden repertoire in 1778–80 and when they failed he abandoned the playhouses and went to Edinburgh as a music teacher. All reference books that mention him repeat erroneous information from Sainsbury; for example the date of his birth cannot be as late as 1762. Butler was a choirboy under Nares, and then studied in Italy for three years under Piccini. In Naples he was patronized by Sir William Hamilton. Back in London he became harpsichordist at Covent Garden. He set first for this theatre a long masque called *Calypso* (CG 20.3.79), and then a dialogue opera, *The Widow of Delphi* (CG 1.2.80), both with words by Richard Cumberland. Cumberland's best-known play was *The West Indian*, and he was currently being represented at Drury Lane as Sir Fretful Plagiary in Sheridan's *The Critic*. He printed *Calypso*, of which no music survives, but not *The Widow of Delphi*, of which there is a vocal score. *Calypso*, with its immense Finales and interminable recitatives, would have been a formidable task for any composer, and it is unlikely that Butler was equal to it. Parke has an anecdote which reflects on his professionalism, or rather the lack of it.[1] Butler,

> who had not studied any instrument but the pianoforte, having in the part for the kettle-drums (which it is well-known give only two different sounds) written all the notes in the octave, on being informed that several could not be played, politely thanked the performer who beat them, and requested he would furnish him with a *scale* of the kettle-drums!!!

Perhaps Butler was indeed a sorry amateur. But it is just possible that after three years with Piccini he knew more about the timpani than anyone at Covent Garden. In Mozart's *Figaro* (1786) the drum part includes every note of the G minor scale except F. (F is hard to find in classical music before Haydn's Symphony no. 98 of 1791; before then, symphonies in F or B flat did not normally have drum parts.) When Butler was at Covent Garden, Britain lagged a little behind Central European countries in the range of her timpani parts Ever since Purcell's time, drummers had scarcely ever been asked to play any notes but D and A. Butler may well have asked for more because he knew more were possible.

This limitation accounts for the very high proportion of clattering symphony-overtures in the key of D, the key that English trumpeters and drummers had come to count on for their music. The following list gives all the overtures Linley and Hook are known to have written between 1776 and 1786; similar examples could easily have been found in the operas of other composers. The key is D major except when shown otherwise.

LINLEY	HOOK
Selima and Azor (1776)	The Lady of the Manor (1778)
The Camp (1778)	Too Civil by Half (1782)
The Carnival of Venice (1781)—in F	The Country Wake (1784)
The Spanish Rivals (1784)—in A	The Double Disguise (1784)
The Strangers at Home (1785)	The Peruvian (1786)

[1] Parke ii, 330.

It can be assumed that the two overtures that are not in D did not have trumpet and drum parts. In the late 1780s Mazzinghi wrote all his ballet overtures for the King's Theatre in D. London's trumpeters and drummers had to learn new techniques when Haydn arrived in 1791.

We can take *The Lady of the Manor* as typical of the clattering D major overture; indeed we can take no other, for no other survives orchestrally. It begins pleasantly with an eight-bar theme for strings *pianissimo*, and this is repeated with some originality by flutes, horns and violins on their own, still *pianissimo*. Then come no less than thirty-two bars of *fortissimo*, with every instrument busying around, though not always meaningfully. There is not a single bar's rest for anyone, not even for the drummer. Here are some characteristic brass and timpani parts (from bar 38):

Hook was so fascinated by the contrast between very soft and very loud that he tried it twice more in the movement, and this meant that he could never get away from the key of D; he scarcely bothered himself about sonata form. He even stayed in D for the slow movement, so that he could keep his brass and drums playing. The Finale is exactly like the first movement in shape and method. No doubt his audience found the loud passages exciting and did not notice how silly they were. It took Haydn to reveal to Londoners that loud music could have just as much intellectual content as soft,[1] though Linley came some way towards showing this too. His overtures are always superior to Hook's.

In the autumn of 1779 Baumgarten started his fifteen-year stint as leader of the Covent Garden band. Of his short village opera, *William and Nanny, or The Cottagers* (CG 12.11.79) only one song seems to survive; a complete vocal score was advertised by Longman & Broderip in some of their other vocal scores, but no copies are listed in BUCEM. Baumgarten was never again asked to compose a whole opera, but he contributed to some of Shield's.

William Shield (1748–1829) was himself edging his way into Harris's favour at this time. His first opera, *The Flitch of Bacon*,[2] had just been a success

[1] He did not always reveal this. The loud music in Symphony 86 near the start of the first Allegro is as silly as Hook's.

[2] See p. 435.

at the Little Theatre, but for Covent Garden he set a libretto by Charles Stuart with no success at all. *The Cobler of Castlebury* (CG 27.4.79) had but one performance. Only two songs from Pilon's *The Deaf Lover* (CG 2.2.80) were published; Shield was sufficiently proud of his orchestration to have them printed in short score. He was eventually to make his reputation in the autumn of 1782, after Dibdin's expulsion; until then his only other work for Covent Garden was *The Siege of Gibraltar* (CG 25.4.80), and we may pause to note a few facts both about this opera and about Shield himself.

The Siege of Gibraltar had topical appeal. Defended by General Sir George Elliott, the Rock was enduring a siege that was to last until 1783. In January 1780 it was temporarily relieved by Admiral Rodney, who sailed into the harbour after defeating the combined French and Spanish fleets, and it was this that sparked off Frederick Pilon's libretto. The plot of this early 'siege' opera is unexpected. The English hero loves an Arab girl called, needless to say, Zayde, but she is about to be shipped to Africa to marry a Jew. Our hero rescues her from this apparently awful fate by disguising himself in a turban and pretending to be drunk. Finally we see the arrival of Rodney's fleet and 'The Spanish Admiral dismasted . . . a small boat is seen to come from one of the ships'. This is accompanied by a stage military band playing a stirring march. Elsewhere there are numerous solos for clarinet, bassoon, horns, and trumpets, and some catchy traditional tunes.

Shield was born at Whickham near Gateshead, and became an apprentice boat-builder at North Shields.[1] He took up the violin as a hobby, and had counterpoint lessons in Newcastle from Avison. After Avison's death in 1770 Shield became a violinist in Bates's theatrical company which toured the North-East. In Stockton about 1774 he became friendly with the eccentric antiquary, Joseph Ritson (1752–1803), who was to have a profound influence on him. He was also friendly with Thomas Holcroft, an actor in the company and later a famous playwright; they once walked together from Durham to Stockton, Holcroft reading aloud all the way from Pope's translation of Homer. When the company was in Scarborough Shield was heard by Giardini who persuaded him to try his luck in London. About 1775 he began playing the viola for the Italian operas at the King's Theatre, and much of his musical education was picked up from what he heard there in operas by Sacchini, Paisiello, and others. Though he never had much technical skill as a composer, he made up for this by a pleasing melodic innocence and a thorough knowledge of orchestral instruments. He was one of the few successful English composers of the century who was universally liked as a man.

Thomas Holcroft (1744–1809) developed astonishingly from the most humble beginnings. His father was a shoemaker and fairground hanger-on, and he himself was brought up at Newmarket as a stable-lad. In his spare time he

---

[1] Busby ii, p. 185; Busby even discovered the name of the firm.

taught himself to sight-read music, and later as shoemaker he taught himself French and mathematics as well. For most of the seventies he was a provincial singing-actor on the Northern circuits, and we have already seen how he sometimes had to supply opera accompaniments on his violin.[1] In 1777 he joined the Drury Lane chorus at twenty shillings a week, and though he was able to offer Sheridan a wide range of opera parts, including Mungo in *The Padlock* and Colonel Oldboy in *Lionel and Clarissa*, he was awkward on the stage and the London playhouses never gave him much encouragement. However he found fame as a playwright. We shall meet him later as the librettist of two full-length operas set by Shield, and as an ardent left-wing Godwinite. Indeed Shield and William Godwin seem to have been his closest friends. His greatest success came in 1792 with *The Road to Ruin*. By this time it was among his favourite diversions to play violin sonatas with his daughter Fanny; she must have been a good pianist for Salomon played sonatas with her too. Clementi was another frequent visitor. By the end of the century Holcroft had to go abroad to escape his debtors, his success declining as his political views became generally abhorrent, but his musical interests persisted, and he was able to express his reasons for preferring Haydn to Mozart with considerable penetration.[2] His own brief autobiographical sketch was developed after his death into a two-volume Life by Hazlitt.

In the same season that saw the productions of *William and Nanny* and *The Siege of Gibraltar*, Dibdin was as active as ever. *Plymouth in an Uproar* (CG 20.10.79) was dismissed as worthless even by its creator. But Dibdin took more trouble over Covent Garden's annual pantomime, *The Mirror, or Harlequin Everywhere* (CG 30.11.79). Its predecessor, *The Touchstone*, had been so liked that one might have expected Harris to revive it, but he would never accept the traditional view that popular pantomimes were as good repertory material as popular plays. From now until the end of the century Covent Garden prided itself on staging a brand-new pantomime every Christmas. *The Mirror* was another 'speaking' pantomime; either the theatre was eager for innovations or they had no dancer equal to the role. The Devil (Reinhold), who has some recitative, is called Belphegor, and he takes Harlequin to Hell. Harlequin is allowed to return only on condition that he brings Pluto a virgin of sixteen years. He is given a Mirror that turns black when any woman who is not a virgin looks into it, and this makes possible the discovery of a girl who is pure 'in thought, word and deed'. Finding her is not easy, and Harlequin has to search in the Antipodes (where gibberish is both spoken and sung), as also in the Garden of Ceres, where he finds a virginal Columbine. The pantomime ended with a short masque in which all the characters are surveyed by Jupiter and other gods raised high in the clouds. The vocal score is far from complete.

Dibdin's full-length opera, *The Shepherdess of the Alps* (CG 18.1.80) was a

---

[1] See p. 295; also p. 301 for his pirated translation of *Le Mariage de Figaro*.
[2] Hazlitt ii, p. 269.

failure, and had only three performances. Londoners were not yet as intrigued with the romance of Swiss mountains and cataracts as they became a decade later. Dibdin got his libretto from *La Bergère des Alpes* (1766), an opera with words by Marmontel and music by Joseph Kohaut. His translation was published, and is fustian at its stagiest. A year or so earlier Holcroft had worked on Marmontel's libretto, cutting it to make an afterpiece;[1] Thomas Linley junior was expected to set it, but achieved only two songs before he died.

In 1780–1 Dibdin fulfilled his quota for Harris with another full-length opera, *The Islanders* (CG 25.11.80) and the usual pantomime, *Harlequin Freemason* (CG 29.12.80). *The Islanders* was mildly successful, and Dibdin later claimed to have made £350 out of it, but he did not think so well of his libretto as to publish it. Harris for his part did not think so well of it as to revive it, except in truncated form; the following season he made Dibdin cut it to an afterpiece, *The Marriage Act* (CG 17.9.81), and in this form the libretto survives. The island turns out to be off the coast of America, the characters being Spaniards and Indians. Yanko and Orra (Reinhold and Mrs. Kennedy) are the Indian hero and heroine, in love with each other. As usual, Dibdin got the plot from a French writer, Saint-Foix. *Harlequin Freemason* touched on a theme of topical interest and proved very popular, with sixty-three performances in a few months. Oulton calls it 'the best and grandest pantomime exhibited in many years', and as with all Dibdin's pantomimes of this period much of its success was due to the 'machinist', Mr. Messink. The music and librettos are very elusive. No vocal score was published, though six songs are to be found in the Royal College of Music. The only librettos I have traced are in the Bodleian and Birmingham Public Library. As well as the song words, there is a nine-page supplement describing masonic ceremony and apparel.

Nothing has been said about the music in Dibdin's Covent Garden operas. This is partly because it is poor in quality and partly because it survives only in fragments. Since 1778 he had written ten musical works in all, but only the first two pantomimes were ever published in vocal score. For the others Dibdin chose the periodical format. It had recently been shown that 'Periodical Overtures' could be published at more or less regular intervals with success, but no one had attempted operatic selections in quite this way. Dibdin started with what he optimistically called *The Monthly Lyrist or Family Concert*. There were to be six numbers, and subscribers would get the lot for 12s. Each number contained an overture, four or five songs, and (perhaps) a catch and a trio. Each of the first three numbers included items from *The Islanders*, together with contributions from *Plymouth in an Uproar*, *The Chelsea Pensioner*, and *Harlequin Freemason*. It looks as though subscribers complained of confusion, and in any case Dibdin found it impossible to keep up the monthly instalments. He therefore started again with the more prudent title of *The Lyrist*, and he now grouped all the

---

[1] Hazlitt i, pp. 274–5.

items from each opera together. Because most of the plates had already been engraved for *The Monthly Lyrist* the result is double pagination. The overture and thirteen vocal items from the full-length *Islanders* now come together, about half of the whole; we would appear to have less than half of the other three works. This is not a matter for much regret. The surviving songs are almost all strophic ballads of little merit, and the overtures are inept.

Many years later in 1799 Dibdin tried his luck with another periodical, *The Lyric Remembrancer*. There were to be two volumes of seven numbers each, and each number was to contain seven items, but of the fourteen numbers and hundred items promised very few ever appeared. It looks as though the venture was a total failure, for copies are rare even of the early numbers. Most of the Covent Garden operas are promised on the title page, together with some 'never before published' that Dibdin wrote later for the Royal Circus. Vol. 1 no. i includes items found in *The Lyrist* together with two from *Rose and Colin* and one from *Clump and Cudden* (RC 1785) that we would not otherwise have.

In October 1781 Harris sacked Dibdin,[1] no doubt because of the stormy gestation and total failure of his last opera, the full-length *Jupiter and Alcmena* (CG 27.10.81). There were only two performances. It had been Harris's idea that Dibdin should make an opera out of Dryden's *Amphitrion*, and the idea seems promising. But Dibdin thought it improper, and wanted Juno to foil Jupiter in his plan for raping Alcmena disguised as her husband. Harris saw that this would rob the plot of all its interest, and Dibdin gave way with as bad a grace as he could. It is significant that Shield had to be roped in to compose 'the favourite frightened song', which he later published with his music for *The Divorce*. No other words or music got into print, but a considerable quantity of the latter survives in chaotic full score in the Southampton Public Library; also there is a duet in the British Museum (Add. 30952; which also contains an air from *The Shepherdess of the Alps*).

Nothing at all is known of the man who compiled Harris's next opera. Distrusting Dibdin, he asked the mysterious J. Markordt[2] to fudge up music for an adaptation by Kane O'Hara of Fielding's *Tom Thumb* (CG 3.10.80). Arne had set the first operatic version nearly fifty years earlier, and he has sometimes been credited with this one, but in fact he died before composition can have been begun, and the only untraced song attributed to him in the vocal score can hardly have been newly written for the occasion. Markordt's competent overture was published in parts. Miss Catley staggered her admirers by singing brilliant coloratura variations on Fischer's famous minuet, and other borrowings include the Leveridge song quoted on page 80, the march in Dibdin's overture *The Recruiting Sergeant* made into a song, and 'The Mallow Fling'. Irish songs were just becoming the rage. The result was fairly successful, and Parke tells us

---

[1] In *The Royal Circus Epitomised* Dibdin says he was out of work from this month onwards.

[2] There was an Amsterdam music publisher at this time called S. Markordt.

that it became a convention to encore Grizzle's death-song, the effect being that he had to get up and die again.

Because of the row over *Jupiter and Alcmena* Dibdin was not asked to provide the annual pantomime, and Harris turned instead to Michael Arne. *The Choice of Harlequin* (CG 26.12.81) was his last work for the theatre, and the score is both fascinating and informative about the action; it includes many orchestral cues. The action was devised by the machinist Messink, and his libretto was published. Harlequin was played by W. Bates, and there was no speaking. The Finale of the two-movement overture has a trick more ingenious than effective. There are two insufficiently contrasted tunes in dotted six-eight, which are later played simultaneously, but because they are so alike in rhythm the lower one has no chance of impinging. However the trick impressed Shield, as we shall see later. Act I begins in a 'Hotel' with Harlequin in oriental dress and encumbered with luggage as though going on a journey. In contrasting songs Virtue and Pleasure pull him in contrary directions; they are the equivalent of the Good Fairy and the Demon King. Pleasure draws Harlequin to 'a Hazard Table', and there is a long and astonishing chorus of gamblers, those winning and those losing singing antiphonally. The cant words are not always comprehensible. Harlequin loses and sweeps all the money off the board in a rage. Outside the Pantheon a prostitute picks him up, takes him to her garret and robs him, but Harlequin conjures up a huge grenadier, in two halves, who transports them to Bridewell. The act ends with the Keeper (Edwin) singing a song with a good folky tune, accompanied by a chorus of ruffianly inmates. In Act II there is a scene in 'Sir Ashton Lever's Museum' of stuffed animals. To save Columbine from some rowdies, Harlequin animates the animals to the accompaniment of wildly rushing scales. An improvident old Lieutenant they meet escapes with a monkey. The bailiffs who come to arrest him arrest the monkey instead. However they are soon all back in prison. Harlequin gets them out by changing them into sailors, and in a sea-front scene a midshipman (Mrs. Kennedy) has a patriotic anti-French song about Admirals Parker and Rodney. Finally Harlequin and the Lieutenant are kind to a beggarwoman who turns out to be Virtue. As a reward she conjures up a grand transformation scene, with a palace, a dance of black girls, and an elephant. The final chorus is given in the libretto, but not in the score.

3　ARNOLD AT THE LITTLE THEATRE 1777–1782

Colman's experiences at Drury Lane with Garrick and at Covent Garden with Harris and Powell had determined him never to return to the theatre except as his own manager. His chance came in 1777. Samuel Foote, his vigour in decline, rented the Little Theatre to Colman and safeguarded his own interests with various provisos. As he died the following year the provisos did not prove onerous.[1] Colman was in sole charge for a decade, and then handed over to his son, another George.

The elder Colman's early friendship with Samuel Arnold has already been mentioned, as also their collaboration for Covent Garden in *The Portrait* and *Mother Skipton*. Colman was much more eager than Foote to include opera in his repertoire, and the more so when, a few weeks after he took over, he decided on nightly performances instead of three a week. For a quarter of a century Arnold wrote nearly all his operas for the Little Theatre. Colman had an eye for talent, and in his very first season he launched the actor John Henderson, as also Edwin and Elisabeth Farren. In his second season, 1778, he discovered Elizabeth Harper, who stayed with him for five summers and who continued to sing for him with her husband, Jack Bannister, even when both had become famous at the winter playhouses. Miss Harper excelled in simple ballad songs, and her sweet unaffected voice did much to make opera popular at the Little Theatre.

Colman also engaged a troupe of child dancers for the intervals, and here standards were not very high. As his son put it in his *Random Records*,

> Monsieur Georgi's infantile pupils . . . were a complete burlesque upon a *Corps de Ballet*. The audience laugh'd, and tolerated the poor little things, when they were push'd on, between acts, to caper and lose their shoes, while Monsieur Georgi was *Peste*-ing and *Sacre Dieu*-ing at them, by the side of the scenes.

Arnold's industry in the last quarter of the century was astonishing. Besides Vauxhall songs and an immense quantity of theatre music, he found time to write eight oratorios, to run the Chapel Royal (from 1783), to attempt a complete edition of Handel (from 1787), to conduct the Academy of Ancient Music (from 1789), and to be organist at Westminster Abbey (from 1793). In the pages that follow it should be remembered that at all times he was attempting two or more careers concurrently. It is not surprising that much of his theatre music is of poor quality. Usually it is less individual than Shield's, though he was quite as adventurous in his scoring. Wind solos abound in both overtures and songs. Both composers were interested in folk tunes, even in the English variety, and examples will be given later. From 1783 onwards Arnold's operas were nearly always published in vocal score. In the earlier period now under discussion his music was less in demand, and few of his operas got into print. He was over forty before he enjoyed much success.

Colman began at the Little Theatre by redressing a wrong of long standing. He staged for the first time Gay's *Polly* (LT 19.6.77). The production confirmed what had long been suspected by its readers that *Polly* was greatly inferior to *The Beggar's Opera*. Arnold added some new songs of his own, but their

---

[1] Foote held the patent for life and it lapsed at his death. The Colmans then ran the theatre under an annual licence from the Lord Chamberlain.

music does not survive. His full-length all-sung burletta, *April Day* (LT 22.8.77), has an amusing libretto by Kane O'Hara, but again the music does not survive. A burletta may well have been too ambitious an undertaking for a new company. Yet this same August the theatre found a lasting musical success in Arnold's *The Spanish Barber* (LT 30.8.77).

Beaumarchais had published *Le Barbier de Seville* the year before, and included in his text the vocal line of the only two songs. 'Vous me l'ordonnez', more usually known as 'Je suis Lindor', became very popular all over Western Europe. The tune has been attributed both to Monsigny and to Beaumarchais himself. Mozart wrote piano variations on it when he was in Paris, and so did Clementi in his B flat piano sonata, op. 12 no. 1. Colman never published his operatic version.[1] According to Genest, he left out the scene in which the Count pretends to be drunk. Figaro, renamed Lazarillo, and Rosina, sometimes inexplicably called Rosara, were played by Edwin and Miss Farren, and though the latter was hardly ever allowed to sing in her more famous days at Drury Lane, Colman gave her five of the ten songs. Some of them are by no means easy. The Count was allowed no songs at all, Palmer being an incompetent musician. There is a good trio for Bartolo and two of his servants, the one sneezing all the time and the other yawning, and this anticipates the similar trio in Paisiello's *Il Barbiere* of 1782. There is also a good 'jealousy' aria, sung, as in both the Paisiello and Rossini settings, by 'Basil'. Most of the music was new-composed, but Arnold did borrow the already popular 'Je suis Lindor'; being unable to give it to the Count, he had it sung by Rosina to new words, 'Tell-tale Eyes'. The overture has only one movement, and perhaps for the first time in English music, a Spanish flavour. It is headed 'El Fandango'.

[1] For a slightly earlier English translation by James Chouquet, see Garrick's Letter 1124.

The first two-and-a-half bars are virtually the same as those in the Fandago quoted by Hawkins in his History of Music (1776).[1] *The Spanish Barber* was in the Little Theatre repertoire for some twenty years.

Shield's first opera, *The Flitch of Bacon* (LT 17.8.78) was equally long-lived. According to Busby[2] Shield led the theatre band that season because 'Mr. Bulkley' was ill, and so got his chance as a composer. It was a pity that he succeeded so early in his career with a sentimental village opera (the libretto was by Henry Bate), for it led to his repeating the recipe at intervals all his life. As will be expected, the opera takes place at Dunmow in Essex. The young couple gain forgiveness for their elopement a year and a day later by winning the flitch given to the happiest married couple in the district. The music is patchy. The overture begins poorly; Shield never enjoyed writing overtures. But there is an original and charming second movement based on the Scots tune 'Up and ware them a', Willie'. Shield seems to have been guided in his borrowings by those in *The Duenna*. The Linleys had preserved no more than the tune of 'Now is the Month of Maying', but Shield kept all three voice parts of East's 'How merrily we live that Shepherds be' (from the Second Set of Madrigals of 1606), though he added string parts and changed 'Shepherds' to 'Soldiers'. One wonders where he came on the original. His arrangement was astonishingly popular, and there were at least six reprints before the end of the century. Perhaps because there is a Giordani aria in *The Duenna*, there is one in *The Flitch*, borrowed from *La vera Costanza* which had just been produced at the King's Theatre for the first time. Shield must have played the viola in it. He also has a traditional tune of real beauty (VS, p. 38), given by Chappell as 'My Lodging is on the cold Ground'.[3] It had just been published for the first time, and Giordani had used it as the slow movement of a piano concerto. The most curious borrowing was 'No, 'twas neither Shape nor Feature', which Shield attributed to J. C. Bach. He got it from a recently published 'Rondeau' called 'Io ti lascio e questo addio' which Tenducci had been singing at Bach-Abel concerts with oboe and piano accompaniment plus unobtrusive strings. Bach wrote several songs about this time with piano obbligato,[4] and in this one it seems he was rearranging an aria by Mortellari. But to make confusion worse, Kelly thought the song was by Schuster, in whose *Didone Abbandonata* he heard it sung by Pacchierotti in Naples.[5] Shield kept Bach's interesting orchestration. Surprisingly his own songs tend to be the most elaborate. 'From Minden's Plains of Glory' has cues for oboes, trumpets, and horns. The orchestral pit at the Little

---

[1] Music example No. 33. For the tune's resemblance to the Fandango in Gluck's *Don Juan* (1761) and Mozart's *Figaro* (1786) see Brian Trowell's letter M&L July 1969.

[2] ii, p. 186.

[3] Moore thought the tune Irish. Bunting and Chappell both thought it English.

[4] See C. B. Oldman's 'Mozart's Scena for Tenducci', M&L Jan. 1961.

[5] Kelly i, p. 71, 2nd ed.

Theatre was tiny, and the trumpets must have been played by the bassoonists or two of the string players; there was never room for more than six wind. The pipe and tabor parts in the opening chorus were played on stage.

A poor all-sung burletta called *Buxom Joan* (LT 25.6.78) had music by Raynor Taylor, a Chelmsford organist who had worked at Marylebone Gardens. The libretto is based on Ben's bawdy song in Act III of Congreve's *Love for Love*, but it is dulled by bowdlerization. The score seems complete. A theme in the overture gets turned upside down, but perhaps only by chance.

Arnold, one of the very few musicians Dibdin always liked, is known to have corresponded with him when he was in France. Dibdin must have sent Arnold from Nancy a libretto called *The Gipsies* (LT 3.8.78), which Arnold set as a favour, but it was not liked and nothing of it was published. A month later Arnold arranged incidental music for a production of *Macbeth* (LT 7.9.78), and the eight pieces were published in full score—for oboes (doubling flutes), horns, and strings. Five of the pieces were Scotch Song Tunes, and they included 'The Berks of Endermay' ('Music before the Play'), 'The Yellow hair'd Laddie', and the nostalgic 'Lochaber' (appropriately for the end of Act III). Arnold composed a minuet for the 'Banquet' and arranged Purcell's still popular 'Britons strike home' from *Bonduca* to provide a rousing end. Leveridge's music was also used.

His full-length pastiche, *Summer Amusement* (LT 1.7.79), was set in Margate and had words by Miles Peter Andrews, who by now was a gunpowder manufacturer. Two-thirds of the music was by Arnold himself; borrowings included the popular sea-song from Dibdin's *The Seraglio* ('Blow high, blow low'), a Giordani aria, and the gavotte from Arne's *Thomas and Sally* overture. *Summer Amusement* had only a limited success.

The Son in Law (LT 14.8.79) was the first of many opera librettos by the Irish dramatist John O'Keeffe (1747–1837), who was inexplicably admired. Hazlitt called him 'the English Molière', and added that 'in light and careless laughter, and the pleasant exaggeration of the humorous, we have had no one to equal him'. Leigh Hunt thought that 'as a farce writer he stands alone'. We today are more likely to agree with Allardyce Nicoll, who wrote that 'mediocrity is the chief characteristic of O'Keeffe's farces', and found him largely responsible for the inanities of nineteenth-century comedy. Modern readers would surely put him far behind both Bickerstaffe and O'Hara for invention and wit, yet he was much more admired in his day. O'Keeffe started as a Dublin actor, and moved to London when his eyesight started to fail. In London he wrote more than fifty dramatic works, and all but two of the first twenty-four were operatic. His farces with music were nearly always much more popular than those without, and one of the most popular of all was *The Agreeable Surprise* which Arnold set in 1781. This was the last piece O'Keeffe wrote with his own hand; the rest, and they are the vast majority, were dictated to an amanuensis. Michael Kelly, who had heard O'Keeffe in Dublin in the 1770s singing in *Lionel and Clarissa*, met him again in 1787.

Alas! how changed I found him!—When he acted Jessamy, he was a fine, sprightly, animated young man; now, poor fellow, broken down, almost blind; but still full of pleasantry and anecdote.

Nevertheless the poor fellow lived to be ninety.

Both music and libretto of *The Son in Law* are rarities. When in 1798 O'Keeffe published his 'Works' by subscription in four volumes, he explained in the Preface that he was unable to print *The Son in Law*, *The Agreeable Surprise*, *The Dead Alive*, and *Peeping Tom* because he had sold the copyright to the elder Colman, 'whereas, if they had been sold to a bookseller and subsequently published, they might have appeared in it (the new edition) at the expiration of fourteen years'. According to Genest, the plot of *The Son in Law* is about a London hop merchant who sets up in the West End as a fine gentleman in order to persuade Cecilia to marry him. Cecilia's father mistakenly thinks a ridiculous Italian castrato called Signor Arionelli is to be his son-in-law, and this role was especially written for the elder Bannister who had for some years been entertaining his friends with a castrato imitation. In York a few years later Tate Wilkinson let Mrs. Jordan play the part, and this gave point to the moment when the Signor declines to marry the girl on the grounds that 'it is quite out of my way'. Rather strangely Arnold makes the Signor sing 'Water parted' from Arne's *Artaxerxes*, and with the original words. Cecilia has a goodish song with oboe and bassoon obbligatos, but most of Arnold's music is undistinguished. Another popular French song had just reached England, 'Lison dormait' from Dezède's opera *Julie*, and Arnold worked it in. A year or two later Clementi was writing variations on it for his piano sonata in F, op. 12, no. 3, and Mozart also used it for piano variations (K. 264).

Colman found no operatic successes for 1780, and Arnold's contributions were never published.[1] However, they had a joint success in a new line with 'An Original, Whimsical, Operatical, Pantomimical, Farcical, Electrical, Naval and Military Extravaganza' called *The Genius of Nonsense* (LT 2.9.80). Following the lead given by Covent Garden, Colman made it a 'speaking pantomime', and the younger Bannister played Harlequin. The Little Theatre could not hope to compete with the winter playhouses in pantomime machinery and effects, but audiences were indulgent. The score was published, and at first glance it appears to be all composed by Arnold; indeed it says so on the title-page. A second glance reveals a number of familiar pieces, and Colman's libretto helps us to identify them. Arnold drew on several Garrick pantomimes of the early fifties, and Burney's 'The Watchman' (*Queen Mab*) becomes a duet for a Watchman and Harlequin. There is a catch by Purcell ('Soldier, soldier, take off thy Wine'), versions of 'Heart of Oak', 'Nancy Dawson', and 'The

---

[1] *Fire and Water* (LT 8.7.80) and *The Wedding Night* (LT 12.8.80). Only one song was published from *The Dead Alive* (LT 16.6.81). This work is not otherwise mentioned, or dated.

Belle-isle March',[1] and a song by J. C. Bach which may have been specially written for the occasion. In the vocal score 'God save the King' forms the Finale, though it is not indicated in the libretto, which also omits 'Heart of Oak'. Much of the fun laying in satirizing a Dr. Graham who was running what he called his 'Temple of Health' and curing his patients mainly by electricity; he had a 'Celestial Bed' which relieved sterility. As Harlequin-Dr. Graham Jack Bannister reproduced his mannerisms. The doctor was not amused and threatened a libel action, but later thought better of it.

Colman had two rewarding successes in 1781. *The Beggar's Opera* was staged with the sexes reversed,[2] and the O'Keeffe-Arnold afterpiece, *The Agreeable Surprise* (LT 4.9.81) introduced Edwin's Lingo, Mrs. Wells's 'beautifully silly' Cowslip, and Mrs. Webb's mountainous Mrs. Cheshire; Londoners took all three characters to their hearts for half-a-century. Though the setting is conventional ('Peasants in rural Merriment after Harvest' is the opening stage direction) and the plot wildly improbable, O'Keeffe is here at his funniest. Years before, Sir Felix Friendly and Compton have agreed to bring up each other's children; these children are now grown-up and in love. But Eugene thinks he is Compton's son and poor, while Laura thinks she is an orphan brought up by the now wealthy Sir Felix. The fathers are delighted the young people should have fallen in love with no thought of the riches they will in fact receive when all is made known. In London Eugene has borrowed money from Mrs. Cheshire, who wants to marry him herself and comes down in a coach with an attorney for the purpose. The rumour flies round the village that she is a Russian princess of terrifying strength and violence. Her plans are foiled and the young couple are given their agreeable surprise. Such a plot could not on its own have made the opera popular. What the audience came for was Edwin's seedy ex-schoolmaster, his speech larded with Latin tags, most of them wrong. He is now Sir Felix's butler, and he loves the moronic farmgirl, Cowslip. Touchstone and Audrey are their distant ancestors, but their backchat would have got by in late Victorian Music-Hall.

> LINGO (*drinking a toast*): Here's that the masculine may never be neuter to the feminine gender.
> COWSLIP: Here's that—ay, here's the masculine to the feminine gender. O Lord! I left out neuter.
> LINGO: You were right. Recte, puella. I know these things, so did Ovid and Caesar.
> COWSLIP: What, Caesar the great dog, Sir?

[1] Written to commemorate a naval victory off the Breton coast in the Seven Years War. The tune is oddly like a chorus in *Il Trovatore*.

[2] Within months Tate Wilkinson was giving similar performances in York, Hull, etc.

LINGO: No, child! Judas Caesar. Romulus and Remus were suckled by a
wolf. They ravished the Sabine girls and found Rome in Italy.
COWSLIP: Ah! such fellows would find room anywhere.

The music in *The Agreeable Surprise* is a little above Arnold's usual hum-
drum level. There is a charming minuet at the end of the overture, a big coloratura aria for Miss Harper as Laura ('The tuneful Lark'), and an ambitious
Quintet at the end of Act I. Lingo's 'Amo, amas, I love a Lass' was so much
liked that in the following century it acquired Student Song status.[1] In most of
his operas O'Keeffe had one or more Irish characters, and for these he wrote
lyrics to fit Irish tunes he'd picked up in his youth; he must have sung them to
his composer to write down and arrange, and we shall see later that O'Keeffe had
some claims to be considered as a Folk Song Collector. Even in *The Agreeable
Surprise*, an opera with no Irish characters, there are three alleged Irish tunes
(though Sir Felix's 'In Jacky Bull' is certainly English). Lingo's first is delightful, his second ('Of all the pretty flowers') an outlandish and fascinating fiddle
tune which Arnold was at a loss to harmonize.

That same season Arnold twice collaborated with Lady Craven. This giddy
but remarkable woman was born in 1750, the youngest daughter of the Earl of
Berkeley; she wrote her own Memoirs as well as a travel book about the Crimea.
Boswell found her 'beautiful, gay, and fascinating', and so at first did Lord
Craven, who married her in 1766. She soon presented him with seven children,
and also found time to build a pastoral 'Cottage' by the Thames. Craven Cottage
has disappeared; the site is now the Fulham football ground. Lady Craven had a
lifelong passion for amateur theatricals and opera. She disapproved of *The
Spanish Barber* on the grounds that a barber should be a subsidiary character; an
author who makes such a man a hero 'deviates from all theatrical rules'. Her
own first play, *The Sleepwalker*, was printed by Horace Walpole on his private
press at Strawberry Hill. In 1779 she dedicated to Walpole 'A Tale for Christmas' about a man with the unmemorable name of Baron Kinkvervankots-
darsprakengotchdern and this was made into an opera libretto which Arnold
set (LT 9.7.81). Nine days later the same collaborators offered *The Silver
Tankard* to an uninterested public. It was never published.

Of much more interest is Lady Craven's share in *The Arcadian Pastoral*
(13.4.82) even though it received only amateur production. It was presented at
Queensbury House in Burlington Gardens by a cast of children stiffened by
well-known professionals, and the music was composed by one of the richest
and strangest men in England, William Beckford. Beckford was still young and
undisgraced. He had not yet written *Vathek* or built Fonthill. He prided himself
on a knowledge of all the arts, and at his coming-of-age party the year before had
produced for the entertainment of his guests a short opera of his own composition
in which, incredibly, Tenducci, Rauzzini, and Pacchierotti were the singers.

---

[1] Arnold identified the tune as 'The Mouse and the Frog'.

Probably Lady Craven was present, and when she had the idea of presenting some of her own children in an opera in London, she asked Beckford to write the music. The dialogue is lost, but Beckford's full score survives in MS.[1] The music is Italianate, *galante*, uninspired, and astonishingly professional; it has been broadcast on the Third Programme. With all the money in the world Beckford could afford the best professional advice and help in London. Barthelemon led the orchestra, and his wife collected a small choral group that sang behind the scenes in support of the diminutive and incompetent choral singers on the stage. The great Pacchierotti himself, the idol of the King's Theatre, was present to lend a hand. John Henderson coached the children in their acting and Bertoni in their singing. Ballet dancers were brought in from Drury Lane. 'Her frolic Ladyship' was much in evidence helping with the clothes, which were sumptuously beautiful, but Beckford did not think highly of her libretto which he altered here and there.[2] The occasion was much talked about, and a very distinguished audience assembled to watch the children and in some cases to hear the music; among those present were a great many Lords, the Archbishop of Canterbury, Horace Walpole, Charles James Fox, and Dr. Burney. The cast need hardly concern us. The Craven children seem to have been less able performers than most. Beckford was characteristically amorous in his praise of the boy hero, and the Barthelemons' daughter was First Fairy; as Mrs. Henslowe she later entertained Haydn.

That summer Arnold was too busy with other work to write more than a pantomime for Colman. *Harlequin Teague* (LT 17.8.82) was a speaking pantomime, and the actor Wewitzer drew large audiences by his performance of Dr. Caterpillar, a take-off of a celebrated quack philosopher of the day called Katterfelt. With Arnold pausing in his work for the Little Theatre we transfer our attention to the winter playhouses.

[1] Beckford's musical MSS are owned by the Duke of Hamilton, whose ancestor married Beckford's eldest daughter.

[2] He described the production in some splendidly vivid letters given in J. W. Oliver's *Life of William Beckford* (London 1932).

13
Shield in the Ascendant
1782–1788

1 LINLEY AND JACKSON AT DRURY LANE

THOUGH Sheridan was in charge at Drury Lane for the rest of the century, he took less and less interest in its running as he got deeper and deeper into politics. During the period covered in this chapter, he delegated most of the administration to Thomas King. John Philip Kemble joined the company in 1783, and when King resigned in 1788 Sheridan made Kemble his manager. But he continued to keep his hands on the purse-strings: salaries at Drury Lane were nearly always in arrears, and Sheridan became slippery when cornered on the subject.

Mrs. Siddons made her mark at Drury Lane the year before Kemble, and together they raised acting standards far above those at Covent Garden. This improvement was not equalled in the field of opera until the end of the decade. The theatre was especially short of tenors, and Kemble himself sang the title role, the only vocal part of his career, in a version of Grétry's *Richard Coeur de Lion*. It was a confession of deplorable weakness that he sang at all. Linley, joint patentee with Sheridan, and the theatre's music director, seems to have been better at training female singers than male. He did not at first realize that he had a promising baritone in John Bannister, son of Covent Garden's Charles Bannister. Jack, as he was always called, had joined the Drury Lane Company in 1779, and he was soon acting Hamlet and Prince Hal. He had an honest cheerful ability, and was extremely popular. In 1783 he married Elizabeth Harper, who had recently won fame by her singing at Covent Garden. When it became apparent that Kemble was supplanting Jack Bannister in the big heroic roles, his wife took him in hand and taught him to sing.

Drury Lane was fairly well provided with sopranos. Anna Maria Phillips made her debut in 1780 while she was still a pupil of Linley's. For her first few seasons she had to give him a percentage of her earnings. She was extremely beautiful, and a competent actress in such roles as Ophelia and Miranda. In 1785 she became Mrs. Crouch, and by this time she had developed into a high coloratura. In vocal display she had a rival in Elizabeth Wrighten, who had been singing leading operatic roles in the company since 1769. Mrs. Wrighten's husband was the Drury Lane prompter (until his death in 1793), and with him and Linley jointly running opera rehearsals there must have been social problems over the casting. They were solved in 1787 when Mrs. Wrighten ran off to America, leaving her husband to cope with their three daughters. Two singers of a quite different sort specialized in simple ballads. One was Miss Romanzini (later Mrs. Bland), who made her debut in *Richard Coeur de Lion* but was no actress. The other was Mrs. Jordan, who joined the company in 1785; she became the leading comedienne of her day.

In the 1780–1 season Linley roused himself from his melancholy to write a pantomime score[1] and to set a fifteen-minute 'Pastoral Interlude' for insertion in a play called *The Generous Impostor* (DL 22.11.80); the Interlude appeared in vocal score complete with recitatives. Linley still felt unequal to a complete opera, and either commissioned or welcomed with gratitude a full-length opera, *The Lord of the Manor* (DL 27.12.80), by 'William Jackson of Exeter'.[2] Linley and Jackson had known each other in Bath in the early 1760s.

The Lord of the Manor is worth treating at some length both because the music is unusual in quality and because it was published in full score. It was the last English opera of the century to be so honoured, and it provides a good deal of such evidence as we have about scoring methods of the time. The words were by General Burgoyne, who has already been mentioned for this work on *The Maid of the Oaks*.[3] Since then he had resigned from the army in disgust at his treatment by the Government; he felt in no way to blame for what had happened at Saratoga. In *The Heiress* he was to achieve a comedy that would be worth staging today, and which has been broadcast in England. His three other dramatic works were all operatic, and *The Lord of the Manor* was outstandingly successful. A revival at Covent Garden in 1812 had additional music by Bishop and others, and according to Loewenberg the last known performance was at the Strand Theatre in 1853.

William Jackson (1730–1803) was the son of an Exeter grocer. He had a few lessons in London from John Travers, but spent most of his life in his home town, where he married a Miss Bartlett by whom he had three children. He published several sets of songs with orchestral accompaniment, and lived mainly by teaching singing. In 1757 he began painting landscapes in oils, and four years later in Bath he became friendly with Thomas Gainsborough. They exchanged lessons in their respective arts. Gainsborough always liked the company of musicians, and besides the Linley family and Jackson he painted portraits of J. C. Bach, Abel, the cellist John Crosdill, and his son-in-law, the oboist Fischer. Jackson's *The Four Ages* (1798) is a prime source of information about the artist.

---

[1] See p. 446.
[2] This is how he always described himself on his title-pages.
[3] See p. 381; also p. 263 for an extract from his Preface to *The Lord of the Manor*.

'You have more of the painter', wrote Gainsborough, 'than half those that get money by it, that I will swear, if you desire it, upon a Church Bible.'[1] But such praise owed more to friendship than truth. As John Hayes has put it in his definitive work on Gainsborough's drawings, 'Apart from a close dependence on Gainsborough, and a tendency to use his ideas and motifs quite unashamedly, the hallmarks of Jackson's style are his thin and overcareful contour lines, fundamental unsureness of drawing, and inability to fuse the different elements in his compositions into a unified whole'.[2] But the same writer shows a little more sympathy when Jackson's landscapes are his main subject, and without question they are, for a composer, remarkably good.[3] In 1771 Jackson exhibited at the Academy, and seriously thought of making his living out of painting rather than music. However two unexpected triumphs caused him to change his mind.

Jackson had first come before the playhouse audience with an unpublished cantata based on Milton's *Lycidas* (CG 4.11.67); he wrote it in memory of the young Duke of York, who had just died, and Mrs. Pinto and Dibdin were among the singers. In 1773 he published in full score a large-scale *Ode to Fancy*, and in the same year some unusual harpsichord sonatas with string quartet accompaniment. He was fifty, or approaching it, when he broke into two musical fields quite new to him. In 1777 he became organist of Exeter Cathedral, a position he held until his death, and in 1780 he composed his first opera, *The Lord of the Manor*. In spite of its success, he does not seem to have hankered after a career in the theatres. In 1785 he made a leisurely tour of Europe, getting as far as North Italy, and thereafter he preferred writing words to music. His review of Burney's *History of Music* had unfortunate consequences. Jackson wrote in *The Critical Review* that the work was a magnificent achievement, but he regretted that the author allowed so little merit to English music.[4] The criticism was just, but Burney was pathologically touchy and never forgave him; in Rees's *Encyclopaedia* he got his own back with the monstrous libel that Jackson's good qualities 'were strongly alloyed by a mixture of selfishness, arrogance, and an insatiable rage of superiority'.

Jackson's innate conservatism comes out in his *Observations on the Present State of Music in London* (1791). He felt strongly that music was going to the dogs. The new symphonies, presumably Haydn's, were 'the ravings of a Bedlamite . . . Sometimes the key is perfectly lost, by wandering so far from

---

[1] Woodall No. 58; and see also No. 103.

[2] *The Drawings of Thomas Gainsborough* (1970) i, p. 69; two landscape drawings thought to be Jackson's are reproduced in Vol. ii (plates 364 and 368).

[3] 'William Jackson of Exeter, organist, composer and amateur artist', *The Connoisseur*, January 1970. The few oils and drawings that can be attributed to Jackson with any confidence are all here reproduced; the three oils are privately owned at Ottery St Mary in Devon.

[4] Lonsdale, pp. 344–6.

it', and he found the discords 'so entangled that it is past the arts of man to untie the knot'. Melody seemed to be vanishing into limbo, and he therefore approved of the way English composers

> very wisely adapt some of the Songs to tunes which were composed when Melody really existed: and it is curious to observe how glad the Audience are to find a little that is congenial to their feelings, after they have been gasping to take in some meaning from the wretched imitations of Italian *bravura*, and pathetic Songs; which, alas! are but 'the Shadows of a Shade'.

The libretto of *The Lord of the Manor* is based on Marmontel's *Silvain*, a one-act libretto set by Grétry. The title role is that operatic rarity, a grandfather, and rather an unobservant one, for he does not know that the son he turned out of his house years ago has been living on his estate disguised as 'Rashly' and successfully bringing up two pretty daughters. Sophia, the elder, is pursued by the Lord of the Manor's younger son, Contrast, who wants love without marriage; he is, of course, unaware that he is pressing his attentions on his own niece. Sophia already has a prospective husband in Truemore. Contrast tries to have Truemore conscripted, but the girls' maid, Peggy, persuades Corporal Drill to conscript Contrast instead. When he deserts, he is brought up before his own father for punishment. All comes out, and the Lord of the Manor is so delighted to find that the pretty girls he has been meeting in the park are his own granddaughters that he gladly forgives their father.

'Rashly' was played by Charles Bannister, on loan from Covent Garden. (This season the two playhouses tried the experiment of pooling their actors, but the administrative chaos that resulted soon brought the experiment to an end.) Miss Farren was Sophia, and her sister, Annette, was taken by Miss Prudom who was French. She had recently sung at the King's Theatre as 'second woman', and Lord Mount-Edgcumbe praised 'the sweetness of her voice, and her chaste good style of singing'. But he added that she was 'too young to be a finished or scientific performer'. Because her English was poor, she was given plenty to sing but very little to say, whereas Miss Farren had plenty to say but only one solo song. Contrast, because he was played by Palmer, was allowed no songs at all. Mrs. Wrighten was Peggy, and Vernon made a somewhat elderly lover of Truemore; he was at the end of his career. Miss Prudom died a few months after the first night.

Much the most popular item in *The Lord of the Manor* was Bannister's 'Encompass'd in an Angel's Frame'. The words offer a foretaste of a popular Victorian emotion, for 'Rashly' was singing of his own dead wife. He ended:

> What now shall fill these widow'd arms?
> Ah me! my Anna's Urn!

Modern lips may curl, but at the time there was not a dry eye in the house. Leigh Hunt wrote in his autobiography that this song 'used to make my mother shed tears, on account of my sister Eliza, who died early'. It was a favourite in the Hunt family because they could 'identify'; also, it must be added, because Jackson's setting is simple, heartfelt, and beautiful. Most of the songs in the first two acts have quality, but there is a slight falling-off in the third, which ends with three consecutive items in E flat. Jackson well understood the voice, and he had lyrical gifts that were rare at the time. There is a fine vigorous hunting song at the end of the first act, with full brass accompaniment as well as a chorus, and though Jackson abhorred 'wretched imitations of Italian bravura', he did allow Miss Prudom some restrained and sensible coloratura in 'So the chill Mist', a beautiful song with interesting bassoon parts.

Only one copy of the published full score is given in BUCEM.[1] In a sense Jackson used a normal Mozart orchestra of eight woodwind, four brass, drums, and strings, but in fact Drury Lane did not have room for such a band; the same two players could have coped with the flute, oboe, and clarinet parts, and no doubt did. The Hunting Song and the Quartet both start with oboe parts which switch to flutes in the middle; in the latter case very little time is given for the change. Jackson treats the clarinets as though unsure of their availability, for he invariably has the flutes doubling them. He could count on clarinets at Drury Lane, but probably not in the provincial theatres for which his full score must have been intended. In flat keys he asked for transposing flutes of two different sizes. Thus the Overture and Finale are both in E flat, but the flute parts are written a semitone down in D.[2] They are again written in D in the Corporal's 'Gallant Comrades of the Blade', a song in F major, and this time the parts sound a minor third higher like E flat clarinets. When songs are in sharp keys, the flutes are 'loco' in the usual way, for instance in Truemore's 'Within this Shade'. This is a beautifully scored piece with no violins, the flutes being supported by solo(?) viola, solo cello, and basses. In the Hunting Song, trumpets and timpani join the horns for the central chorus section; needless to say the song is in the trumpet-and-drum key of D major. There is a side-drum in the Corporal's 'Gallant Comrades' but the part is not notated; the player is directed to beat 'only in the Symphonies', presumably in the rhythm of the bass line, but when the chorus joins in he is to beat all the time. The Overture has two rather dull movements and then a delightfully vivid one at the end with high written Cs for the E flat horns.

Jackson's only other opera was a failure. *The Metamorphosis* (DL 5.12.83), a full-lengther, had a libretto said to be by Jackson himself, though Richard

---

[1] Unclearly as 'another edition'; it is in the Euing Library at Glasgow University.

[2] Today we would describe such flutes, if they were still used, as being in D flat to indicate that they transposed up a semitone. But in the late eighteenth century they were said to be in E flat—the sound that resulted when you played the bottom note (written D). Similarly the flutes in 'Gallant Comrades of the Blade' were said to be in F, and again this was the sound produced when you played written D. On the normal one-keyed flute of the time it was hard to play in flat keys.

Tickell wrote the lyrics. The dialogue was never published. The vocal score has a good minor-key song for Mrs. Wrighten ('To be sure') and a coloratura one for Miss Phillips. Act II ends with a well-developed Dibdin-style Finale that keeps the plot going and is in several contrasted sections. It would seem that deficiencies in the libretto sank the opera. There is a synopsis of the plot in the *London Magazine* for December 1783.

It may have been noticed that *The Lord of the Manor* had its first night on Boxing Day. At Covent Garden this was becoming the conventional day for launching the new pantomime. Drury Lane scarcely attempted to compete in this field. Four new or allegedly new pantomimes were produced annually from the winter of 1781; thereafter for the rest of the century the theatre relied almost entirely on revivals. A lack-lustre attitude is shown by the second of these four, *Lun's Ghost* (DL 3.1.82), which was a dish-up of *Harlequin Jacket* (1775), itself a dish-up of earlier pantomimes. No music from it was ever published, and apparently only one song from *Harlequin Junior, or The Magic Cestus* (DL 7.1.84), even though this pantomime was often revived. We are left with two examples for which Linley composed the music, *Robinson Crusoe* (DL 29.1.81) and *The Triumph of Mirth* (DL 26.12.82), and both appeared in unusually informative vocal score.

Sheridan himself wrote much of the scenario of *Robinson Crusoe*, and the 'Short Account' was published. The first act takes place on the island and tells the familiar story in mime. Crusoe's costume is described at length, as is also the house he has built. We see him making a boat, and at the point where 'He sees the mark of the foot' in the sand Linley's music, though not striking in itself, is descriptive in a new way:

Crusoe rescues Friday from the 'Savages', whose music is wholly European in style, and they in turn are rescued by sailors. The act ends with Mr. Gaudry singing 'The Midnight Watch' before a drop curtain, thus allowing the stage 'carpenters' to strike the Act I scene and set up the one for Act II. Kelly[1] describes how, when this scene-changing problem arose, Sheridan dashed off the words on the back of a playbill for Linley to set immediately. So far there have been nearly thirty Comic Tunes and this one song, and there were even more instrumental pieces in Act II.

The 'Short Account' prefaces Act II with the words

> The *Story* being no longer pursued in the remainder of the representation, it is only necessary to add that *Friday*, being invested with the powers of Harlequin, after many fanciful distresses and the usual pantomimic revolutions, receives his final reward in the hand of Columbine.

The act starts with Crusoe leaving his friends at the quayside in England; we do not see him again. By confining the harlequinade to the second half and divorcing it from the main plot, Drury Lane had hit on a new formula that was to become conventional in the next century. At the time not everyone was enthusiastic. Horace Walpole much preferred 'the pantomimes of Rich, which are full of wit, and coherent, and carried on a story'.

Linley's score is remarkable not so much for the music, which is often poor, as for the amount of information it provides about the action. With this and the 'Short Account' it would be quite easy to re-create the whole entertainment, though a modern audience would miss the humour of the musical quotations. For the entrance of some Friars Linley has his own Friars' Glee from *The Duenna*, and for a mill scene he quotes the song about the miller in the 1760 version of *The Jovial Crew* (No. 37). No doubt I have missed other quotations.

The Triumph of Mirth starts with a one-movement overture salvaged from something by Tom Linley. Besides a large number of Comic Tunes, there are four songs, a glee, and a final chorus; also, for the first time in a Drury Lane pantomime, spoken dialogue. We begin with a Magician telling Mirth (in song, recitative, and speech) why he has buried Harlequin, whose tomb is visible in the Magician's cave. Mirth turns out to be Harlequin's mother, and she insists on her son being re-animated. Thereafter Harlequin is chased all over London in the usual way, the audience being regaled with views of Cornhill, St. Paul's Church-Yard, and Westminster Bridge. In the end Harlequin and Columbine are married in the Magician's cave to the sounds of a final Chorus. At its best the music is gay and pert in a way that was becoming characteristic. Mrs. Wrighten, as Diana, had a difficult coloratura song with elaborate horn parts.

During these pantomime years Linley was accepting at least one new opera a season from an outside source. Thomas Carter's *The Fair American* (DL 18.5.82) had been turned down by Covent Garden, and though Drury Lane audiences were at first enthusiastic it did not last. Pilon, the librettist, absconded

<hr/>

[1] ii, p. 309, 2nd ed.

with his share of the takings and without paying his composer. As in several operas of this period, there is less music than usual (the opera is full-length) because so many of the cast could not sing. Miss Phillips played the fair American, Angelica, who has recently been rescued by a British officer at 'Charlestown'. She has one lovely Da Capo song, 'Ah cease, fond Youth', with interesting modulations in the middle section. Parts of the score suggests the influence of Haydn, though this may be illusory.

The next 'outside' opera was Hook's afterpiece, *Too Civil by Half* (DL 5.11.82). There are only six songs, but they are all rather good. Miss Phillips sang three of them, one being a big three-section fast-slow-fast aria; another was one of those imitation Scotch Songs Hook could write so well:

Hook

In___ youth_when__ a___ lo - ver we meet_ that__ is___ ten - der,

Who could tell from the notes alone if that is genuine or not? Most of the characters in this 'opera' have no songs at all. The libretto starts well though it fails to sustain the interest. Sir Toby Treacle has ships on the brain, more particularly the one being built at his own expense. His daughter's lover dresses up as a sea-captain in order to ingratiate himself but is handicapped by his ignorance of all things nautical. There is much heavy humour with him talking about the girl when Sir Toby thinks he is talking about the ship.

The following season Drury Lane accepted another afterpiece opera from Hook, *The Double Disguise* (DL 8.3.84); it has a dreadful libretto by Hook's first wife, 'Harriet Horncastle', who, says Parke, was a genteel officer's daughter who painted miniatures. There is a pleasant bassoon solo in the slow movement of the overture and concertante parts for oboe and bassoon in one of the songs, but nothing else holds the interest. Hook cooked his goose with this unsuccessful piece; he did not write again for Drury Lane until 1795.

Dibdin's afterpiece *Liberty Hall* (DL 8.2.85) can hardly have been accepted on merit. Drury Lane must have felt sorry for an ex-employee in financial distress. Much the most popular song was 'The high mettled Racer', which tells the story of a horse once supreme in the hunting field but now dying, old and broken.[1] Hogarth, writing in 1842, thought, wrongly, that this song would 'retain its popularity as long as the language shall be understood in which it is written'. Certainly the long rolling melody is splendidly sustained. Dibdin never wrote again for Drury Lane, and there were no more 'outside' operas there until Storace started contributing to the repertoire at the end of 1788.

Linley himself composed three full-length operas in the 1780s and one after-piece, and their overtures are especially interesting for the way they reflect

---

[1] Was this song the origin of the popular children's novel, *Black Beauty*?

Haydn's mounting influence. Sets of Haydn string quartets (op. 1, 2, and 17) had been published in London as early as 1772, and about that time there were Paris editions of some of the early symphonies, but it is most improbable that English composers were either interested or influenced. It was the London publications in 1782 of Symphonies 53 and 73 ('L'Impériale' and 'La Chasse') that made Haydn suddenly popular. One cannot easily distinguish between the influence of Haydn and that of other continental composers using much the same idiom; for instance Vanhal, whose symphonies were much played in England from about 1775. But ten years later Haydn's influence was undoubtedly stronger than that of any other instrumental composer, especially as regards the intellectual content of development sections and the balance of phrases.

Linley begins his overture to *The Carnival of Venice* (DL 13.12.81) with the following unpromising theme

The middle parts are not given in the vocal score, and this may result in an unfair picture of what Linley intended, but the passage must always have sounded clumsy and directionless. There is no balance of phrase either melodically or harmonically. Yet the movement has occasional points of interesting invention, mostly as regards key shifts. We have already found Linley, alone of English composers, shifting out of key and then back again, and the habit was to grow on him. There is no Haydn influence in this overture, and we would hardly expect there to be. But in *The Strangers at Home* (DL 8.12.85), an intelligent awareness of new continental trends is already battling with Linley's rather clumsy technique. The first theme in the overture, though not individual, does at least have balance:

Linley knew that Haydn would juggle with his main tune in a kaleidoscope of keys, and made a brave attempt to do the same:

The overture to his last opera is much his best. *Love in the East* (DL 25.2.88) starts with a vivid and assured first movement, and though at first we suspect that the momentary shifting out of key and back again reflects incompetence, it soon becomes clear that Linley liked the effect and knew what he was about. Here is a passage in which he is developing his main tune.

The slow movement is a sad little violin solo in G minor. The Finale shows how closely Linley at his best could ape Haydn's style

Not much need be said of the vocal items in these operas. *The Carnival of Venice* has a superfluity of not-very-good strophic ballads, much the prettiest being Mrs. Cargill's[1] 'Young Lubin was a Shepherd Boy'. Miss Phillips has some more meaty arias in which she could show off her technique, and Act I ends with Linley's most Italianate and 'conversational' Finale. Though there were twenty-four performances the first season, Richard Tickell's libretto was never published, perhaps so that he could protect his rights.

The Spanish Rivals (DL 4.11.84), an afterpiece, was remarkable mainly for an astonishing character dreamed up by the librettist, Mark Lonsdale. Though the plot is set in Spain, a rich old gentleman called Don Narcisso de Medicis has an English servant from Cumberland; which, by no coincidence, was Lonsdale's home county. The servant is called Peter, and he is an ex-naval rating who keeps saying 'By Gosh' and talking Cumberland dialect to uncomprehending Spaniards. More to our purpose, he astonishes them with a couple of Cumberland songs which Lonsdale must have sung to Linley. The first is obviously a fiddle tune, and highly unvocal.

[over a pedal C]   *etc.*

Years later (1839) Lonsdale published his *Dialogues, Poems, Songs and Ballads in the Westmoreland and Cumberland Dialects.* He seems to have come from Great Orton, west of Carlisle, which makes it unlikely that he was a close connection of the Lonsdales of Lowther Castle for whom Wordsworth's father was steward. His libretto for *The Spanish Rivals* found little favour in its day, but it was lively and inventive compared to the librettos Linley set next.

James Cobb (1756–1818) had been working for the East India Company since he was fifteen, but he must always have nursed dramatic ambitions. He was encouraged because he was liked, but he had no talent for writing natural dialogue, and he later provided some terrible librettos for Storace. His *Strangers at Home* was set in Florence, and the wordy story was barely comprehensible; much of it had to be cut in rehearsal. Among other improbabilities, we are asked

---

[1] Miss Brown had just become Mrs. Cargill. She left the company at the end of the season and went to India, though not with Mr. Cargill.

to believe that Viola does not recognize her own brother when he is 'redeemed from slavery' in North Africa. Jack Bannister made his operatic debut, as did Mrs. Jordan so far as London was concerned; she spent most of the opera disguised as a boy. Charles Dignum, a recent arrival, was proving a useful tenor; he was twenty, rather stout, and a Linley pupil. Suddenly Drury Lane had plenty of singers, though there was still no heroic tenor. Mrs. Crouch and Miss Field sang some extremely difficult but not very interesting songs, and Mrs. Jordan brought the house down with 'When first I began, Sir to ogle the Ladies', sung to the tune of 'Ally Croaker'. This popular tune had a strange history. In Limerick about 1725 a simple young 'gentleman piper' named Larry Grogan unsuccessfully courted an artful jilt named Alicia Croaker. The affair became famous, and both had songs written about them with simple but excellent tunes. 'Larry Grogan', which must be Irish, was borrowed for *Love in a Village*; 'Ally Croaker' occurs in *Midas* as well as in *The Strangers at Home*.[1]

Linley's last opera, *Love in the East*, also had a libretto by Cobb, and the action was laid in Calcutta, a place Cobb probably knew. (Later on he wrote another libretto about India, *Ramah Droog*.) The endless plotting that goes on among the English residents has a certain probability, but there is little to admire in the way the situations are handled. Mrs. Crouch and Michael Kelly had the best songs, and the former sang long coloratura passages full of high Cs. Linley was earlier quoted as saying he thought opera composers should write all the music themselves, yet in his last two operas he borrowed several items. Thus in *Love in the East* a three-part glee near the start is taken from 'We be three poor Mariners' (*Deuteromelia*, 1609), and 'Let no accusing Sigh' from a song in Linley's own 'Twelve Ballads' (1780). He was probably driven against his own principles by the fact that he was falling into a melancholy that today would demand medical attention. There are other signs of flagging energy. More than half the songs in *The Strangers at Home* are simple strophic ballads, and though there are not so many in *Love in the East* (which contains much better music all through), there are no complex ensembles or Finales of the type that are troublesome to write.

Linley had good reason for his dejection. In 1784 Maria had died, aged only twenty-two, and in 1787 Richard Tickell's wife Mary died too, leaving no active musicians among the younger members of the family. Sheridan's sister Betsy gives a sad picture of the Linley home in her *Journal*. By 1784 Mrs. Linley had lost all her teeth 'and looks a compleat Witch'; also she never stopped talking, and Betsy attributed Thomas Linley's headaches in part to his wife's 'incessant prate'. Soon after finishing *Love in the East* he had a 'kind of paralitic attack in the head—so violent that his life was in the greatest danger . . . He will not leave the Chimney Corner'. By 1790 he was too shattered for the

---

[1] See *The Muses Delight* (1754), p. 218, for the tune with the original words; also p. 99 for a simpler version called 'The Kettlebender'; also Chappell, pp. 713–14, for further information, though not for the facts given here.

heavy work of composing and organizing the music of a busy theatre, and delegated such work to Storace and Kelly.

It has already been mentioned that Michael Kelly sang in Linley's last opera. He had arrived in England, for the very first time in his life, in March 1787, and his performance a few weeks later of Lionel in Dibdin's *Lionel and Clarissa* revealed that Drury Lane had a heroic tenor at last.

2 SHIELD AT COVENT GARDEN

On the last day of 1782 Covent Garden staged one of the most successful afterpiece operas of the century, *Rosina*. It established Shield overnight, and until he quarrelled with the theatre in 1791 he enjoyed a virtual monopoly in its operas, which became the most profitable items in the repertoire. Throughout this period Harris remained the manager, and the prompter-producer was James Wild. Baumgarten led the band, which included two notable players in William Parke, the leading oboist from 1783, and the trumpeter Sarjeant. Many of Shield's operas have difficult obbligato parts designed to show off their skill.

A new generation of singers was taking over. Vernon had just left, and Mr. and Mrs. Mattocks were soon to go. Arne's pupil Mrs. Kennedy (Mrs. Farrel) was almost alone in being inherited from the previous decade. Mrs. Martyr was a recent arrival, and being petite and 'a neat breeches figure' can be thought of as the equivalent of Mrs. Jordan; though less of an actress and more of a singer. Miss Harper, for five years a summer attraction at the Little Theatre, established herself in 1782 as Covent Garden's leading soprano by her performances in *The Castle of Andalusia*, *Rosina*, and various standard works. The following year she became Mrs. Jack Bannister. Covent Garden was not much better equipped with male singers than Drury Lane. For a year or so the theatre made do for its opera heroes with the aging and volatile Charles Bannister. In the autumn of 1783 it acquired the Dublin tenor John Johnstone, who proved a godsend in O'Keeffe's Irish roles. Hazlitt wrote of 'his lubricated brogue, curling round the ear like a well-oiled moustache'. His falsetto was admired, though not by Haydn, who thought it overdone. For comedy roles the theatre relied on Edwin, who was a surprisingly able singer.

Harris's first opera in 1782 was not by Shield but by Arnold, and it was Covent Garden's first big success in this field since *The Duenna* seven years before. Arnold took more than his usual trouble over *The Castle of Andalusia* (CG 2.11.82), and must have hoped thereby to graduate from the summer playhouse to the more glamorous winter ones. Yet he never composed for Covent Garden again. Non-encouragement after such a success is unique in playhouse history, and only extraordinary reasons can account for it. We can refer to Haydn's *London Notebook* for the probable explanation. Arnold told Haydn he had once written an opera, and because 'the backers' (presumably the management) had no confidence in it, he financed the production himself to the tune of £700. The backers then paid a claque to hiss the opera, and it failed. So he sold the opera, costumes and all, to the backers, for £200, and they subsequently restaged it with prodigious success and made £20,000 pounds out of it. Haydn does not name the opera, and gives the theatre as Drury Lane. But there is no Drury Lane opera by Arnold to which the story can apply, and it would be understandable for Haydn to forget which playhouse was involved. It seems certain that the opera was *The Castle of Andalusia*, which had been staged the previous season as *The Banditti* (CG 28.11.81), when it had failed utterly. O'Keeffe mentions in his Recollections that he had to rewrite the libretto several times before Harris was satisfied. It is quite likely that Arnold had been siding with the recently-disgraced Dibdin, and that Harris, apart from thinking the libretto could be bettered, wanted to be rid of both composers. In such circumstances he would not have approached Arnold again however successful *The Castle of Andalusia* proved. (But O'Keeffe makes no mention of such scheming in his *Reminiscences*.)

To a modern reader O'Keeffe's libretto reads like stage fustian at its worst, but historically it was ahead of its time. The first stage direction runs as follows:

> A Cavern with winding Stairs, and Recesses cut in the Rock; a large Lamp hanging in the Center, a Table, Wine, Fruits, etc., in disorder—At the head Don Caesar . . . and others of the Banditti.

Then follows a tale of complex intrigue laced with impenetrable disguises, a tale that might well have served Donizetti or even Verdi in his younger days. Romantic Opera was in gestation, and audiences were fascinated by its dark novelty. Bandits were superseding beggars as the symbol of freedom and defiance, and had recently been popularized in the paintings and drawings of John Henry Mortimer (1740–79). As late as the 1830s Berlioz was portraying them as heroes rather than villains, for instance in his *Lélio* and *Harold in Italy*.

The overture of *The Castle of Andalusia* is one of Arnold's best. Structural landmarks are pointed with the same clattering dominant-tonic alternation as Mozart used in his 'Paris' Symphony of 1778, and inevitably the key is D major. Arnold's first movement can be compared with Mozart's without his appearing ridiculous. An early song, 'Flow, thou regal purple stream' (Ramirez is holding up a glass of wine), was still popular in Victorian times in spite of the dreadful words. Miss Harper, making her Covent Garden debut, had a full-scale aria with flute obbligato, and the middle section shows Arnold at his rare best. The borrowings are listed in an appendix, but one deserves mention here. The tune of 'In the Forest here hard by' is a version of a folk-song Cecil Sharp 'discovered' and published as 'The Poacher'. Arnold called it 'All among the leaves so green O', and this is his refrain:

Vivace

Dam-me Sir, if you stir, Sluice your veins, Blow your brains, Hey down ho down der-ry der-ry down, All a - mongst the leaves so___ green - O.

I shall have more to say later about Arnold's unusual interest in English folk-song. Lorenza was played by Giovanna Sestini, who had recently sung at the King's Theatre in operas by Bertoni and Giordani; hence the borrowings from these operas. Though she had spent only a year or two in England, she also sang later for Colman at the Little Theatre and for Daly in Dublin, where she played Jessamy, the male fop in *Lionel and Clarissa*. Lord Mount-Edgcumbe thought her 'a handsome, sprightly actress', but he found her voice 'gritty', which may explain why she did not sing more often at the King's Theatre. She had a small son who also performed at the playhouses, and she remained in Britain for the rest of her life.

The British Museum has a book of the song-words in *The Banditti*, a great rarity. It reveals that nine of the fourteen borrowings in *The Castle of Andalusia* were not sung in its predecessor. Perhaps Harris, or some member of his staff, ditched most of the songs Arnold had chosen, and replaced them with music from other sources. But the rewriting of *The Banditti* is full of puzzles. Whoever saw the vocal score of *The Castle of Andalusia* through the press had little to be proud of. It includes two items which are not to be found in the librettos and which were presumably never sung: 'The Prado I resorted' and 'Severe the Pangs'. One might conclude that Arnold sent the music to the engraver without finding out what Covent Garden was doing in his absence. But he wasn't absent. O'Keeffe states that Arnold did work on the revision,[1] and this is supported by the fact that the vocal score of *The Castle of Andalusia* includes two new numbers by Arnold himself: one of these was the Quintetto Finale in Act I. Other music in the score seems to have been ignored in 1782 but sung in the 1790s. I can throw no light on the confusion.

Covent Garden had several big successes in opera at this time, but the word is imprecise and some statistics will clarify it. The list below shows those operas that had more than fifty performances in their first two seasons; all but the first notched a hundred in five or six years:

The Castle of Andalusia (1782)	Full-length	Arnold	50
Rosina (1782)	Afterpiece	Shield	70
The Poor Soldier (1783)	Afterpiece	Shield	63
The Farmer (1787)	Afterpiece	Shield	65

[1] ii, p. 33.

No Drury Lane opera in this decade had equal success until Storace's *The Haunted Tower* reversed the see-saw in 1789. From then on there were comparable operatic successes at Drury Lane, but none at Covent Garden.

Rosina was liked for its music rather than for its insipid libretto. Frances Brooke, who wrote it, was an able, cross-eyed woman of sixty. She had spent the end of the Seven Years War in Quebec because her husband was the Governor's chaplain, and she had written a novel about the experience. Earlier still she had run *The Old Maid*, a weekly paper full of theatrical gossip.[1] She got the plot of *Rosina* from the Book of Ruth and from Favart's *Les Moissonneurs*, which Duni had set in 1768. The action takes place in 'A Village in the North'. Rosina and Phoebe are thought to be sisters living in the cottage of their mother, Dorcas. The brothers Belville are the local bigwigs, and Captain Belville has villainous tendencies. They see Rosina gleaning in the cornfield and both fall in love with her. The Captain tries to gain an advantage by wickedly leaving a purse of money for her. He then throws discretion to the winds and makes his servants abduct her. Meanwhile the good Belville has learnt from Dorcas that Rosina is 'nobly-born' and not her daughter. Irish labourers rescue her and bring her back by river. She steps from the boat and confronts the Captain with his misdeeds. He is stunned into contrition. 'Allow me to retire, brother,' he says, 'and learn at a distance from you to correct those errors into which the fire of youth and bad example have hurried me.' No man could say more in the circumstances. Rosina marries Belville, and Phoebe marries the farm-hand William, whom she has been courting. Belville and Rosina were played by the middle-aged Charles Bannister and his daughter-in-law, Miss Harper; William and Phoebe by Mrs. Kennedy and Mrs. Martyr. The opera was much loved for nearly a century. A Victorian edition of the vocal score by J. L. Hatton and John Oxenford maltreated it without popularizing it, and in 1967 Decca recorded the music and some of the dialogue with Richard Bonynge conducting.

Influenced by the old-fashioned plot, Shield devised a score with ballad opera characteristics. Of the eighteen vocal items, six have identifiable ballad tunes and another six are composed more or less in ballad style. Unusually, there are no large-scale arias; even the Sacchini borrowing is only a short lyrical air. The first few songs are undistinguished, but the music comes to life with Belville's 'Her mouth', which begins:

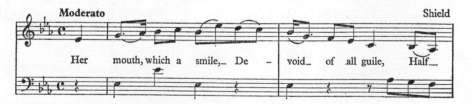

Moderato   Shield

Her   mouth, which a   smile,— De - void— of all guile, Half—

[1] See Gwendolen B. Needham's article in *Theatre Notebook*, Winter 1960-1.

o - pens to view,— is the bud of the rose.

This beautifully-shaped melody is by Shield himself, writing in sublimated folk style. There is a similar song of equal quality at the start of Act II, 'Sweet Transports'; as there is no ascription we cannot tell for certain whether Shield made it up or purloined it. As in *The Castle of Andalusia*, the inclusion of an Irish tune, though not justified by the plot, reflects a growing trend. The longer songs are not much longer. The Captain has a spirited 'Shooting Song' with amusing imitations of the chase, and Rosina's 'Light as Thistledown' is a deliciously orchestrated trifle.

One can comment on the orchestration because the British Museum has an early nineteenth-century set of manuscript parts of the whole opera. They are in a chaotic state, with cuts made and rescinded, and disquieting string parts that are almost innocent of bowings. Even the notes that are slurred in the published vocal score are not slurred in these parts, and it would seem that phrasing, so far as there was any at all, was left to the whim of each individual player. There are a few minor changes. Belville's 'Her Mouth', originally placed so that Bannister could sing it without falsetto, is raised a fourth to make it a tenor song. Phoebe's 'When William at Eve' is lowered a third because the then singer could not manage the high Ds that Mrs. Martyr was eager to display. Trumpets and drums occur only in the D major 'Shooting Song'. Clarinets in the first movement of the overture become flutes in the last, one of the flutes being a piccolo.[1] It is not a good overture, Shield having little to say. In the middle of the first movement there is a deplorable octave passage, immediately followed by some pleasant writing for wind instruments alone. The slow movement is a pretty oboe solo. The most striking moment comes in the coda of the Finale. This is unrelated to the rest of the movement, and it starts with the second oboe, bassoons, and horns holding octave Cs like a bagpipe drone; Shield had first used this effect in a Scotch Song in *The Siege of Gibraltar*. Above the drone the first oboe plays a variant of the tune we know as 'Auld lang syne'.

The origins of this tune have often been investigated, sometimes with due mention of the *Rosina* overture, but full justice has never been done to Shield's influence on its popularity and final form. The title comes from a poem by Allan Ramsay, 'Should auld acquaintance be forgot'; it appeared in *Orpheus Caledonius* with a tune no one today would be likely to recognize. But the tune was then popular, and in 1788 the publisher Johnson put a version of it in *The Scots Musical Museum*, Vol. 1. It was for this collection that Burns wrote many of his best-known song-words. But when Burns sent Johnson his first very free

[1] 'Octave flute' in the parts, 'small flute' in the much earlier vocal score.

revision of Ramsay's words, Johnson did not print it because he had already printed the only tune that was then associated with the title. Burns never associated his words with the tune popular today. However he knew it, for early in 1796 he wrote 'Comin' through the Rye' to fit a variant of it that he had found,[1] a variant he described as 'The Miller's Wedding'.

'The Miller's Wedding' was first published about 1765 as a strathspey in Bremner's *Scots Reels*, and Scottish writers have always clung to this as the origin of their most jealously-loved tune. In fact the Bremner collection contains a number of English tunes in spite of its title, for instance 'Elsie Marlie', and it was certainly not Shield's source. The only possible reason for his introducing a similar, but much better version of this tune at the end of his *Rosina* overture was that he wanted to prepare his audience for the setting, 'a Village in the North'. Nothing in the libretto suggests Scotland. Shield, I believe, was adapting a Northumbrian pipe tune he remembered from his youth. Its inclusion in *Rosina* made it popular all over Britain, and but for Shield we would probably not know it today. We would certainly not know the second half, which in its present-day form derives almost entirely from Shield. Burns himself must have known *Rosina*, and in 1792 he wrote for Johnson's *Museum* 'I fee'd a man at Martinmass' to fit the version of the tune with the improved second half. After his death in 1796, George Thomson wedded Burns's final revision of the 'Auld lang syne' words to this same tune, and he himself made slight alterations in the first half. Only then was the song printed as we know it today.

Long before the tune was worked on in Scotland, Shield came out with another version of it in his overture to *The Nunnery* (1785). It forms the main theme of the Finale, as also of the sung Finale to the whole opera. There is no drone bass and no Scottish or North Country associations. *The Nunnery* was not a success, and the score cannot have affected the popularity of the tune, but it may be of interest to give both of Shield's versions, together with the original strathspey as printed by Bremner about 1765. I have transposed the latter up a seventh.

[1] Much the same variant occurs in Sanderson's pantomime, *Harlequin Mariner* (RC 28.5.96), but Sanderson can hardly have got it from Burns. Burns died in the middle of 1796.

The Poor Soldier (CG 4.11.83) was a calculated success.[1] If *Rosina*, with its ballad opera leanings, was liked, then something even more like a ballad opera would be liked even more, especially if it cashed in on the vogue for Irish songs. With Johnstone and Mrs. Kennedy in the company, Covent Garden could do full justice to an Irish opera. Of the seventeen vocal items, six may be by Shield, but the number is probably less. Most of the tunes were Irish, and audiences found them irresistible.

The libretto is undistinguished, but occasionally it gives a foretaste of Synge, as when Kathleen, serenaded by both Dermot (Johnstone) and the ridiculous Darby (Edwin), remarks 'It's a fine thing, that people can't take their rest of a morning, but you must come roaring under their windows'. The village has another courting couple as well. Fitzroy (Charles Bannister) is pursuing Norah (Mrs. Jack Bannister), though Norah regrets that a year or so earlier she spurned Patrick—who enlisted for America in his disappointment. However Patrick turns up, and when Fitzroy discovers he is the man who saved his life in the American Wars, he magnanimously relinquishes his claim on Norah. Dermot marries Kathleen (Mrs. Martyr). So bare a summary does not do the story justice, but even in full it is not much more interesting. Patrick was played

---

[1] An earlier version, *The Shamrock, or The Anniversary of St. Patrick* (CG 7.4.83), had failed. O'Keeffe (ii, p. 49) said it was 'made up of Irish characters and customs, pipers, and fairies, foot-ball players, and gay hurlers'. The revision was made to preserve the songs.

as a breeches part by Mrs. Kennedy, and later by Mrs. Jordan who did much to keep the opera in public favour.

O'Keeffe claimed in his *Recollections* that he provided the tunes in *The Poor Soldier* by singing 'the airs of Carolan' to Shield,[1] and though I have identified only one item by Carolan we can hardly blame O'Keeffe for mistaking the origin of the tunes he had learnt in childhood. Carolan (1670–1738) was much the most famous Irish harper within living memory. He drew for his tunes not only on Irish tradition but also on the instrumental music of Corelli, but we have little idea of how he played them, for his compositions survive only in melody-line versions for violin or flute, together with a bass-line provided by the publisher. Harpists passed their compositions on by ear without writing them down, and in any case Carolan was blind. A few of his tunes were published in Dublin in the 1720s, but they were so incompetently engraved that the publication is of little practical value. The first important collection of Irish tunes was the one Burk Thumoth edited about 1745; it contained twenty-four Irish tunes and twenty-four Scots ones. Thumoth, who played the flute, the trumpet, and the harpsichord, had been employed at Goodman's Fields in 1729 when he was only twelve years old. He must have relied for his melodies either on very youthful memories or on what he gathered when he (presumably) returned to his native Ireland in the 1730s. Only two of his Irish tunes are widely familiar today, 'Eileen Aroon' and 'The Mallow Fling', and they were widely familiar in the eighteenth century as well. At least two others were by Carolan, and one of these, 'Thomas Birk', is of high quality. About 1780 a Dublin firm, S. Lee, published a new collection of Carolan tunes, and one of them occurs in *The Castle of Andalusia*; O'Keeffe had probably known it for years. The later pieces in the Lee collection look as though they had been harmonized by the office boy after one lesson.

In 1792 it was widely feared that Irish harp traditions were dying. A conference of harpers was organized at Belfast, and a youth named Edward Bunting (1773–1843) was engaged to write down what they played. The occasion made him a folk-music enthusiast for life, and he published admirable collections of 'Ancient Irish Music' in 1796, 1809, and 1840. Only the first of these concerns us here. It contains sixty-six tunes arranged for keyboard, and the titles are given bilingually. Between 1808 and 1836 Thomas Moore published his best-seller, the ten lavish volumes of *Irish Melodies*; there were about 120 songs in all, and a few piano duet arrangements. Moore wrote new lyrics for every tune, either because the original had only Irish words or because it appeared to have no words at all. He found some of the tunes in print, remembered others from his youth, and was sent some by friends and well-wishers. In the first volume most of the tunes are from Bunting; in all he used some two dozen of Bunting's sixty-six. Moore also drew freely on the Irish tunes that O'Keeffe had introduced into his London operas.

[1] O'Keeffe ii, p. 70.

It is surprising that English and Irish folk-song specialists seem so indifferent to the work of eighteenth-century collectors. One might think that an early source would be more valuable than a version transmitted to Cecil Sharp by Uncle Tom Cobley and all; indeed Cecil Sharp's versions must quite often derive from eighteenth-century publications. Bunting is venerated in Dublin, and rightly so, but not Thumoth. Yet three of Bunting's tunes occur in Thumoth in versions that seem to me quite as interesting. O'Keeffe was not perhaps the most reliable of collectors. His version in Act II of *The Poor Soldier* of the tune Thumoth calls 'Balin a mone' is far inferior to Thumoth's, which has strange and fascinating modal implications. But he did provide material for Moore. There are about ten Irish melodies in *The Poor Soldier* (in one or two cases the nationality is in doubt), and five had never before been published. Of these Moore took four. He had good reason to know *The Poor Soldier* because in 1790 at the age of ten he himself played Patrick in an amateur performance. He was even influenced by O'Keeffe's words. Thus Dermot's 'Sleep on, sleep on, my Kathleen dear' becomes 'Weep on, weep on, your hour is past'.[1] The popular tune still known as 'The Rose Tree' is so called because of the words O'Keeffe wrote for it in *The Poor Soldier*.

It is sometimes difficult to tell if a tune is Irish or Scottish. The one for which Burns wrote 'O whistle and I'll come to you' is usually thought to be the latter, but O'Keeffe and Shield were so sure it was Irish that it occurs both as a song in *The Poor Soldier* and as the main theme of the Finale in the overture. The opera also has a tune, probably Irish, that *The National Song Book* puts in its Scottish section as 'The Piper of Dundee'.

Shield showed little skill in the way he arranged these tunes, but at least he felt their character sufficiently to leave alone such modalisms as the flattened seventh; for instance in the beautiful 'Farewell, ye Groves'. The most popular song was Patrick's 'How happy the Soldier', a typical six-eight moto perpetuo. According to Boaden, 'it walked through every street, before you or behind you'. This is one of the tunes Shield may have composed himself.

Vocal scores of *The Poor Soldier* correspond well with each other, but very ill with such librettos as I have seen. Extra songs seem to have been included from very early on. The vocal scores allow Charles Bannister no songs at all, perhaps because he was a late choice for Fitzroy, but the librettos give him two, and they also allow Patrick some additional songs. Some of these were published separately.

The Poor Soldier was so successful that O'Keeffe and Shield devised a sequel, *Love in a Camp, or Patrick in Prussia* (CG 17.2.86). It was similar in style, and though less successful it did much better than most sequels. Patrick and Darby enlist in the Prussian service and are followed by Norah. Patrick was played

[1] This tune occurs in O'Sullivan as 'The fair Hills of Eire O', and he gives an 1888 source for it. But Shield's version is as good, and none the worse for being slightly decorated.

not by a woman but by Johnstone. Perhaps the reasoning was that by this time he must have grown up.

Shield had not found much credit or satisfaction in the success of *The Poor Soldier*, and he now set about trying to establish himself as a serious opera composer. In under two years he achieved four full-length operas:

Robin Hood (CG 17.4.84)
The Noble Peasant (LT 2.8.84)
Fontainbleau (CG 16.11.84)
The Choleric Fathers (CG 10.11.85)

The second and fourth of these were near-failures, but the other two had a gratifying success and remained in the repertoire for most of Shield's lifetime.

Robin Hood received some sixty performances and was then shortened to an afterpiece (1789). The main plot is predictable. The secondary plot was derived from Oliver Goldsmith's ballad *Edwin and Angelina*; the duet that these two characters sing near the end of the opera makes use of the last two verses. Most of the libretto is 'ye olde' in style, and it was written by Leonard Mac-Nally, an Irishman who, years later, turned out to have been spying for the English against his own countrymen. *The Noble Peasant* was the only opera Shield ever wrote for the Colmans. The libretto was by his friend Thomas Holcroft, and it tells an uninteresting tale of romance and intrigue in Saxon times. *Fontainbleau* has an O'Keeffe libretto about the growing craze for crossing the Channel to France—either on holiday or, in the hero's case, because he wrongly thinks he has killed someone in a duel. The score is one of Shield's best, and the opera had a steady if unspectacular success, with some fifty performances spread over twelve years. John Addison wrote additional music for a Drury Lane revival in 1813, and the opera was still popular in Bath in the 1820s. Holcroft's libretto for *The Choleric Fathers* seems to have been influenced by that of *The Duenna*. Two passionate old men in Madrid are prepared to sacrifice the happiness of their children for the sake of their foolish squabble. As in *Così fan tutte* there are references to Mesmer; Pedro, a penniless unemployed servant, pretends to mesmerize Jaquelina, the heroine's maid.

We can conveniently consider the music of these full-length operas together. Of the overtures, that to *The Choleric Fathers* is probably not Shield's, and that to *Robin Hood* is certainly by Baumgarten.[1] The latter has a very long and shapeless first movement and a briefly beautiful slow one. Shield's overture to *Fontainbleau* is a feeble medley of French tunes; they include 'Marlbrook' and 'Je suis Lindor'.

The Noble Peasant is different from its fellows in two respects. Because at the Little Theatre Shield could not count on expert oboe and trumpet players, there are no concertante arias of the type described below. On the other hand there are Italianate Finales of some elaboration. This suggests that the simple

---

[1] He took it from his *William and Nanny* overture (*LS* Part 5, ii, p. 696).

glees which so often ended an act at Covent Garden were not so much Shield's choice as Harris's. The Finale to Act III is omitted because, the vocal score says, it was by Dr. Cooke, and a glance at the libretto reveals that a few other items Shield borrowed were also omitted. Both this score and that of *The Choleric Fathers* are said on their title pages to be 'composed by William Shield', as opposed to his usual 'selected and composed'. One item in *The Noble Peasant* appears to have been accompanied only by piccolo, flute, oboe, and bassoon.

Each of the other three operas includes a long aria in C major with a very difficult oboe obbligato and a very difficult soprano line. There had been somewhat similar songs before, for instance 'Adieu, thou noble Pile' in *The Duenna*, which had originally been written by Sacchini when in London for Fischer to play. But Shield, writing for William Parke, allowed the oboe a much longer introduction, with two contrasted themes and a pause near the end inviting a cadenza. In *Robin Hood* Mrs. Bannister had to stand around waiting for nearly as long as Mozart's soprano in 'Martern aller Arten'. This *Robin Hood* aria is poorly organized in that the tunes of the introduction never recur later. Shield must have realized that this was unsatisfying, for in *Fontainbleau* and *The Choleric Fathers* he made the opening theme the foundation of the whole; also he cut the introductions down to about a minute. In all three of these 'oboe' songs a vocal cadenza is allowed for near the end. The *Robin Hood* and *Fontainbleu* examples take both singer and oboe up to high E; in *The Choleric Fathers* Parke was able to show off his newly-discovered high F. All these arias would be easy to orchestrate from the vocal score, and the task would be worth the trouble for they are unusual and effectively written, especially 'Search all the wide Creation round' in *Fontainbleau*. This has a further point of interest in the horn parts. In the middle of the lyric O'Keeffe wrote

> Why, Phoebus, smile upon the morn,
> Why lend a Ray to Dian's horn?

But C major, the key Parke wanted, is a poor one for horns, so for this middle section Shield modulated into F. Thus the horns are crooked in a key other than that of the song; there appears to be an earlier example of this in Dibdin's *The Ephesian Matron* (p. 29 of the score).

There were arias with a trumpet obbligato for Sarjeant in both *Robin Hood* and *Fontainbleau*. The former was in E flat, an unusual key for an English trumpet at that time. The part was almost certainly played on the newly-invented double trumpet with which Clagget's name is associated.[1] Charles Bannister was the singer, and it was so written that he did not need his falsetto notes. But 'Fame, sound the Trumpet' in *Fontainbleau* took Johnstone up to high D, and a good deal of the vocal line was certainly sung falsetto. Though the vocal score indicates two trumpets, Covent Garden's second trumpeter was

[1] See p. 407.

not very good, for in both arias, whenever anything difficult is called for below the first trumpet, it is given to an oboe.

Trumpet songs are the only ones of the period that retain Handelian influence.

Besides composing full-length arias for these operas, Shield borrowed a few from Italian composers. *Robin Hood* has one from Bertoni's *Demofoonte*, which had been given at the King's Theatre in 1778. Even so, simple strophic songs predominate in nearly all Shield's operas. There are more than a dozen in *Robin Hood*, as against a mere half-dozen of Italianate length. Irish songs are featured even when, as in *Robin Hood*, there was no dramatic justification for them. In *Fontainbleau* Mrs. Kennedy was allowed to play a female role for once—an Irish hotel-keeper called Mrs. Casey—and she sang an Irish tune I have not identified, accompanied only by oboes and bassoons. For less reason Edwin had an Irish song in the same opera. He had originally been cast as a Welsh traveller, Sir Shenkin ap Griffin, but his Welsh accent was so atrocious that the character was changed into a Yorkshire squire. According to Parke, Edwin's 'In London my Life is a Ring of Delight' was 'the *ne plus ultra* of comic singing', and 'The Morning we're married' must have had even more obvious Music Hall undertones. To nonsense syllables Edwin imitated in turn the sounds of a violin, an oboe, fife and drum, harp, cymbals, double basses, marrow bones and cleavers, horn, and trumpet. In each case the imitation was followed by the real sound from the orchestra pit. Again the trumpet must have been in E flat. There were at least two musical quotations: from an oboe concerto by Fischer, and, inexplicably, 'Lison dormait' by Dezède for the cymbals. On a higher musical level are Mrs. Martyr's delightful 'Indeed, I'll do the best I can' (she was the heroine's maid) and Johnstone's charming 'Through circling sweets', which contrasts clarinets and oboes in the accompaniment.

The glees that end the first two acts of *Robin Hood* are of some interest. 'Lord Mornington's Waterfall', as it was usually called ('Here in cool grot'), was still a favourite when George IV was king, and it was a pity that Shield thought fit to fill the prettily effective silences near the end with piccolo bird-song. For the end of Act II he borrowed a glee by John Stafford Smith (1750–1836), and *The Noble Peasant* begins with another by the same composer.[1] The Finales in *Fontainbleau* were un-final to a degree. One was Edwin's song in imitation of orchestral instruments, and another was 'A Negro Duet' borrowed from Corri's *Select Collection*, Vol. III, p. 19, complete with Corri's accompaniment. The tune seems purely European in style. As it has French words in the *Select Collection* it was probably sung by negro characters in some French opera.

The Act II Finale in *The Choleric Fathers* is unusual. Mrs. Bannister and Mrs. Martyr, who play the heroine and her servant, have successive songs; the first is in two-four and accompanied by strings, the second in six-eight and accompanied by flute, two clarinets, bassoon, and two horns; the songs are then sung simultaneously. Another duet is full of many-syllabled words of a Gilbertian cast:

Pimento: Be so kind as to call when you're in the vicinity.
Pedro: This vast honorificabilitudinity
        Commands my esteem . . .

In the period of these full-length operas, Shield composed only one afterpiece, *The Nunnery* (CG 12.4.85), and in this he collaborated for the first time with William Pearce.[2] One of Edwin's ballads in *The Nunnery* shows Shield's ability to achieve real quality within a tiny compass:

Moderato   Shield

My   friend the hon - est   Cu - rate's dead;   His mer - ry jokes the

Neighbours tell;   The___ Men all praise his___ learn - ed Head, And the

Wo-men say   he___ knew things well.

[1] Yet a third glee by Smith was turned into 'The Star-spangled Banner'. Smith later became one of our first musicologists.

[2] Pearce rose later to be Chief Clerk of the Admiralty; Gainsborough painted his portrait.

The accompaniment has echoing phrases on a mournful bassoon.

The operas of Grétry were becoming increasingly popular in Paris, and some of this popularity rubbed off on the London playhouses. The opening Glee in *The Nunnery* was taken from the March in *Les Mariages Samnites*; it was a theme on which Mozart wrote variations for piano (K.352). Though Hook did not use any of Grétry's music in his full-length *The Peruvian* (CG 18.3.86), the plot was taken from *L'Amitié à l'Épreuve*. Marmontel had set his version of the Noble Savage theme in London. Coralie has been brought back from Peru by an English sailor who loves her, and when he leaves on another voyage he puts her in the care of a friend called Lord Nelson (Belville in Hook's version). On his return he realizes that the girl is now in love with the friend; magnanimously he gives up all claim on her. Coraly (Hook's spelling) was the first part created by Mrs. Billington; she had just made her début at Covent Garden in *Love in a Village*.

Another Grétry opera with an English theme was *Richard Coeur de Lion* (1784), and both London playhouses prepared an adaptation at the same time. Sheridan asked General Burgoyne to translate Sedaine's libretto. Less wisely Harris approached MacNally, who according to Parke knew no French. The Covent Garden version (16.10.86) reached the stage first, and the vocal score claimed, inaccurately, to contain 'Almost the Whole of the original French Music'. MacNally had been able to discover very little about Sedaine's libretto, and his version is quite different from and very inferior to Burgoyne's. The Drury Lane *Richard* (24.10.86) was much the more successful. In brief, Richard is imprisoned in a castle. Matilda his mistress and Blondel his minstrel come separately to rescue him, the former disguised as a boy and pretending to be blind. The governor of the castle loves a Welsh girl called Lauretta, and is himself imprisoned when he goes to court her. While he is away, Richard is rescued. At Covent Garden it was Blondel who pretended to be blind, and there was no Matilda; more decorously, Richard's queen, Berengaria, comes in search of him.

The Covent Garden score organized by Shield claimed to have been composed by 'Grétry, Anfossi, Bertoni, Dr. Hayes, Dr. Wilson, Carolan and William Shield', and there were fifteen intrusions for which Grétry was not responsible. The last of these was a monster aria Shield wrote for Mrs. Billington 'Accompanied on the Flute by Mr. W. Parke', and the reason for this is clear. French operas never had coloratura arias, and Mrs. Billington (Berengaria) was a coloratura singer. Shield took her up to high F sharp and allowed her to improvise a cadenza at the end. In shape and scale the aria is just like those in *Fontainbleau* and *The Choleric Fathers* in which Parke had played the oboe, and it is remarkable that he should have been equally expert on the flute. Shield also contributed two shorter songs and a glee, and there were several Scotch and Irish ballads which Harris perhaps insisted on. It is not surprising that a good deal of Grétry was omitted. Mrs. Martyr as Lauretta gave the first performance in Britain of the lovely song Tchaikovsky later borrowed for *Pique Dame*.

The Drury Lane score organized by Linley included virtually all Grétry's music except for the Trio at the beginning of Act I and Richard's song at the beginning of Act II. The latter was omitted because Kemble was singing Richard. But it would have been impossible to omit the most famous song in the opera, Blondel's 'Une fièvre brulante'.[1] Because Blondel sings this song Richard knows he is outside the castle walls, and later Richard joins in, making it a duet. This was the only exposed vocal line Kemble had to sing, and he managed to be out both in tune and in time.[2] Mrs. Crouch was Laurette and Mrs. Jordan Matilda. The latter had a boy to guide her across Europe, and Miss Romanzini was the boy; Lauretta had a younger sister, and in this part Miss De Camp made her operatic début. She was a very young Viennese dancer who later became Mrs. Charles Kemble and the mother of Fanny Kemble.

Richard Coeur de Lion seems to be the first 'Escape Opera'. The genre was increasingly cultivated in Paris during and just after the Revolution, and examples like Cherubini's *Lodoiska* and *Faniska* made possible Beethoven's *Fidelio*. The subject is best left for the time when Drury Lane staged their own version of *Lodoiska* in 1794.

Nina (CG 24.4.87) also derived music and plot from a very recent French opera, this time by Dalayrac. The translation by Peter Pindar, whose real name was John Wolcot, was never published, and the score is a rarity. The afterpiece was presented for Mrs. Martyr's benefit. She had just transferred her fickle affections to William Parke, and it was Parke who adapted Dalayrac's original. He tells us in his *Musical Memoirs*[3] that the plot was based on the story of Maria in Sterne's *The Sentimental Journey*. Two years later Paisiello wrote another *Nina* based on the same story and much the same libretto.

The Farmer (CG 31.10.87) was a prodigious success, and another afterpiece later that season, *Marian* (CG 22.5.88) was also well liked. In both Shield reverted to the country setting that had answered so well in *Rosina*. *The Farmer* contains the only song he wrote that is well known today, 'The Ploughboy'. It has been arranged by Benjamin Britten as part of his series of folk-song arrangements, though it is not a folk-song and the arrangement ignores the pretty solo for 'small flute' that represents the boy's whistling. In its own day the song was immensely popular, and Dussek used it as a Rondo theme in his Piano Concerto in E flat, op. 15. Infuriatingly the vocal score of *The Farmer* does not indicate the composer of each item. Such borrowings as I have identified are given in Appendix D. Mrs. Martyr's 'Send him to me, Let him woo me' is a curiosity. Shield had just heard it sung at the King's Theatre as 'Chi mi mostra' in Paisiello's *Gli Schiavi per amore*, but most of it is also to be found in the Finale of Mozart's Flute Quartet in A, K.298. Köchel thought this quartet dated from the

---

[1] Beethoven later wrote variations on it.
[2] Kelly i, p. 290, 2nd ed.
[3] i, p. 95.

1770s, in which case Paisiello was the borrower, but Saint-Foix has convincingly suggested that Mozart knocked it up in 1786 as a joke for a party given in Vienna at the Storaces' house. Because Hoffmeister and Paisiello were both present, he based the first movement on a Hoffmeister song, the Minuet and Trio perhaps on something by Stephen Storace, and the Finale on a Paisiello aria Nancy Storace had just been singing at the Court Theatre. That Mozart was hardly serious over the Finale is shown by its tempo marking: *Allegretto grazioso, ma non troppo presto, però non troppo adagio, così, così, con molto giusto ed espressione.*

O'Keeffe's libretto had started as a full-length comedy, *The Plague of Riches*; Colman made him cut it down and add songs. It had a moneylending theme, began on a farm in Kent, and ended in London. Mrs. Mattocks came out of a brief retirement to play Betty Blackberry, and Edwin found one of his funniest roles as a stay-maker called Jemmy Jumps. His 'Gad a mercy' was one of London's first patter songs. A cheerful overture by Giordani and attractive vocal music helped *The Farmer* to its long-lasting popularity.

Marian also had attractive music, though this was offset by another insipid libretto by Mrs. Brooke. Marian's mother won't let her marry Edward because she is better off than he is. In the end Edward's family suddenly becomes affluent. Mrs. Billington as Marian had another of Shield's vast 'oboe' arias in C major, and was joined in it by William Parke. She asserted her pre-eminence with a high G, one tone higher than anything the Queen of the Night had to face in Vienna three years later. There is no cadenza for the oboe in the comparatively modest introduction, but there is one for the singer near the end. Elsewhere in *Marian* there are unexpected borrowings, including the duet, 'Joys in gentle trains appearing'[1] from Handel's *Athalia*, an item by Salieri that I have not identified, and a big Paisiello aria for Mrs. Billington. There is a piquant ensemble by Shield himself with a scherzando theme in six-bar phrases over repeated E flats:

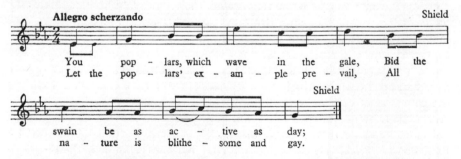

The final Vaudeville was based on the anonymous final Vaudeville in *Le Mariage de Figaro* by Beaumarchais. As already mentioned, the play had only

----

[1] It had previously been borrowed by Henry Carey for *The Honest Yorkshireman.*

two musical items, the other being Cherubino's song to the Countess. It had been given at Covent Garden as *The Follies of a Day* (14.12.84) but without the Vaudeville, because the cast contained so few singers. Cherubino, re-christened Hannibal, sang 'Ah weladay my poor Heart' by Shield, for which Longman the publisher paid him 'three and twenty dozen of wine', more in effect than he had ever had for a song. The part was played by Mrs. Martyr.

3 SHIELD AND PANTOMIME

Every Christmas Shield wrote the music for the new Covent Garden panto-mime; the titles are listed with the author of the song-words and dialogue (if any):

> *The Lord Mayor's Day, or a Flight from Lapland* (25.11.82)—O'Keeffe.
> *Friar Bacon, or Harlequin Rambler* (23.12.83)—O'Keeffe.
> *The Magic Cavern* (27.12.84)—Pilon.
> *Omai, or A Trip round the World* (20.12.85)—O'Keeffe.
> *The Enchanted Castle* (26.12.86)—Miles Peter Andrews.

Thereafter Shield lost interest in pantomimes. *The Dumb Cake* (26.12.87) was composed by Clagget, and although Shield wrote the new songs in *Aladdin* (26.12.88), he left the selecting and the overture to others. No music from these two pantomimes was published. Most of Shield's pantomimes were so popular that they were revived in later seasons. According to Tate Wilkinson, Christmas audiences at this period were so besotted at the thought of the panto-mime that they paid no attention whatever to the preceding play, which they made inaudible with their continuous excited chatter.

    The Lord Mayor's Day, a speaking pantomime, began[1] with a representa-tion of Lapland, the cliffs hung with icicles and glowing with the light of the Aurora Borealis. Harlequin and Whalebone come in on a sledge drawn by an elk. The elk appears to die (to music and in the unusual key of B flat minor), but rises again imbued with the spirit of a magician. There are some recitatives and half a dozen songs, one sung by Gobble, 'Oh what a charming thing's our dinner', parodied 'Oh what a charming thing's a battle' in Dibdin's *The Recruiting Sergeant*. In this, as in other pantomimes by Shield, folk tunes are more often English than Scottish or Irish, and there are some remarkable examples. Here is one known today as a Northumbrian song, 'O the Bonny Fisher Lad'. Shield calls it 'The Rolling Taylor', and though some of the verses are probably by O'Keeffe, the earlier ones could be words Shield remembered from his youth.

---

[1] See 'McCready Prompt Books at Bristol', TN iv, p. 77.

I'm the toast of half the ci - ty, For my shape I
Tom the tai - lor swears I'm pret - ty, Tom him - self looks

bear the belle;   O the lit - tle roll - ing tai - lor,
pret - ty well.

None can roll it so like he!   Blithe and mer - ry may he be.

2. Once a jolly roving Sailor
   Ask'd if I his Wife would be:
   No, says I, the little Taylor
   Is the Lad that's made for me.
   Oh the little rolling Taylor, etc.

Edwin has a song whose refrain is either nonsensical or lewd, and in either case a folk origin seems certain.

There was an old wo - man liv'd un - der a hill,

Green and air - y round,   There was an old wo - man liv'd

un - der a hill And she had good beer__ and ale to sell, With her

clack, her co - ry air - y whack!   Jack and her hair - y round.

There are five more verses.

Two similar folk-songs can be found in *Omai*. One is, so far as I am aware, the earliest sea-shanty to get into print. Again one suspects that Shield picked it up in his Northumbrian youth, and again, though the later verses smack of O'Keeffe, the earlier ones are surely genuine. The tune is bursting with salty vigour.

Another song in this pantomime, 'In der big canoe' (Edwin was representing a Polynesian warrior with scant English), has a tune that Shield probably got from O'Keeffe for he labelled it 'Irish'. It may well be a distant relative of the one Stanford arranged as 'Trottin' to the fair', but Victorians knew it as a Scottish song, 'The Massacre of Macpherson'.

The music in these pantomime scores is often unexpected. *Friar Bacon* contains four marches played while various characters 'march down the stage', and their strange scoring results from the fact that they are ultimately played simultaneously.

1. The Judges. Violins (1st?) and Bassi in ponderous unison.
2. Columbine. Flutes and violas.
3. The Chevaliers. Violins (2nd?), clarinet in D (!), and trumpets.
4. Harlequin. 'Violin' (solo?), horns, and pizzicato cello (solo?).

All these marches are in common time except the last, which dances in six-four with typical snap rhythms. *Friar Bacon* also had an overture thick with woodwind cues, and a splendid opening chorus of students questioning the two friars about the brazen head they have made. Friar Bacon is surly (Reinhold), and Friar Bungay cheerful (Bannister). The latter sings a song while a thunderstorm is raging, and this reveals that the automaton they have created becomes Harlequin. There is the usual chasing when, like Frankenstein, he gets out of hand. A peacock, presumably moved by clockwork, and 'a real balloon was for a few

nights introduced; but, being offensive to the audience, was soon laid aside.'
Montgolfier was being much talked of at the time, and in the following summer
Michael Arne wrote a song called 'The Balloon' for Vauxhall Gardens. A
Comic Tune of undeclared purpose was based on part of the Finale in Haydn's
String Quartet, op. 33, no. 4. This had been composed only two years before,
and it was probably the first music by Haydn that playhouse audiences had
heard.

I have not found a word-book or Description for *The Magic Cavern*. The
score contains a calm Comic Tune headed 'Horns and Clarinetts under the
Stage', and a chorus with triple echo effects 'accompanied by a small organ in
shape of a pianoforte, tho' not two-thirds of its size, manufactured by Longman
& Broderip', who, by no coincidence, were the publishers of the score.

Two folk-tunes in *Omai* have already been mentioned. Omai (he was also
called Omiah) was a native of Tahiti (or Otaheite) who had been brought to
England in 1774 on the sloop *Adventure*. He stayed two years, and was then
taken home by Captain Cook. He was handsome and popular, though almost
wholly inarticulate, and there are a number of references to him in the letters
and memoirs of Horace Walpole, Fanny Burney, and others.[1] The longest
account known to me is in the *Random Records* of George Colman the younger.
Though only about twelve years old at the time, Colman claimed to have taught
Omai such English as he knew, and to have learnt from him a smattering of the
Tahiti tongue. They used to go bathing together off the Yorkshire coast, Omai
swimming with the boy on his back. According to William Gardiner, Omai was
taken to an oratorio performance at Leicester, and 'stood up all the time in wild
amazement at what was going on'. George III financed most of his stay in
England, and when they first met Omai is said to have greeted him with the
words 'Howdy, King Tosh'. Sir Joshua Reynolds painted Omai's portrait, and
it is now at Castle Howard in Yorkshire.

As early as 1775 Garrick 'had some thoughts' of putting Omai on the stage
as an 'arlequin sauvage'.[2] The pantomime that O'Keeffe devised for Covent
Garden did not reach the stage until ten years after Omai had returned to Tahiti.
Genest quotes from a Description, but I have not found a copy. Harlequin-
Omai, the king's son, has a rival in Oediddee (Mrs. Kennedy with her face
blackened). Brought to England, he is chased round London and Margate. The
pantomime ended with Omai's coronation in Tahiti and an Ode to Captain
Cook, who had recently died in the Sandwich Islands. Wewitzer as a Tahitian
warrior astonished the audience with a flow of 'Tahitian' that in fact was
gibberish; a sham English translation was provided in the word-book.

Some of Shield's music was very original. In the following song, Tahitian
percussion instruments, real or imitation, were used, and the tune has a strange
exotic flavour.

[1] See my article, 'A Covent Garden Pantomime', *MT*, Aug. 1963.
[2] Letter 936 (29.8.75), written to the elder Colman.

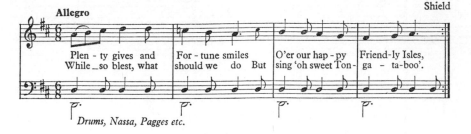

Shield

Allegro

Plen - ty gives and
While so blest, what

For - tune smiles
should we do But

O'er our hap - py
sing 'oh sweet Ton-

Friend-ly Isles,
ga - ta-boo'.

Drums, Nassa, Pagges etc.

The Enchanted Castle was equally original in its setting. According to Andrews' Preface in the Song-Words, it took

> its Rise from the Writings of Miss Aikin and the Hon. Horace Walpole. *The Castle of Otranto* and *The Fragment of Sir Bertrand* form the Bass of an Endeavour to bring upon the Stage somewhat of the Effects which may be produced by Midnight Horror, and Agency Supernatural . . . the Clank of Chains, the Whistling of hollow Winds, the Clapping of Door, Gigantic Form, and visionary Gleam of Light . . . mix'd up with lighter Things to counteract the Gloom.

The vogue for the Gothic Horror novels of 'Monk' Lewis and Mrs. Radcliffe was yet to come, and it owed more to Pantomimes such as *The Enchanted Castle* than has been realized. The central theme is about a Necromancer who keeps a beautiful Indian girl in a trance; periodically he wakes her with proposals of love which she spurns. A scene in America allowed Mr. Gaudry to sing 'Yankee Doodle', which had recently been popularized in Arnold's *Two to One* (1784). In the middle there is some very un-Gothic chasing in the streets of London. A Comic Tune called 'Billingsgate' is marked 'to be played in a slang style', and 'For the Jew' quotes Isaac Mendoza's song from *The Duenna*, 'Give Isaac the Nymph'. Some of the other Comic Tunes would also have been familiar to the original audience, notably some Scotch Songs. A great many animals took part.

The remaining years of the century produced no pantomimes as interesting as those Shield composed in the early eighties, and they will receive only an occasional brief comment.

4 ARNOLD AT THE LITTLE THEATRE

At this period Arnold's operas are often most notable for their English folk tunes and for tunes he composed himself with an English flavour. But he also pandered to contemporary liking for songs from other parts of Britain. After an unimportant compliment to the Prince of Wales on his coming-of-age, *The Birthday, or the Prince of Arragon*, (LT 12.8.83), he contrived what was virtually a ballad opera in *Gretna Green* (LT 28.8.83). Most of the songs had Scotch tunes; even the overture was based on them. O'Keeffe, who wrote the lyrics but not the dialogue, managed to work in an Irish tune, and somewhere or other Arnold found the lovely melody that we now associate with 'O My love's like a red, red Rose'. At the start there is a curious 'Begging Prologue' cleverly built out of tiny snatches of tunes from *The Beggar's Opera*.

It is ironic that in the following season the elder Colman was still making money from this afterpiece when, unknown to him, his son was in Gretna Green getting married. The elder Colman had had a good deal of trouble with George junior. A year at Oxford left the boy with such mountainous debts that he was packed off to the most distant university in the country, Aberdeen; the theatre treasurer went with him to make sure he got there. Partly in Aberdeen and partly in Montrose the younger Colman wrote the libretto of a full-length opera and sent it to his father in time for production in 1783. For reasons the son claimed never to have understood, the father did nothing about it. However the following summer *Two to One* (LT 19.6.84) was produced with Arnold's music and a gracious Prologue by the elder Colman. The latter was determined to think London a bad influence on his boy, and when he started chasing a certain Miss Morris, the father sent him off to France. It was at this point that the younger Colman took control of events and married Miss Morris on the quiet. The event was not disclosed for four years.

Two to One is one of Arnold's most interesting scores. About half of it consists of his own compositions, and they are above his usual level. The other half consists of folk tunes, most of them English, and they are all identified with a title. What Arnold calls 'Peggy of Derby O' is known today as a sea-song, 'Shannon and Chesapeake'[1] and it is mentioned in *Tom Brown's Schooldays* as popular at Rugby. 'Adzooks, so crusty' is sung to a version of 'Yankee Doodle', and this is the first time the tune was printed in recognizable form. Frank Kidson, writing in *The Musical Quarterly* in 1917, quoted a debased version he found in Volume I of Aird's *Selection of Scotch, English, Irish and Foreign Airs, for the Fife, Violin, or German Flute* and he dates this 1775. Strange to say, this volume is not mentioned in *The British Union-Catalogue of Early Music*, though there are entries for volumes ii and iii which are dated '*c.* 1795'. It is most unlikely that Volume I was as much as twenty years earlier. Arnold calls the tune 'Yankee Doodle' and must have known other words for it. Its subsequent popularity must be due in large measure to its appearance in this opera. Other interesting English folk-tunes are described as 'Herring and Salt', 'Little Bingo', and 'As Roger came tapping at Dolly's Window'.

Another full-length opera produced that same summer was Shield's *The Noble Peasant*,[2] and there were two new afterpieces for which Arnold provided the music. *Hunt the Slipper* (LT 21.8.84) had a silly plot and only four songs; it failed. But *Peeping Tom of Coventry* (LT 6.9.84) was a lasting success, presumably because people found its undertones intriguing. O'Keeffe's libretto reads

[1] See *Ships, Sea Songs and Shanties*, by W. B. Whall, p. 59.
[2] See p. 462.

poorly today, and it is significant that Lady Godiva should be often talked about but never seen. The moral climate was changing fast. The second movement of the overture broke new ground with a medley of 'tunes used in the opera'. There are cues for every wind instrument then in use, and several players must have doubled to make this variety possible. There are no attributions for the various songs, but the most striking is so modal that it must be of folk origin. The Mayor of Coventry is making advances to Peeping Tom's wife:

Michael Kelly[1] says this is a Scotch tune and that when the composer Meyer chanced to hear it in Italy, he liked it so much that he made it into a chorus for his opera *La Virgine del Sole*. Thompson got Haydn to arrange it as 'Could I find a bonny Glen', these new words being by Mrs. Grant; he called the tune 'The Wish'. Burns and Hector MacNeill also thought it Scotch, and wrote new words for a very inferior version of it.[2] Arnold's version could easily be English rather than Scottish.

In four consecutive seasons Arnold composed a full-length opera, and in 1785 it was *Turk and No Turk* (LT 9.7.85). The younger Colman's libretto was never printed; later, when manager of the Little Theatre, he found the MS in the 'Prompter's closet', blushed, and tore it up. But Arnold at least had taken trouble, and the overture is the best he wrote. An unusual feature is that the second subject of the Finale is the same as the first subject of the opening movement. Most of the songs were new-composed, and some of these allowed Miss George, a singer with an unusually high voice, to show off her coloratura

[1] ii, p. 193, 2nd ed.
[2] 'Ye Jacobites by Name' (Burns) and 'My Love's in Germany' (MacNeill). See *Pills* vi, p. 251, for a possible origin.

up to top D. But the borrowed songs were even more fascinating. Emily sings Maurice Greene's imitation Scotch Song, 'Sweet Annie frae the Sea'. There is an interesting folk tune with flattened sevenths identified as 'The Tailor done over', and there is an early version of 'The British Grenadiers' which begins 'Some talk of Cherokees, Sir, and some of Catabaw'. O'Keeffe must have known the words we know today, which date from the latter half of the seventeenth century. The antiquity of the familiar tune is less certain. Attempts have been made to derive it from 'Nancie', No. 12 in *The Fitzwilliam Virginal Book*, but such likeness as there is must be due to chance rather than influence. The version we know today is the one Chappell printed; he may have had an undisclosed source which he tidied up. Arnold's version is the earliest I have found, and preferable to Chappell's.

Turk and No Turk also has a song that is very like 'Hunting the Hare'. Until the late nineties, Welsh tunes are very rare indeed in playhouse music. Edinburgh and Dublin had lively theatres, and between them and London there was a constant interchange of actors and musicians. There was no comparable theatre in Wales. The country was remote and seldom visited, and there was no easy way for Welsh songs to reach the capital. In 1784 Edward Jones, minor composer and official 'Bard to the Prince of Wales', published a small collection of his country's music called *Musical and Poetical Relicks of the Welsh Bards*. A second edition ten years later included far more music as well as a book-length 'Historical Account', and this was soon followed by a second volume. Jones is the source of such tunes as 'All through the Night' and 'Men of Harlech'. Some that he printed, for instance 'The Ash Grove', were probably his own composition, for he was not always a very scrupulous scholar. It was perhaps from Jones's collection that Arnold got 'Hunting the Hare', but no spate of Welsh tunes followed the publication. Wales was not chic as Ireland was.

Arnold's next full-length opera was *The Siege of Curzola* (LT 12.8.86).[1] Again it was not very successful, and O'Keeffe's libretto was never published. O'Keeffe himself says that the plot was based on events of 1588 when the Turks were fighting the Venetians. According to Genest, the Turks besieged the island which was defended by the women inhabitants because all the men were in hiding. Baba, the heroine, was sung by Signora Sestini, whose part included a Cherubini aria; Cherubini had spent the last two seasons at the King's Theatre without attracting any notice. Arnold's own music for *The Siege of Curzola* is above his usual level, and more interesting than the music he borrowed. There is an excellent Trio at the end of Act I.

Inkle and Yarico (LT 4.8.87) was no better musically than *The Siege of Curzola*, but it was incomparably more successful. Loewenberg noted performances in Jamaica a year later, in Calcutta in 1791, in New York from 1789 to 1844, and it was popular in Britain for fifty years. It was the younger

---

[1] *Grove*'s spelling is wrong. The island is now called Korcula, and it is in Dalmatia just south of Split.

Colman's libretto that was the attraction. In Ligon's *True Exact History of the Island of Barbadoes* (1673) there is a story, presumably true and exact, of a beautiful naked Indian girl called Yarico who is got with child and has her baby by the side of a pond. Three hours later, carrying the baby in her arms, she meets a young English merchant running away from some Indian warriors. She hides him in a cave, feeds him, and falls in love with him. When it is safe, he takes her back to his ship and, instead of rewarding her, sells her into slavery Steele repeated this shocking story in *The Spectator* (No. 11; 13.3.11), invented the name of Thomas Inkle for the young trader, and made him the baby's father. He only discovers she is with child when he is about to sell her. 'He made use of that Information, to rise in his Demands upon the Purchaser.' Steele rather oddly thought the story 'a Counterpart to the *Ephesian Matron*' of Petronius, and was moved to tears by the gross ingratitude shown in both stories. We have found several plays and operas that pointed the moral superiority of the savage over the educated European, most notably *Polly*, but *Inkle and Yarico* was much the most successful, partly because it was better written, and partly because slavery had suddenly become a national problem. It was well known that during the previous winter two go-ahead young politicians, William Pitt and William Wilberforce, had been having frequent discussions as to how the Slave Trade might be abolished, and those who found it financially rewarding began to prepare their defence. Wilberforce was to have introduced the necessary Bill, but in the spring of 1787 he became seriously ill, and as a stop-gap device Pitt successfully carried a resolution on 9 May that the House should commit itself to a full discussion of slavery early in the next session. The ethics of slavery thus began to be widely debated, and as a result Colman wrote *Inkle and Yarico*. It was one of our first problem plays.

Inkle states, rather badly, the case for a colour bar ('Hear me, Yarico. My countrymen and yours differ as much in minds as in complexions'), and the Governor of the Barbadoes fumbles towards the case for equality ('The only excuse for buying our fellow creatures is to rescue 'em from those who are unfeeling enough to bring them to market'). More to the purpose, Trudge demonstrates that integration can work.

Colman gave both his main characters a servant, the cockney Trudge for Inkle and the negress Wowski for Yarico. Conventions of the time forced him to leave out the baby, which should have been one of the main elements in the plot. He made Inkle betrothed to Narcissa, the Governor's daughter. When Inkle reaches the Barbadoes in Act II, he tries to sell Yarico to a stranger who in fact is the Governor; Inkle is unaware that he is debasing himself in the eyes of his future father-in-law, and this is an effective piece of invention. Jack Bannister, who created Inkle, disliked the part so much that he asked Colman to make Inkle reform at the end. It might seem that this would ruin the plot, but in fact it hardly affects it. Inkle agrees to marry Yarico only because he has discovered that Narcissa wants to marry someone else (Campley) and because he has been so slated by the Governor that he fears for his future prospects. We do not think the better of him for his 'reform'. The change in the last scene resulted in a very long slab of dialogue without music, for Colman rightly felt that he must make Inkle consider marriage with Yarico near the start, then decide to sell her, and then finally agree to marriage when pressed. If he had not first worried at the problem, his 'reform' at the end would have seemed too improbable. Trudge, on the other hand, never questions that it will be as much a pleasure as a duty to marry Wowski, his 'dingy Wows' as he affectionately calls her. These 'lower class' parts are written with great charm; indeed Trudge has both the most sympathetic and the longest part in the opera.

Edwin and Miss George played Trudge and Wowski, and when, a few months later, Edwin suddenly died, Jack Bannister jumped at the chance of taking over Trudge. At Covent Garden Johnstone and Mrs. Billington played the title roles, and Mrs. Martyr was Wowski. It was unprecedented for a winter playhouse to take over a piece written for the Little Theatre, and Covent Garden could only stage it 'by permission of Mr. Colman'; almost certainly they had to pay him for the privilege. Arnold composed two new songs for Johnstone, and they were published in full score. 'What Citadel so proud' is a curiosity in that it is written for clarinets that transpose down a semitone and must therefore be in B major.[1] Mrs. Billington, finding herself without any display pieces, incongruously added 'Sweet Bird' from Handel's *L'Allegro* and for good measure 'Ah, will no change of clime' by Paisiello, which as 'Nel cor più' had just been heard in *La Molinara*. In ten years Covent Garden gave some fifty performances, and to these must be added nearly a hundred at the Little Theatre and even four or five, on benefit nights, at Drury Lane.

The songs as given in the vocal score are unambitious and tuneful. A number of phrases end with a cadential formula which, because it occurs in our most famous hornpipe, suggests sailors, though it may not have done so to Arnold:

That little tag occurs in the opening song sung on the American mainland by the Mate of the *Achilles* (the ship that inadvertently leaves Inkle behind), and in 'Wowski's 'Remember when we walked alone'; and more prominently in both the first and the last movements of the overture. The main tune of the overture's slow movement is played by 'Octave Flute and Bassoon Unis.', which means that they played two octaves apart. One wonders if Arnold thought of this Mozartean device for himself or found it in music by some other composer. The Finale, much the best movement, has an irresistible main tune which recurs at the end of the opera in the Vaudeville-Finale; it is the original of our children's song, 'Have you seen the muffin man?':

---

[1] The song is in A major; the clarinet parts are written in B flat.

The Finale of the overture has a difficult bassoon solo in one of the episodes.

Perhaps the most beautiful of the songs is one that Inkle and Yarico sing together outside her cave in the first act, 'O say, simple maid'. It is a folk-song whose phrases end pleasingly in the wrong key, and Arnold found it in a recently-published duet, 'O say, bonny Lass', which had been sung at Covent Garden. One of the singers there was Elizabeth Satchell, who then became Mrs. Stephen Kemble and created Yarico at the Little Theatre; thus it may be due to her rather than to Arnold that this lovely tune gained wider currency:

The tune has been described as a Scotch reel, though it does not look Scotch and cannot be a reel. If its anonymous arranger at Covent Garden was Shield, then it may well have been Northumbrian. *Inkle and Yarico* made it famous, and in the following decade Haydn arranged it with appreciative care for George Thomson. Narcissa's 'Fresh and strong the Breeze is blowing' has an accompaniment intended to suggest waves, and Wowski's 'Remember when we walk'd alone' one that suggests a lion roaring. The libretto gives two songs in Act II that are not in the score; one of them had an 'American Tune'.

That summer Arnold issued proposals for his great Handel edition, and it is hardly surprising that in the following year he composed nothing. About this time the Little Theatre was imperceptibly changing its manager. Back in 1786 the elder Colman and Arnold had been in Margate mainly for a holiday, and just before they were to set out together for Canterbury Colman ran upstairs for something he'd forgotten and had a stroke. For a year or two he was able to keep much of the theatre management in his own hands, but by 1789 he was incapable of decisions and was judged, perhaps unfairly, to be out of his wits. It had always been assumed that the younger Colman would take over the theatre, and he had done so long before the fact was officially announced. He remained the manager for the rest of the century.

An afterpiece opera produced just before *Inkle and Yarico* has not yet been mentioned. *Harvest Home* (LT 16.5.87) by Dibdin was allowed only seven performances, and deserved no more. We shall now explore, briefly, his activities in the middle eighties at one of London's fringe theatres.

5 THE ROYAL CIRCUS AND ROYALTY THEATRES

In the winter of 1781–2 Dibdin was in debt and out of work, and he must have wondered if the time had come for another trip abroad. However he never lacked initiative, and he teamed up with Charles Hughes, owner of a riding-school, and together they talked a group of business men into putting up £15,000 for a new theatre in St. George's Fields. The plan was to offer entertainments that consisted in part of horse-shows organized by Hughes and in part of short operas, pantomimes, and ballets organized by Dibdin. No one seemed certain whether or not the Lord Chamberlain had jurisdiction south of the Thames. They applied to him for a licence but he refused to grant it, and an application to the Surrey magistrates was equally unsuccessful. They then decided to risk going ahead without a licence, in the hope that opposition would fall away when people saw how respectable the entertainments were. The Royal Circus Theatre was built at the usual break-neck speed and opened in October 1782; almost immediately it had to close, but in the following March it opened again. The Surrey magistrates granted a licence in October 1783, and when the theatre closed three months later it was because of the chaotic state of its finances.

Dibdin's energy was prodigious. Besides composing a large and varied repertoire he engaged the performers, directed the performances, and mismanaged the business side of the theatre. Most of those who appeared on the stage seem to have been children. There were twenty child ballet dancers, and Dibdin engaged Grimaldi, father of the famous clown, to train them; they were apprenticed to him for five years. An opera called *The Graces* was certainly sung by an all-child cast, most of them Dibdin pupils. In his *Professional Life* Dibdin says there were as many as sixty children on the books.

By the summer of 1783 Dibdin had reduced his debts to £400. Yet in the closing months of that year his troubles multiplied. Debt collectors were for ever on his doorstep, and the children's parents kept coming to complain of the way Grimaldi was exploiting them; the local magistrates had to intervene. Dibdin tried to relieve the worst of his worries by borrowing from the proprietors, choosing to go to them at the precise moment when they were most jittery about losing all they had invested. He was furious when they refused his request, and even more furious when he was put in the King's Bench and they sacked him.

In prison in February 1784, Dibdin wrote a short and extraordinary little book from which most of this information is drawn. It is called *The Royal Circus Epitomized*, and it does not appear to have been noticed before. Though burning with indignation, Dibdin is completely frank about his own failings, and the result is that the book has the opposite effect to the one he intended; the reader finishes it sympathizing rather more with the proprietors than with the author. It begins with one of the bitterest pieces of invective ever penned by a composer, and astonishingly it takes the form of a six-page parody of the Athanasian Creed. The five proprietors are identified by their professions or interests rather than by their names. Here is a short extract:

> Whosoever would belong to the Royal Circus, before all things it is necessary that he hold the proprietors infallible . . .
> The merchant stupid, the surgeon stupid, the sportsman stupid, the courtier stupid, the attorney stupid.
> The merchant absurd, the surgeon absurd, the sportsman absurd, the courtier absurd, the attorney absurd.
> The merchant incomprehensible, the surgeon incomprehensible, the sportsman incomprehensible, the courtier incomprehensible, the attorney incomprehensible.
> And yet not only one is stupid, they are all stupid.
> Neither is only one absurd, or one incomprehensible; they are all absurd, and all incomprehensible.

Then follows an angry account of how the theatre had been financed, built, and opened, with vitriol thrown at Grimaldi as well as at the proprietors. For some reason Hughes is treated almost amicably, though in the *Professional Life* he is 'a noxious reptile'. The publishers inserted a footnote to tell their readers that since writing the book Dibdin had been taken off to the Fleet. In his later autobiographical writings he makes no mention of going to prison, and I have not discovered when or how he got out. It is possible that in 1785 he had another spell back at the Royal Circus, and if so William Davis, the leading proprietor, must have been very forgiving.

I have not felt equal to a thorough investigation of the music and librettos Dibdin wrote for this theatre. They survive in scattered and confused state, and most of what I have seen is of very poor quality. Another deterrent is the impossibility of finding or making a complete list of what was given, for items were not normally advertised in the press. All the dates below are from Allardyce Nicoll, but some may well be of performances later than the first. Dibdin estimated the number of his Royal Circus compositions variously as 'nearly sixty pieces of which I am author and composer' and 'twenty-eight performances twenty-one of which were entirely new' (both in *The Royal Circus Epitomized*), and (in *The Musical Tour*, p. 307) as fifteen named operas or pantomimes, 'two or three other pantomimes, four or five *intermezzi* of a more trifling kind, and at least fifteen ballads (a misprint for ballets?) with a variety of other matter'.

Only *The Cestus* (1783) was published in vocal score, and then without the linking recitatives. There was of course no spoken dialogue in any of the Royal Circus operas, but the fringe theatres were beginning to bend the law in this respect. As the younger Colman put it, they

> made their Recitative appear like Prose, by the actor running one line into another, and slurring over the rhyme;—soon after, a harpsichord was touch'd *now and then*, as an accompaniment to the actor; sometimes once in a minute;—then once in five minutes; at last—not at all; till, in the process of time, musical and rhyming dialogue had been abandoned.[1]

One cannot but regret that no judge or jury has ever had to pronounce on what is and what is not recitative.

In *The Cestus* Jupiter was played by 'Master Sestini', whose mother had sung in *The Castle of Andalusia*, and Juno was taken by Dibdin's pupil, Miss Romanzini, who was about thirteen. He gave her both coloratura and high Cs, though when she sang at Drury Lane as Mrs. Bland she was never given either. Baker found a libretto of *The Cestus*, but I have not. If it was no better than the music, its loss can be endured.

In Southampton Public Library there is a large quantity of manuscript music that appears to belong to a Royal Circus pantomime called *Pandora* and to other unnamed pieces by Dibdin for this theatre. Such other Royal Circus information as I have come upon follows in note form.

Librettos I have seen

> *The Graces*. Lib. pub. 1782, and presumably performed that October. Written in France, perhaps on a French model, but turned down by Harris. It is about three nymphs who tie Cupid up when he makes advances.
> *The Long Odds* (RC 13.11.83), a burletta. Lib. in BM Add. 30964; other librettos in this and 30963 may also have been written for the Royal Circus. Baker says lib. was published. The music of seven or more songs is in BM Add. 30951–3.
> *The Benevolent Tar*. Lib. pub. 1785; if first performance was that year, then Dibdin must have returned to the theatre after his imprisonment. A simple tale, but it could not have been done by children. Some agreeable sea-songs given in Hogarth. Some of the songs survive in manuscript in BM Add. 30951, 30952, and 30955.

Librettos apparently published but not in BM or Bodleian

> *The Saloon*. 'not printed' (Baker) but it may have been, for Hogarth gives

---

[1] Colman i, pp. 52–3.

three lyrics. Like *The Graces*, written in France and turned down by
Harris.

The Talisman of Orosmanes (RC 28.3.83); pantomime, originally called *The
Magic of Orosmanes*. Lib. pub. (Nicoll), but it is not mentioned by Baker.
Recit and aria in BM Add. 30951; one lyric in Hogarth.

The Lancashire Witches (RC 27.12.83), pantomime; song-words pub.
(Baker); one lyric in Hogarth, and a Comic Tune for woodwind in BM
Add. 30952.

Clump and Cudden; pub. 1785 as 'Com. Mus. Piece' (Baker). Hogarth may
have seen lib., for he gives four lyrics. One song in *Lyric Remembrancer*
(see p. 431); also manuscript songs in BM Add. 30954/5.

Life, Death and Renovation of Tom Thumb (RC 28.3.85); lib. pub. (Nicoll);
Hogarth gives seven lyrics; some of the music is in BM Add. 30952.

All the MSS mentioned above appear to be in Dibdin's hand. Much of their
contents is difficult or impossible to identify.[1]

As already mentioned, in 1787 John Palmer built the Royalty Theatre near
the Tower of London, thinking that he could present spoken plays there; being
no singer, he did not want to present anything else. When he found that the law
was against him, he tried to recoup some of his losses with a desperate season of
musical pieces and recitations. The music was in the hands of Thomas Carter
and William Reeve, and Carter composed two all-sung operas for the Theatre.
The Birthday, or The Arcadian Contest was a short pastoral, of which both the
anonymous libretto and the vocal score were published. A passage in the overture is worth quoting:

Carter

[1] In *The Musical Tour* Dibdin gives the following additional Royal Circus titles:
The Barrier of Parnassus; *The Milkmaid*; *The Refusal of Harlequin*; *The Land of
Simplicity*; *The Passions*; *The Statue*; *The Regions of Accomplishment*.

Eccentric modulations were to become common in the 1790s, notably in Dussek's piano sonatas, but Carter's example is perhaps the most remarkable of the time. He also wrote *The Constant Maid, or Poll of Plympton* (RC 16.1.88), but only one song was published.

William Reeve (1757–1815) had until recently been organist of Totnes in Devon, and he was now singing in the chorus at Covent Garden. He wrote his first theatre music for the Royalty, and both *Hero and Leander* and *Hobson's Choice* were burlesques; Isaac Jackman and W. C. Oulton respectively wrote the words. The overture and two songs from *Hero and Leander* were published, but like nearly all Reeve's music they are very poor indeed. He also composed the greater part of a ballet with songs called *Don Juan*, in which Palmer himself mimed the title role. It has been said that the music was mostly taken from Gluck's ballet of the same name, but this is not so. Barthelemon had borrowed a few items from Gluck's ballet for his *Il Convitata di Pietro* (KT 1785), but he too composed most of the score himself. Barthelemon's version of the famous Fandango is even further removed from Gluck than the one in Act III of Mozart's *Figaro*.[1]

The Royalty also presented established afterpieces such as Carey's *True Blue* and Dibdin's *The Recruiting Sergeant*; these and other librettos, together with some song-words, were published in a book called *The Royalty Songster*. In February 1788, shortly before the theatre closed, Palmer staged Dibdin's *The Deserter*, presumably with the dialogue sung as recitatives. According to the *General Magazine*, there were nearly a hundred soldiers on the stage in the last scene. Throughout this venture Palmer, a popular man, was loyally supported by a number of playhouse singers, including Charles Bannister and Miss George.

We must now take leave of Dibdin. In 1786 he ran a periodical called *The Devil*, most of which he wrote himself. Despairing of success, he decided to emigrate to India. To raise money for the passage, he made a concert tour all round England, and in 1788 published a very readable account of it, *The Musical Tour*. His voyage to India was a lamentable failure. He, the famous composer of sea-songs, found he had no taste for the sea, and he prudently disembarked at Torbay. For the rest of his life he lived by his wits. He found some measure of self-adjustment and of success in his own tiny one-man theatre off the Strand. From this period in the 1790s comes the great spate of songs, some of which are still remembered today. Many are charming, but they are small recompense for the operas he should have been writing. 'His manner of coming upon the stage was in happy style; he ran on sprightly and with nearly a laughing face, like a friend who enters hastily to impart to you some good news',[2] and he then sat down at a piano which had stops like a barrel-organ for adding such percussion

---

[1] The confused history of this theme has already been touched on with reference to Arnold's *The Spanish Barber* (p. 434).

[2] O'Keeffe ii, p. 322.

instruments as drum, cymbals, and triangle. Sea-songs, and songs in cockney and Jewish dialects were interrupted with spoken patter between the verses. The Victorian music-hall was in gestation.

Somehow he found time for other activities as well; in particular he wrote three three-volume novels. *The Younger Brother* (1793) is said to show Fielding influence and to be partly autobiographical. No one thinks the worse of the hero for keeping mistresses and getting into debt, and there is a description of an opera rehearsal.[1] For years on end words poured from Dibdin's pen in barely credible profusion. *Hannah Hewit* (1796) was based on a comparatively recent event, the wreck of the East-Indiaman *Grosvenor* on the coast of South Africa. The wreck and the appalling sufferings of the survivors also inspired novels by Captain Marryat and Conan Doyle. Dibdin's novels are so hard to come by that they cannot have had any success. He also wrote an unhelpful musical textbook, a very second-hand *History of the Stage*, another *Tour* of Britain which he illustrated himself with surprising ability, and his *Professional Life*, but their publication did not prevent him from continually falling into debt. In old age he tried once more for playhouse esteem with two dreadful afterpiece operas. The last was *Round Robin* (LT 21.6.11). By now he was heavy and ill and tired. He had by his own wish severed all connection with his sons. Thomas Dibdin told Holcroft that 'he had seen his father so seldom that, having weak eyes, he should not know him if he met him in the street'.[2] However he had married Miss Wilde when his first wife died, and she and their daughter looked after him in his decline. It was not Dibdin's fault that the bad music of his middle and old age should survive[3] rather than the lively opera music of his twenties, but if he had been easier as a man he might have written lively opera music to the end, and secured for himself a better reputation. He must have known he had squandered his abilities. At least the government granted him a small pension for his sea-songs, which were said to have done more for recruiting during the Napoleonic Wars than the pressgangs.

6 ITALIAN OPERA

In 1955 the Society for Theatrical Research published *Italian Opera and Contemporary Ballet in London 1789–1820* 'compiled' by William C. Smith, and this has lit up many dark corners. Mr. Smith began his list of performances in 1789 because Burney's History had taken the story of 'Italian Opera in England'[4] up to the previous season, but he might with advantage have begun a decade earlier, for Burney is quite unreliable about recent opera. He seems to

---

[1] See 'Charles Dibdin as a Writer' by Edward Rimbault Dibdin, *M&L* April 1938.

[2] Holcroft iii, p. 133.

[3] It is not altogether surprising that the large and chaotic MS collections in the British Museum and Southampton Public Library should have had very little work done on them.

[4] Book IV, ch. 6.

have lost his relish for it once his idol Sacchini had begun to deteriorate, and it may be that there was less to relish. Sacchini's departure in 1781 followed closely on an impassioned row with his one-time friend Rauzzini, who accused him of wholesale musical thieving. Burney thought it likely that Sacchini had indeed got Rauzzini to fill in parts of his London opera scores; Rauzzini claimed that Sacchini had filched whole arias without acknowledgement. The following season Sacchini was replaced as official composer by Anfossi, and he in turn in 1784 by Cherubini, but neither of these appointments was much noticed. At the time Cherubini was virtually unknown, and the operas he composed for London were not generally liked nor ever published. But Burney had the perspicacity to describe him as 'a young man of genius, who had no opportunity, while he was here, of displaying his abilities'; Cherubini's *Giulio Sabino* (1787) was 'murdered in its birth, for want of capital singers'. Cherubini did not attempt to reanimate *opera seria* until he moved to Revolutionary Paris, where he was a major influence on the 'Escape' opera, with its exciting new-style plot. In London the *opera seria* remained hide-bound; only the comic opera was go-ahead and, within operatic limits, realistic. It is not surprising that comic operas were much the more popular. Cimarosa was just beginning to make headway in London, and Cherubini had revised his *Giannina e Bernadoni* (KT 9.1.87). Paisiello was also bringing a warmer and more urbane invention to the buffo plot than opera-goers expected, though it took London longer than most other European capitals to appreciate his merits.[1] We shall later have occasion to mention a very free revision of Gluck's *Orfeo* in 1785,[2] and in 1787 there was even a revival of what purported to be Handel's *Giulio Cesare*, but, as Burney pointed out, it was really no such thing for almost all the arias were inexplicably borrowed from other Handel operas.

Only two new singers need be mentioned. In the spring of 1786 a German soprano named Elisabeth Mara made her stage début in the title role of *Didone abbandonata*, a pasticcio, and in the following spring an equally remarkable singer, Nancy Storace, made her London début in Paisiello's *Gli schiavi per amore*. But during the years that followed, both were to play a more important part in English opera than in Italian.

[1] Paisiello's *La Fraschetana* was the first of his operas to be heard in London—in November 1776 (In Italy it was usually called *La Frascatana*).
[2] See p. 547.

14
Storace in the Ascendant
1788–1796

1 THE NEW CLIMATE

IN the last decade of the eighteenth century there was almost as much new
thinking in the arts, philosophy, and industry as in all the other decades put
together. Though we are not here directly concerned with the Romantic
Movement, we may note that some of those who worked at its centre were
born no more than eight to a dozen years after Storace.

Wordsworth	b. 1770
Walter Scott	b. 1771
Coleridge	b. 1772
Southey	b. 1774
Jane Austen	
Charles Lamb	b. 1775
J. M. W. Turner	
Constable	b. 1776

This generation of writers and painters was to change the artistic scene to an
exceptional extent, and all of them but Jane Austen had at least sixty years of
living in which to do so. Storace was probably born too soon (in 1762) and he
certainly died too soon (in 1796), when he was only thirty-three. His own
generation included a similarly short-lived genius in Robert Burns, and more
humdrum writers such as William Cobbett, Samuel Rogers, and Mrs. Radcliffe. He can never have heard of any of those listed above as Romantics, and
in any case music lagged behind the other arts in all countries when it came to
applying the new principles. We shall find in his operas occasional instances of a
heroic brashness that anticipates a quality we associate with early Verdi; also
examples of Gothic Horror and of last-minute Escapes, both of which can be
classed as Romantic themes. But the purely musical innovations that Storace
learnt from Mozart are both more obvious and more interesting.

The London playhouses were inevitably influenced by the new philosophy epitomized in the French Revolution. The storming of the Bastille on 14 July 1789, though it resulted in the release of only seven prisoners, was widely seen as a portent of vast significance. The Bastille was a symbol of absolute monarchy, and its overthrow was a matter for unbridled enthusiasm. The French Parliament, meeting for the first time in 175 years, abolished the feudal system and issued a Declaration of the Rights of Man, and in every country of Europe people began wondering if they too could improve their lot by sudden means.

> Bliss was it in that dawn to be alive,
> But to be young was very heaven.

Shield's pantomime-ballet, *The Picture of Paris* (CG 20.12.90), is full of such lines as 'The gay Monsieur, a slave no more', 'To be blest we must be free', and

> Hence Slavery, afar;
> Controul thy baleful Star
> That fiercely glares in the Red sphere.
> Drop not from venom'd breath
> A Horror worse than Death,
> Nor shed again thy influence here.

The libretto was never published, but its principal author,[1] Charles Bonnor, took the trouble of going over to Paris in the summer of 1790 to ensure its verisimilitude. As a modern writer puts it, a visit to Paris at that time 'was as obligatory on the Left as a visit to Russia in the nineteen-thirties',[2] and a remarkable number of middle-class intellectuals made the trip. It is astonishing how long they were allowed in. The guillotine began its work in August 1792, though the full blast of the Reign of Terror was not felt until after the execution of the King in January 1793. Yet even when France declared war on Britain a month later enemy travellers were virtually unrestricted. Not until the summer were they ordered to leave the country, and not until October were those who stayed arrested. Because she was living with an American citizen Mary Wolstonecraft survived unmolested right up to April 1795, when she returned to London after two and a half years in France.

Enthusiasm in Britain for the new freedom was greatly weakened by the horrors of the guillotine and the subsequent Napoleonic Wars, and those who later wrote of their visits to Paris in the early nineties were usually at pains to conceal their real motives. Even the honest Wordsworth maintained that he had been

> Led thither chiefly by a personal wish
> To speak the language more familiarly,[3]

[1] Robert Merry wrote the lyrics.
[2] Rosalie Glynn Grylls in *William Godwin and his World*.
[3] *Prelude* (1805 ed.) IX, 36–7.

but in 1791 this cannot have been anyone's 'chief' motive. Michael Kelly, dictating his *Reminiscences* in 1826 to Theodore Hook,[1] declared that he went to Paris 'to see what I could pick up in the way of dramatic novelty for Drury Lane', but by this time he was on dining-out terms with George IV at the Brighton Pavilion, and he could hardly have confessed that his main reason was to sample life in a republic. On his visit in 1791 or 1792 he scarcely went to the theatre, and in old age he was a little too anxious to appear shocked at having seen the King and Queen brought back after their attempted escape; as also at the enthusiasm with which his then companion, Tom Paine, greeted this event.[2] It is only fair to add that in the summer of 1790 he, Mr. and Mrs. Crouch, and the singer Johnstone had spent almost every night in the theatre, and Drury Lane did indeed profit from the music and librettos that Kelly brought back, but it can hardly be doubted that he had left-wing tendencies at the time and that it was mainly these which drew him to Paris.

Shield went to Paris in August 1791 with Joseph Ritson and he was there again early the following year, and though the main motive for his visits was the trip to Italy that filled the time between them, his close friendship with Holcroft and Ritson showed that he too was 'progressive' in his views. A more extreme revolutionary was John Thelwall, who later had to hide in Coleridge's cottage at Nether Stowey to escape arrest. His opera libretto, *The Incas*, does not survive, but it certainly stressed the moral superiority of the non-Europeans over their Spanish aggressors. Robert Merry was another who wrote an opera libretto with a purpose; again *The Magician no Conjuror* (CG 2.2.92) does not survive, though Mazzinghi's music was published. Merry was an upper-class poet, gambler, and *bon viveur* who, within months of penning an Ode for the King's Recovery which Mrs. Siddons recited, had his opinions suddenly turned upside down by the Fall of the Bastille. He then spent as much time as possible in Paris, and when he could stay there no longer he took his actress wife to the freedom of America.

The views of these and other non-conformists were crystallized and developed by William Godwin in his *Enquiry concerning Political Justice and its influence on Morals and Happiness* (1793). The influence of this book was tremendous, and those who kindled to its message included not only 'advanced' thinkers like Holcroft, Mrs. Inchbald, and Robert Owen, but even men who ended their lives die-hard Tories like Wordsworth and Southey. Godwin did not believe in

---

[1] A son of James Hook. See *English Wits* by A. J. A. Symons for an amusing account of his flamboyant taste in practical jokes.

[2] Kelly states that his second visit was in 1792, and Storace's use of a tune from *Les Visitandines* supports this (see p. 518). But if so, he cannot have seen the royal couple brought back in 1791. Perhaps he made three trips to Paris. Paine's *The Rights of Man*, Part 1 (1791), had advocated equal rights and true democracy; Part 2 (1792) went further and asked for the suppression of the monarchy and the peerage. See Kelly i, 342–9; ii, 22–5, 2nd ed.

violence, and had there been a revolution in England he would doubtless have
been a Girondin, massacred by the second-wave revolutionaries. Many of his
ideas are still in the air today. He was against all forms of association (even
orchestras) and he hoped that eventually the State would wither away. He was
against religion, and (in the normal sense) marriage, and he thought that universal benevolence should supersede all family ties. Every man should be 'the
ingenuous censor of his neighbour' and practise absolute sincerity in all his relationships. A loaf 'should belong to him who most wants it'; charity and gratitude, being degrading, should be done away with. He did not think that men
had equal rights, for they differed in their usefulness to the community, but they
should have equal duties and equal justice. These ideals should be suggested
rather than forced; appealing to reason, they would inevitably snowball.

Not all Godwin's theories worked well in practice. Holcroft's son was so
miserable in a Godwinian home that he killed himself. Basil Montagu,[1] with
absolute sincerity as his beacon, told Coleridge exactly what Wordsworth had
said of his drug-taking habits, and thereby wrecked our most profitable literary
friendship. At a frivolous level, Montagu, when travelling through the Mid-
lands with Godwin, removed their horse's bit and bridle so that it could eat its
corn more pleasurably; it ran away and was not seen again. Shield was inspired
with similar Godwinian sentiments on the Mont Cenis pass and described them
in a letter to Holcroft:

> I thought it degraded the race of men too much to suffer them to carry me
> in a sedan over this immense mountain: in consequence of which we had
> mules; and after riding about one mile, reflection told me that I was
> shortening the life of the animal . . . and as I saw women walking I was
> resolved to do the same.[2]

Godwin himself found it impossible to live up to one at least of his own precepts.
In 1796 he married Mary Wolstonecraft as unobtrusively as possible in St.
Pancras Church; their daughter, it is hardly necessary to add, later wrote
Frankenstein and married Shelley.

Inevitably Godwin was a republican, though he did not feel able to write
freely on the subject in *Political Justice*. But the authorities were soon seeing
republicans in every doorway, and in 1794 they charged twelve of Godwin's
followers with High Treason. Only Thomas Hardy, a shoemaker, and Horne
Tooke were actually tried; when they were acquitted the charges against the
others were dropped, as indeed was proper, for no violence had been planned.
Holcroft's would have been the third case, and Thelwall was also among the
twelve. Godwin himself was not arraigned, but he attended the case, as did

---

[1] A natural son of Lord Sandwich, the man who started the Concerts of Ancient
Music.

[2] Holcroft iii, p. 297; letter from Turin dated 22.9.91.

Francis Place.[1] Charles James Fox was a witness for Tooke, and so was Sheridan.

Though the case did much to advertise Godwin's views, his followers were already a dwindling minority even in the progressive world of the theatre. Burke's reactionary *Reflections on the Revolution in France* (1790) had prophesied the excesses in Paris that in fact occurred, with the result that the book was soon swaying the waverers. Storace must have been a royalist, for in 1792 he composed a song called 'Captivity, a Ballad supposed to be sung by the Unfortunate Marie Antoinette, during her Imprisonment in the Temple'. A footnote in the score added the loaded information:

> The Hair of this once lovely Woman WAS of a bright flaxen colour—We say WAS, because three years of Sorrow have brought on a premature old age. The unfortunate Antoinette is now grey headed, wan, and wrinkled.

A few months later Storace composed another song, this time a 'Lamentation of Marie Antoinette, late Queen of France, on the Morning of her Execution'. Personal feelings were involved in these songs, and they may well have been strong. Storace had known well Marie Antoinette's brother, the Emperor of Austria, and he had probably met Marie Antoinette herself. It is significant that he never accompanied Kelly to Paris.

The establishment of our national anthem in the early nineties was due about equally to concern for the King in his illness, to fear that the Treason Trials heralded an English Revolution, and to patriotism induced by the Napoleonic Wars. Those in the cheaper seats at the playhouses were vociferous in their demands for its performance every night, preferably sung by the entire cast lined up across the stage. Theatres complied to prevent rioting, and thus a tradition was established. Holcroft was all too aware that whenever he put Godwinian views into one of his plays, it failed. In *Love's Frailties* (1794), someone says 'I was bred to the most useless, and often the most worthless, of professions, that of a gentleman', but, as Baker put it,

> Such democratic sentiments incautiously, or, as it was believed, intentionally introduced, at a time when the general opinion was, that the encouragement of such sentiments might be attended with pernicious consequences, occasioned an opposition to this play . . .

The stage could not yet be used as a pulpit for any but the most orthodox views.

Thus we shall find liberty lauded in the early nineties, and patriotism taking its place once the war started. Nevertheless when Godwin followed up his *Political Justice* with a novel that exhibited some of his precepts in action, Colman turned it into a successful opera which Storace was setting on his deathbed. The novel was called *Caleb Williams*, the opera *The Iron Chest*.

---

[1] Place and Hardy did much to establish the trade-union movement. And see p. 121.

2 STORACE'S ITALIAN OPERAS

Michael Kelly's *Reminiscences* are the chief source of our information about the Storaces' years abroad, and an important source for Mozart's career in the middle eighties. Unfortunately they are far from accurate. Kelly dictated them in old age, relying on an Irish memory that tended to sacrifice truth for the sake of a good story, and he was not helped by an amanuensis who made mistakes and even additions on his own account.[1] Kelly is said to have been horrified when he read some of the statements Theodore Hook had made him make. There is no evidence that Kelly ever kept a diary, and the book is mostly devoid of dates except such as Hook could come on in London. In what follows, the events are sometimes from Kelly, the dates always from elsewhere.

The Storace parents laid what should have been a good foundation for their son's career by being friendly with the Sheridan family. Stephen Storace the elder had known Thomas Sheridan in Dublin in the 1750s, and in the sixties he was friendly with the Linley family as well, for he arranged all Elizabeth's dates at the Three Choirs Festivals. (He was what today would be called a fixer.) When Richard Brinsley Sheridan married Elizabeth in 1773, they honeymooned at East Bergholt and then stayed with the Storaces in Marylebone High Street while they looked for a London house. They found one not far away in Orchard Street.

The boy Stephen was eleven at the time, and he was showing promise as a violinist. By 1776 he was a pupil at the San Onofrio Conservatoire in Naples where so many well-known Italian composers had been trained, and he lodged with an uncle who is said to have been a bishop. It may be remembered that in the autumn of 1775 Sheridan was in despair because he had no one to rehearse the singers for *The Duenna*, and the situation was resolved only when Linley agreed to come to London. This may mean that the elder Storace was not available because he had already left for Italy with his son. The boy spent some three years studying in Naples. He became friendly with the Welsh landscape painter Thomas Jones, who was his senior by twenty years. Jones described in his *Memoirs* how they climbed Vesuvius together and how they made a four-day trip across the Bay to Sorrento. He thought Stephen

a giddy and thoughtless young fellow who apply'd very little to his Musical Studies and being tired of the restraints he felt under his Uncle's

---

[1] One of these additions was almost certainly the story that Storace's name had originally been Sorace, and that he changed it because of its vulgar implications if pronounced with a French accent. In spite of *Grove*, there is no evidence for this. The father was called Storace in Dublin as early as 1749; it was quite a common name in the Naples area, and I can find no evidence that the name Sorace ever existed. It was just the sort of story that Theodore Hook would have found irresistible. See Kelly i, p. 95, 2nd ed. (The pagination differs from that of the 1st ed., though both came out in the same year.)

roof, lived entirely with the English, and as he was fond of Drawing, was almost always of our parties.

Later in Vienna Stephen might easily and profitably have passed for an Italian composer, but in fact he insisted on being described on the playbills of his operas as 'Ein Engländer'. Jones was so determinedly 'English' that he organized Country Dancing and cricket matches in the Borghese Park.

At Christmas 1778 Mr. and Mrs. Storace arrived in Naples with Nancy, no doubt to judge for themselves if reports of Stephen's dinolence were true. Nancy had had singing lessons in England from both Rauzzini and Sacchini, and she may have studied further in Italy in 1779. There is no evidence that either she or her mother returned to England before 1787. Stephen on the other hand preferred to live in England and to travel abroad only when he had to; he made at least three more foreign 'tours' in the 1780s, all of them short. In Naples that winter the parents must have decided their son was wasting his time, and they removed him from the conservatoire. Making their leisurely way north they met two young artists in Florence, James Northcote and Prince Hoare. The latter was the son of William Hoare, a Bath painter who had himself studied in Italy.[1] Prince Hoare never had much success with the brush; he made his modest reputation first as Storace's librettist and later as an art critic. He became a lifelong friend of Nancy's.

While Nancy was starting her incredible career as a singer—at fifteen she sang in Florence, at sixteen in Parma and at seventeen in Milan at La Scala— Stephen back in England dithered between music and painting. About 1782 he published a set of Canzonets, one of them a setting of verses from Gray's *Elegy*, and they seem to be the first English songs that were engraved in the modern way with a two-stave accompaniment. But Stephen's heart was not then in music, and he tried to set up in Bath as an artist. It is strange that with so many friends in the right place he did not compose for Drury Lane. Perhaps he was reacting passionately against his father's plans for his career.

About 1783 his father died, probably in Italy. Stephen spent that spring in Leghorn where Nancy was singing. Michael Kelly first met them there, and in his memoirs he described how they happened to see him come ashore in the harbour dressed in Sicilian clothes. He had long flowing hair at the time, and Nancy said to Stephen in English: 'Look at that girl dressed in boy's clothes.' Kelly replied disconcertingly: 'You are mistaken, miss; I am a very proper he animal, and quite at your service.'[2] It was the start of a life-long friendship. Stephen heard Kelly sing in Leghorn, and when he was back in London a month later he told Linley he had found the tenor Drury Lane so badly needed. That summer Linley wrote to Kelly in Venice and offered him a contract.

[1] Many of his paintings and one by his son can be seen at Stourhead, Wiltshire.
[2] The *General Magazine* for May 1788 says more banally that they met at a Leghorn concert.

Kelly refused, says the *General Magazine*, but years later he maintained that it was his father who prevented an agreement being reached.

By the late summer of 1783 Nancy was in Vienna, chaperoned as ever by her mother. She sang leading parts there for four years, and as already mentioned she made the mistake of marrying John Abraham Fisher. Kelly calls him 'a very ugly Christian . . . and a bit of a quack and an inordinate prattler who related strange things of himself'. He won Nancy mainly by drinking endless cups of tea with her mother, and that autumn Lord Mount-Edgcumbe as best man led her to the altar in the chapel of the Dutch ambassador. A surprising number of English lords were present to see Nancy become Mrs. Fisher, and the British ambassador, Sir Robert Keith, gave the wedding dinner.

The approximate date of the wedding is proved by the MS of Mozart's comic opera, *Lo sposo deluso*, which he abandoned unfinished in December 1783; he wrote the part of Emilia for 'Signora Fischer'.[1] Some time in the following year the marriage broke down, partly because Fisher was both silly and ill-tempered, mainly because the Emperor Joseph II had himself become aware of Nancy's attractions. She did not complain when he ordered Fisher out of Vienna and made her his mistress. She never saw her husband again, and never married anyone else.

Kelly states in his *Memoirs* that he started his own career in Vienna at the same time as Nancy and the Italians Benucci and Mandini, but for various reasons this cannot be so. However he certainly took a rather small part in the première of Paisiello's *Il re Teodoro* (23.8.84), and from then on he appeared regularly until he and the Storaces left Vienna for good in February 1787. Operas at this period were commissioned or their choice approved by the Emperor himself; like most of the Hapsburgs, he was intensely musical. Nancy had such a hold over him that she talked him into commissioning an opera by her brother. This was a risky thing to have done, for Stephen had never written theatre music even in his own country, and it is most unlikely that the Emperor had ever met him. Probably he was shown and liked the two piano quintets and sextet that Stephen had just published in London. *Gli sposi malcontenti* (1.6.85) had a libretto by Stephen Brunati, and in spite of a first-night calamity, it was surprisingly successful. Loewenberg records subsequent performances in Prague, Leipzig, Dresden, Hanover, Berlin, Breslau, and at two theatres in Paris; needless to say it has never been given in London, and the music seems never to have been published. However, there are manuscript full scores in Dresden and elsewhere, and these reveal that Stephen already had melodic gifts and knew how to score with an almost Mozartian sense of colour.

It has sometimes been said that Storace took lessons from Mozart, and though I have found no definite evidence of this it is likely enough. His style is quite often Mozartian in flavour, and the Storaces and the Mozarts were certainly

---

[1] Einstein, p. 423.

close friends. Perhaps the disastrous first night of *Gli sposi malcontenti* brought them together. Right in the middle of the first act, and with the Duke of York in the audience next to the Emperor, Nancy completely lost her voice. Kelly, who had the chief male part, says he never forgot her despair, especially as the whole occasion had been engineered by herself to encourage her brother in his musical career. Her place was taken by Celestine Coltellini,[1] and Nancy did not sing again for three months. Her recovery in September was celebrated by a cantata, *Per la ricuperata salute di Ophelia,* in which Mozart, Salieri, and Cornetti all collaborated; the music was published but no copy is known to survive.[2] I have not discovered why Nancy was referred to as Ophelia.

It must be emphasized that Nancy was not just one of many singers in the Vienna company; she was *the* singer, the *prima donna.* Though she had no great talent for serious opera, the taste of the time was for *opera buffa* in which she excelled. She was Vienna's first Rosina in Paisiello's *Il Barbiere di Siviglia* (Kelly and Mandini alternated as Almaviva), and it was naturally thought that when Mozart set Beaumarchais' sequel, *Le Nozze di Figaro,* she would keep to the same character and sing the Countess. But Rosina is much more mature and dignified in the sequel, and dignity was not within Nancy's range. At a comparatively early stage in the writing of the opera she was switched to Susanna; Mozart naturally made sure that she should sing above the Countess in the ensembles. Susanna must have suited her down to the ground, and a study of the part tells one a great deal about her personality and style of singing. Kelly doubled Don Basilio and the lawyer. Stephen was probably not present on the first night, but he saw subsequent performances and was very much influenced by them.

Stephen's second opera, *Gli Equivoci* (27.12.86), had the advantage of an excellent libretto by Da Ponte. 'Directly I had finished Figaro', he says in his Reminiscences, 'Storace's brother had obtained the Emperor's permission for me to write a libretto for him. So to please him and get the matter out of the way as quickly as possible, I adapted one of Shakespeare's comedies.' Kelly says Stephen chose the subject, which was *The Comedy of Errors.* The playbills[3] described the opera as 'Ein italienisches Singspiel', which may mean that it had spoken dialogue, but the Dresden score, the only one I have seen, has the usual sung recitatives. Da Ponte changed most of the names. The twins become Eufemio instead of Antipholus, Eufemio of Ephesus (Kelly) being married to Sofronia (Nancy), whom Shakespeare had called Adriana. The opera begins splendidly. As the G minor Storm Overture is subsiding[4] the curtain rises on the seashore of Ephesus where the Syracusan Eufemio and Dromio have just been shipwrecked. During their duet the violins imitate the lapping of the waves. The

[1] Her father wrote the libretto for Mozart's *La finta semplice.*
[2] See Hyatt King's *Mozart in Retrospect,* pp. 223–4.
[3] One is reproduced in Eric Walter White's *The Rise of English Opera.*
[4] See p.503.

plot followed Shakespeare fairly closely, except that Da Ponte invented a wife for the shipwrecked Dromio and a little son, Dromioncino, of whose existence he had been unaware. Also Da Ponte cut the Abbess and the courtesan. Like *Figaro*, the opera is very long, and it has an unusually high proportion of ensembles. The first act ends with an immense and spirited Finale in which Eufemio of Ephesus is trying to get into his own house while his brother is snugly inside drinking with his wife. When the Watch arrives and asks what all the rumpus is about, everyone tells him at once in a quick fugue of great brilliance; there is a similar moment in the Act II Finale of Rossini's *Il barbiere*.

Photostats apart, there is no copy of this libretto in Britain. It was first described by Einstein in *The Monthly Musical Record* (March–April 1936), who compared it, not to its disadvantage, with the libretto of *Figaro*. In other words it is first-rate. Much of Storace's vocal writing has a decided Viennese flavour. One short example must suffice. In Mozart's ensembles there is sometimes an incidental but endearing 'codetta' theme, introduced quite late on; here is such a theme from the Act I Finale of *Gli equivoci*, a theme Shield or Arnold could not possibly have written:

There is a good duet earlier in this first act for Sofronia and her sister Sosostra (Luciana) with basset-horns featured in the accompaniment, and there are second act arias with cello and clarinet obbligatos. The scoring is professional and interesting. Manuscript full scores survive in Vienna and Dresden. The Vienna score, though not the one in Dresden, contains two arias by Süssmayr and one headed 'Bach'. Like all English singers Nancy had a number of Scotch Songs in her repertoire, most of them slow and emotional, and one of her party pieces in Vienna was 'The Yellow-hair'd Laddie', which she must have sung in an arrangement by J. C. Bach.[1] Nancy must have brought it from England in manuscript form. It was so liked in Vienna that she substituted it for one of Stephen's arias in the second act, but because the simple tune did not cover all Da Ponte's words someone, presumably Stephen, composed a dramatic contrasting section for the middle. There cannot be very much of Bach's invention left in the finished product.

Gli equivoci has never been performed in Britain. It would be at least as entertaining as any comic opera by Paisiello or Cimarosa, and had it been written by either of those composers we would no doubt have staged it long ago.

[1] Though four Scotch Song arrangements by Bach survive in print, 'The Yellow-hair'd Laddie' is not among them. But he used the tune in the Finale of his Piano Concerto op. 13 no. 4.

The three Storaces left Vienna for England in February 1787, accompanied by Kelly and twenty-one-year-old Thomas Attwood, whose lessons with Mozart are much better documented than Stephen's. By now Mozart was in love with Nancy and wanted to come too; they all expected his arrival in London later that year, and Stephen was confident he could arrange a contract for him at the King's Theatre. However, what with improved conjugal feelings and the death of his father Mozart never came.

On arrival in London the travellers went straight to Linley's house in Norfolk Street off the Strand, and somehow they found energy that night to go to Drury Lane where Kemble was playing Richard Coeur de Lion. They had seen Grétry's opera in Paris on their way home, and Linley, who had renewed by post his offer of a contract, wanted Kelly to see how little competition he would have if he accepted it. Kelly did, of course, notice Kemble's inadequacy, but what he noticed much more was Mrs. Crouch's performance as Laurette. 'She seemed to aggregate in herself, like the Venus Apelles, all that was exquisite and charming', he wrote in 1826. She was the most potent reason for his joining the Drury Lane company, and he loved her dearly until her death. Within a month he was singing Lionel and Young Meadows; Drury Lane had found the tenor the theatre needed so badly.

There is no evidence as to whether or not Linley tried to recruit the Storaces for his theatre; if he did they must have refused, for in their innocence they both expected to be welcomed at the King's Theatre. Nancy, one of the best-known singers in Europe, had sung all over Italy as well as in Vienna. Stephen had had much more continental experience and success than the official Italian composer in London that season, even if his name were Cherubini. In fact the welcome was grudging in the extreme. As Stephen put it in a letter to the British Ambassador in Vienna:

> My sister's success in London upon the whole has been as much as we could expect, though she has had great opposition from the Italians, who consider it as an infringement on their rights that any person should be able to sing that was not born in Italy . . .[1]

Nevertheless for some years the Storaces had a good deal of influence at the King's Theatre.

Just before their arrival in London a new manager had been appointed. He was an Italian dancing-master who had been working in London or Dublin for more than twenty-five years, and his name was Gallini; perhaps because he had done well for himself, he was known as 'Sir John' Gallini. He showed both personal taste and good sense when he appointed the great Noverre as the King's Theatre dancing-master; Noverre devised the ballets there for some eight years. Gallini also appointed Mazzinghi as his music director and harpsichordist, and this was a less happy choice, though with the experienced Cramer

[1] BM Add. 35538; the letter, the only one of Storace's to survive, is dated 3.7.87.

still leading the violins the newcomer's youth and inexperience may not have mattered very much. Joseph Mazzinghi (1765–1841) was an anglicized Corsican brought up in London. His father, a wine-merchant, had played the violin in Marylebone Gardens and published some violin sonatas. Joseph had lessons from J. C. Bach. His appointment at the King's Theatre when he was only twenty-one should have led to a successful career, but Mazzinghi was always an unimaginative composer, and he seems to have lacked authority as a director. The result was that his stints at the King's Theatre were never very long, and he had to supplement his income by teaching and an increasing quantity of work for the playhouses.[1]

It is not likely to have been Gallini or Mazzinghi who objected to Nancy Storace's arrival at the tail-end of the London season. Objections surely came from rival singers. But her immediate triumph in Paisiello's *Gli schiavi per amore* silenced most of the criticism, and she was soon repeating some of her other Viennese successes as well; for instance in Paisiello's *Il re Teodoro,* and in the same composer's *Il barbiere di Siviglia* which she chose for her benefit in 1789 and sang with Kelly.[2] Stephen composed an additional aria for *Il re Teodoro,* and it was published in full score.[3]

Nancy must also have proposed a production of Mozart's *Figaro,* for it is virtually certain that she and Stephen brought back from Vienna a copy of the full score with this very purpose in mind. Yet neither this nor any other Mozart opera was staged in London until Mrs. Billington sang in *La clemenza di Tito* in 1805. The most likely reason for *Figaro* not being given is that it proved impossible to cast. At no time in the eighteenth century was the King's Theatre equipped to stage operas in which all the chief male parts were baritones. It was assumed that Londoners wanted male soprano heroes in their serious operas, and tenor heroes in their comic ones. Perhaps for the same reason Gallini asked Stephen Storace to write a new comic opera, instead of accepting *Gli equivoci* or *Gli sposi malcontenti.*

It is not known who wrote the words of *La cameriera astuta* (KT 4.3.88). The libretto was published in the usual way with the Italian on one side and an English translation on the other, but the only copy I know of is in the Library of Congress. Two of Nancy's songs appeared in full score and also a quartet; the overture was published in a piano arrangement; the rest of the music is lost. There were only three performances and they were not much liked. The *Spectator* for 6 March found the music insufficiently Italian; 'The Overture

---

[1] In the 1830s he visited Corsica, and established to his own satisfaction that he was a Count. He died in Bath.

[2] In Vienna *Gli schiavi per amore* had been called *Le gare generose.* The British Museum has MS full scores both of this opera (Add. 16075) and of *Il re Teodoro* (Add. 16076–8).

[3] 'Care donne che bramate'; the main tune also appears in his C major piano trio; and see p. 501.

announces a French author, and the Finales are in the German style of Gluck, loaded with harsh, terrifying music of trumpetting and drumming.' Similar remarks had been made in Vienna about Mozart's *Die Entführung* by another critic who saw orchestras purely as a background to the singing. In fact Storace's overture would not sound French at all to our ears; the second subject is decidedly Viennese:

But one of the surviving arias *was* supposed to be French. Nancy, the astute chambermaid of the title, had at one point to disguise herself as a French society lady, and the recitative at the start of 'Beaux yeux' imitated 'the distracted manner of singing in French serious operas'. (In Paris in 1787 Storace had seen *Phèdre* by Le Moyne, as also Sacchini's *Oedipe à Colone*.)[1] 'As to melodious and soft Italian music', the critic went on, 'there is very little', and inadvertently he makes the opera sound unusually interesting, but in fact such vocal music as survives is rather characterless and disappointing.

In Vienna Stephen had collected a large amount of material both in print and in manuscript for a grandiose publication he had envisaged, *Storace's Collection of Harpsichord Music*; in fact all the music was much better suited to the piano. The Collection was published in twelve instalments between November 1787 and December 1789, and it included every type of keyboard music from concertos through chamber works to piano solos. There were separate parts for all the stringed and wind instruments. The chamber works included three Mozartean piano trios by Storace himself. Mozart's E flat Piano Quartet appeared within a few weeks of its Viennese publication, and Storace must have brought a manuscript copy of it with him. He managed to publish Mozart's Piano Trio in G (K.564) for the first time anywhere, and as the trio was not written until after his return to London he must have corresponded on the subject with Mozart. It is sad that these letters are lost, and sadder still that shortly before her death Nancy apparently burnt the love-letters Mozart is thought to have written to her.

[1] Kelly i, p. 285.

The Collection was doubly important to Storace in that it brought him a wife. The vignettes on the title pages were the work of John Hall, who had just been appointed Historical Engraver to the King. Storace married his third daughter, Mary, on 23 August 1788. Their only child, Brinsley John Storace, had perhaps been born already, for when he died early in 1807 (he was a pupil of Sir John Soane's) *The Gentleman's Magazine* described him as nineteen. One might reasonably guess from his christian names that Sheridan was his godfather.

3 STORACE AT OLD DRURY

In the summer of 1788 Thomas King retired from running Drury Lane, and John Philip Kemble took over as Sheridan's henchman; also, though this was not at first realized, Linley gave up writing operas and Storace in effect took over as theatre composer. He made an inconspicuous start with an afterpiece called *The Doctor and the Apothecary* (DL 25.10.88). Eighteen months earlier he had arrived in London with high hopes of composing for and even running the King's Theatre, yet by now with a wife and child to consider he was grateful for any theatre work. He had seen Dittersdorf's *Der Apotheker und Doktor* at the Kärntnertor Theatre in Vienna (first performed on 11 July 1786), and he had acquired a published vocal score and no doubt a libretto. He got James Cobb to knock up a concise and very free version of this extremely long opera, and he composed a good half of the settings himself. Roughly a third of the items are by Dittersdorf, and most of these Storace cut heavily and scored himself. He gave Kelly an aria from Paisiello's *I filosofi immaginarii* which Kelly had probably sung in Vienna; Mozart had written piano variations on the theme (K.398).

The doctor and the apothecary each think the other a rogue who kills more than he cures, and they will not hear of a marriage between their children, Carlos and Anna. The apothecary plans to marry Anna to a garrulous middle-aged sot with a wooden leg called Captain Sturmwald. Carlos teams up with Juan, who himself has designs on Anna's companion, Isabella, and together they lure the apothecary out of his house by night and climb in at one of his windows. In the confusion that follows Juan disguises himself first in the Captain's clothes (and is 'married' to Anna in front of her father by Carlos disguised as a notary), and then as the apothecary's wife (and is treated for a trumped-up ailment by the doctor). All ends predictably.

It will be apparent that Juan has much more to do than the alleged hero, and as in all Storace's operas the best acting part was written for John Bannister. Kelly and Mrs. Crouch played the young couple, Suett and Parsons the title roles. *The London Chronicle* praised 'the first view of the Apothecary's shop, and a distant convent with its spires illuminated by the sun in its gradual descent', and Storace accompanied this effect with a charming nineteen-bar 'Symphony play'd during the Sun sett'. The overture was the first one-movement example on the modern Viennese plan that playhouse audiences had heard, and several of the songs are of unusual quality. The first, sung by Anna when miserable about her enforced engagement to the Captain, had an elaborate bassoon obbligato intended to give the music a flavour of sadness. Near the end there is a written-out cadenza for voice and instrument, and both here and earlier the bassoon is taken up to a high B flat. This note is most unusual at this early period, and it argues an exceptional bassoonist in the Drury Lane orchestra. Two of the best songs come near the end. Carlos's love song 'Am I beloved' is full of Viennese touches, and Isabella's 'How mistaken is the lover' (sung by Miss Romanzini) is more Mozartian still, and one of the most delightful songs Storace ever wrote. The music was not new; he took it from 'Care donne che bramate' which he had written for inclusion in *Il re Teodoro*, and it thus survives in full score.[1] Here is the preparation for the reprise:

The Dittersdorf items in this afterpiece seem decidedly inferior to those by Storace.

The Doctor and the Apothecary enjoyed a mild success, and there had been more than fifty performances by the time Storace died.

On 17 June 1789 the King's Theatre was burnt to the ground. In the following season Italian opera had to make do with the quite inadequate Little Theatre, and Nancy was glad to join Kelly at Drury Lane. It can hardly have been coincidence that her brother was immediately commissioned to write his first full-length English opera, *The Haunted Tower* (DL 24.11.89), and it was the most successful full-length opera that Drury Lane staged in the entire century. There were eighty-four performances in the first two seasons, and for half a century it was sung all over Britain and in the States.

It was generally recognized that this success was due much more to the music

[1] See p. 498.

than to the libretto, which Tate Wilkinson and Genest both thought very poor. The confused plot is laid unpromisingly in the days of William the Conqueror. Before the curtain rises, the true Baron Oakland has been wrongfully banished, and when later his innocence is proved he cannot be found, so the king has created another Baron Oakland. Edward, the son of this boorish upstart, is an unpretentious youth with charm but no brains, and he secretly loves a village girl called Adela, but his father wants him to marry Lady Elinor whom they have never met. The opera begins on the seacoast of Kent with Elinor's arrival from Normandy; she has a secret lover of her own, Sir Palomede, who has followed her from France. When they learn that Edward is a rough simple fellow, Lady Elinor disguises herself as her maid, Cicely, so that she can watch him more easily; Sir Palomede pretends to be a jester. At the near-by castle they find there is already an accepted Lady Elinor; this in fact is Adela, disguised above her station by Edward who hopes to marry her before the deception is uncovered. The real Lady Elinor is only too willing for the deception to succeed. At a big wedding party an ox is roasted whole. In Act III we see the haunted tower, with the sea in the distance and an improbable lighthouse. Hugo, an old retainer, recognizes Sir Palomede as Lord William, the true Baron's son and thus the rightful owner of the castle. He tells Lord William that his father's armour is in the tower. They see lights flickering inside and Lord William goes in to investigate. While he is up in the armour room, three of the Baron's servants emerge from below. For months they have been stealing wine from the cellar, and their lights have led to the belief that the tower is haunted by the old Baron. They are then terrified by the appearance from the tower of what they all think is the ghost of the old Baron in full armour; in fact Lord William. All comes out. Lord William marries Elinor.

No doubt James Cobb took pride in having worked out a situation in which a mistress disguised herself as a maid, and a maid disguised herself as a mistress, but much more to the audience's taste was the spectacular ox-roasting scene and the Gothic horrors of the last act. There were to be several more operatic ghosts before the end of the century, and *The Haunted Tower* is a minor historical landmark; Mrs. Radcliffe did not publish *The Romance of the Forest* until 1791, while *The Mysteries of Udolpho*, Catherine Morland's favourite novel, dates from three years later still. With good dialogue the plot of *The Haunted Tower* might have served well enough, but Cobb's dialogue was seldom easy or natural. 'To what a wayward fate am I subjected!' remarks Sir Palomede, and Cobb's characters are all too liable to talk in that style. The combination of plot and dialogue would probably prove too much of a bad thing today, however likable the music.

Inevitably Mrs. Crouch played the aristocratic Elinor and 'Signora Storace' the working-class Adela, and inevitably Kelly and John Bannister were their respective swains. The upstart Baron was a non-singing part designed for Baddeley, but his wine-stealing servant Robert has several songs because the role was taken by Dignum. Drury Lane had recently acquired a solid bass singer called Sedgwick who was a very poor actor. Storace needed such a voice for ensembles, and in all his operas (Sedgwick made his début in *The Doctor and the Apothecary*) he gave him at least one slow and rather beautiful song even though the role was usually of no importance dramatically. In *The Haunted Tower* Sedgwick played a totally inactive servant called Charles and sang two of the best songs.

Storace must have told Cobb to start the libretto on the coast so that he could drag in the storm overture he had written in Vienna for *Gli equivoci*. For some reason he added a new, long, and not noticeably slow introduction with storm effects of its own and some forward-looking harmony. He shortened the main section to its advantage, for the overture to *Gli equivoci* has the second-subject group three times over and is inclined to be diffuse. But it is a strikingly original conception. In both versions thunder and lightning are cued into the music from the start of the recapitulation, at which point the curtain rises. The stage direction reads:

> The Coast of Kent at a distance. Oakland Castle is seen at the top of a hill. A storm, thunder and lightning—a boat appears, from which several Attendants on Lady Elinor land.

The overture subsides into a quiet coda with good bassoon writing, and immediately there is a chorus of fishermen, peasants, and attendants to the music of the overture's new introduction. Sir Palomede has a big aria with oboe obbligato, and the maid Cicely (Miss Romanzini) a simple ballad to what is described as a 'Welch tune'; in fact it is Irish. Storace is here pandering to playhouse taste, but he does so much less often than Shield or Arnold. The audience was next entertained with an elaborate chorus of hunters led by the Baron's servant, Robert. There are trumpets in the orchestral pit echoed by horns behind the scenes, as also a male-voice chorus on the stage echoed by another out of sight. Such writing must have seemed excitingly effective to anyone used to Shield's simple little glees. Storace did not risk an elaborate Finale to Act I; the trio sung by the 'French' party is nicely written but short. Near the start of Act II Adela has her biggest song, 'Be mine, tender passion', sung when she is first embarrassed by the disguise of fashionable clothes. The music is strikingly Mozartian in both plan and style. As in 'Dove sono', there is a long *Andantino* section followed by an agitated *Allegro* that ends with long-held high notes. The aria begins as follows:

Storace

Here is the opening of the *Allegro* and a later fragment:

The song ends with the kind of pyrotechnics Mozart used to write for his sister-in-law. The vocal score gives none of the orchestral detail.

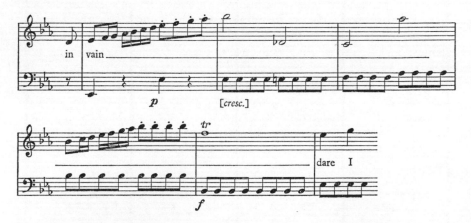

As a sop to Linley, Storace borrowed a song from *The Carnival of Venice* for Miss Romanzini, and broke new ground with a little French song for Edward; the libretto reveals that at the pauses in the music Jack Bannister spoke a few random remarks to the servants preparing the wedding banquet. Next came an elaborate Sextet in which varied emotions were effectively expressed. Inevitably at the ox-roasting Robert obliged the gallery with Leveridge's 'Roast Beef' song, but the act ended well with a brisk Finale.

It cannot be said that Storace made any attempt to create an atmosphere of horror in the last act, but the librettist gave him scarcely any opportunities. Mrs. Crouch had a big coloratura song borrowed from Sarti,[1] and Miss Romanzini, who specialized in charm, was given a particularly charming item by Storace himself. Lord William's 'Spirit of my sainted Sire' has already been mentioned for the fact that Kelly sang the high As without resorting to falsetto. He delivered this vigorous aria from the steps of the Haunted Tower itself, just before going in to look for his father's armour, and we can get some idea of the stage picture from the frontispiece of the vocal score, which shows the setting for this last scene. No music publisher had ever before offered his customers this attraction, and it may well be that the idea came from Storace himself. It caught on, with the result that in effect we have backcloths for a number of operas written in the following decade.

It was generally recognized that the music of *The Haunted Tower* included a number of elements that were new to the playhouses. 'The specimens of adopted ballads', wrote Bannister's biographer, John Adolphus, 'can no longer be essayed; the improvements effected in *Love in a Village*, *The Duenna*, and even in *Rosina* are no longer sufficient to satisfy the scientific ear.' According to Baker, 'our author, aided by the ever-to-be lamented Stephen Storace, formed the bold idea of telling the story of the scene in music', and though this is much more obviously true of his later full-length operas, Baker recognized that Storace's great contribution to English opera was that he raised the importance of the music in proportion to the words.

The success of *The Haunted Tower* established Storace's reputation in the playhouses: overnight he was recognized as our leading theatre composer. But a backlog of commitments affected Drury Lane's other musical novelties that season. Throughout Storace's time at this theatre the orchestra was led by Thomas Shaw.[2] A few days before the first night of *The Haunted Tower* an afterpiece opera called *The Island of St. Marguerite* (DL 13.11.89) was given with music composed or 'selected' by Shaw. The libretto by the Hon. John St. John was based on the story of the Man in the Iron Mask, and this was the first English opera to be inspired by the Fall of the Bastille the previous July. The Prisoner in the Iron Mask (Kelly) is released from confinement by the mob, and the castle is destroyed; from its ruins rises the Temple of Liberty. In some ways the score is remarkable. The overture is in three linked sections, the first and last the exposition and recap of a sonata-form movement, the middle one slow.

---

[1] The Storaces had met him in Vienna and probably brought back some of his music. Sarti's *Giulio Sabino* had been given at the King's Theatre in 1788.

[2] See p. 280.

Mozart adopted the same plan in his overture to *Die Entführung aus dem Serail*. Published orchestral parts were advertised on the piano arrangement of Shaw's *Cymon* overture, but I have not found a set. In a roundabout way Shaw borrowed 'Crudel! perchè finora' from Act III of *Figaro*. Mozart's opera had not then been published either whole or in part. Shaw found the music in a Birchall & Andrews full score of that summer (1789) described as 'a favorite Duet . . . sung in the comic opera of La Vendemmia' by Gazzaniga. Nancy Storace, who had sung in the *Figaro* duet, also sang in the *Vendemmia* borrowing at the King's Theatre, and she must have suggested the interpolation and supplied the music. It thus came about that London, which later published the first full scores of any Mozart symphony, also published a *Figaro* item in accurate full score several years before any continental firm did so.

As already suggested, the Storaces must have brought with them from Vienna a MS full score of *Figaro* in its entirety. Alfred Loewenberg has shown[1] that a few months later Nancy, as Mandina in Bianchi's *La villanella rapita* (LT 27.2.90), sang not only 'Deh vieni' from *Figaro* but also 'Batti, batti' from *Don Giovanni*. The latter had not then been published, and Mozart must have sent it by post because he thought it would be in Nancy's line. We shall come upon other *Figaro* borrowings later.

Another curious borrowing in Shaw's *Island of St. Marguerite* was the song for Miss Hagley based on the first half of Haydn's 'Menuet al Rovescio' from an A major piano sonata (Hob. XVI/26); Shaw changed the bass and destroyed the whole point of the piece by composing a new second half.

When Sheridan was first offered *No Song No Supper*, he turned it down. What he turned down was Prince Hoare's libretto; the music can have meant nothing to him. But he must have known who had written the settings, and it is strange that he did not encourage a very experienced young composer who had been a family friend for years. Perhaps Storace had annoyed Sheridan by parading his abilities too aggressively. Boaden described him as 'a rough honesty', and though the implication of the expression is not clear, it can hardly be complimentary. Was he in some way unlikeable? Yet Kelly spoke warmly enough of him 'He was the most gifted creature I ever met with: an enthusiast and a genius. But in music and painting he was positively occult.' We know much less about Storace's character than about Shield's or Arnold's. There is not even a portrait of him, apart from the posthumous and unreliable one on the vocal score of *Mahmoud*.

No Song No Supper (DL 16.4.90) was eventually staged for Kelly's benefit, and it thus appeared after *The Haunted Tower* though it had been composed before. It was immediately 'adopted', and became the most successful London afterpiece of its decade; there had been more than a hundred performances by the end of Storace's short life, and of his other operas only *The Haunted Tower*

---

[1] 'Don Giovanni in London', *M&L*, July 1943.

reached three figures by 1796. There were performances all over Britain and in the States for half a century.

There is something familiar about the opening: Frederick and Robin are on the coast of Cornwall, having just survived shipwreck in a storm. Storace must have told Prince Hoare to start in this way so that he could work in the *Gli equivoci* storm overture of which he was so proud, and then, when *No Song* was refused, he gave the same instructions to his *Haunted Tower* librettist. Thus when Kelly chose *No Song* for his benefit, Storace had to compose or dig up another overture. The one in the score is in E flat, in one movement with a slow introduction, and not in the least storm-bound. The main section is headed 'Chacone' [*sic*] and in style it is very like Jomelli's much-played 'Celebrated Chaconne' in the same key, which is also in sonata form. Storace did achieve some effective sea music in the first aria, sung by Frederick.

No Song is the only opera of its decade to survive in full score. There is no need to describe at length its charming music or the naïve plot; both can be studied in my Musica Britannica edition. It contains Storace's most popular song, 'With lowly Suit', given to Margaretta (Nancy Storace) when disguised as a beggar-woman. Sung quietly, the voice floating over a hushed auditorium, it can still sound thrilling. A third of the music was borrowed, and some two-thirds of the songs are strophic; such proportions suggest that Storace and Hoare were consciously trying to ape the simple but popular afterpieces on which Shield's reputation was based. Nevertheless Act I ended elaborately. The second half of the Finale had previously been used in both *Gli equivoci* and *La cameriera astuta*, and the spirited action Trio earlier in the same act was also freely adapted from the first of these operas. The two Grétry borrowings reveal unexpected aspects of Storace's methods. Kelly records that in Strasbourg on their way home from Vienna he and Storace heard someone sing 'the popular ballad of "Mon bon André" ',[1] of which there were several sheet music versions with just the melody line. In fact it is the song that begins 'Bon Dieu' in Grétry's *L'Épreuve villageoise*. No doubt Storace bought a melody line copy in Strasbourg, for when he came to compose Margaretta's 'A miser bid to have and hold me' he made up, indeed had to make up, his own harmonies and orchestration. In both his Grétry borrowings he improved considerably on the hastily-written original.

In the Finale of *No Song No Supper* there is a part for 'Carillons', written in the MS full score on two staves of which the top one is obviously a cue that has got in by mistake. Most of the part consists of a single line of notes that never go below the D above Middle C, but there are two four-note chords at the end:

Storace

Allegro

[1] Kelly i, p. 283, 2nd ed.

Such writing could hardly be played with sticks as on a glockenspiel, and though the instrument cannot have been exactly the same as the one used for Papageno's song in *Zauberflöte* (Mozart took the part an octave lower and wrote for it on two staves) it must have had a keyboard and been similar. The Storaces probably brought it back with them from Vienna; Mozart's father, who saw them pass through Salzburg, reported that they were travelling with a prodigious quantity of luggage. Storace liked the instrument sufficiently to introduce it into *The Haunted Tower* (Act II Finale) and *The Siege of Belgrade* ('All will hail the joyous day').

The Siege of Belgrade (DL 1.1.91) had its première on the night Haydn first set foot in London. Unusually, Storace contrived a full-length opera that was almost as much borrowed as composed. Much of the plot and about a third of the music was taken from *Una cosa rara* by 'Martini';[1] Kelly and Nancy Storace had sung in the first performance, which was in Vienna in 1786. The first act looks like a straight English adaptation. But in the other two acts nearly all the music is new, and it looks as though Storace had become impatient with the original, thinking he could improve on it. Indeed the music in Act II shows him at his best, and it is far superior to the 'Martini' music in Act I.

The story is involved in the extreme, and it is never quite clear who is besieging whom or why. It will be enough to say that there are two young couples of 'Servian' villagers who get caught up in political and military events. The most prominent couple consists of Leopold (whose character it is to be constantly angry because people keep accusing him of being constantly angry) and Lilla, and these parts were played by Bannister and Nancy Storace; Peter and Ghita were played by Dignum and Mrs. Bland,[2] Peter being Lilla's brother. The opposing factions are represented on the one hand by the Seraskier in charge of the Turkish army (Kelly), and on the other by an Austrian Colonel and his wife Catherine (Mrs. Crouch). Catherine spends most of the opera as a Turkish prisoner in the Seraskier's harem, and Colonel Cohenberg (a speaking part for Palmer) is consistently unsuccessful at rescuing her. Fortunately for her, the Seraskier is more interested in pursuing the village girl, Lilla. The opera ends with a scene that consists of a long stage direction, a single line of dialogue and a final chorus:

> *Castle and view of Belgrade—the siege commences. Guns firing balls of fire, supposed to be thrown to fire the citadel. A party of Turks are repulsed by a party of Austrians. An Austrian soldier fights some time sword in hand with a Turkish soldier; but, losing his sword, takes a pistol from his belt, and fires*

[1] There had been a production at the King's Theatre in 1789 (called *La cosa rara*), and there were London revivals in 1805 and 1816. The Spanish composer Martin y Soler was known as Martini in every European country but his own; he himself worked at the King's Theatre in 1795.

[2] Miss Romanzini as was; she had just married Mrs. Jordan's brother.

at him; the Turk falls and is thrown into a ditch that surrounds the Castle—
Enter the Seraskier and Cohenberg fighting. The Seraskier falls—Peter,
Leopold etc. fight with the Turkish soldiers. Useph enters and flourishes his
sword on the side of the Turks; but finding they are sure to be conquered joins
the Austrians. Drums and Trumpets heard all the time.

At this point the Colonel says to the Seraskier, 'Rise and learn Christian revenge', and after this moment of conventional magnanimity everyone launches into the last chorus.

This is presumably the scene shown on the title page of the vocal score, and it is disquieting to learn from the *Theatrical Guardian* that though 'the siege was carried on with spirit by all parties' some of the soldiers were made of 'pasteboard'. Nevertheless the press was full of praise for Greenwood's fourteen new sets, as also for the music, and the opera remained popular for many years. Crabbe Robinson took Charles Lamb to a performance in 1811, but the latter seems to have been struck only by the rotund figures of Mrs. Bland and Dignum; they were the only surviving members of the original cast. Braham chose the opera for his farewell performance in New York in 1840.

The vocal score was the last by Storace to indicate the composer or origin of each item, and on the few occasions when it does not do so one can usually suggest a reason. In the overture he reverted to the three-movement form still for some reason favoured by the playhouses. The first movement he wrote himself, and it has an excellent development section, full of energy. The charming movement in the middle is labelled 'Spanish Tune', but in fact it is the Cavatina in *Una cosa rara*; perhaps in Vienna 'Martini' had told Stephen or Nancy that he had used a folk tune for this item. For his Finale Storace wanted something with a Turkish atmosphere, and so he borrowed the second subject (the one in the major) from Mozart's 'Alla Turca'; he had published the sonata from which it comes in his *Harpsichord Collection*, with violin and cello accompaniments. He did not put Mozart's name over the Finale presumably because he wrote all the episodes himself. The movement has a written-out cadenza which must have been for either harp or piano, and it leads without a break into the opening Chorus of Turks, which uses Mozart's minor key theme as well as the major one. The first act includes a good action trio (with brief chorus interjections) in which Useph, the village magistrate, tries to arrest Peter and there is a fight during the music; also a slow and deservedly popular song, 'The sapling Oak', that was sung alternately by Sedgwick and a new bass called Cook (who could not act either). Martini's Finale has the theme Mozart quoted in the last scene of *Don Giovanni*.

Act II begins with a splendid aria for Catherine, with a long and elaborately scored introduction, and this is followed by a Letter Duet modelled on the one in Act II of *Figaro*. Storace must have been very alive to what might be called the non-musical charms of this opera when he saw it in Vienna, especially those of the duets. In three different operas he imitated a Da Ponte-Mozart device that encouraged the two characters to act at each other, as opposed to the usual English way of facing the audience and just singing. In *The Pirates* he had a love duet in which the girl keeps answering no when she means yes (or *vice versa*), and in *The Cherokee* another in which the philandering servants keep being interrupted by their mistress ringing the bell. In no case are Mozart's notes made use of; it is the dramatic device rather than the musical content that Storace apes, and his object, of course, was to make his duets more interesting visually. Here is the start of the Letter Duet in *The Siege of Belgrade*; for complicated reasons the imprisoned Catherine is dictating a letter which the Seraskier is writing down.

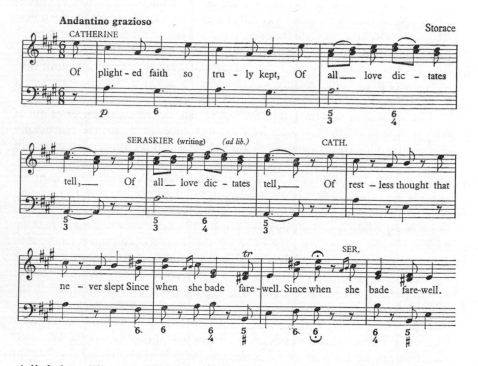

A little later Thomas Attwood, who had also seen *Figaro* in Vienna, borrowed Mozart's Letter Duet for his afterpiece opera, *Caernarvon Castle*.

A year or two after his return from Vienna Attwood had published some interesting piano trios that he had probably written under Mozart's tuition, and in one of them (op. 2, no. 2) he used a perky minuet theme that he took from Salieri. In *The Siege of Belgrade* the same music is turned into a song with which Lilla charms her moody lover out of his dumps, and on the first night it was twice encored. I have not traced its source. A 'March of Turkish Soldiers' is in the conventionally Turkish key of A minor, and the scoring must have included

Turkish cymbals, triangle, and bass drum. The over-simple and patriotic Finale to Act II leans too heavily on Boyce's 'Heart of Oak'.

In Act III Nancy Storace and Kelly both sang their longest and most difficult arias. For contrast, and to please the gallery, Useph (Suett) had a folksy tune that sounds like an amalgam of 'Dargazon' and 'Lilliburlero'. The main *Allegretto* section of the Finale was by Martini, and its delightful music has been hailed both as a very early example of the waltz and, more probably, as a Spanish jota.

That May Storace and Prince Hoare contrived an afterpiece opera for Mrs. Crouch's benefit called *The Cave of Trophonius* (DL 3.5.91). Salieri had composed an opera on the same story called *La Grotta di Trofonio*, and Loewenberg and others have jumped to the conclusion that Drury Lane's opera was a version of Vienna's. But the published song-words show that none of the music was by Salieri and that nearly all of it was by Storace; it does not survive. The opera failed because of its uninteresting plot for which Pausanias must take some of the blame.[1] Aristo has two daughters, the one quiet and the other vivacious, and they are loved respectively by a vivacious youth and a quiet one. Those who enter Trophonius's cave have their characters changed to the opposite. Against orders the two girls go in, and some tedious confusion results. The plot can be found in more detail in the *European Magazine* for May 1791. As Aristo's servant, Suett sang a wildly inappropriate song of his own invention about four girls who get tipped out of a coach; it ended:

> Whose legs are those, said I, with the shoes so fine?
> Oh lord, cried one below, if they're crooked they are mine.
> > Hey! hoity toity,
> > Up with 'em,
> > Hey!
> > Hoity, toity, hoh!

Though Hoare himself might not have sunk so low, he seldom showed either ambition or talent when writing his librettos. In his vigorous, candid autobiography Benjamin Haydon described him as

> a delicate, feeble-looking man, with a timid expression of face, and when he laughed heartily, he almost seemed to be crying. His father was a bad painter at Bath, who, having a high notion of Prince's genius, sent him with a valet to Italy, to get what nature had denied him in the Capella Sistina. He went through the whole routine of labouring for natural talents, by copying Michel Angelo, copying Raffaele, copying Titian— came home to be the rival of Reynolds, found his own talents for Art were of the feeblest order, and being well educated took refuge in writing farces and adaptations of Spanish and French pieces, which his friends Storace

[1] See *Spectators* 598-9.

and Kelly fitted with music. He was an amiable but disappointed man, the companion of the democrats Godwin and Holcroft.[1]

As we have seen, the Storaces had got to know him in Florence. He can have had no illusions about his librettos, and it must have irked him that they were so much more popular than his paintings.

In the summer of 1791 Drury Lane was pulled down. The building had been surveyed and judged unsafe; in any case Sheridan had long wanted a larger theatre. For the last night, a sentimental occasion, *The Country Wife* with Mrs. Jordan was chosen as the mainpiece; the afterpiece, the last dramatic work of any kind to be performed in Wren's much-loved theatre, was *No Song No Supper* by Prince Hoare and Stephen Storace.

4 THE DRURY LANE COMPANY IN EXILE

It will be remembered that in 1789 the King's Theatre, home of Italian Opera, was burnt to the ground. A new theatre had risen from the ashes, but could not be opened for its intended purpose on account of a legal wrangle.[2] However there was no objection to Sheridan's making use of it while his own theatre was being rebuilt, and in September 1791 the Drury Lane company moved in. This was the first time that the King's Theatre had been used for anything other than concerts, and public interest was considerable. Kelly declared that it was the best theatre for sound that he ever sang in, and on the first night he sang in *The Haunted Tower*. Some people complained that the ox-roasting scene lost much of its effect on the much larger stage, and there must have been some desperate problems for the scenery-makers; nothing from Old Drury can have fitted. But Sheridan and Kemble soon realized that what they lost in intimacy might be gained through elaborate spectacle, and in December they revived Garrick's *Cymon*. This had always relied on spectacle, but much more grandiose effects were now possible. The Duke of York lent his military band, which appeared on the stage clad in armour borrowed from Carlton House; the Duke himself attended rehearsals, and selected the marches that his band played. There was also a tournament with knights on horseback jousting and unseating one another, and at one point there were three horses on the stage at once. Foot-soldiers fought each other with lances and battle-axes, and 'a small female warrior' subdued a Highlander.[3]

The published song words show that nearly half the music was taken from the original score by Michael Arne. Storace contributed nine items, but none of the new music was published except that written by Thomas Shaw. His overture appeared in keyboard arrangement, and was advertised as available 'in Parts for

---

[1] Haydon's Autobiography, ch. 2
[2] See p. 523
[3] Also see Kelly ii, pp. 17–19, 2nd ed.

full Band', and two marches by Shaw and a song for Urganda (Mrs. Crouch) were published in full score. No one pretended that the success of this nonsense had anything to do with its music.

Because the theatre had been designed for Italian opera, it occurred to Storace to compose an English *opera seria*. His choice of a Metastasio libretto was unfortunate, but unless he aped the new French style there was still no other kind of serious opera he could have written. Ten months earlier Mozart had submitted to a Metastasio libretto for the same reason in *La clemenza di Tito*. Hoare translated *Didone abbandonata*,[1] and *Dido, Queen of Carthage* (KT 23.5.92) had five performances at the tail-end of the season. It was never revived. Critics reported well of the set pieces, but everyone found the recitatives very long and boring, and the evening was not saved by a grand Masque at the end which had no recitatives at all; in it Neptune prophesied a thriving future for Ascanius. The libretto was published, but not a note of the music survives.

The production was expensive. According to advertisements, the dresses of the Tyrians, Trojans, and Africans were 'entirely new and taken from the most accurate descriptions', and one critic thought that 'the destruction of the city of Carthage was well imagined and well executed'. At one point, according to the *Morning Herald*, 'an Ostrich, a Dromedary and an Elephant marched to slow music', but they can hardly have been real ones. At this period the Drury Lane company had a notable 'machinist' called Johnstone, who was famous for his 'wooden children to be toss'd over battlements, and straw heroines to be hurl'd down precipices:- he was, further, famous for wicker-work lions, paste-board swans, and all the sham birds and beasts appertaining to a theatrical menagerie'.[2] Johnstone is known to have demonstrated these skills in *Cymon* and *Lodoiska*, and no doubt the animals in *Dido* were his handiwork.

The opera suffered from the disadvantage of having Madam Mara as Dido. She was a stout German of forty-three, and an atrocious actress. According to Burney, who met her in Berlin, her teeth stuck out. He thought her a magnificent singer, and that of course is why she was engaged at Drury Lane (she also sang, for this theatre, Mandane in Arne's *Artaxerxes*), but her dreadful English must have been a contributory cause of the recitatives being disliked. Boaden says she was incapable of assuming majesty, and with her as Dido there can have been no hope of any dramatic tension. Mrs. Crouch was described as 'exceedingly happy as Aeneas', and an eleven-years-old protégé of Linley's was a success as Ascanius in the final Masque. His name was Thomas Walsh (it was often spelt Welsh or Welch), and he was the most remarkable boy soprano of the

---

[1] Sacchini's setting had been given at the King's Theatre in 1775; one of Dido's arias was borrowed by Storace.

[2] Colman i, p. 228. When a friend took Johnstone to see a real elephant on the Covent Garden stage and challenged him to make one as good, Johnstone replied, 'I should be very sorry if I could not make a better elephant than that.'

century. Storace wrote parts especially for him in several of his later operas, and in *The Cherokee* he was virtually the hero.

The Drury Lane company spent more than two seasons and a half in exile. The second of these (1792–3) began, like the first, at the King's Theatre, but ended in unhappy compromise. The Pantheon had been burnt down in January 1792, and the subsequent season of Italian Opera had again been given at the Little Theatre, where facilities were hopelessly inadequate. Because the situation was felt to be intolerable, the King withdrew his objection to Gallini's theatre being used for its intended purpose. At this period Italian opera seasons did not usually begin until January, and until January 1793 the Drury Lane company had the sole use of the King's Theatre. Thereafter the Italians were allotted it on Tuesdays and Saturdays, and on these days and these alone the Drury Lane company had to move over the road to the Little Theatre. The arrangement must have been costly both in man-hours and tempers, but there was no alternative, and to make it work as smoothly as possible Sheridan managed to arrange that Storace and Kelly should run the Italian opera season.

Because Storace would not be able to spend so much time with the Drury Lane company, Attwood was brought in as his assistant. The musical novelties that season consisted of three afterpieces by Attwood, and one full-length opera by Storace. *The Pirates* (KT 21.11.92) was his finest English opera, and the plot, though attributed to Cobb, must have been largely devised by Storace, as it is laid in and around Naples and shows many signs of local knowledge. All Greenwood's scenery was new, and according to Kelly it was painted 'from designs taken on the spot by Stephen Storace, at Naples'. The engraving of the Bay of Naples on the title-page of the vocal score is obviously the back-cloth for the opening scene, and it may well be based on one of Storace's drawings. The first night was something of a sensation; the critics complained only that the performance started at 5.45 and did not end till 10.15. Amongst the items encored were, astonishingly, the overture and Mrs. Crouch's allegedly Irish ballad in Act III, 'As wrapt in sleep I lay'.

Before the opera begins, Don Altador, in love with Donna Aurora (both are Spaniards), has had to fly from Spain when on the point of marrying her because of a duel. Since then, Aurora has come under the protection of Don Gaspero, a pirate operating in the Naples area who wants her to marry his nephew Guillermo. Act I begins with Altador landing at Naples and learning of Aurora's plight from her maid, Fabulina. His servant, Blazio, who combines impudence with a rather charming brand of cowardice, falls for Fabulina. (These parts were written for Bannister and Nancy Storace; the upper class lovers were played by Kelly and Mrs. Crouch.) Though tongue-tied in her presence, Blazio sings 'O the pretty, pretty creature' when Fabulina has gone.[1] The scene changes to the courtyard outside Gaspero's house; Aurora is inside. Gaspero, returning home

---

[1] Heavily arranged by H. Lane Wilson, the song became popular in late Victorian and Edwardian times.

unexpectedly, catches Altador trying to get in. Thinking he has chased him away he later goes, leaving an elderly pirate called Sotillo guarding the door with a blunderbuss. The long Finale begins with Fabulina singing Sotillo to sleep with his favourite song, a sailor's lullaby (still sometimes sung today) that begins 'Peaceful slumb'ring on the ocean'. Fabulina then plans Aurora's escape, and Sotillo is overpowered by Altador. Again Gaspero returns too soon, and when a fight develops he sends for the Guard. On the Guard's arrival everyone explains at once what has been happening in a long chattering fugue, and this music is a slightly cut version of the Act I Finale in *Gli equivoci*.

Act II starts with an excellent trio in which the girls plead with Gaspero for forgiveness; the vocal parts are well characterized. Pretending to relent, Gaspero offers to take the girls to the Fair, but in fact he is planning to lock them up in his pirate hide-out in a castle at Pausilippo. When Blazio arrives with a message from his master, Fabulina has to pretend not to know him, and she sings 'A saucy Knave'. In some surprisingly well-written dialogue Gaspero worms out of Blazio his master's plan for Aurora's rescue; Blazio foolishly lets out that Altador knows Gaspero to be a pirate. Then follows the Fair Scene, which has four consecutive dances. One of them is the first example I have found in English music of a waltz; it is in three-eight time. (Kelly reports that when he and Storace were in Vienna the city was just beginning to be waltz-mad.) During the bustle Altador snatches a few words with Aurora, but Gaspero soon hurries her away. The last scene of the act is on the sea-shore. Altador and Blazio have planned to rescue Aurora as she is being taken over the bay to Gaspero's castle, and as the Finale begins they leap out from their hiding-place and attack the pirates. But the pirates are prepared and overpower the two men who are taken off in a boat. Aurora is taken off in another, and we hear the sailors singing unaccompanied as the two boats recede into the distance. Fabulina is left on shore to join in a storm chorus that sounds like early Verdi.

Act III begins in a vineyard within sight of Gaspero's castle. Fidelia, a childhood friend of Aurora's (she appeared earlier disguised as a boy) plans to rescue Aurora. The King's men capture the pirate ship and rescue Altador and Blazio, who once again plan Aurora's rescue with Fabulina's help. In the great hall of the castle the unsuspecting Gaspero is told there is a troupe of Savoyards at the door who offer a magic lantern show about Hero and Leander. The audience has no difficulty in penetrating their disguise, but not Gaspero, who even allows Aurora to be present at the entertainment. The stage direction now reads:

Alt. places Lanthorn on table—lights it up—turns it towards the Flat— Two Servants enter O.P. and take candles away—Lamps sink—Stage dark —part of scene draws up and discovers a Circular Transparency.
ALT: And now attend.
A view of the Hellespont moves slowly P.S.
TRIO: O softly flow

When the lights come up, the hall is full of the King's sailors. The pirates are seized and all ends happily.

This is a good plot, full of incident, and the final *coup de théâtre* is striking. The magic lantern was not quite a novelty. The actor Baddeley had been giving humorous lectures with its aid at least as early as 1775,[1] but this may well have been its first use in a London theatre. The stage direction quoted above is not such as would have been published. In fact no libretto ever was published, for the then usual reason that Drury Lane hoped to prevent other theatres from staging the opera. However the British Museum has a MS libretto (Add. 25913) that appears to have been used by whoever was in charge of the lights. The dialogue, though often stilted, is far above Cobb's usual level, and the story suggests nineteenth-century opera rather than eighteenth.

The Pirates was England's first Escape Opera. The genre had just been established in Paris, where Kelly had seen an example, *Lodoiska*, in the summer of 1791; perhaps Storace and Cobb had been fired by his description of it. A great deal of money was spent on the production, and the opera was a notable success, but the number of performances it received was limited because it could not be staged when the Drury Lane company was at the Little Theatre; apart from scenery problems, the orchestral pit at the Little Theatre was not large enough for the full Mozartian orchestra that the score demanded.

Nearly all the music of *The Pirates* is of high quality. Kelly remembered that 'both the songs sung by me' came out of *Gli equivoci*, but he remembered wrong. His first two songs were from Storace's *Gli sposi malcontenti*,[2] and the third was new. Aurora's 'Love, like the opening flower' had a cello obbligato printed an octave up. The ensembles are outstandingly good, especially the first two Finales which are very long, full of action, and continuously interesting as music. Here is the start of the fugue in the Act I Finale; a very quick tempo is required.

[1] See advertisement in the *Morning Post* for 17.3.75.
[2] They are slightly cut; in 'Some device' the vocal score of *The Pirates* leaves out a good deal of the counterpoint.

In a more forward-looking style, here is part of the Finale to Act II. Modulating to allow a differently-placed voice to have the tune was to be a typical nineteenth-century device.

Later this theme is sung in close four-part imitation, and the orchestra contributes continuous triplet quavers to suggest the rising storm.

The part of Fidelia was dramatically superfluous, and it was fudged up to give Mrs. Bland something to sing. She had an unexpected song in Act II:

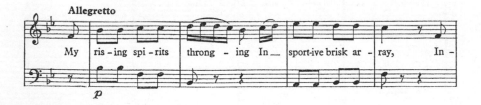

The resemblance to Papageno's 'Ein Mädchen' can hardly be coincidence, yet *Zauberflöte*, produced in Vienna just over a year before, had not been published long enough for Storace to borrow from it. In any case had he ever seen Mozart's music he would have written in Common Time and not made so many mistakes. It is virtually certain that he thought he was borrowing a French melody. In Paris the previous summer Kelly had heard the tune in the first act of *Les Visitandines* by Devienne. Either he sang it to Storace from memory or he brought back a melody-line copy. Devienne may also have relied on memory, for he cannot have seen Mozart's music in print either. His version is also in two-four time with many mistakes of detail. In the early advertisements *The Pirates* was said to include borrowed material by Anfossi, Bianchi and Guglielmi; Storace did not mention Devienne no doubt because he had had to harmonize the tune himself and compose all the episodes. But when later he saw a copy of *Zauberflöte* some quirk of conscience or friendship made him add Mozart's name to the composers on whom he had drawn.[1] These borrowings were advertised because they attracted Italian opera lovers, but in fact *The Pirates* contained fewer borrowings than any other of Storace's full-length English operas,[2] as also fewer strophic ballads. In scale and in degree of elaboration it resembles *Die Entführung aus dem Serail*.

Thomas Attwood showed his affection and admiration for Mozart by including one of his songs in nearly all the operas he wrote as a young man. During the 1792–3 season he composed the following afterpieces for Drury Lane:

The Prisoner (KT 18.10.92). Another Escape Opera; it gave Kelly a big aria about Liberty, as also a good sombre arioso in C minor with trumpets that distinguished dramatically between utter despair and mere melancholy. Sedgwick sang Figaro's 'Non più andrai' to the words 'Where the Banners of Glory are streaming'. Libretto by John Rose.

Osmyn and Daraxa (KT 7.3.93). Only five performances; unpublished except for the song-words which show two borrowings from Mozart, one of them a Fandango (no doubt the one in *Figaro*). Libretto by James Boaden.

---

[1] A playbill of 1796 with Mozart's name included can be seen in the Nag's Head near the stage door of Covent Garden Opera House.

[2] See Appendix E.

The Mariners (KT 10.5.93). Written for Sedgwick's benefit; he sang Sarastro's 'In diesen heil'gen Hallen', for which his voice was well suited. The music was published but not Samuel Birch's libretto. Shaw wrote the overture.

Figaro's famous song was published for the first time anywhere in *The Prisoner*, though only in vocal score; Attwood got it from the MS score that the Storaces had brought back. It must have caught on, for within weeks Longman & Broderip published it as 'The Duke of York's new march, as performed by His Royal Highness's new Band in the Coldstream Regt of Guards . . . arranged . . . by C. F. Eley'. Presumably Attwood had to orchestrate Sarastro's song, for it had been published only in vocal score.

In those months when the Drury Lane company was playing some nights each week in the Little Theatre and some in the much larger King's, it was common sense to have a different repertoire for each theatre. *No song No Supper* was ideal for the one, *The Pirates* for the other. The less scenery, clothes and props that had to be carried across the Haymarket, the better for everyone. Storace somehow found time to write music for *The Prize* (KT 11.3.93), an afterpiece intended for the smaller theatre but given a prestige first performance over the road for Nancy's benefit. It was immediately liked and quickly taken into the repertoire. Storace had not given himself much trouble, and the words are more interesting than the music. To save himself time he began cleverly with a short guitar solo (or perhaps with pizzicato strings imitating a guitar) and this was justified because the curtain rose on Juba, a black page, playing the guitar for his master Lenitive. Lenitive, a country apothecary, learns he has won a lottery and transforms himself into a beau the better to court Caroline. Later he discovers there has been a clerical error; he has won nothing.

The music is pretty, but what the audience enjoyed more was hearing Bannister continually fail to keep up his assumption of good breeding and slip into chemist's lingo. Juba was sung first by Mrs. Bland, and later by Master Walsh. Nancy Storace played Caroline and had most of the songs. At one point she disguised herself as her own French cousin the better to observe Lenitive, and this allowed Stephen to resurrect 'Beaux Yeux', the dramatic accompanied recitative he had written for the similarly-disguised heroine in *La cameriera astuta*. (The *Andante* section in the middle was new.)

It had been expected that Sheridan's vast new theatre would be finished by the summer of 1793, but work was far behind schedule. It was therefore agreed that Colman should rent Drury Lane's patent during the following winter season and keep the Little Theatre open until New Drury was ready. Kemble spent the autumn in Newcastle and Edinburgh, Mrs Siddons was also on tour, and Mrs Jordan refused to act because of pregnancy. As the weeks stretched into months, nearly forty small-part actors, chorus singers, and orchestral players had to be sacked because there was no room for them in the tiny theatre. New Drury did not open until the following March, and all this time large-scale operas had to be shelved, their place taken by simple afterpieces such as *Thomas and Sally*, *The Quaker*, *No Song No Supper*, and *The Prize*. Even Shield's *Rosina* was given a dozen performances.

Fortunately this lean period was enlivened by one of the most popular short operas of the decade, Arnold's *The Children in the Wood* (LT 1.10.93). Thomas Morton's libretto has much the same story as 'The Babes in the Wood', which was not then thought of as pantomime material. Jack Bannister's performance as Walter was considered the best of his career. By nature Walter is a coward, but he forces himself to resist the wicked Baron and save the Babes. Like all Bannister's varied repertoire of cowards, the part was a sympathetic one. The praise lavished on his acting was fulsome beyond belief. Even the cautious Baker went so far as to say that it 'perhaps exceeds every other effort of the modern drama'. Audiences were ripe for plots of this nature. The plight of the Babes (played by Miss and Master Menage) brought tears of pleasurable horror to every eye; Morton had precisely judged the degree of sentimentality to which people were prepared to react. He scored another bull's-eye in 1800 with a comedy called *Speed the Plough* in which the characters keep asking each other what the disapproving Mrs. Grundy would say.

Arnold's music could hardly hope to compete with Bannister's acting and the plight of the forlorn infants, but it is not without interest. The overture started a playhouse fashion for sombre D minor introductions, and though Arnold had been anticipated by Mozart's *Don Giovanni* overture and Kreutzer's *Lodoiska* he cannot have known either work. In the next two or three years at least six playhouse overtures started with a slow D minor slow introduction leading into a D major *Allegro*. Like Kreutzer Arnold began splendidly and then lapsed into nonsense. The second movement of his overture is appropriately based on 'O ponder well' from *The Beggar's Opera*, played first by two horns; the tune was often known as 'The Children in the Wood'.[1] The trumpet theme in the Finale recurs in the Finale of the opera.

Both children sang, Miss Menage a good deal more than her brother. One of her songs was printed in full score with a 'flagelet' imitating bird-song and three-part string accompaniment. Near the end of the opera there were two striking folk tunes. The children's father (Dignum) had a version of the lovely Scotch song 'Ay wakin oh', also known as 'Jess Macpharlane'; the charm of it lies in the unexpectedly short line at the end. Next Mrs. Bland, representing the children's governess, sang what Arnold called 'The Ditty':

Moderato

A Yeo-man of ⌐ no mean de - gree, For thirst of

---

[1] Chappell, p. 200.

Gain ___ and ___ lu - cre he A pret - ty babe did mur - der straight. By rea - son of its large Es - tate.

This is a version of the folk carol Vaughan Williams collected in Herefordshire, 'The Truth from above' (*Oxford Book of Carols*, no. 68). We may deplore the sharpened sevenths and the regular rhythms, but Arnold's version could easily be nearer the original than Vaughan Williams's. As we have noted before, there was some source of English folk-song to which Arnold had access, and it was certainly not a published source.

By March *The Children in the Wood* had been given fifty-five times; both in England and America it was played constantly for some forty years.

Almost as popular was *My Grandmother* (LT 16.12.93) by Storace and Hoare, though again the music was a subsidiary attraction. None of Storace's later afterpieces depend on their music as *The Doctor and the Apothecary* and *No Song No Supper* had done. They contain no action ensembles, and most of the songs are strophic ballads. *No Song* could not be performed without its music, but *My Grandmother* could. Indeed it was considered for presentation at Mansfield Park by the Bertram family, though Jane Austen mentions no musical facilities. *The Prize, My Grandmother*, and another Storace afterpiece to be mentioned later all succeeded, as did *The Children in the Wood*, mainly because of Jack Bannister's engaging performance in the chief role. Hoare's librettos were ahead of their day in that they read like Victorian curtain-raisers, and they gave Bannister every opportunity of charming and amusing an audience that in fact was on his side before he ever came in. He was much the most likable actor of his day.

In *My Grandmother* Bannister had a rival in Richard Suett, who had the part of his life; he was called Dicky Gossip ever after. The character was distantly derived from the Barber of Baghdad in *The Arabian Nights*, but broadened into the village barber, dentist, carpenter, and undertaker all in one.[1] The plot concerns Vapour (Bannister) who is travelling to the house of a friend called Medley when, in an inn, he falls in love with the miniature of a girl dressed in the style of long ago. Love makes him look so unkempt that he has to be spruced up by Dicky Gossip, who infuriates him with his slowness and interminable monologues. Medley has a daughter called Florella (Nancy Storace). The miniature at the inn shows her at a masquerade in her grandmother's clothes, and there is a life-size portrait of her similarly dressed in Medley's hall.

[1] There is a good portrait of Suett in this role in the Ashmolean Museum at Oxford.

Florella gets Gossip to make this portrait slide to and fro behind its frame. She then dresses up in the masquerade clothes and astonishes Vapour by sitting in the frame and making the 'picture' come to life. Originally there was also a sub-plot that allowed Sedgwick and Mrs. Bland to sing a song each and join in the simple ensembles, but later their parts were usually cut.

We shall see in the next section that Storace was grossly overworking himself at this period, and he can never have had as much time as he would have liked for his playhouse work. He began his overture with a new slow introduction, and then made do with a Polonaise from a ballet he had just written for the King's Theatre.[1] The songs are more substantial and interesting than those in *The Prize*, and Dicky Gossip's 'When I was a younker' is delightful. The next song, 'Say, how can words a passion feign?' was sung by Nancy in the picture frame; she may well have played the guitar accompaniment herself.

5 ITALIAN OPERA IN LONDON: PAISIELLO

After the King's Theatre was burnt down in June 1789, Gallini moved his company into Covent Garden, vacant during the summer recess, and in the last fortnight of the season he presented two additional performances of two operas, one of them Paisiello's *Il barbiere di Siviglia*. Nancy Storace again sang Rosina, but Kelly had gone to Ireland on a concert tour with Mrs. Crouch and was not available for Almaviva. Most of the theatre's music had been destroyed, and the score of *Il barbiere* had to be reconstructed from memory by Mazzinghi, who must have worked the clock round for several nights to get it done in time. The music of Cherubini's *Ifigenia in Aulide* seems to have been lost for good; this and *La cosa rara* had been the season's most successful operas. Indeed the latter was being adored all over western Europe, and it would have surprised those who saw it to learn that Mozart's comic operas would be much preferred by their descendants. Those who heard 'Crudel perchè' from *Figaro* sung in Gazzaniga's *La vendemmia* (KT 9.5.89) seem to have noticed no outstanding quality in the music.

In 1790 Gallini was forced to play in the Little Theatre, but managed to keep the better-known members of his company. Nancy Storace and Kelly sang at the end of the season when the Drury Lane repertoire was demanding less of their time, and earlier on Gallini had re-engaged the great castrato Marchesi. Unfortunately Pacchierotti was currently singing at the Pantheon in New Oxford Street, and Londoners preferred to hear his arias in the exquisite surroundings of Wyatt's rotunda to opera in London's most cramped and charmless theatre. For Gallini it was a season of anxiety and near-failure. Cramer continued to lead the band, but Gallini ousted Mazzinghi and brought in Giardini, who by now was old and rheumaticky and had difficulty in raising his arms sufficiently for violin-playing. A ballet compiled by another of the theatre's

[1] See p. 524.

violinists, Blake, had as many as thirty performances; it was called *La Bergère des Alpes*, and by this period almost anything Alpine had an emotional effect.[1] Throughout the 1790s the evening's entertainment almost always included a ballet as well as an opera.

In 1791 the Pantheon attempted opera for the first time, though the building was quite unsuited to dramatic performances. By now the King's Theatre had been rebuilt, and Haydn had been invited to London partly to compose for it; he spent his first months there working on his Orpheus opera, *L'anima del filosofo*. But O'Reilly, the manager of the Pantheon, disputed Gallini's right to open the King's Theatre for Italian Opera, and he was supported by George III. Gallini had the less effective patronage of the Prince of Wales. The result of this squabble was that the Drury Lane company moved into the new building, and Haydn's new opera was never produced.

O'Reilly made good use of his rather surprising monopoly. He brought over Paisiello as the season's composer, re-engaged Pacchierotti, and added Mara to the company. Cramer led the band, Shield had his last season among the violas, someone called Attwood played the trumpet (can this have been the composer?), and Mazzinghi was back at the harpsichord. Paisiello's *La molinara*[2] was much liked, especially the song 'Nel cor più' (which became widely known as 'Hope told a flattering tale'), and *La locanda*, specially composed for the Pantheon by Paisiello, had an immediate success. Also very popular was Guglielmi's *La bella pescatrice*, which had more performances in the 1790s than any other Italian opera—thirty-five in three seasons. But throughout this decade Paisiello was the most represented composer. It was usual at this period for comic operas to outnumber serious ones by about two to one.

There were to have been more Italian operas at the Pantheon in 1792, but on 14 January the building was gutted by fire and for the rest of the season O'Reilly's company had to share the Little Theatre with the Drury Lane company; it was thought best to present only comic operas. There was no longer any good reason for opposing Italian Opera at the King's Theatre, and in 1793 it was at last used for its intended purpose. The directors decided to dispense with Gallini, who by now was in his middle sixties, and in his place they engaged Storace and Kelly as joint managers. It was not immediately possible to assemble as impressive a group of singers as they would have liked, and they must have been appallingly handicapped by their continuing work with the Drury Lane company. Storace got rid of Mazzinghi, played the harpsichord himself, and tried to organize a more rigorous system of rehearsals. Mara was engaged for the serious operas (by Paisiello and Sarti), Nancy Storace for the comic ones (also by Paisiello and Sarti). Kelly himself sang frequently, and with both managers taking an active part in the performances the administration of the theatre must have suffered.

[1] See also p. 551.
[2] There is a MS full score in the British Museum, Eg. 2510/1.

When Sarti's *Fra due litiganti* was put on (under a new title, *Le nozze di Dorina*), Storace composed an additional aria for it; 'Io non era' was published in full score, and is suavely beautiful.

On the same night as the Sarti, Storace's only ballet received its first performance. *Venus and Adonis* (KT 26.2.93) had Mlle Hilligsburg as Venus, and Noverre as choreographer. 'The naïve, the natural Hilligsberg', wrote Boaden, 'had a lovely expression of innocent apprehension or pure festivity with a wild, elastic spring; danced entirely from her feelings.' One critic complained of the way Jupiter (James d'Egville, an English dancer) gave lecherous glances at every girl who went by; 'the Thunderer should preserve some dignity in his pleasure'. The music was published in keyboard arrangement, and consisted of a poor overture and twenty-five dances, some of them borrowed. The one in A major on page 23 was taken from Kreutzer's opera *Lodoiska*, which Kemble was translating for Drury Lane. It was from this ballet that Storace borrowed the Polonaise that forms the main part of the overture to *My Grandmother*. *Venus and Adonis* had thirteen performances, but other ballets that season had more, and it was never revived.

For the next season Storace and Kelly engaged the most entrancing operatic soprano of the day, Brigida Banti. She made her London début in the title role of a serious opera, *Semiramide* (KT 26.4.94), and her success was prodigious. She was, wrote Lord Mount-Edgcumbe, 'far the most delightful singer I ever heard', but, he added, 'an idle scholar'. She commanded an enormous salary, and remained at the King's Theatre for the rest of the century, not uninfluenced by the danger and difficulty of returning to Italy in time of war. The music of *Semiramide* was by Bianchi, one of two official composers to the King's Theatre this season. The other was 'Martini', whose new opera, *Il burbero di buon cuore* (KT 17.5.94) was not greatly liked. Both composers directed the first few performances of their operas from the harpsichord. Banti also sang in Paisiello's *La serva padrona*,[1] which was put on as an afterpiece in place of the usual ballet. The season had opened with Cimarosa's masterpiece, *Il matrimonio segreto*[2] (KT 11.1.94), and it ended with Noverre's last ballet for this theatre.[3]

Banti was not a woman to suffer gladly any colleagues with whom she felt at odds, and at a slightly later date she is known to have had Cramer replaced by Viotti as leader of the band. It is all too likely that she did not relish Storace's new-style rehearsal methods. Whatever the reason, he took no further part in the running of the King's Theatre from the summer of 1794 onwards. No doubt he was glad to be able to tackle one job properly—at Drury Lane—instead of trying to do two at once.

The two following seasons both began earlier than usual at the beginning of

[1] Written in 1781 when Paisiello was in St. Petersburg. He wrote his *Barbiere di Siviglia* in Russia the following year.

[2] BM Add. 31736/7 and 16003/4.

[3] He worked at Covent Garden in the following season; see p. 555.

December, and lasted to the end of the following July. They were remarkable for the production of no less than three non-Italian operas, and as Banti sang in all of them she must have had unusually catholic tastes. Much the most successful was Gluck's *Alceste* (KT 30.4.95). Kelly, who had recently been singing with Banti in revivals of *Semiramide*, was Admeto. He must have thought Gluck's music a major cause of the audience's enthusiasm, but when the same composer's *Ifigenia in Tauride* was staged in the following season (KT 7.4.96) there were only five performances. There had been several mutilated productions of *Orfeo*,[1] but these were the first Gluck masterpieces to be presented in this country in a form of which the composer would have approved. Banti also sang in the only Grétry opera to be staged in eighteenth-century London, *Zemira ed Azor* (KT 23.7.96).[2] It was revived the following season under its French title, *Zémire et Azor*, though it was still sung in an Italian translation. This perhaps was by Da Ponte, who had been doing desultory work at the King's Theatre since 1794. We shall see later that in this revival of Grétry's opera Banti was joined by a remarkable young English tenor named John Braham.

Banti's preference for Viotti over Cramer was by no means to her discredit. Though he was averse to giving solo performances, Viotti was the greatest teacher of his day and a composer who should be better known in ours. Brahms rightly admired the romantic undertones of his A minor Violin Concerto, which was probably written in London at this time. Supported by Banti's patronage, Viotti even joined Kelly as one of the manager's of the King's Theatre, but in the spring of 1798 he was suspected of sympathizing with the French and had to fly from the country.

6 STORACE AT NEW DRURY

The King's Theatre had taken twenty-one months to rebuild. Drury Lane took nearly three years,[3] and this dilatoriness was symptomatic of the way the building was to be run. The architect was Henry Holland, designer of the Brighton Pavilion in its original form, and the cost was £130,000. This was far more than had been expected, and the theatre started life in the state to which it later became accustomed—deep in debt. The enormous auditorium held 3,600 people, and when full, which it seldom was, it brought in some £800 a night. There were over a hundred boxes arranged in five tiers, and in the third and fourth tiers from the top they ran continuously all round the house. The colour scheme was blue and white, and *The Thespian Magazine* thought the effect 'astonishingly light and airy'. Because of what had happened to the King's Theatre and the Pantheon, a large water tank was placed in the roof, and a

---

[1] They are listed on p. 547–8.

[2] It has been given earlier at the King's Theatre in 1779; see p. 327.

[3] When Covent Garden was burnt down in 1808 a new theatre was put up and opened in just under a year.

metal-covered safety-curtain separated the stage from the front of the house. It was generally but incorrectly believed that the theatre was incombustible.

The Drury Lane company found their new home hard to love. Bannister's biographer, no doubt expressing Bannister's views, complained of the unnatural distances, with actors

> delivering ordinary comic dialogue in tones adapted to the harangue of a general addressing his army . . . It is monstrous to see a breakfast-table at an inn or private dwelling, in a room that looks like the vestibule of a temple; to see a cottage with the furniture and utensils so placed that high ladders would be required to reach them.

Furthermore scene-changing took much longer on the bigger stage,

> like the putting about of a large vessel heavily laden. The impressive alteration of countenance, the minute by-play, and, above all, the exquisite power of the eye, are now utterly lost; nothing remains but energetic declamation, boisterous mirth, and forced dumb-show.

The new theatre opened with Kemble and Mrs. Siddons in *Macbeth*, and their brother Charles made his first London appearance as Malcolm. Because of the unusual circumstances the season was prolonged, and Drury Lane did not close until July. *The Pirates* and *The Siege of Belgrade*, shelved while the company was at the Little Theatre, were brought back into the repertoire, and two new musical pieces were staged. The first of these was *Lodoiska*, of which Kelly had seen two versions in Paris. Cherubini's was first staged at the Théâtre Feydeau in the middle of July 1791, and Kreutzer's a fortnight later at the Comédie Italienne. The French Revolution was having a profound effect on opera in Paris. Audiences were becoming attuned to melodramatic excitement of a new kind, and the stories demanded a much more dramatic contribution from the orchestra. Méhul and Cherubini were the leading exponents of the new style, but in fact it was two non-French composers, Cherubini and Kreutzer, who established in *Lodoiska* a long line of 'Escape' operas that culminated in *Fidelio*. This was neither the first nor the last time that French opera was reshaped by foreigners. Kreutzer was notorious for losing at roulette such money as he earned from his music, and he later acquired immortality by having a violin sonata dedicated to him. Parisians preferred his *Lodoiska* to Cherubini's, and certainly his music at its best shows a forward-looking excitement, but to modern eyes Cherubini's looks to have more quality. Both versions, needless to say, have spoken dialogue in the usual French way.

Kelly brought back from Paris full scores of both *Lodoiskas*, as also a libretto, and Kemble did not hurry himself over the translation. Drury Lane's *Lodoiska* (9.6.94) achieved twenty performances in a month, and some seventy in three seasons. In London as in Paris it was the story rather than the music that got the opera talked about, and audiences were thrilled by Floreski, a new type of romantic hero who was to be repeated in countless operas. He is the prototype of Verdi's Manrico.

The action takes place in Poland. The wicked Baron Lovinski has imprisoned the lovely Lodoiska in his castle for his own fell purposes, and the brave Count Floreski in trying to rescue her is ensnared himself; all would be lost but for the warlike Tartars, natural enemies of the Poles, who storm the castle. Because of kindnesses received in Act I they spare Floreski and his bride. The stage direction at the climax anticipates the type of action that was to make Drury Lane melodramas famous a century and more later:

> Shouts, Drums, Trumpets, and Cannon. An engagement commences between the Polanders and the Tartars; the Tartars having stormed the castle, which they fire in various places, the battlements and towers fall in the midst of loud explosions. Lupauski and Lodoiska are discovered in a blazing tower; Floreski rushes through the flames, and rescues them. During this action Lovinski and Kera Khan meet hand to hand, and, after a desperate conflict, the Baron is killed. The Tartars are victorious. Loud shouts of victory.

On one occasion a stage hand prematurely removed one of the supports of the tower, precipitating Lodoiska in earnest; Floreski caught her as she fell, and carried her to the front of the stage in his arms. The applause was deafening, and ever afterwards Kelly and Mrs. Crouch repeated the 'catastrophe'.[1]

The vocal score that Storace put together gives no attributions, but in fact the overture and the other three purely orchestral items are Kreutzer's, as also the attractive song 'Adieu, my Floreski, for ever'. Only the Quintet and the Trio in Act I are by Cherubini, and both were considerably shortened. One item out of the remaining six solo songs and the quartet is apparently by Andreozzi; the rest must be by Storace. There is much less music than in either of the Paris operas, yet it can hardly have been the extent of the original scores that frightened Storace, for he had written as extensively himself in *The Pirates*. One must presume that he found the music of Kreutzer and Cherubini rather dull. Unfortunately he did not replace it with anything better, and it was absurd to allow Master Walsh, representing the Baron's page, the most difficult coloratura aria in the opera.

In the early part of 1794 the French War had been going badly, with France retaking the Netherlands and leaving Britain no allies within easy reach. But on 1 June off Ushant Admiral Howe defeated the French fleet, and as soon as the news reached London Sheridan determined on staging a grand patriotic 'musical entertainment' to celebrate the victory. *The Glorious First of June* (DL 2.7.94) was contrived, incredibly, in a mere three days. Sheridan roughed out a scenario (given in Moore's Life of him), and engaged Cobb to write the libretto and

---

[1] There are amusing differences between Mrs. Crouch's account of this event and Kelly's in their respective Memoirs.

Storace to provide the music. His scenario demanded a sea-fight between model ships, the very thing he had ridiculed in *The Critic*. The stage-hands told him it was impossible in the time available to construct two mobile fleets capable of firing at each other; Sheridan said they must, and they did. The vocal score shows the fleets in action on the title-page. Unlike the music, the words were never published, and this is not wholly surprising for they were the work of many pens, and alterations were still being made after the first performance. Indeed, if Bannister's biographer is to be believed, the closing dialogue was still being written after the curtain had risen on the first act. Lyrics were contributed by the Duke of Leeds, Lord Mulgrave, Mrs. Robinson ('Perdita'), and Joseph Richardson. Cobb cannot much have relished the task of linking them with dialogue, for the scenario was very dull, and he must have liked it even less when someone, probably Storace, suggested reshaping the story to make it a sequel to *No Song No Supper*; the libretto of *No Song* was by his rival, Prince Hoare. But the idea breathed some life into the project. Robin and his wife Margaretta were dragged in, the hero's name was changed to William, and Suett repeated his always popular role of Endless, the lawyer. These last-minute alterations explain why Kelly in his Memoirs claimed to have been Frederick, the hero in *No Song*, though the vocal score called him Splic'em and *The European Magazine* Bowling.

The gist of the plot was something as follows. William and Robin enlist on the spur of the moment in Lord Howe's fleet. Before he goes, Robin leaves a purse with William's fiancée, Susan, to give to Margaretta (Nancy Storace), but the latter has secretly followed him to Susan's cottage, and suspects the worst. 'Never, never, when you've won us, can we trust in faithless men', she sings, to the music of the Mengozzi aria Nancy had sung in Paisiello's *Gli Schiavi*.[1] However, suspicions are allayed, the lovers part, the sea-fight is won,[2] and all are reunited in a grand celebratory fête organized by Endless. A great many fireworks were let off, and the entertainment ended with everyone on both sides of the footlights singing 'Rule, Britannia'.

The music is rather better than might be expected, though nothing can be said in favour of the one-movement overture; it can only have had point if, as is possible, it was based on some sea-song I have not identified. Kelly wrote of the entertainment 'Storace and myself gave it some new songs; but the music was chiefly old'. Even when it was old Storace may have had to orchestrate it; for instance the glee by Joseph Baildon that was used for the first vocal item was originally unaccompanied. Storace must also have scored any contribution by Kelly, whose composing was usually limited to humming a tune for someone else to write down. There seems no way of telling who wrote what, except that 'When 'tis night and the mid-watch is come' has music that Linley composed

---

[1] It is the one Shield borrowed for *The Farmer*.

[2] 'The spectators coughed and enjoyed the powder' (Boaden's *Mrs. Jordan* i, p. 266).

about 1780 for a revival of the pantomime *Fortunatus* and words that Sheridan dashed off on the same distant occasion. The following song, sung by Miss Leake as Susan, is surely by Storace, for it is very similar in style and rhythm to 'With lowly suit' in *No Song*. 'When in war on the ocean' was taken from a twenty-years-old Anacreontic song, but so inaccurately that someone must have relied on a very hazy memory. *The Glorious First of June* was a sensation. It took well over a thousand pounds the first night, and though there could not be much repetition of so ephemeral a piece, it raised a considerable sum of money for the widows and children of those who had been killed in the battle.

Storace spent the summer of 1794 writing a new full-length opera for the new theatre, and he took more trouble over it than over anything he had written since *The Pirates*. He had learnt his lesson from *Dido*, and realized that from now on new operas must be new in spirit and subject-matter if they were to succeed. *The Cherokees* (DL 20.12.94), the first English opera on a 'Western' theme,[1] promised well. Of all Red Indian tribes the Cherokees were much the best-known in Britain, for parties of them had been brought to London in 1762 and again twenty years later. They are mentioned in the dialogue of *Love in a Village*, and more than one publisher had a Cherokee love-song or funeral dirge in his catalogue. It is a pity that Cobb never met any of these visitors. He had no idea how they behaved or spoke, and though he need not be blamed for making them the villains—conventionally Red Indians were to be villains for many years to come—there was no good reason for his giving them such stilted dialogue. Malooko, the Cherokee chief, keeps making such remarks as 'Lovely enchantress, if thou would'st pity move, show by thy feelings what thou would'st inspire', and 'My lips are locked by policy's insidious bands'. Furthermore Cobb devised a plot that almost defies comprehension.

Colonel Blandford (Kelly) is in charge of an expedition sent to suppress a squabble between two groups of Cherokees whose leaders think they are rivals for the hand of the mysterious Zelipha (Mrs. Crouch). In fact Zelipha is an Englishwoman living very quietly under an assumed name with her small son Henry (Master Walsh) and her Welsh maid Winifred (Mrs. Bland). There is a sub-plot about Jack Average (Bannister) who has come to America to meet his cousin Eleanor (Nancy Storace) to whom he is espoused; their servants Jeremy and Fanny (Suett and Miss Leake) are soon courting too. The action develops when Malooko kidnaps Henry hoping thereby to lure his mother to the Cherokee camp. The ruse succeeds, but a pro-British Cherokee rescues the boy and brings him to Eleanor. When a council of peace is called, Malooko is furious at seeing the boy with Eleanor and breaks off the parley. The splendidly original Finale starts with a trio of 'whites' (p. 22), and later Malooko calls for vengeance, speaking dramatically over a stormy orchestral passage in C minor; the act ends with a spirited Indian chorus, 'Revenge, revenge, we ask no more'.

[1] J. C. F. Bach, one of Johann Sebastian's sons, had written *Die Amerikanerin* in 1776.

In Act II it is revealed that Zelipha is really Colonel Blandford's wife; a lawsuit has kept them apart for years. They are reunited. But in the Finale they are both captured by the Indians. Meanwhile Jack Average is being truculent and contrary, refusing to marry Eleanor because his father wants him to. But in the last act his father changes his ground and tries to persuade Jack to sign away his rights in Eleanor; this makes him love her in earnest, especially as little Henry is eager to bring them together. Henry persuades Jeremy and another soldier (old Charles Bannister) to come with him by a secret path to the cave where he thinks his mother is held prisoner. Outside the cave Henry shoots an Indian who is about to shoot Colonel Blandford. Blandford stabs Malooko, and all are rescued and reunited.

As so often, Jack Bannister had the only part with any dramatic interest; all the others are sticks. But much of the music is splendid. Storace borrowed the one-movement overture from his own *Gli sposi malcontenti*, adding the now obligatory slow introduction in D minor. He did not attempt local colour, but the Indian chorus is full of vigorous and almost Handelian counterpoint, and unlike anything else in English opera of the period. The C minor orchestral introduction over which Malooko calls for vengeance even has a foretaste of Beethoven:

Act II also ends with a good Finale in several sections. Mozart's influence is most apparent in the arias modelled on 'Dove sono' in which an *Andante* leads into an *Allegro*. There are three of these two-movement arias in the last act alone.

The most popular song was Mrs. Bland's 'A Shepherd once had lost his love'.

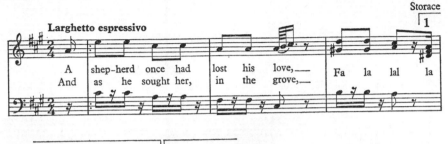

There is nothing in the score to suggest that this charming song was not by Storace, but it was later published on its own as 'the favourite Welch air'. Dussek and Field chose the theme for piano variations, and George Thomson sent it to Beethoven, whose arrangement of it can be found in his volume of Welsh Songs (WoO 155/3). Thomson did not send Storace's bass, which in fact is much more interesting than Beethoven's. When in 1818 he asked Beethoven to write piano variations with an optional flute or violin part on any airs he especially liked, Beethoven chose Mrs. Bland's song among others. The result was published as op. 105, no. 1, and the Finale of the set consists of a fugato on the first two bars put into G minor. Beethoven described the tune rather inaccurately as 'The Shepherdess' and wholly inaccurately as Scottish. It may not be Welsh either. It does not occur in the collections of Welsh tunes by John Parry or Edward Jones, and there were no other published sources. The tune does not sound in the least Welsh. It will be remembered that Mrs. Bland was portraying a Welsh maid. I suggest that Storace himself composed the song, and that it became known as 'the Welch air' merely because Mrs. Bland sang it with a Welsh accent. It is sweetly pretty, but Blandford showed astonishing restraint in sitting it out while waiting to be reunited with a wife he had not seen for years.

Like nearly all Storace's operas, *The Cherokee* was tailor-made to fit the Drury Lane company, and this in fact proved its undoing. Because Master Walsh was thought to have considerable drawing-power, the plot had been devised round a boy-hero. But when this remarkable boy-hero's voice broke, the opera could no longer be given. It received eighteen performances that first season and one more the next, but it then had to wait until 1802 when Mrs. Billington revived it in truncated form as an afterpiece called *Algonah*. It thus happens that *The Cherokee* was much the least performed of Storace's full-length English operas, and this in turn has resulted in vocal scores being a great rarity today.

So much admiration was lavished on Master Walsh at this period that he was even granted a benefit, and he commissioned for the occasion an afterpiece by Attwood called *The Adopted Child* (DL 1.5.95). Attwood, it will be remembered, had been cold-shouldered by Drury Lane since the failure of his early afterpiece operas, but the theatre had no control over what was given on benefit nights. The libretto of *The Adopted Child* was by Samuel Birch, later a Lord Mayor of London, and concerns a boy left in charge of a ferryman and his wife. The boy has a mysterious trunk that may not be opened until after the death of Sir Edmond of Milford Castle. In fact the trunk contains evidence that the boy is really heir to the domains of Milford. The ferryman averts a plot to kidnap him, and has his title recognized. Such a story would have been inconceivable twenty years earlier in Arne's day, or ten years earlier for that matter. In England as elsewhere opera plots were changing out of recognition.

Though advertisements mention music by Mozart, there is no such music in the vocal score, but a big two-section aria for Miss Leake, 'In Seclusion's sacred Bower', is decidedly Mozartian in style. Most of the songs are strophic and of no more than mild interest, but Sedgwick was given a remarkable aria, 'Down the rugged Mountain's steep', with the orchestra imitating first the waters 'leaping and rushing' and then 'the Derwent's gentler course'. Since the setting is described as 'A remote Part in the North' it seems likely that Samuel Birch had in mind Borrowdale in the Lake District.[1]

Five days after *The Adopted Child* the hard-worked Drury Lane company somehow managed to put on a new full-length opera by Hook, *Jack of Newbury* (DL 6.5.95). The libretto, by Hook's son James (who later did well in the Church), was never published; it is said to have been wholly without interest. The first chorus began:

> Hail, Commerce, Britain's glory, hail!
> To Industry thy sons invite.

Miss Leake had a coloratura song that took her up to high D, and the opera ended with a masque in honour of the nuptials of the Prince and Princess of Wales—a marriage which turned out to be as unsuccessful as Hook's opera.

That summer Storace composed *The Three and the Deuce* (LT 2.9.95). As *The Prize* and *My Grandmother* were also being given there, Storace and Hoare

---

[1] This part of England was just beginning to attract tourists. An anonymous full-length opera libretto called *The Lakers*, published in 1798 and in fact by the Rev. James Plumtre, seems never to have been set or produced.

had three afterpieces running at the same time. Most of the action takes place on the landing of a Cheltenham inn, with three bedroom doors visible. The bedrooms are occupied by triplets, three brothers identical in appearance and each unaware that the others are in the vicinity. Bannister played all three, shooting in at one door as the Frenchified fop Peregrine and out of another as the simpleton Percival, and changing his mannerisms with each change of name. As the *European Magazine* put it, 'he got complete possession of the audience, to the utter extinction of all interest in the progress of the drama and of all attention to the other characters'. The latter included three men-servants in a permanent state of confusion and Phoebe (Miss Leake), who finds herself loved and scorned alternately and inexplicably.

The one-movement overture, the best in Storace's later afterpieces, is frothy and clever, with some interesting modulations. The main theme, taken from a piano sonatina he had published five years earlier, reappears in the finale. Other English composers sometimes linked the first and last items in their score, but this is the only example of Storace doing so. All the songs are musicianly and charming, tiny though some of them are. Miss Leake has the more lyrical ones; also an agreeable duet with Suett, representing Justice Touchit. Johnstone as one of the three servants sang an exuberant patter song in the Irish style, and Mrs. Bland as Taffline repeated with success the Welsh maid she had first revealed in *The Cherokee*. *Three and the Deuce* has a better score than *My Grandmother*, and a much better score than *The Prize*, though it was never quite as popular. It would make delightful entertainment today.

That autumn Storace was in Bath, where he heard the début of a young tenor named John Braham. Like Nancy Storace, Braham was a pupil of Rauzzini, and no doubt Rauzzini had arranged this 'audition'. Stephen reported back to Kemble that Braham's voice was of exceptional quality, and that he would like him for his next full-length opera, *Mahmoud*; Prince Hoare was already at work on the libretto. But Kemble was anxious for Storace to turn his energies in another direction. During the years of exile Kemble had become friendly with the younger Colman at the Little Theatre, and had even played the lead in Colman's semi-operatic *The Mountaineers*. He invited Colman to submit a semi-opera for production at the new Drury Lane, and Colman based his contribution on Godwin's novel, *Caleb Williams*. The result was at first a notorious failure. The libretto arrived in dribs and drabs, and Kemble's enthusiasm waned as Colman's procrastination increased. Rehearsals were scrappy because no one was able to get a picture of the whole, and Storace could not complete and rehearse the music with enough care because half the lyrics had not arrived. He became ill worrying about it. The production should have been postponed, but Kemble was curiously obstinate about accepting this solution, even though he had not yet learnt his words. On the first night of *The Iron Chest* (DL 12.3.96) he walked through his part in a daze, fluffing half his lines. The audience became increasingly restive at the obvious lack of preparation, and took especial exception to Dodd's playing of a boring old manservant called Adam Winterton. His speeches are larded with such supposed Shakespeareanisms as 'Why, what! why, Wilford! alas! what, Wilford, I say', and 'Out on thee! thou has sunk my spirits into my heels. Who calls merry old Adam Winterton?' Nobody in the audience was in any mood to call him, or indeed to put up with Kemble's casual indifference. There was such a clamour that he came before the curtain and attempted an apology. Afterwards he said he had taken too much opium and felt ill.

Storace was a great deal iller. Against all advice, he attended rehearsals wrapped in blankets and carried in a sedan chair, but he never quite finished the music. Kelly improbably claimed to have composed all but the first twelve bars of 'When the robber his victim has noted', but wrongly remembered it as occurring in *Mahmoud*. Two days after the disastrous first night, the *True Briton* reported 'Poor Storace is so ill with gout and fever that it is hardly supposed he will recover. He is principally attacked in the head, and it is said that on Saturday (the first night of *The Iron Chest*) his disorder was so violent as to deprive him wholly of sight.' Kelly says he died of gout which crept to his stomach. Gout in the stomach is not now recognized as a disease, but it was thought to be a common cause of death right up to Victorian times.[1] Storace was only thirty-three. His absence at the final rehearsals must have resulted in dreadful singing and playing. Nancy refused to take part in *The Iron Chest* any more. After three despondent and much-cut repeats, Drury Lane wrote the work off as a failure.

Colman was not beaten so easily. That summer he put on *The Iron Chest* at his own theatre, and everyone who could went to see it. Mrs. Bland took over Nancy's part, Fawcett made Adam Winterton tolerable, and the leading role, Sir Edward Mortimer, was played by an unknown actor named Elliston. His triumphant success in a part that had defeated Kemble made him for life. By now rampantly aggressive, Colman published the play, adding one of the most scurrilous prefaces in the language. He attacked Kemble at length in splendid passionate prose, far more readable than anything in the play itself, accusing him of incompetence, of not attempting to learn his lines, and of wanting the play to fail out of sheer malice. A few years later this first edition had become a collector's item, selling at twenty times its original cost; the attraction was the preface, omitted in all later editions. *The Iron Chest*, with more and more of the music cut, was popular for many years, the last known production being Irving's at the Lyceum in 1879. Like Kemble, Irving embarked on it with enthusiasm and then lost interest. Sir Edward was not among his successes.

Godwin complained to Samuel Rogers that no one sent him a ticket for the first night, but he would not much have enjoyed what Colman made of *Caleb Williams*. The novel had been written to illustrate one of the main contentions

---

[1] Among those said to have died of it were Boyce, Robert Owenson, and a minor political character in Trollope's *Phineas Finn* of 1869.

in *Political Justice*, namely that justice was not the same for the poor as for the rich. Caleb, an upright young man of humble origin, becomes secretary to a rich but gloomy land-owner, Mr. Falkland, whom he admires in spite of all that happens. Falkland's old steward tells Caleb that Falkland had been cheerful enough when younger, but his life had been blighted by a feud with an insanely jealous neighbouring squire, Barnabas Tyrrel. Falkland had wanted to marry Tyrrel's ward, Emily Melville, but to prevent this Tyrrel tried to make the girl marry an oaf called Grimes; when she refused he hounded her to her death. After an assembly attended by both squires, Tyrrel was found dead in the road outside. Blame was put on an ex-tenant, Hawkins, who had been turned out of his cottage by Tyrrel and therefore had a motive. Falkland, though generally thought to be guilty, was examined superficially and let off. Hawkins and his son, though known to have been thirty miles away at the time, were tried and executed. These events had turned Falkland into a gloomy recluse.

Caleb cannot help probing his idol's secret, and in a rash but almost affectionate moment Falkland admits that he killed Tyrrel. He then tells Caleb that because he knows too much he must never leave him. Terrified, Caleb runs away but soon returns. Jewellery from Falkland's iron chest is planted in his luggage, he is accused of stealing it, imprisoned for months, but not tried. Eventually he escapes and lives in the woods with a gang of robbers. Falkland engages one of the robbers, Gines, to pursue Caleb relentlessly all over England, never letting him settle to any job. When at last they meet again, Falkland is gaunt, mad, and dying. In the iron chest is the true account of his crime.

Caleb Williams is powerful and readable, and the love-hate relationship between the two leading characters has a stark originality. But one could not so easily admit to liking it in 1796 as when it came out two years before. The climate of opinion was changing rapidly as a result of the Reign of Terror in Paris and the subsequent wars, and changing against Godwin's leftist theories. Colman surely began his adaptation because he admired the book, but lost his enthusiasm when he realized he would have to suppress its message. Kemble no doubt suffered a similar change of heart. Hence Colman's procrastination and Kemble's careless indifference. Years later Colman wrote, with understandable prudence: 'I had nothing to do with the political tendency in the book; which is thought by many to inculcate levelling principles, and disrespect for the Laws of our Country.'[1]

Presumably as a safety precaution Colman set the plot back in the reign of Charles I and changed all the names. The guilty landowner became Sir Edward Mortimer, his secretary Wilford, the robber-informant Orson. The girl in love with Sir Edward was kept alive and called Helen. For mainly musical reasons Colman invented a family of amiable poachers living on Sir Edward's estate; Rawbold has a daughter called Barbara who is in love with Wilford, a zany son called Samson, and two small children one of whom, needless to say, was played

[1] Colman the younger ii, p. 183.

by Master Walsh. Bannister and Nancy Storace were Wilford and Barbara. Sir Edward and Helen were non-singing roles for Kemble and Miss Farren. Kelly was the well-meaning robber, Armstrong, and Suett sang the poacher's zany son, Samson. A robber chorus was supported by Dignum, Sedgwick, old Bannister, and Miss De Camp. There is no Tyrrel, no prison scene, and no trial, though old Adam mentions that Sir Edward was once tried for murdering Helen's uncle.

The first scene shows Rawbold's cottage in the New Forest (Godwin had been less specific). It is revealed that Sir Edward up at the big house nurses a terrible secret, and in the next scene he confesses to Wilford that he once murdered someone. In a compound of terror, curiosity, and affection, Wilford searches the iron chest for evidence and is caught. Escaping, he makes for the poacher's cottage where his Barbara lives, but is captured on the way by the robbers. Orson sells him to Sir Edward, who plants jewellery in his luggage and accuses him of theft. Because he has sworn never to reveal the secret, Wilford keeps silent, earning Sir Edward's affection. But Sir Edward's half-brother Fitzharding, the Good Fairy of the story, discovers the incriminating account of the murder. Sir Edward has a stroke, Helen has four lines of tragedy-queenery, and Wilford gets his Barbara.

The plot is not so powerful as that of the novel, and the characters are not so absorbingly obsessive. Much of the dialogue consists of such fustian as 'My bosom is unclogged with crime' (for 'I am innocent'). Yet there are the makings of high drama, and the events are interesting. Furthermore most of the music is first-rate. For once Storace wrote a completely new overture, the best he ever achieved. The first movement, a slow introduction leading to an *Allegro*, is entirely in D minor, and admirably portrays the titanic gloom of the principal character. It prepares the audience for what follows in a way we associate with the nineteenth century rather than the eighteenth.

The second movement, an *Andante* in free variation form, is pleasant but superfluous. The Quintet at the end of the first scene is another forward-looking piece, in which Storace differentiated musically between Wilford and Barbara singing loving farewells, the poacher's small children screaming for their supper, and Samson trying to shush them; he even made some attempt to combine these disparate themes. As a Finale to Act I he wrote a charming duet for Wilford and Barbara in which he drew heavily on 'Se vuol ballare' in *Figaro*:

Kelly's only song, 'When the robber his victim has noted', is Mozartian in form rather than melody; the two sections, rather slow and rather fast, are both good of their kind. Near the end of Act II there is a long and very imaginative ensemble for the robbers, 'Listen, it is the owl that hoots upon the mouldering tower'; the actual Finale, as in Act III, is short and uninteresting. But Act III also contains a curiously attractive duet for Barbara and her brother Samson which combines quiet lyricism and buffoonery in a most unusual way, and later, when she thinks her Wilford gone for ever, Barbara has a most touching ballad as she contemplates suicide:

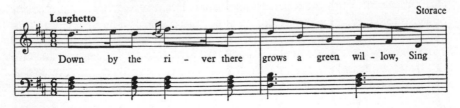

O!   for   my   true   love,   my   true____ love   O!

The melody is very long and very well organized. Colman had Ophelia in mind:

> Make me a Grave, all while the wind's blowing
> Close to the stream, where my tears once were flowing;
> And over my corse keep the green willow growing,
>   'Tis all for my true love, my true love, O!

As we shall see in the next chapter, Colman had recently had a big success with a would-be Shakespearean style of writing in *The Mountaineers*, and this too had been a semi-opera. In *The Iron Chest* he again chose blank verse for the upper-class characters and prose for the others, and he may well have set the story back in Stuart times partly because a modern plot would not have suited the kind of blank verse he wanted to write. It was also the kind of blank verse Kemble wanted to spout. Neither *The Mountaineers* nor *The Iron Chest* is a true opera in that the leading character never sings and the solo aria is not emphasized. The only full-scale aria in the latter, Kelly's 'When the robber his victim has noted', was cut after the Drury Lane performances; the words do not occur in later editions of the libretto. The only other solo songs are in ballad style. On the other hand there is a striking emphasis on the ensemble. There are seven examples, most of them long and fascinating. There is no pigeon-hole for this particular proportion of speech and singing.

Like Allan Ramsay, Charles Wesley, and George Stubbs, Storace was buried in the tiny church at the top of Marylebone High Street, within yards of where his mother had sold her 'rich seed and plum cakes'. The church was demolished in 1949 and Storace's memorial was moved to the near-by parish church where the Brownings were married; it is just outside the door of the gallery. The memorial is incorrect both as to the date of his death (19 March, not 16) and his age (33, not 34). Storace left nearly £5,000 and a solid rather Moorish-looking house at Hayes; it was used for council offices until about 1960 when it was pulled down. Everyone at Drury Lane felt sorry for his widow and son, and on their behalf Nancy Storace and Kelly contrived enough music to stage *Mahmoud* (DL 30.4.96). With great generosity Prince Hoare gave all his share of the proceeds to Mary, on whose behalf the music was published by subscription, together with that of *The Iron Chest*, at the high price of 25s. The keyboard arrangements were made by Mazzinghi. The picture of Storace on the joint title-page seems to have been drawn from memory after his death. Subscribers included most of the Drury Lane singers; also Braham, Colman, Hoare,

Sheridan, and Shield. Notable absentees were Attwood, Burney, and Mrs. Bland. According to the author of *Nollekens and his Times*, John Hall never got over the sudden loss of his son-in-law, and he himself died a year later.

George Hogarth thought *Mahmoud* the finest of Storace's operas, but in fact, of the full-length examples, it is much the least interesting. Perhaps only Braham's songs were new, and they are all good; most of the score was hurriedly assembled from unsuitable sources. The long three-movement overture is well below Storace's usual level and was probably written in youth. About half the music in Act II and III, including most of the very long Act II Finale, was pillaged from *Gli sposi malcontenti*. Some of the remainder may have been taken from *Dido, Queen of Carthage*. With little time at their disposal, Kelly and Nancy Storace must have chosen so far as possible arias they already knew. Advertisements mention borrowings from Paisiello, Sarti, and Haydn; one item came from Haydn's *Orlando Paladino* of 1782.

Hoare's libretto was never published. He took his plot from *The Arabian Nights*, and it is given in the *True Briton* for 2 May 1796. The title role, a speaking part, was played by Kemble; Braham was his younger brother, Noureddin.

Kelly does not seem to have sung at the King's Theatre after the summer of 1796, and he must have wondered if his days as a Drury Lane tenor were nearly over, for Braham's voice was far superior. However he was temporarily reprieved in unexpected circumstances. Nancy Storace, after mothering Braham through his first big roles, fell in love with him; he was the younger of the two by nine years. At much the same time, with Stephen dead and gone, she took an aversion against Drury Lane. In the following season she and Braham were both at the King's Theatre. Braham sang with Banti in Gretry's *Zémire et Azor* and in a very popular opera called *Evelina*,[1] while Nancy appeared in Paisiello's ever popular *Gli schiavi* and in an opera by 'Martini' that was new to London, *L'arbore di Diana*. In the summer of 1797 they left England for a prolonged tour of Italy and Germany, where they were welcomed with enthusiasm. There was no one at Drury Lane who could take their place, and several Storace operas, *Mahmoud* for one, could no longer be given. In addition Mrs. Crouch was fast losing her voice. Operatic standards fell suddenly and lamentably, not least because the theatre no longer had a competent music director. Kelly found himself having to fill a gap for which he was quite the wrong shape.

[1] Adapted by Federici and Da Ponte from Sacchini's French opera, *Arvire et Evelina*. There is a MS full score in the British Museum, Add. 16117; also of *L'arbore di Diana* (Add. 16046/7).

15

Decline
1788–1800

1 SHIELD AT COVENT GARDEN, 1788–1791

IN the middle eighties Shield had been consistently successful, but he found success much harder to come by once Drury Lane had raised its musical standards. Also he made the mistake of looking backwards instead of forwards. *The Highland Reel* (CG. 6.11.88) was little more than an old-fashioned ballad opera, and though its Scottish airs were well liked, nobody felt that Shield deserved much of the credit. O'Keeffe set the action in Coll and Raasay, and admitted to being influenced by the much-publicized Hebridean Tour of Dr. Johnson and Boswell. He also says that he chose for this opera 'two or three' Grétry airs that his son had sent him from Paris, but I cannot trace them. There is an unusual Handel borrowing: 'For soldiers the feast prepare' comes from a march in *Judas Macabbaeus*. The slow movement of the overture is based on 'Roslin Castle', and the Finale is an artless 'Scotch Medley'.

A few weeks later Shield assembled a pastiche called *The Prophet* (CG 13.12.88), but in spite of some difficult and showy arias for Mrs. Billington by Sacchini, Salieri, Cimarosa, and others, it failed, and no libretto was published. 'Fear no danger' from Purcell's *Dido and Aeneas* was sung as a three-part glee, and can have done nothing to give the score a unity of style. As the pantomime *Aladdin* (CG 26.12.88) also had little success, Shield had cause for despondency, and in 1789 he did no more than cut *The Prophet* to an afterpiece. That failed too.

The British Sailor (CG 22.5.89) was a curiosity. It was staged for the benefit of a Mr. Bernard who had probably written the libretto, but the vocal score had been in print for several years, for this short opera had already been produced at Bath (18.4.86). The music was by William Boyton, of whom little is known; he had published his Second Harpsichord Concerto some ten years before. The sailor hero had an aria more notable for difficulty than interest, but the overture looks competent. Incledon, then unknown, was in the Bath production as was one William Wordsworth who sang the hero's role.

Shield reached his nadir with the failure of *The Czar* (CG 8.3.90). He had composed quite half this full-length opera himself, yet the music was not thought worth publishing. O'Keeffe chose the story of Peter the Great working in a Deptford shipyard, the same story that Lortzing later set in his *Czar und Zimmerman*. Always interested in folk music and local colour, Shield acquired some Russian folk tunes, and his MS source survives in the British Museum (Add. 34007). The MS seems to be in Clementi's hand, for it includes sketches of Clementi's two-piano sonatas. Shield and Clementi often met for musical evenings at Holcroft's house, and no doubt elsewhere. Most of the Russian tunes, though not all, had been published in St. Petersburg in 1778 in the first of all Russian song collections. Clementi added bass lines to some, including the well-known 'Birch Tree'. Unfortunately we do not know which tunes Shield chose or how he treated them. *The Czar* also included a duet sung by Charles Bannister as Peter and Mrs. Billington as Ottokesa (O'Keeffe was uncertain on the subject of Russian names), and this item, 'Should worldly cares oppressing', was published as 'Composed by Sig. Mozart, adapted by Mr. Shield'; the music is that of 'La ci darem' from *Don Giovanni*, and one wonders how Shield got hold of it, for *Don Giovanni* had not yet been published.

In the spring of 1790 the Lord Chamberlain refused to license an opera about the Fall of the Bastille. Not wishing to waste the scenery and music that had been prepared, Harris got his staff to botch up *The Crusade* (CG 6.5.90), using whatever could be salvaged. Shield, attracted as always by the possibilities of exotic flavouring, showed his knowledge of Turkish percussion in such music as 'The Saracens March'; this is entirely in unison, with cymbal clashes shown here by crosses.

Handel choruses were sung by 'Performers from the Concert of Ancient Music'.

At the end of the opera there was a good 'March after Victory', printed in lavish full score. Elsewhere Edwin, as a Crusader, sang a burlesque of 'The Soldier tir'd' from *Artaxerxes* and a version of the folk tune Percy Grainger popularized as 'Country Gardens'.[1] *The Crusade* achieved a mere seventeen performances in three seasons.

[1] Edwin died the following October and was greatly missed.

Soon after turning down the Bastille opera, the Lord Chancellor sanctioned *The Picture of Paris* (CG 20.12.90), which must have been at least as inflammatory.[1] Shield based his one-movement 'Introduction' (the overture) on the famous revolutionary song 'Ah, ça ira', and it came again in the sung Finale. It looks as though sympathy with the French rebels was becoming more acceptable to the authorities, but it was soon being stifled. In a letter of December 1792 Joseph Ritson wrote to a friend:

> I know I was to send you the song or tune of *Ça ira*, but as it has become high treason either to sing or whistle it and, I presume, . . . to communicate or speak of it, you will excuse my breach of promise for the present.

Baker calls *The Picture of Paris* a pantomime, but it had elements of ballet. The story was devised by Charles Bonnor; he had tried to found an English theatre in Paris in 1784 but the French Queen had refused her permission. In 1790 he was in Paris again, this time with Robert Merry who was writing the lyrics for him, and together they 'collected materials' for their pantomime.

The British Museum has a rare copy of the *Airs, duetts, and chorusses, arrangements of scenery and sketch of the pantomime*, and this reveals that Harlequin was a working-class silversmith, and Columbine the Marquis's daughter; the Clown (named Grotesque) is Columbine's servant. Scenes include 'The Convent of the Jacobins, now a Guard House', the 'Hotel de Ville with the fatal Lanterne', and the new bridge over the Seine. There is an operatic plot running alongside the pantomime one, and in this the Captain (Incledon) has come to Paris with his Irish servant (Johnstone) to rescue a nun with whom he is in love. He succeeds. Meanwhile Harlequin has been changing magistrates into 'Figures of Justice, Mercy and Truth', and a 'Grand Assembly' of squabbling members into a 'Temple of Concord'. The Finale is set in the 'Champ de Mars' with everyone welcoming their new-found liberty and attributing it in part to Britain. Great store was set by the accuracy of the scenery.

Shield's score includes only the numerous vocal items. There must have been a large number of Comic Tunes, but they do not survive and we cannot be certain that Shield wrote them. He had recently acquired a vocal score of J. H. Naumann's *Amphion*, first produced in 1776 in Stockholm, and from this opera he borrowed two ensembles (those on pp. 12 and 19), and acknowledged the debt with apparent pride on the title page. Presumably he composed the other songs himself; no attributions are given. Shield wrote rather more solidly than usual, and in several items insisted on an extra stave to show orchestral detail. Two seasons later he borrowed the long three-movement overture of *Amphion* for an afterpiece called *The Midnight Wanderers* (CG 25.2.93). This also had a French setting, described as 'The Mountains of Biscay', and William Pearce provided a good deal of local colour. In the preface to his libretto he praised

[1] See p. 488.

Shield for the songs sung by Mrs. Clendining and for Mrs. Martyr's 'The Waving Willow' and 'The Rosary'; the last-named was very popular, and Dussek used its tune for a piano rondo. Much of the remainder must be by Paisiello and Grétry, whose names are given on the title page as prominently as Shield's.

We now return to the 1790–1 season, when Shield wiped out the memory of his failures with a successful full-length opera, *The Woodman* (CG 26.2.91). The words were by Sir Henry Bate Dudley, now rector of Bradwell in Essex; he had written the libretto of Shield's very first opera. They took for their subject the craze of the season, female archery, and the final scene with all the girls shooting their arrows across the stage must have been effective. Emily, the heroine, gets the first bull's-eye. There is an even more extraordinary stage effect when Sir Walter and his mountainous cousin and housekeeper Di Clacket are tricked into entering a hopfield to meet their supposed lovers and in fact meet only each other. As they wander round among the tangled hops, a sharp shower of rain soaks them to the skin, to the delight of the presumably sheltered onlookers. These events are accompanied by a short, imaginatively-scored ensemble, 'Mark how the cooing pair draw near!'. The music in this last act is all rather good, with two elaborate arias for Incledon as the hero, Shield's first big-scale chorus (of hop-pickers), and an unusually complex octet for six girl-archers and two of the male characters ('O sweet Mr. Medly'). But in the earlier acts there are too many glees (five in all) and too many simple strophic songs, good though some of them are. The libretto is impossibly drab, with scarcely any characterization, and a plot that is little more than a re-hash of *Rosina*.

Because Mrs. Billington refused to draw a bow in public, Covent Garden engaged Madame Pieltain as Emily. She had sung at the King's Theatre in 1789, when the *Morning Post* thought her 'a very pretty woman', but two years later she was not a happy choice; a fortnight after the first night she was discharged for being drunk.[1] At a moment's notice Emily was sung by Miss Dahl, and it is not surprising that she was criticized for showing nervousness. Her father, Nicholas Dahl, was a Danish artist who for a time had been a Covent Garden scene-painter. The following season Mrs. Billington had second thoughts about an opera that, against her expectations, was doing very well, and her return banished Miss Dahl to Tate Wilkinson's company in York. As usual Mrs. Billington insisted on introducing music of her own choice, and when Haydn saw *The Woodman* in December 1791 the duet he admired in the last act[2] was in fact 'Together let us range the fields' from Boyce's *Solomon*. Haydn also confided to his diary the opinion that Incledon had a good voice but used

---

[1] She must have been the wife either of Dieudonné Pieltain, the Belgian composer and violinist, or of his brother who played the horn at the King's Theatre. See Parke i, p. 147; and the *Morning Post* for 19.2.89.

[2] H. C. Robbins Landon, *The Collected Correspondence . . . of Joseph Haydn*, p. 273.

too much falsetto, and that Johnstone had no sense of time 'but the cast is used to him'. Later Haydn became friendly with Shield, and visited him at his home in Taplow, where he presented him with the autograph of a remarkable Terzetto for voices and orchestra; it includes a solo horn part of unbelievable difficulty.[1]

Most of the overture to *The Woodman* is poor. According to Parke[2] 'the adagio and difficult rondo were entirely obligato [*sic*] for me on the oboe'. The charming engraving on the title-page of the score shows Act I, scene ii, with Emily and Dolly (Mrs. Martyr) having their breakfast outside the woodman's cottage. Dolly has a good aria in Act II with concertante parts for oboe and piano, but her song in Act I was criticized by the *Theatrical Guardian* for gross indecency. This was what shocked:

> There's something in kissing—I cannot tell why,
> Makes my heart in a tumult jump more than breast high:
> > For nine times in ten,
> > So teazing,
> > And pleasing,
> We find those rude creatures—the dear kissing men,
> That we wish it repeated again, and again!

We are apt to think that high moral principles did not stifle the theatres until Victorian times; there were critics who wished they would do so in the 1790s.

The Act III octet mentioned above ('Sestetto' in the libretto) has an eight-bar introduction, and the libretto appears to show that there was speech over it; I have found no earlier example of this. In his preface Bate Dudley remarked that 'the words adapted to two or three old Airs unavoidably partake of a broken, irregular measure', and though there is nothing to show which airs were borrowed there must have been fewer borrowings than usual; indeed the title-page of the vocal score describes the music as 'chiefly' composed by Shield. The libretto includes a sixth glee in Act II, 'Oh Mistress Coy! where art thou roving?', and a footnote reveals that rather than write new words the author 'slightly altered' Shakespeare's lyric to preserve 'the melody of this charming Glee'. The music is not given in Shield's score, and it must have been a pre-existing setting of Feste's song; no doubt the recent one by R. J. S. Stevens.

That summer Shield quarrelled with Harris and went abroad for nearly a year. His purpose was twofold: to see Paris under the revolution and to study Italian opera and singing in Italy. His companion at first was his old friend Joseph Ritson, and they left in the last week of August, 1791.[3] Ritson, previously a Jacobite and now a republican, was in Paris until October admiring the libraries

---

[1] The MS is now in the British Museum, Add. 34073; Mrs. Billington was one of the singers.

[2] i, p. 136.

[3] See Ritson's letter to Mr. Walker dated 20 August.

Jackson by Gainsborough.

Arnold by Hardy.

Shield by Opie (1787).

Landscape by
William Jackson.

and even more the freedom of the Parisians. 'You may now consider their government as completely settled', he wrote in November after he got back, 'and a counter-revolution as utterly impossible: They are more than a match for all the slaves in Europe.' Shield spent nearly two months in his inflammatory company, and when Ritson returned to London Shield went over the Mont Cenis pass to Italy. Sainsbury lists a number of towns where he saw operas, including Turin, Milan, Bologna, Florence, and Siena; he spent most of the winter in Rome.

It is easy to set Ritson up as the most venomous scholar of all time, and he was certainly warped in his last years, ending his life in a madhouse. But there were exceptionally good qualities as well as exceptionally bad in his tiny frame. His troubles stemmed mainly from his becoming in youth a vociferous vegetarian, one of the first in this country. His last and craziest book was about vegetarianism. It was much harder in his day than it is now to plan a non-animal protein diet, and his growing moroseness was largely due to constant undernourishment. Shield too had the reputation of being something of a food-faddist, and he seems at some periods to have avoided meat under Ritson's influence. Much more important, Ritson turned Shield into an antiquary, and it may well have been these months in Paris that confirmed his growing taste for research.

Ritson's main contribution to knowledge was in the field of ballads. His research into Robin Hood ballads may well have suggested Shield's opera on the subject.[1] He was extremely hard-working, and meticulously thorough, and he did not find these qualities in his rivals. Dr. Percy had 'improved' most of the poems in his *Reliques* of 1765, and John Pinkerton invented whole ballads for his *Select Scotish Ballads* of 1783. It had been generally accepted that old poems were faulty; only 'improvements' would render them viable. As one critic wrote, 'Dr. Percy's reading is preferable to the *true one*, and should therefore remain undisturbed.' Though modern scholarship has acquired different tenets, few today would attack Burns for rewriting almost every old song that he found.

Ritson left Burns alone, but he was frequently and excessively rude about Percy and Pinkerton, in print and in letters. He was the first British scholar in this field who believed passionately that an editor's only consideration was accuracy. He was, as Southey once put it, 'the oddest, but the most honest of our antiquaries'.

He was also alone in thinking that the music mattered, though he was not equipped to take tunes down in notation. In 1783 he had brought out his *Select Collection of English Songs* in three volumes, the last of which consisted of the tunes. He and Shield worked together on the project. Less than half were traditional. Of the composed songs, twenty-five were by Arne and a dozen by Carey; Dowland and Wilson rated one each, Purcell two, and Blow three. By the end of the century Shield would have insisted on more early songs. The

---

[1] MacNally dedicated the libretto to Shield, which suggests it was the composer's idea.

collection may seem unoriginal, but it set new standards of accuracy. Ritson complained that Arne and Jackson made many mistakes when transcribing the poems they set. From associating with Ritson Shield learnt to be careful. In 1794 they brought out their four volumes of *Scotish Songs*, both traditional and otherwise, and again the emphasis is on accuracy and taste rather than originality; in fact most of the tunes came from Oswald or from Johnson's *Museum*. Even so, Ritson and Shield were eager to uncover what we today would call folksongs. We have already seen that Shield took down a number of Irish tunes from the singing of his librettist, O'Keeffe, and we know that on the Mont Cenis Pass he met a Russian and seized the opportunity of 'collecting' some Russian tunes. One of Ritson's last letters (May 1802) was to ask Shield to transcribe for him some Welsh songs sung by 'Edward Williams, the Welsh bard' who was then in London. There must have been many unrecorded instances of Shield 'collecting' folk-tunes in this way, and there must be many examples of what he found in his operas.

Ritson was not without other friends. His last miserable years were brightened by Walter Scott, who gladly accepted his help over his *Border Minstrelsy* and welcomed him at Lasswade. But his enemies were legion, his quarrels public property. Not only was he disliked for slanging such respected figures as Percy, Warton, and Malone; in addition he was an avowed republican and atheist. No reputation could then survive under such handicaps. His decline when only fifty-one into madness and death was seen by Percy, now a bishop, as divine retribution.

'Mr. Shield did not accept any public engagement after his return from the continent, and devoted himself to study.'[1] His enthusiasm for playhouse opera certainly declined sharply, and by 1800 he was ready to capitalize on the music he had brought back from abroad or acquired in London, transcribing it with an accuracy learnt of Ritson in two fascinating anthologies disguised as textbooks.

2 COVENT GARDEN AND SHIELD, 1791–1797

Before his quarrel with Harris, Shield had worked without enthusiasm on *Oscar and Malvina* (CG 20.10.91), a 'grand pantomime ballet' based on Ossian. Ritson thought there never was such a poet as Ossian, and Shield must have known of his suspicions. What he composed does not survive. When he went abroad the bulk of the work was transferred to William Reeve, already mentioned as a deplorable composer in the Covent Garden chorus; he may have caught Harris's eye before Harris had had time to think of anyone better.

As M. J. Young put it,

> Lovers of Ossian felt a kind of enthusiastic rapture when they beheld the
> guests seated and the bards arranged in the flower-decked hall of Fingal;

[1] Parke ii, p. 276.

when they heard the sweet harmony of the harps and union pipes (bag-pipes), and the songs of the bards—they heard, also, the warlike sound of the shield of the Hall of Fingal.

No libretto was published, but the plot is given in the *European Magazine* for October 1791. Oscar's love for Malvina, only hinted at in Ossian, was largely a fabrication. In one scene Oscar, who was Ossian's son, leapt from the top of a tower and was caught below on the shields of his followers. There are some choruses with very un-Ossianic words, but most of the story was mimed or danced; Mlle Armand was brought over from Paris especially to dance Malvina. Some of the Comic Tunes were apparently performed by bagpipes and drums only, and the effect may well have been stirring, but they look very banal on paper. *Oscar and Malvina* was undeservedly successful, so much so that twelve years later Clementi's firm republished the music.

Reeve was now known as a composer, but Harris must have had his suspicions of him, for later that season he called on Mazzinghi and Carter for operas. Mazzinghi was a much more capable composer than Reeve, though he had no individuality or imagination. He was first engaged by Harris to write incidental music for *A Day in Turkey* (CG 3.12.91), a five-act 'harem' play by Mrs. Cowley that required no more than a Turkish March and six vocal items. When he attempted a full-length opera, *The Magician no Conjuror* (CG 2.2.92), it was not much liked.[1] The Overture is rather good, the Act I finale elaborate. There are few strophic songs. In the big aria 'Mark, mournful Night', Mrs. Billington was joined by Parke on the oboe, and both are taken up to high F; the introduction has contrasting subjects like a sonata exposition, and there is the usual cadenza at the end. Robert Merry's libretto was not published.[2]

A few weeks later Mrs. Billington bravely chose for her benefit a full-length all-sung opera, *Orpheus and Euridice* (CG 28.2.92). Apart from *Artaxerxes*, Covent Garden patrons had not heard such a thing within living memory, and they did not much care for it; there were only two performances. Whatever Mrs. Billington's reason for the choice, it was not a desire to sing Gluck, a composer who did little to show off voices such as hers. But she had no objection to other people doing so, and the plot was thought to have perennial interest. We have already seen that Lampe's pantomime of 1740 was extremely popular, and it was frequently revived right up to 1768. Gluck could easily have seen it when living in London. His own *Orfeo* was first performed in Vienna in October 1762, and in 1770 the King's Theatre staged a version of it for Guadagni, who had created the title role in Vienna. Additional characters were added to lengthen the plot, and J. C. Bach wrote seven fine arias for them.

---

[1] An unexplored aspect of provincial life is revealed by the BM copy, which once belonged to 'Burgess's Musical Circulating Library of Ramsgate'. This firm also hired out pianos and other instruments 'by the Week, Month or Year'.

[2] The plot can be found in *The General Magazine* for 1792, p. 77.

Guglielmi's wife sang Euridice, and Guglielmi himself contributed two arias for her. All this music, together with six items Gluck had written for Guadagni, was published by Bremner in full score. Bach also wrote some new choruses, but they do not survive, and there is no way of telling which, if any, of Gluck's choruses and dances were preserved. 'Che faro' was taken up by Tenducci and became the rage. The Epilogue to *She stoops to conquer* (1773) tells how 'Madam'

> Pretends to taste, at Operas cries caro,
> And quits her Nancy Dawson for Che Faro.

Somewhat altered versions of this pastiche were given in the eighties in both London and Dublin, but no scores were published and it is not known if advantage was taken of Gluck's revised Paris version of 1774, with its many beautiful additions.

There is both a vocal score and a libretto of the Covent Garden version of 1792. The anonymous libretto, not mentioned by Baker, was 'translated from the Italian', and though Hymen and Pluto were added to the original characters the words were closer to Calzabigi's than those sung at the King's Theatre in 1770. The vocal score is complete except for the recitatives and dances. The title-page promises music by Gluck, Handel, Bach, Sacchini, and Weichsel 'with additional new music by W. Reeve'. Just under half of the score was Gluck's, and the selection was different from that found in the 1770 'Favourite Songs'. Several items were freely altered, and some, including 'Che faro', were con-considerably cut. Act I ended with a long sequence of almost unadulterated Gluck, this being the first of the scenes in Hades. The overture was not the one familiar today; it consisted of the first movement of the one played at the King's Theatre in 1770, and almost certainly it was the J. C. Bach item indicated on the title-page of the vocal score.[1]

It was presumably Sacchini who wrote Mrs. Billington's 'Comfortless is every thought', which is very long and very difficult. The violin obbligato in it was played by 'Mr. Weichsell', Mrs. Billington's brother, and there is a complete concerto exposition with contrasting subjects before the singer comes in. The unremarkable song at the beginning of Act II was composed for Mrs. Billington by her brother, and this was the only item the score identified. The ten remaining songs must mostly be by Reeve. Three are strophic, and Hymen's 'When cruel Fates' is incongruously English in style. Taken as a whole the score is a travesty of what Gluck wrote, though it may be that the playhouse audience would have disliked undiluted Gluck even more. The opera was unlucky in that Holcroft's *Road to Ruin* had been produced a few nights earlier, and this play was so successful that it crowded everything else out of the repertoire. But it is unlikely that Londoners would have accorded success to a

---

[1] Advertisements offered an 'entirely new' overture by Gyrowetz, but this cannot be the one in the vocal score.

version of the Orpheus story that had a great deal of recitative and none of the old familiar pantomime tricks.

There was some merit in Covent Garden's next full-length opera, *Just in Time* (CG 10.5.92). The critics liked Carter's music but not Thomas Hurlstone's libretto, and though 'judicious alterations' were made next season, the opera soon fell out of the repertoire. Hurlstone was one of the proprietors of the *Morning Herald*, and the other papers may have decided on his fate in advance. He had originally submitted the libretto to the elder Colman, who asked for it to be made into an opera. By the time Hurlstone had done so, Colman was irrecoverably ill, and there was thus a long delay between the writing and the performing. In the end Munden chose it for his benefit. Johnstone helped with O'Liffey's dialogue, and wrote both words and music of one of his songs. Hurlstone's preface, from which most of this information is taken, does not mention Carter.

The libretto is in the Bickerstaffe style and may have seemed a little old-fashioned, but it is well above average in quality and interest. Sir Solomon Oddly is a wholesale grocer who has made a fortune, retired into the country, and taken up crazy historical writing. He is currently engaged on showing analogies between the characters in Plutarch's *Lives* and successive Lord Mayors of London. He plans to wed his daughter Augusta to a rather charming quack doctor who is after her money. Doctor Camomile, a forerunner of Alfred Jingle, butters up Lady Oddly with beguiling insincerity:

> I love Augusta, faith, 'tis true,
> But 'tis because she's so like you.

Augusta has a secret lover of her own, Melville, who is in the habit of disguising himself for their meetings in the cottage of Stave, the young parish clerk. All is resolved when Maria, who has been lodging mysteriously in Stave's cottage, is revealed as the quack doctor's wife. The characterization is alive, the dialogue well written.

Munden played Stave and Mrs. Martyr Augusta's servant Judith. Fawcett was the doctor, Incledon the hero, and Miss Dahl Augusta. Augusta had been intended for Mrs. Billington, who suddenly refused to learn a new part for a mere benefit performance, especially when the composer was of little repute. At the last moment Miss Dahl was summoned from York and, says the *Thespian Dictionary*, took the part 'declining all emoluments'.

The overture to *Just in Time* is so solidly written that one wonders why Thomas Carter never had more success. The first movement is spirited and there is a strong development section in the middle. Ending on the dominant, it leads straight into the only other movement, a rondo on the theme of the opera's Finale. Hurlstone had allowed for plenty of ensembles, but Carter, never at his best in such music, hurried through them with no verbal repetition and no distinction. However there is a charming duet for Stave and Judith, 'Too gay deceiver'. Carter's lyrical airs are better than his animated ones, and Miss Dahl's slow bird song with flageolet obbligato is lovely. Her 'Fancy paints the flatt'ring scene' in the last act is of quite unusual length and difficulty, and it was obviously intended for Mrs. Billington; there is at least a minute of quick orchestral music at the start, a great deal of coloratura later, and a cadenza near the end. But Carter was not at home in such music, and Incledon's trumpet song, 'Fell War', is positively banal. He wrote best when least ambitious, and Melville's previous song, 'The mind oppress'd by sleep', has much more musicality. 'Such Symmetry and Grace', Melville sings elsewhere of Augusta. Today we take it for granted that girls are symmetrical, but in late eighteenth-century operas and indeed novels it is the most remarked-on ingredient of beauty.

Carter did not compose again for playhouses. He is a shadowy figure who never seems to have enjoyed regular employment, and he was often hard up. According to Busby,[1] when he was desperate he used to forge Handel MSS and live on the proceeds. He was nearly sixty when he composed *Just in Time*, and he died in 1804.

From 1792 until the end of the century Covent Garden averaged at least six new operas a season, and at least one was full-length. Had Harris found more successes he would not have staged so many. There is a clear decline in quality, and only published operas will be mentioned in what follows. Shield returned from abroad to compose one of his most successful afterpieces, *Hartford Bridge*, but from now on he neither had nor wished to have a monopoly in the theatre's operas.

Hartford Bridge (CG 3.11.92), described as an 'Operatic Farce', had words by William Pearce, who wrote most of Shield's librettos after his return. The title refers to a place between Camberwell and Basingstoke where there was a military camp, and Shield's 'Preludio' established the right atmosphere with an opening 'Marcia'. (He had picked up some Italian on his travels.) The other movement, a 'Quick Step' has a tune like 'The Ash Grove', but perhaps by coincidence. This is an animated score, with a good deal of fifing and drumming and more quotations than usual. An early chorus, 'In rain and in sunshine', borrows the tune of 'O say, bonny lass', which was also associated with the weather in *Inkle and Yarico*. 'Thro' France, thro' all the German regions', sung by the much-travelled Peregrine Forester (Munden), is a medley of quotations, including the ubiquitous Fandango first found in Gluck's *Don Juan*, 'Nel cor più' from Paisiello's *La molinara*, and the Russian folk-tune immortalized in Glinka's *Kamarinskaya*. This is not in the British Museum collection of Russian songs that Shield had drawn on for *The Czar*, and he probably got it from the Russian he had met on the Mont Cenis Pass the previous autumn. In his *Introduction to Harmony* (p. 17) he later printed another 'Russian Air' which he had 'frequently heard an accomplished Russian sing, as we travelled together, who was more desirous to please than astonish'. It is pleasant to think of Shield

[1] Busby iii, p. 13.

scribbling these tunes in his notebook amid such romantic and exciting scenery.

Much the most popular song in *Hartford Bridge* was Incledon's 'The Heaving of the Lead'. Some of the others are given almost in full score, notably a big aria with modest coloratura for a newcomer to the company, Mrs. Clendining. Clara was her first London role. She had been recommended by Mrs. Billington, who had left Covent Garden to go to Italy. According to *The Thespian Dictionary*, Mrs. Clendining was a Rauzzini pupil and, by implication, approaching middle age.

The pantomime that Christmas is of some interest not because of its merit but because we know so much about it. A detailed anonymous 'Description' was published,[1] as also a vocal score, and it was called *Harlequin's Museum, or Mother Shipton Triumphant* (CG 20.12.92). It will be remembered that there had been an earlier pantomime about Mother Shipton with music by Arnold. Shield wrote a little new music for *Harlequin's Museum*, but could not be bothered with the drudgery of selecting, and this was done by T. Goodwin, of whom I know nothing. The overture and finale are attributed to Salieri, but he can hardly have written more of the overture than its slow introduction; the rest consists of a ternary-form allegro based on the 'Kamarinskaya' theme introduced into *Hartford Bridge* six weeks earlier. Unhelpfully the songs are all placed together at the beginning, and all the Comic Tunes together at the end, but the Description reveals where most of them occurred. The pantomime made a virtue of its unoriginality, 'being partly new, and partly a Selection of Scenery, Machinery, Tricks, and Business, from the most approved Pantomimic Productions of *Lunn, Rich, Woodward, Messink, Rosoman, Lalauze* etc.' Of the scene in Whimsey's house the libretto boasts that 'no less than seven of the best *pantomime tricks* are introduced', and these included Harlequin jumping through a clock, and the Clown 'charging a Blunderbus with tea, sugar, bread, butter, milk etc.' The Clown is called Hawtie Clodpole, and the emphasis on him is unusual and significant; by 1806 Grimaldi was making the part more fascinating than Harlequin's. The time-honoured tricks must have had a nostalgic appeal, and the music had to be older than usual too. The title-page of the score names Pepusch, Galliard, Vincent, Boyce ('Heart of Oak'), Fisher, and Arnold, but very few of the items that follow are identified. Some spice of newness was provided with a skating scene and the launching of a ship at Deptford; 'The Stage is completely full of performers', says the Description, boasting again, and a number of cannon were fired to general satisfaction.

In *Sprigs of Laurel* (CG 11.5.93) Shield again collaborated with O'Keeffe, but he took little trouble over this hastily-patched afterpiece. The last opera he composed with care was *The Travellers in Switzerland* (CG 22.2.94), and it was full-length. Switzerland was suddenly in fashion, mainly because the Alps were becoming a symbol of romanticism. Later that year Parisians were to see Cherubini's *Eliza, ou le Mont Saint-Bernard*, in which the mountains seem

[1] BM 11621.e.2.(29).

almost a chorus influencing the action; as indeed they do when an avalanche falls. By comparison Bate Dudley's plot is sadly conventional, being centred on the attempts of Dorimond (Johnstone) to achieve matrimony by means of disguise. He follows Lady Philippa Sidney (Mrs. Mattocks) to Switzerland and becomes her 'Swiss' servant in order to be near her daughter Julia (Mrs. Clendining). Her husband (Munden) disguises himself as a Swiss Guide to keep track of her suspected affair with Count Friponi (Fawcett), but in fact the Count is after Julia. Yet another plot concerns Miss Somerville (Miss Poole), who has taken a Swiss castle because she thinks, wrongly, that Dalton (Incledon) is after her money. In a melodramatic but botched last act he saves her from being abducted.

The music of this, as of all Shield's later operas, is especially hard to write about because there is no way of distinguishing between the items he selected and those he composed. Before his Italian trip his scores usually name the composer of each item and so do the published Song Words. Furthermore one can discover what Italian operas Shield could have seen in London and what books of Scotch or Irish songs he could have owned. With effort his borrowings can mostly be identified in detail. But we know nothing at all about what operas he saw abroad or what scores he brought back. With his own opera scores and the published Song Words offering no help, identification is a despairing business. There were certainly more borrowed items in *The Travellers in Switzerland* than in *The Woodman*, and like so many eighteenth-century librettists Bate Dudley complains in his preface of the difficulty of finding words to fit them. One should not assume that the simple songs are Shield's and the Italianate ones by continental composers, for in his earlier operas the precise opposite is often the case.

The overture, though fairly ambitious, is probably Shield's. The slow D minor Introduction recurs after the main *Allegro,* and by finishing on the dominant provides a bridge to the rondo finale; the latter is based on the tune sung at the end of the opera. The first movement *Allegro* starts banally rather like Sibelius's Third Symphony but develops contrapuntal energy later.

The curtain rises on the Sidney family booking rooms in a Swiss hotel, and this opening ensemble is unlike anything else in Shield's operas. After a twenty-bar introduction, Daniel, the Sidney's servant tries to make contact with the staff:

Landlord! [*f*   *p*] Land-lady, I

LANDLADY

say! Land-la-dy, I say! Qui va là?

(One wonders if the composer had recently seen *Figaro*.) The conversational ensemble that develops is a delight. Shield must have known the elaborate ensembles in Storace's very successful operas, and it would not be surprising if he were attempting such music himself. The first act ends with an unaccompanied glee, but there is a more elaborate ensemble at the end of Act II, and, as in *The Woodman*, the most operatic writing is kept for the end. Indeed the parallels between these two scores are striking. There is an exciting ensemble, 'Surrender', when Miss Somerville's castle is beset by soldiers, and this includes another elaborate chorus with rushing triplets on the violins; it has less musical substance than the similar chorus in *The Woodman*, but the very next item looks far ahead into the nineteenth century, anticipating those nocturnal ensembles in early Verdi. The pace is slow and the music is sung conspiratorially in detached chords. It is most unlikely that Shield wrote it.

Among the numerous strophic songs there is at least one Scotch Song, 'Gae to the kye wi' me, Johnnie' (p. 10). But the most memorable solo is the Count's patter song in which he claims to be able to captivate girls of all nationalities with his 'Canto bello'. 'Spanish or Danish or Russian or Prussian, Florentine, Algerine, American, Belgican, Corsican, Mexican, Hollander, Polander' he sings, and he ends this bowdlerized 'Madamina' with a list of all the great musicians he thinks inferior to himself:

> Mara, Banti, Pacchierotti,
> Billingtoni, sweet Menghotti . . .
> Giornovichi, or Giardini,
> Bold Pasquali, or Nardini,
> Caporalli, or Viotti,
> Paisiello, or Mingotti,
> Sarti, Bruni, Boccherini,
> Haydn, Pleyel, San Martini
> Grétry, Ditters, fat Jomelli,
> Bach, Clementi or Corelli . . .

The song was always encored, and it was certainly by Shield. *The Travellers in Switzerland* had twenty-one performances the first season, which was creditable for a full-length opera, but after two seasons it was laid aside for good.

Netley Abbey (CG 10.4.94) had a naval setting and was named after the Cistercian ruin on Southampton Water. William Pearce, the librettist, praised Richards for providing in the last act 'the most pictoresque Portrait of a Gothic Ruin that the hand of Science ever produced'. Parke wrote the overture and a jolly 'Yo heave ho' song that Mrs. Martyr, his mistress, sang as a sailor boy. Baumgarten, still the band leader, contributed an air for Incledon, and one William Howard composed the Finale. Shield's contribution was unremarkable. Near the start Johnstone had yet another version of 'O say, bonny Lass' which he ended curiously; as the stage direction puts it, 'He tunes his fiddle, while he sustains the note with his voice', the note being a long-held A.

Hercules and Omphale (CG 17.11.94) was virtually a ballet and will be considered later. A vocal score survives of *Mago and Dago, or Harlequin the Hero* (CG 26.12.94) and it was compiled by T. Goodwin. It took six English composers to achieve the six songs and the only two Comic Tunes that were published, and the overture was lifted from Grétry's *Les Événemens imprévus*. Mark Lonsdale's libretto was never printed.[1]

More interesting was *The Mysteries of the Castle* (CG 31.1.95), a Gothic Horror opera. Miles Peter Andrews had started by trying to adapt Mrs. Radcliffe's *The Mysteries of Udolpho*,[2] but was soon diverging so much that he ended by altering all the names. The action depends on an underground passage leading to a castle in Sicily; by its means Julia is saved in the nick of time from being stabbed by the wicked Count. Shield's score contained no overture and some goodish songs, one with spoken patter between the verses. The idea of a 'Glee sung by the Boatman rowing to Shore' came from Storace's *The Pirates*. Just before the glee, the orchestra played 'The Sicilian Mariners', a tune that became so popular as a hymn that it was given an entry in the first edition of *Grove*; Sir George, who wrote the entry himself, was unable to suggest an origin. No doubt Shield was struck by the coincidence of the title, and took the tune from a famous publication perhaps of the same year—famous because it also included the first known version of 'Adeste fideles'.[3]

On 8 April 1795 the Prince of Wales very unwillingly married Caroline, Princess of Brunswick, and Covent Garden celebrated the event with *Windsor Castle, or The Fair Maid of Kent* (CG 6.4.95). Such plot as there was ran its course in Act I, in which the Black Prince married the Fair Maid. Act II had no dialogue and consisted entirely of an entertainment put on for the pleasure

---

[1] See *LS* Part 5, iii, p. 1714 for the action.

[2] Reynolds ii, p. 198; Reynolds says he wrote half the libretto himself. He gives a lot of information about Andrews.

[3] The earlier date given in BUCEM for its first entry is impossible; Thomas Preston, the publisher, was not in business until 1798. The exact date is unknown.

of the young couple. Pearce, the librettist, had wanted a tournament like the famous one in *Cymon*, but Noverre who had been engaged for the occasion over-ruled this suggestion in favour of a ballet he had been planning on the Peleus and Thetis story. The vocal score and libretto call the entertainment a masque, but it is nothing of the kind; the song-words booklet correctly calls it a ballet. Peleus and Thetis were dancers and mimed the story.[1] Vocal items were limited to one song (for Cupid), one duet, and some simple choruses. The music was continuous.

Act I originally included an overture and eight vocal items, but perhaps was found too long, for six of the vocal items were cut before the score was published, and are indicated only in the libretto. One of the casualties was a chorus 'accompanied by Mr. Jones on the harp', and he must have been the 'official Bard to the Prince of Wales' who had published the Welsh song collection. The only vocal items that got into the vocal score were both by Reginald Spofforth, well known at the time for his glees. Although the score implies that all the music was by Salomon, this is not borne out by its contents.

Salomon is best known as the man who persuaded Haydn to come to London and compose symphonies for his concerts there. He was a good violinist, but he had no reputation as a composer, and it is unbelievable that he should have been preferred to Shield for an occasion of such national importance. The problem of this opera's commissioning is allied, I suggest, to the problem of its overture. The one played on the first night was not the feeble one by Salomon, given in the vocal score, but Haydn's so-called 'Overture to an English Opera',[2] first published in 1951. Much the most probable explanation of a mystery that no one so far has claimed to solve is that Covent Garden originally turned to Haydn for this afterpiece as being the greatest composer alive, and that Haydn got so far with it as to complete the overture. He then backed out of the commission either because of the pressure of other work or because he disliked Pearce's libretto. He may well have told Harris, when it was too late for objections, that he had asked his friend Salomon to step into the breach. Harris would certainly have disliked the substitution, and his dislike would explain why Spofforth's music in Act I was kept and Salomon's jettisoned, and why Haydn's overture was preferred once Harris had discovered its existence. Haydn went to the first night, and, perhaps a little on the defensive, thought Salomon's music

> quite passable. The decorations—costumes—scenery, and the enormous amount of people on the stage are exaggerated. All the Gods of Heaven and Hell, and everything that lives on the earth are in the piece.

He does not seem to have been impressed by Noverre.

Covent Garden lagged well behind Drury Lane and the Little Theatre in its

---

[1] See *LS* Part 5, iii, p. 1741–2 for the action.
[2] See *The Symphonies of Joseph Haydn* by H. C. Robbins Landon, pp. 541–2.

search for a new type of opera plot. Shield's afterpiece, *Lock and Key* (CG 2.2.96) was on the hoary theme of an old guardian locking up a girl to prevent her marrying. Parke again wrote the overture, no doubt to Shield's relief, and Incledon thrilled the house with 'The Arethusa'. A century later Gratton Flood suggested that Shield got this popular and indeed magnificent tune from 'The Princess Royal' by Carolan, and more recently he has been supported by Donal O'Sullivan,[1] but it is not certain that Carolan was the composer; there are English versions of the early 1730s that might be earlier. It is sad to find that Shield did not write what has often been thought of as his finest song.

This was a busy year for Shield, for he also composed two full-length operas. *The Lad of the Hills* (CG 9.4.96) had a dreary libretto by O'Keeffe, who was at the end of his career and about to publish his Complete Works. The hero finds some pieces of gold in the Wicklow Mountains near Dublin and is accused of stealing them. The opera failed, and the next season it was cut to an afterpiece called *The Wicklow Mountains*, which also failed. O'Keeffe changed all the characters' names. Most of the tunes are or look Irish. Parke claimed to have composed the Act II Finale.

Abroad and at Home (CG 19.11.96) had the best libretto Shield had worked on for years. It was by Joseph Holman, who had played Romeo at Covent Garden at the age of twenty, studied at Oxford, and then returned to theatre life. The plot is about two old men, joint guardians of Miss Hartley, each of whom wants her to marry his son. One of the sons is thought to be abroad, but in fact he is languishing in the King's Bench, the debtors' prison. As a lot of money is involved as well as a pretty girl, he manages to get a 'Rule for the day', in other words a pass, so that he can stake his claim. But it is a condition that one of the prison keepers accompanies him while he is out, so he dresses the keeper up as a foreign Count. The other son also arrives, but makes love to the maid thinking that she is Miss Hartley. In the subsequent confusion he gets hauled off to prison in mistake for the debtor son. The published score claimed to be 'composed by and selected from Grétry, Giornovichi etc., and William Shield'. Shield must surely have written the charmingly silly duet sung by the debtor son and his very puzzled keeper:

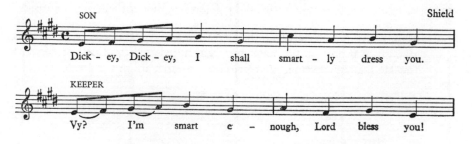

SON — Shield

Dick - ey, Dick - ey, I shall smart - ly dress you.

KEEPER

Vy? I'm smart e - nough, Lord bless you!

[1] See No. 87 in O'Sullivan's *Carolan*.

The most interesting borrowing was 'Ah, Divinité', sung by Banti in the recent King's Theatre production of Gluck's *Alceste*. Incledon, assisted by Sarjeant, sang one of Shield's least successful trumpet songs. The absence of glees and the fewness of strophic songs shows some seriousness of purpose.

Shield wrote one more full-length opera that season, *The Italian Villagers* (CG 25.4.97), but it failed and no score or libretto was published. He then had a 'misunderstanding' with Harris, says Parke, and 'withdrew himself at the end of the season'. He had written himself out in the dramatic field, and must have been glad to get away from Covent Garden. During his thirty years of retirement he made one misguided return to theatre music in collaboration with Thomas Dibdin, but *Two Faces under one Hood* (CG 17.11.07) was too old-fashioned to have much success.

In other directions Shield still had something to offer. In 1796 he had published a piquant set of string trios, notable for some charming and original movements in five-four time, and he was soon busy with the two remarkable anthologies disguised as textbooks. *Introduction to Harmony* appeared in 1800 and was revised with very minor additions in 1815, while *Rudiments of Thorough Bass* also appeared in 1815. Both contain much intelligent and agreeably written instruction, but their chief interest lies in the music examples. On principle Shield refused to identify them, on the grounds that readers should be allowed to judge their value without being prejudiced by the composer's name. The result is a continuous series of Quiz questions to which no answers are provided. The examples are often complete movements and often in full or at least short score. Shield must have been drawing on a considerable music library, and it was described as extremely valuable when he died.

Much the most remarkable item in the 1800 volume is the D minor Prelude from Book I of Bach's '48'. This was the very first time that any piece from this collection had been published anywhere. In 1801 publication of the whole set began simultaneously in Zürich, Bonn, and Leipzig, and very soon afterwards in London, but Shield of all people was first in the field. He must have got the music from the MS that aroused Samuel Wesley's famous enthusiasm for Bach.[1]

As stated earlier, Shield's *Harmony* also shows various ways of accompanying a Russian folk-song. *Thorough Bass* has several examples of decoration (pp. 18–19), specimens of folk-song accompaniments,[2] and a very proper and Ritsonian warning against accepting Mozart's Additional Accompaniments for *Messiah*. One of Beethoven's preludes for piano through every key finds a place, as also some lute tablature.

[1] This had been brought to London by C. E. Horn, whose son later composed 'Cherry Ripe'. Clementi owned an autograph of Book II of the '48', part of it in the hand of Anna Magdalena; this MS is now in the British Museum.

[2] The striking example on p. 32 with concertante parts for violin, cello, oboe, and piano is by J. C. Bach.

In 1817 Shield, by now very stout, became Master of the King's Musick; with Southey he produced the last of all Birthday Odes, and the autograph survives in the Royal Music Library. In 1829 Shield died, aged eighty, and was buried in Westminster Abbey. He left all his possessions to his 'beloved partner Ann (Stokes), Mrs. Shield upwards of forty years'. The portrait by Opie (Plate xiii) is from an engraving; the original has not been seen for a century. The Royal College of Music has a good portrait of Shield in old age. In Brightling Church (north-west of Battle in Sussex) there is a lavish memorial to Shield put up by the eccentric John Fuller, owner of the local mansion.

3 ARNOLD AT THE LITTLE THEATRE, 1789–1800

In spite of his other work, Arnold continued writing for the Little Theatre to the end of the century and beyond, and he had no rivals. He cannot have needed the money. Perhaps he valued his theatre days for their cheerful contrast with his organ-playing and Handel-editing. After a year's respite in 1788, he composed an all-sung afterpiece, *The Enraged Musician* (LT 18.5.89); the published vocal score includes all the recitatives and is complete. The libretto was by the elder Colman, who was incapacitated with brain injury by the time it appeared. He himself had called it, forbiddingly, *Ut Pictora Poesis!*, and it aimed to bring alive Hogarth's famous print of a noisy London street and a musician at the window enraged by the racket. He is said to have been Pietro Castrucci, the violinist who often led Handel's opera orchestra. Colman made him an Italian singing-teacher called Castruccio.

After a dull overture, we see Castruccio at the harpsichord teaching Castruccina and Piccolina (Mrs. Bannister and Mrs. Plomer). One girl sings an Italianate aria and has it damned as a feeble 'madrigal from Wales', while the other sings a folk-song and has it praised as opera at its most 'divino'; in other words Castruccio cannot tell the difference. The laborious joke takes half the scene to make its point, and it is the more stupid in that Castruccio has started the opera by singing, falsetto, part of 'Non temer' from Bertoni's *Demofoonte*. (The audience would probably have known this aria from its inclusion in Shield's *Robin Hood*.) The outdoor scene is much better. Quaver addresses an amusing serenade to Castruccina, and the Finale is splendidly Hogarthian, with its elaborate and noisy ensemble of street-cries: 'Knives to grind', 'Milk below', 'Pots to mend', 'New Mackarel', and so on.

The scenery was by Rooker, who had been Drury Lane's Harlequin twenty years earlier. Critics much admired his sets for another opera that season, *The Battle of Hexham*. The British Museum has an unusual and interesting watercolour he made of the attic in the Little Theatre where he did his work. It looks unnaturally tidy.

Genest summed up *The Battle of Hexham* (LT 11.8.89) as 'a jumble of

Tragedy, Comedy and Opera—the language is unnatural'. But it proved so successful a recipe that the younger Colman tried it again and again. He deserves much of the blame for the unrealistic stage fustian of Victorian times. He gave his serious characters blank verse that reads like a parody of Shakespeare at his most bombastic, while his comic characters speak like the Gobbos at their dreariest. Because his best actors were not singers, he limited the singing to the subsidiary characters, and the result was an entertainment with too much music for a play but not enough for an opera; the vocal scores are of afterpiece length, but belong to full-length entertainments. We have already met an example of this hybrid form, Colman's *The Iron Chest*, given so disastrously at Drury Lane in 1796.

Hexham's battle belonged to the Wars of the Roses. Adeline follows her lover, Gondibert, to the battle disguised as a youth; Gondibert rescues Queen Margaret and her small son Henry. John Bannister, who played Gondibert, thought this opera Colman's best work, and one must add in its defence that it was popular for twenty years.

It is never wise to flip through Arnold's scores too superficially. There is plenty to repel the modern score-reader in *The Battle of Hexham*; for instance the overture, and Edwin's moronic 'In an old quiet Parish', which, incredibly, was always encored. Yet the very first song, sung by Adeline as she considers how to comport herself in male garb, is very good indeed, and there is unusual virility in one for Charles Bannister as a Forest Robber; the following is part of the introduction:

There are also some soldiers' choruses, and even a simple song for the unmusical Palmer. His recent experiences at the Royalty Theatre must have increased his confidence and ability. There is seldom much borrowing in an Arnold score, but he did include a glee, words and music, by J. W. Callcott (1766–1821), the most popular of all glee-writers.

Arnold had just been asked to 'select, adapt, and compose' a large collection called *The Psalms of David, for the Use of Parish Churches*, and he persuaded Callcott to do most of the work; they became close friends. Though Callcott composed little else but glees, he had had operatic ambitions as a young man, for the British Museum has the autograph full score of an afterpiece by him called *The Mistakes of a Day*. Baker lists it as a farce given in Norwich in 1786 or 1787, but he does not suggest an author, and I have not found the spoken dialogue. Callcott wrote the music in ten days, and noted on the score that he completed it 'past midnight' on 3 December 1785. The three-movement overture fills a third of the pages and it is mildly charming, though some of the accompaniment figures are rather pianistic. There are several good songs, notably a sea-song for Hardy, 'The sail-yards whistle in the wind'. The end of the score looks incomplete, but only because the sheets have been bound in the wrong order.

New Spain, or Love in Mexico (LT 16.7.90) had a libretto by an army officer named John Scawen, and he described it as an 'opera'. Arnold described his music as 'intirely new', but it is also intirely dull and needs no comment. The plot is curious. In Spain before the curtain rises Leonora muffs an elopement by waiting in the wrong place. Don Garcia, thinking himself rejected, has come in despair to New Mexico, where the entire opera takes place. Leonora has followed him with her servant Flora, both in male disguise, and when we first see her she has had two years in the army and risen to be a colonel. By Act II she has been promoted to Lieutenant-Governor, a position that allows her to effect a happy ending. The travesty roles were played by Mrs. Goodall and the diminutive Miss Fontenelle, for whom Robert Burns wrote poems.

Arnold collaborated again with his manager in another historical hybrid, *The Surrender of Calais* (LT 30.7.91), and he provided a military-style overture and a very long chorus of English soldiers. Part of the lyric for this ran: 'When the soldier marches o'er the crimson field knee-deep in gore'; Colman was never one for understatement. Act II ended with a good five-part chorus for the inhabitants of Calais, and later Johnstone had a song to the cheerful tune we know as 'The Irish Washerwoman'.

More unusual, but less successful, was *The Enchanted Wood* (LT 25.7.92). Baker thought the author of the anonymous libretto was 'Francis', but lists no other plays from his pen. In the preface the author states that he originally wrote the work 'as a legendary poem in dialogue' when he was only fifteen; he had not meant it to be acted; more recently he had added 'some of the lighter parts'. As Baker noticed, he got many of his ideas from *The Tempest* and *A Midsummer Night's Dream*, but the actual poetry, partly in heroic couplets and partly in blank verse, is not especially derivative and surprisingly good. One would guess that the author must later have written other works under his own name and become fairly well known.

The main characters do not sing, as was now usual at the Little Theatre.

Miss Brown (Mrs. Cargill) as Clara
in Linley's *The Duenna* (1775).

Mrs. Crouch by Romney.

Nancy Storace.

THE PIRATES.

an Opera

in Three Acts,

As Performed at the

Theatre Royal Drury Lane

the Music

Composed

By STEPHEN STORACE.

Price 12ˢ

Entered at Stationers Hall

LONDON Printed & Sold by J. DALE, at Nº 19. Cornhill & at Nº 132. Oxford Street opposite Hanover Square.

Title-page,
1792.

Una is uncertain whether to marry Ethelred, who is handsome but selfish, or Julian, who is noble in mind but deformed in body. Her problem is eventually resolved for her by Orion, who puts them both in a magic cauldron that reverses their physical attributes. Orion is Prospero and Oberon in one, his attendant Cymbriel Puck and Ariel. The singing was mainly done by two fairies, Transit and Sylphina (Mrs. Bland and Miss De Camp) who quarrel and make it up. John Bannister as a cottager who speaks prose was roughly the equivalent of Bottom, and at one point had a cuckold's horns fixed to his head. The libretto was outspoken for its day. The words strumpet and cuckold are bandied about, and in an unfortunate couplet that would surprise from a grown-up, let alone a boy of fifteen, Transit tells Sylphina that he has been watching her bathe naked in the Stream :

> Transform'd into a bee, with honey prest,
> I flew, and stung thee on the heaving breast.

There is a faint suggestion of Mendelssohn's *A Midsummer Night's Dream* in the way Arnold tried to conjure up the fairy world in the first movement of the overture. The middle movement is a duet for horn and bassoon; Arnold may have associated horns and forests as Weber later did. Transit and Sylphina have a rather beautiful duet, 'Mortal Man, learn to hear', and several songs show a fairy-tale innocence. Act I ends with a ballet for fairies in several sections. One of the tunes is a version of 'Baa, Baa, Black Sheep', and some of the others could be nursery rhymes too. I do not know of a collection of such songs with their music before Hook's *Christmas Box* of 1797. It will be clear that *The Enchanted Wood* was one of Arnold's most original scores.

The Mountaineers (LT 3.8.93) was a sensation because of the appearance for the first time at the Little Theatre of John Kemble. Colman and Arnold concocted for the occasion one of their usual hybrid entertainments—a play for the chief characters but an opera for the subsidiary ones. The plot came from two intertwined stories in *Don Quixote*, the one about the Captive who escapes from slavery in Algiers with a Moorish girl turned Christian, and the one about Cardenio living in desolate mountains because of his bride being forced to 'marry' another man. All the names were changed except that of the Moorish girl, Zorayda. Kemble played Cardenio, renamed Octavian. He did not appear until the middle of Act II, but then his slightly mad behaviour and the unfairness with which he was treated wrung tears from every eye. Baker was not alone in finding 'a high degree of poetic genius' in the words, and in not noticing the music, but in fact there were as many as nine vocal items spread over the three acts. Four of these were choruses sung by goatherds or muleteers. A duet, 'O happy tawny Moor', became deservedly popular, for the rhythmic structure is individual. The accompaniment must have been for guitar or pizzicato strings in imitation, and this was fitting for Sadi and his Christian slave were about to set off 'over the mountains to Andalusia'. Their duet in the

last act, 'Faint and wearily', was parodied by Goethe as 'Matt und besch-
werlich', his title being 'Hochländisch' or 'Der Wanderer'.[1] Quite as extraordinary as Goethe's interest in this obscure lyric is the fact that someone
noticed it.

Arnold had no further big summer successes at the Little Theatre, though
he composed one the following winter, *The Children in the Wood*.[2] His theatre
music was becoming slapdash. Most summers he wrote one or more unsuccessful
afterpieces that were never published; they will not be mentioned here.

Auld Robin Gray (LT 26.7.94) was a pastiche based on the popular pseudo-
ballad of the same name. Two different tunes were known, neither of them
traditional. The later one seems to have been first published by Corri about 1779,
and it was the one Arnold used. According to Parke, both the words and this
tune were by Lady Caroline Fordyce.[3] The words tell a typical ballad tale.
Jenny thinks her sailor lover Jemmy has been drowned, so she married a kindly
old man she does not love in order to provide for her ailing parents. Jemmy
comes back—too late in the song, but just in time in the opera. This is the first
libretto I have noticed in which there is some attempt at 'Scotch' dialogue, and
it was written by Arnold's son. Charles Kemble and Miss Leake played the
young lovers, Suett the title role. The piece had only a moderate success.

Arnold's overture included an inane medley of fourteen identified Scotch
song tunes, among them 'Auld Robin Gray' and 'The Mallow Fling' (which in
fact is Irish). The first song has genuine ballad affiliations, for the words are a
debased version of 'Our Goodman' (Child No. 274). Father comes home and
finds a sword he does not recognize; Mother says 'Lovee, 'tis a poker Auntie
sent to me'. When he finds a man in the bedroom, she says it's her milkmaid,
and his whip is her stay lace. He uses it to whip her out of the house. Ballads
were a burning subject at this time, with Ritson quarrelling about their texts
with Percy, Pinkerton, and others. The tune, also found in *The Jovial Crew* and
The Gentle Shepherd, has already been mentioned as a version of the one Cecil
Sharp called 'Dance to your Daddy'.

The young lovers sing the tune of 'Auld Robin Gray' to new words, there
is a glee version of 'Begone, dull Care', and a Finale in which 'The Mallow
Fling' is the recurring rondo theme; 'Tweedside' and 'Lochaber' are the episodes. Most of the airs are strophic and very simple. Act II begins elaborately
with an orchestral piece called 'The Shipwreck'; the stage direction runs as
follows: 'A Storm at Sea and Shipwreck—Prelude of Music as the Scene is discovered. Enter Jemmy as from the Wreck'. The 'Prelude of Music' is in fact
the earthquake movement from Haydn's *Seven Last Words*.

Haydn saw *Auld Robin Gray*, presumably on Arnold's invitation, and very

---

[1] See F. W. Sternfeld's *Goethe and Music* (New York 1954), p. 34.
[2] See p. 520.
[3] Parke i, p. 249. The more beautiful earlier tune was probably by the Rev.
William Leeves. Corri gives both tunes in his *Select Collection* iii, p. 85 (*c.* 1779).

much disliked it. His diary provides the best account we have of the costumes then used in operas on a Scottish theme:

> The men were dressed in flesh-coloured breeches, with white and red ribbons twisted round their stockings, a short, brightly-coloured, striped mason's apron [he meant a kilt], brown coat and waistcoat, over the coat a large broad ensign's sash in the same style as the apron, and a black cap shaped like a shoe and trimmed with ribbons. The women all in white muslin, brightly coloured ribbons in their hair, very broad bands in the same style round their bodies, also for their hats.[1]

Haydn did not complain in his diary that for trivial purposes Arnold had pillaged his most profound sacred work.

In *Zorinski* (LT 20.6.95) Arnold returned to the hybrid form, sensibly described on the vocal score as 'Musical Play'. Thomas Morton based his plot on the recent abduction of Stanislaus, King of Poland, but changed the names because the king was still alive. Zorinski is too noble to kill King Casimir, yet so disgusted with his policy that he prefers to live in some salt-mines. Johnstone, who had often been an Irish servant in Spain, had the new experience of being one in Poland. Mrs. Bland sang a beautiful Scotch Song called 'Donald'.

The playhouses could seldom resist anything on a Scottish theme. *Love and Money, or The Fair Caledonian* (LT 29.8.95) was an afterpiece ballad opera on the lines of *Auld Robin Gray*, and this time the intruder in the Medley Overture was not Irish but Welsh, 'All through the Night'. Later in the opera Miss De Camp sang the refrain to the correct Welsh words, 'Ar hyd y nos'; she was playing a breeches part of little interest.

Bannian Day (LT 11.6.96) had abysmal music. The title was a naval term meaning one on which no meat was served, and it was a naval man, George Brewer, who wrote the libretto. Johnstone repeated his eternal Irishman, and Suett had a song with spoken patter between the verses.

In the following winter Drury Lane, impoverished by Storace's death, engaged the Arnolds, father and son, to create an afterpiece opera called *The Shipwreck* (DL 10.12.96). Writing for a more esteemed theatre and a larger orchestra than usual, Arnold produced one of his best scores. The overture begins with some quick storm music in D minor, and this returns after a central Andante section, and leads without a break into a long male chorus of Wreckers. Then comes a stage direction:

> During the chorus a ship appears tossing on the sea, and is wreck'd—the plunderers, smugglers, etc. then leave the rocks, and crowd down to the shore, watching the waves and taking up goods, etc. that are supposed to be thrown ashore from the wreck.

[1] *The Collected Correspondence and London Notebooks of Joseph Haydn*, ed. H. C. Robbins Landon, p. 294.

The influence of the similar scene in *Auld Robin Gray* is obvious. We are not told if the plunderers have lured the ship onto the rocks by means of false lights, as in Ethel Smyth's *The Wreckers*, and we are not told if the sea coast is in Cornwall. Nevertheless this is a splendid beginning, and an exceptional opera should have followed. Unfortunately the plot crumbles into futilities about a girl disguised as a boy. What should have been the main subject—the attempts of the surviving sailors to get back their property from the villagers—is stated but never developed. Angelica, the heroine, is appalled that her own father should sink to these illicit practices, especially as her lover is one of the surviving sailors, but nothing is made of this confrontation either. Hazlitt wrote later that Samuel Arnold (the son) 'writes with the fewest ideas possible . . . he fails to offend through downright imbecility'. The title-page of the score is unique in that it depicts two stage sets—the ship being wrecked, and the pub where the wreckers divide their spoils.

The Italian Monk (LT 15.8.97) was a full-length play by James Boaden, and there were only four lyrics for Arnold to set. Boaden failed first as an actor and then as a playwright, but he won success with his biographies of Mrs. Siddons, John Philip Kemble, and Mrs. Jordan. He took his plot from Mrs. Radcliffe's novel of the same name. The hero, imprisoned by the Inquisition, was called Vivaldi.

Wrongful imprisonment was beginning to be rivalled as a popular theme by events so far back in history as to justify a great deal of harp playing, and usually the events were Welsh. Boaden's full-length *Cambro-Britons* (LT 21.7.98) was about the war between Edward I and Llewellyn. Arnold's four-movement overture dispensed with the usual sonata-form opening and began with a march. Then came a duet for two harps, printed in full score, and then a kind of jig played by the unlikely combination of bagpipes and harp. The final rondo is conventionally scored as to its main theme, but returns to the two-harp formula for its episodes. The theatre got full value from the harpists, who had very elaborate parts in a Chorus of Welsh Bards and provided the sole accompaniment in a Trio. Much of the orchestration looks novel and interesting. The very first song, given in full score, is described as a waltz and accompanied by flute, one harp, triangle, and tambourine. A march for the English army is also given in full score. Patrons of the Little Theatre were not surprised to find a well-known Irish singer established in the Welsh countryside. Johnstone's admirers were further satisfied that season by an opera called *False and True, or The Irishman in Italy* (LT 11.8.98), but Arnold's music was not interesting.

In the autumn Arnold was so unlucky as to fall off the steps in his library; he injured himself severely. While convalescing in 1799 he wrote an oratorio called *Elisha*, but no theatre music. Busby, who gives the best account of Arnold's career,[1] described his final illness as follows:

---

[1] Busby iii, pp. 148–55; he wrongly called the oratorio *Elijah*.

Doctor Arnold's general habits were not the most abstemious; and a train of disorders brought upon his constitution, already enfeebled by the long confinement to which he had been subjected by the accident just mentioned, hastened his dissolution. After an illness of many months, too severe to admit the hope of his recovery, he expired at his house in Duke-street, Westminster, on the 22nd of October, 1802.

Busby went to the funeral, and can hardly have got his main facts wrong, yet Arnold was active to the end. In January 1802 he finished a short oratorio called *The Hymn of Adam and Eve*,[1] and in his last two years he composed as many as six stage works, three of them of unusual length. He may have been bed-ridden, but he cannot have been as enfeebled, or indeed as inebriated, as Busby made out. Arnold's nineteenth-century stage works will be discussed below.

4 BALLET AT THE ROYAL CIRCUS AND LITTLE THEATRE

There is very little information as to what went on at the Royal Circus immediately after Dibdin left it. The theatre was in an unfashionable part of London, and was not visited by people likely to record their impressions. However, in the late 1790s it gradually improved its status until it became famous in the following century under Elliston.

In 1789 a composer called Richard Chapman was employed there, but he is not mentioned by any writer I have come on. He published in one volume a few items from *The Bastile* and *The Naval Review*; no librettos are known. The one-movement overture to *The Bastile* is more interesting than any overture by Reeve, but that is not high praise.

Chapman cannot have lasted long. For the 1793 season the theatre engaged as its composer James Sanderson (1769–*c*.1841), and in the next thirty years he is said to have composed as many as 154 stage works. Like Shield, Sanderson came from County Durham, and he was playing the violin in the Sunderland theatre when only fourteen and even teaching the instrument a few months later. In 1788 he came to London to play the violin at Astley's Royal Grove, which was near the present-day County Hall. Astley is mainly remembered for his Amphitheatre in Westminster, opened in 1803, but he had been putting on equestrian shows south of the river since the 1770s. For a brief period he included burlettas and pantomimes in his programmes, and that no doubt is why he engaged Sanderson. The latter had composition lessons with Shield, and *Harlequin in Ireland, or Apollo and Daphne* (R.C. 17.2.92) is said to have been his first stage music. Nothing of it survives.

For much of his career Sanderson worked with an unsuccessful but ambitious actor named J. C. Cross. Baker gives his christian name as James, but in fact it

---

[1] The score is in the Royal College of Music, RCM 739.

was John. Cross devised *Harlequin Mariner, or The Witch of the Oaks* (RC 28.5.96), in which 'If [Gin] a body meet a body' was sung for the first time.[1] The first movement of Sanderson's overture is long and unexpectedly good. Though he lacked individuality and often wrote boringly, he was far from being incompetent. As a result of this production Cross met the daughter of James Jones, the Royal Circus proprietor. In 1798 she became his second wife and he became joint proprietor and acting manager. He immediately set about transforming the repertoire with an infusion of ballet.

Back in the 1740s short ballets had often filled the intervals at the playhouses, but most of them were divertissements with very little story. In the last quarter of the century the King's Theatre regularly presented ballets that told a mythological story in dance and mime, and Noverre, the prime originator of ballet d'action, had even devised an entirely mimed version of *Macbeth*. Other London theatres were first driven into presenting ballet because they did not know what else to present. At the Royalty Theatre in 1787, it will be remembered, Palmer had mimed the role of Don Juan to music by Reeve, but only because the theatre was not licensed for spoken dialogue. Such experiments showed that pantomime had scarcely touched the latent possibilities of serious miming, and the possibilities were made even clearer by *Oscar and Malvina* (1791).[2] This was a landmark of historical importance, however lame its artistic merits. Covent Garden had proved that an audience's attention could be held by an hour-long entertainment with no dialogue, no harlequin tricks or horseplay, and very few songs; an alternation of serious miming and pure dancing could be enough. English ballet had made a leap forward.

Three years later Covent Garden tried again. *Hercules and Omphale* (CG 17.11.94) was much less successful, and made Harris doubt the wisdom of continuing such experiments. Tate Wilkinson on the other hand fully realized its importance. In his *Wandering Patentee*[3] he reproduced an elaborate and fascinating playbill, and devoted three pages to the action. This is as well, for the 'Description' and music do not survive. The story is wholly serious. In Part I Omphale, Queen of Lydia, is carried off by one of her suitors, the Prince of Mycene, while another of them, Hercules, is temporarily distracted by having to deal with a monster. In a fury Hercules besieges Mycene, and with the help of a battering ram he carries off the gates of the city, kills the prince, and rescues Omphale. Part II has little action and ends with a masque of the gods in the old pantomime tradition. Covent Garden never called the piece a ballet; it was a 'Grand Pantomimic Spectacle'. The music was 'Partly new, by Mr. Shield, and partly selected from Haydn, Mazzinghi, Gluck, Baumgarten, Grétry, Martini, Dezede, Eloy, etc.' Also there was an overture by Reeve for 'double orchestra'.

The failure of *Hercules and Omphale* led Cross to the truth that plots based

[1] See p. 458.
[2] See p. 546.
[3] iv, p. 140.

on Greek mythology were played out. But perhaps British mythology might have more appeal. *The Round Tower, or The Chieftains of Ireland* (CG 24.11.97), described as a 'Ballet Pantomime', had despicable music by Reeve. The plot was laid in pre-historic Ireland, and centred on who should be King of Munster. *Raymond and Agnes* (CG 16.3.97) and *Joan of Arc* (CG 12.2.98) were also ballets with no spoken dialogue, had poor music by Reeve, and failed, but their much more dramatic plots pointed the way to the success Cross found in this field when he transferred to the Royal Circus.

The answer was a modern or nearly modern plot with romantic undertones, and in *Blackbeard or The Captive Princess* (RC Easter Monday 1798) Cross and Sanderson scored a vital success. There were nearly a hundred performances in the first season. Years later in 1809 Cross published what he clumsily called *Circusiana*, a two-volume collection of 'The most favourite Ballets, Spectacles, Melo-dramas, etc., performed at the Royal Circus, St. George's Fields'. He gave a brief history of the theatre and some dozen scripts. In these the action is set out in clearly-written prose with the song words inserted in the proper place, exactly as in the better pantomime Descriptions. Most of the ballets fall outside our period. Cross included *The Round Tower* because it was revived at the Royal Circus in 1803. He reveals that he got its plot from O'Halloran's *History of Ireland*, and that he used *The History of the Buccaneers of America* for *Blackbeard*.

'Blackbeard' is the alias of a pirate called Captain Teach. He was danced by Crossville; James d'Egville was his faithful negro servant, Caesar.[1] In the first scene Blackbeard's men board and plunder another ship; they take from her a 'Mogul' princess called Ismene and her lover Abdullah. On the coast of Madagascar we see Blackbeard's wife Orra (Madame de la Croix), as also his ship towing in its prize. There is another ill-starred love affair between William and Nancy, the latter being disguised as a pirate. In the end the good ship Revenge, under Captain Maynard, captures the pirate ship and its crew, and the lovers find happiness. The originality of this ballet scenario is striking, and its success is not surprising.

Alone of Sanderson's eighteenth-century scores, *Blackbeard* was published complete, the music 'entirely new'. The overture was avowedly in imitation of the one by Kreutzer used in Drury Lane's *Lodoiska*, and it is odd that Sanderson should have written the slow introduction in a major key, for it was the minor-key opening in the Kreutzer overture that had been so influential. William and Nancy did most of the singing, and the latter's 'My Willie was a sailor bold' is given in full score. Like countless sailor songs of the eighteenth century, it has a rather slow tune in three-four time starting on the fourth quaver; the prototype seems to have been Greene's 'Fair Sally'. Of the nine vocal items five are duets

---

[1] D'Egville, who was English, had danced at the King's Theatre in Storace's *Venus and Adonis*. In 1799 he became choreographer there, and later he founded an Academy of Dancing to train English dancers.

or choruses, and there is an increasing tendency in these ballets to cut down on the solo song. It would be untrue to describe Sanderson's music as enthralling, but the long and elaborate 'Battle Piece' that accompanies the sea-fight at the beginning is something new in English theatre music, and there are moments of interest later as well.

Because *Blackbeard* was so successful, the Royal Circus concentrated on ballets until the building was burnt to the ground in 1805, when all the music, scenery, and costumes were destroyed. The theatre was quickly rebuilt, renamed the Surrey Theatre, and eventually pulled down in 1934. We know little of Sanderson's music for the ballets that followed *Blackbeard*. *Cora* (1799) had some success and may have influenced Sheridan next year when he chose Pizarro as a subject for a play. Cross took the plot of *Cora* from Kotzebue's *The Virgin of the Sun*. Sanderson's overture was published; also one song. The 1800 novelty was a ballet called *Sir Francis Drake*. Sanderson's later activities need not concern us, except that he must share the blame with Thomas Dibdin for the first English production of Mozart's *Don Giovanni* in 1817. It is arguable that no musical masterpiece has ever been massacred so outrageously.

George Colman had been watching the success of Cross's Pantomime Spectacles, and in 1800 he decided to try the recipe at the Little Theatre. The result was that Arnold ended his career with three ballet scores of far more interest than the three conventional operas he scribbled at much the same time.[1] The most remarkable was also the first, *Obi, or Three-finger'd Jack* (LT 2.7.00). The story, which Baker says was taken from Dr. Moseley's *Treatise on Sugar*, is astonishingly modern and might still excite an audience today. It was, as the Description puts it, 'invented by Mr. Fawcett' the actor, and before the 'Prospectus of the Action' there is some useful background information. The story, it appears, was founded on something that occurred in Jamaica in 1780, and Dr. Moseley is much quoted though not named. Obi (or more correctly Obeah) is African in origin, perhaps Egyptian, and seems to be both a cult related to Voodoo and a substance used in that cult for the purpose of bewitching people. The substance 'is made of grave dirt, hair, teeth of sharks and other animals, blood, feathers, egg shells, images in wax, the hearts of birds', etc., and any negro who thought himself bewitched by it applied for help to the Obi-man or Obi-woman. The help does not seem to have been successful. The huts of these witch-doctors became the haunts of outcasts who took to robbery. The most notorious of them, Three-fingered Jack, terrified his fellow negroes, plundering as he liked and always killing his pursuers. Eventually two negroes called Quashee and Sam managed to trap him.

Arnold's overture was mainly based on 'The Savage Dance' in Linley's pantomime of *Robinson Crusoe*. The curtain rises on a good negro duet and chorus about the miseries of slavery. The negroes are given a holiday to celebrate

[1] Of the operas, *The Veteran Tar* (DL 29.1.01) alone was published in vocal score, but the music is without interest.

the arrival from England of Captain Orford, who is in love with their master's daughter, Rosa. Off-stage Orford is stunned by a blow from Three-fingered Jack (or shot, according to the score), and the negroes are terrified at the nearness of the island's notorious villain. When the Captain staggers in, the orchestra unexpectedly plays the Andante from Mozart's String Quartet in D (K.575); or rather they play about half of it. Arnold must have been studying Mozart's quartets during his final illness, for soon afterwards he quotes the theme of the finale of the D minor. This accompanies a sombre scene inside the Obi-Woman's Cave, where Three-fingered Jack expresses fury because there is now an order for his arrest. However, concealed by 'a Promontory with a view of the Sea', he ambushes those sent to arrest him, throws a negro boy called Tuckey into the sea, and captures Orford, who is dragged into a cave and locked up. Back at 'Montago Bay' Tuckey tells Rosa and her father what has happened. Rosa faints. A reward is offered for killing Jack, and Quashee is baptized to give him a better chance of success. At a Negro Ball there is general though premature rejoicing.

Act II starts inside 'A Slave's Hut'; the details were guaranteed to be correct. Quashee and Sam bid farewell to their families and friends. Rosa arrives disguised as a boy, and asks to be allowed to accompany them. Back at Three-fingered Jack's Cave the villains are prowling to the music of Haydn's 'Surprise' Symphony. Nearly all the slow movement is played, and the action fits surprisingly well. At bar 107 there is some shooting between the good negroes and the bad; in bars 115–16 Jack escapes by climbing a tree. A violent storm springs up and Rosa is so exhausted that she goes into Jack's cave to rest. He makes her his servant. Inside the cave we see her singing Jack to sleep so that she can release Orford. However, he wakes up as she does so, and ties them both up. She escapes by the now familiar pain-defying method of burning the rope that binds her wrists. (Had this ever been done before?) She releases Orford, Quashee kills Jack, the Obi-Woman is captured, and this time the negro rejoicings are fully justified. The final dance comes from Kotzwara's famous piano piece, *The Battle of Prague*. Three-fingered Jack was mimed by Charles Kemble, Rosa by his future wife, Miss de Camp, and the Obi-Woman by a man, Mr. Abbot. Quashee's wife (Mrs. Mountain) had a song with the line 'Go dance to the Banja, just like mad!' (the word is glossed in a footnote as 'a rude musical instrument'), but there is very little singing. Song-words for negroes are mostly in 'coon' English. Almost all the score is orchestral. I have emphasized the borrowings, but most of the music is Arnold's. The movements are much longer than those found in pantomime scores, and there is intelligent repetition, a piece being played again if the story warrants it. Arnold was never blessed with anything approaching genius, but in this ballet he rose at least to some of the occasions.

The Corsair, or The Italian Nuptials (LT 29.7.01) has a more involved but less exciting plot, in which revenge is the mainspring. Not for the first time in our playhouses, there was a representation of Vesuvius erupting. Of the fifty-two separate items, only three were vocal—two choruses and a duet for fisher-men. The score is thus very close to ballet in the modern sense. In the overture there are solos for 'village bells' playing a scale of C. At this date tubular bells are said not to have been invented, but Covent Garden must have had some similar instrument. As always with Arnold, much of the music is shoddy, but some of it surprises with dramatic touches.

There is better music in *Fairies' Revels, or Love in the Highlands* (LT 14.8.02), but judged by length this must have been an afterpiece. Again it was Fawcett who 'invented' the action, but I have not found a copy of the Description. It appears from the score that Donald loves Isabel, that her father disappears, and that a witch called Film is at the bottom of their troubles. Both music and story have the pretty simplicity and some of the basic characteristics later found in Romantic Ballet. The overture begins with a movement based on the opening song, and then sets the atmosphere with Mrs. Jordan's 'Bluebells of Scotland', played first by two cellos on their own and then by two bassoons. Other well-known Scottish tunes are introduced into the mimed and danced scenes, including 'Tweedside' and 'Saw you my Father'. Donald is melancholy to part of the slow movement of Haydn's Symphony No. 93. Arnold's contribution frequently shows him at his most inventive. Two months after the first night he was dead.

LOOSE ENDS, 1796–1800

The last years of the century are a desert in which the view seldom interests. As we have seen, when Storace died in 1796 Drury Lane invited Arnold to compose *The Shipwreck*, but he cannot have given satisfaction, for he was not asked again. Other stopgap composers were William Linley and Attwood.

William Linley (1771–1835) was the youngest of Thomas Linley's twelve children, and his only claim to musical fame lies in his two-volume anthology, *Shakespeare's Dramatic Songs* (1815); when he could not find a setting, he wrote one himself. He spent much of his life in India as the servant of the East India Company, but he was back in England between 1796 and 1800, and composed two never-published afterpieces and a pantomime for Drury Lane. Kelly says they failed 'owing to an unjust cabal'. The pantomime, *Harlequin Captive, or The Magic Fire* (DL 18.1.96) survives in MS in London's Guildhall Library, and this gives it a special interest. Unfortunately the sheets were badly bound in Victorian times, and some of the top staves have been sliced off; also the order is chaotic. But for anyone in pursuit of pantomime music this is a rarity not to be missed, even though the music itself lacks quality. Some of the Comic Tunes and one of the songs are ascribed to Thomas Linley. The music is catalogued under its alternative title.

An afterpiece by this uninteresting composer has also been preserved in full.

The British Museum has a manuscript score of *The Pavilion*,[1] which was performed without success at Drury Lane (16.1.99), and then turned into *The Ring* which was performed without success two months later. Only the song words survive of the first version, but there is a published libretto of *The Ring*. Linley wrote the words as well as the music, and they treat the familiar harem theme without often arousing one's interest. Kelly was the Caliph, and a selection of Arab maidens was played by Miss De Camp, Mrs. Bland, and Mrs. Crouch. The first-named had a good song in C minor in the vein of 'When the night wind howls' in *Ruddigore*:

> Over my head the flitting owl,
> Ravens and bats appear,
> And now a shriek and now a howl
> By turns assail mine ear.

It is significant that Linley did not take Mrs. Crouch above the F at the top of the treble stave. A few years earlier she could have managed the octave above, but by now her voice was finished. One item has a trumpet solo played 'behind the scenes', an original touch.

If Attwood had had any real aptitude for opera he would now have made his mark. By the autumn of 1797 no playhouse could call on any other composer with half his ability. Yet he failed utterly, and the reason is obscure. It is true that he was beset with other work. In 1796 he became organist of St. Paul's and Composer to the Chapel Royal; he even taught the piano to Caroline of Brunswick, the ill-starred wife of the Prince Regent. Yet amid all these activities his theatre music, so far from declining, increased in quantity. Perhaps he lacked interest in the theatre, but needed the money for his wife and growing family.[2]

Attwood's second stint at Drury Lane was even shorter than the first. His afterpiece, *The Smugglers* (DL 13.4.96), had some success and the music was published, but the all-sung *Fairy Festival* (DL 13.5.97) was not much liked, while *Fast Asleep* (DL 28.10.97) collapsed after only three performances. All-sung masques had little hope of success at this period, even when written in honour of the Princess Royal's wedding. Next season Attwood transferred to Covent Garden, and, incredibly, Michael Kelly was Drury Lane's composer for the rest of the century.

As Tom Moore put it when writing to his mother (18.7.02), 'Poor Mick is rather an *im*poser than a composer. He cannot mark the time in writing three bars of music: his understrappers, however, do all that for him, and he has the knack of pleasing the many.' Kelly once admitted to Parke that 'he merely

[1] Eg. 2494. It is bound with Act II of *The Woodcutters*, about which I have no information.

[2] He married Mary Denton in 1793. His eldest son was assassinated in Madrid in 1821.

wrote the melodies, and the old Italian, Mazzanti, did the rest'.[1] In short he hummed tunes for Mazzanti to write down, harmonize, and score. Some of them were pretty in a tum-ti-tum way; for instance 'Yes, Beda, thus' in *Blue Beard*, which became very popular as a Country Dance called 'Tink-a-tink'. But Kelly was in no way equipped for composing dramatic music.

To the credit of the Drury Lane audience, his first two afterpieces failed. He was then so fortunate as to be associated with the highly successful *Castle Spectre* (DL 14.12.97). There were forty-six performances that season, and though there was very little music, and most of that was not by Kelly, what there was was memorable and he was allowed some of the credit. The emotional impact of *The Castle Spectre* was prodigious. As James Boaden put it,

> The set scene had an oratory with a perforated door of pure Gothic, over which was a window of rich tracery, and Mrs. Jordan, who played Angela, being on the stage, a brilliant illumination suddenly took place, and the doors of the oratory opened—the light was perfectly celestial, and a majestic and lovely, but melancholy image stood before us; at this moment, in a low but sweet and thrilling harmony, the band played the strain of Jomelli's *Chaconne*, in his celebrated overture in three flats . . . And the figure began slowly to advance; it was the spirit of Angela's mother, Mrs. Powell, in all her beauty, with long sweeping envelopments of muslin attached to the wrist.[2]

'Monk' Lewis's plot concerned the monstrous Osmond, who has killed Angela's mother before the piece begins, and now wants to marry Angela. The ghost prevents Osmond from killing Angela's father too; he is languishing in the castle dungeon. The ghost is finally laid when Angela stabs Osmond. But it was Mrs. Powell's entrance that everyone remembered, and the background music played a vital part in the effect. Here for instance is Thomas Peacock in his novel *Gryll Grange* (1861), putting his own boyhood memories into the mouth of Miss Ilex:

> In my young days ghosts were so popular that the first question asked about any new play was, Is there a ghost in it? *The Castle Spectre* had set this fashion . . . The opening of the folding-doors disclosing the illuminated oratory; the extreme beauty of the actress who personated the ghost; the solemn music to which she moved slowly forward to give a silent blessing to her kneeling daughter; and the chorus of female voices chanting *Jubilate*; made an impression on me which no other scene of the kind ever made.

In fact the *Jubilate* consisted of no more than four bars of conventional four-part harmony; yet they were remembered.

[1] Parke ii, p. 127. Ferdinando Mazzanti was a minor Italian composer, praised of course by Burney, who published some sets of songs in London.

[2] *Mrs. Jordan* i, p. 347.

Background music usually has an unconscious effect on an audience; Kelly's is of interest because its effect was widely noticed. Jomelli's Chaconne begins:

Music from the Oratory while the Ghost appears

Jomelli

Kelly borrowed eight more bars, perhaps a tenth of the whole movement (which is not a Chaconne but in sonata form). In the theatre the simplest devices are often the most effective.

Kelly was a simple soul. Years later when returning from Dublin he found himself on the ferry by Conway Castle. This was where *The Castle Spectre* was supposed to have happened, and as he crossed the water Kelly sang the only considerable item he had composed himself, a glee called 'Megan oh'. The other passengers, he rather naïvely remarked, 'seemed much astonished, and, by their silence, not ill pleased at the animated manner in which I was singing'.

Blue Beard (DL 16.1.98) was much the biggest score to which Kelly put his name. Perrault's tale had been made into an opera by Grétry in 1789; Kelly had seen *Barbe Bleue* in Paris, and he brought back what he described as a programme of it. He paid Colman £200 to make a libretto out of the synopsis. Colman kept the title, but turned the French villain into a Turkish one, Abomelique. So many effects went wrong on the first night that Kelly was in despair, but Miss De Camp's spirited singing of 'I see them galloping' was generally agreed to have saved the day. This was part of a quartet in which the latest wife, Fatima (Mrs. Crouch), also sang, and the splendid stage set given on the vocal score show this very ensemble, with the brothers in the far distance galloping to their rescue. There had been an unsuccessful Covent Garden pantomime called *Blue Beard* in 1791, with unpublished music[1] by Baumgarten, but it was Kelly's opera that first popularized the story in Britain.

Unusually for the time, the score names the composer of each item, giving Kelly's name for eleven of the fifteen. As the eleven include a good many elaborate ensembles and choruses, loud doubts were expressed as to the truth of the ascriptions, but this had no effect on the popularity of this 'Grand Dramatic Romance', which held the stage for the rest of Kelly's life. The quartet near the end with Fatima and Irene on the castle walls is the most interesting part of the score, and the threatening trombone notes are unusual. According to

[1] A quartet from this pantomime survives in BM Add. 25075.

Kelly, the military march near the start 'where Blue Beard comes over the mountain' was scored for military band by 'Mr. Eley', the German bandmaster. He needed more than one understrapper to keep him going.

In the cast was Kelly's seven-year-old niece, Fanny Kelly, who later became a popular actress and singer. In 1819 Charles Lamb wrote her a memorably charming letter which, in a round-about way, proposed marriage, but she refused him.

The only other Drury Lane opera of any interest was an afterpiece called *The Captive of Spilburg* (DL 14.11.98). It had a Czech subject, and a Czech composer was entrusted with the music. Jan Ladislav Dussek (1760–1812) was astonishingly gifted, and sadly limited. A virtuoso pianist who lived in London throughout the 1790s, he played concertos in several of the Haydn-Salomon concerts. Almost all his compositions have a piano part, and he was not at home in any other medium. It would be hard to exaggerate the brilliance and excitement of his piano writing at its best. The fiery development sections, the astonishing modulations, the anticipations of such unlikely composers as Chopin and Brahms, should have put him among the very great. But almost all his music is flawed by banal patches; he had no powers of self-criticism. Nevertheless Dussek addicts today are not uncommon; his music can still exercise an extraordinary fascination.

Prince Hoare derived the libretto of *The Captive of Spilburg* from Dalayrac's *Camille, ou le Souterrain* (1791), and Genest found it 'rather too serious for a musical piece'. Eugenia (Mrs. Crouch) has secretly married Korowitz. She is rescued from robbers by her husband's nephew, Canzemar (Kelly), who does not know of the marriage. He tries to seduce her, fails, and lets her go on condition that she swears never to reveal his advances. Thus she cannot tell her husband where she has been; thinking her false, he puts her in a dungeon. All comes right in the end.

Dussek had no great gift for vocal writing, or for that matter experience of it, and he felt he could not tax his singers with the difficulties of his famous modulations. The result is that though there are some fairly successful imitations of the sort of traditional air on which he sometimes wrote piano variations, the music as a whole lacks individuality. Dussek showed most of himself in the one-movement overture. The main theme of the Allegro is trivial, but there is a striking switch from C major to D flat in the slow introduction, and some splendid passages later. The following transition is typical:

Pizarro (DL 24.5.99) finds scarcely any readers today, but it was the talk of London when it was first produced. Sheridan had not written a play for twenty years, and perhaps was no longer capable of writing one of his own; he preferred to refurbish a bombastic melodrama by Kotzebue.[1] The result is stage fustian at its most turgid, but it accorded with the taste of its time. Kelly was called on for a good deal of incidental music, about half of it in Act II scene ii, 'The Temple of the Sun', which is operatic in its emphasis. The play as printed mentions several choruses of priests and priestesses, as well as a dirge at the very end sung over Rolla's corpse, yet it does not provide any words for them. The words are of course in the vocal score, and they should be in modern editions of the play as well. Sheridan had been dilatory beyond belief, finishing the dialogue on the morning of the first night, and no doubt he had given Kelly the chorus words on odd scraps of paper that he later forgot when sending the text to the printer. The text does include the only solo song, sung in the fifth act by Cora (Mrs. Jordan); this was originally to have been set by William Linley, but the score attributes it to Kelly. In Act II scene ii Kelly wrote the march at the start, Thomas Shaw the one at the end; no doubt Shaw was still leading the orchestra. For the middle of the scene Kelly borrowed 'The March of the Priestesses' from Act III of Gluck's *Iphigénie en Tauride* ('Chaste fille') and a 'Chorus of Priests' from Sacchini, adding some music of his own. He took the choral 'Song of Victory' in Act III scene i from Cherubini. Throughout the play only the Peruvians sing. Kelly himself composed their final Lamentation on the Death of Rolla, ending it with a few bars for oboes and trombone. As well as Mrs. Jordan, John and Charles Kemble were in the cast, and also Mrs. Siddons. The occasion was thought so important that Kelly, Dignum, Sedgwick, Mrs. Crouch, Miss De Camp, and Miss Leake all helped to swell the chorus, though none had a speaking part. Dussek wrote the overture which does not survive.

[1] Some fifteen years later Kotzebue was writing two short operatic librettos for Beethoven, *Die Ruinen von Athen* and *König Stephan.*

Drury Lane's musical standards were declining because the theatre had no adequate composer or music director, and no influx of young singers. Covent Garden was in no better state. In the last four years of the century this theatre staged at least six new operas a season, but they were slapdash affairs, forgotten as soon as seen, and hardly any lingered in the repertoire. Reeve's pantomimes, ballets, and afterpieces have abysmal music, but *Raymond and Agnes* is worth a mention. Half a century later, the story was reworked by Edward Fitzball for an interesting opera by Edward Loder which was given at Cambridge in May 1966. Reeve's twelve-page score consisted of no more than the overture and three vocal items; the presumably dramatic music that accompanied all the mimed action was never published. Agnes, the heroine, had a song that began:

> Full fifteen years have passed away
> Since first within these walls
> Appear'd the Ghost whose gliding form
> The stoutest heart appals.
> Long time here nightly stalk'd this bleeding Nun,
> Her entrance at the awful hour of one.

The libretto derived from the famous Horror Novel, *The Monk*, which gave Matthew Lewis his nickname. Three songs from Reeve's *Joan of Arc* were published in virtual full score, but again none of the actual ballet music survives.

For Mrs. Mountain's benefit James Hook intruded again into the playhouses with an afterpiece opera called *Diamond cut Diamond* (CG 23.5.97), but it was rightly thought not worth adopting. Baker attributed the libretto to Theodore Hook, who was eleven at the time; perhaps his brother wrote it. Hook composed more operas in the first two decades of the next century but learnt nothing of dramatic writing in the process.

Because he did not care to trust Reeve with a full-length opera, Harris persuaded him to collaborate with Mazzinghi. The result was *Ramah Droog* (CG 12.11.98), the name of the hill-fort in India depicted on the title-page of the score. Genest found Cobb's main plot 'dull to the last degree', and it also suffers from racialist undertones. Not all the items in the score are attributed, but those that are show that Mazzinghi was a much better composer than Reeve. His three-movement overture is spirited and inventive, and it was published in parts. The elaborate ensembles in this opera do not repay study.

The same composers collaborated in a poor afterpiece called *The Turnpike Gate* (CG 14.11. 99) which had a libretto by Thomas Knight. For insufficient reasons Reeve's overture was published in parts. *Paul and Virginia* (CG 1.5.00) by the same composers was based on a famous desert island romance that had already been made into an opera by Kreutzer and Lesueur; as also into a King's Theatre ballet with music by Mazzinghi himself (KT 26.3.95). Cobb's libretto was never published. Mazzinghi's overture is disappointing, but Reeve's ballad songs are more memorable than usual. His 'Negro March' has a tinge of local colour, and the following Dance (also for negroes?) starts with twenty-four bars of 'Solo Bells', written on two staves with chords in the bass. Near the end of the opera there is an elaborate 'Storm Scene' by Mazzinghi that apes the ones by Arnold; during a chorus Paul carries 'his lovely Prize' (Virginia) through the waves to the shore.

Meanwhile Attwood had had a long innings at Covent Garden, though he should have been dismissed several times. In 1798 he contrived five failures in a row, and none of their music was published.[1] In *The Magic Oak, or Harlequin Woodcutter* (CG 29.1.99) there was a return to past techniques, with Attwood writing the overture, marches, and songs (which were published), and Mountain and Eley supplying the Comic Tunes (which were not). No description survives of Tom Dibdin's action. Some of these Attwood scores are great rarities, which probably means that very few copies were sold. BUCEM lists only one copy of *The Old Cloathsman* (CG 2.4.99) and *The Red Cross Knights* (LT 21.8.99), and none at all of *True Friends* (CG 19.2.00), though a vocal score turned up at a sale in 1964. The first of these had a libretto by Holcroft, and there is a great deal of information about it in his *Reminiscences*. Holcroft claimed to have composed the first number himself, with help from Shield. *The Red Cross Knights* was a full-length play by Holman based on Schiller's *Die Räuber*, and there was not much music. As usual Attwood included something by his revered master, Mozart, and this time it was 'Bei Männern' from *Die Zauberflöte*. In *Il Bondocani* (CG 15.11.00) it was the rather uninteresting end to the Finale in *Die Entführung*; Thomas Dibdin's title was the name assumed by Haroun al Raschid as he roamed Baghdad by night in disguise. Attwood collaborated with John Moorehead, whose overture is surprisingly good.

Moorehead was an Irish violinist who joined the Covent Garden band in 1798; he died in 1804. He compiled a pastiche afterpiece called *The Naval Pillar* (CG 7.10.99) and a pantomime called *The Volcano* (CG 23.12.99), and in both cases the music was published. The former was fulsomely patriotic, and had a Finale based on 'The Star-spangled Banner' (described as an 'Old Air'). The latter anticipated Arnold's *The Corsair* in showing Vesuvius in action; the overture depicts it both 'in its Quiet State' and erupting furiously. Moorehead had some talent for orchestral music, but none at all for songs. The deplorable state to which playhouse music sank can be exemplified by his hugely-enjoyed *Perouse* (1801), in which the chief character was a chimpanzee on a desert island. London audiences were suddenly animal-mad, and Reeve's *The Cabinet* was prodigiously successful entirely because, at the climax, a small boy was rescued from a waterfall by a Newfoundland dog called Carlo. It was described as an opera.

Attwood churned out yet another secret-passage afterpiece for Colman called *The Castle of Sorrento* (LT 13.7.99); the libretto derived from Della Maria's

[1] See MT December 1965 for a list in a useful article by C. B. Oldman.

opera *Le Prisonnier*, and C. B. Oldman has described the Trio and Chorus as 'some of Attwood's most ambitious writing for the stage'. Attwood also concocted the first Welsh ballad opera, *St. David's Day* (CG 25.3.00), and dedicated the score to his first patron, the Prince of Wales. The dedicatory letter has biographical interest. The plot is about an honest Welshman who finds a pocket-book containing £100, and keeps it safely until he is able to restore it to its owner twenty years later. Such a subject could hardly be other than boring. 'Men of Harlech' is among the Welsh tunes in the overture. Attwood wrote three more short operas in 1801, and for the remaining thirty-seven years of his life devoted very much less time to the theatre. He did however contribute in 1816 to Bishop's *Guy Mannering*. He ended his life an admired composer of anthems for St. Paul's and a close friend of Mendelssohn.

Little need be said of Sadler's Wells in the 1790s. The type of entertainment offered had scarcely changed in a quarter of a century. In 1791 Wordsworth went several times to 'half-rural Sadler's Wells', and

> Saw Singers, Rope-dancers, Giants and Dwarfs,
> Clowns, Conjurors, Posture-Masters, Harlequins,
> Amid the uproar of the rabblement
> Perform their feats.

They were still staging naval battles fought between model ships, and, a charming touch of naïveté, Wordsworth saw Jack the Giant-killer 'conceal' himself by donning 'his Coat of Darkness'.

> How is it wrought? His garb is black, the word
> INVISIBLE flames forth upon his chest.[1]

Mark Lonsdale was the manager and wrote most of the librettos. They were usually set by Reeve. The British Museum has a volume of his overtures,[2] and many individual songs by Reeve and others were published, but I have found only two vocal scores. Reeve's *Tippoo Saib* (sic; July 1791) is one. Lonsdale's libretto does not seem to survive in print. Tippoo Sahib had recently invaded Travancore, but he was defeated by Lord Cornwallis aided by the Mahrattas and the Nizam. The Sadler's Wells production was described as spectacular. Covent Garden had staged an unsuccessful and unpublished 'pantomime ballet' on the same theme a month earlier.

In 1796 Lonsdale handed over the management of Sadler's Wells to Thomas Dibdin, who brought in Alexander Moorehead to lead the orchestra and his brother, John Moorehead, to compose. Two years later John was lured away by Covent Garden; some of the music he wrote for that theatre has already been mentioned. In his place Dibdin engaged V. de Cleeve, about whom I have no

[1] *The Prelude* (1805 ed.) VII, 280–345.
[2] BM g. 137.

information.[1] His 'Comic, Pastoral, Burletta', *The Bird-Catcher* (1799) was published in vocal score, and is of interest because, although it omits the music of the recitatives, it gives the words on the last page in the form of dialogue. Dibdin's father had composed precisely similar little operas for Sadler's Wells a quarter of a century earlier. The four characters are all working-class. Robin, a bird-catcher, and Peter, a fisherman, both love Nancy, who sells watercress. To further his cause, Peter brings a writ for debt against Robin, but Snatchem, the apparently unprincipled bailiff, is won over by Nancy's charms, and generously lends the money. Peter was played by Grimaldi. The overture has two movements, the second a likeable rondo. The songs are well above the contemptible. There is a short orchestral interlude headed 'The Fisherman rowing in his boat'.

[1] He was no longer at Sadler's Wells in 1800 when Charles Dibdin Junior took over the management. See *Memoirs of Charles Dibdin The Younger*, ch. v.

16

Debits and Credits

DURING the Napoleonic Wars, English theatre music plumbed the lowest level of all time, and it is not much consolation to realize that, Beethoven apart, music was in a low state all over Europe.[1] As there was a renaissance in most countries from about 1815 it does look as though widespread war has a debilitating effect on composers; though not, apparently, on writers. So far as London was concerned, the renaissance exemplified in the music of Henry Bishop may not have been very startling in its degree, but it is real enough to anyone who studies Bishop's predecessors.

The trouble is that our eighteenth-century composers were often deficient even when there was no widespread war, and in these final pages I must try to put as good a face on this fact as possible. I hope not to overstate my case. I am well aware that much of the music described in this book is near-rubbish, and not worth ever playing again. It is impossible to look at the later music of Dibdin or any music by Reeve without wondering how anyone could write such stuff; or indeed listen to it. One must suppose that then as now theatre music often got by because the audience was enjoying what it saw, and not listening at all.

The absence of music schools in England has sometimes been put forward as a reason for our composers' inadequacies, but it does not carry very much weight. Had Dibdin been to one, his harmony and counterpoint would have been better, but he might easily have lost his vitality and sense of the theatre. Very few of the better eighteenth-century composers learnt their craft in a conservatoire, and those Italian opera composers who did tended within any given period all to write alike. Tradition in Italian conservatoires was so strong that composers seemed able to break away from it only if they spent most of their working lives abroad; as did Boccherini, Clementi, and Cherubini. Paisiello and Sacchini both wrote much better music out of Italy than in, and those who stayed behind or ventured abroad but seldom tended to compose like computers. The eighteenth century was not one that encouraged experiment, but it does seem to me that English opera music, with all its faults, has at its

---

[1] Was it coincidence that Beethoven's only serious rivals between 1800 and 1815 all worked in exile? Who else was there besides Clementi, Dussek, Cherubini, and Field? Even Beethoven was hardly on home ground in Vienna.

best more individuality than the Italian opera music that Burney praised so lavishly. Indeed one could not now support his judgements, for the composers he admired have not lasted as well as Boyce and Arne. How many of us today could hum a tune by Burney's idol, Sacchini?

The truth is that at all periods all countries produce a high proportion of poor music. Anyone who wrote a comprehensive book about late eighteenth-century French opera would find himself describing quite as many rubbishy works as I have done, and the generalization would be almost as true if the subject were Italian opera. (And perhaps I should add that bad music is as much a part of history as good, and no apology is needed because of its inclusion here.)

But if we are to form any worthwhile judgements bad music is a red herring. The question is not why there is so much bad music in the English theatres, for that is inevitable, but why there is not more that is good. Those who wrote the best music on the Continent usually learnt their technique in the family or in a music-filled environment; for instance all the Bachs and Mozart. In this respect English composers, and for that matter French, were at a sad disadvantage. The rage for Italian opera early in the century destroyed any tradition that might have stemmed from Purcell, and deprived our composers of any hope of a music-filled environment. We had no system of private patronage such as composers enjoyed in central Europe. A dozen or so princelings and archbishops, in geographically close rivalry, are much more likely to encourage composers than a single king in a unified kingdom. In England, as in France, for want of any other employer composers relied on the theatres, more especially in the second half of the century. But in the theatres, it so happened, the emphasis was on the acting rather than on what was said or sung. It is the actors who were famous, rather than the dramatists or composers. It is the actors that we today can most easily name; very few indeed of our theatre-lovers could call to mind any dramatists between Congreve and Gilbert other than Sheridan and Goldsmith. In the days of Garrick, Mrs. Siddons, and the Kembles, dramatists had to write what the theatres wanted or their plays would not be staged. Our composers were similarly circumscribed. Experiment and novelty were not in demand.

But a number of factors have conspired to make us think worse of English composers than they deserved, and the chief of these is sheer ignorance. We do not know the music partly because so little of it survives orchestrally. In 1808 Covent Garden and in 1809 Drury Lane were burnt to the ground and their music libraries totally destroyed. MS full scores and orchestral parts of such operas as *Artaxerxes* and *The Pirates* vanished overnight for ever. In France such a loss might have been reparable, for throughout the last forty years of the century French all-sung and dialogue operas, many of them much less interesting than the best English examples, were published complete in full score. London publishers had been wretchedly cautious in their concentration on vocal scores, and it is partly their fault that our opera inheritance survives in so maimed a state. Yet some of our eighteenth-century operas continued to be staged after the theatre fires. Either they were rescored by hacks, or MS parts survived in the provinces. It would seem that we must also blame Victorian librarians for throwing away tattered scores and parts of operas they thought would never be produced again.

Our historians, failing to find the music in a form that did it justice, have been confirmed in their indifference to it by what they read in Burney. Burney was a magnificent historian, but he suffered from the common national defect of believing that only foreigners could compose, sing, or play. Until recently his judgements, even the most biased, have scarcely ever been questioned, and they have done untold damage to the cause of English music.

Those who have wanted reasons for the alleged failure of our composers have sometimes blamed Handel's all-pervasive influence. It is true enough that early in the century our composers were silenced by the clamour for Italian Opera, but they would have been silenced if Handel had never lived. In whatever country he had settled, he would have outshone all rivals; Arne and Boyce are not of no account merely because they were lesser figures. Indeed they held their own reasonably well. It is quite untrue that later composers failed through aping Handel's style. His influence (except in oratorios) was very slight in the 1750s and precisely nil from the 1760s onwards.

It should be remembered that until quite recently the lesser figures in eighteenth-century music were not well thought of whatever their country of birth. Concert giveis and goers believed that Bach, Handel, Haydn, and Mozart were so superior to any of their contemporaries that their music alone was worth playing. It is still not sufficiently realized that the best symphonies of, say, Beck and Vanhal are more interesting than the worst of Haydn and Mozart. But at last we are beginning to value the music of second-rank composers. Before the last war it would have been virtually impossible to interest people in the music of C. P. E. and J. C. Bach, but broadcasts and long-playing records have revealed many minor masterpieces in what they wrote, and these same media are at last beginning to do the same for such English composers as Boyce. Today we are ready to enjoy our own musical heritage as never before.

I do not myself believe that our composers were markedly inferior to our creative artists in other fields. None was the equal of Fielding, Sterne, or Gainsborough, but had the younger Thomas Linley not died at twenty-two he would surely have been a composer of similar calibre. No country can expect *many* such creative artists. As for Arne and Boyce and Greene and Storace, they were surely the equal of the Thomsons and Cowpers of poetry, and the Haymans and Wilsons of painting. They have suffered from ill luck and prejudice rather than natural deficiency.

Even in the worst times there was talent just below the surface, and I end with an example by a composer who has not so far been mentioned, a composer whose gifts would surely have got him into the history books if he had lived in

Vienna rather than in London. John Davy (1763–1824) is remembered, if at all, for his song, 'The Bay of Biscay', though in fact the tune was a shanty he picked up from Incledon. Davy had been a pupil of Jackson's, and was at least thirty by the time he reached London and became a Covent Garden violinist. As a composer he must have been a late starter (a national characteristic?), and as a man he may have lacked personality, for his own theatre did not at first notice his potentialities. It was Colman who staged his first opera, the full-length *What a Blunder!* (LT 14.8.00). The libretto by Joseph Holman had the twin advantages of a Spanish setting and a heroine named Leonora, but I am here concerned only with the one-movement overture, which has an energy and drive that make one think of Beethoven. If a full score survived, it would surely be played regularly. The slow introduction in D minor is full of feeling, and has some good writing for flutes and bassoons. (There are instrumental cues in the vocal score arrangement.) The main Allegro starts pianissimo in octaves, and soon develops interesting syncopations:

The pretty second subject is shared by flute and bassoon in alternation. The development starts by treating the first subject; I include the final bar of the exposition:

The theme is so fully discussed that it is omitted at the beginning of the recapitulation. The coda, quiet and resigned, is lovely, but the impression given by the overture as a whole is one of controlled strength.

Yet the man who wrote this music was given no real encouragement until he was thirty-seven. What a blunder, one might say, as so often where English opera is concerned. It is both sad and significant that, theatrical conditions being what they were, so gifted a composer never grew to eminence. As so often the talent was there but not the conditions in which it could ripen.

APPENDIX A

Operas that Survive Orchestrally
(complete or nearly so)

Titles in CAPITALS: Full-length Operas
Titles in lower case: Afterpieces
All have spoken dialogue unless marked 'All-sung'
C in right-hand margin indicates complete survival
PFS: Published Full Score (locations as in BUCEM)
PP: Published (orchestral) Parts
MSFS: Manuscript Full Score (locations as in BUCEM)
MSOP: Manuscript Orchestral Parts (locations as in BUCEM)
Published librettos are in BM unless otherwise stated

Arne, T. A.
    COMUS (Milton–Dalton), 1738: PFS lacking recits and choruses;   C
        MSFS (L Add. 11518) virtually complete; mod. ed. Musica
        Britannica
    The Judgment of Paris (Congreve), 1742, all-sung: PFS lacking 1st
        recit and final chorus; end of chorus MSFS (L Add. 29370)
    ALFRED (Thompson–Mallet–Arne), 1753, all-sung: PFS lacking
        recits and the 8 choruses
    ELIZA (Rolt), 1754, all-sung: PFS lacking recits, 2 dances, and 5
        short choral endings to songs
    Thomas and Sally (Bickerstaffe), 1760, all-sung: PFS   C
    LOVE IN A VILLAGE (Bickerstaffe), 1762: MSFS (LCM 342)   C
    ARTAXERXES (Arne), 1762, all-sung: PFS lacking recits (but
        see p. 309) and final chorus
Bates
    THE JOVIAL CREW (many hands), 1760, PFS   C
Battishill–Potter
    The Rites of Hecate (Love), 1763, pantomime (no speech): MSFS of
        Battishill's vocal items (L Add. 31812); PFS Potter's Comic Tunes;
        no libretto
Beckford
    The Arcadian Pastoral (Lady Craven), 1782: MSFS (in private
        hands; copy in BBC Music Library): no libretto

Boyce
>   Peleus and Thetis (Lansdowne), *c.* 1736, all-sung: MSFS (O Mus.   C
>   d. 24, the autograph, and c. 113 MSOP and vocal parts)
>   The Secular Masque (Dryden), *c.* 1745, all-sung: MSFS (LCM 93   C
>   autograph?)
>   The Chaplet (Mendez), 1749, all-sung: PFS and MSFS (LK)   C
>   The Shepherds' Lottery (Mendez), 1751, all-sung: PFS   C

Burney
>   ALFRED (Thompson–Mallet), 1751: PFS lacking dances and three
>   songs that end with choral sections

Callcott
>   The Mistakes of a Day (anon), 1785: MSFS (L Add. 27638)   C

Clayton
>   ARSINOE (Motteux), 1705, all-sung: PFS lacking recits and sug-
>   gesting only continuo accompaniments for arias
>   ROSAMOND (Addison), 1707, all-sung: PFS lacking recits and
>   suggesting only continuo accompaniments for arias

Dibdin
>   The Recruiting Sergeant (Bickerstaffe), 1769, all-sung: PFS but with   C
>   only str. parts for airs; MSFS of 2 airs with wind parts included
>   (L Add. 30951)

Eccles, J.
>   EUROPE'S REVELLS (Motteux), 1697: MSFS (L Add. 29378)   C
>   RINALDO AND ARMIDA (Dennis), 1698: MSFS (L Add.
>   29378)
>   The Judgment of Paris (Congreve) 1701, all-sung: PFS; nearly full-   C
>   length
>   SEMELE (Congreve), 1707, all-sung: MSFS (LCM 183) for str.
>   only, lacking overture, start of first scene, dances in Act II, one
>   page in Act III, and several at the end.

Finger
>   THE VIRGIN PROPHETESS (Settle) 1701: PFS of selected   C
>   songs; PP of instrumental items; MSFS (CFM 23.H.12, and
>   LCM 862)

Galliard
>   CALYPSO AND TELEMACHUS (Hughes), 1712, all-sung:
>   PFS lacking recits and final chorus
>   Pan and Syrinx (Theobald), 1718, all-sung: MSFS (L Add. 31588)   C

Greene
>   (FLORIMEL OR) LOVE'S REVENGE (J. Hoadly), 1734, all-sung:
>   MSFS (LK 22.d.14; LCM 226; L Add. 5325; L Add. 15980 has
>   Part II only in Boyce's hand; LCM 227 is MS VS)

PHOEBE (J. Hoadly), 1747, all-sung: MSFS (O Mus. d. 53 is   C
    autograph; L Add. 5324)

Hayes, P.
  Telemachus (Graham), 1763, all-sung: MSFS (O Mus. d.77 lack-
    ing last few pages)

Hayes, W.
  Peleus and Thetis (Lansdowne), 1749 or earlier, all-sung: MSFS (O   C
    Mus.d.79/80, MSOP O Mus. d.126/7)

Jackson
  THE LORD OF THE MANOR (Burgoyne), 1780: PFS (GE   C
    only)

Lampe
  THE DRAGON OF WANTLEY (Carey), 1737, all-sung: PFS,   C
    2 vols, lacking recits; MSFS (LCM 927)
  MARGERY (Carey), 1738, all-sung: PFS, 2 vols, lacking recits
  The Sham Conjuror (?), 1741: PFS lacking dances; no libretto
  Pyramus and Thisbe (Shakespeare etc.), 1745: PFS lacking recits;
    libretto O Malone 151

Linley, T. and T.
  THE DUENNA (Sheridan), 1775: PP of overture; MSFS of new
    items (but not overture) by younger Linley (L Eg.2493); MSFS of
    Act III (LGC Gresham 376) lacking glee and finale

Linley, T., jun.
  The Cady of Bagdad (Portal), 1778: MSFS (L Add. 29297)   C

Linley, W.
  (Harlequin Captive or) Fire and Water (?), 1796, Panto: MSFS
    (LGC); no libretto
  The Pavilion (W. Linley), 1799: MSFS (L Eg.2494); Song words   C
    pub. but no libretto (but see p. 571)

Nares
  The Royal Pastoral (anon.), 1769, all-sung: PFS; no known perfs.   C
    and no known libretto

Pepusch
  Venus and Adonis (Cibber), 1715, all-sung; PFS lacking recits and final   C
    chorus; MSFS (LCM) includes recits and final chorus; also MSOP
    (LCM)
  Apollo and Daphne (Cibber), 1716, all-sung: MSFS (LCM 976)   C

Purcell, D.
  (with Clarke and Leveridge) THE ISLAND PRINCESS (Fletcher   C
    and Tate), 1698: MSFS (L Add. 15318)
  THE GROVE (Oldmixon), 1700: PFS of selected songs; MSFS
    (LCM 988) lacking overture

(with Finger) The Secular Masque (Dryden), 1700: MSFS of first half L Add. 29378

The Judgment of Paris (Congreve), 1701, all-sung: PFS and MSFS (CFM 23. H. 12 and L Add. 29398); nearly full-length

(with Finger) THE RIVAL QUEENS (Lee), 1701: MSFS (CFM   C
23. H. 12)

Sammartini, Giuseppe

The Judgment of Paris (Congreve), 1740, all-sung: (LK 23.b.21 and   C
23.b.22; L Add. 17860)

Shield

Rosina (Frances Brooke), 1782: MSOP (L Add. 33815)   C

Smith, J. C.

TERAMINTA (Carey), 1732, all-sung: MSFS (LCM 1020)   C

ULYSSES (Humphreys), 1733, all-sung: MSFS autograph (Ham-   C
burg Staats- und Universitätsbibliothek MA/279)

ISSIPILE (Metastasio), 1743, all-sung to It. words: MSFS (L Add.   C
31700) lacking recits

IL CIRO RICONOSCIUTO (Metastasio), 1745, all-sung to It.
words: MSFS (Hamburg Staats- und Universitätsbibliothek MA/
668) lacking recits

THE FAIRIES (Shakespeare, etc.), 1755, all-sung: PFS lacking
recits, dances, and one song that ends chorally

THE TEMPEST (Shakespeare etc.), 1756, all-sung: PFS lacking
recits and choruses

The Enchanter (Garrick), 1769, all-sung: PFS lacking recits, a dance,
and two choruses

Stanley

Arcadia (Lloyd), 1761, all-sung: MSFS (LCM 1022)   C

Storace

GLI SPOSI MALCONTENTI (Brunati), 1785, all sung to It.
words: MSFS (Dresden Sächsisches Landeshauptarchiv Mus.
4109 F/2); no libretto known

GLI EQUIVOCI (Shakespeare–da Ponte), 1786, all-sung to It.   C
words: MSFS (Vienna, K.T. 133; Dresden, Mus. 4109/F/1);
Libretto in Munich etc., but no known copy in Britain

No Song no Supper (Hoare), 1790; MSFS (LCM 597); modern   C
Musica Britannica ed.

Weldon

The Judgment of Paris (Congreve), 1701, all-sung: MSFS Folger   C
Library, Washington; nearly full-length

Yates

The Choice of Apollo (Potter), 1765, all-sung: MSFS (LCM 645)   C

Early Italianate Operas

Saggione (Fedelli)
> THE TEMPLE OF LOVE (Motteux), 1706, all-sung: PFS of most
> songs

Bononcini, M.A.
> CAMILLA (Swiney), 1706, all-sung: PFS of songs; also PFS and
> PP of overture and songs for 1719 revival (CFM); also MSFS
> (LCM 779); a great deal survives

(Pastiche)
> THOMYRIS (Motteux), 1707, all-sung: PFS of selected songs; PP
> of 'Symphonies or instrumental Parts'; PP of G. Bononcini's overture

Gasparini, etc.
> LOVE'S TRIUMPH (Motteux), 1708, all-sung: PFS of most
> songs; PP of 'Symphonies or instrumental Parts'

Scarlatti, A., etc.
> PYRRHUS AND DEMETRIUS (Haym), 1708, all-sung: PFS of
> most songs; PP of 'Symphonies or instrumental Parts'

Conti
> CLOTILDA (Heidegger), 1709, all-sung: PFS of most songs; PP of
> 'Symphonies or instrumental Parts'

Scores for which I cannot account

?
> THE ENTERTAINMENT (?), MSFS (LCM 2231), lacking   C
> spoken dialogue. I can find no libretto. Act II includes 'A comical
> Mask representing the five senses', and Harlequin is among the
> dancers. The Act III masque, 'Bacchusses Revells', has jovial
> working-class characters and an overture by Kremberg, who came
> to London in 1697. The score must date from the next ten years,
> and probably from the next three.

Legnani
> ELMIRA (?), MSFS (Tenbury 1074) has English words only, and   C
> includes the recits. Characters: Elmira, Gobrina, Arsinda, Ferindo
> (the hero, a counter-tenor), Teramene, and Frulla (a comic 'cor-
> poral', bass). Elmira is made tyrannical by a spell, removed even-
> tually by Pan; she has a good tragic aria. Several scenes are comic.
> The score could have been prepared for London production just
> before Handel's arrival.

Giordani, T.

Un-named afterpiece (?), MSFS (LGC) includes a few borrowed   C
items, apparently from Italian operas. Cues show there was spoken
dialogue. Characters; Eudosia, Mariana, Sir Jonh (*sic*), Mellifont,
Pagliano, Lord Wiffler. No such opera was given in London; performances, if any, must have been in Dublin.

This Appendix could also have included Handel's *Acis and Galatea, Semele,*
and *Hercules*; also those Ballad Operas that were published with basses to the
airs.

APPENDIX B

Theatre Overtures and Ayres Published in Parts 1698–1708

(See pp. 24–5)

The list that follows may well be far from complete. It does not include the sets of untitled theatre music that John Eccles published in 1698, 1699, and 1700; these survive only in Durham. The items I have listed are of such rarity that I have given locations. All are for four-part string band.

Locations as in BUCEM (see p. xiii)

HA: *Harmonia Anglicana*, pub. 1701

* An incomplete set of parts; L(HA)* consists of VI.I only

LCM: A complete set of four part books (xxix A 11)

LCM*: A set of part books (xxix A 12) lacking VI.I, the part in L(HA)*

Allnott
 Phaedra and Hippolitus (Smith) QT 21.4.07   L
Barrett
 The Pilgrim (Fletcher–Dryden) DL 29.4.00   L*; L(HA)*; LCM*
 The Generous Conqueror   DL Dec. 1701   L(HA)*; LCM*
  (Higgons)
 Tunbridge Walks (Thomas   DL 27.1.03   L*; L(HA)*; LCM
  Baker)
 Mary Queen of Scots (?)   DL? 1704   L*; L(HA)*; LCM
 The Fine Lady's Airs   DL 14.12.08   L
  (Thomas Baker)
Clarke
 All for the Better (Manning) DL Nov. 1702   L*; L(HA)*
Corbett
 Henry the Fourth, or The   Oxford *c.* 1700   L*; LCM
  Humours of Falstaff
 Love Betray'd or The Agreeable LIF Jan. 1703   LCM
  Disappointment (Burnaby)
 As you find it (Boyle)   LIF 28.4.03   L*; LCM
 The British Enchanters   QT 21.2.06   L*
  (Lord Lansdowne)
 'For the Theatre'   ?   L

Croft
Courtship à la mode (Crauford)   DL 9.7.00   L*; LCM
The Funeral (Steel)   DL Dec. 1701   L*; L(HA)*; LCM
The Twin Rivals (Farquhar)   DL 14.12.02   LCM
The Lying Lover (Steele)   DL 2.12.03   L; L*; LCM
Deane, Thomas
The Governor of Cyprus   LIF Dec. 1702   LCM
(Oldmixon)
Eccles
The Italian Husband   LIF 1697   O MS 26437
(Ravenscroft)
The Mad Lover (Fletcher)   LIF 1700?   L*; LCM
The Queen's Coronation   LIF April 1702   L(HA)*; LCM*
Finger
Love at a Loss (Mrs. Trotter)   DL 23.11.00   L*; L(HA)*; LCM
Love makes a Man (Cibber)   DL 9.12.00   L*; L(HA)*; LCM
The Humours of the Age   DL 1.3.01   LCM
(Baker)
Sir Harry Wildair (Farquhar)   DL April 1701   L*; L(HA)*; LCM
The Virgin Prophetess (Settle)   DL May 1701   L*; LCM

Also Love for Love (Congreve) and The City Lady (Dilke) and two others
without a title: Bodleian MS 26437

Gillier
(no title)   QT 1706?   L
The (Beaux') Stratagem   QT 8.3.07   L
(Farquhar)
Lenton
The Ambitious Stepmother   LIF Dec. 1700   L*; L(HA)*; LCM
(Rowe)
Tamerlaine (Rowe)   LIF Dec. 1702   L(HA)*; LCM
The Royal Captive (?)   LIF? 1702?   L*
The Fair Penitent (Rowe)   LIF May 1703   L; LCM
Abra Mule (Trapp)   LIF Jan. 1704   LCM
Liberty asserted (Dennis)   LIF 24.2.04   L*; LCM
The Gamester (Mrs.   LIF Jan. 1705   L
Centilevre)

Also a set without title: Bodleian MS 26437

Paisible
King Edward III (Bancroft)   revival c. 1700   L(HA)*; LCM
The Humours of Sir John   DL April 1702   L ;L(HA)*; LCM
Falstaff (Dennis) (i.e. The
Comical Gallant)

She would and she would not (Cibber)	DL 26.11.02	LCM
Love's Stratagem (?)	? 1702?	L; L(HA)*
A Person of Quality		
The False Friend (Vanbrugh)	DL Jan. 1702	L(HA)*; LCM
Purcell, Daniel		
(The Relapse, or) Vertue in Danger (Vanbrugh)	DL 21.11.96	L
The Unhappy Penitent (Mrs. Trotter)	DL 4.2.01	L*; L(HA)*; LCM; LCM*
The Inconstant (Farquhar)	DL Feb. 1702	LCM
The Faithful Bride of Granada (Taverner)	DL May 1704	LCM*
The Patriot, or The Italian Conspiracy (Gildon)	DL Nov. 1702	L*; L(HA)*; LCM*
The Northern Lass (Brome)	DL 8.11.04 (revival)	L*
Smith, John		
The Wonders in the Sun (Durfey)	QT 5.4.06	L
Tollett		
A set without title: Bodleian MS 26437		

All the sets published between 1705 and 1708 will be found together in the same box at the BM (g. 15).

APPENDIX C

Theatre Overtures Published in Parts 1740–1800

Unless otherwise indicated, these overtures were published separately
All dates are of publication
6 FOs (7 in most sets): 'Abel, Arne and Smith's six Favourite
  Overtures'
6 MOs: Six Medley Overtures
PO: Periodical Overture
Locations (as in BUCEM) are given for rarities (see p. xiii).

Abel
 Love in a Village (6 FOs)   1762–3
Arne, T. A.
 Comus (Arne's 'Eight Overtures' no. 7) *c.* 1751
 The Judgment of Paris ('Eight Overtures' no. 8) *c.* 1751
 Harlequin Restor'd (6 MOs no. 1) *c.* 1763
 Eliza (6 FOs)   1762–3
 Thomas and Sally (6 FOs) 1762–3
 Artaxerxes   1765
 The Guardian Outwitted (PO no. 27) 1770
 The Fairy Prince *c.* 1771 (O)
 The Cooper ('no. 9'?) *c.* 1772 (no set seems
        to survive)
 King Arthur ('no. 10') *c.* 1772
 Elfrida ('no. 11') *c.* 1772 (L)
 The Rose ('no. 12') = The Trip to Portsmouth 1773 (L)
Boyce
 The Chaplet (Eight Symphonies no. 3) 1760
 The Shepherds' Lottery (ditto no. 4) 1760
 The Secular Masque (Twelve Overtures no. 6) 1770
Charke
 Harlequin Restor'd (6 MOs no. 3) *c.* 1763
Collet
 Midas (Collet's 6 Symphonies, op. 2 no. 3) *c.* 1765 (LAM)
 The Hermit, or Harlequin at Rhodes *c.* 1766 (O)

Dibdin
    The Padlock   *c.* 1768
    The Institution of the Garter   *c.* 1771 (no set seems
                                           to survive)

    The Blackamoor   *c.* 1776 (no set seems
                                           to survive)

Fisher, J. A.
    The Syrens   1777 (L)
Giordani, T.
    The Elopement   *c.* 1770 (LH)
Hook
    The Lady of the Manor   1778 (M)
Howard
    The Amorous Goddess (also 6 MOs no. 4)   *c.* 1745
Kellie
    The Maid of the Mill (PO no. 28)   1770
Lampe
    Columbine Courtezan (also 6 MOs no. 2)   *c.* 1740
Linley jun.
    The Duenna   *c.* 1775 (CUM)
Markordt
    Tom Thumb   1780 (M)
Mazzinghi
    Ramah Droog   *c.* 1800 (M)
Moze
    The Witches   *c.* 1770 (M)
Pasquali
    The Nymphs of the Spring (12 Ov. no. 1)   *c.* 1755
    The Triumphs of Hibernia (12 Ov. no. 3)   *c.* 1755
    Venus and Adonis (12 Ov. no. 5)   *c.* 1755
    Apollo and Daphne (12 Ov. no. 7)   *c.* 1755
    The Temple of Peace (12 Ov. no. 11)   *c.* 1755
Prelleur
    The Emperor of the Moon (6 MOs nos. 5 or 6)   *c.* 1763
Reeve
    The Turnpike Gate   *c.* 1801 (M)
    Harlequin and Oberon   *c.* 1801 (M)
Rush
    The Royal Shepherd   *c.* 1764
    The Capricious Lovers   *c.* 1764 (no set seems
                                           to survive)

Shaw
    The Island of St. Marguerite   *c*. 1789 (no set seems
                                                          to survive)

    Cymon   *c*. 1791 (no set seems
                                                          to survive)

Smith, J. C.
    The Fairies (6 FOs)   1762–3
    The Tempest (6 FOs) (no. 7 in 2nd ed.)   1763
    The Enchanter (6 FOs)   1762–3

Many other overtures are recoverable in orchestral form:

a. from the operas listed in Appendix A

b. from the four ballad operas listed on pages 114–15

c. in MS. e.g.: Dibdin's *The Wedding Ring* and *Liberty Hall* (L Add.
30950);
Storace's *The Cherokee* from MS of *Gli sposi malcontenti* (except for the
slow introduction). The Dibdin MS includes several other untitled
overtures in autograph full score.

Collet's overture *The Hermit* also survives in MS (L Add. 31576), and so
does Dibdin's *The Recruiting Sergeant* (Southampton Public Library).

APPENDIX D

Ballad Operas Published with their Airs
1728–1736

The order is chronological
CAPITAL LETTERS denote full-length ballad operas
AV: afterpiece version
S: lasting success
F: failure with less than ten performances

THE BEGGAR'S OPERA (LIF 29.1.28) by John Gay; Ov. and 69 airs arr. Pepusch; S

The Cobler's Opera (LIF 26.4.28) by Lacy Ryan; Ov. and 31 airs; F

PENELOPE (LT 8.5.28) by Thomas Cooke and John Mottley; Ov, and 14 airs; F

THE QUAKER'S OPERA (BF 24.9.28) by Thomas Walker; 26 airs (arr. Carey?)

POLLY by John Gay; not performed; 54 airs

LOVE IN A RIDDLE (DL 7.1.29) by Colley Cibber; 18 airs (arr. Carey?); F, but AV *Damon and Phillida* (LT 16.8.29) S. Latter not pub, with airs till 1765

THE VILLAGE OPERA (DL 6.2.29) by Charles Johnson; 62 airs; F. AV, *The Chambermaid* (10.2.30) also pub., 28 airs, also F

Flora, or Hob's Opera (LIF 17.4.29) by John Hippisley, from Dogget's *Hob. or The Country Wake* (1711); 24 airs; S

The Wedding (LIF 6.5.29) by Essex Hawker; Ov. and 23 airs arr. Pepusch; F; Later at DL as *The Country Wedding and Skimmington* (18.7.29); also F

The Patron, or The Statesman's Opera (LT 7.5.29) by Thomas Odell; 20 airs; F (only one perf.)

The Lovers Opera (DL 14.5.29) by William Chetwood; 32 airs; S

THE BEGGAR'S WEDDING (LT 29.5.29, and earlier in Dublin) by Charles Coffey; 55 airs; S. AV at both LT and DL, sometimes called *Phebe*, also S

MOMUS TURNED FABULIST (LIF 3.12.29) by Ebenezer Forrest; 42 airs

The Fashionable Lady, or Harlequin's Opera (GF 2.4.30) by James Ralph

Patie and Peggy (DL 20.4.30) by Theophilus Cibber, from Ramsay's *The Gentle Shepherd* (much altered); latter not pub. with airs till *c.* 1758

THE FEMALE PARSON (LT 27.4.30) by Coffey; 28 airs; F

The Generous Freemason (BF 20.8.30) by Chetwood; 25 airs (arr. Carey?)

Robin Hood (BF 24.8.30) by ?; 19 airs

SYLVIA (LIF 10.11.30) by George Lillo; 53 airs; F. AV (CG. 18.3.36) also F

The Jealous Clown (GF 16.12.30) by Thomas Gataker; 12 airs; F

THE JOVIAL CREW (DL 8.2.31) by ?; taken from still popular comedy by Richard Brome (1641); AV 5.4.31: both versions revived later

THE HIGHLAND FAIR (DL 20.3.31) by Joseph Mitchell; 51 airs; F

THE DEVIL TO PAY (DL 6.8.31) by Coffey and others, partly from Jevon's *The Devil of a Wife* (1686); 42 airs; F. AV (16.8.31) by T. Cibber with 16 airs (arr. Seedo); S

The Lottery (DL 1.1.32) by Henry Fielding; 19 airs comp. or arr. Seedo; S

A Sequel to Flora (LIF 20.3.32) by Hippisley; 15 airs; F

The Mock Doctor (DL 23.6.32) by Fielding from Molière; 9 airs arr. Seedo; S

The Devil of a Duke (DL 17.8.32) by Robert Drury, from Tate's *A Duke and no Duke* (1684); 21 airs arr. Seedo; F

The Boarding School, or The Sham Captain (DL 29.1.33) by Coffey, from D'Urfey's *Love for Money* (1691) 12, F

THE DECOY (GF 5.2.33) by Henry Potter; 52 airs; F

ACHILLES (CG 10.2.33) by Gay; 54 airs

The Livery Rake (DL 5.5.33; libretto wrongly says LT) by Edward Phillips; 18 airs, some with several verses

The Intriguing Chambermaid (DL 15.1.34) by Fielding, from a French farce; 12 airs; S

DON QUIXOTE IN ENGLAND (LT 5.4.34) by Fielding; 15 airs

The Whim, or The Miser's Retreat (GF ?) from *La maison rustique* by ?; 13 airs; F (pub 1734)

An Old Man Taught Wisdom, also called *The Virgin Unmasked* (DL 6.1.35) by Fielding; 12 airs; S. (*Miss Lucy in Town* (1742) a sequel, but not pub. with airs, and F)

The Plot (DL 22.1.35) by John Kelly; 10 airs; F

The Merry Cobler (DL 6.5.35) by Coffey, a sequel to *The Devil to pay*; 17 airs; F

Trick for Trick (DL 10.5.35) by R. Fabian; 10 airs; F, only one perf., just after which Macklin killed Hallam, one of the cast. 3 more perfs. GF 1741

The Honest Yorkshireman (LT 15.7.35) by Carey, who also comp. or arr. the 21 airs; S

The Lover his own Rival (GF 10.2.36) by Abraham Langford; 17 airs, one comp. by John Stanley

———————

The Prisoner's Opera (SW) by Edward Ward; 11 airs and no dialogue; pub. 1730

Borrowings 1760–1800

Only the most successful operas are included. To save space, items are identified by the first two words, however senseless. Page numbers refer to the original vocal score. Dates of Italian operas are of the first London production.

THE CASTLE OF ANDALUSIA

The vocal score attributes the overture and most of the first act to Samuel Arnold, but allows him less than half of the other two. Only the borrowed items are listed below. Those marked with asterisks were new; they do not occur in the book of the song-words for *The Banditti*. Some of the others were slightly rewritten for *The Castle of Andalusia*.

I 18* (Come ye): 'Se fidi siete' by Vento, from pastiche *Zenocrita* (1764)

    25* (Like my): Trad. Scotch Song, 'The Braes aboon Bonaw' or 'Wilt thou go, my bonnie Lassie'

    26 (New graces): Trad. Irish Song, 'The Humours of Balamagairy'; later set by Beethoven

II 34* (In the): Trad. English Song, 'All amongst the Leaves so green O' (Cecil Sharp's 'The Keeper')

    35 (The Prado): Trad. Scotch Song, 'Where hae ye been a' the day, bonny Laddie?'

    38* (I have): Trad. Scotch Song, 'There's nae Luck about the House'

    39 (By woes): 'Scotch Song' probably by Oswald, 'The Braes of Ballenden'

    40 (Idalian Queen): from Arnold's oratorio *Abimelech* (Busby i, p. 59)

    42 (Severe the): Trad. Scotch Song, 'The Flowers of the Forest' (the elaborate version; the simple one known today came to light in 1838)

    44* (So faithful): Irish, 'Carolan's Receipt for Drinking', also known as 'Dr. John Stafford's Receipt' (O'Sullivan No. 161)

    46 (Love soft): 'La verginella' from Bertoni's *La Governante* (1779)

III 48* (Hey for): Arne's song to the same words in *The Guardian Outwitted* (1764); O'Keeffe added verse 2

51* (My fair): Giardini's 'madrigal' 'For me my fair' in *The Universal Magazine* lxi p. 370 (1775)

55* (Heart beating): 'Sento che in seno' by Giordani, sung in Piccini's *Il Barone di Torre Forte* (1781)

58* (Love sweet): 'Verdi prati' from Handel's *Alcina*

THE DUENNA

I attempted identifications in M&L, April 1961, but made some errors; this article can be consulted for sources of decorated versions of the airs. In what follows TL¹ is the elder Linley, TL² his son. Eg. 2493 is a BM MS, LGC a MS in the younger Linley's hand of Act III only in London's Guildhall Library (Gresham 376).

Overture: TL². Pub. in parts; only known set in Pendelbury Lib., Cambridge

I 6   (Tell me): by TL²; FS Eg. 2493

8–11 (The Crimson—What vagabonds): by TL¹? Two continuous items

12   (Could I): by TL²; FS Eg. 2493

13   (I could): by TL¹?

14   (Friendship is): by TL²: FS Eg. 2493

16   (Though cause): by William Jackson; FS in his *Third Set of Songs* op. 7 (*c.* 1769)

18   (Thou canst): by TL¹?

19   (If a): Scotch Air, 'Hooly and Fairly', 1st pub. 1757; Beard sang it at Ranelagh Gardens. Later arr. Haydn for Thomson

20   (When sable): Scotch or more probably English Air, 'De'il tak' the wars'; *Pills* i, p. 294

21   (Had I): Irish tune, 'Gramachree Molly'; Moore later wrote for it 'The Harp that once through Tara's Halls'. Intro. an oboe solo (Parke ii, p. 14)

22–5 (My mistress—Gentle Maid—May'st thou): Finale in three sections, all by TL²; FS Eg. 2493

II 26 (Give Isaac): by TL¹?

28   (When the): Unidentified. In no libretto; came at end of 1st scene

30   (When a): 'On a Bank of Flowers' by Galliard, sung in Settle's *The Lady's Triumph* (1718). Thomson thought it was Scotch and got Kozeluch to arr. it

31   (Ah sure): 'The Highland Laddie' by Michael Arne, from *The Floweret* (1750)

32   (Believe me): freely arr. by TL² from John Travers's canon 'When Bibo thought fit', one of his *Eighteen Canzonets*. FS Eg. 2493

34   (A Bumper): by TL¹? Virtually in FS in the pub. score of *The Duenna*

36   (What bard): from T. Giordani's *La Marchesa Giardiniera* (1775);
        FS in 'Favourite Songs'.

38   (O had): Scotch Song, 'The Bush aboon Traquair'; in *Orpheus
        Caledonius*, 1726

39   (Soft pity): 'Epitaph on Sophocles', a catch by William Hayes

III 40 (O the): by TL¹ but source untraced (see Moore's Life of Sheridan);
        FS in LGC

41   (Ah cruel): 'My days have been so wondrous free' by William
        Jackson; FS in his Op. 1 Songs (*c.* 1755), and in LGC

44   (Sharp is): by TL²; FS Eg. 2493 and LGC. Not in mod. eds. of
        play; should end Scene ii

47   (By him): from Rauzzini's *Piramo e Tisbe* (1775); FS in 'Favourite
        Songs' and LGC

50   (How oft): Scotch Song, 'The Birks of Endermay' (or Invermay);
        In *Orph. Cal.* ii; FS arr. TL² in LGC. Not in mod. eds. of play;
        should come just before the maid's entrance

51   (Adieu thou): ascr. Sacchini, by 1835 VS ed. Philips. FS in LGC

54   (This bottle's): by TL¹; ascribed to him by Ritson and Shield in
        Select Collection of English Songs iii (1783); FS *not* in LGC

55   (Turn thee): by TL²; FS Eg.2493 and LGC

56   (Oft does): 'Geminiani's Minuet', first (?) pub. 1725 as 'Gently
        touch the warbling Lyre'; FS arr. TL² in LGC

57   Finale: Melody from Morley's 'Now is the Month of Maying';
        FS *not* in LGC

THE FARMER

The Vocal Score does not show which items Shield composed and which he
selected. Those on pp. 8, 10, 12, 26, and 32 are ascribed to Shield in contemporary sheet-song editions. Those on pp. 14, 24, 30, 38, and 40 are probably
his too.

Overture: by T. Giordani

I 16   (My Daddy): Scotch Song, 'O'er the muir to Katie'

18   (Look dear): 'Great Lord Frog' (*Pills* i, p. 14)

20   (Send him): 'Chi mi mostra' from Paisiello's *Gli schiavi per amore*
        (1787); also borrowed by Mozart for the Finale of his Flute
        Quartet in A, K.298

22   (My dear): perhaps a version of Scotch Song, 'Saw ye Johnnie
        comin', known also as 'Fee him, Father'. Shield had used a more
        orthodox version in *The Siege of Gibraltar*

II 34   (Lovely Ladies): 'Donne, donne' by Mengozzi, sung in Paisiello's
        Gli schiavi per amore

See O'Keeffe ii, p. 129 for 'Ere round the huge Oak' by Michael Arne, which was added to later productions. First-night advertisements wrongly gave the 'selected' music as by Paisiello, Storace, and Morelli; in fact Nancy Storace and Morelli had sung the Paisiello items at the King's Theatre.

THE HAUNTED TOWER

All items not mentioned below are by Storace

Overture: *Allegro assai* = Storace's *Gli equivoci* overture shortened

I 13   (Tho' pity): Pleyel's song 'My little blithsom Sparrow' with words by George Saville Carey. Storace improved the accompaniment

14   (Nature to): 'Welch tune', but in fact Irish, 'Lacrum Cush'. Perhaps from Giordani's overture *The Isle of Saints* (1789), and see *Midas* p. 54

22   (Whither my): 'La Rachelina' from Paisiello's *La molinara*, shortened

II 32   (Hush hush): Sarti, but not in his then published operas

33   (Tho' time): 'On doit soixante mille francs' from *Les Dettes* (1787) by Champein

34   (What blest): 'The Song of thy love' from Linley's *The Carnival of Venice*, slightly shortened and with two bars of coloratura cut

36   (Now all): 'French Tune', untraced. Bannister's biographer says it it is 'Qui veut ouir, qui veut savoir'

43   (Now mighty): Leveridge's 'The roast Beef of old England'

III 50   (Love from): 'Sereno raggio' from Martini's *L'arbore di Diana* (not then published). Coloratura cut; C minor episode (p. 51) apparently by Storace

52, 54
     (Dangers unknown) (Dread parent): Sarti, but not in his then published operas

66   (As now): Purcell's catch 'I gave her cakes'

67   (Tho' banish'd): 'Vivent les fillettes', probably by P. J. Meyer; used by Krumpholz in Finale of 6th Harp Concerto which Storace published in his *Harpsichord Collection* with the solo part adapted for keyboard. Episodes by Storace

LIONEL AND CLARISSA

When follows is based on the DL score of 1770, in which three-quarters of the music is Dibdin's; the title-page emphasizes the sub-title, *The School for Fathers*. (In the rare 1768 CG score just under half the music is Dibdin's and the title-page emphasizes *Lionel and Clarissa*.) In 1770 the printer used the old plates where possible and changed the order when this helped him to fit in single-page songs. Apart from the wrong order, the 'Table of the Songs' or Index omits two items that are given, includes one that isn't, and attributes two songs to the wrong composers. Miss Macklin, the CG Clarissa, is incorrectly named as the DL one on pp. 48 and 49.

I have kept the order of the later librettos, correcting mistakes and indicating the changes between the two versions. The later librettos give some of the 1768 lyrics, but I think by mistake for they are omitted in the index.

Overture: Dibdin (new). (1768: a different overture by Dibdin)

I 6   Quartetto (Ah how): Scolari. Unidentified. (1768: same music is labelled Duet and sung by the two girls.) Probably accompanied only by the harpsichord on the stage

8   (To rob): Dibdin (new). (1768: same words with music by Ciampi)

12   (To tell): Dibdin (new). (1768: another setting by Dibdin for a higher voice)

14   (Zounds sir): Dibdin

20   (When a): Dibdin

49   (Immortal Powers): Dibdin

17   (I'm but): Dibdin (new). (1768: same words set by Arne)

22   (You ask): Dibdin

24   (Ah prithee): 'Se io ritorno' from Galuppi's *Il filosofo di campagna* (1761)

27   (Ye gloomy): Dibdin (new music and words). (1768: 'Hope and fear' by Dibdin—accidentally included in the 1770 score on p. 48)

30   Quintetto (Finale): Dibdin

II 34   (Oh talk): 'Conserva costante' from Vento's *La Conquista del Messico* (1767). (1768: a different setting of the same words, also by Vento)

35   (Indeed forsooth): Scolari. From pastiche, *Gli Stravaganti* (1766), where it is anon

37   (How cursedly): Arne. Perhaps written specially for *Lionel and Clarissa*

40   (Come then): 'Pastorella io guire' from Ciampi's 'Arie 8' (c. 1755)

43   (To fear): Dibdin (new): see ref. for p. 60. (1768: 'Hence with caution' with music by Galuppi; given in many later librettos)

44   (Ladies, pray): Dibdin (new music and words). (1768: 'I wonder, I swear' set by Arne)

—   (Poor panting Heart): Dibdin (new music and words). Given in index but replaced in error (p. 48) by 1768 'Hope and Fear'. Given in librettos. The music is in Harrison's 1797 edition

50   (In Italy): Dibdin

52   (We all): Dibdin (new music and words. No equiv. in 1768)

54   (Go and): from Vento's *La Conquista del Messico* (1767)
55   Quintetto (Finale): Dibdin
III 60   (How can): Dibdin (new words and music). (1768: 'Ah how cruel'
     by Pescetti). NB. 1768 score puts next 'To fear a stranger'
     (Galuppi); in 1770 these words, new-set by Dibdin, were trans-
     ferred to Act II (see p. 43 above), but librettos continued to put
     them in Act III
62   (I wonder): Dibdin (new). (1768: same words set by Arne)
64   (Hist, soft): Dibdin (new music and words). (1768: 'Bear oh bear
     me' by Dibdin)
67   (A rascal): Dibdin (new music and words). (1768: 'Girls like
     squirrels' by Dibdin)
70   (Why with): by Potenza from pastiche *Creso* (1758). NB. 1768
     score puts next 'When love gets into a youthful brain' by Dibdin
     and 'O dry those tears' by Galuppi. Some librettos put them here
     too.
71   (O Bliss): Dibdin (new). (1768: same words set differently by
     Dibdin)
74   Vaudeville (Finale): Dibdin

LOVE IN A VILLAGE

Overture: Abel (new)
I 7   (Hope thou): 'Let Ambition' from Weldon's *The Judgment of
     Paris* (1701) with new accompaniment (by Arne?)
9   (Whence can): 'Non son le lacrime' from *Tito Manlio* (1756) by
     Abos. (VS incorrectly attributes it to Arne.) In A in MS
11   (My Heart's): 'The Female Phaeton' from Arne's *Favourite
     Collection* i (1757)
12   (When once): 'The generous distress'd from Arne's *Lyric Harmony*
     (c. 1745)
13   (O had): Samuel Howard (new)
14   (Gentle Youth): 'The fond Appeal' from Arne's *Lyric Harmony*
15   (Still in): Arne (new)
16   (There was): Trad. English, 'The Budgeon' (Chappell, p. 666);
     in *The Devil to pay* etc.; now known as 'The Jolly Miller' from
     Love in a Village words
17   (Let gay): 'Hark, the Horn calls' by Baildon; in his *The Laurel*
     (c. 1750)
18   (The honest): 'The Morning fresh' from Festing's *Collection* (1750)
19   (Well well): Trad. Irish, 'Larry Grogan'
     (Cupid God): 'Voi amante' by Giardini (an isolated song); in A in MS
21   (How happy): 'Bonny Broom' from Arne's *Vocal Melody* iii (c. 1750)

22   Medley: a. 'Nancy Dawson'; b. 'Your humble Servant, Madam'; c. 'Roast Beef' by Leveridge; d. 'Gee ho, Dobbin' (Chappell p. 691); e. by Arne and new (?)

II 25   (We women): 'Quel ruscelletto' from Paradies' *La Forza d'amore* (1751); in *Delizie* vi, p. 14

27   (Think my): 'Advice to Sylvia' by Arne; in his *Blind Beggar* vol. (*c.* 1742)

        (Believe me): Arne (new)

29   (When I): Trad. English, 'Joan's Placket' (Chappell p. 518)

30   (Let Rakes): 'Ask if yon damask rose be sweet' from Handel's *Susanna* (1749)

32   (How blest): 'La Pastorella' from Galuppi's *Il filosofo di campagna* (1761)

33   (In vain): 'The Stream that glides' from Arne's cantata *Cymon and Iphigenia* (*c.* 1750)

34   (Begone I): 'A Pastoral' from Arne's *Agreeable Musical Choice* vii

36   (Oh how): 'The Power of Beauty' by Henry Carey (*c.* 1740)

37   (Young I): 'Son troppo vezzose' from Galuppi's *Enrico* (1743)

39   (Oons neighbour): 'Ye Prigs' from Arne's *Vocal Melody* i (1746)

40   (My Dolly): 'Let me wander' from Handel's *L'Allegro* (1740)

41   (Was ever): by Agus; untraced

42   (Cease gay): 'Jockey and Mary' from Arne's *Agreeable Musical Choice* viii (*c.* 1757)

44   (Since Hodge): by Arne; untraced. In A in MS

45   (In Love): by George III under pseudonym of 'Mr. Barnard'

47   (Well come): by Arne (new)

III 50   (The world): 'A Touch on the Times' from Arne's *Agreeable Musical Choice* viii

51   ('Tis not): 'Quanto mai felici', No. 6 of Giardini's *Sei Arie* (1762)

52   (The traveller): by Arne (new)

54   (If ever): from finale of Geminiani's Concerto Grosso in C mi, Op. 2/1. In G minor in MS

55   (A Plague): Trad. Irish, 'St. Patrick's Day'

56   (How much): 'I like the Man whose soaring Soul', a 'Vauxhall' song by Howard. In A in MS

57   (When we): by Arne (new)

58   (All I): 'O the Raptures of possessing', duet from Arne's *Agreeable Musical Choice* viii

59   (If ever): 'An Answer to Orpheus and Euridice', a song by Boyce (1740)

60   (Go naughty): by Arne (new)

62   (Hence with): 'Rail no more' from Boyce's *Lyra Britannica* v (*c.* 1751)

THE MAID OF THE MILL

Overture: The Earl of Kellie (new). Pub. in parts

I 6   Chorus (Free from): Rinaldo da Capua; untraced

8   (If that's): Abos; untraced

9   (In love): The Elector of Saxony (Friedrich August II); untraced

10   (What are): Ciampi; given in *Delizie* vii 152 as a minuet for strings

12   (Hark 'tis): from *Tre cicisbei ridicoli* (1749), a pastiche. Libretto and score give Laschi which may be a mistake for Latilla. The six-eight section is from Philidor's *Le Soldat magicien* (c. 1760) p. 68

14   (Ah why): from pastiche *Il tutore e la pupilla* (1762), where it is anon; libretto and score have Piccini which is probable

16   (With the): 'La bella che adoro' from Galuppi's *Il filosofo di campagna* (1761)

18   (Why how): Pergolesi; untraced

20   (Odd's my): Rinaldo da Capua; untraced

22   (The Madman): Monsigny; untraced

24   (I am): Vinci; untraced

25   (Why quits): Scarlatti; untraced

27   Finale (Lye still): Arnold (new)

II 31   (Ah how): from Cocchi's *La clemenza di Tito* (1760)

32   (My passion): from Cocchi's *Tito Manlio* (1761) but cutting the long intro.

34   (Was I): 'Una donna come me' given in Oswald's 'Favourite Songs' from *La serva padrona*. Libretto and score give Pergolesi, but it is not in authentic scores. Also in Favart's *Les Jeunes Mariés* (1751)

37   (When a): Arnold (new)

38   (Trust me): 'Se velete' from J. C. Bach's *Orione* (1763)

40   (Ye vile): Galuppi; untraced

42   (Hist, hist): Arnold (new)

44   (Yes 'tis): 'Si mon ardeur' from Monsigny's *Le Roi et le Fermier* (1762)

46   (Lord sir): Pergolesi; untraced

49   (An they): Hasse; untraced

50   (Zooks why): from Duni's *Les deux Chasseurs* (1763) p. 31

52   (Cease oh): Giardini; perhaps new

54   Finale (The quarrels): Arnold (new)

III 57   (To speak): 'La garde d'une jeune fille' from Duni's *La Fille mal gardée* (1758)

58   (Let me): 'Agité' from Duni's *Ninette à la Cour* (1755). Libretto
       and VS give Jomelli, from whom Duni may perhaps have got the
       music

61   (When you): Hasse; untraced

62   (O what): Pergolesi; untraced

64   (Women's tongues): from Duni's *Les deux Chasseurs* (1763)

65   (Oh leave): 'Rende mi il figlio mio' from Cocchi's *Il Ciro riconosciuto*
       (1759)

66   (Who'll buy): from Duni's *Les deux Chasseurs* (1763)

67   (Who upon): Martini, i.e. the 'English' Giuseppe Sammartini.
       Probably a minuet from an instrumental work

68   (Then hey): 'Ah quel jour heureux' from Monsigny's *Le Cadi
       dupé* (c. 1760)

70   (My life): J. C. Bach; probably new

72   Finale (Yield who): from Philidor's *Le Sorcier* (1764) without final
       ensemble

MIDAS

Vocal scores give the music for the original three-act version, but most librettos
show the afterpiece version that made the burletta popular. The rare three-act
librettos identify each item, often unhelpfully; these identifications, when used,
are in double quotes. Asterisks denote items kept in the afterpiece version.

Overture: Collet, from *Six Symphonies* Op. 2/3; PP (LAM)

I —*   (Jove in): 'The King of Prussia's March' by Nicolini (1758); a two-
        part chorus, not given in VS but pub. separately (L)

7   (To happy): "New", but in fact derived from *Venetian Ballads* i, p. 27
        by Hasse etc.

8*   (Think not): "Shaan Bwee", Trad. Irish (?); also called 'Shawn Boy',
        'Marquis of Granby' and (in Scotland) 'Over the Water to
        Charlie'; cf. p. 54 below for similar tune

9   (No difference): Trad. English, 'There was a jolly Beggar' (*Pills*
        iii, p. 265)

10*   (Be by): "New", but see *Venetian Ballads* i p. 18 by Hasse etc.;
        'Apollo's drunken song' (Kelly ii 181)

11   (With fun): 'Hang me if I'll marry' from Boyce's *The Chaplet* (1749)

12*   (Since you): "New", but first bars from *Comic Tunes* i, p. 16 by
        Hasse etc.

14   (If the): 'Nature fram'd thee' from Arne's *The Judgment of Paris*
        (1742)
        (If I): "Mirleton"

15*   (Girls are): "Three Sheepskins" (See Chappell p. 614)

16* (Pray Goody): 'Fairy Dance' from Burney's pantomime *Queen Mab* (See Kelly ii 182 for attribution to Rousseau)

* (Mama how): "Non, non, votelle n'est point trompeuse" (sic)

19 (Wretched he): "Fanny's fairer than a Flower"

20* (Shall a): "A la santé du Père d'Oleron"

* (Jupiter wenches): Trad. Irish, "Shela na Gig," (or Girig)

21* (All around): Comic Tune, 'The Laundry' from pantomime *Fortunatus* (1753)

22 (Shall he): Trad. Scots, 'My Wife's a wanton wee thing' (rewritten by Burns with 'winsome' for 'wanton')

* (Sure I): Trad. Irish, 'Chiling o'Guiry'; in Thumoth; Moore called it 'Sheela na Guira' and wrote for it 'Oh had we some bright little Isle'

23 (When at): 'Planxty Johnstone' by Carolan (O'Sullivan No. 62)

24 (This rash): Gavotte from Handel's *Ottone* overture (1723)

26 (Oh fye): Trad. English (*Pills* i, p. 332) or Scots ('Cock up your Beaver')

27 (To blast): Lib. "From tree to tree", but VS has 'Come let us all be blith and gay' from Arne's *The Winter's Amusement* (c. 1762)

* (He's as): "Quand on scait aimer"

29* (Lovely Nymph): Lib. "When on thy dear Bosom lying", but apparently by Rousseau; pub. separately in VS and FS

30* (If you): Trad. Irish? "The Priest in his Boots" (see Crosby's *Irish Musical Repository* p. 81)

31 (Neatest compleatest): 'Semplici amanti' by Pescetti from pastiche, *Alessandro in Persia* (1741)

32* (My Minikin): Trad. English, 'Bobbing Joan' (*Dancing Master* 1651)

II 33* (In these): Lib. "Assis sur l'herbette"; but VS has 'The Fields and the Groves' by Worgan in collection called *Amaryllis* (1746). Put later in afterpiece version

(O what): Comic Tune in pantomime *Perseus and Andromeda* (by Galliard?)

34* (Ne'er will): "A pantomime Tune"

36* (When into): 'Princess Royal' from *Country Dancing Master* 1731; lib. has different words labelled 'Larry Grogan'

37 (Strip him): Comic Tune, 'The Milkmaids' from pantomime *Fortunatus* (1753), with new 'symphonies'

38 (Since first): 'Nanny of the Hill' by Worgan (*The Muses Delight* p. 68)

40 (Yes your): "Torteuille"

(By whining): 'The Country Girl's Farewell' in *Calliope* (1737) and other collections

41 (When gathering): 'When that I was and a little tiny boy' by Vernon

42   (The Wolf): "An Italian Opera Tune"

44   (When fairies): 'When fairies' from Boyce's *The Shepherds' Lottery* (1751) p. 26

      (My heart): "New"

47   (O yes): apparently a Medley; no attribution in lib.

48   (Fine Times): "Kiss me fast, my Mother's coming"; a version of trad. Scots tune 'O where wad bonnie Annie lye'

50   (The Gods): English Country Dance, 'Nancy Dawson'

      (A Monarch): 'When Daisies pied' by Arne

53   (Mark what): Trad. Irish? or Scots? "Baaltiorough"

54   (If in): "New"

      (As soon): Trad. Irish, "Ligurum Cuss" or 'Lacrum Cush'; cf. p. 8

55*   (Master Pol): Trad. Irish, 'Cold and raw' or 'The Irish Ho-hoane' (*Pills* iv, p. 152)

56*   (If a): 'The Modern Beau' from Carey's *The Honest Yorkshireman* (1735)

58*   (Mother sure): "Viens l'examine" (and another tune too?)

62*   (What the): Trad. English (?) 'The Kettlebender' in *The Muses Delight* (p. 99) etc.; and see Chappell p. 713 for other titles. But perhaps Irish; it is very like 'Ally Croaker'

  *   (Now I'm): "New"; but 1st two bars from *Venetian Ballads* ii, p. 31

64*   (A pox): Trad. English, 'Liberty Hall' or 'Derry Down' (Chappell p. 677)

  *   (Ah happy): "New"

65*   (See triumphant): 'See the conquering Hero comes' from Handel's *Judas Macabbaeus* (1747)

66*   (Dunce): "To various tunes". The rondo theme is from Boyce's *The Chaplet* (1749); the one in Common Time is 'The Watchman' from Burney's pantomime *Queen Mab* (1750)

THE PIRATES

Overture: 2nd and 3rd mvts from Storace's Piano Quintet in D, transposed.

I 16   (Some device): from Storace's *Gli sposi malcontenti*, shortened

   34   (Hear Oh): from Act I finale of Storace's *Gli equivoci*, shortened

II 52   (What shall): 1st 4 bars from Anfossi's *L'Inconnue persécutée*; Anfossi's aria has similar words

   58   (Mem'ry repeating): from Storace's *Gli sposi malcontenti*

III 72   (My rising): main tune from 'Ein Mädchen' in Mozart's *Die Zauberflöte* via *Les Visitandines* by Devienne

   87   (Oh softly): from Quintet 'Al suon soave' in Guglielmi's *La bella pescatrice*. (The original has two further sections)

THE POOR SOLDIER

The vocal score attributes the overture to Shield, but is silent about the sung items. The first London libretto (1798) cuts several songs and adds others; by then many changes had been adopted. Additions are asterisked below.

Overture: by Shield; Finale based on 'The Irish Lover's Morning Walk' (see p. 8 below)

I 6   (Sleep on): Irish song. O'Sullivan (*Songs of the Irish* p. 91) calls it 'The Fair Hills of Eire O', and has a note on its history. Moore called the tune 'The Song of Sorrow' and wrote for it 'Weep on, weep on'

7   (Dear Kathleen): perhaps Irish but now associated with Scottish words and known as 'The Piper of Dundee'; possibly from Scottish reel 'The Drummer'

8   (Since Love): Irish song, 'The Irish Lover's Morning Walk' (pub. *c.* 1780), but Burns thought it was Scottish and wrote for it 'O whistle and I'll come to you'. In the overture

9   (Out of): Irish song? Untraced

*   (The Twins of Latona): not in VS; pub *c.* 1785 as by Shield, and very popular

*   (An humble Curate am I): not in VS; I have not found the music

10   (The Meadows): probably by Shield

*   (For you, dearest maiden): not in VS; I have not found the music

11   (How happy): untraced. Not in libretto, but obviously sung by Patrick on his first entrance. O'Keeffe (ii, p. 70) disliked it, and says the words were not his and the music not Shield's

12   (The wealthy): untraced. Also in *Love finds a Way* (1777) with words by Hull

14   (A Rose Tree): Irish song? Moore later wrote for this tune 'I'd mourn the Hopes that leave me'; as he called the tune 'The Rose Tree', he probably got it from *The Poor Soldier*; it may be by Shield, and not Irish at all

II *   (Why breathe so rude): not in VS; I have not found the music

16   (Dermot's welcome): Irish song; Moore later wrote for the tune 'Oh for the Swords of former time', calling it 'Name unknown'; he probably got it from *The Poor Soldier*

17   (Though late): not in most librettos; by Shield?

18   (Farewell, ye Groves): Irish song, 'Savourneen Deelish'; Moore later wrote for the tune ''Tis gone and for ever'. Libretto has different song for Norah, 'Dearest Youth'

19   (The spring): not in libretto; almost certainly by Shield

20   (Tho' Leixlip): Irish song, 'The Humours of Glen' (a village near Clonmel); first pub. in McLean's *Scots Tunes* (*c.* 1773); Burns, who knew it was Irish, wrote for it 'Their Groves o' sweet Myrtle'

*   (Farewell, my dear Norah): not in VS; I have not found the music

*   (Thou little Cheat): not in VS; I have not found the music

22   (You know): Irish song, 'Balin a mone'; in Thumoth's collection (1745–6)

24   (Dear Sir): probably by Shield: later replaced by 'My sheep feast on Flowers'.

25   (You the): Irish song, 'Pease upon a Trencher', from Aird's *Selection* of 1782; Moore later wrote for the tune 'The Time I've lost in wooing'

26   (Since Kathleen): Irish song? Untraced

28   (What true): Carolan's 'John (or Planxty) O'Connor' (O'Sullivan No. 114); in Thumoth as 'Planks of Connaught'; O'Keeffe (i, p. 355) says he was sent the tune by Robert Owenson

ROSINA

Items *not* mentioned are ascribed to Shield in the vocal score

I 6   (When the): from Catch, 'Care, thou canker' (anon; 1780). Chappell (p. 722) says it was by John Garth of Durham, whom Shield must have known

10   (The morn): 'Published by Permission of Mr. Paxton', i.e. Stephen Paxton, cellist and composer. Origin not traced; perhaps written specially for *Rosina*

11   (See ye): 'French Tune'. Untraced

20   Finale (By this): Irish Song, 'The Brown Irish Girl', probably 1st pub. in *Rosina*. Moore later wrote for it 'By that Lake whose gloomy Shore'. Rather like 'The Brown Maid' (Bunting 1796 p. 18); both may stem from same original

II 26   (Henry cull'd): from Sacchini's *Rinaldo* (KT 1780); in 'Favourite Songs'

28   (When bidden): Scotch Song, 'My Nannie O' (*Orph. Cal.* i, 1726). Thumoth (1745) has it as an Irish tune

35   (How blest): Scotch Song, 'I wish my Love were in a Mire' (*Orph. Cal.* i)

36   Finale (To bless): 'French Tune'. Untraced

APPENDIX F

Arne's 'The Fairy Prince'

(See pp. 360–3)

The published score of 1771 gives the music in an unworkable order, with all the orchestral pieces placed together at the end. As reference to the published libretto shows, most of the recitative music is omitted as also one or two other items. What follows is an attempt to place such music as survives in its correct order. Keys are mentioned only when significant. '?' implies some doubt about the placing, its absence a reasonable degree of confidence. I have failed to find a home for the five bars on p. 44 of the score headed 'When St. George descends'. In any modern revival the words of the missing recitatives must be spoken.

Part I (starts in E flat)

VS p.2–9	Continuous. Next recit. missing in score.
10–12	Song for Silenus in D. Chorus at end of it missing.
38	'Figure Dance' for Satyrs in A (?). Lib. has no such dance anywhere, but the first dance in the score's appendix was probably the first to be played. Next recit. missing
13–14	'Air divided among the Satyrs'. Lib. (but not score) shows that 2nd, 4th, 3rd, and 1st Satyrs sing successive phrases. Next two lines of recit. missing
	The Rock now opens to reveal the West Front of St. George's with the Sylvans asleep before the gates. Thus the next music must be
38–9	'For the Entrance of the Sylvans'; the plaintive phrases (oboes and bassoons) must represent the sleeping Sylvans. The final switch to B flat must prepare for
40–1	'Chacoon' in E flat, the full revelation of St. George's. Next recit. missing
15	Catch for the Satyrs. Next recit. missing
15–18	Air for Wood-Nymph. A short missing recit. invites dancing
41–2	Two dances for Sylvans and Wood-Nymphs (shown in lib.). Next recit. missing
19–27	Continuous as in score

Part 2 (basically in B flat)

28 Introduction in B flat, 'A Troop of Fairies'. Next recit. missing

29–31 Air for 1st Fairy. Next recit. missing

32–4 Duet for Fairies. Next recit. missing

34–5 Air for 2nd Fairy in B flat

43   'The Fairies Country Dance by the children in the 2nd Act' in B flat (?). Not in lib

43–4 Two Marches 'at the Procession' (i.e. 'to St. George's Chapel, of the Sovereign, Knights Companions etc.'), both for two trumpets in E flat. No doubt there were drums as well

44   'Orchestra March' in B flat; it restores tonality and ends Part 2.

Part 3 (ends in E flat, the key of the overture)

    Recit. missing

36–8 Duet for Fairies in F

    Lib.: 'A Dance for Fairies'. Perhaps the one on p. 43 (see above), but if so '2nd act' is a misprint in the VS, and here alone the order of the dances is wrong. Placed here, it provides a useful key transition, being in B flat

45   'The first Air' and 'The favourite Minuet', both 'play'd at the Dinner' and both in E flat. The missing final chorus must have been in the same key. As suggested on p. 362, Grabu's setting of the same words in *Albion and Albanius* might be used.

APPENDIX G

The Singers

ARNE, Mrs. Cecilia (1711–89), soprano, was the daughter of Charles Young, a London organist; her grandfather, Anthony Young, composed some of the songs in *Pills*, and her two sisters were professional singers (see LAMPE). Like Susanna Arne, she made her debut in the 'English Opera' season of 1732–3, appearing first in the title role of Lampe's *Britannia* and singing Penelope in *Ulysses*. She had 'a good natural voice and fine shake . . . her style of singing was infinitely superior to that of any other English woman of her time' (Burney), and for her alone composers were prepared to write high As and B flats. In 1735 Handel engaged her (and Beard) to sing in *Ariodante* and *Alcina*, as well as in the first London performance of *Athalia*—an honour he had paid no other English singers in recent years. She married Arne in March 1737, and thereafter sang conscientiously in her husband's works as well as in Handel oratorios, for instance in *Comus*, the Cliveden *Alfred*, the revision of *Rosamond*, and *The Judgment of Paris*. As an actress she was so diffident or so incompetent that she seems never to have undertaken a speaking role; thus she never appeared in ballad opera. In 1742–4 she was in Dublin with her husband, and besides singing in his masques she attempted a comic role for the only time in her career, Margery in *The Dragon of Wantley*. Back in London she won the affection of Burney when he lodged with her as a student apprentice, but by this time she was being abominably treated by her husband who was constantly unfaithful to her. Her last London appearances were in *Harlequin Sorcerer* for which Arne had written new songs, and as Britannia in his *Eliza* (LT 29.7.54). In 1755 the Arnes were again in Dublin, their success tarnished by domestic misery. When Arne returned to London, Cecilia preferred to stay on in Dublin. By now her career as a singer was over. She bore her misfortunes with courage, returned to London to further the singing careers of her nieces, and was so Christian as to look after her erring husband when he returned to her in old age. After his death she lived with her niece Polly, the wife of the composer Barthelemon.

ARNE, Susanna. See Mrs. Cibber.

BADDELEY, Mrs. Sophia (1745–86), was the daughter of Valentine Snow, the trumpeter. At eighteen she eloped with Robert Baddeley, and soon afterwards made her stage debut as Ophelia at Drury Lane. Her husband then took to the stage and became famous. Mrs. Baddeley combined striking beauty with unreliability in private life and an ability to read music. At first she kept mainly to spoken roles, but in 1769 her singing of Dibdin's Stratford Jubilee song, 'Sweet Willy O', drew crowds to the theatre (see Boaden's *Mrs. Jordan* i 94), and the following year she sang Clarissa in the revision of *Lionel and Clarissa*. Her speciality was the slow pathetic song, but she was also a good comedienne and sang the feminine lead in both of Dibdin's Ranelagh operas, *The Ephesian Matron* and *The Recruiting Sergeant*. From 1771 to 1774 she disappeared from the playhouses. After her return she sang in *The Maid of the Oaks, Selima and Azor, The Milesian*, etc. By 1778 her addiction to men, jewellery, and alcohol had driven her first into the provinces and then into futureless poverty and disease. As Boaden put it, 'Extraordinary beauty on the stage commonly seals the fate of the victim'.

BANNISTER, Charles (1741–1804), was born at Newland in Gloucestershire; Lee Lewis said he was the illegitimate son of Leveridge, who would have been sixty-nine at the time of conception. Bannister acted occasionally for Foote at the unlicensed Little Theatre and had his first operatic role as Merlin in *Cymon* (DL 1767). He was a baritone whose falsetto was later much admired, but, says his son's biographer, 'a singer of the untaught class'. He was famous for his imitations of well-known castrati, yet he was seldom encouraged as a straight actor. His Caliban was praised, and for his DL benefit in 1776 he essayed Jacques in *As you like it*, but such parts were exceptional. His most popular role was Tom Tug in *The Waterman*, and he was also much liked as the hero in *Rosina* and *The Poor Soldier*; in all these parts a rough good humour put him on friendly terms with his audience. Boaden calls him 'a Hercules in bulk' (*Mrs. Jordan* ii, p. 128), and Parke perpetuated a number of his not-very-funny *bons mots*. He was something of a *bon viveur* and often in debt; unlike almost every other singer of his time, he never settled anywhere, switching theatres with bewildering suddenness. Kindliness led him to sing with little reward at Palmer's ill-fated Royalty Theatre in 1787. In the 1790s he worked increasingly in the provinces, and retired in 1800.

BANNISTER, Mrs. See Miss Harper.

BANNISTER, John (1760–1836), born in Deptford, was only nineteen years younger than his father, Charles. Nothing is known of his mother. After training as an artist with Rowlandson he turned to the theatre, and we know a great deal about his career from the excellent two-volume *Memoirs* by John Adolphus (1839). Here can be found a long vivid account of his audition as a youth with Garrick, whom he always regarded as his mentor.

His début was at the Little Theatre in 1778, and in the following autumn he joined the Drury Lane company, creating the part of Don Whiskerandos in *The Critic*, playing Hamlet at twenty, Orlando, Cassio, etc. Yet by 1782–3 he had little to do. Kemble's arrival at Drury Lane in the autumn of 1783 further limited his choice of serious roles. However there was a lack of presentable young opera singers, and after his marriage in 1783 to Miss Harper (q.v.), he was able to switch to less competitive roles. 'All the merit he possesses as a singer, is to be attributed to the instructions of Mrs. Bannister' (Oxberry iv). His first vocal part was in Linley's *The Strangers at Home* (1785), and though he continued to play straight parts such as Tony Lumpkin—and he was an outstanding success as the sailor, Ben, in *Love for Love* (1788)—he concentrated more and more on operatic roles both at Drury Lane and, in the summer months, at the Little Theatre. In all Storace's operas he had the best acting part, creating Blazio ('O the pretty, pretty Creature') in *The Pirates* (1791). His Walter in Arnold's *The Children in the Wood* (LT 1793) was a sensation. It 'perhaps exceeds every other effort of the modern drama' (Baker). Leigh Hunt remembered him as 'a handsome specimen of the best kind of Englishman, jovial, manly, good-humoured, unaffected . . . and this was his real character'. Hazlitt said his good humour shone through all his parts. 'He did not go out of himself to take possession of a part, but put it on over his ordinary dress, like a surtout, warm and comfortable. He let his personal character appear through . . . Most of his characters were exactly fitted for him, and no one else could do them so well because no one else could play Jack Bannister.' According to Parke (i, p. 33) he 'never sang out of time or out of tune, but did not know one note of music'. He had all his operatic roles 'parroted' to him by Griffith Jones, the Covent Garden pianist.

BARBIER, 'Mrs.' Jane (*c.* 1691–1757), mezzo-soprano and 'a native of England' (Hawkins), made her début singing in Italian in *Almahide* (QT 1710). She sang for Handel from 1712 to 1714, usually in travesty roles, for instance in revivals of *Rinaldo* and in *Il Pastor fido* and *Teseo*. She was the hero in Galliard's *Calypso and Telemachus* and the heroine in Pepusch's *Apollo and Daphne*, and in 1717 John Hughes, the librettist of the last-named works, publicized her recent elopement in his poem 'The Hue and Cry', his stated object being 'to bring the vagrant beauty Back to her mother and her duty'. He also sketched her character:

> Some wit, more folly, and no care,
> Thoughtless her conduct, free her air;
> Gay, thoughtful, sober, indiscreet,
> In whom all contradictions meet;
> Civil, affronting, peevish, easy,

> Form'd both to charm you and displease you;
> Much want of judgment, none of pride,
> Modish her dress, her hoop full wide;
> Brown skin, her eyes of sable hue,
> Angel when pleas'd, when vex'd a shrew;
> Genteel her motion, when she walks,
> Sweetly she sings, and loudly talks.

Already the conventions of prima donna behaviour were established. From John, Earl of Corke, we learn that 'she could never rest long in a place; her affectations increased with her years . . . She loved change so well that she liked to change her sex.' On her return from wherever it was her first role was the heroine in *Pan and Syrinx* (LIF 1718), and she continued to sing for Rich for many years, notably as the hero in his successful revivals of *Thomyris* and *Camilla*, and in the masque sections of his most successful pantomimes. On countless occasions she was Proserpine in *Harlequin Sorcerer*, Ceres in *The Rape of Proserpine*, and Perseus in *Perseus and Andromeda*. During the 'English Opera' seasons (1732–3) there was still no adequate tenor for the male leads, and Mrs. Barbier played Xarino in *Teraminta*, the title role in *Ulysses*, and King Henry in *Rosamond*. Her last part was Britannia in Arne's *Love and Glory* (DL 1734). Some twenty years later she described herself in her Will as a spinster, and left 50s. to every debtor in Whitechapel Prison.

BEARD, John (1716–91), England's first great tenor, was brought up in the Chapel Royal, and engaged by Handel when still very young. After his début in a revival of *Il Pastor fido* (1734) he sang in several Handel operas and, for some thirty years, in most of his oratorios. 'The whole direction of English oratorio was changed by his choice of Beard's tenor voice for the part of Samson' (Dean), and Beard's high ability also changed the direction of English opera, pushing the soprano hero into limbo. Burney thought him less naturally gifted than Lowe, but Lowe was musically illiterate, whereas Beard 'constantly possessed the favour of the public by his superior conduct, knowledge of music, and intelligence as an actor'. Like Mrs. Cibber, he learned to act only after he had succeeded as a singer. He had won playhouse fame overnight by his singing of Galliard's 'The early Horn' in *The Royal Chace* (1736): he was no more than a huntsman, but because of the novelty of his tenor voice the song filled Covent Garden for months. When Rich would not let him branch out he moved to Drury Lane, where he had his first speaking role, Sir John Loverule in *The Devil to pay* (1737). He now alternated between Handel operas and oratorios, and playhouse masques and ballad operas, singing in *Comus*, Paris in *The Judgment of Paris*, Macheath, Pyramus in Lampe's burlesque (during a return to Covent Garden 1744–8), and two shepherds in *The Chaplet* and *The Sheperds' Lottery*. He sang in

Garrick's pantomimes, in various versions of *Alfred*, and in Smith's *The Fairies* and *The Tempest* (Theseus and Prospero). His penchant for marrying well helped to raise the social status of the English singer. In 1739 he married Lady Henrietta, widow of Lord Edward Herbert and an earl's daughter, and after her death he married Rich's daughter, Charlotte. This prudent step led to his becoming the virtual manager of Covent Garden when Rich died in 1761. Beard had crossed over to this theatre on his marriage two years before, and he was soon sweeping the cobwebs out of the repertoire, reducing the proportion of pantomime, and increasing that of opera. This daring policy succeeded because he had enough tact to push Arne into creating two very successful novelties, *Artaxerxes* and *Love in a Village* (both 1762). Beard contributed to their success by singing Artabanes in the one and Hawthorn in the other (artfully accompanied by his own spaniel). His last appearance was as Hawthorn on 23 May 1767. By then he was going deaf. That summer he sold his share in Covent Garden and retired to a comfortable house in Hampton near Garrick's. As late as 1790 he was to be seen in the audience at Drury Lane sporting an ear-trumpet.

BILLINGTON, Mrs. Elizabeth (1765–1818), was one of the great coloratura singers of all time. Everyone thought her father was the German oboist Carl Weichsel, long resident in London, but years later Lady Morgan suggested that her own father, the Irish singer Robert Owenson, had sired Mrs. Billington as well. Either way, her mother was the popular English Vauxhall Gardens singer, Mrs. Weichsel. Even as a child, Elizabeth was a good keyboard player with a gift for composition. She played a piano concerto in Bath in March 1780. In 1783, very young, she married the double-bass player, James Billington, and that same year she was singing in Dublin with Tenducci, who probably gave her lessons. She also claimed to have been taught in Paris by Sacchini, who died in 1786. In that year Mrs. Billington made her début at Covent Garden as Rosetta in *Love in a Village*; her success was instant, and in no time she commanded enormous fees. She sang Clara in *The Duenna*, Mandane in *Artaxerxes*, roles in operas by Shield, and, less probably, Polly. For her benefit in 1790 she played Ophelia, in which part she threw in a performance of Purcell's 'Mad Bess'. When Lord Mount-Edgcumbe first heard her, 'she was very young and pretty, had a delightful fresh voice of very high compass . . . in its very high tones it resembled a flute or flageolet. Its agility was very great, and everything she sung was executed in the neatest manner, and with the utmost precision.' She could sing with ease up to F and G in alt. According to Burney, 'the natural tone of her voice is exquisitely sweet, her knowledge of music so considerable, her shake so true, her closes and embellishments so various, and her expression so grateful, that nothing but envy and apathy can hear her without delight'. But others thought that she lacked expression, that her embellishments (published by

Thomas Busby) were extravagant, and that she was a very bad actress. Her private life was so criticized (a scurrilous 'Life' was published) that in 1794 she fled to Italy. In Naples she was patronized by Sir William Hamilton and Emma, and she was a prodigious success at the San Carlo and later in other Italian opera houses. She had a European reputation when she returned to London in 1801. By this time her first husband had died, some said mysteriously, and she had married a turbulent Frenchman called Félissent. The years had made her plump and pudding-faced, yet she was much more popular than before as a person. In 1805 she revived *La clemenza di Scipione* by J. C. Bach (her harpsichord teacher when a child), and in the following year *La clemenza di Tito*; she sang Vitellia, and this was the first Mozart opera ever given in London. She then retired to Venice, where she died after constant rows with her husband. The year of her birth is given incorrectly in all reference books.

BLAND, Mrs. Maria Theresa (1769–1838), was known as Miss Romanzini until her marriage in 1790 to Mrs. Jordan's brother. According to Mollie Sands, her original name was Ida Romanzi, and 'Romanzini' resulted from her short stature. A plump, charming, illegitimate Italian-Jewess, she was a pupil of Dibdin's at the Royal Circus, and her first adult role at Drury Lane was in Grétry's *Richard Coeur de Lion* in 1786. She became famous for simple ballads rather than elaborate arias, and yet when she deputized in 1798 at short notice at the King's Theatre (in Paisiello's *Gli schiavi per amore* and *La Frascatana*), Lord Mount-Edgcumbe reported that though she was 'only a singer of the second class, few, if any, English singers who have appeared at the opera sung [*sic*] with such pure Italian taste, or equalled her in recitative and pronunciation of the language'. Her English words were very clear as well. She was a success as Wowski in *Inkle and Yarico*, and sang secondary roles in nearly all Storace's operas. Kelly took Haydn and Pleyel to the *Cherokee* especially that they might hear her sing 'A little Bird sang on the Spray', which she did 'with great simplicity and truth' as the Welsh maid. 'The favourite little singer', wrote Leigh Hunt, 'with a voice like her name, and a short thick person, and dark face to match, whose sweet ballads made her ever welcome.' Her marriage broke up in the middle nineties, and she later had several illegitimate children. In a temper, she locked one of them out in the cold, and later found it dead on the doorstep; thereafter she had bouts of melancholia, and periods of wretched poverty. Her son Charles Bland created the title role in Weber's *Oberon* in 1826.

BRACEGIRDLE, 'Mrs.' Anne (*c.* 1673–1748), soprano, was the daughter of a Northampton gentleman, but she was brought up by the actor-manager Thomas Betterton ('whose Tenderness she always acknowledges to have been Paternal'). The greatest actress of her day (and the original Emmeline in Purcell's *King Arthur*), she was also an excellent singer, specializing in the songs of Eccles. She was probably Congreve's mistress; as well as acting leads in all his plays, she sang Venus in the various versions of his *Judgment of Paris* (1701). She was at her peak when Betterton was running the old Lincoln's Inn Fields Theatre (1695–1705), and it was thought she would shine as brightly at the new Queen's Theatre, of which Congreve was joint manager. She did sing in the Italianate opera *The Temple of Love* (1706) by Fedelli, but the next year she suddenly retired, thus ruining the prospects of *Semele*, which Congreve and Eccles had written for her. Her retirement followed on Congreve's refusal to have anything more to do with the new theatre, or indeed with any other. In comfortable affluence she lived to enjoy the earlier performances of Garrick, and to breakfast with Horace Walpole.

BRAHAM, John (1774–1856), was a Jew of German extraction brought up and taught by a fellow Jew, Leoni, who was his uncle. His real name was Abraham, but when he sang at the Royalty as a boy soprano, Palmer advised him to clip the first letter. As a tenor he made his début in Bath in 1794, and Rauzzini was so impressed that he took him into his house and taught him; also he asked Storace to audition him for Drury Lane. Storace, equally impressed, began writing *Mahmoud* for him, but died in March 1796 before completing the score. In spite of a sensational London début in this opera, Braham went abroad in the summer with Nancy Storace; they had become lovers. For five years they sang with acclaim in Paris, all over Italy, and in Hamburg. Back in London in 1801, Braham astonished everyone with his brilliant execution, great power, and sweetness in soft passages. His average earnings in the next twenty-five years are said to have been about £14,000 p.a. Leigh Hunt found him wonderfully animated when singing, but 'a remarkably insipid performer' when he wasn't; his voice had 'that nasal tone which has been observed in Jews . . . (and) in Americans', but it was 'a veritable trumpet of grandeur and exaltation' in Handel. It was less admired in simple ballads, which he 'italianized' with too much ornamentation. He composed a number of operas with a great deal of help from others, and his song 'The Death of Nelson' was a sensational onslaught on the audience's feelings, with its imitation of gun-fire and emotive subject. 'The public', wrote Leigh Hunt, 'were enchanted with a style which enabled them to fancy that they enjoyed the highest form of art, while it required only the vulgarest of their perceptions.' Charles Lamb, whose ear was less educated, wrote in a letter of 1808, 'Braham's singing, when it is impassioned, is finer than Mrs. Siddons' or Mr. Kemble's acting, and when it is not impassioned is as good as hearing a person of fine sense talking. The brave little Jew!' (Braham was 5 feet 3 inches in height.) In 1816 his liaison with Nancy Storace broke up and he started a family by a legal wife. Later he sang under Weber in *Der Freischütz* and *Oberon*.

BRENT, Miss Charlotte (Mrs. Pinto) (*c.* 1735–1802), was the outstanding English soprano of the 1760s. Her father was a fencing-master who sometimes sang small roles, for instance Hamor in Handel's *Jephtha* (1752). She became an articled pupil of Thomas Arne, and in 1755–6 she accompanied him and his wife to Dublin where she played Ariel in *The Tempest* and sang in *Alfred* and *Eliza*. Arne and his pupil were soon living together, and Mrs. Arne preferred to stay on in Dublin rather than return with them to London. Garrick was unimpressed by what he heard of Miss Brent's singing, but her début at Covent Garden as Polly (1759) established her fame overnight. From then on she sang all the leading operatic roles, creating Mandane in *Artaxerxes*, Rosetta in *Love in a Village*, Patty in *The Maid of the Mill*, etc. Her voice was expressive, wide in range, agile in coloratura. She also sang frequently in oratorios by Handel and in Arne's *Judith*, and she was engaged at the Three Choirs Festival from 1765 to 1768. In November 1766 she became the second wife of the violinist Thomas Pinto; earlier that year she had still been Arne's mistress, and the marriage antagonized Arne and may account for his ceasing to write playhouse operas at this period. In *Thespis* Hugh Kelly laments her shortcomings as an actress, but calls her 'matchless Pinto' and adds that her voice

> Melts the whole breast divinely while it storms,
> Pains with delight, and wounds us as it charms.

About 1770 Pinto got into financial difficulties and took his wife to Ireland. Her career was virtually over. In 1773 Thomas Snagg heard her in Dublin, where her husband was leading the band, and described her as 'the ruins of the once celebrated Miss Brent'. She grew old before her time. In 1784 she sang in a benefit performance of *Comus* and had aged so much that William Parke, who played the obbligato in 'Sweet Echo' with her, thought she was in her seventies. She died in poverty in Vauxhall. She does not seem to have had any children; George Frederic Pinto (1786–1806), who composed an astonishing piano sonata and other promising music, was the grandson of Thomas Pinto and his first wife.

BROWN, Miss (Mrs. Cargill) (*c.* 1756–84), was the daughter of a coal-merchant who disapproved of her stage career. He twice tried to abduct her, on one occasion carrying her by force into the country purposing to ship her to America, but as a result of her cries 'the peasants released her, when she ran to town across country' (*Morning Post* 5.1.76). Later he tried to seize her as she was arriving at Covent Garden to play Polly, and she was saved only when 'the theatrical garrison sallied out in great numbers, headed by Messrs. M—, B—, W—, and S—, to relieve the distressed damsel. The thieves in the Beggar's Opera, armed with pistols etc., made a formidable appearance, and the crowd was so numerous that for a considerable time the street was impassable' (*Morning Chronicle* 7.10.76). Her rescuers presumably included Mattocks, du Bellamy, and Wewitzer. Miss Brown seems to have appeared first as a child in Arne's *The Fairy Prince* (1771). Her greatest success was as Clara, the most difficult vocal part in *The Duenna* (1775), and it is clear from the way the part is written that Sheridan did not think much of her as an actress. She must have improved with experience for *The Gazetteer* of 27.9.77 especially praised the way she spoke the dialogue as Rosetta in *Love in a Village*, and Sheridan allowed her to create Lauretta in his *St. Patrick's Day* though she had only one song (by Hook). She sang both coloratura roles and lyrical songs. Her marriage in 1780 to Mr. Cargill was unsuccessful, and in 1782 she set off for India with an army officer. A subscription theatre had been erected in Calcutta in 1775. At first all the characters were played by gentlemen amateurs, but women soon joined in. Mrs. Cargill had a sensational success both in *Messiah* and in several operas, and at her benefit she cleared 12,000 rupees. She did not live to spend many of them. The East-India packet *Nancy*, on which she was returning to England, was wrecked in a storm, and 'She was found on the rocks of Scilly floating in her shift, and an infant in her arms' (*The Thespian Dictionary*).

CARGILL, Mrs. See Miss Brown.

CATLEY, Miss Anne (1745–89), was the daughter of a London coachman and a washerwoman. About 1760 she was apprenticed to William Bates as a singing pupil, and made her stage début as the Pastoral Nymph in *Comus* (CG 8.10.62). Her beauty soon got her into a scrape which ended with her lover paying Bates £200 for the rest of her apprenticeship. She then sang mainly in Dublin. O'Keeffe described her as 'one of the most beautiful women I ever saw . . . she was eccentric, but had an excellent heart'. Boaden thought her both handsome and arch. 'She aimed at an almost manly frankness of speech, and acted as one superior to censure.' She first sang at Covent Garden as a star in the 1770–1 season. Her Rosetta (*Love in a Village*) was outstanding, as also her Rachel (*The Jovial Crew*), Polly, and Juno (*The Golden Pippin*). She had frequent absences from the stage, and it is curious that she was not at first in *The Duenna*, but she took over the part of Clara in 1780 when Miss Brown left the company. Next year she sang Macheath, and in 1784 she retired. Parke (ii, p. 252), writing of Sontag's stunt in 1828 of singing difficult variations intended for the violin, said 'the staccato style of singing was practised with equal success fifty years ago . . . by Miss Catley. That lady . . . sang the whole of Fischer's Minuet staccato, in the burlesque opera of "Tom Thumb", first performed 1780, with most extraordinary power of voice and articulation.' At some period General Lascelles 'took her from the stage', and after she had presented him with a son and four daughters, 'he married her for her really good conduct' (Mrs.

Papendiek ii, p. 158). Not everyone thought her conduct as good as all that. In 1888 an anonymous Life was published in which her misdemeanours were stressed in salaciously guarded but uninteresting terms. Mrs. Papendiek, a reliable writer, goes out of her way to mention her numerous charities after retirement. 'In every respect she was a truly good woman.'

CHAMBERS, Mrs. Isabella, soprano, was perhaps the most active and successful singer of the century of whom nothing seems to be known. She joined Rich's company at Lincoln's Inn Fields in the autumn of 1724, and in *Harlequin Sorcerer* she got nothing better than Fifth Witch. The following season she was singing leads; presumably it was her high voice and feminine appearance that kept her out of travesty roles. She sang Lavinia in the revival of *Camilla* and several pantomime heroines, for instance Proserpine in *The Rape of Proserpine* and Andromeda in *Perseus and Andromeda*. In the 'English Opera' seasons of 1732–3 she was limited to such 'second lady' parts as Ardelia in *Teraminta* and Grideline in *Rosamond*, her eclipse resulting from the rise to fame of Susanna Arne and Cecilia Young. Mrs. Chambers had no more success, though Rich continued to give her small parts, for instance a Nymph in the pantomime *Orpheus* (1740). A 'Mrs.' Chambers was singing for Rich in the 1750s, making her début as Polly to Lowe's Macheath (27.10.51). This perhaps was a daughter; she survived the same shipwreck on the south coast of Scotland that drowned Theophilus Cibber in 1758.

CIBBER, Mrs. Susanna (1714–66), mezzo-soprano and tragedienne, was Thomas Arne's sister. She made her début as Amelia in Lampe's opera of that name (1732), and sang in most of the English Operas her father staged, including Galatea in Handel's *Acis and Galatea* (she was then a soprano) and the title role in her brother's *Rosamond*. Huncamunca in *Tom Thumb* was among her very few comedy parts. In April 1734 she unwisely married Theophilus Cibber, whose first wife had just died. Their affairs soon became notorious. In 1737 Cibber fled the country in debt. Next year he returned, found his wife living with a Mr. Sloper, and brought an action against him. But it transpired that Cibber had connived at the relationship from the first, and he was given negligible damages. Mrs. Cibber lived with Sloper for the rest of her life. She had joined the Drury Lane company in 1734, and in 1736 she first attempted tragedy in Aaron Hill's *Zara*. Whereas Mrs. Clive was an actress who learned to sing, Mrs. Cibber was the supreme example of a singer who learned to act. Mrs. Siddons excepted, she became the outstanding tragedienne of the century. She preserved her slight youthful figure to the end, and with her low voice and emotional feeling she was supreme in such roles as Juliet, Hermione, and (her favourite) Constance in *King John*. She was still playing Ophelia and Cordelia at forty, Celia at fifty. By 1750 she had more or less given up singing; until then she ran two careers with astonishing success. She was the original contralto soloist in *Messiah*, the original Micah in *Samson*. (Handel like her company and visited her house regularly on Sunday evenings.) Burney says her voice was 'but a thread', but he agreed with the general view that her singing depended on expression rather than vocal quality. In slow melancholy songs she could move an audience to tears, and Handel surely had her in mind when he wrote 'He was despised'. Vivacity was beyond her powers. For a decade from 1736 she sang Polly, setting new vocal standards for the part, but Polly is the one *Beggar's Opera* character that demands plaintiveness rather than gaiety. When Mrs. Cibber died Garrick remarked, 'Then Tragedy has expired with her.' He added that 'she was the greatest female plague belonging to my house. I could parry the thrusts, and despise the coarse language of some of my other heroines but whatever was Cibber's object, a new part or a new dress, she was always sure to carry her point.' They were in fact fond of each other. The likeness between Garrick and one of her daughters was much commented on, but she and Garrick were themselves rather alike. There is a large and striking portrait of her as Cordelia by Pieter van Bleeck (*c.* 1754); her hair was dark, and she had a long narrow face a little like her brother's. (See May 1968 Catalogue of P. & D. Colnaghi, 14 Old Bond Street, W.1.) For her last illness see Cradock iv, p. 101, and for a list of her parts and some interesting eulogies see Genest v, pp. 99–102.

CLIVE, Mrs. Catharine, *née* Raftor (1711–85), was London's first soubrette. Her father, a Kilkenny gentleman, lost his property through supporting James II, but got a pardon in London where he married well. Kitty Raftor was friendly with one Jenny Johnson; both were stage-struck, and when Jenny got engaged to Theophilus Cibber, Kitty was soon being auditioned by Colley. After hearing her sing, he offered her a contract at 20s. a week. 'She flew to Perfection like a Bullet in the Air' (Chetwood). Joining the Drury Lane company in the autumn of 1728, she remained in it, with very few absences, for over forty years. Among her first parts were Minerva in *Perseus and Andromeda* and Phillida in *Love in a Riddle*; at the time she was only seventeen. A delightful comedienne with a charming though untrained voice (she had a few lessons from Carey), she was ideally equipped for ballad opera. Her first big success was as Nell in *The Devil to pay*, a part in which she delighted Londoners for more than a quarter of a century. In 1732 she married George Clive, a lawyer, but they soon separated. For some years Mrs. Clive aimed no higher than ballad opera, but in the 1740s she grew more ambitious, singing Emma in *Alfred* at Cliveden, and Pallas in Arne's *The Judgment of Paris*. In 1743 Handel wrote for her the part of Dalila in *Samson* and that same season she sang some of the solos in *Messiah* and *L'Allegro*. Burney thought she had aimed too high; he found her singing 'intolerable when she meant it to be fine', though 'in ballad farces and songs of humour it was, like her comic acting, everything it should be'. It would seem that Handel wanted Dalila sung in a way that had no appeal for Burney —in character. Boyce wrote songs especially for Mrs. Clive in *The Chaplet* and *The Shepherds' Lottery*, but, like Arne, he was careful not to overtax her. A Mrs. Clive song was usually strophic, gay, and not much more sophisticated than the ballads she sang so entrancingly as Chloe in *The Lottery* and as Nell. The pert charm she radiated in performance was not always evident at rehearsal. Burney records her habit of blaming the orchestra for her own lapses, and once when she came in wrong and cried out 'Why don't the fellows mind out what they are about?' Arne, goaded beyond endurance, remonstrated, got slapped, and proceeded to put her over his knee and spank her (Lonsdale, p. 17). But Garrick was said to have been in awe of her. She was Dr. Johnson's favourite actress; 'Clive, Sir, is a good thing to sit by, she always understands what you say'. In 1769 she left the stage and retired to Strawberry Hill where she had had a house for many years; she and Horace Walpole much enjoyed each other's company. She lived long enough to see Mrs. Siddons perform at Drury Lane, and remarked that 'it was all Truth and Daylight'. One of her sidelines was to sing Irish songs in the theatre intervals; for instance 'Eileen Aroon' (DL 8.3.42). I have not found an earlier example by any singer.

CROUCH, Mrs. Anna Maria (1763–1805), was the daughter of Peregrine Phillips, a Mr. Turveydrop who gave public readings that very few wanted to hear. She was articled to Linley for three years, during which time she made her début at Drury Lane as Mandane in *Artaxerxes* (1780–1) and had her first speaking role as Clarissa. She was soon a competent actress in lyrical or sentimental roles (she was never animated), being much helped by her beauty and grace. She was a natural choice for Olivia to Mrs. Jordan's Viola, and made a charming Perdita, but she was best in those parts that needed good singing as well as acting; for instance Ophelia and Miranda. She was the first notable actress who accepted regular summer engagements. She played Liverpool in 1781 and Dublin from 1782, taking such roles as Polly, Sabrina in *Comus*, Clara in *The Duenna*, Rosetta in *Love in a Village*. Her love life was varied. She nearly married Kemble in 1783. Next year she eloped while touring in Ireland, and the couple actually got as far as the altar, but the R.C. priest delayed matters until her father caught them up. These events were so well publicized that when she married a naval lieutenant called Rollings Edward Crouch (Twickenham, 9.1.85), she thought it best to do so secretly. Pregnancy forced her to reveal the marriage; the baby born that summer died. When Michael Kelly joined the Drury Lane company in March 1787, Mr. Crouch unwisely proposed that he should live with them. Kelly taught Mrs. Crouch to sing in a more Italianate style, she taught him 'to give proper expression to the dialogue', and they fell in love. Every summer

Kelly went with the Crouches to Liverpool or Ireland, but when he proposed they should go to Paris in 1791, Mr. Crouch felt the time had come to leave his wife. Soon after the split, Mrs. Crouch had a brief liaison with the Prince of Wales; she used to entertain him, Sheridan, and other notables at her house in Pall Mall, often dressed in the clothes she had just been wearing on the stage. By this time she was singing the upper-class heroine in most of Storace's operas—as opposed to the servant-class heroines taken by Nancy Storace. Her voice, which was described as 'particularly sweet and soft', could easily reach E and F in alt, and she always looked agreeable while singing, 'not betraying those struggling emotions, those horrid italian gestures which are so visible in many great singers, and must disgust the eye'. She was also much in demand for Handel oratorios. Kelly signed a contract on what he described as their wedding-day, undertaking to marry her should she ever be a widow, but she never was. He remained faithful to her in spite of her becoming an alcoholic in her last years. She made her farewell to the stage in 1801 as Celia in *As you like it* (her singing voice by then had gone), and she died in Brighton. In 1806 her *Memoirs* by M. J. Young were published; this is an ill-written book in which no character has any reality, but it contains useful information. See also *Thespian Magazine*, June 1792; *Gentleman's Magazine*, Oct. 1805, *European Magazine*, Nov. 1805.

DE CAMP, Miss Maria Theresa (*c.* 1774–1838), is mainly remembered as the wife of Charles Kemble and the mother of Fanny. In Fanny's enchanting *Record of a Girlhood* she is portrayed in detail. I give the usual spelling of her surname, but Fanny preferred Decamp, and thought her much younger than she really was. In fact she was in London at least by 1781. The daughter of a French army officer and a Swiss farm girl, she had been born in Vienna and named after the Empress. Aged six, she was dancing in ballets at the King's Theatre, London, as was her aunt, Mme Simonet. A titled lady took her up, and had her taught English. Absurdly young, she made her début at Drury Lane as Julie in *Richard Coeur de Lion* (1786), and for the rest of the century sang small parts in nearly all this theatre's operas. When Mrs. Bannister retired in the early nineties, she took over operatic leads at the Little Theatre, where her slim figure was much admired in Macheath. (This was a travesty production, with Incledon and Johnstone as Polly and Lucy.) She continued to dance on occasion. *The Thespian Magazine* (Feb. 1794) admired her versatility and clear articulation, and Leigh Hunt her 'fine, large dark eyes'. She played several Shakespearean heroines, simple roles in most of Storace's and Kelly's operas, and in 1803 was Britain's first Cinderella. After resisting assault in the Drury Lane dressing-room by J. P. Kemble, she married his brother in 1806 when she was over thirty. By this time she had had several plays performed. In 1829 she came out of retirement to play Lady Capulet when Fanny made her astonishing début as Juliet. Her husband staged

London's first *Der Freischütz*, commissioned Weber's *Oberon*, and made it possible for Berlioz to meet Harriet Smithson. The whole family had perfect French. Fanny says her mother loathed London, loved the country, collected antiques, and had manias for re-arranging the furniture in their cottage ('crimson and dishevelled') and for fishing.

FARREL(L), Mrs. (*c.* 1755–93), was born Margaret Doyle in Ireland. According to Parke (i, p. 27) she was heard by some Covent Garden performers singing in the pub where she worked near St. Giles, and they were so impressed that they told Arne about her. It seems she was already married. Arne gave her lessons and introduced her in *The Sot* (16.2.75), the main item in one of the 'Pupils' Evenings' he organized at the Little Theatre. He wrote his famous 'A-Hunting we will go' for Mrs. Farrell to sing in this work, and she later introduced it in *The Beggar's Opera* in the notable Covent Garden revision of 1777, when she was Macheath. She is described as 'tall, large and raw-boned' and plain of face, and inevitably she specialized in breeches parts. There was something 'attracting notice' in her Irish features, and she was both 'courteous and chatty'. In January 1779, having been recently widowed, she married Morgan Hugh Kennedy, a doctor, at St. Paul's, Covent Garden, and from then on she sang as Mrs. Kennedy. She was Don Alphonso in Arnold's *The Castle of Andalusia*, and she appeared in almost all Shield's earlier operas. Her Patrick in *The Poor Soldier* was thought outstanding, her Irish accent helping her both in this part and as Mrs. Casey in *Fontainbleau* (one of her few female roles). Parke described her as having 'one of the finest counter-tenor voices ever heard'; in fact she was a mezzo; Shield seldom took her above F, and never (I think) above G. She had 'a rich tone and perfect intonation' (Parke again) and latterly tended to drink too much. She retired from Covent Garden in 1788.

HARPER, Elizabeth (Mrs. Bannister) (*c.* 1757–1849), was the daughter of a mantua-maker in Bath. She began her career rather older than most sopranos, unless the ninety-two years with which she was credited at her death are an exaggeration. She made her début as Rosetta at the Little Theatre (1778), and the same season she sang Polly, Wilhelmina in *The Waterman*, and Eliza in *The Flitch of Bacon*. For five summers she was the Little Theatre's leading soprano, and her singing was one reason for the emphasis on opera there. Occasionally she took straight roles, such as Olivia in *Twelfth Night*, and Ophelia to John Bannister's *Hamlet* (LT 17.8.80), but she was more liked for her Clarissa and her singing in Arnold's numerous operas. All this time there was no place for her either at Drury Lane, where Linley wished to hear only his pupils, or at Covent Garden, where Miss Brown and Miss Catley held sway. When the last-named singer left the theatre, Miss Harper was engaged at Covent Garden and was an immediate success in *Rosina*

(CG 1782). In the following spring she married John Bannister and changed him from a straight actor into a reliable baritone and from a rake into a good family man; she herself was famous for her virtuous behaviour. They had a son and three daughters. Though she often tossed off difficult coloratura arias in Shield's operas, she was most admired for her expressive singing of simple lyrical ballads. In 1786 Mrs. Billington joined the company and in bravura arias outclassed Mrs. Bannister. Her tactful husband encouraged her to spend more time with her family and less at Covent Garden, though she continued to sing in the summer at the Little Theatre. She does not seem to have sung professionally after 1792.

INCLEDON, Charles (1763–1826), was a Cornishman and sang as a choir-boy at Exeter under Jackson. He spent some four years in the Navy where his singing attracted attention. By 1784 he was ashore for good and in Collins's company at Southampton. Next year he was taking opera roles in Bath and having lessons with Rauzzini. His progress was slow; in spite of being popular at Vauxhall Gardens, he did not have any real success until he was engaged by Covent Garden in the autumn of 1790. The first role he created was in *The Woodman*. For the next thirty years he was one of our leading tenors, being gifted with a beautiful voice (his shake was admired) but not with much musicianship or intelligence. As an actor he was clumsy, and his conceit made him unlikable. Parke, who shared lodgings with Incledon and Shield, thought him 'a singular compound of contrarieties, amongst which frugality and extravagance were conspicuous' (ii, p. 56). Leigh Hunt was less charitable: 'It is a pity I cannot put upon paper the singular gabblings of that actor, the lax and sailor-like twist of mind, with which everything hung upon him, and his profane pieties in quoting the Bible; for which, and swearing, he seemed to have an equal reverence.' See p. 271 for his falsetto.

JOHNSTONE, John (1759–1828), was a self-taught rough-and-ready Irish tenor with an extensive falsetto. The son of an army riding-master, he him-self was briefly in the army, but when threatened with a court-martial in Clonmel for duelling, he deserted. In 1776 he sang Lionel at Smock Alley Theatre, Dublin, and two years later he married Maria Poitier, niece of the Miss Poitier that Vernon 'married'. For some five years they sang together all over Ireland. On Macklin's recommendation Johnstone was engaged by Covent Garden, and *The Poor Soldier* (4.11.83) was so successful that all subsequent operas by Shield had an Irish character, usually a servant; John-stone's accent was so thick that he could take no other role. His singing coupled with O'Keeffe's lyrics made Irish songs popular in London. John-stone sang at both Covent Garden and the Little Theatre for the rest of the century. He had a likable stage personality and 'won you before he spoke'. He sang 'without the slightest affectation or mixture of the foreign graces', but, as Haydn noticed when seeing him in *The Woodman*, he was no musician. He was also unreliable as a husband; his infidelities were thought to have driven his first wife to the grave (in 1784). In 1791 he married a 'Miss Bolton of Bond Street' with whom he had been living for some time. (See *The General Magazine*, 1792, pp. 299 and 332; *The Thespian Magazine*, Sept. 1793; Tate Wilkinson i, p. 219; Boaden's *Kemble* i, p. 122.)

KELLY, Michael (1762–1826), was the son of the Deputy Master of Ceremonies at Dublin Castle. He had lessons from Michael Arne, and when sixteen sang Lionel so promisingly that he was shipped off to Naples with letters of recommendation to Sir William Hamilton. He studied singing for some four years, mainly at Palermo under Aprile; he climbed Mount Etna among other activities. Early in 1783 he met the Storaces in Leghorn, and they became close friends. Kelly sang briefly in several North Italian opera houses, for four months in Venice, in Graz, and (according to *The General Magazine*) in Warsaw and Berlin. In 1784 Nancy Storace got him into the Vienna company, where he was known as Ochelly; he created Don Basilio in Mozart's *Figaro* and roles in operas by Paisiello. In March 1787 he came to London with the Storaces and was immediately engaged by Linley at Drury Lane; Linley had been making him offers for a year or more. He had never been in England before. When he made his début as Lionel, *The European Magazine* found him 'so much the disciple of the Italian school, in reciting as well as singing, that he does not personate an English character'. He was always considered a poor actor, though in Vienna his character parts (especially his old men) had been admired. His vocal quality was unremarkable, but he had style, and he was the first playhouse tenor who never sang falsetto. He took the lead in most of Storace's Drury Lane operas, and small parts sometimes at the King's Theatre, where he had a share in the management on and off from 1793. After Storace's death he masqueraded as a composer, singing less and less, and not at all after 1811. Thereafter he ran both a wine shop and a music shop in Pall Mall. Leigh Hunt described his 'quick, snappish, but not ill-natured voice, and a flushed, handsome, and good-humoured face, with the hair about the ears. The look was a little rakish or so, but very agreeable.' His only known passion was for Mrs. Crouch, with whom he lived from about 1789 until her death. In old age he supplied material for his vivid, delightful, and inaccurate *Reminiscences*, ghosted by James Hook's son, Theodore. Retired in Brighton, Kelly enjoyed the friendship of George IV. (See *The European Magazine*, April 1787; *The General Magazine*, May 1788; *The Thespian Magazine*, July 1794.)

KENNEDY, Mrs. See Mrs. Farrel.

LAGUERRE, Jean or John (*c.* 1702–48), singer, scene-painter, and perhaps dancer, whose name was usually mis-spelt Legar. He was the son of Louis Laguerre, who came to England about 1683 and stayed for the rest of his life, painting halls, staircases, and ceilings at Burleigh House, Petworth, Chatsworth, Cannons, Blenheim, etc. William III gave him apartments at Hampton Court, where he painted the Labours of Hercules in the Fountain Court. Of his two wives, one was the daughter of a French iron-worker employed at Hampton Court, while the other was probably English. It is unknown which was the singer's mother. In 1721 Louis Laguerre went to Lincoln's Inn Fields to see *The Island Princess*, in which his son was singing a small and unadvertized role, and died in the theatre. John Laguerre, employed by Rich throughout his working life, was prominent in all his most famous pantomimes, playing Mercury in no less than three of them, *Jupiter and Europa*, *The Rape of Proserpine*, and *Perseus and Andromeda*. The *London Stage* lists him among Rich's dancers for the four seasons 1722–6 (thereafter as a singer), and he may have played miming roles, but usually in pantomimes (and perhaps always) he sang in the masque sections. He must have had perfect English, for he was a success as the countryman Hob in the ballad opera *Flora*. He also produced a popular series of illustrations of this piece. Later parts included Diomedes in Gay's *Achilles*, Gubbins in *The Dragon of Wantley*, Dreadnought in *Nancy*, and finally Wall in *Pyramus and Thisbe* (1745). For many years he had helped Lambert with the scene-painting at Covent Garden, and by the 1740s this activity provided most of his rather meagre living. On 29.3.48 Cross recorded that 'Jack Laguerre dy'd', and *The General Advertiser* obituary described him as 'an eminent Painter belonging to . . . Covent Garden; a facetious companion [the epithet was not then derogatory], universally esteem'd in every Scene of Life'. Vocally his most ambitious part had been Coridon in the staged version of *Acis and Galatea* (1731) but he was never on Handel's mailing-list. He is not to be confused with Lagarde, a mysterious bass who occasionally sang for Handel in the early 1720s.

LAMPE, Mrs. Isabella, *née* Young, and a sister of Mrs. Arne, seems to have made her first appearance as Margery in *The Dragon of Wantley* (LT 1737); in the middle of the run she married its composer. Thereafter she sang in everything that he wrote, going with him to Dublin (1748–50) and Edinburgh, where he died in 1751. Early in her career she had created the part of Nancy in Carey's little piece and sang Rhodope in Rich's last important pantomime, *Orpheus*; her sister Esther, a contralto, was Euridice. Soon after this Rich's wife converted the Lampes to Methodism, and they became friendly with Charles Wesley, the hymn-writer. After her husband's death Mrs. Lampe sang at Covent Garden in *Harlequin Sorcerer* (1752) and two years later she was Rosamond in a revival of Arne's opera of that name. The

Isabella Young who sang in Arne's *Eliza* and *Britannia* at this period was a niece. A Mrs. Lampe was still singing chorus parts at Covent Garden, for instance in the *Romeo and Juliet* dirge, as late as 1775, but this was probably the wife of her son Charles, a minor composer and organist.

LEONI, Michael (*c.* 1755–97), a Jewish tenor, made his début as Arbaces in *Artaxerxes* (CG 25.4.75) and had his greatest success the following October as Don Carlos in *The Duenna*. But his career in the playhouses, though brilliant, was short. Perhaps because he had made himself very unpopular with his fellow Jews for singing in *Messiah*, he left for Dublin in 1778, where he went into partnership with Tommaso Giordani. Their operatic schemes did not prosper, and back in London Leoni sang briefly for Palmer at the Royalty. He later went to Jamaica, where he died. He was the uncle of John Braham, and when the boy's parents died Leoni brought him up.

L'EPINE, Margherita de (*c.* 1670–1746), soprano, in spite of her name (which was variously spelt) is more likely to have been Italian than French. She seems to have first sung in London in the winter of 1692–3, and may well have been the first Italian vocalist to visit England professionally. On later visits she brought with her a sister, Maria Gallia, who was also an excellent soprano. Margherita (as she was often called) became the mistress of a German violinist working in London called Greber, and on page 34 I have discussed the evidence for thinking that she organized the opening production at the Queen's Theatre in 1705—Greber's *The Loves of Ergasto*. Margherita also sang in some of the macaronic operas that followed, for instance *Thomyris*, but she found in Mrs. Tofts an unscrupulous rival, and perhaps she was not sorry that her sister rather than she had to face Mrs. Tofts in *Rosamond*. In 1712–13 she sang for Handel, notably in a revival of *Rinaldo*, but this association collapsed when she became friendly with Pepusch, who regarded Handel with both dislike and jealousy. At the time when Cibber was making some attempt to popularize the masque at Drury Lane, Margherita sang in three examples with music by Pepusch—Adonis in *Venus and Adonis*, the title role in *Myrtillo*, and Dido in *The Death of Dido*; she was also Apollo in Galliard's *Apollo and Daphne*. Three of the four were travesty roles, and it should perhaps be remembered that at this time Margherita must have been at least in her middle forties, and handicapped by being 'outlandish . . . swarthy and ill-favoured' (Burney). In spite of this she married Pepusch in 1718 (he was fifty-one at the time), and no doubt her money and her amiable temper were sufficient compensation. She did not sing again, devoting herself to her husband until her death, which seems to have been in 1746. Burney remarks that her vocal technique must have been unusually good to allow for so long a career. She was an excellent harpsichordist.

LEVERIDGE, Richard (*c.* 1671–1758), bass, was on the London stage for at least fifty-six years. His career as a composer has been outlined on pp. 26–27. He sang at Drury Lane in Purcell's *The Indian Queen* (1695), and in such Italianate operas as *Arsinoe, Rosamond,* and *Thomyris.* At this time he had aspirations as an opera composer, and trifled with the Italianate style on occasions. He contributed to the very successful *Island Princess* (1699), and wrote music for *Macbeth* (1702) which was constantly given for 170 years and in which he sang the part of Hecate for nearly fifty. In his 1712–13 season Handel engaged Leveridge for *Il Pastor fido* and *Teseo* (in which, incredibly, he sang Minerva), and for a revival of *Rinaldo,* and he also sang at this time in Galliard's full-length opera, *Calypso and Telemachus.* He seemed all set for a career of increasing distinction. However, in 1714 he joined Rich's company at the new Lincoln's Inn Fields, and thereafter lost all ambition to sing or compose anything better than the strophic popular song. He built up for himself the image of a jovial, hard-drinking, boon companion, and in Rich's pantomimes he was constantly being type-cast, playing such parts as Charon, Merlin, and Pluto, the latter everlastingly turning up in *Harlequin Sorcerer, The Rape of Proserpine,* and *Orpheus.* However, Leveridge did also sing Pan in Pepusch's masque, *Pan and Syrinx,* Polyphemus in the 1731 *Acis and Galatea,* and Sir Trusty in Arne's *Rosamond.* It is significant that Handel himself showed no further interest in him after 1713. 'He had no notion of elegance in singing; it was all strength and compass' (Hawkins). About 1726 he opened a coffee-house in Tavistock Street. He continued to sing in pantomimes, ballad operas, and *Macbeth* for so long that he became the sort of institution that seems lovable to the elderly and maddening to the young. He sang in *Macbeth* as late as November 1750, and at his benefit on 24 April 1751 he appeared for the last time, singing interval songs and an 'Epilogue of thanks'. He lived on with his daughter in High Holborn, and died there 'in his eighty-eighth year'. He may have been the father of Charles Bannister (q.v.).

LOWE, Thomas (*c.* 1719–83), tenor, started life as a Spitalfields weaver (Busby ii, 122). He never learned to read music. Burney thought he had the finest tenor voice he had ever heard, but 'for want of diligence and cultivation, he never could be safely trusted with any thing better than a ballad, which he constantly learned by ear'. In fact he sang a number of small oratorio roles for Handel, though Handel never wrote for him regularly and lavishly as he did for Beard. Lowe made his name singing 'Rule, Britannia' in the Cliveden *Alfred* (1740), and he was Mercury in Arne's *The Judgment of Paris.* He had some success at Drury Lane as Macheath and as other favourite ballad opera characters, but he was not much of an actor, and his greatest successes came at Vauxhall Gardens, where he was a regular attraction for nearly twenty years. In 1748 he left Drury Lane for Covent

Garden, where he sang pantomime parts such as Perseus as well as in ballad operas, but on Beard's arrival in 1759 he returned to Drury Lane. After 1763 he was not re-engaged, Vernon being preferred as leading tenor. For six years Lowe was proprietor of Marylebone Gardens, where he brought out his pupil, Miss Catley, but he lost all his money, and in the 1770s he had to rely on the kindness of Thomas King, who gave him dates at Sadler's Wells; for instance the title role in Dibdin's 'dialogue', *The Grenadier*. He died in poverty.

MATTOCKS, George (*c.* 1738–1804), made his stage début as a small boy in Arne's *The Triumph of Peace* (DL 1749) and later that year played one of the leads in *The Chaplet*. After 1751 he is lost sight of, no doubt because his voice broke. When he returned it was to Covent Garden, where he sang from 1758 to 1780, creating Rimines in *Artaxerxes*, Young Meadows in *Love in a Village*, Lionel in *Lionel and Clarissa*, and many other parts. In 1764 he eloped to France with Miss Hallam, whom he married. Her parents had disapproved of the match because of his notorious affair with Miss Pitt just previously. (Miss Pitt later lived with Dibdin.) Mattocks was an uninspiring actor, and *The Theatrical Biographer* mentions his unmanly appearance. 'We are often led to imagine, that we are listening to the notes of a *Castrato*, than to those of a British singer.' In fact he sang mainly falsetto. In *Thespis* Hugh Kelly summed him up as one

> Whose tender strain, so delicately clear,
> Steals, ever honied, on the heaviest ear;
> With sweet-toned softness exquisitely warms,
> Fires without force, and without vigour charms.

His last Covent Garden season was in 1783–4; latterly he had sung only minor roles. He had already paved the way for his retirement as a London singer by acting regularly in the provinces in the summer, notably in Liverpool. After short spells managing the theatres in Portsmouth and Birmingham, he spent most of his later years in charge of the Liverpool theatre.

MATTOCKS, Mrs. Isabella (1746–1826), though overshadowed vocally by Miss Brent, was superior as an actress. After Mrs. Cibber, she is the most notable example in the century of a woman who shone equally in plays and operas. Her grandfather had been killed in a notorious duel by Macklin, her uncle (William Hallam) ran Goodman's Fields for many years, and her father fled to America in the early 1750s to escape his debts; he later managed theatres in New York, Charlestown, and Philadelphia. Miss Hallam was brought up in London by an aunt. Helped by a distant relationship with John Rich, she played her first part in Gay's *The What d'ye call it* (CG 2.10.52) aged six and a half (four and a half according to *The Thespian*

Dictionary). At fifteen she was Juliet, at seventeen Lucinda in *Love in a Village*, and she sang in numerous Covent Garden operas until 1780, playing Theodosia in *The Maid of the Mill*, Priscilla the 'Creole' in *Love in the City*, Venus in *The Golden Pippin*, Louisa in *The Duenna*.Her marriage in 1764 to George Mattocks was intermittently happy. She was soon having an affair with the actor Bensley, but later returned to her husband. They spent most of their summers acting together in Liverpool, and Genest (V. 384, etc.) lists an astonishing range of parts she played there in 1773: Lady Macbeth, Cordelia, Portia, Constance, Juliet, Angelica in *Love for Love*, and parts in Dryden's *All for Love*, Congreve's *The Mourning Bride*, and many less-remembered plays. The following summer she added Imogen and Olivia to her Shakespeare roles, and sang Leonora in *The Padlock*. Back at Covent Garden she was still playing Ophelia as late as 1781, and in that same year she was Kate Hardcastle and Mistress Ford. After a brief retirement spent mainly in Liverpool, she returned to Covent Garden to create Betty Blackberry in Shield's *The Farmer* (1786), and for the next twenty years she was quite often to be seen in 'older woman' parts.

NORRIS, Miss (born *c.* 1730), mezzo-soprano, is ignored in all reference books, but must have had a good voice, for Boyce gave her all the best serious songs in *The Chaplet* and *The Shepherds' Lottery*. She made her début at Covent Garden (10.12.48) as Euphrosyne in *Comus* (Peg Woffington was The Lady), but from the following September she sang at Drury Lane for the rest of her short career. She was Sabrina in *Comus* ('with the Echo Song'), the heroine in *Robin Hood* (Burney) and *Alfred* (Mallet, Burney, etc.), and Polly in *The Beggar's Opera*. After 23.10.52 she disappears from the advertisements. For five weeks all operas in which she appeared were dropped; thereafter she was replaced, mainly by Miss Thomas. Only serious illness, perhaps death, can account for this. (Perhaps I should add that she does *not* reappear under a married name.) Significantly she was never given parts that required more acting than singing.

PHILLIPS, Miss Anna Maria. See Mrs. Crouch.

PINTO, Mrs. See Miss Brent.

POITIER, Miss. See Vernon.

ROMANZINI, Miss. See Mrs. Bland.

STORACE, Ann Selina (1765–1817), was incorrectly known as Anna, and commonly as Nancy. Because her early career ran parallel with her brother's, it has already been covered in Chapter 14. When Stephen died in 1796,

Nancy went abroad for five years, singing and living with John Braham, who was by nine years her junior. In 1802 they had a son, Spencer. Nancy retired in 1808, and by 1816 her liaison had broken up. (Until 1806 she could not have married Braham because her husband, J. A. Fisher, was still alive.) The split is poignantly recorded in numerous letters at the Sir John Soane Museum, London; they vividly reveal the personalities of all concerned, especially of Spencer Braham, who became a psychological case. (He later changed his name to Meadows, and ended his days a Minor Canon at Canterbury Cathedral.) The letters reflect no credit on John Braham, though it was understandable that he should want a legitimate family; he later married and had six sons. Nancy had some consolation from her many friends, who included the Duke of Sussex and Prince Hoare. She was survived by her old mother. English singers are often more praised abroad than at home, but for Nancy the difference was exaggerated by her affair with Braham. After her death writers ignored or underpraised her in order not to offend the leading tenor of the day, who by then was a respectable family man. Yet Nancy received unstinted praise during the ten or twelve years that she sang in Italy, Vienna, and Paris. Burney just caught her London début of 1787 in time to get a snap judgement into his *History of Music*: 'Though a lively and intelligent actress, and an excellent performer in comic operas, her voice, in spite of all her care, does not favour her ambition to appear as a *serious* singer. There is a certain crack and roughness.' In fact this ambition was never very strong. Nancy was short and inclined to be plump, and she knew she was incapable of dignity on the stage. Lord Mount-Edgcumbe thought she had 'a clumsiness of figure and a vulgarity of manner that totally unfitted her for the serious opera', but he added that she sounded magnificent in oratorio in Westminster Abbey 'for in that space the harsh part of her voice was lost, while its power and clearness filled the whole of it'. Like everyone else, he thought her an excellent actress; indeed, both in Vienna and in London, she set new standards in comic opera by her vivacity and infectious good humour. As one writer puts it, 'Her brisk, *degagée* and dancing air . . . infused life and spirit into every scene'. She was far from smart. Of her performance in *My Grandmother* the *Thespian Magazine* (12.5.94) remarked 'and what is extraordinary for *her*, she was dressed with neatness and taste'. Yet she attracted friends at all social levels, and could count both an Austrian Emperor and Mozart among her lovers.

TENDUCCI, Giusto Ferdinando (*c.* 1734–1790), sometimes known as Senesino, was a castrato from Siena who sang mainly in Britain. He was first in London in 1758, singing at the King's Theatre. He was extravagant, and spent part of 1760 in a debtors' prison, but in 1762 he was widely acclaimed for his Arbaces in Arne's *Artaxerxes*. Thereafter he sang mainly in Edinburgh and Dublin. In Ireland he made an extraordinary marriage with Dora

Maunsell of Limerick, who wrote (or is alleged to have written) an account of the ignominy with which she and her husband were later treated. They are said to have had two children. For Dublin Tenducci shortened Rush's *The Royal Shepherd* into an afterpiece (*Amintas*), and he later sang in this version at Covent Garden. Also for Dublin he compiled a pastiche called *Athridates* (1767). Back in London he sang regularly at Ranelagh and at the Bach-Abel concerts, composing many of the songs himself. He specialized in Scotch Songs, singing some arranged for him by J. C. Bach. Mozart met him in Paris in 1778 and wrote for him a scena, now lost, with concertante parts for piano, oboe, bassoon, and horn. Tenducci spent much of the eighties back in Dublin, and wrote a short English opera, *The Campaign, or Love in the East Indies*. Shield adapted it for Covent Garden (May 1785) but there were only three performances. Tenducci also published a singing manual. 'A thing from Italy', wrote Liddy Melford after a visit to Ranelagh. 'It looks for all the world like a man, though they say it is not. The voice, to be sure, is neither man's nor woman's; but it is more melodious than either; and it warbled so divinely, that, while I listened, I really thought myself in Paradise.' (Smollett's *Humphry Clinker*, letter of May 31.) It has recently been discovered that Tenducci died at Genoa in 1790.

TOFTS, 'Mrs.' Catherine (*c.* 1684–1756), soprano, 'endeared herself to an English audience by her voice, figure, and performance, more than any preceding singer of our own Country' (Burney), yet her meteoric career lasted little more than five years. She was singing songs in English in 1703 and in Italian by March 1704. When Italian singers began to arrive, she not only held her own, but demanded and got far higher salaries. Her first stage part seems to have been in the 1704 revival of Weldon's *The Judgment of Paris*. Later she sang in many of the transitional operas, including both of Clayton's (she was Queen Eleanor in *Rosamond*), *Thomyris*, *Camilla*, and *Clothilda*. There can be no doubt that it was her beauty and personality that misled people into thinking well of Clayton's wretched music. In his *Apology* Cibber writes of her having 'charms that few of the most learned singers ever arrive at. The beauty of her finely proportioned figure, and the exquisitely sweet, silver tone of her voice, with that peculiar, rapt swiftness of her throat, were perfections not to be imitated by art or labour.' Less to be admired was her disputatiousness about money. According to Hawkins it was Pope who wrote of her:

> So bright is thy Beauty, so charming thy Song,
> As had drawn both the Beasts and their Orpheus along;
> But such is thy Avarice, and such is thy Pride,
> That the Beasts must have starv'd, and the Poets have died.

Even so her fate was severe. 'In the meridian of her beauty' she began to be afflicted with mental troubles. In March 1709 she made the most of a party at which thirty gentlemen were present by offering kisses at a guinea a time. Every gentleman accepted the offer, some of them as many as five times, and it seems reasonable to put the day's takings at about £100. This perhaps was little more than high spirits and an eye for the main chance, but two months later Steele was hinting in *The Tatler* (No. 20) at megalomania. After the summer of 1709 she never sang in England again. Loaded with money and a clouded mind, she made her way to Venice where she married a banker called Joseph Smith; later he became the English consul in Venice. As the years went by she became increasingly unhinged, and was said to spend much of her time wandering round her Venetian garden singing in a frenzy. Her husband collected Canalettos, most of which are now in Windsor Castle.

VERNON, Joseph (*c.* 1739–82), tenor, was illegitimate and grew up in a Coventry Charity School (Cradock iv, p. 178). He became a choirboy at St. Paul's Cathedral, and as 'Master Vernon' sang at Drury Lane in *Queen Mab* (26.12.50), *Alfred* (Burney), and *The Shepherds' Lottery*. His voice broke in 1753, but next autumn he was back as an actor and playing Donalbain. In January 1755 he made a notorious and precocious marriage with Miss Poitier, who had just sung in *Eliza* and perhaps was the Jenny Poitier who had danced as a child at the King's Theatre in 1748 with her father. One at least of them being under age, the wedding took place at the Savoy Chapel, which until the Marriage Act of 1754 had been outside the reach of the law and was wrongly thought to be so still. The marriage was annulled and the officiating chaplain and curate were deported. Vernon had given evidence against them and, the Drury Lane audience disapproving of this, he prudently spent a year in Ireland. Many details can be found in Vol. 1 of the *Memoirs* of Tate Wilkinson, his father being the chaplain concerned. He wrote of the young couple: 'Infidelity was so demonstrative on both sides, that the archbishop's licence would have had very little effect in tying faster the marriage noose.' 'Mrs. Vernon' continued to sing at Drury Lane, creating Helena in *The Fairies* and Miranda, a coloratura part, in Smith's *The Tempest*. Late in 1756 Vernon returned to Drury Lane, but not to his 'wife'. He was now primarily an actor, Beard and then Lowe being preferred as tenors. His voice, though expressively used, was unappealing in quality, but his acting was admired in such parts as Feste and Autolycus. He composed what is still the best-known setting of Feste's 'When that I was and a little tiny boy'. When Lowe left Drury Lane in 1763, Vernon was pushed into the leading operatic roles. As well as Macheath he played the hero in *Almena* and the title roles in *Pharnaces* and *Cymon*. Miss Poitier spent the sixties at Covent Garden, creating roles in *Thomas and Sally*, *Midas*, and *The Maid of the Mill*. When she sang at Ranelagh in *The Recruiting Sergeant* and *The Ephesian Matron* she had just become Mrs. Thompson, but she was soon having an affair with

Charles Bannister while both were singing at Marylebone Gardens (1770–3). Later she joined Tate Wilkinson's company at York. Vernon sang in most of Dibdin's Drury Lane operas and was Selim in *Selim and Azor*. When he asked Garrick for a rise of £2 a week, he got a severely-written refusal (Letter 863 of 11.9.74). In *The School for Scandal* Vernon sang Linley's 'Here's to the Maiden of bashful fifteen'. His last role was Truemore in *The Lord of the Manor* (DL 27.12.80). In Hugh Kelly's *Thespis* Vernon is praised for his masculinity; it is implied that the quality was unusual in a singer. The same poem reveals that Miss Poitier ('the liveliest baggage on the modern stage') anglicized her name, accenting the second syllable. In 1773 Vernon married, legally, Margaret Wilkinson.

WALKER, Thomas (1698–1744), known as Tom Walker, was the original Macheath, though he seems to have done no singing previously. Born in Soho, he first appeared at Drury Lane as Lorenzo in Lord Lansdowne's version of *The Merchant of Venice* (1716), but soon transferred to Lincoln's Inn Fields. His handsome, manly appearance helped him in such parts as Hotspur, and the Bastard in *King John*. He knew nothing of music, but 'supported his singing by so much expression of countenance and inimitable action, as rendered him in Macheath, a great favourite with the public' (Baker). He wrote *The Quaker's Opera* in imitation of *The Beggar's Opera*, and two other theatrical pieces, but his sudden and unexpected success went to his head. Unable to say no when being lionized, he became an inebriate. When Rich discharged him, he tried his luck in Dublin, but it did not hold, and he died in distress.

WALSH, Thomas (c. 1781–1848), often known as Master Welsh, was the most remarkable boy soprano of the century. He had been a choirboy at Wells, where his singing filled both the cathedral nave and the local hotels. When New Drury opened, Linley had him brought to London, and he made his début as a page in *Lodoiska* (9.6.94). From then until early in 1797 most Drury Lane operas were designed to show off his remarkable high coloratura, and in *The Cherokee* he was virtually the hero. Attwood wrote *The Adopted Child* for his benefit. The last part he created was in Arnold's *The Shipwreck*. He had no success as an adult singer, but was respected as a teacher; C. E. Horn and Miss Stephens were among his pupils.

WALTZ, Gustavus, bass, was a German who lived in London on and off for over thirty years, starting there, according to Hawkins, as Handel's cook. He took a prominent part in the 'English Opera' experiment of 1732–3, making his début as Osmyn in *Amelia*, and also singing Polyphemus in *Acis and Galatea*, and doubling Grizzle and the Ghost in *Tom Thumb*. According to Burney he had 'a coarse figure, and still coarser voice', and though 'as an actor, he had a great deal of humour' he does not seem ever to have been entrusted with a speaking part at the playhouses, which made use of him, if at all, mainly as a chorus singer. He was still singing in choruses in the Foundling Hospital performances of *Messiah* in the 1750s. There is a chapter about him in W. C. Smith's *Concerning Handel,* and a picture of him playing the cello.

YOUNG, Cecilia. See Mrs. Arne.

YOUNG, Isabella. See Mrs. Lampe.

Bibliography

Abbreviations: M&L   Music and Letters
           MT   Musical Times
           RMA   Royal Music Association Proceedings
           STR   Society for Theatre Research

All books listed below were published in London unless otherwise stated.

Addison, Joseph, etc. *The Spectator*, 7 vols, 12th ed, 1739

Adolphus, John. *Memoirs of John Bannister*, 2 vols, 1839

Algarotti, *Essay on Opera*, 1768 (anon translation)

Angelo, Reminiscences of Henry, 2 vols, 1828

Arundell, Dennis. *The Story of Sadler's Wells*, 1965

Avison, Charles. *An Essay on Musical Expression*, 1751

Baker, *Biographia Dramatica*, 3 vols (one is in two parts), 1812

Boaden, James. *Memoirs of the Life of John Philip Kemble*, 2 vols, 1825

Boaden, James. *The Life of Mrs. Jordan*, 2 vols, 1831

Black, Clementina. *The Linleys of Bath*, revised ed. 1926

British Union-Catalogue of Early Music, 2 vols, 1957

Bronson, Bertrand H. *Joseph Ritson, Scholar-at-Arms*, 2 vols, University of California 1938

Brown, Dr. John. *Dissertation on Poetry and Music*, 1763

Brownsmith, John. *The Dramatic Timepiece*, 1767

Burgoyne, Gen. John. Preface to *The Lord of the Manor*, 1780

Burney, Charles. *A General History of Music*, 4 vols, 1789

Burney, Charles. *MS Memoirs*, BM Add. 48345

Burney, Fanny. *Evelina*, 1778

Burney, Fanny. *Cecilia*, 1782

Burney, Fanny. *Diary and Letters of Madame d'Arblay*, 7 vols, 1854

Busby, Thomas. *Concert Room and Orchestra Anecdotes*, 3 vols, 1825

Carey, Henry. *Poems* ed. Frederick T. Wood, 1930

Carse, Adam, *The History of Orchestration*, 1925

Chappell, William. *Popular Music of the Olden Time*, 1855–7

Charke, Mrs. *A Narrative of her Life*, written by herself, 1755

Chetwood, William. *A General History of the Stage*, 1749

Cibber, An Apology for the Life of Mr. Colley, 2nd ed, 1749

Clark, William Smith. *The Irish Stage in the County Towns 1720–1800*, 1965

Clinton-Baddeley, V.C. *The Burlesque Tradition in the English Theatre*, 1952

Colman, George (the Younger). Preface to *The Iron Chest*, 1796
Colman, George (the Younger). *Random Records*, 2 vols, 1830
Cooke, William. *The Elements of Dramatic Criticism*, 1775
Churchill, Charles. *The Rosciad*, 1761
Coxe, William. *The Life of John Gay*, 1797
Coxe, William. *Anecdotes of G. F. Handel and J. C. Smith*, 1799
Cradock, J. *Literary and Miscellaneous Memoirs*, 4 vols, 1828 (i and iv are of musical interest)
Craven, Lady. *Memoirs of the Margravine of Anspach, written by herself*, 2 vols, 1826
Croft-Murray, Edward. 'John Devoto', *STR*, 1953
Cross, Diaries of Richard (Drury Lane Prompter), Folger Shakespeare Library
Cudworth, Charles. 'English Eighteenth Century Symphonies', *RMA* 1951–2
Cummings, W. H. *Dr Arne and Rule, Britannia*, 1912
Dean, Winton. *Handel's Dramatic Oratorios and Masques*, 1959
Dean, Winton. 'Opera under the French Revolution', *RMA* 1967–8
Delaney, Autobiography and Correspondence of Mrs., 3 vols, 1861
Deutsch, Otto Erich. *Handel, A Documentary Biography*, 1955
Dibdin, Charles. *The Royal Circus Epitomised*, 1784
Dibdin, Charles. *The Musical Tour*, 1788
Dibdin, Charles. *The Professional Life of*, 4 vols, 1803
Dibdin the Younger, Memoirs of Charles. STR 1956
Dibdin, Edward Rimbault. 'Charles Dibdin as a Writer', *M & L* April 1938
D'Urfey, Thomas. (*Wit and Mirth or*) *Pills to Purge Melancholy*, 6 vols, 1719 (Facsimile ed. New York 1959)
Dutton, Thomas. *The Dramatic Censor*, 1800
Dobrée, Bonamy. *English Literature in the Early Eighteenth Century*, 1959
Einstein, Alfred. *Mozart*, 1946
European Magazine, The, a monthly started in 1782
Fiske, Roger. 'The Operas of Stephen Storace', *RMA* 1959–60
Fiske, Roger. 'A Score for "The Duenna"', *M&L* April 1961
Fiske, Roger. 'The Macbeth Music', *M&L* April 1964
Fiske, Roger. 'A Cliveden Setting', *M&L* April 1966
Gagey, Edmond McAdoo. *Ballad Opera*, Columbia University Press 1937
Gainsborough, The Letters of Thomas, ed. Mary Woodall, 1963
Galliard (trans.). *Tosi's Obersvations on the Florid Song*, 1743
Galpin, Canon Francis. *Old English Instruments of Music*, 1965
Gardiner, William. *Music and Friends*, 3 vols, 1838
Garrick, The letters of David, 3 vols, ed. D. M. Little & G. M. Kahl, New York and London 1963
Gaye, Phoebe Fenwick. *John Gay*, 1938
General Magazine, The, 1787–92
Gentleman's Magazine, The, 1731–1833

Genest, John. *Some Account of the English Stage*, 10 vols, Bath 1832

Gibbs, Lewis. *Sheridan*, 1947

Girdlestone, Cuthbert. *Rameau*, 1957

Goldsmith, Oliver. *The Bee*, c. 1760

Grylls, Rosalie Glynn. *William Godwin and his World*, 1953

Hartnoll, Phyllis (ed.). *Shakespeare in Music*, 1964

Hawkins, Sir John. *General History of . . . Music*, 5 vols, 1776

Hayes, John. 'William Jackson of Exeter', *The Connoisseur*, January 1970

Hazlitt, William. *Complete Works*, ed. P. P. Howe, 21 vols, 1930–4

Heriot, Angus. *The Castrati in Opera*, 1956

Hill, Aaron. *Works*, 4 vols, 1754

Hogarth, George. *Memoirs of the Musical Drama*, 2 vols, 1838

Hogarth, George. 'Memoir of Charles Dibdin' in *The Songs of Charles Dibdin*, 1842

Holcroft, Memoirs of the Late Thomas, 3 vols, 1816 (completed by Hazlitt)

Hopkins, The Diaries of William (Drury Lane Prompter), Folger Shakespeare Library

Hughes, John. Preface to *Calypso and Telemachus*, 1712

Humphries, Charles, and Smith, W.C. *Music Publishing in the British Isles*, 1954

Hunt, Leigh The Autobiography of, ed. J. E. Morpurgo, 1949

Jackson, William. *Thirty Letters*, 1782 (four are about music)

Jackson, William. *Observations on the Present State of Music in London*, 1791

Jackson, William. *The Four Ages*, 1798

Johnson, Dr. Samuel. *Lives of the English Poets* (in particular of John Hughes)

Jones, Memoirs of Thomas. Walpole Society vol. XXXII, 1951

Kavanagh, Peter. *The Irish Theatre*, Tralee, 1946

Kelly, Hugh. *Thespis*, 1766

Kelly, Michael, Reminscences of, 2 vols, 2nd ed. 1826

Kemble, Fanny. *Recollections of a Girlhood*, Vol. 1, 1878

Knapp, J. Merrill. 'A Forgotten Chapter in English 18th c. Opera' (about Galliard), *M & L* January 1961

Lamb, Charles. *Essays of Elia*, 1818

Landon, H. C. Robbins. *The Symphonies of Joseph Haydn*, 1955

Landon, H. C. Robbins. *The Collected Correspondence and London Notebooks of Joseph Haydn*, 1959

Larsen, J. P. *Handel's Messiah*, 1957 (see especially Chapter Four for information about the two J. C. Smiths)

Laurie, Margaret. 'Did Purcell set "The Tempest"?', *RMA* 1963–4

Lincoln, Stoddart. 'The First Setting of Congreve's *Semele*', *M & L* April 1963

Lloyd, Robert. Poetical Works, 1774, especially 'The Actor'

London Stage, The (1660–1776), Southern Illinois University Press, 1960–70 (11 vols)

Loewenberg, Alfred. *Annals of Opera*, 3rd ed., 1955

Lonsdale, Roger. *Dr. Charles Burney*, 1965

Lysons, Rev. Daniel. *History of . . . the meeting of the Three Choirs*, Gloucester 1812

MacMillan, Douglas. *The Drury Lane Calendar*, 1938

Manifold, J. S. *The Music in English Drama from Shakespeare to Purcell*, 1956

McCredie, Andrew. 'John Christopher Smith as a Dramatic composer', *M & L* January 1964

Meyerstein, E. W. H. *A Life of Thomas Chatterton*, 1930

Moore, Thomas. *Memoirs of . . . Richard Brinsley Sheridan*, 2 vols, 3rd ed. 1825

Moore, Thomas. *Memoirs, Journals and Correspondence*, 4 vols, 1853

Morgan, The Memoirs of Lady, 2 vols, 1862

Mount-Edgcumbe, Musical Reminiscences of the Earl of, 3rd ed. 1829

Nicholl, Allardyce. *A History of English Drama; Early Eighteenth Century Drama*, London 1955; *Late Eighteenth Century Drama*, 1955

O'Keeffe, Recollections of the Life of John, 2 vols, 1826

Oliver, J. W. *Life of William Beckford*, 1932

Oman, Carola. *David Garrick*, 1958

O'Sullivan, Donal. *Carolan*, 2 vols, 1958

O'Sullivan, Donal. *Songs of the Irish*, Dublin 1960

Oulton, W. C. *History of the Theatres of London from 1771 to 1795*, 2 vols, 1796

Oxberry's Dramatic Biography, 5 vols, 1825 (originally a monthly magazine)

Page, Eugene R. *George Colman the Elder*, New York 1935

Papendiek, The Journals of Mrs., 2 vols, 1887

Parke, W. T. *Musical Memoirs*, 2 vols, 1830

Peake, R. B. *Memoirs of the Colman Family*, 2 vols, 1841

Pedicord, Harry William. *The Theatrical Public in the Time of Garrick*, New York 1954

Pope, Alexander. *The Dunciad* (first version of 1728)

Potter, John. *Observations on the Present State of Music and Musicians*, 1763

Reynolds, The Life and Times of Frederick, 2 vols, 1826

Ritson, The Letters of Joseph, 2 vols, 1833

Rosenfeld, Sybil. *The Theatre of the London Fairs in the 18th Century*, 1960

(Sainsbury). *A Biographical Dictionary of Musicians*, 2 vols, 2nd ed. 1827

Sands, Mollie. *Invitation to Ranelagh, 1742–1803*, 1946

Sands, Mollie. 'The Problem of "Teraminta"', *M & L* July 1952

Scholes, Percy. *The Great Dr. Burney*, 2 vols, 1948

Sheldon, Esther K. *Thomas Sheridan of Smock-Alley*, Princeton 1967

Sheridan, Betsy. *Betsy Sheridan's Journal*, ed. W. Le Fanu, 1960

Shield, William. *Introduction to Harmony*, 1800, revised 1815

Shield, William. *Rudiments of Thoroughbass*, 1815

Sichel, Walter. *Sheridan*, 2 vols, 1909

Simpson, Claude M. *The British Broadside Ballad and Its Music*, Rutgers University 1966

Smith, William C. *The Italian Opera and Contemporary Ballet in London, 1789—1820*, STR 1954

Smithers, Peter. *The Life of Joseph Addison*, 1954

Snagg, Thomas. *Recollections of Occurrences*, reprinted 1951

Stockholm, Johanne M. *Garrick's Folly*, 1964

Strong, Roy. 'Festival Designs by Inigo Jones', Introduction to the Chatsworth Collection Catalogue, 1967–8

Symons, A. J. A. *English Wits*, 1940 (for chapter on Theodore Hook)

Taylor, John. *Records of my Life*, 1832

Terry, C. Sanford. *John Christian Bach*, 1929, revised 1967

Thespian Dictionary, The, 1805

Thespian Magazine, The, a monthly of the 1790s

Tilmouth, Michael. *RMA Research Chronicle I*: 'A Calendar of References to Music in Newspapers, 1660–1719', 1961

Troubridge, St. Vincent. *The Benefit System in the British Theatre*, STR 1967

Victor, Benjamin. *A History of the Theatres in London and Dublin from 1730 to the present time*, 2 vols, 1761

Walker, Ernest (revised J. A. Westrup). *A History of Music in England*, 1952

Walpole, Horace. *Memoirs of the last ten years of the Reign of King George II*, 1822

Westrup, J. A. *Purcell*, 1937, revised 1960

White, Eric Walter. *The Rise of English Opera*, 1951

Wilkinson, Tate. *Memoirs*, 4 vols, 1790

Wilkinson, Tate. *The Wandering Patentee*, 4 vols, 1795

Willey, Basil. *The Eighteenth Century Background*, 1940

Wilson, John. *Roger North on Music*, 1959

Young, M. J. *Memoirs of Mrs. Crouch*, 2 vols, 1806

Young, Percy. *A History of British Music*, 1967

Index A

ENGLISH THEATRE MUSIC AND
ITS COMPOSERS

This Index includes, it is hoped, all works that survive in full or vocal score from 1695, Purcell's death, to 1800; some fifteen of these have been given precise dates etc. because they have not been mentioned in the text. It also includes works of interest that were produced but never published; virtually all omissions date from the last twenty-five years of the century.

The following categories have also been included:
1. English operatic works before 1695, but only under the composer
2. The very few operatic works written after 1800 by Arnold, Dibdin, and Shield
3. Italian operas by Arne, J. C. Smith, and Storace
4. Italian and French operas staged with English words
5. Non-operatic works by the more important English composers.

For Italian operas by foreign composers, including Handel, see General Index.

CAPS: a full length work; others are afterpieces
BO: Ballad Opera
Pant.: Pantomime
Past.: Pastiche, less than half the music being by one composer
NS: No score. This usually means that no music survives, but in some cases the overture and one or two songs will have been published.

Index B

GENERAL INDEX

The indexing of the Appendices has been selective to reduce repetition of information.